European Patent Law
The Unified Patent Court and the European Patent Convention
De Gruyter Handbook

European Patent Law

The Unified Patent Court and
the European Patent Convention

Edited by
Duncan Matthews and Paul Torremans

DE GRUYTER

ISBN 978-3-11-077401-6
e-ISBN (PDF) 978-3-11-078168-7
e-ISBN (EPUB) 978-3-11-078171-7

Library of Congress Control Number: 2023936127

Bibliographic information published by the Deutsche Nationalbibliothek
The Deutsche Nationalbibliothek lists this publication in the Deutsche Nationalbibliografie; detailed bibliographic data are available on the Internet at http://dnb.dnb.de.

© 2023 Walter de Gruyter GmbH, Berlin/Boston
Cover Image: tashechka / iStock / Getty Images Plus
Typsetting: jürgen ullrich typosatz, Nördlingen
Printing and binding: CPI books GmbH, Leck

www.degruyter.com

Foreword

Our decision to compile and edit this book came at a critical time for the evolution of European patent law. With the imminent coming into effect of the Unitary Patent Package and the Unified Patent Court (UPC), the legal landscape of European patent law was about to change forever. The European Patent with unitary effect and the jurisdiction of the UPC, operating alongside the patent regime established five decades previously by the European Patent Convention (EPC), would lead to significant change, and we wanted to reflect this exciting prospect in the book's overall approach.

What interested us most was the opportunity to compile and edit a volume that reflected the diversity of patent law traditions in Europe, with authors from a multitude of countries, together with the opportunity to blend a mix of experts from legal practice, the judiciary and academia, and to provide a voice for both established legal scholarship and new, vibrant, thinkers in the field. By Summer 2021 we had a concept for the book and a list of authors, which we then shared with De Gruyter.

Faye Leerink, our Commissioning Editor at De Gruyter, and Birte Treder, Acquisitions Editor, were both incredibly supportive of what we had in mind. The book was not merely to focus on the changes brought about by the European Patent with unitary effect and the Unified Patent Court, but also a chance to reflect to reflect on how the most significant changes to the European patent regime in half a century would impact more widely on patent law practice and legal scholarship over the entire European continent.

By early 2022 we had curated a list of topics and potential authors that reflected our vision of a unique and timely volume that would contribute to the ongoing debate about the future of European patent law. Thanks to the generosity of our contributors, who were willing to accept our invitations to write chapters for the book despite their incredibly busy schedules, the final version of the manuscript that you see here mirrors almost exactly what we initially had in mind. In that respect, it is the book's contributing authors who have made this project possible and we remain indebted to them for sharing their expertise and vision of the future of patent law in Europe.

During the writing phase of the book project, we were fortunate to have the editorial support of Maciej Padamczyk, a talented Research Associate based at the Queen Mary Intellectual Property Research Institute in the Centre for Commercial Law Studies, Queen Mary University of London. Maciej's meticulous project management skills ensured that the book remained on track and that the manuscript was submitted to the publishers on time and in good shape.

On behalf of De Gruyter, Claudia Loehr, our Project Editor, provided invaluable guidance and encouragement throughout. We would also like to thank our colleagues at Queen Mary University of London and the University of Nottingham for their support. An edited book is, by its very nature, a team effort and this project has shown that when teamwork goes well, the results are eminently worthwhile.

We are also incredibly grateful to Lord Justice Birss of the Court of Appeal of England and Wales for writing the Preface to the book, and for his kind words of support.

We hope you will enjoy reading the book, and find it useful, as we enter a new and exciting phase of development for patent law and practice in Europe.

Duncan Matthews and Paul Torremans
23 April 2023

Preface

Despite the success of the European Patent Convention and the system it has created, it is a still a surprisingly rare thing in the patent world for all three groups of academics, and senior practitioners, and judges, from a variety of European countries, to get together with each other and share their ideas and their experience. Some of the major international conferences achieve this at a global level, but at the European level the conversation is less complete. For many years in Europe there have been international dialogues inside each of these groups, and quite a few occasions to join pairs of them together such as judges with academics and so on. However at least in my experience, having all three groups, each at a European level, around the same table at the same time is not as common as it ought to be.

The introduction of the Unified Patent Court and the Unitary Patent is a perfect justification for redoubling efforts to increase these kinds of interactions. This work, which is a collection of essays on European patent law, covering the EPC, the UPC, and the Unitary European patent; by authors from all three groups, is to be welcomed. The collection forms a Research Handbook and I recommend dipping into the essays. You will find inciteful and up to date thinking on the most current legal and practical problems arising the European patent system today. Three personal favourites of mine are a very clear judge's (personal) perspective on the rules of procedure of the UPC by Sam Granata (Chapter 18), a thought provoking piece on the likely interaction of the new UPC with the national courts and the EPO Boards of Appeal by Heinz Goddar and Konstantin Werner (Chapter 2), and a really interesting examination of future litigation strategy in Germany, drawing on experience in Japan, by Matthias Lamping and Christoph Rademacher (Chapter 26).

The authors of the individual essays are thought leaders in Europe today in this field, and the editors Duncan Matthews and Paul Torremans are to be congratulated for the work they have done in bringing this material together and making the Handbook a reality. Well done!

Lord Justice Colin Birss
Judge of the Court of Appeal of England and Wales

Table of contents

Duncan Matthews, Paul Torremans
Foreword —— V

Lord Justice Colin Birss
Preface —— VII

List of contributors —— XXIII

Duncan Matthews, Paul Torremans
Introduction —— XXV

Part 1: The existing system: the EPC

Jean-Christophe Galloux
1   The role of EPO Boards of Appeal in shaping of patent law in Europe —— 3
1.1   Boards of Appeal's characters —— 4
1.2   BoA's role —— 6
1.2.1   BoA's ways in shaping European patent law —— 6
1.2.2   BoA's real influence on contracting states jurisdictions —— 9
1.3   BoA's limits in shaping of patent law in Europe —— 11
1.3.1   Limits inherent to the European law system —— 11
1.3.2   Dialog of judges: a necessity —— 14

Heinz Goddar, Konstantin Werner
2   The interaction between the UPC, national courts, and the EPO Boards of Appeal —— 17
2.1   Introduction —— 17
2.2   Initial situation —— 17
2.2.1   Obtaining patent protection in Europe – the present system —— 17
2.2.2   Future UPs and the role of national courts vs. UPC —— 19
2.3   The interplay between national courts, UPC, and Boards of Appeal ('BoA') of EPO in future —— 20
2.4   The best filing strategy in Europe in the future —— 22
2.4.1   "Category A" —— 22
2.4.2   "Category B" —— 24
2.4.3   "Category C" —— 24
2.5   Conclusions —— 25

Żaneta Zemła-Pacud, Tomasz Targosz
3 Cross-border patent litigation under the EPC — 27
3.1 Introduction — 27
3.2 Existing rules of cross-border patent litigation in the EU – jurisdiction — 28
3.3 Unfair tactical litigation — 36
3.4 Infringing acts in multiple countries — 37
3.5 Practical ramifications of the status quo: inconsistency of decision-making, high costs, forum shopping — 38
3.6 Concluding thoughts — 40
3.7 References — 41

Alison Slade
4 Plausibility: a route to stronger and more robust patents? — 43
4.1 Introduction — 43
4.2 Why a plausibility test? — 45
4.3 Filling the legislative lacuna — 46
4.4 Defining the plausibility standard — 48
4.5 Which approach would secure stronger and more robust patents? — 52
4.6 Implications for the UPC: a lack of legal coherency — 55
4.7 Conclusion — 57

Amandine Léonard
5 Wrongful preliminary injunctions and EU procedural law — 59
5.1 Introduction — 59
5.2 Wrongful preliminary injunctions – liability with or without fault? — 60
5.2.1 The case — 63
5.2.2 Analysis — 64
5.3 'Appropriate compensation' and the meaning of 'abuse' under IPRED — 67
5.3.1 A uniform interpretation of 'appropriate compensation' — 67
5.3.2 The question of 'abuse' under article 3(2) IPRED — 70
5.4 EU procedural law and patent litigation — 72
5.4.1 IP enforcement and vertical harmonisation — 72
5.4.2 Reflections for patent litigation and civil procedural law — 74
5.5 Conclusion — 76
5.6 References — 76
5.6.1 Legislation — 76
5.6.2 Case law — 76
5.6.3 Secondary sources — 77

Maciej Padamczyk, Duncan Matthews
6 Proportionality and patent injunctions —— 79
6.1 Introduction: proportionality and enforcement of patent rights —— 79
6.2 Injunctions: policy considerations —— 80
6.3 Injunctions and proportionality: an outline of the debate —— 83
6.4 Injunctions and proportionality in national and international law —— 85
6.4.1 International law —— 85
6.4.2 United States —— 87
6.4.3 United Kingdom —— 89
6.4.4 Germany —— 89
6.4.5 Final injunctions in the UPC —— 90
6.5 Preliminary injunctions —— 91
6.6 Concluding remarks —— 93

Part 2: The European Patent with unitary effect and the Unified Patent Court

Frantzeska Papadopoulou
7 The novelty and inventive step requirement in Europe and under the UPP —— 97
7.1 Background —— 97
7.2 Novelty and inventive step requirement in Europe a fragmentised view? —— 99
7.2.1 Novelty requirement in Europe —— 99
7.2.2 Inventive step in Europe —— 100
7.3 Unitary patent but disharmonised European patent law? —— 103
7.3.1 The role of the EPO towards a European substantive patent law —— 103
7.3.2 The Unitary Patent, the Unitary Patent Court and the CJEU —— 105
7.4 Concluding remarks —— 106

Ana Nordberg
8 Exceptions and limitations (27 UPCA) —— 109
8.1 Introduction: historical origin of UPCA limitations —— 109
8.2 Legal nature and scope of Article 27 UPC —— 111
8.2.1 Legal nature of limitations —— 111
8.2.2 A closed list or does the provision allow for further limitations? —— 112
8.2.3 Analogy and extensive interpretation —— 113
8.3 Harmonization and uniformity of patent limitations —— 114
8.4 Article 27 limitations to the effects of a patent —— 116
8.4.1 Limitations based on international law —— 116
8.4.2 Limitations based on EU policy (Community Patent Convention) —— 117
8.4.2.1 Acts done privately and for non-commercial purposes —— 117

8.4.2.2 Acts done for experimental purposes —— 119
8.4.2.3 Extemporaneous preparation of medicines —— 121
8.4.3 Limitations based on EU Law —— 122
8.4.3.1 Use in the context of regulatory approval procedures: 'Bolar exemption' —— 122
8.4.3.2 Plant and animal related patent Limitations —— 125
8.4.3.3 Computer-implemented inventions decompilation and interoperability —— 126
8.5 Conclusion —— 127

Jacques de Werra
9 Patent Arbitration under the Agreement on a Unified Patent Court —— 129
9.1 Introduction —— 129
9.2 The Patent Mediation and Arbitration Centre instituted by the UPCA —— 131
9.2.1 Introduction —— 131
9.2.2 Substantive scope of the arbitration services offered by the Centre —— 134
9.2.3 No exclusivity for arbitration instituted by the Centre —— 137
9.2.4 Interactions between arbitration proceedings and court proceedings before the Court —— 138
9.2.5 No right to revoke or limit patents in arbitration proceedings —— 141
9.2.6 Improved enforceability of settlements reached through the use of the facilities of the Centre —— 144
9.2.7 Double seat of the Centre and provision of 'facilities' by the Centre —— 146
9.2.8 List of arbitrators —— 148
9.3 Concluding remarks —— 148

Justyna Ożegalska-Trybalska
10 Supplementary Protection Certificates (Article 30) —— 153
10.1 Introduction —— 153
10.2 General overview of the SPC system in the EU – in fitting with or conflicting with unitary protection concept? —— 155
10.3 The SPC under UPCA – the present —— 156
10.3.1 The subject matter application of Article 30 —— 157
10.3.2 The scope of Article 30 —— 158
10.3.3 Effects of SPC – unitary or not? —— 159
10.4 The SPC under UPCA – the future —— 160
10.4.1 Towards a unitary SPC —— 161
10.4.4.1 Centralised granting procedure —— 162
10.4.4.2 Marketing authorisation for a unitary SPC —— 164
10.5 Final remarks —— 166

Phillip Johnson
11 Liability for infringement of EU law —— 169
11.1 Introduction —— 169
11.2 The extent of EU law before the UPC —— 170
11.3 Compelling compliance —— 174
11.3.1 'Infraction' proceedings —— 175
11.3.2 Köbler liability —— 175
11.4 Ways in which the UPC can breach EU law —— 177
11.4.1 Failure to give direct effect to an EU law —— 178
11.4.2 Incompatible rules —— 178
11.4.3 Failure to give conforming interpretation —— 180
11.4.4 Failure to request a preliminary reference —— 180
11.5 How real is the risk? —— 181
11.6 Conclusion —— 183

Paul LC Torremans
12 Regulation 542/2014 on jurisdiction —— 185
12.1 Introduction —— 185
12.2 The insertion of a common court: a mere clarification in Article 71(a) —— 186
12.3 The new rules on international jurisdiction: Article 71b —— 188
12.4 Article 71c: *lis pendens* —— 194
12.5 Recognition and enforcement —— 196
12.6 Conclusion —— 196

Paul LC Torremans
13 Exclusive jurisdiction and competence —— 197
13.1 Introduction —— 197
13.2 The exclusive jurisdiction of the UPC: registration and validity —— 197
13.2.1 Applying Article 24(4) Brussels I Regulation —— 197
13.2.2 The transition period as a complicating factor —— 198
13.2.3 Other grounds of jurisdiction —— 199
13.3 The competence rules —— 200
13.3.1 An action for the revocation of a patent —— 200
13.3.2 Infringement and other actions —— 201
13.4 *Lis pendens* —— 203
13.5 Conclusion —— 203

Fernand de Visscher
14 Constitutional aspects of the Unitary Patent Package (UPP) and the Unified Patent Court (UPC) – question marks remain — 205
14.1 Regulation 1257/2012 — 206
14.2 The UPCA — 213
14.3 What about the Court of Justice? — 216

Esther van Zimmeren
15 Trusting the Unified Patent Court: the importance of the institutional design of the UPC and its judges — 221
15.1 Introduction — 221
15.2 The one-of-its kind unique nature of the UPC — 224
15.3 Translating key concepts from the trust literature to the UPC setting — 229
15.3.1 Defining trust, identifying the trust relationship and understanding the multilevel nature of trust within the context of the UPC — 229
15.3.2 Trust and uncertainty — 231
15.3.3 Trust, trustworthiness and the ABI-model — 232
15.4 Concluding remarks — 233

Stefan Luginbuehl, Matilda Titeca
16 The EPO within the unitary patent system — 235
16.1 Introduction — 235
16.2 Legal framework — 237
16.2.1 The Unitary Patent Regulations — 237
16.2.2 Agreement on a Unified Patent Court (UPCA) — 238
16.2.3 Secondary legislation — 238
16.3 Role of the EPO from a governance perspective — 239
16.3.1 Select Committee of the Administrative Council of the European Patent Organisation — 239
16.3.2 Unified Patent Court (UPC) — 240
16.4 Role of the EPO with regard to the Unitary Patent Procedure — 241
16.4.1 Additional tasks for the European Patent Office — 241
16.4.2 Request for Unitary Effect — 242
16.4.3 Payment of fees — 242
16.5 Correlation of European Patent, Unitary Patent and national patent systems — 243
16.5.1 From a true Community patent to an alternatively available patent for a group of EU member states — 243
16.5.2 Co-existing EPO opposition and appeals proceedings before the EPO and the EPO Boards of Appeal, the Unified Patent Court and national courts — 244

16.5.3 Role of the Court of Justice of the European Union (CJEU) and impact on the EPO and the European Patent System —— 246
16.5.3.1 The impact of rulings of the CJEU on the EPO —— 246
16.5.3.2 The interpretation of substantive patent law provided for in the UPC Agreement by the CJEU —— 247
16.6 Conclusion —— 249

Hanns Ullrich
17 The Role of the Court of Justice of the European Union —— 251
17.1 The general role of the Court of Justice —— 251
17.1.1 The provisions of the Treaties —— 251
17.1.2 The role of the Court of Justice under Reg. 1257/2012 and under other EU intellectual property regulations compared. —— 252
17.1.2.1 Review of the grant and of the validity of EU intellectual property rights —— 252
17.1.2.2 Interpretation of the rules of substantive law of EU intellectual property protection —— 255
17.2 The role of the Court of Justice in the interpretation of the rules of substantive law of the unitary patent and the European bundle patent —— 257
17.2.1 The law covered by Art. 267 TFEU —— 257
17.2.1.1 Union law —— 257
17.2.1.2 The interdependence of Reg. 1257/2012 and Art. 25 to 27 UPCA —— 267
17.2.2 The relationship between the Court of Justice and the Unified Patent Court —— 276
17.2.2.1 On the application of Art. 267 TFEU by the UPC —— 276
17.2.2.2 A division of labor —— 281
17.3 Outlook —— 285

Sam Granata
18 Rules of procedure of the UPC, a judge's perspective —— 287
18.1 Introduction —— 287
18.2 Levels of rules of procedure of the UPC —— 288
18.2.1 Hierarchy between the rules of procedure of the UPC —— 288
18.2.2 The UPCA —— 289
18.2.3 The Statute —— 290
18.2.4 The Rules of Procedure —— 292
18.3 The driving principles of 'proportionality' and 'fairness' as a matter of trust in the UPC judge —— 293
18.4 Pragmatic versus legalistic approach —— 296
18.5 The Judge-Rapporteur —— 297
18.6 The UPC as one-stop-shop for patent disputes —— 298
18.7 Conclusion —— 299

Guillaume Dubos, Stéphanie Rollin de Chambonas, Thomas Leconte
19 The user in the UPC —— 301
19.1 Opting out and in: beware of the torpedoes —— 301
19.2 Procedural aspects: the devil is in the details —— 303
19.3 The UPC as a 'one-stop shop' for users —— 305
19.4 National patents: not (yet?) out of the picture —— 306
19.5 Forum shopping with the UPC and its impact on its users' actions —— 307
19.6 Means of evidence: a large and complete toolbox for users —— 309
19.7 UPC-style *saisie*: less powerful than the French *saisie-contrefaçon*? —— 311
19.8 Access to decisions, orders, and written pleadings: some lingering question marks —— 313
19.9 Conclusion —— 313

Klara Polackova Van der Ploeg
20 Unified Patent Court and international law —— 315
20.1 Introduction —— 315
20.2 UPC as an international court —— 317
20.3 International law as the UPC's governing law —— 318
20.4 UPC's interpretative autonomy —— 326
20.5 Patent law and other international law: from regime-conflict to regime-cooperation —— 328
20.6 Functions and authority of international courts: strengthening the UPC's decision-making —— 331
20.7 Obligations of commercial patentees and other businesses —— 335
20.8 Conclusion: building a new international court —— 338

Miłosz Malaga
21 The patent with unitary effect and competition law —— 339
21.1 Introduction —— 339
21.2 Intellectual property rights in the internal market —— 339
21.3 EU Competition legal framework —— 341
21.4 EU Competition law and intellectual property rights —— 344
21.4.1 Principles —— 344
21.4.2 IPRs and anti-competitive agreements —— 345
21.4.3 IPRs and abuse of dominant position —— 346
21.4.3.1 Refusal to supply and licence —— 347
21.4.3.2 Tying —— 347
21.4.3.3 Excessive pricing —— 348
21.4.3.4 Regulatory and litigation abuses —— 348
21.4.3.5 Patent hold-ups and patent trolling —— 349
21.5 The Unitary Patent and EU competition law —— 349
21.6 Conclusions —— 352

Thomas Jaeger, Johannes Lukan
22 A system fit for innovation? Part I: (Dis-)incentives for potential patentees in the UP legal framework —— 355
22.1 Introduction —— 355
22.2 Easy, fast and legally secure access to UPs? —— 356
22.2.1 Easy access: the EPO as a central granting authority and the language regime —— 356
22.2.1.1 The request for unitary effect as a replacement of national validation —— 356
22.2.1.2 Downsides to the language regime? —— 357
22.2.1.3 Centralised collection of renewal fees —— 358
22.2.2 Value for money: costs and territorial scope of protection —— 358
22.2.2.1 What is an 'average' EP? —— 359
22.2.2.2 Dependence of territorial coverage on the status of ratifications —— 360
22.2.2.3 Who will use the system? —— 361
22.2.2.4 The compensation scheme —— 362
22.2.2.5 Licenses of right —— 362
22.2.3 Duration of the granting procedure and temporal scope of protection —— 363
22.2.3.1 The EPO's improved timeliness —— 364
22.2.3.2 The importance of patent quality —— 364
22.2.3.3 The unheard call for a differentiated approach —— 366
22.2.3.4 The UP and SPCs —— 367
22.2.4 Uncertainties regarding the law applicable to the UPC as an object of property —— 368
22.2.4.1 Disadvantages of the available interpretative options —— 369
22.2.4.2 Impact on patent value —— 370
22.2.4.3 Which alternatives would have been available? —— 370
22.3 Interim conclusion —— 371

Thomas Jaeger, Johannes Lukan
23 A system fit for innovation? Part II: (Dis-)advantages for follow-on inventors in the UP legal framework —— 373
23.1 Introduction —— 373
23.2 Substantive scope of protection and applicable limitations – a functional balance? —— 374
23.2.1 No changes with regard to patentability? —— 375
23.2.2 A case for a purpose-bound compound protection —— 376
23.2.2.1 How could such adaptions be made? —— 378
23.2.3 The applicable limitations – more of the same —— 379
23.2.3.1 Limitations stemming from the CPCs —— 379
23.2.3.2 Limitations stemming from EU directives —— 380
23.2.3.3 The breeder's privilege – why not also exempt new animal breeds? —— 381
23.2.3.4 The Bolar- and the general research exceptions: a race to the bottom? —— 382

23.2.4 Compulsory licenses and limitations to injunctive relief under the UP legal framework —— 388
23.2.4.1 The relation between individual and general limitations to patent holders' rights —— 388
23.2.4.2 The link between compulsory licenses and limitations to injunctive relief —— 388
23.2.4.3 Compulsory licences left untouched —— 389
23.2.4.4 A missed opportunity —— 390
23.2.4.5 A proportionality requirement for injunctions —— 391
23.2.4.6 Presumed incompatibility with EU law of individual restraints of patent protection —— 394
23.3 Overall conclusion: a system fit for innovation? —— 395

Maximilian Haedicke
24 Patent mediation —— 397
24.1 Introduction —— 397
24.1.1 Definition and legal basis —— 397
24.1.2 Guiding principles —— 398
24.1.2.1 Confidentiality —— 399
24.1.2.2 Voluntariness —— 399
24.1.2.3 Openness —— 399
24.1.2.4 All-partiality / neutrality —— 399
24.1.2.5 Legal information —— 399
24.1.3 The course of IP mediation proceedings —— 400
24.1.3.1 First contact —— 400
24.1.3.2 Preparation —— 400
24.1.3.3 Opening – Phase I —— 401
24.1.3.4 Exploration of facts and identification of issues – Phase II —— 402
24.1.3.5 Working through the areas of conflict – Phase III —— 402
24.1.3.6 Negotiation and problem solving – Phase IV —— 403
24.1.3.7 Drafting a final agreement – Phase V —— 404
24.1.3.8 Enforcement of mediation settlements —— 404
24.1.4 The role of the mediator —— 405
24.1.4.1 General —— 405
24.1.4.2 The mediator's techniques for conflict resolution —— 405
24.1.4.3 Special requirements for mediators in patent disputes —— 406
24.1.5 Opportunities and challenges of mediation in general —— 406
24.2 Patent conflicts suitable for mediation —— 407
24.2.1 Licence agreements —— 407
24.2.2 International and complex disputes —— 408
24.2.3 Disputes requiring confidentiality —— 408
24.2.4 Further advantages of mediation —— 409
24.3 Conclusion —— 410

Alan Johnson
25 Litigation strategies and bifurcation — 411
25.1 Introduction — 411
25.2 Forum shopping within the UPC — 413
25.2.1 The claimant perspective — 414
25.2.2 The non-patentee defendant perspective — 417
25.2.3 The patentee defendant perspective — 417
25.2.4 Conclusions on the 'balance of power' — 418
25.3 Forum shopping between national and UPC jurisdictions in the transitional period — 418
25.4 Anti-suit injunctions — 420
25.5 Conclusions – a more uncertain world for European patent litigation — 422

Matthias Lamping, Christoph Rademacher
26 Patent litigation strategies in Germany: maneuvering the evolving landscape of bifurcation — 423
26.1 Bifurcation of proceedings — 423
26.1.1 Germany — 423
26.1.1.1 Basic structure, legal basis and effect — 423
26.1.1.2 Requirements for a stay of the infringement procedure — 425
26.1.1.3 Communication between Patent Court and infringement courts — 427
26.1.2 Unified Patent Court — 431
26.1.2.1 Institutional structure of the UPC — 431
26.1.2.2 Jurisdiction of the UPC — 432
26.1.3 Japan — 436
26.2 Implications for litigation — 439
26.2.1 General remarks — 439
26.2.2 Litigating in Germany — 440
26.2.2.1 Timing of revocation and infringement actions — 440
26.2.2.2 Stay of infringement proceedings — 441
26.2.2.3 Compensation for injury caused by enforcement — 442
26.2.3 Litigating before the UPC — 442
26.2.3.1 Infringement actions brought by licensees — 443
26.2.3.2 Parallel revocation and counterclaim — 444
26.2.3.3 Compensation for injury caused by enforcement — 444
26.3 Concluding remarks — 445

Part 3: Co-existence and alternatives

Marc Mimler
27 The co-existence between EPC and patents with unitary effect —— 449
27.1 Introduction —— 449
27.2 Main body —— 450
27.2.1 Historical background —— 450
27.2.2 Occurrence —— 452
27.2.2.1 European Patents with unitary effect (i.e. UPs) —— 453
27.2.2.2 Classical European Patents falling within the jurisdiction of the UPC —— 454
27.2.2.3 European Patents which do not fall within the jurisdiction of the UPC —— 454
27.2.2.4 National patents —— 458
27.2.3 Adjudication and substantive law —— 459
27.2.3.1 The UPC's exclusive competence —— 459
27.2.3.2 Competence of national courts and applicable law —— 460
27.3 Conclusion —— 461

Karen Walsh
28 Institutional coexistence: the necessity of judicial dialogue and cooperation in the UPC —— 463
28.1 Introduction —— 463
28.2 The UPC —— 464
28.3 Harmonisation and the UPC —— 468
28.4 The necessity of judicial dialogue and cooperation in the UPC —— 471
28.5 Conclusion —— 474

Tamar Khuchua
29 The role of the CJEU in European patent law from a procedural perspective —— 477
Introductions —— 477
29.1 EU legislation in patent law and the CJEU's current role in the patent field —— 478
29.2 Avenues leading to CJEU judgments on patent enforcement and available case law —— 480
29.3 Guaranteeing an EU-law compliant patent enforcement procedure within national courts based on the Enforcement Directive —— 483
29.3.1 CJEU rulings on interim and provisional measures in patent enforcement —— 485
29.3.2 The issue of reimbursement of legal costs in patent proceedings clarified by the CJEU —— 489
29.3.3 CJEU providing guidance on procedural guarantees in patent enforcement in the light of EU competition law —— 491
29.4 The future role of the CJEU in procedural aspects of patent enforcement at the UPC —— 493
29.5 Conclusion —— 495

Naomi Hawkins
30 Gene patents in the EPC and the European Patent with unitary effect — 497
30.1 Introduction — 497
30.1.1 Definition of gene patents — 498
30.1.2 Current technical landscape — 499
30.2 Patents on genes – the historical concerns — 502
30.3 Gene patents in European patent law – current pressing questions — 504
30.3.1 Ethics and morality – the application of the morality exclusion — 504
30.3.2 Addressing access concerns — 508
30.3.3 Divergence of approaches – does the UPC offer possibilities for increased harmonisation? — 511
30.3.3.1 A single forum — 513
30.3.3.2 The role of the CJEU — 513
30.3.3.3 Persuasive standards — 514
30.4 Conclusion — 515

Aisling McMahon
31 Decision-Makers, institutional influences and the role of ethical issues in the patenting of biotechnological inventions in Europe: enter the unitary patent system — 517
Introduction — 517
31.1 Patenting biotechnological inventions in Europe: the embedding of ethical considerations within the Biotechnology Directive 98/44/EC — 519
31.1.1 Drafting of the Biotechnological Directive and ethic — 520
31.1.2 Ethical provisions and the Directive — 521
31.2 Applying the Directive's ethical provisions in Europe: interpretative communities, institutional overlaps & influences — 522
31.2.1 Ethical provisions within the Directive & practical interpretation – pre-UPC — 522
31.2.2 Institutional overlaps & ethical considerations – enter the UPC — 523
31.2.3 Interpretative communities and the UPC's role in interpreting ethical provisions within the Directive — 525
31.2.3.1 Ethical issues, discretion & the interpretative role of decision-makers in the European patent system — 526
31.2.3.2 Institutional influences and overlapping EPO, CJEU and UPC functions: interpretating ethical provisions in the Directive — 527
31.3 Technological developments and the need for a renewed conversation on the role ethical issues should play within the European patent system — 529
31.4 Concluding thoughts — 530

Gail E Evans
32 The UPC and the FRAND injunction —— 533
32.1 The discretion of the UPC to grant a final injunction —— 536
32.1.1 The English courts and the discretionary grant of an injunction —— 537
32.2 The FRAND undertaking and the court's discretion to grant a final injunction —— 539
32.2.1 Use of the FRAND injunction to defeat hold-out strategies —— 541
32.3 The discretion to award damages as an alternate and adequate remedy —— 543
32.4 Withholding an injunction based on the FRAND defence of abuse of dominance —— 545
32.4.1 Huawei v ZTE: a 'safe harbour' from abuse of dominance —— 547
32.4.2 The importance of giving the implementer notice of patent infringement —— 548
32.4.3 Assessing 'abuse of dominance' —— 549
32.4.3.1 Offering a global licence —— 550
32.4.3.2 Bundling SEPs and non-SEPs —— 550
32.4.3.3 The reasonableness of the royalty rate —— 551
32.5 No entitlement to an injunction where the defendant is a willing licensee —— 552
32.5.1 Proof of an implementer's 'willingness' to enter into a FRAND licence —— 553
32.6 Conclusion: FRAND injunctions, consistency of decision-making and arbitration —— 555

Index —— 557

List of contributors

Lord Justice Colin Birss, Court of Appeal England and Wales
Guillaume Dubos, Partner, Abello IP Firm, Paris
Gail E. Evans, Reader in the Licensing of Intellectual Property, Queen Mary University of London
Jean-Christophe Galloux, professor, Sorbonne-Assas Law School
Heinz Goddar, partner, BOEHMERT & BOEHMERT, honorary Professor for Intellectual Property, the University of Bremen and the Munich Intellectual Property Law Center (MIPLC)
Sam Granata, Judge, Court of Appeal Antwerp, Belgium and the Benelux Court
Maximilian Haedicke, Professor of Intellectual Property Law, University of Freiburg and Judge, Unified Patent Court, Central Division, Paris
Naomi Hawkins, Professor in Intellectual Property Law, University of Sheffield
Thomas Jaeger, Professor of European Law, University of Vienna
Alan Johnson, Consultant, Hogan Lovells International, London
Phillip Johnson, Professor of Commercial Law, Cardiff University
Tamar Khuchua, Post-doctoral Researcher, SciencesPo University, Paris
Matthias Lamping, Senior Research Fellow, Max Planck Institute for Innovation and Competition, Munich
Thomas Leconte, European Patent Attorney, Abello IP Firm, Paris
Amandine Léonard, Early Career Fellow in Intellectual Property Law, University of Edinburgh.
Stefan Luginbuehl, PhD, Lawyer, Head of Department, European Patent Office.
Johannes Lukan, University Assistant (prae doc) at the Department of European, International and Comparative Law, University of Vienna
Miłosz Malaga, PhD, Assistant Professor, Chair of European Law, Faculty of Law and Administration, Adam Mickiewicz University in Poznań
Aisling McMahon, Professor of Law, Maynooth University
Marc Mimler, Senior Lecturer, City University of London
Duncan Matthews, Professor of Intellectual Property Law, Queen Mary University of London
Ana Nordberg, Associate Professor and Senior Lecturer, Faculty of Law, Lund University
Justyna Ożegalska-Trybalska, Assistant Professor, Intellectual Property Law Chair, Jagiellonian University in Kraków
Maciej Padamczyk, Research Associate and PhD Candidate, Queen Mary University of London
Frantzeska Papadopoulou, Private Law, Stockholm University.
Klara Polackova Van der Ploeg, Assistant Professor, University of Nottingham
Christoph Rademacher, Professor, Waseda University, Tokyo
Stéphanie Rollin de Chambonas, Lawyer, Abello IP Firm, Paris
Alison Slade, Associate Professor, University of Leicester
Tomasz Targosz, Assistant Professor Jagiellonian University in Kraków, Partner TKP, Kraków
Matilda Titeca, Trainee, European Patent Office
Paul Torremans, Professor of Intellectual Property Law, University of Nottingham
Hanns Ullrich, Honorary Professor, College of Europe, Bruges
Fernand de Visscher, partner, Simont Braun LLP, Brussels, and Scientific associate CRIDES (UCLouvain)
Karen Walsh, Assistant Professor in Law, Maynooth University
Konstantin Werner, PhD candidate, Humboldt University Berlin
Jacques de Werra, Professor of Intellectual Property Law and Contract Law, Director of the Digital Law Centre, University of Geneva
Żaneta Zemła-Pacud, Assistant Professor in the Institute of Law Studies, Polish Academy of Science, Of Counsel in TKP, Warsaw.
Esther van Zimmeren, Professor in Intellectual Property Law & Governance University of Antwerp, coordinator of the GOVTRUST Centre of Excellence of the University of Antwerp

Duncan Matthews, Paul Torremans
Introduction

Patent law in Europe is going through a period of significant change. After decades of often futile negotiations, the European Patent with unitary effect and the complementary Unified Patent Court (UPC) are finally materialising. The time is therefore right for patent scholars and practitioners to look in detail at the emerging landscape in European patent law from their unique legal perspectives. The new legal landscape shows a significant degree of complexity, as the new elements do not produce a tabula rasa effect. On the contrary, they build extensively on the existing system of European patent law and create new layers of complexity, new threats and new opportunities.

The Unitary Patent Package raises important questions about how the current system may evolve in the future, having due regard to its relationship to European Union (EU) law. In chapter 1 Jean-Christophe Galloux reflects on the role that the European Patent Office (EPO) Boards of Appeal have so far played in shaping European patent law as an independent and final appellate jurisdiction with no further mechanism for challenging their judgments by way of appeal. The Boards of Appeal not only construe and apply the European Patent Convention (EPC), but also interpret and adapt its spirit and intent to ever-changing legal and technical circumstances and, in this way, play a crucial role in the evolving European patent system.

In the context of the Unitary Patent Package, the interplay between the UPC, national courts and the EPO Boards of Appeal raises new possibilities for innovative patent filing and enforcement strategies. The Unitary Patent Package creates, by virtue of the European Patent with unitary effect, a third way to obtain patent protection in European countries alongside the existing national and 'classical' European Patent routes. In chapter 2 Heinz Goddar and Konstantin Werner highlight the strategic importance of filing and enforcement possibilities that lie ahead.

Cross-border patent litigation will also change as a result of the Unitary Patent Package. In chapter 3, Żaneta Zemła-Pacud, Tomasz Targosz explain why, despite the coming into force of the UPC Agreement, serious reform of the cross-border litigation system is still needed, since the existing system is characterised as being fragmented, expensive and complicated to navigate. Reform of cross-border litigation will be crucial for the enforcement of European patents for many coming years.

In European patent law the principle of plausibility requires that all valid patents must demonstrate that the technical problem underlying the invention was at least remove underlining solved at the filing date. In chapter 4 Alison Slade explains how, despite lacking direct acknowledgement by the EPO, plausibility appears aimed at addres-

---

Duncan Matthews, is Professor of Intellectual Property Law, Queen Mary University of London.
Paul Torremans, is Professor of Intellectual Property Law, University of Nottingham.

sing deficiencies in the legal framework of the EPC that open the window to bad or unjustified patenting. Yet even plausibility seeks to uphold objectives that should be reflected in any well-functioning patent system, and uncertainties remain that may well be amplified by the new European patent system's legal architecture.

The relationship between EU procedural law, the EU Enforcement Directive and national procedural autonomy raises important questions in the context of patent litigation, particularly when defining what constitutes appropriate compensation and what should be considered 'abuse' of the injunction system. In chapter 5 Amandine Léonard assesses the scope for wrongful preliminary injunctions and EU procedural law, in a manner which is particularly timely given the arrival of the UPC.

The advent of the UPC has raised concerns that the issuance of final and preliminary injunctions may lead to undesirable outcomes. The UPC will be issuing injunctions covering the territories of all Contracting Member States of the EU and, in chapter 6, Maciej Padamczyk and Duncan Matthews assess how the concept of proportionality might be applied in such instances, based on the chapter's review of established practice in the United States (US), the United Kingdom (UK) and Germany.

The harmonisation of European patent law remains a work in progress and, as Frantzeska Papadopoulou explains in in chapter 7, the Unitary Patent Package creates a unique opportunity to reconsider the novelty and inventive step requirements in Europe. Significant differences exist when assessing novelty in the EPC member states, while the EPO approach to inventive step also differs from the various national approaches. The role of the UPC, and potentially an increased role for the Court of Justice of the European Union (CJEU) will be crucial in terms of how these patentability criteria are in the future defined.

The UPC Agreement for the first time establishes harmonised exceptions and limitations to patent rights in Europe. In chapter 8, Ana Nordberg analyses the exceptions and limitations established by Article 27 of the UPC Agreement. As Nordberg explains, the possibility remains for divergences and variations concerning applicable limitations depending on the type of patent and whether these are to be litigated under the jurisdiction of the UPC, and to some extent the approach taken will be difficult to predict.

Given the complexities and risks of litigation before national courts the advantages of alternative methods of dispute resolution help explain why arbitration is increasingly considered as an alternative. In chapter 9, Jacques de Werra assesses the patent arbitration arrangements set up under the Unified Patent Court Agreement, concluding that the success of the system will, ultimately, depend on the willingness of parties to use it.

The Unified Patent Court Agreement also impacts the regime of Supplementary Protection Certificates (SPCs) for patented medicinal products and plant protection products subject to additional regulatory requirements. In chapter 10 Justyna Ożegalska-Trybalska explains that the fact that the UPC has jurisdiction in SPC cases does not mean that unitary protection under the SPC will be available even after the unitary patent system is operational. While the logical next step would be to create a unitary SPC to sit alongside the Unitary Patent, Justyna Ożegalska-Trybalska outlines the complexities and obstacles that may lie ahead.

The creation of the Unified Patent Court also raises important questions about proceedings which can be brought in the Court of Justice of the European Union (CJEU) against Contracting EU Member States where they have not complied with EU law. In chapter 11 Phillip Johnson explains that the UPCA includes rules that subject Contracting Member States to infraction proceedings before the CJEU. As Phillip Johnson points out, the fact that the UPC is not a Member State of the EU adds complexity to the task of ascertaining where liability should lie in such instances, but that the UPCA nonetheless includes various safety valves to ensure it was compatible with EU law and, in doing so, minimises such risks.

The creation of a new court that is operating as a court of the member states does of course raise the question of the jurisdiction of that court. On what basis can a defendant in cases that have by definition an international element to them be brought before the UPC? This issue is examined by Paul Torremans in chapter 12 on Regulation 542/2014. In order to comply with EU law the UPC Agreement does not deal with jurisdiction and reliance had to be placed on the Brussels I Regulation. The latter was amended to accommodate the special nature of the UPC by Regulation 542/2014.

In chapter 13 the book Paul Torremans looks at the internal division of labour in the UPC, i.e. the issue of competence. It does so against the backdrop of the particularly complex question of exclusive jurisdiction. For many years attempts to bring cross-border infringement cases in patent law before a single court have been frustrated by counterclaims on the basis of invalidity that led to the exclusive jurisdiction of the court of the state granting the patent. That made it impossible to continue with the infringement case in a single court. The chapter analyses whether the UPC has overcome this hurdle.

It is clear that the Unitary Patent Package (UPP) and the Unified Patent Court (UPC) are about to become part, not just of European patent law, but also of the European legal framework. But when looked at from a constitutional perspective question marks remain. In Chapter 14 Fernand de Vischer therefore looks at the debate on the legality of Regulation 1257/2012 and the even more controversial legality of the UPC Agreement and the UPC as a court it establishes.

In that controversial constitutional framework it will be of crucial importance for the UPC to build up trust. In Chapter 15 Esther van Zimmeren looks at this aspect from the perspective of the importance of the institutional design of the court and its judges. The one-of-its kind unique nature of the UPC is of course an important factor in this respect, but it is one that brings both risks and opportunities. The chapter therefore turns to the risk literature and asks the question how some of its key concepts can be translated to the UPC setting. One needs to define trust, identify the trust relationship and understanding the multilevel nature of trust within the context of the UPC. But trust also comes with an element of uncertainty about the trustee's future behaviour and that leap of faith needs to be given a place in the UPC context. Things are greatly helped if the trustee is seen as trustworthy and the combination of ability, benevolence and integrity is crucial in this respect.

The new system will not depend solely on the UPC. There is also after all, aside from the infringement and validity litigation, the crucial element of the examination and the grant of the European Patent with unitary effect. This is where the EPO comes in and the organisation will play an important role in the shaping and the operation of the unitary patent system. In Chapter 16 Stefan Luginbuehl and Matilda Titeca look at the legislative framework before turning to the role of the EPO from a governance perspective. Attention then turns to the unitary patent procedure and the correlation of European Patent, Unitary Patent and national patent systems.

Much ink has been spilled on the role of the Court of Justice of the European Union in the process of enhanced cooperation in the area of patent law and lots of political capital has been invested in keeping that role as limited as possible. It is therefore important to take a step back and to look 'neutrally' at that role as it emerges from the agreed framework. In Chapter 17 Hanns Ullrich undertakes that crucial task by looking first of all at the role of the Court of Justice of the European Union in EU intellectual property matters in general. That analysis starts with the Treaty provisions and then compares the court's role under the EU intellectual property regulations with that under Regulation (EU) No 1257/2012 of the European Parliament and of the Council of 17 December 2012 implementing enhanced cooperation in the area of the creation of unitary patent protection. It is however equally important to analyse the role of the Court of Justice of the European Union in the interpretation of the rules of substantive law of the unitary patent and the European bundle patent.

Chapter 18 Sam Granata offers a judge's perspective to the rules of procedure of the UPC. It is important to note that there are different levels in those rules of procedure and with that comes a certain hierarchy. At the top of this hierarchy one finds the procedural rules contained in the UPC Agreement itself. These are then in the first place supplemented by the procedural rules in the Statute of the Court, as that is defined in Article 2 UPC Agreement. And then there are the rule of procedure themselves. The rules give the UPC judge a relatively high level of discretion and trust that his or her decisions will be based on standards of fairness and proportionality. The whole framework also takes a very pragmatic approach.

The creation of the UPC rather inevitably puts the focus of the debate on the court, its structure and functioning. That does not detract from the fact that the success or the failure of the UPC will depend on how well it serves or rather is able to serve its users. In Chapter 19 Guillaume Dubos, Thomas Leconte and Stéphanie Rollin de Chambonas look therefore at the UPC through the eyes of the users. Such an analysis cannot avoid starting by noting the complexities and the confusion that arise from the opportunity for the users to opt in and out. There is a risk of torpedoes here. Leaving these temporary concerns to one side, there is also the introduction of a new procedural framework and as always the devil will be in the details and undue reliance on previous national habits may prove risky. On the other hand there is the attraction of being able to use the UPC as a one-stop shop. National courts are however not yet out of the picture and there are therefore issues of forum shopping to be contended with. Evidence and the availability and format of procedural tools are, of course, also of crucial importance to the users.

The introduction of the UPC brings with it the challenge to build a new international court. Public international law provides the backdrop for such an exercise and, in chapter 20, Klara Polackova Van der Ploeg turns attention to that aspect of the creation of the UPC. She looks at the status of the UPC as an international court and at international law as the UPC's governing law. Against that backdrop it is critical to examine how much interpretative autonomy the UPC will have. The UPC may, however, be required under international law to consider or even apply international legal rules beyond those that may have traditionally been viewed as 'patent law', which bring us to the issue of regime interplay. Narrow subject matter and the specialisation of its staff may in this context turn out to involve risks for the UPC, but the topic will need to be addressed as modern public international law puts obligations on the shoulders of commercial patentees and other businesses.

They may not be monopolies properly speaking, but as exclusive rights patents do have an impact on competition. They affect and regulate competition at a structural level. The introduction of the European Patent with unitary effect will have an impact in this respect, as a single right is stronger and more effective than a bundle of national rights (or a bundle of the equivalents of national rights). Competition law on the other hands deals with behavioural aspects of the operation of exclusive rights. They can be used in unacceptable ways, turning such use into an abuse (of rights). In chapter 21 Miłosz Malaga looks at the impact of the introduction of European Patents with unitary effect on the operation of competition law in the European Union and pays particular attention, not only to the impact of the translation regime, but also to the potential redefinition of the geographical market.

A patent system can only be justified if it supports and encourages innovation. That raises the intriguing question of when a patent system is fit for innovation. Therefore, against the background that the key objective of patent regulation is to encourage investments in innovation in an optimal and functional manner, in chapters 22 and 23 Thomas Jaeger and Johannes Lukan make the argument that a balance must be struck between two main interests in order to attain this goal: on the one hand, easy, fast, legally secure and inexpensive access to patent protection and to a solid substantive, territorial and temporal scope of patent protection will provide incentives for investment in R&D. On the other hand, access to patentable knowledge for follow-on research also needs to be ensured within a patent system. The first part of this bipartite contribution will therefore be dedicated to an analysis of the incentives and obstacles the UP legal framework provides in this respect. The second Jaeger and Lukan chapter deals with the second question and concludes with an overall assessment of whether the UP and its surrounding legal framework succeed in striking a fair balance between these two interests, ie a balance between protecting a patented 'senior' invention on the one hand and facilitating a 'junior' invention on the other.

The emergence of the European Patent with unitary effect has directed a lot of attention to the UPC and the idea of streamlining patent litigation in Europe. That should however not obscure the increasingly important role that is played by mediation in the patent arena. Guided by principles such as confidentiality, voluntariness and openness it is easy to see why certain types of conflict are better addressed in this way and away from the open courts and the conflictual approach and why certain parties prefer mediation. Licence agreements and SEP/FRAND disputes are obvious examples that come to mind. But international and complex disputes are maybe also better served by mediation, rather than risk potentially conflicting proceedings in national courts and/or the UPC. In chapter 24 Maximilian Haedicke examines the rise and potential of patent mediation in full detail.

If, however, litigation is the preferred option, the topic of litigation strategies surfaces immediately. In chapter 25 Alan Johnson looks at these strategies in the light of the additional options that the emergence of the UPC offers. The key idea is centralisation, but that also raises the stakes. Much more depends potentially on the outcome of a single case. There are forum shopping options within the UPC and these require careful consideration. And there is still a role for bifurcation, but is it an option worth considering? The transitional period comes with its own forum shopping problems, this time between the UPC and the national courts. In that context, but also in the relationship with the courts of third countries the potential for anti-suit injunctions also needs to be taken into account and it further adds to the creation of what looks at least for the initial period like a more uncertain world for European patent litigation.

The creation of the UPC as a single court system obviously required the contracting parties to take a view on the concept of bifurcation. The German approach on this point was often a topic for discussion, as it differed significantly from the approach in most other contracting states. In chapter 26 Matthias Lamping & Christoph Rademacher therefore look in depth at bifurcation in the context of litigation strategies. The chapter first of all analyses the German approach in depth and then goes into the place and role of bifurcation in the new UPC approach. The balance between the divisions of the court of first instance on the one hand and the central division on the other hand takes centre stage in this debate and it will be interesting to see how this unfolds over the coming years.

Leaving litigation strategies to one side, the creation of the UPC and European Patents with unitary effect adds another layer of complexity. Indeed, national and (traditional) European Patents remain an option and will still be the preferred option in a number of scenarios. That complexity of the European patent framework at large is expressed through various forms of fragmentation. This fragmentation occurs within the applicable legal rules, but also will be seen along territorial and institutional lines and moreover within that of markets in Europe. The key issue here is the co-existence between the EPC and its (traditional) European Patents on the one hand and European Patents with unitary effect of the other hand. In chapter 27 Mark Mimler examines the rules in this respect and tries to clarify some of the complexity.

Co-existence issues arise in a sense also inside the added layer of the European Patent with unitary effect and the UPC. The latter is after all made up of many different divisions. There exists therefore a necessity of judicial dialogue and cooperation in the UPC. In chapter 28 Karen Walsh focusses mainly on post-grant matters, and particularly on the functioning of the UPC, and argues that the post-grant harmonisation of patent law in Europe, to the extent that this is possible and desirable, cannot rely solely on the EU unitary patent system. To assist with the development of a consistent system overall, communication between divisions within the UPC, and between the UPC and external institutions will be key. Judicial dialogue and cooperation, that is, the process of judges considering or discussing relevant decisions and interpretations of other courts, and taking a coordinated approach where possible, will be essential in achieving this goal.

In the arduous process that eventually led to the creation of the European Patent with unitary effect and the UPC the role of the Court of Justice of the European Union was often seen as a major stumbling block. In chapter 29 Tamar Khuchua therefore looks in detail at the role of the Court of Justice of the European Union in the area of patent law. She does so from a procedural point of view, as in the almost complete absence of substantive patent law at EU level the enforcement directive and its various measures takes centre stage. Preliminary measures, the reimbursement of legal costs and final injunctions will of course also remain important in the UPC era and that will in practice require a smooth and fruitful cooperation between the two courts.

Gene patents are a fascinating topic, but also one of considerable complexity. In chapter 30 Naomi Hawkins examines the concept of gene patents in depth and looks at the way the EPC and the national legal systems and courts have dealt with them. It is fair to say that a certain form of divergence in approach to key questions around gene patent eligibility and scope has opened up in recent years. The chapter then turns to the UPC and asks the question whether it may arguably provide scope for this divergence to be explored, and for some degree of consistency and coherence in approach to be developed.

Taking a small step back from the practical issues involving gene patents, it becomes clear rather easily that ethical issues remain important in the context of the patenting of biotechnological inventions in Europe. In chapter 31 Aisling McMahon explains how ethical considerations play a role in patent decision-making for biotechnological inventions in Europe and that is reflected in legislative instruments such as the biotech directive and an additional layer of complexity is added by the fact that multiple adjudicative bodies are involved in the interpretation of these ethical provisions across the EU, European Patent Organisation (EPOrg), and now the UPC contexts. The addition of the latter creates the need for a proper discussion all the more urgent, as it re-enforces the need for a single harmonised approach.

Not only ethical harmonisation may end up on the UPC's plate. The Court may also soon be asked to deal with the FRAND issue. In chapter 32 Gail Evans therefore examines on the basis of recent case law in the UK and Germany whether and how the UPC may determine whether a SEP holder, who has undertaken to grant licences on FRAND terms, is entitled to a prohibitory injunction. The analysis shows that despite the courts having some discretion in the grant of an injunction, once there is a finding of patent infringement, the court is unlikely to refuse a FRAND injunction.

We hope that our team of contributors has been able to offer a comprehensive and in depth analysis of patent law in Europe at this historical point in its development. The future will of course tell us if all of this was worth the decades of waiting and whether the European patent system will really emerge in far better shape from all of this.

Part 1: The existing system: the EPC

Jean-Christophe Galloux

1 The role of EPO Boards of Appeal in shaping of patent law in Europe

Patent law is the only Industrial Property (IP) right which is not subject to either the harmonization of EU's substantive law, or to a unitary title valid throughout its territory, and offering its holder the same scope in each of the Member States[1]. The Unitary Patent established by Regulations n° 1257/2012 and 1260/2012 of 17 December 2012[2], and the Unified Patent Court Agreement (UCPA) of February 2013 will be implemented on June 1, 2023. Importantly, it only concerns 17 of the 27 EU country members among which three are not part to the agreement. This system allows European patents—an issue which escapes EU law—to persist. It thus furthers the complex relationships between these two legal orders. Born outside of the European Community, European patent law is not integrated to the EU's legal order, that is a set of standards which form a legal order distinct from the national legal orders. EU law's relationship to the latter is marked by three principles: autonomy without separation, primacy and direct effect. This is not the case of European patent law, which can also be considered as a specific legal order in the sense given to it by Santi Romano[3]: it is the set of rules and norms that govern a given place and time.

Indeed, European Patent Law is a non-state legal order, stemming from international law, endowed with its own rules based on the European Patent Convention (EPC). It has its own governance and jurisdictions, its own Board of Directors which enacts implementing regulations, a President who takes administrative and financial measures, as well as produces its own law through jurisdictional bodies' case law. This unique architecture explains the role (2) and the limits of the EPO Boards of Appeal in shaping Patent Law in Europe[4] (3). But let us start with a short reminder of theses bodies and of their characters.

---

[1] See: Hans Ullrich, Harmonizing patent law: The untamable Union Patent, in Harmonization of European IP Law: from European rules to Belgian law and practice, Contributions in honor of Frank Gotzen, Bruylant-Larcier, 2012 p. 245; Winfried Tilman, Harmonization invalidity and scope-of-protection practice of national courts of EPC Member States, E.I.P.R. 2006, 28(3), 169–173; Legislative and judicial powers in Europe – how far is harmonization of patent law and practice possible and desirable? E.I.P.R. 1988, 10(5), 138–142.
[2] OG 31 December 2012 n° L. 361 p. 1 à 8.
[3] Santi Romano, The Legal Order, Routledge 2018, p. 2 et sq.
[4] Attempts to "shape" Patent law are quite common: Andrei Iancu, The role of the courts in shaping patent law & policy, Georgetown Law Technology Review, 2019, Vol. 3, 526.; Chris Murphy, Supreme Court Isn't Done Re-Shaping Patent Law, InformationWeek 4 may 2007; Christophe Geiger and Elena Izyumen-

---

Jean-Christophe Galloux, is professor at Sorbonne-Assas Law School.

https://doi.org/10.1515/9783110781687-001

1.1 Boards of Appeal's characters

The original intention of the 1974 Munich Diplomatic Conference was to set up a real European appeal body, and therefore to separate it administratively from the rest of the EPO. For 40 years, cost and other factors dictated that the Boards of Appeal was be housed in the EPO headquarters in Munich; since November 2017 it is no longer the case. The Boards of Appeal constitute the judicial body of the EPO and are competent to carry out a substantive review of the decisions of the first instance departments within the scope of an appealing party's request.

The Boards of Appeal (BoA) are the first and final judicial instance in the procedures before the European Patent Office. They are independent of the Office in their decisions and are bound only by the EPC. The Boards of Appeal provide an independent review of decisions taken by the Receiving Section, Examining Divisions, Opposition Divisions and the Legal Division of the EPO. In this role, the Boards of Appeal strives to apply their procedures in a consistent and predictable manner and maintain consistency in their jurisprudence, The Boards of Appeal consist of: the Enlarged Board of Appeal, the Technical Boards of Appeal, the Legal Board of Appeal, and the Disciplinary Board of Appeal. The role of the later lays beyond of the scope of our study: The Disciplinary Board of Appeal decides on appeals in cases relating to the European qualifying examination (EQE) for professional representatives before the EPO and in cases concerning breaches by professional representatives of their Rules of Professional Conduct. It is composed of two legally qualified members of the BoA, one European professional representative in EQE cases, and of three legally qualified members of the BoA and two European professional representatives in disciplinary cases.

The 28 technical Boards of Appeal, in a composition of two technically qualified members and one legally qualified member, hear appeals from decisions concerning the refusal of a patent application or the grant, limitation or revocation of a European patent, i.e. decisions of the Examining Divisions in the context of ex-parte proceedings (one party involved) or decisions of the Opposition Divisions in the context of inter-partes proceedings (two or more parties involved in contentious proceedings). The EPC system with technically and legally qualified judges are of equal status, is well suited to deciding patent issues, involving as these do both technical and legal matters. This system has been partly adopted by the UCPA. Among the BoA, work is allocated according to the International Patent Classification.

The Legal Board, with three legally qualified members, hears appeals against decisions of the namely Receiving Sections: the Opposition Divisions; the Legal Division and in rare cases, the formalities section of the Examining Divisions. The Board is principally

---

ko, Shaping intellectual property rights through human rights adjudication: the example of the European court of human rights, Mitchel Hamline Law review, vol. 46 n° 3 (2020).

concerned with deciding whether the complex procedural requirements of the EPC have been fulfilled.

The decisions of the Boards of Appeal are final with a binding effect on the refusal or maintenance of a European patent, unless they become subject to a review by the Enlarged Board of Appeal on the ground that a fundamental procedural defect has occurred or that a criminal act may have had an impact on the decision[5].

BoA exercise independent and final appellate jurisdiction and since there is no further mechanism for challenging their judgments by way of appeal (national actions or claims for revocation of European Patents are not appeals from the Board's decisions to grant them) it is essential to the credibility of their jurisdiction that the members of the Boards should be independent of the first instances of the Office. EPC does provide a detailed and clear-cut framework of independence for the judges serving on the BoA and consequently for the BoA themselves as judicial organisations[6]. This independence mirrors that enjoyed by other judges and courts in the Contracting States[7]. The NoA have the status of an internationally recognised judicial authority, even if they are integrated in the organisational structure of the EPO.

The Enlarged Board of Appeal (EBA) decides important questions of law referred to it either by a BoA or by the President of the EPO. Its decisions are key to ensuring the uniform application of the EPC, thereby promoting legal harmonization and certainty which are vital for the European Patent system. EBA consists of five legally and two technically qualified judges, reflecting the predominantly legal nature of the questions they have to decide. One of the legally qualified judges acts as the Chairman, and at least four of its members are drawn from judges who took no part in the proceedings of the BoA from which the point of law to be decided had originated. The proceedings of the EBA are not appeals as such from decisions handed down by the BoA: their purpose is to settle points of law on which a BoA requires definitive guidance, or a point of law on which at least two BoA have given different decisions[8]. The role of the EBA is increasingly important for harmonization and certainty of the law under the EPC.

---

5 Petition for review according to Art. 112a EPC.
6 E. Waage, L'application de principes généraux de procédure en droit européen des brevets, preface. D. Stauder, LITEC/CEIPI, 2000.
7 The key functions of appointment (Article 11(3) EPC), dismissal (Article 23(1) EPC) and discipline (Article 11(4) EPC) of Board members lie in the final jurisdiction of the Administrative Council itself – the ultimate authority on the European Patent Organization. It is also expressly provided by the Convention that members of the BoA may not belong to any EPO departments of first instance (Article 23(2) EPC). Furthermore, their independence of judicial operation is expressly safeguarded in Article 23(3) EPC, which provides that they must, in their decisions, comply only with the EPC, and shall not be bound by any instructions.
8 Article 112(1)(b) EPC.

BoA and BoA has been recognized as a "Tribunal" according to the definition laid down by the European Court of Human Rights[9] by this latter[10] and some national courts[11]. Consequently, in its decision R 8/13 of 20 March 2015 the Enlarged Board of Appeal stated that it was established case law of the Enlarged Board (R 2/14 of 17 February 2015: and of the boards of appeal) that the EPC, must be applied in a way which supports the fundamental principles of Art. 6(1) ECHR[12].

1.2 BoA's role

BoA and the EBA not only construe and apply the strict letter of the EPC, but also interpret and adapt its spirit and intent to the ever-changing legal, especially technical circumstances. Accordingly, a decision of the EBA on a point of law is open to reasoned challenge during a subsequent appeal to a BoA on the self-same point of law. For example , this can be done on the basis that fresh legal or technical developments make it desirable in the public interest to have the point reconsidered. This mechanism of legal flexibility and adaptability is more important in the European Patent System than in national patent systems because the latter can be readily changed by amending national legislation, while in practice the substantive provisions of the EPC are immutable (except if case of revision of the Convention; the last and unique one occurred in 2000).

1.2.1 BoA's ways in shaping European patent law

In the shaping patent law in Europe, this legal flexibility and adaptability confer to the BoA case law first great advantage over national case law. Several other factors may also explain this phenomenon: the fact that the EPC provisions are mirrored by national patent laws in the contracting states, the quantitative importance of these case law and, their actuality and the large diffusion of these case law throughout Europe and beyond. Besides, BoA case law feeds the Guidelines for Examination in the European Patent Office. Over 42 years of existence (1980–2022) the Boards of Appeal have developed a substantial body of case law. During this time, they have dealt with more than 55 000 cases and issued over 41 000 decisions. In the same period, the Enlarged Board of Appeal has handed down more than 100 decisions and opinions under Article 112 EPC, in order to

---

9 See: Campbell and Fell v. the United Kingdom (28 June 1984, No 7819/77, paragraph 76): and: ECHR, Rolf Gustafson v. Sweden, 1 July 1997, No. 23196/94, paragraph 45.
10 ECHR, British-American Tobacco Company Ltd c. Pays-Bas – 19589/92, 2 nov. 1995.
11 House of Lords' decision of 26 October 1995 in Merrel Dow v. Norton, [1996] R.P.C. 76, and to the decision of the United Kingdom High Court of Justice dated 20 December 1996, Lenzing AG's European Patent (UK), [1997] R.P.C., 245.
12 G 1/05, OJ 2007, 362, point 22 of the Reasons; G 2/08 of 15 June 2009, point 3.3 of the Reasons.

clarify legal points of fundamental importance and ensure a uniform application of the law. According to the BoA's annual report (2022), in 2021, the Boards settled 2938 cases with action, which constitutes a 11%.1% increase over 2020 (but this figure is comparable to the years before the Pandemia) 7131 pending cases). 38,4% of these almost 3000 yearly decisions come from examination procedures (ex parte). Opposition procedures (inter partes) count for 61,6%.

This mass of decisions is unparalleled in the world and, of course, in the contracting states of the EPC. Delivered by highly specialized jurisdictions, it is an incomparable source for all patent law specialists, counsel, lawyers and judges. It is all the more remarkable in that it obviously covers all technical areas, and it makes it possible to follow the evolution of legal solutions over a significant period of time (forty years).

Unlike court case law, the case law of the Boards of Appeal intervenes fairly quickly upon the emergence of new techniques likely to challenge patent law. This is because the litigation experienced by BoAs arises from the rejection of a patent application or as soon as it is granted, in the event of an opposition. In this sense, the case law of the BoAs unquestionably plays a pioneering role likely to inspire national case law. This was the case in the field of biotechnology with the first patents on animal chimeras[13], stem cells[14], or in that of artificial intelligence[15]. In other terms, in the process of producing legal norms (to the extent that we may consider that case law is a legal norm), BoA' case law comes first and it is carefully watched by the patent community and beyond.

The frequent intervention of NGOs or lobbies in opposition procedures before the EPO aiming to challenge the patentability of inventions which they do not consider legitimate, further illustrates the central role played by BoAs in the development of the patent law in Europe[16].

Influence needs communication. BoA's case law must be known by all practitioners. The decisions of the BoA are readily accessible. Before the development of digital means, the most important of the EPO's decisions were published in the three official languages of the EPC in its Official Journal. In addition, a systematic summary of the case law of the BoA appeared annually. EPO edits the "Case Law of the Boards of Appeal" which is the Bible to the specialists: its 10th edition of July 2022 is worth 2000 pages.

By comparison, case law of the national courts is less accessible. The Official Journal of the EPO published on the past a very limited volume of decisions of national courts in the three languages; it is no longer the case as most national case law are accessible through private data bases, but at high costs and without translation.

---

[13] *Harvard/Onco-Mouse* Dec. T 19/90 [1991] EPOR 525.
[14] Decision G 2/06, 25 November 2008 of the Enlarged Board of Appeal.
[15] In cases J 8/20 and J 9/20 (21 December 2021) the Legal Board of Appeal confirmed the decisions to refuse the applications in which an artificial intelligence system was designated as inventor.
[16] For ex: Dec. T 0356/93, 21 feb. 1995, Plant Genetic System, for the patentability of plant GMO's (Greenpeace); patent No. 2430454 for a method of selecting embryos for implantation using the results of time-lapse microscopy:

Shaping patent law consists also -to some extent- in shaping national judges in charge of patent litigation. Cooperation between national judges and members of the BoA is a way also to promote EPO's work but also legal analysis[17]. Two major initiatives have been planned by the EPO to this end. To avoid "divergent outcomes" in the various jurisdictions of the EPC contracting states and "to ensure a uniform interpretation of European patent law" EPO decided to establish the biennial European Patent Judges Symposium as an opportunity for judges specialized in patent law and patent litigation to come together and exchange their views on patent law topics. The first Patent Judges' Symposium was held in Munich in 1982.

Besides, the EPO offers internships at its Boards of Appeal for national judges of the contracting states to the European Patent Convention (EPC) with the objectives to promote of equal access to training opportunities in the field of European patent law and practice across all current and future EPC contracting states. In addition, national patent judges may be appointed as members of BoA or even the EBA for one or more terms, before turning back to their original jurisdiction. For instance, Carl Josefsson became the first President of the Boards of Appeal on 1 March 2017. He was used to belong to the Swedish judiciary.

The last means to shape European patent law is the systematic reference to BoA and EBA's case law in the EPO's Guidelines for Examination[18]. Guidelines provide guidance in respect of the practice in proceedings before the EPO in accordance with the EPC and its Implementing Regulations. They are addressed primarily to examiners and formalities officers of the EPO. They are also intended to serve the parties to the proceedings and patent practitioners as a basis for illustrating the law and practice in proceedings before the EPO. They do not constitute legal provisions: the authority on practice in the EPO refers firstly to the EPC itself including the Implementing Regulations, but secondly to the interpretation put upon the EPC by the boards of appeal and the Enlarged Board of Appeal. Where decisions or an opinion of the Enlarged Board of Appeal or decisions of the Legal Board of Appeal or technical boards of appeal are referred to, this is to inform the reader that the practice described has been adopted to take account of the decision or opinion referred to. In case of diverging decisions of theBoA, EPO examiners and formalities officers will, as a rule, follow the common practice as described in the Guidelines, which applies until further notice. By principle, the Guidelines reflect only those decisions of the BoA incorporated into the EPO's general practice due to their general procedural significance; they do not take into account any deviating decisions taken in the individual case, given that the binding effect referred to in Art. 111(2) EPC applies to that specific case only. Therefore, integration of BoA and EBA's case law in the Guidelines of Examination before the EPO constitutes the most powerful instrument for shap-

---

[17] J. Brinkhof, The desirability, necessity and feasibility of co-operation between courts in the field of European Law, E.I.P.R. 1997, 19(5), 226–229.

[18] Pursuant to Article 10(2) EPC, the Guidelines for Examination have been amended by decision of 16 december 2021 (OJ EPO 2022, A10), the new Guidelines apply as from 1 March 2022.

ing patent law in Europe. In addition, national courts often refer to these guidelines to justify their decision, even if they do not rely on them as a direct source of law[19].

1.2.2 BoA's real influence on contracting states jurisdictions

After having analyzed the ways BoA and EBA may shape European patent law, we have to measure this influence on contracting states case law and practice. As a preamble, two elements deserve to be recalled. First, because of the ratification of the EPC by the signatory states, national patent laws present a high degree of harmonization, at least regarding the conditions of patentability. Then, most of the signatory states directly apply the provisions of the EPC to national part of European patents. Although differences between national legislation and the EPC are not excluded in this respect by art. 2(2) EPC 1973 or Art. 66 EPC 1973.

The influence of BoA and EBA case law in national case law is clearly expressed by the reference to it in national decisions, especially when they share their reasoning and solution.

Global alignment on BoA case law or previous decision is exceptional and when punctually adopted, it is linked with a set of parallel national judgments for the same case: for an example the Swiss Federal Patent Court[20], noting that parallel proceedings on this case had already been brought before an EPO board of appeal and before Germany's Federal Patent Court, observed that any related judgments by foreign courts should be taken into account, in the interests of harmonization within Europe.

The general impression given by the comparison of European case law and the decisions of EPO departments is both an overall convergence which is expressed by the quasi-identity of the provisions to be interpreted, many nuances and a few differences[21]. These latter may be considered as limits to the shaping of European Patent law by BoA and EBA case law.

Convergence comprises all range of the pre-granting legal questions[22]. Exceptions to patentability: Business methods[23]; surgical methods[24] for example. Novelty: the judg-

---

19 For ex.: House of Lords of 14 October 2004 – Sabaf SpA v MFI Furniture Centres Ltd et al. [2004] UKHL 45 Cour d'appel de Paris, Pôle 5 – chambre 1, 21 mai 2019, n° 18/19669; Mons Commercial Court of 23 October 2014 (14/5716) – Oliver Funderingstechnieken v Votquenne Foundations.
20 German Federal Patent Court, 7 October 2015 (O2013_006).
21 F. Pollaud-Dulian, La brevetabilité des inventions: étude comparative de la jurisprudence France-OEB, IRPI/LITEC 1997.
22 See: H. Ullrich, Standards of Patentability for European Inventions, IIC Studies 1980.
23 German Federal Patents Court of 10 February 2005 (17 W (pat) 46/02), with reference to T 258/03, OJ EPO 2004, 575.
24 Federal Court of Justice of 31 August 2010 (X ZB 9/09) The Court shared the view taken by the EBA in G 1/07 that Art. 53(c) EPC precluded the patenting of surgical methods but not the patenting of processes which might be conducted in connection with such a method.

ment by the German Federal Supreme Court dated 16 December 2008 in the olanzapine case, the German concept of novelty had been brought into line with the standard applied by the EPO; the Norwegian Board of Appeal of the Patent Office of 7 January 2010[25] abandoned the old concept of novelty and adhered to the EPO standard; Barcelona Court of Appeal (Section 15 of the Barcelona Court of Appeal in its decision of 18 October 2007 held that selection patent was novel and did not depart from the general criteria on novelty developed by the EPO boards of appeal[26]; in its judgment of 10 June 2016, the Federal Patent Court[27] novelty aligned on EPO board of appeal case law[28] holding that technical information sent to a client would not normally be considered secret; the Swiss Federal Court of 28 February 2007[29] stated that the manufacture of a known substance in an especially pure form was patentable only exceptionally, if conventional purification methods did not enable the skilled person to manufacture the substance with the degree of purity claimed[30]. Inventive step[31], with the choice of the closest prior art by Federal Patent Court, 27 May 2015[32] which ruled that inventive step could be acknowledged only if it held good against all the documents cited as potentially being the closest prior art[33]. Clarity of the claims: the Federal Court of Justice, 27 October 2015[34] refers to the Enlarged Board of Appeal decision G 3/14, or the control of amendments to claims: UK Patents Court, 22 September 2014[35]. Priority: the concept of "same invention": Austrian Supreme Patent and Trademark Chamber of 27 June 2007[36] and the Paris District Court, 15 January 2016[37] referred to the relevant jurisprudence of the EPO boards of appeal and concluded that the scope of the right to priority extended to the same invention; transfer of priority rights: Patents Court of 23 June 2010[38], held that even if the agreement was not effective to convey the legal title to the invention, it was effective to transfer the entire beneficial interest in it.

Convergence does not exclude nuances. Stating that here was no basis in the EPC for basing the assessment on the "closest" prior art alone, the London Court of Appeal in its

---

25 Case no. 7886, Laminaria hyperborea.
26 Audiencia Provincial, appeal no. 116/2007 – LEK Pharmaceuticals v Warner-Lambert Company.
27 O2012_043.
28 T 173/83, T 958/91 and T 602/91.
29 4C.403/2005, Citalopram.
30 T 990/96, OJ EPO 1998, 489.
31 See: J. Bochnovic, The Inventive Step, IIC Studies vol. 5, 1982; L'activité inventive (de la loi de 1968 à la JUB, un demi-siècle d'évaluation de l'activité inventive en France et en Europe, Galloux (Dir.), IRPI 2019.
32 O2013_11.
33 Décision T 967/97.
34 X ZR 11/13.
35 CompactGTL v Velocys plc & Ors [2014] EWHC 2951 (Pat).
36 Op 7/06.
37 13/17432, Time Sport v Decathlon.
38 KCI Licensing Inc et al. v Smith & Nephew plc et al. [2010] EWHC 1487 (Pat) Referring to decision J 19/87 of the Legal Board of Appeal.

judgment of 13 October 2016[39] and the Federal Court of Justice of 18 June 2009[40] decided that prior art could not always be taken as the sole basis for deciding whether patented subject-matter was obvious. Rather, the choice of starting point (or starting points) had to be specially justified, the basis generally being the skilled person's efforts to find a better or even simply different solution to a particular problem than that existing in the prior art.

The Problem-Solution approach, methodology privileged by the EPO for evaluating inventive step, still raises some doubts among national courts. The UK Supreme Court[41] stated that there was no single method, but that one must be followed which would ensure that the evaluation considered the decisive factors. On the same line, Paris District Court[42] noted that Art. 56 EPC did not prescribe the problem-solution approach, in which the first step was to identify the prior art closest to the contested patent, as the method of ascertaining whether the patent involved an inventive step.

Sometimes, these nuances or doubts are due to the rapid -and then not always coherent- evolution of the BoA case law. In its decision of 12 October 2007[43] the UK Patents Court Judge Warren did not feel able to deviate from the Bristol-Myers decision (precedent on Swiss claims admissibility) as this decision considered itself whether to deviate from its previous approach given the evolving case law at the EPO.

Beyond, there are limits to the shaping of European Patent law by BoA and EBA case law.

1.3 BoA's limits in shaping of patent law in Europe

These limits lie in differences with national patent court case law and sometimes, with legal texts, national legislation, or European Union law. There are inherent to the European patent law system, and they might be difficult to overcome.

1.3.1 Limits inherent to the European law system

The limits to the "shaping power" of the BoA's case law come, firstly from the national case law: some national case law diverge form the BoA's case law and sometimes maintain their position.

---

[39] Warner-Lambert Company LLC v Generics (UK) Ltd (t/a Mylan) & Ors [2016] EWCA Civ 1006.
[40] Xa ZR 138/05.
[41] 14 April 2015 (182/2015) – Aventis Pharma SA, May & Baker Ltd & Sanofi Aventis SA v Hospira Productos Farmacéuticos y Hospitalities.
[42] 21 November 2014 (10/14073) – Ethypharm v AstraZeneca AB & Cipla Ltd.
[43] Teva Pharmaceutical Industries Ltd & Teva UK Ltd v Merrell Pharmaceuticals Inc, Aventis Inc & Sepracor [2007] EWHC 2276 (Ch).

Firstly, BoA case law evolves and and there is no binding precedents within the EPO's judicial system. In its decision R 0014/11[44], the Enlarged Board stated that, like any other decisions of boards of appeal, its decisions in petition for review cases do not have the legal nature of creating a precedent in the sense that it would have to show in which respect a later decision differs from an earlier one for that latter decision to be legally justified. Furthermore, the EBA, in G 003/19[45] stated that a particular interpretation which has been given to a legal provision can never be taken as carved in stone, because the meaning of the provision may change or evolve over time. This aspect is intrinsic to the ongoing development of the law by way of judicial decision-making. In general, the bar for overturning long established case law and practice should be a high one because of the disruptive effects a change may have; the weight of habit can lead BoAs, unsatisfactorily, to justify their decision by this circumstance alone rather than carrying out a more in-depth legal analysis, as the CRISPR-Broad Institute case has unfortunately shown[46]. We must admit that an administrative organization such as the EPO (even its judicial emanations) is keener to see the continuation of long-standing based practices as a major aspect of legal certainty, and to wait sign of change coming from outside, than a judicial body. This consideration reinforces and justifies the need for a dialogue between judges.

Secondly proceedings before the boards are independent and decisions of national courts are not binding in law[47]. Before the boards of appeal, questions of patentability are decided solely in accordance with the EPC. As regards decisions made in contracting states, these are not to be cited as if they were binding upon the boards of appeal, and claims should not be refused because their patentability cannot be upheld under the jurisdiction of one member state[48]. Even if national case law does not bind EPO's judicial system, these case laws are carefully watched and remain a source of inspiration for BoA and the EBA of the highest national courts and when the legal question at stake is controversial or as no precedent in EPO's case law. The same apply to the European Court of Justice (ECJ): as an international organization independent of state authorities and courts, EPO is not bound by the case law of national courts when interpreting the foreign law to be applied, and the case law of the ECJ but, if aware of such case law, it should nevertheless consider and evaluate it in coming to its decision.

Thirdly, by principle the established case law of the EPO boards of appeal, it was not binding upon the national courts, for the same reasons as discussed below[49]. Computer

---

44 5 July 2012, Objection under Rule 106 EPC/Celanese International.
45 14 May 2020, Tomato and Brocoli, OJ 2020, A119.
46 Dec. T 0844/18 of 16 January 2020.
47 See Dec. R 21/09, and Board's decisions: T 1904/12, T 885/02, T 202/13, T 231/13, T 488/16.
48 Dec. T. 0452/91 of 5 July 1995.
49 See for ex.: Paris District Court, 21 November 2014 (10/14073) – Ethypharm v AstraZeneca AB & Cipla Ltd.

implemented inventions and in the field of biology are usually technical fields where conflicts may happen between EPO's and national's case law.

The resistance of UK Courts against the evolution of the BoA's case law applied to Computer implemented inventions perfectly illustrates this independence between EPO and national jurisdiction. The UK Court of Appeal of 27 October 2006[50] the case law of the boards of appeal of the EPO and national courts in other European countries but found the decisions of the boards of appeal mutually contradictory, revealing at least four different approaches. The Court of Appeal considered a referral of this point of law by the President of the EPO to the Enlarged Board of Appeal to be desirable and even formulated possible referral questions. What was done by the President of the EPO (a British citizen)[51] when ulterior decisions pushed to that end[52].

Patentability of the dosage and formulation patents is another example. In its decision of 19 December 2006, the Federal Court of Justice[53], in contrast to EPO case law, left open whether a patent claim including such a recommendation was non-patentable in its entirety. Paris Court of Appeal[54] went further and revoked the French part of an EP Patent comprising three claims directed to low-dosage oral administration of a drug.

The question of procedural stays, when national proceedings and opposition proceeding are pending, is also questionable. According to BoA's case law[55] the question when proceedings became pending is to be assessed under the (national) procedural law of the state in question. The Legal Board further pointed out that, in the interests of a uniform European standard of interpretation, recourse could be had to the ECJ's case law on Art. 21 of the Brussels Convention, which not only matched Article 8 of the Protocol on Recognition.

To conclude, besides the necessary harmonization and legal security for which the BoA's case law plays a major role, Patent Offices, requires counterbalancing courts (or Court)[56] and it is questionable that BoAs and EBA replace this judicial function. It has to do with the culture of the members of these boards: "their culture as 'examiners' must be reconsidered in the light of judicial requirements. It may be difficult for the Boards of Appeal being able to re-engineer themselves in this light, simply owing to the force of

---

50 Aerotel Ltd v Telco Holdings/Re Macrossan's Application [2006] EWCA Civ 1371.
51 Dec. G 003/08, 12 May 2010, OJ EPO 2011, 10.
52 Court of Appeal of 8 October 2008 – Symbian Ltd v Comptroller General of Patents [2008] EWCA Civ 1066 the Court of Appeal found that recent decisions of the boards of appeal appeared to have adopted an analysis which appeared substantially more restrictive of the exclusion (T 931/95, T 258/03 and T 424/03). These decisions were rejected.
53 X ZR 236/01 – Carvedilol II.
54 TGI Paris, 3ème ch., 1ère sect., 28 September 2010, Actavis Group, Alfred E. Tiefenbacher GmbH c. Merck Sharp & Dohme Corp.
55 Dec. J. 0014/19 of 19 April 2021.
56 See: Philip Leith, Revision of the EPC, the Community Patent Regulation and "European technical judges" E.I.P.R. 2001, 23(5), 250–254.

the engineering/examining culture which dominates their thinking"[57], and more, with the "public interest" in the patent system. That is, that if there is a monopoly, then the public may have an interest in its breadth and operation. As is had been said of the way US Supreme Court shaped US patent law: "The court is realizing it's not just about the patents, it's about how people work"[58]. National courts and EPO's judicial bodies may not always judge the same way: the latter are some distance removed from litigation and the pressure on judges to decide in a 'just' manner. There must be a tension between individual economic needs and "public good": this is the very nature of National courts (or UPC) to carry out this balance.

1.3.2 Dialog of judges: a necessity

Limits to the BoA "shaping power" toward European patent law lie also in legal texts. Obviously, BoA case law is limited to the pre granting phase, and essentially to conditions for patentability. Rules related to exploitation and defense of the patent rights are out of the reach of this case law because outside of the EPC's scope. However, one question is evoked by EPC in relation with the scope of rights: the Protocol of interpretation of article 69 (which is an integral part of the EPC). This provision links the scope of protection conferred by a patent to its claims. It clarifies that courts should interpret the claims adopting an approach that combines a fair protection for the patentee with a reasonable degree of certainty for third parties. In this perspective, the claims should not be interpreted strictly, nor should they be treated as mere guidelines. In the absence of any case law from the EPO, National courts have taken different paths towards the application of Article 69 EPC. It's up to the UPC to build a coherent approach, seeking common grounds between the various national approaches and identifying appropriate solutions for areas of divergence[59] National and European legislations may be also shaped by the BoA's case law: European and national legislator may be tempted to endorse it or to refute it.

The question of the patentability of computer-implemented inventions is a good example of the relevance of European patent law for EU law[60]. The legal protection of computer-implemented inventions giving rise to major discrepancies between the case law of certain Member States and the bodies of the EPO due to differences in the interpretation of the exclusion from patentability, the European Commission has tried to harmo-

---

57 Ibid.
58 Chris Murphy, Supreme Court Isn't Done Re-Shaping Patent Law, InformationWeek 4 may 2007.
59 See: Pagenberg and Cornish, Interpretation of Patents in Europe, Applications of art. 69 EPC, Heymanns, 2006; Paul England, The scope of protection of patent claims in Europe and the UPC, *Journal of Intellectual Property Law & Practice*, Volume 11, Issue 9, September 2016, Pages 689–697.
60 See: Justine Pila, What patent law for the European Union? Lessons from the jurisprudence of the CJUE, in "Quel droit des brevets pour l'Union européenne?" CEIPI 2013, p. 247.

nize positions. The proposal for a directive on the patentability of computer-implemented inventions of February 20, 2002[61], aimed to secure this issue at Community level. The cornerstone of the initial proposal merely endorsed the EPO's jurisprudential advances[62]. The reluctance vis-à-vis this project led to the development of a modified proposal dated 24 May 2004. These adjustments did not disarm the opposition in principle to the text: the European parliament finally rejected the proposal in the vote on 6 July 2005. The Commission did not present a new proposal. As for the practice of the EPO, it has not been affected by these community upheavals: despite of national reluctance in the process of standardization, the case law of the EPO has largely unified the law of the countries of the Union.

Conversely, the relevance of EPO's case law to European and national legislations can take the form of opposition: the Union has been able to take measures to oppose EPO case law. In March 2015, the EBA decided that products derived from the use of essentially biological processes could be patentable even if the process used to obtain the product (selection and crossing of plants) was essentially biological and therefore not patentable[63]. On December 17, 2015, the European Parliament, moved by the situation created by this decision, adopted a resolution in which it asked the Commission to examine the patentability of products derived from essentially biological processes. It published an opinion on November 8, 2016, in which it condemns the EPA's position[64]. To counter EPA's questionable interpretation, several countries, including Germany and the United Kingdom, have decided to amend their patent laws to expressly exclude the patentability of plants obtained by an essentially biological process. On June 29, 2017, the Administrative Council of the EPO decided to align itself with the position of the Commission and the main countries of the Union on the interpretation of Article 53(b) EPC, by modifying the rules 27(b) and 28 EPC to exclude from patentability plants and animals obtained exclusively by an essentially biological process. The Guidelines for Examination have been adapted before the entry into force of the November 2017 edition, with this modified practice.

This alignment of EPC law with that of certain countries has been received to varying degrees. In a decision of 5 December 2018 no. T 1063/18, a Technical Board of Appeal of the EPO questioned the modification of Rule 28 by the Administrative Council based

---

61 COM (2002) 92 final, *JOCE* C 151 du 25 juin 2002.
62 It consisted in affirming that the innovations implemented work by a computer a priori fell within a technical field a sine qua non condition for the recognition of their quality of invention. It also reaffirmed the central role of the "technical contribution" criterion for the patentability of these inventions (Art. 4.2. of the draft), a rather obscure concept drawn from the Office's case law.
63 Decisions G 2/12 et G 2/13, JO OEB 2016, A27 et A28.; However, the patentability of these products comes into potential conflict with the legal protection granted to plant varieties under European Union plant variety law: Regulation (CE) no 2100/94 of 27 july 1994 (OG n° L 227 of 1rst september 1994, p. 1).
64 N° 2016/C 411/03: "According to the Commission, the intention of the European Union legislator when adopting Directive 98/44/EC was to exclude from patentability of products (plants/animals and parts of plants/animals) obtained by an essentially biological process".

on a simple opinion of the Committee European Union and not a legislative act of the Union as required by Article 33 of the EPC. On April 5, 2019, the EPA was seized of this new difficulty (case G 03/19): to what extent should European patent law align with Union law to offer applicants to the EPO the legal certainty to which they are entitled? A decisive issue for the dualism of the right of patents in Europe. In its decision of May 14, 2020, the EPA sacrificed its previous case law on the altar of relevance. It concludes that new Rule 28(2) calls for a "dynamic" interpretation of Article 53(b) EPC. By adopting this dynamic interpretation, the EPA abandoned its earlier interpretation of Article 53(b) EPC in decisions G 2/12 and G 2/13 of 2015. A tribute paid to harmonization but by the EPO's case law: a lesson to be remembered in the time where the "dialog of the judges"[65] is a necessity with the UPC next start…

---

65 Comp.: Vassilios Kondylis, The Dialogue of the Judges – National Courts and European Courts: Case Study, European Review of Public Law, 2012 / Vol. 24, No. 1, (83).

Heinz Goddar, Konstantin Werner

2 The interaction between the UPC, national courts, and the EPO Boards of Appeal

2.1 Introduction

Questions of territoriality and transnational use of inventions are of steadily growing importance in considerations concerning patent filing and enforcing strategies all over the world.[1] That is particularly true regarding the forthcoming Unitary Patent ("UP") and Unified Patent Court ("UPC") system[2] in Europe. Insofar, with the UPC probably starting its work already in June 2023[3] and a preceding "Sunrise Period" possibly starting already in March 2022, it might be not the worst time to revisit the questions connected to territoriality and transnational use of inventions, together with specific tactical advice on how a patent portfolio could be structured in the future.

2.2 Initial situation

A few facts, insofar, describing the present situation in Europe, might be useful.

2.2.1 Obtaining patent protection in Europe – the present system

Presently, there are two ways to obtain patent protection in European countries: Via the "national route" as well as via the European Patent Office ("EPO"). This applies to all member states of the European Patent Convention ("EPC"). They include all member states of the European Union ("EU") as well as additional countries, such as Nor-

---

[1] An example of the global importance of not only patent law, but intellectual property in general is e.g. the very current contribution *Grosse Ruse-Kahn/Metzger* (Eds.), Intellectual Property Beyond Borders, Cambridge University Press, 2022.
[2] The UP/UPC system or "European Patent Package" in the sense of this contribution consists of the Regulations (EU) 1257/2012 and 1260/2012 as well as the Agreement on a Unified Patent Court (UPCA).
[3] See the announced timeline on the official UPC-website, https://www.unified-patent-court.org/en/news/adjustment-timeline-start-sunrise-period-1-march-2023 (accessed 03.02.2023).

Heinz Goddar, is partner at BOEHMERT & BOEHMERT, honorary Professor for Intellectual Property at the University of Bremen and at the Munich Intellectual Property Law Center (MIPLC).
Konstantin Werner, is PhD candidate at Humboldt University Berlin.

way and Switzerland. The United Kingdom also remains a member of the EPC despite Brexit.[4]

As already mentioned above, the first possibility to obtain national patents in each country is, as it has "always" been, filing a national patent application at the respective national patent office, such as the German Patent and Trademark Office (GPTO) for Germany.[5] Such a filing can either be made by an independent patent application at the respective national patent office, either as a first filing or by claiming Paris Convention ("PC") priority[6], or by "deriving" a respective national patent application from a Patent Cooperation Treaty ("PCT") application by entering the respective national phase of the PCT-application[7]. In any case, the aforementioned procedure leads, after national treatment at the respective national patent office, to a national patent in the respective country. The territory of protection thereof is restricted to the country in and for which, resp., the respective patent has been granted.[8] For Switzerland and Liechtenstein there is just the specificity that regarding the "national route" these two countries are covered by one single "transnational" patent.[9]

As an alternative to filing national patent applications, the EPC-System set up the possibility to file a patent application centrally at the EPO with the designation of member countries of the EPC, essentially, as "countries of wish" wherein the patent applicant later on wishes to have patent protection.[10] Again, this filing can take place either directly, claiming Paris Convention (PC) priority (or not)[11], or out of a PCT application by entering the European Patent Regional Phase[12]. In any case, at the time of grant of such a "European patent application", which better should be called an "EPC application"[13] and often is referred to as "bundle patent application", *is not* a regional patent or the

---

4 For an overview regarding the impact of "Brexit" on the UP/UPC system, see e.g., *Leistner/Simon*, GRUR Int. 2017, 825 et seq.; *Jaeger*, IIC 2017, 254 et seq.
5 For a general overview regarding an application at the national (German) Patent Office: *Haedicke*, Patenrecht, 6th Edition 2022, p. 343 et seq; *Ann*, Patentrecht, 8th Edition 2022, p. 510 et seq.
6 *Haedicke*, Patenrecht, 6th Edition 2022, p. 95–96; *Ann*, Patentrecht, 8th Edition 2022, p. 538 et seq.
7 *Haedicke*, Patenrecht, 6th Edition 2022, p. 41–42; *Ann*, Patentrecht, 8th Edition 2022, p. 86–87; *Köllner*, PCT-Handbuch, 16th Edition 2022, Einleitung p. XVII et seq.
8 General regarding the principle of territoriality of a national patent application: *Haedicke*, Patentrecht, 6th Edition 2022, p. 35–37; *Ann*, Patentrecht, 8th Edition 2022, p. 84.
9 Treaty between the Swiss Confederation and the Principality of Liechtenstein on Patent Protection (Patent Treaty) of 22 December 1978. Below, it will be refrained from specifically mentioning Liechtenstein, rather consider Liechtenstein/Switzerland – for the purpose of this article – as *one* country.
10 For a general overview regarding an application at the EPO: *Haedicke*, Patenrecht, 6th Edition 2022, p. 354 et seq; *Ann*, Patentrecht, 8th Edition 2022, p. 510 et seq.
11 See *Moufang* in *Schulte*, Patentgesetz mit EPÜ, 11th Edition 2022, § 41 Paragraph 13 et seq.
12 *Landry* in *Haedicke/Timmann*, Handbuch des Patentrechts, 2nd Edition 2020, p. 363 et seq.
13 The reason is to differentiate: The less informed reader is confused by just saying "European patent application". "EPC", which refers to the "old"/existing bundle patent and UP, which refers to the new unitary patent are both are in a way "European patents". That's why one should precisely name the correct patent application.

like, which could be enforced centrally for all or some member countries of EPC results. It is rather a "bundle" of national patents, each of which covers a single territory, namely the territory of the respective member country of EPC which has been designated by the applicant/patentee.[14]

Both national patents obtained via the "national route" from national patent offices in Europe, and the "fragments" of the bundle patent, each of which creates a national patent in a designated country chosen by the applicant, are, and this point cannot be emphasised too often, national patents: The protection is restricted to the respective territory, for instance a German patent to Germany. All these national patents, whether obtained at national patent offices or as fragments of an EPC-based bundle patent, can essentially only be enforced in the respective country, for example in German courts for the national German patent, etc.

This current territorial restriction of the effect of the patents described above has been the main motivation for the efforts to create a European patent with unitary effect.[15]

2.2.2 Future UPs and the role of national courts vs. UPC

With the coming into force of the UP/UPC system, there will be a third way to obtain patent protection for European countries: The UP. The grant of a UP will be achieved by selecting, at the time of grant of a patent by the EPO a single UP, covering the respective countries which have joined the UP/UPC system[16]. Additionally, for countries that are EPC member states but not part of the UP/UPC system, for example the United Kingdom, Turkey or Switzerland, 'Classical' European Patent protection will still be required, with national parts of the bundle of patents treated in the same way as nation patents after grant.[17]

The new UP/UPC system applies, in principle, not only to new UPs but also to (existing) bundle patents. A characteristic of the new UP/UPC system is, however, the seven year long transitional period provided in Art. 83.1 UPCA: A patentee has the choice to opt-out of the new UP/UPC system with his existing bundle patents (and thereby exclude the UPC).[18] After an opt-out, the patentee has the option to withdraw his opt-out until the date of a pending national action (Art. 83.4 UPCA). The UPCA reserves the possibility of extending the transitional period for a further seven years (Art. 83.5 UPCA).

---

14 *Haedicke*, Patenrecht, 6th Edition 2022, p. 46–47.
15 See just Recital 7 of Regulation (EU) 1257/2012.
16 *Ann*, Patentrecht, 8th Edition 2022, p. 755.
17 For strategic consideration regarding the relation between a UP and/or national patents and which application to choose, see *Hüttermann*, Einheitspatent und Einheitliches Patentgericht, 1st Edition 2016, p. 48 et seq.
18 For further information regarding the opt-out, see *Hüttermann*, Einheitspatent und Einheitliches Patentgericht, 1st Edition 2016, p. 76 et. seq.

2.3 The interplay between national courts, UPC, and Boards of Appeal ("BoA") of EPO in future

At the time of grant at the EPO, the applicant has to make a decision as to whether to take a UP covering all member states participating in the UP or, alternatively, to use the 'Classical' route for obtaining a European Patent in those states by relying on a bundle patent covering certain EPC member countries. The applicant therefore will have to take into consideration the following facts.

Leaving aside whether or not the patentee chooses to validate the patent in with or without using the UP/UPC system, an opposition can be filed at against European Patents post-grant at the EPO, with the possibility of an appeal to the Boards of Appeals (BoAs) of the EPO.[19] This creates the possibility of "re-examination" of the decision to grant the patent both for UPs, and for 'Classical' European patents which will become a bundle of national patents post grant. Furthermore, in the case of UPs, it will be possible to launch a central attack with the aim of invalidating UPs, centrally at the UPC.[20]

Taken together this opens up two possible different ways to attack the validity of UPs centrally which will effect the validity of the patent in all countries covered by the UP. In addition to UPs, bundle patents not opted out of the UPC during the transitional period will be subject to both EPO opposition proceedings and invalidity proceedings centrally at the UPC.

In the future, it will be instructive to see whether the speed of the invalidation procedure against an UP at the Central Division of the UPC, with appeal to the appeal stage of the UPC[21] will lead to the result that the first decision on the validity of an UP will be made by a court, namely UPC[22], that does not fully exist yet and has no case law. As can be seen from the the Rules of procedure of the UPC, the aim is to finish an invalidation procedure in the first instance of the UPC within one year.[23]

Given that the speed of EPO opposition proceedings have been accelerated in recent years,[24] with the EPO aiming to complete a first instance opposition procedure within

---

19 The possibility to file an opposition against an UP at the EPO is obvious – because the UP is granted by the EPO. This is also to be read from Art. 33.8 and Art. 33.10 S. 1 UPCA.
20 See Art. 32.1 litt. f) UPCA.
21 See Art. 73 UPCA.
22 An argument therefore is Art. 33.8 UPCA which states explicitly that revocation actions and actions for declaration of invalidity can be brought to the UPC without the applicant having to file notice of opposition with the European Patent Office.
23 See the Rules of Procedure UPC, Preamble Nr. 7.
24 EPO Quality Report 2019, p. 26: *"By the end of 2019 95 % of all opposition cases were completed within 28.6 months."* If one looks at the corresponding timeline, one sees the improvement regarding the duration https://documents.epo.org/projects/babylon/eponet.nsf/0/626FCEF63B72E852C1258593002640F4/$FILE/quality_report_2019_en.pdf (accessed 03.02.2023). In 2020 with 74 % of the cases completed within 18 months, see the EPO Quality Report 2020, p. 37, https://documents.epo.org/projects/babylon/eponet.nsf/0/66A4055

about 15 months[25], it remains to be seen whether or not by the aforementioned double-way invalidation possibilities against UPs will lead to the UPC taking the "driver's seat" in invalidation procedures against UPs. This remains an unknown for the UPC, as is the possibly that the EPO may give deference to earlier decisions of the UPC concerning the validity of a certain bundle patent.[26]

The aforementioned situation may be a reason for applicants to decide not to opt out from the UP/UPC system but to file a divisional patent application immediately before patent grant of the respective EPC-based bundle patent at the EPO. Divisional patent applications contain all or parts of the subject matter of a previously filed patent application (parent application).[27] They are a common tool for obtaining patents with different scopes of protection for the same or a similar invention, which facilitates prosecution.[28] Practically, divisional patent applications are also often used to avoid that the examination procedure leads to a narrowly defined patent claim or a rejection.[29] Such a divisional patent application might be a viable strategy if a patent is not opted out of the UP/UPC, system or because the transitional period has come to an end or because the patent is granted after the coming into force of the UP/UPC system.

If a divisional patent application is filed, the first patent granted could be attacked by an unsolicited invalidation action at the UPC, but in the "divisional case" there would still be the chance to get essentially similar protection by bundle patents which later on could _not_ be attacked by invalidation action at the UPC. This is an interesting consequence, indeed, and is already now carefully observed particularly in case of "crown-jewels" in the portfolio of certain patentees.[30]

46212DDF4C12586FC00330A90/$FILE/quality_report_2020_en.pdf (accessed 03.02.2023). Nevertheless, the duration is still too long.
25 See the EPO on streamlined opposition proceedings in May 2016, https://www.epo.org/law-practice/legal-texts/official-journal/2016/05/a43.html? (accessed 03.02.2023).
26 Such a "watchdog" function of the UPC in relation to the EPO is desirable *Schovsbo/Riis/Salung Petersen*, The Unified Patent Court: Pros and Cons of Specialization – Is There a Light at the End of the Tunnel (Vision)?, International Review of Intellectual Property and Competition Law (Springer), 46 (3), 2015, p. 271 (272); *De Lange*, EU patent harmonization policy: reconsidering the consequences of the UPCA, Journal of Intellectual Property Law & Practice, 2021, Vol. 16, No. 10, p. 1078 (1081).
27 *Harhoff*, Patent Quality and Examination in Europe, American Economic Review Papers and Proceedings 2016, 106 (5), 193 et. seq., Footnote 1. The divisional patent application has the same filing and priority date as its parents application.
28 *Gleiter/Fischer* in BeckOK PatR, 26th Edition (15.10.2022), § 39 PatG, Paragraphs 11, 12.
29 *Harhoff*, Patent Quality and Examination in Europe, American Economic Review Papers and Proceedings 2016, 106 (5), 193 et. seq., Footnote 1.
30 The law firm of the author *Prof. Dr. Goddar* is bounded to, *Boehmert and Boehmert*, often advises patentees in this direction: https://www.boehmert.de/patentportfolio-auf-das-einheitspatent-vorbereiten/ (accessed 03.02.2023).

2.4 The best filing strategy in Europe in the future

Already today, the authors consider several recommendations concerning best filing and prosecution strategies in Europe to be essential.

First of all, it is recommended that applicants wishing to get patent protection in Europe might in future wish to categorize their inventions into categories "A"-highest priority, "B"- medium/normal priority; and "C"- cases of minor priority.

2.4.1 "Category A"

With regard to category "A", one should think of filing, in parallel to an EPC application, whether via the PCT or directly at the EPO, a patent application at a national patent office, particularly the GPTO, with the same priority and filing date.

At this point, the attention should be drawn to a special aspect regarding the future UPC system. National German patents will be in a position to co-exist with UPs or bundle patents which are not opted out.[31] This possibility is called "double protection". It can certainly be seen as a paradigm shift, because up to now, which means with regard to the bundle patents, there is a prohibition of double protection *de lege lata*.[32] That each member state may decide on its own now whether to allow a double protection is deduced from a contrary reading of Recitals 26 and Art. 4.2 of Regulation 1257/2012 and Art. 139.3 EPC.[33] The German legislator[34] has made use of this opportunity and regulated it in the new version of Art. II, § 8 (1) IntPatÜbkG[35] which will enter into force together with the UPCA. Accordingly, the prohibition of double protection in the future will only apply to bundle patents, which are opted-out of the new UPC-System. This is per se convincing, because opted-out bundle patents have the same territorial scope and are under the same jurisdiction as national patents– unlike future UPs and not opted-out bundle patents.

---

[31] Regarding the possibility of double protection in Germany, see *Goddar/Werner*, The lack of harmonization and consequently fragmentation in the patent field, in: The Unified Patent Court – Problems, Possible Improvements and Alternatives (Eds. *Strowel* et al.), expected publication: early 2023, Ledizioni (open access); *Makoski*, Die Einrede der doppelten Inanspruchnahme, Berlin 2021; *Zilly/Vollmer*, GRUR 2022, 1401 et seq.
[32] *Makoski*, Die Einrede der doppelten Inanspruchnahme, Berlin 2021, A. II. 1. and 2; Overview in the Brochure „National law relating to the EPC, https://documents.epo.org/projects/babylon/eponet.nsf/0/32A79B8E16750D76C12584D5005ABF91/$File/national_law_relating_to_the_epc_20th_edition_en.pdf, p. 344ff. (accessed 03.02.2023).
[33] *Makoski*, Die Einrede der doppelten Inanspruchnahme, Berlin 2021, p. 95ff.
[34] Regarding the legislative process https://dip.bundestag.de/vorgang/.../74552 (accessed 03.02.2023).
[35] The IntPatÜbkG is a national law regulating the consequences of international agreements at the national level.

With the introduction of double protection, Germany has opened the door for strategic considerations on how to benefit from the opportunity to apply for double protection.

However, if, as it is normally the case, the EPC application is in English language, the same English text could be used for filing a national German patent application at the GPTO, which would be accompanied, essentially, or supplemented shortly after filing, by a relatively cheap machine translation of the English text into German.

No request for examination would be filed at the GPTO at that time.[36] From the effective filing date for the German national patent application at the GPTO, very little cost will arise, for instance annuities start only in the 3rd effective year of the lifetime of the German patent application[37]. In the meantime, the search/examination procedure at the EPO, for the application co-pending there, would go forward. If at the time of grant of the application by the EPO, perhaps 3–4 years after the effective filing date at the EPO, the applicant is satisfied with the result of search/examination at EPO and is also satisfied by the then certainly available first "solid" information concerning effectiveness and practice of UPC, it might be a valid consideration not to go forward with the national German patent application. The applicant has the option to "hold" his national application and to wait until the end of the term during which a request for examination at GPTO still can be filed, i.e. seven years after effective filing date.[38] In the case described above, the applicant could simply withdraw or allow the national German patent application to become abandoned by not filing request for examination[39].

If, however, the experiences with either the examination/grant procedure at the EPO did not lead to a grant of a patent, which could be opted out or not, due to the satisfaction of the applicant, a request for examination for the co-pending German patent application can be filed at any time before the expiration of the aforementioned seven-year period. At that time, the original machine translation might best be replaced by a "fresh" human translation, with a wording which would be considered as useful by the applicant for patent grant of a national patent at the GPTO.

The advantage of obtaining a national German patent at the GPTO would be that such a patent "forever" will remain within the jurisdiction of the national courts of Germany, namely the patent dispute litigation courts (district courts) in the first instance, with appeal to the district appeal courts, and with final legal review to the German Federal Court of Justice (GFCJ) as the highest instance. The UPC would never play a role for such national German patents.

---

36 See § 44.2 German Patent Act.
37 See § 17 German Patent Act.
38 See again § 44.2 German Patent Act.
39 See § 58.3 German Patent Act.

2.4.2 "Category B"

As far as category "B" of inventions, as discussed above are concerned, it might be sufficient simply to file an EPC application as applicants have done in the past. At the time of grant of such a bundle of patent applications it should carefully be considered whether to opt out or not to opt out. Of course, after the transitional period of seven – or probably 14 years – comes to an end[40] – starting with the coming into force of the UPC, opted out bundle patents will be under the sole jurisdiction of the UPC like UPs. One possibility at that time that could be considered would be to file a divisional patent application just before the grant of the respective bundle patent. The divisional patent application would be treated as a separate patent application for the purpose of conversion to UP and/or an opt-out later on. In such a case, the UP could be taken for EU countries, and other selected countries could be covered by fragments of the bundle patent (the divisional patent application). However, where divisional patents are possible, the risks associated with central enforcement and/or revocation in the UPC may be spread by treating the divisional application differently for parents for the purpose of conversion to UPs and an eventual opt-out.

Similarly, at the time of grant of the divisional patent application, a decision will need to be taken about whether to opt out or not, with even the possibility to consider filing a further "secondary divisional", so that practically to the end of the 20 years term after effective filing date of the primary bundle patent application, the option would be kept open to obtain, if desired, a UP.

2.4.3 "Category C"

For category "C" it might be worth considering, instead of filing an application at the EPO, only applying for national patent applications, e.g., and particularly, in Germany. The reason is that, over the past few years, around 50–70 % of all patent litigation that has started in EU countries has been in Germany, including also the U.K.[41]. This largely is due to the fact that, by obtaining injunctive relief in Germany, nearly 25 % of the GDP of all EU countries are covered.[42] Consequently, a German patent litigation procedure

---

40 See Art. 83.5 UPCA.
41 Germany attracts between 50 and 70 % of all patent litigation activity in Europe, see *Harhoff*, Economic Cost-Benefit Analysis of a Unified and Integrated European Patent Litigation System, Final Report to the European Commission, 2009, p. 13; *Hüttermann*, Einheitspatent und Europäisches Patentgericht, 1st Edition 2016, p. 84f.
42 Germany's share of the EU's GDP was approx. 25 % in 2021, see https://de.statista.com/statistik/daten/studie/347262/umfrage/anteile-der-laender-am-bruttoinlandsprodukt-bip-in-eu-und-euro-zone/#:~:text=Deutschland%20als%20gr%C3%B6%C3%9Fte%20europ%C3%A4ische%20Volkswirtschaft,am%20Bruttoinlandsprodukt%20der%20Euro%2DZone. (accessed 03.02.2023).

based on a national German patent, with the threat of its enforcement is, usually, the basis for an EU-wide settlement of all and any patent disputes in Europe.[43] As has been stated previously, only in about 2 % of all patents litigated in Germany subsequently or simultaneously additional (parallel) patent litigation has been initiated in other EU countries.[44]

2.5 Conclusions

The foregoing explanation sets out clearly why even some big patent filers, such as in those in the semiconductor sector, have essentially never filed any EPC patent applications in the past, but rather have relied only German patent applications. Another reason is the huge differences in Patent Office fees. For the price of a single EPC bundle patent it is possible to cover all fees, attorneys' honorarium, etc., for about three German national patents.[45] The resulting portfolio, consisting only, in such cases, of German national patents, in settlement negotiations, cross-licensing discussions etc., would be of huge practical significance – and would apply to most applicants of bundle patents. In other words, the nationally obtained "isolated" German patent is as important and effective as if parallel patents in other European countries would also exist.[46]

In the future, various institutions will decide on infringement as well invalidation questions relating to patents in Europe. On the one hand, for bundle patents (and in general, for EPC-based patent applications, whether they lead to bundle patents or to UPs or to a mixture thereof), the opposition divisions and Boards of Appeals of the EPO will play an important role. Parallel to that, the UPC, after coming into force, will have a significant impact in its decision practice concerning validity questions of UPs, but later on, at the latest after the end of a transition period in which opted-out EPC applications still will be handled nationally, also regarding "normal" EPC bundle patents. All this will lead to the fact that two different institutions, namely EPO and its BoAs, on the one hand, and UPC on the other, will decide on not-opted-out, and later on all, including opted-out, "fragments" of bundle patents and their validity.

In the case of following the strategy discussed above for category "B", but also in case of category "C" to a certain extent, the practice and case law of Germany, the Feder-

---

[43] *Hüttermann*, Einheitspatent und Europäisches Patentgericht, 1st Edition 2016, p 65 (Footnote 133).
[44] *Cremers* et. al., Discussion Paper No. 13–072, Patent Litigation in Europe, Zentrum für Europäische Wirtschaftsforschung GmbH, 2013, p. 50.
[45] For cost calculations regarding the question which patent protection to choose in general, see *Hüttermann*, Einheitspatent und Europäisches Patentgericht, 1st Edition 2016, p. 49 et seq, especially p. 61–62.
[46] Of course, this is an exaggeration, but it can be taken by following the above mentioned thoughts on the importance of a German patent (or certainly the significance of patent protection in the "TOP 3" countries Germany, France and the U.K.), well presented in *Hüttermann*, Einheitspatent und Europäisches Patentgericht, 1st Edition 2016, p. 49 et seq.

al Patent Court ("GFPC") and German Federal Court of Justice ("GFCJ"), will continue to develop their own case law concerning validity questions. Furthermore, the claim construction and its consequences might be very different at the UPC and for national courts systems such as in Germany.

It will take probably many years until a full harmonization of case law and practice concerning validity, but even more concerning claim construction and scope of protection etc., within the European countries will be realized.

Last but not least, it should be mentioned that the UP/UPC system is still incomplete insofar as it is not clear yet where, finally, the technical fields originally intended to be handled by a separate division of UPC in London should be located. Italy and Spain apparently are competing to "get" such division for their country[47], and it is even rumoured that in case of "getting" such division onto their territory, such countries would join the UPC/UP system.[48]

---

[47] https://www.gje.com/resources/from-london-to-milan-the-unified-patent-courts-journey/ (accessed 03.02.2023).
[48] Regarding the current development on Italy winning this "race" see https://www.juve-patent.com/people-and-business/italian-government-confirms-milan-will-host-third-upc-central-division/ (accessed 22.05.2023).

Żaneta Zemła-Pacud, Tomasz Targosz
3 Cross-border patent litigation under the EPC

3.1 Introduction

Even though the Unitary Patent Court Agreement brings a revolutionary change to the cross-border patent litigation rules in Europe, this change will initially affect only an insignificant number of unitary patents and will only gain importance over time. In the meantime, the existing rules will still apply to many European and domestic patents.

First, the rules will apply to all patents already granted or applied for. Moreover, within seven years after the UPCA comes into force, European Patents granted or applied for within the period may be opted-out from the UPC jurisdiction. Finally, a considerable number of countries – members of the European Patent system will remain outside the realm of the unitary patent and the jurisdiction of the UPC. These will include three relatively big EU economies: Spain, Poland and Croatia, and many non-EU countries, including Switzerland, Norway, and the United Kingdom. Entrepreneurs from these countries will still be able to use the unitary patents and the UPC to protect their inventions within the contracting EU countries. They also will be open to litigation within the UPC based on actions they undertake within the contracting EU countries if they infringe existing rights. However, within their territories, they will only have the option of protecting their inventions using European or national patents and domestic courts.

This paper presents the outline of the current *status quo* in cross-border patent litigation in Europe. This *status quo* results from an interplay of different factors, primarily jurisdictional rules, private international law rules and, to some extent, the extraterritorial scope of national patent rights. It elaborates on the submission that the current litigation system of cross-border conflicts regarding a single European patent in different jurisdictions has many drawbacks. Sometimes it results in contradictory decisions; other times, it encourages abuse of the litigation system by the parties, both on the attacking and defending side. While some features of the current system could be improved[1], in a mosaic of many jurisdictions and patents, no ideal solutions can be found.

---

[1] See eg. The European Max Planck Group on Conflict of Laws in Intellectual Property (CLIP), *Principles on Conflict of Laws in Intellectual Property*, 1 December 2011, available at: https://www.ip.mpg.de/fileadmin/ipmpg/content/clip/Final_Text_1_December_2011.pdf, accessed 27.10.2022.

Żaneta Zemła-Pacud, PhD, Assistant Professor in the Institute of Law Studies, Polish Academy of Science, Of Counsel in TKP, Warsaw.
Tomasz Targosz, PhD, Assistant professor Jagiellonian University in Kraków, partner in TKP, Kraków.

Cross-border litigation will be understood here as a scenario in which a patent infringement action is brought before the courts of a country different from the one in which the allegedly infringed patent has been issued. This may also include cases in which the court seized with such a dispute issues an injunction that is supposed to apply in another jurisdiction. Cross-border litigation is usually motivated by the advantages of consolidation. These are typically beneficial to the plaintiff who prefers to conduct one proceeding instead of several and in different countries to boot. There may be, however, other reasons. For example, the plaintiff may trust the competence or efficiency of the courts of the selected jurisdiction more than those of the alternative ones. Certainly, in some cases, cross-border enforcement of patent rights can be to the defendant's advantage too[2]. Still, we would argue that it is principally an option valued by patent owners.

3.2 Existing rules of cross-border patent litigation in the EU – jurisdiction

The starting point for cross-border patent litigation in the sense described above must be the establishment of international jurisdiction. In the EU, the rules governing international jurisdiction in civil and commercial matters were first harmonised by the Brussels Convention on jurisdiction and the enforcement of judgments in civil and commercial matters of 1968, later replaced by Regulation (EC) No 44/2001 and finally repealed by Regulation (EU) No 1215/2012 on jurisdiction and the recognition and enforcement of judgments in civil and commercial matters, also sometimes referred to as the Brussels Ia or *Ibis* Regulation[3]. Brussels I applies to all legal proceedings instituted after 10 January 2015.

The application of Brussels I Regulation provisions for establishing jurisdiction in cross-border intellectual property disputes comes into play if the parties themselves have not chosen a forum (*see* Article 25 of Brussels I). The parties' freedom of contractual choice of jurisdiction is excluded in cases of exclusive jurisdiction, listed in Article 24. Importantly, Article 22(4) of Brussels I provides that, regardless of the domicile of the parties and irrespective of whether the issue is raised by way of an action or as a defence, the exclusive jurisdiction in proceedings concerned with the registration or validity of patents shall lie with the courts of the Member State in which the deposit or registration has been applied for (or has taken place, or is deemed to have taken place under an instrument of the Union or an international convention). This rule is without preju-

---

2 It would be simplistic to say that all defendants favour judicial obstruction.
3 Regulation (EU) No 1215/2012 of the European Parliament and of the Council of 12 December 2012 on jurisdiction and the recognition and enforcement of judgments in civil and commercial matters (recast), [2012] OJ L 351, 20.12.2012, p. 1–32.

dice to the EPO jurisdiction on the revocation or maintenance of a European Patent in the opposition procedure initiated on the grounds of the EPC[4].

Where parties have not determined jurisdiction contractually, and a dispute in question does not belong to the realm of the exclusive jurisdiction, the general principle of *actor sequitur forum rei applies.* The criterion for determining national jurisdiction is the defendant's domicile, habitual residence, or seat (Article 4 of Brussels I). Neither citizenship nor incidental residence of the defendant plays a role here.

Above that, two specific jurisdiction rules are further provided in Article 7 (1) of Brussels I for matters relating to a contract and in Article 7(2) for disputes relating to a tort (delict) or an act similar to a tort (*quasi*-delict). Article 7 is not construed as *lex specialis* but rather as a provision complementing the basic principle discussed above. Specifically, it indicates alternate jurisdiction in addition to the jurisdiction determined based on the defendant's domicile, who can also be sued, respectively, where the performance of the contract took place or where the harmful event occurred or may occur.

Other cases of specific jurisdiction are provided for in Article 8 (1) of Brussels I, according to which a person domiciled in a Member State may also be sued in situations where there are several defendants in the courts for the place where one of the defendants is domiciled, provided that the cases are so closely connected that it is expedient to hear and determine them together to avoid irreconcilable judgments resulting from separate proceedings.

Art. 35 of Brussels I gives jurisdiction regarding provisional measures to the courts of a Member State even if the courts of another Member State have jurisdiction as to the substance of the matter. This means that courts of any Member State could decide provisional measures, such as e.g. preliminary injunctions.

The final piece of the puzzle are the rules on *lis pendens*. Art. 29 (1) of the Regulation 1215/2012 states that where proceedings involving the same cause of action and between the same parties are brought in the courts of different Member States, any court other than the court first seized shall of its own motion stay its proceedings[5] until the jurisdiction of the court first seized is established. The concept of "the same cause of action" is understood as including both infringement proceedings and proceedings in which a declaration of non-infringement[6] is sought[7].

It should be noted here that once the competent jurisdiction has been established, the applicable law must be determined. As this issue falls outside the scope of this chap-

---

[4] Art. 22 (4) of the 44/2001 Regulation did not contain an express mention that it applies "irrespective of whether the issue [of validity] is raised by way of an action or as a defence."
[5] Art. 33 (2) provides some relief in that it allows the court to continue the proceedings under certain conditions.
[6] *See* Italian Supreme Court Cass. 19.12.2003, n. 19550, Societe BLMacchine Automatiche v. Windmoeller & Holscher KG, in GRUR Int [2005] 264.
[7] Judgement of the CJEU of 6 December 1994, Case C-406/92 *Tatry v the owners of the ship "Maciej Rataj"*, ECLI:EU:C:1994:400.

ter, it suffices to mention that the Rome II Regulation[8] foresees the *lex loci protectionis* as the law applicable to actions in IP disputes with cross-borders elements.

In practice, cross-border litigation can occur in patent cases in four ways, one of which is limited to preliminary injunction proceedings.

Firstly, a court of the defendant's domicile is competent to decide any cases against this defendant, including those that pertain to other jurisdictions. Consequently, if a company has infringed patents in several EU Member States, it can be sued before the Court of its domicile in line with art. 4 of the Brussels I Regulation. These claims can include both injunctions and monetary claims (damages, restitution of profits) covering all jurisdictions where the infringement happened. The court of the defendant's general jurisdiction is not limited to adjudicating damages sustained in the country of its seat but can decide on such measures appropriate for the other jurisdictions where, for example, the derivatives of the same European patents have been infringed[9]. There are, however, two factors diminishing the significance of this type of cross-border litigation. The first is that for art. 4 to apply there must be the same defendant. In other words, the same defendant must have infringed (European) patents in all jurisdictions pursued by the plaintiff. This may of course happen, but if the infringers in other jurisdictions are separate legal entities (even subsidiaries or otherwise connected), then the *actor sequitur forum rei* rule points in the direction of each of these jurisdictions individually. Whereas a single case in a single court can pertain to the EU-wide infringing activity of a single infringer, in a case where there are multiple infringers, the matter will be split into as many cases as there are the Member States in which the defendant is based[10].

The second obstacle is the exclusive jurisdiction concerning validity. Whenever the issue of validity is raised as a defence (not necessarily as a counterclaim), the issues of infringement and validity become inextricably linked and the infringement court cannot decide on the validity of the right granted in another jurisdiction, even with an *intra partes* effect. A significant role in this respect is accorded to the CJEU's judgement C-4/03 in *GAT v LuK*[11]. The ECJ held in this decision that the exclusive jurisdiction stipulated in Article 24(4) of the Brussels I is not limited to proceedings that have already been initiated to declare a patent invalid. Instead, the exclusive jurisdiction provision of Article 24(4) takes full effect as soon as foreign invalidity is invoked as a defence. The infringement court cannot consider, let alone rule, on that invalidity defence. In other words, a court has no jurisdiction over the infringement of the foreign parts of a EP as soon as

---

8 Regulation (EC) No 864/2007 of the European Parliament and of the Council of 11 July 2007 on the law applicable to non-contractual obligations (Rome II), [2007] OJ L 199, 31.7.2007, p. 40–49.
9 P. England, *Cross-border actions in the CJEU and English Patents Court: Ten years on from GAT v LuK*, Journal of Intellectual Property Law & Practice, 2017, Vol. 12, No. 2, p. 107.
10 P. Torremans, Jurisdiction for cross-border intellectual property infringement cases in Europe, Common Market Law Review, 53(6), 2016, p. 4.
11 Judgment of the Court (First Chamber) of 13 July 2006 in case C-4/03 *GAT v LuK*, ECLI:EU:C:2006:457.

the validity of such parts is questioned or challenged by the defendant. Effectively, this has restricted cross-border decisions on the merits, as the invalidity of the patent in suit is nearly always argued by the alleged infringer as a defence against cross-border infringement claims.

Even after *GAT v. LuK* it is not entirely clear how far this connection goes. There are decisions by English courts that seem to imply that all infringements involve validity assessments[12] even when not raised by the defendant. Should this reasoning be accepted, it is difficult to imagine an infringement case in which the issue of validity was not relevant, except perhaps when the defendant explicitly waives the right to challenge the patent's validity. It would seem, though, that while the issue at hand is about jurisdiction and should be settled before any discussion of the case's merits, procedural laws of the seized court may play a part in determining the extent of art. 24 (4) operation. For example, in a bifurcated system, the mere defence of invalidity may be insufficient. Some procedural laws are quite strict as to when certain defences can be introduced. If the defendant does not initially invoke invalidity in such a system, he or she may be barred from introducing this issue at a later stage and the once-established jurisdiction can survive. Nevertheless, it remains true that if the defendant wants to attack validity precisely because of its impact on the jurisdiction, it will be easy to do so. Even a blatantly unfounded challenge will be sufficient to trigger art. 24 (4) of the Regulation because no substantive evaluation of the merits of such a claim is permitted. The response of the infringement court could theoretically be twofold. It could either declare that it lacks jurisdiction and the whole case must be "transferred" to the country where the patent was granted and where its validity can be decided, or it could stay the infringement case and wait for the decision regarding validity. Although the latter option seems reasonable and has been applied by e.g. Swiss courts[13], it does not agree with the literal interpretation of art. 24 (4) of the Brussels I Regulation since when invalidity is invoked by the defendant, this transforms infringement proceedings into "proceedings concerned with the registration or validity of patent" and with respect to such proceedings only the court of the patent country has jurisdiction. If so, any mention of invalidity would lead to the exclusive jurisdiction of the country of the patent's court. A defendant would have to purposefully give up on such a defence for the infringement court to retain jurisdiction.

The second way of initiating cross-border litigation in patent cases is to rely on art. 7 (2) of the Brussels I Regulation. Since, for the purpose of establishing jurisdiction, patent infringement is a tort[14], the defendant can be sued in the courts of the place

---

12 Patents Court, Coin Controls Ltd v Suzo International (UK) Ltd [1999] Ch 33 (26 March 1997), Patents Court, Anan Kasei Co, Ltd & Rhodia Opérations SAS v Molycorp Chemicals & Oxides (Europe) Ltd [2016] EWHC 1722 (Pat).
13 P. Torremans, *Jurisdiction in Intellectual Property Cases* (in) P. Torremans (ed) *Research Handbook on Cross-Border Enforcement of Intellectual Property*. Edward Elgar 2014, p. 398.
14 Judgement of the CJEU of 19 April 2012, *Folien Fischer AG & Anor v Ritrama SpA*, C-133/11, ECLI:EU: C:2012:664.

where the harmful event occurred[15]. The latter can principally be the place of the event giving rise to damages, as well as the place where the damage occurred. The first alternative is usually the country where the patent is in force (as only actions in that country can, in principle, infringe it)[16]. Because of the above-described issue with the exclusive jurisdiction in all matters concerning validity, this is a reasonable choice as courts of the country of the patent will not lose jurisdiction under art. 24 (4) of the Regulation. The second alternative (where the damage occurred) is relevant when the right holder sustained losses (or other types of damage) in a different country from the one where the infringing action took place. As correctly noticed by *Torremans*,[17] contrary to "typical" torts, infringements of intellectual property rights do not depend on the existence of "damage". The very encroachment upon the exclusive competencies of the right holder is illegal, irrespective of the consequences. While this distinction may appear clear at first glance, there remain some unresolved issues. The landmark CJEU case cited in this context is the *Pinckney* judgment.[18] Mr Pinckney argued that he suffered damage in France due to a copyright infringement committed in Austria[19], because the illegally manufactured copies were accessible in France (the mere possibility of damage, even small, suffices). However, selling these copies in France would have infringed his copyright in France. In patent cases one can imagine a scenario in which a patent owner in Austria residing in France, where no patent is in force, would argue that the importation of illegally manufactured (in Austria) copies causes damage in France because this is the place of the owner's residence and the location of his/her assets[20]. Would it be possible to argue that what is a lawful act in France causes damage to the Austrian patent owner residing in France, because products illegally manufactured in Austria could not have entered the French market, but for the infringement in Austria?[21]

---

[15] It may be argued that this also applies to non-infringement declarations: *Folien Fischer AG & Anor v Ritrama SpA*, C-133/11, Ibid.; P. England, *Cross-border actions...* supra n. 9, pp. 109–110.
[16] OLG Düsseldorf, 9.6.2022 – 15 U 50/21, GRUR-RS 2022, 14773.
[17] P. Torremans, *Jurisdiction for...*, supra n. 10, p. 1632.
[18] Judgment of the Court (Fourth Chamber) of 3 October 2013 in case C-170/12 *Pinckney v.Mediatech*, ECLI:EU:C:2013:635.
[19] P. Torremans, *Jurisdiction for...*, supra n. 10, p. 1633–34.
[20] In our opinion there is certain similarity here to cases where financial damage had to be localised (See eg. Judgment of the Court (First Chamber) of 12 September 2018 in caseC-304/17 *Helga Löber v Barclays Bank PLC*, ECLI:EU:C:2018:701; Judgment of the Court (First Chamber) of 12 May 2021 in caseC-709/19, Vereniging van Effectenbezitters v BP plc, ECLI:EU:C:2021:377)
[21] Based on *Wintersteiner* (Case C-523/10, Wintersteiner v. Products4U, EU:C:2012:220) the answer ought to be negative, however whether there is real justification to distinguish copyright and industrial property in this way seems doubtful (O. Vrins, M. Schneider, *Cross-border Enforcement of Intellectual Property: the European Union* (in:) P. Torremans (ed) *Research Handbook on Cross-Border Enforcement of Intellectual Property*, Edward Elgar 2014, p. 201).

Unlike in the case of personality rights (harm as mental suffering), harm in patent infringement cases cannot be tied directly to the person of the patent owner[22]. The place of residence/domicile of the plaintiff is therefore as such insufficient to establish jurisdiction[23].

The CJEU restricted the potential of forum shopping resulting from the application of art. 7 (2) in its decision in *Shevill* (C-68/93)[24], developing a mosaic principle regarding damages known as the 'Shevill doctrine'. Accordingly, proceedings in the courts of the place where the damage occurred can be brought only in respect of damage that actually occurred within that forum. If the claimant wants to concentrate all proceedings before a single court, he needs to address the courts of the place where the defendant is domiciled or where he has acted. The potential for abuse has not been removed, though. It may not be financially reasonable for the right holder to initiate proceedings in countries where the amount of damages possible to claim would be minimal. That does not mean that it could not be beneficial for tactical reasons (e.g. generating huge costs for the defendant who has been forced to litigate in several jurisdictions). Fortunately for defendants in patent matters, even if it were assumed that the place of the harm can be different from the place where the infringement happened, they would still be able to invoke invalidity and the jurisdiction of the country of the place of harm (damage, not infringement) would be thwarted. Jurisdiction established on the basis of art. 7 (2) of the Regulation does not allow courts to issue cross-border injunctions, i.e. injunctions going beyond the territory of the country of protection.

The third way of initiating a cross-border infringement case is through Art. 8 (1) of the Brussels I Regulation, i.e. by suing several defendants in the country of domicile of one of them. This method has the greatest "consolidating" potential since while it is possible to use art. 7 (2) to join cases against different infringers (e.g. against one defendant jurisdiction is based on domicile, against the other on art. 7 (2)), the number of defendants the patent owner could realistically hope to sue together before one court will usually be limited. In a fairly typical case, in which different entities infringe iterations of the same European patent in their respective jurisdictions, only art. 8 (1) could offer some hope. However, the application of this provision to patent cases is rather narrow. In *Roche v Primus*[25] the CJEU held that claims relating to the infringement of various national parts of an EP were not to be considered "so closely connected that it is expedient to hear and determine them together to avoid the risk of irreconcilable judgments resulting from separate proceedings" as required by Article 8(1). The main argument in fa-

---

22 See also Case C-523/10, Wintersteiner (ibid.); P. Torremans, *Jurisdiction for...*, supra n. 10, p. 1632. See also O. Vrins, M. Schneider, *Cross-border Enforcement...*, ibid.,, p. 198–199.
23 Case C-523/10, Wintersteiner, supra n. 22.
24 Judgment of the Court of 7 March 1995 in case C-68/93 *Shevill and others v Presse Alliance* [1995] (Rec. 1995, p. I–415), ECLI:EU:C:1995:61.
25 Case C-539/03 Roche Nederland BV and Others v Frederick Primus and Milton Goldenberg [2006], ECLI:EU:C:2006:458.

vour of this position was the fact that European patents are – in the eyes of the law – separate national patents, and consequently, cases concerning their infringements are also separate. However, later decisions called this reasoning into question[26]. Whereas the judgment in *Solvay*[27] could be perhaps reconciled with *Roche* (the defendants were accused – each of them[28] – of infringing the plaintiff's rights in two countries which meant that the court had to decide infringement with regard to each company and each national patent)[29], it is more difficult to say the same about the decision in the *Painer*[30] case. *Painer* concerned copyright[31], however, again looking through the eyes of the law, copyright is no less territorial than patents[32]. One could therefore argue that *Painer* has relaxed the conditions imposed by *Roche* and made them more flexible. On the other hand *Solvay* does not refer to *Painer*. Looking at the above cited cases it would appear that it should be possible to sue several defendants based on art. 8 (1) when they have all acted (infringed) in the same jurisdiction[33]. To what extent *Painer* overrides or corrects *Roche* remains open[34]. Interestingly, in a quite recent judgment in *Novartis v. Mylan*, a Dutch District Court decided that the condition of "closely connected" was met because both defendants were accused of tortious interference with infringement of patent and the alleged acts "showed significant overlap both in a legal and a factual sense"[35], which suggests that national courts are indeed ready for a laxer approach to art. 8 (1).

Finally, the fourth opening for cross-border litigation is provided by art. 35 of the Regulation. If any Member State court can issue provisional measures even if it would not have jurisdiction in the case on the merits, this can of course apply in intellectual

---

[26] P. Torremans, *Jurisdiction for...*, supra n. 10, p. 1640 ff.

[27] Judgment of the Court (Third Chamber) of 12 July 2012 in case C-616/10 *Solvay SA v Honeywell Fluorine Products Europe BV & Ors*, ECLI:EU:C:2012:445.

[28] It has been convincingly argued that the mere fact that two companies, A and B, sell an identical infringing product in the same country does not necessairly justify joint jurisdiction. This can be a purely coincidental action and the prospect for A of being sued in the country of B's seat is not predictable: H. Schacht, *Neues zum internationalen Gerichtsstand der Streitgenossen bei Patentverletzungen Besprechung zu EuGH*, Urt. v. 12. 7. 2012 – C-616/10 – Solvay, GRUR 2012, p. 1112–1113.

[29] P. England, *Cross-border actions...*, supra n. 9, p. 105.

[30] Order of the Court (Third Chamber) of 7 March 2013 in case C-145/10, *Eva-Maria Painer v Standard VerlagsGmbH and Others*, ECLI:EU:C:2013:138; P. Torremans, *Intellectual property puts art.6(1) Brussels I Regulation to the test*, I.P.Q. 2014, p. 4 ff.

[31] Copyright in a portrait photograph.

[32] The lack of registration or even harmonisation (almost identical – par. 82 does not change the nature of these rights. In *Painer* though (par. 80) the identical legal base of the claim is reduced to only one of the relevant factors.

[33] H. Schacht, *Neues zum...*, supra n. 29, p. 1111.

[34] Since Solvay was handed down later, P. Torremans argues that it "represents a revival of the Roche Nederland doctrine" (P. Torremans, *Intellectual property puts...*, supra n. 31, p. 9).

[35] Decision of the Hague District Court dated 29 September 2020 in case C/09/595262/KG ZA 20-605 *Novartis v. Mylan*, available in Dutch at <https://drive.google.com/file/d/1p7swxIrTWwineJtn7CGdJzFAUTfAXwad/view> accessed 17.10.2022.

property cases. The obvious problem regarding this provision is its relationship with art. 24 (4). In *Solvay*[36] the CJEU decided that, when a court considers the validity of the patent[37] in the context of preliminary injunction proceedings, it does not concern itself with the registration or validity of that patent. Its assessment in that regard is only done to properly balance the interests of the parties and has no impact on patent registers, nor does it create *erga omnes* effects. It may be added that unlike in a case on the merits when a defence of invalidity is raised (with the effect only between the parties), a preliminary decision does not even decide the issue of validity in this sense, let alone create the state of *res iudicata*[38].

Although art. 35 of the Brussels I Regulation is very general and does not seem to introduce any additional requirements, the interpretation of this provision has limited its scope by demanding a connection between the jurisdiction where the measure is to be issued and the jurisdiction where it is supposed to take effect[39]. These connecting factors aside, the usefulness of obtaining cross-border preliminary injunctions is also tempered[40] by the relationship between such injunctions and proceedings on the merits. Art. 9 (5) of the Enforcement Directive provides that provisional measures such as preliminary injunctions "are revoked or otherwise cease to have effect, upon request of the defendant, if the applicant does not institute, within a reasonable period, proceedings leading to a decision on the merits of the case before the competent judicial authority". The plaintiff, who has been granted a preliminary injunction by a court deriving its jurisdiction from art. 35 of the Regulation, will have to initiate proceedings on the merits within a relatively short period of time. If not, the preliminary injunction will expire and the defendant may even claim damages. These actions on the merits will have to be filed according to the jurisdictional rules described above, which make a consolidation in the jurisdiction that issued the preliminary injunction unlikely. Finally, even if the court has jurisdiction, it will have to apply foreign patent law and in some countries this is seen as problematic at the preliminary stage of proceedings[41]

Despite that fact that the severity of the CJEU's decisions may have been slightly diluted by subsequent cases, the Court's judgments in *GAT v Luk* and *Roche v Primus* re-

---

36 Case C-616/10 *Solvay SA v Honeywell Fluorine Products Europe BV & Ors*, supra n. 28.
37 This is common in most countries, but e.g. not in the EU – P. England, *Can the English Patents Court award a cross-border preliminary injunction?* Journal of Intellectual Property Law & Practice, 2022, Vol. 17, No. 4, p. 371.
38 See P. Torremans, *Jurisdiction for...*, supra n. 10 at 394 argues that in such cases decisions valid inter partes should not by covered by the exclusive jurisdiction.
39 Judgment of the Court of 17 November 1998 in case C-391/95 *Van Uden Maritime BV, trading as Van Uden Africa Line v Kommanditgesellschaft in Firma Deco-Line and Another*, ECLI:EU:C:1998:543.
40 One additional disadvantage is that a preliminary injunctions cen be enforced when it has been properly served on the defendant. Often this process of service takes a long time and the plaintiff would have been able to act sooner had he/she applied for a PI in the country where it should be enforced.
41 E.g. in Germany it is unlikely that a court will consider equivalent infringement – P. Mes, *Patentgesetz. Gebrauchsmustergesetz*, C.H. Beck 2020, § 14 no. 152, 153.

presented a watershed moment for cross-border patent litigation. The number of cross-border patent litigation cases on the merits has been smaller ever since.

When taking a look at the litigation statistics, it is clear that the vast majority of patent disputes in Europe are concentrated in just a few selected venues. According to statistics published in 2013[42], of the 1,500 to 2,000 patent infringement proceedings tried every year by European courts, 66% are brought in Germany, 15% in France, 14% in Italy, 3% in the United Kingdom and 2% in the Netherlands. As to the outcome of patent infringement proceedings initiated in Germany over the past years, on average, roughly 40% of infringement actions resulted in an injunction, 40% were dismissed due to non-infringement, and 20% were suspended pending the outcome of invalidity proceedings before the Federal Patent Court and the Federal Supreme Court. However, cross-border litigation cases make up only a very small percentage of these 1,500 to 2,000 patent infringement proceedings.

This concentration of cases in a handful of litigation venues cannot be explained by there being any need to sue in other countries. As explained above, in light of the CJEU's case law, cross-border verdicts are largely unavailable in patent cases today. Rather, the small number of popular venues is due to companies deciding to enforce their patents in only a few jurisdictions based on a cost-benefit analysis. It is often sufficient to obtain an injunction in the most important economic markets (e.g., Germany, France, or the United Kingdom) or in a defendant's home court in order to effectively shut down the infringement. The popularity of German courts can also be explained by their high level of specialisation in patent matters, which leads to greater predictability for plaintiffs and quicker patent infringement proceedings (it takes about one year from filing the complaint to obtain a first-instance decision in Germany).

3.3 Unfair tactical litigation

Multiple jurisdictions may have diverging consequences. Often patent owners would prefer a consolidation of almost identical infringement cases, especially before a court they consider to be experienced and competent. On the other hand, a plaintiff with larger financial resources will have the possibility to exhaust a smaller defendant, as the latter may not have the resources to litigate in several jurisdictions[43].

The current system also allows delaying infringement cases by commencing a dispute (especially a non-infringement declaration type of action) in a state that is known for ineffective proceedings, giving the result that the competent court in the infringe-

---

42 Statistics referred to by Ralph Minderop Arwed Burrichter and Natalie Kirchhofer, 'Cross-border patent litigation in Europe: change is coming' (*I AM Media Blog*, 17 June 2015), <https://www.iam-media.com/article/cross-border-patent-litigation-in-europe-change-coming> accessed 17.10.2022.
43 A broader understanding of art. 8 (1) of the Brussels I regulation would not change much in that regard as it would only give to the plaintiff an option to sue before one court.

ment case has to stop the proceeding and await the other state's court, which can take years (torpedoes)[44]. From the perspective of procedural economy, fairness and the aim for consistent judgements, the current system is not favourable.

Finally, it has to be mentioned that the aggregate costs of enforcing patent rights in multiple jurisdictions can be enormous. A February 2009 report requested by the European Commission cites the average legal costs parties must bear in patent litigation in four countries, namely, France, Germany, the Netherlands and the UK. The report estimates that, in big commercial cases, at first instance, party costs amount to €200,000 in both France and the Netherlands, €250,000 in Germany and €1.5 million in the UK[45]. Average litigation costs in just four European countries count to about €3.6 million ($4.6 million in 2012)[46]. Such costs often prevent small and medium-sized enterprises (SMEs) from enforcing their patent rights in all the jurisdictions in which a pan-European patent infringement might take place[47].

More recently, another pathology seems to have arisen in SEP litigation, where some courts, including UK courts, issue anti suit-injunctions, anti-anti suit injunctions, etc.[48] While this practice it not necessarily caused by European jurisdictional rules, it would appear that a unified European patent court would be better placed to defend the interests of EU actors in such cases.

3.4 Infringing acts in multiple countries

An important cross-border context arises when the infringement itself occurs or is deemed to occur across borders, i.e., concurrently in many countries. This can result from today's mode of operations, where large multinational companies frequently divide work between their different national subsidiaries. Ubiquitous infringement of patents can also easily occur in the Internet and AI environments. Such contexts can give

---

44 M. Franzosi, *Torpedos are here to stay*, IIC 2002, p. 154ff.
45 See also K. Cremers, et al. (2016), *Patent Litigation in Europe*, European Journal of Law and Economics, available at <https://openaccess.city.ac.uk/id/eprint/16392/8/Published%20article.pdf> accessed 18.10.2022, who refer to estimations of litigation costs across Europe from 2013 (C. Helmers, L. McDonagh (2013) *Patent litigation in England and Wales and the issue-based approach to costs*, Civil Justice Quarterly, 32(3), 369–384). Costs of litigation in Great Britain, the most expensive jurisdiction in Europe, range from GBP 1 to 6 million.
46 Malwina Mejer & Bruno van Pottelsberghe de la Potterie, *Beyond the Prohibitive Cost of Patent Protection in Europe*, VOX (10 April, 2009), available at <http://voxeu.org/index.php?q=node/3440> accessed 18.20.2022. *See also* K. Cremers et al., ibid.
47 Alejandro I. Garcia, 'A Single Patent Court for Europe: Dream or Reality?' (*WIPO Magazine* February 2010) available at <https://www.wipo.int/wipo_magazine/en/2010/01/article_0005.html>, accessed 18.10. 2022.
48 D. Grading, D.Katsifis, The Use and Abuse of Anti-Suit Injunctions in SEP Litigation: Is There a Way Forward?, GRUR International, 71(7), 2022, 603–617.

rise to complex patent infringement scenarios in which only some steps of a patented method are performed within one country[49]. These business realities stay in contrast to the enforcement rules traditionally based on territoriality rules.

A to a certain extent similar, yet distinct issue is the extensive interpretation of the territorial scope of patents by courts in some Member States (in particular in Germany)[50], so that actions taken outside the protection territory, such as offering or selling, are considered infringements of the national patent when they have effect on its territory. This in essence introduces a duty of care for foreign entities who must take into account that e.g. a website with their offerings is available in another Member State, even though it has not been directed at that territory[51]. Although such overreach seems to have a long tradition in Germany, it is perhaps not unlikely that one of the factors contributing to such decisions could be the fact that establishing jurisdiction and consolidating infringement proceedings in one court would be difficult. Hence, what in some cases could be better characterised as infringements of two national patents (e.g. one in the exporting and the other in the importing country) is pursued as an infringement of only one of them (in the importing country).

In such cases, not only the choice of the right jurisdiction but also the rules relating to the applicable law are problematic. In complex factual settings, especially in cases of infringing acts happening in multiple locations, the rule on the *lex loci protectionis*, provided in the Rome II Regulation and closely following the choice of jurisdiction, will not be adequate[52].

3.5 Practical ramifications of the *status quo*: inconsistency of decision-making, high costs, forum shopping

The current system for jurisdiction rules regarding patent litigations in the Brussels I Regulation gives a plaintiff the possibility to sue the defendant in an infringement case where the defendant is domiciled, has its establishment or where the harmful event occurred. These rules also apply in cases concerning declaratory claims. However, several alleged patent infringers cannot be sued within the same jurisdiction unless they have acted in the same state (unless one accepts that this requirement has been relaxed in *Painer*). If the issue of revocation/validity arises, the plaintiff has to sue the right holder

---

49 R. Minderop et al, supra n. 43.
50 M. Trimble, *Global Patents*, OUP 2012, p. 120 f.
51 Judgement of German Federal Constitutional Court of 21 April 2016, BGH GRUR 2016, 1048 – Evening with Marlene Dietrich.
52 *See* A. Kur, U. Maunsbach, *Choice of Law and Intellectual Property Rights*, OLR 2019, vol. 6, p. 61. M. Husovec, *Injunctions against innocet third parties: case of website blocking*, JIPITEC 2013, Vol 4, p. 116.

in the Member State where the patent is protected. It affects an infringement suit regarding the same patent in different Member States[53]. which will have to stay. As a result, the current system is fragmented, and disputes regarding basically the same patent (only formally split into national rights) between more than two parties or disputes regarding infringement actions in different states have to be litigated in more than one state. This, in turn, leads to different approaches and different final conclusions that are likely to be taken by differential national courts[54].

Selective analysis of major European jurisdictions in the field of patent law – Germany, France and the UK – indeed proves the diversity between the institutional elements of competent patent courts in these countries, such as centralised (France and the UK) vs decentralised court systems (France and the UK), general legal (France) vs specialised patent (Germany and the UK) expertise of the judges, separation of infringement and validity issues, i.e. 'bifurcation' (Germany) vs single treatment of these issues (France and the UK)[55].

Due to the existence of bifurcation, a regional court in Germany can grant an injunction against a potential infringer of a patent which is later found to be invalid by the EPO, DPMA or the Federal Patent Court. Another potential issue is that regional courts, which decide on infringement, and the Federal Patent Court, which decides on validity, construct claims independently of each other. This might lead to inconsistent claim constructions in the infringement and revocation procedures. This is often referred to as the Angora cat problem, where the patentee applies the broadest possible interpretation of the patent claims in infringement procedures (a fluffy, blow-dried cat) and the narrowest possible interpretation in revocation proceedings (a wet, rolled-up cat). This creates the problem that an infringement court might issue an injunction against a defendant based on a broad claim construction which would inevitably lead to the invalidation given a certain piece of the prior art.

Moreover, the analysis of the cases that have been litigated in Europe in the cross-border context also proves that in addition to institutional differences, substantive patent law provisions related to infringement by equivalent (*Improver Corp. v. Remington Consumer Products Ltd* [1989][56]; *Samsung Electronics Co. Limited v. Apple Retail UK Ltd.*

---

[53] Case C-68/93 *Shevill and others v Presse Alliance*, supra n. 25..
[54] AG Alba Betancourt, *Cross-Border Patent Disputes: Unified Patent Court or International Commercial Arbitration?*, Utrecht Journal of International and European Law, 32(82), 2016, p. 45.
[55] IGIR, 'European patent judiciary in the light of the emergence of the unified patent court: challenges and debates' (*Maastricht University Blog*, 28 May 2021), https://www.maastrichtuniversity.nl/blog/2021/05/european-patent-judiciary-light-emergence-unified-patent-court-challenges-and-debates>, accessed 18.10.2022. See also Brian Jacobsmeyer, *Forum Shopping in Patent Cases: Lessons for the Unified Patent Court*, 25 Michigan Technology Law Review 131 (2018), available at: <https://repository.law.umich.edu/cgi/viewcontent.cgi?article=1008&context=mtlr>, accessed 18.10.2022.
[56] *Improver Corporation v Remington Consumer Product Limited* [1990] FSR 181.

and Apple Sales International [2013])[57] *Samsung Electronics Co. Limited v. Apple Retail UK Ltd. and Apple Sales International* [2013] EWHC 467 (Pat)., obviousness and common general knowledge *(Angiotech Pharmaceuticals Inc. and others v. Conor Medsystems Incorporated* [2007][58]; *Pozzoli v. BDMO SA* [2007])[59], added matter *(Document Security Systems v. European Central Bank* [2008][60]), insufficiency *(Novartis AG and Cibavision AG v. Johnson & Johnson Medical Ltd and others* [2010][61]), etc., are often understood and treated differently by national courts and judges.

Empirical data shows that a considerable number of patents are litigated across multiple European jurisdictions and, further, that in the majority of these cases, divergent case outcomes are reached across the different jurisdictions, suggesting that the long-suspected problem of inconsistency of decision-making in European patent litigation is in fact real[62].

3.6 Concluding thoughts

The reality of cross-border patent litigation does not correspond to the idea of a single market with a homogenous IP/patent regime. The current system has been criticised for being fragmented, expensive and complicated[63] and for enabling tactical litigation, which remains a central feature of the regime[64]. Duplicative litigation results in a substantial waste of judicial resources, but perhaps the greatest casualty of all is the European patent system itself, as confusing and contradictory rulings damage its credibility and standing amongst present and future patent proprietors[65]. From the perspective of global competition, such a fragmented patent system is detrimental to the European economy[66].

To sum up, the use of general instruments anchored in the Brussels I Regulation shows its limitations when applied to IP rights cases. This calls for more tailor-made leg-

---

57 *Samsung Electronics Co. Limited v. Apple Retail UK Ltd. and Apple Sales International* [2013] EWHC 467 (Pat).
58 *Angiotech Pharmaceuticals Inc. and others v. Conor Medsystems Incorporated* [2007] EWCA Civ 5.
59 *Pozzoli v. BDMO SA* [2007] EWCA Civ 588.
60 *Document Security Systems v. European Central Bank* [2008] EWCA Civ 192.
61 *Novartis AG and Cibavision AG v. Johnson & Johnson Medical Ltd and others* [2010] EWCA Civ 1039.
62 K. Cremers, et al. (2016), *Patent litigation...*, supra n. 48.
63 *See* for example Rodriguez Victor, *From National to Supranational Enforcement in the European patent System*, EIPR, 2012 34(6), p. 402.
64 C. Nyombi and M. Oruaze Dickson, 2017. *Tactical litigation in the post-Recast Brussels Regulation era*, European Competition Law Review. 38 (10), pp. 457–469.
65 Philip P. Soo, *Enforcing a Unitary Patent in Europe: What the US Federal Courts and Community Design Courts Teach Us*, 35 Loy. LA Int'l & Comp. L. Rev. 55 (2012).
66 Bruno van Pottelsberghe & Jérôme Danguy, E*conomic Cost-Benefits Analysis of the Community Patent*, 7, EUR. COMM'N (7 September, 2012), available at <http://ec.europa.eu/internal_market/indprop/docs/patent/studies/compact-cost%20-benefit-study- final_en.pdf> accessed 18.10.2022.

islation that is adequate for the specificities of intellectual property[67]. The European legislator should reconsider modifying the undesired status by reference to the CLIP principles[68]. But a broader availability of consolidation instruments is not without issues, either. While it may be more cost-effective and avoid diverging judgments in almost identical cases, it would sometimes be to the detriment of defendants who could be sued in jurisdictions where they have not acted and where litigation is more expensive.

Parties to a multi-jurisdictional patent dispute may conclude arbitration agreements whereby they agree to resolve their dispute before a single arbitral forum. In such "consolidated" cases, arbitration is often cheaper and quicker than resorting to litigation in several jurisdictions, but arbitration requires the consent of all parties involved, an unlikely prospect in many patent infringement cases.

The concluding thought is that, despite the UPC coming into force, serious reform of the cross-border litigation system is still very much needed, as this system will be crucial for the enforcement of European patents for many coming years. It should allow consolidation of claims and automatic enforcement of injunctions or other judicial decisions across Europe[69]. It also should better correspond to technological advancement or complex business setups[70].

3.7 References

Betancourt, AG A., *Cross-Border Patent Disputes: Unified Patent Court or International Commercial Arbitration?*, Utrecht Journal of International and European Law, 32(82), 2016, pp. 44–58.

CLIP (2013), Conflict of Laws in Intellectual Property: The CLIP Principles and Commentary, OUP, pp. 308–313.

The European Max Planck Group on Conflict of Laws in Intellectual Property (CLIP), *Principles on Conflict of Laws in Intellectual Property*, 1 December 2011, https://www.ip.mpg.de/fileadmin/ipmpg/content/clip/Final_Text_1_December_2011.pdf.

Cremers, K., Ernicke, M., Gaessler, F., Harhoff, D., Helmers, C., McDonagh, L., Schliessler, P. and van Zeebroeck, N. (2016). Patent Litigation in Europe. European Journal of Law and Economics, https://openaccess.city.ac.uk/id/eprint/16392/8/Published%20article.pdf.

England, P. (2022) *Can the English Patents Court award a cross-border preliminary injunction?* Journal of Intellectual Property Law & Practice, 2022, Vol. 17, No. 4.

England, P., (2017). *Cross-border actions in the CJEU and English Patents Court:Ten years on from GAT v LuK*, Journal of Intellectual Property Law & Practice, 2017, Vol. 12, No. 2.

Franzosi, M., (2002) *Torpedos are here to stay*, IIC 2002.

Garcia, A.I., (2010) 'A Single Patent Court for Europe: Dream or Reality?' (*WIPO Magazine* February 2010) available at <https://www.wipo.int/wipo_magazine/en/2010/01/article_0005.html>.

---

[67] P. Torremans, supra n. 10.
[68] *Ibidem.* See also CLIP (2013), Conflict of Laws in Intellectual Property: The CLIP Principles and Commentary, OUP, pp. 308–313.
[69] P. Torremans (eds.), *Research Handbook on Cross-Border Enforcement of Intellectual Property*, Edward Elgar Pub 2015, p. 191.
[70] Ibidem, p. 57. A. Kur, *Farewell to Cross-Border Injunctions? The ECJ Decisions GAT v. LuK and Roche Nederland v. Primus and Goldenberg*, IIC 2006, 844.

Grading, D. & Katsifis, D. (2022) *The Use and Abuse of Anti-Suit Injunctions in SEP Litigation: Is There a Way Forward?*, GRUR International, 71(7), 2022, 603–617.

Helmers, C., McDonagh, L. (2013) *Patent litigation in England and Wales and the issue-based approach to costs*, Civil Justice Quarterly, 32(3), 369–384.

Husovec, M. (2013) *Injunctions against innocet third parties: case of website blocking*, JIPITEC 2013, Vol 4.

Jacobsmeyer, B., *Forum Shopping in Patent Cases: Lessons for the Unified Patent Court*, 25.

Mes, P., (2020) *Patentgesetz. Gebrauchsmustergesetz*, C.H. Beck.

Michigan Technology Law Review 131 (2018), available at: <https://repository.law.umich.edu/cgi/viewcontent.cgi?article=1008&context=mtlr>.

Kur, A., Maunsbach, U., *Choice of Law and Intellectual Property Rights*, OLR 2019, vol. 6, 61.

Kur, A., *Farewell to Cross-Border Injunctions? The ECJ Decisions GAT v. LuK and Roche Nederland v. Primus and Goldenberg*, IIC 2006, 844.

Mejer M. & van Pottelsberghe de la Potterie B., *Beyond the Prohibitive Cost of Patent Protection in Europe*, VOX (10 April, 2009), http://voxeu.org/index.php?q=node/3440.

Nyombi, C. and Oruaze Dickson, M. 2017. Tactical litigation in the post-Recast Brussels Regulation era. *European Competition Law Review*. 38 (10), pp. 457–469.

van Pottelsberghe B. & Danguy J., *Economic Cost-Benefits Analysis of the Community Patent* 7, EUR. COMM'N (7 September, 2012), <http://ec.europa.eu/internal_market/indprop/docs/patent/studies/compact-cost%20-benefit-study- final_en.pdf>.

Rodriguez V., *From National to Supranational Enforcement in the European patent System*, EIPR, 2012 34(6), p. 402–409.

Schacht, H., *Neues zum internationalen Gerichtsstand der Streitgenossen bei Patentverletzungen Besprechung zu EuGH*, Urt. v. 12. 7. 2012 – C-616/10 – Solvay, GRUR 2012.

Soo, P., *Enforcing a Unitary Patent in Europe: What the US Federal Courts and Community Design Courts Teach Us*, 35 Loy. LA Int'l & Comp. L. Rev. 55 (2012).

Torremans, P., *Jurisdiction for cross-border intellectual property infringement cases in Europe*, Common Market Law Review, 53(6), 2016.

Torremans, P. (eds.), *Research Handbook on Cross-Border Enforcement of Intellectual Property*, Edward Elgar Pub 2015.

Torremans, P. (2014) *Intellectual property puts art.6(1) Brussels I Regulation to the test*, I.P.Q. 2014.

Trimble, M. (2012) *Global Patents*, OUP.

Alison Slade
4 Plausibility: a route to stronger and more robust patents?

4.1 Introduction

It is a principle of European Patent Office jurisprudence that 'the patent monopoly should correspond to and be justified by the technical contribution to the art'.[1] This principle has been recognised as the 'foundation of modern patent law'.[2] It justifies the grant of monopolistic patent rights in return for the inventor's contribution to the technical field and for the disclosure of knowledge to the public. It also operates to ensure that the scope of the patent right is proportionate to the inventor's contribution. Notably, it also underpins the introduction of the *plausibility test* into the EPC legal framework and defines its role.[3]

Plausibility has its origins in the case law of the EPO's Technical Boards of Appeal (TBA).[4] It requires that all valid patents must demonstrate that 'the technical problem underlying the invention was at least plausibly solved at the filing date.'[5] The test seeks to prevent speculative patenting and, thus, avoid patent monopolies being granted on products or process that do not work and to discourage over-broad or arbitrary claiming. In line with the principle above, plausibility's objective, is to secure stronger and more robust patents by excluding applications that do not disclose sufficient technical information to be useful. This objective is uncontroversial. Patents are granted over inventions to advance technical progress. Technical contributions that are unworkable and/or unsubstantiated clearly fail in this regard.

Yet, deciding how plausibility should operate to secure the robustness of the patent system is not as quite so straightforward. What should be the situation, for example, when the invention does achieve the purported technical effect, but this is only evidenced in documentation submitted after the filing date – i.e., in post-published/post-filed evidence? It is certainly debatable whether a patent is justified when the purported

---

1 T 409/91 *EXXON/Fuel Oils* [1994] EPOR 149 [3.3]-[3.4].
2 Warner-Lambert Co. v Generics (UK) Ltd t/a/Mylan [2018] UKSC 56 [17].
3 T 939/92 AGREVO/Triazole sulphonamides [1996] EPOR 171 [2.4.2]. In this case the Board of Appeal drew upon the earlier decisions in T 409/91 EXXON/Fuel Oils (n 1) and T 435/91UNILEVER/Hexagonal liquid crystal gel [1995] EPOR 314, where this legal principle was applied in the context of article 84 and article 83 of the European Patent Convention (EPC) respectively, to subsequently assert its relevance in the context of article 56.
4 T 939/92 *AGREVO* (n 3).
5 T 488/16 *BRISTOL-MYERS SQUIBB/Dasatinib* [2019] EPOR 24 [4.9] (emphasis added).

Alison Slade, is Associate Professor at the University of Leicester.

technical contribution is only evidenced in later filed supplementary data. However, as observed by Sir Robin Jacob, 'The days are long gone when patents can only be granted for Dragon's Tooth inventions. To be patentable an idea does not have to be 'oven-ready' anymore.'[6]

In deciding how plausibility should operate within the modern system two requirements central to its operation must be aligned. The first, as stated above, is fundamental to the quid pro quo character of the law – the patent must be proportionate to the technical contribution to the art. The second is fundamental to what is an 'invention' for the purpose of patent law. As pondered by Mark Lemley in the opening to his 2015 article, Ready for Patenting,

> We give patents to inventors to reward and therefore encourage innovation. But what is the act of invention? Am I an inventor when I think of an idea? Or am I an inventor only when I actually get my invention to work?[7]

Accordingly, the technical teaching of the patent specification identifies the contribution made to the art, but the adequacy of that teaching must be judged considering patent law's understanding of the act of 'invention'. This raises the following questions: Should plausibility require that 'the applicant was actually in possession of the invention at the time of filing'[8], and thus align itself with the traditional 'backward-looking' incentive rationales that only protect inventions made prior to patenting? Or should plausibility require something less, thereby finding support in the 'forward-looking' theories that aim to incentive innovation 'prospecting' post-grant?[9] While a more robust approach safeguards the disclosure requirement of the system, it may also undermine its incentive effect.

A further difficulty is plausibility's compatibility or, more properly, incompatibility with the current legal framework. Plausibility's role in securing stronger and more robust patents is undermined by a lack of legislative basis. Its origin is the case law of the EPO where it has been developed to find application in the context of inventive step,[10] sufficiency[11] and industrial application.[12] It appears to have arisen to address deficiencies in the current legislative system, but its alignment with the patentability criteria lacks doctrinal coherency. The rationale for its use is, at best, contrived and, at worst, 'positively Humpty Dumpty-ish'.[13]

---

6 Robin Jacob, 'Plausibility and Policy' (2020) 17 Bio-Science Law Review 223, 230.
7 Mark A Lemley, 'Ready for Patenting' (2016) 96 Boston University Law Review 1171, 1171.
8 T 0116/18 *SUMITOMO/Insecticide compositions* (11 October 2021) [13.4.1].
9 The 'backward-looking' and 'forward-looking' terminology is adopted from the work of John F Duffy, 'Rethinking the Prospect Theory of Patents' (2004) 71 Uni Chi L Rev 439, 440.
10 T 1329/04 *JOHN HOPKINS/FACTOR-9* [2006] EPOR 8.
11 T 609/02 *SALK INSTITUTE FOR BIOLOGICAL STUDIES/AP-I complex* (27 October 2004).
12 T 898/05 *ZYMOGENETICS/ Hematopoietic cytokine receptor* [2007] EPOR 2.
13 Jacob (n 6) 223.

Some coherency may emerge from a recent referral made to the EPO's Enlarged Board of Appeal (EBA) in October 2021 in T 0116/18 *SUMITOMO/Insecticide compositions*.[14] Referral G 2/21[15], while framed in terms of the applicability of post-published evidence, looks set to address some, but not all, of the problems presented above. These include whether plausibility is a legitimate part of EPO jurisprudence, and what evidence is required at the filing date to support an application. These and other practical, legal and conceptual difficulties will need to be tackled if plausibility is to establish itself a credible part of EPO jurisprudence and have a role in securing a strong and robust system.

4.2 Why a plausibility test?

Although lacking direct acknowledgement by the EPO, plausibility appears aimed at addressing deficiencies in the legal framework of the EPC that open the window to bad or unjustified patenting.[16] From an inventive step perspective, it is possible for an invention to satisfy a formal and rigid interpretation of the law, i.e. be non-obvious to the skilled person, while at the same time failing to provide any advance over the prior art. For example, a combination of known features may be considered non-obvious, but they would fail to advance the art if they do not interact to solve a technical problem. Likewise, the structural originality of a chemical compound, in and of itself, cannot give rise to a patent. It must be shown to produce an effect or an increase in an effect in order to demonstrate inventive ingenuity.[17] The application of the problem-solution approach to inventive step, which now includes a requirement for the interaction or technical contribution to be at least plausible, addresses these anomalies.

In terms of Article 83 and the requirement for sufficient disclosure, plausibility finds application where the use or function is an essential feature of the claim, e.g., new and second medical use claims. When read literally, an application for a patent will be 'sufficiently clear and complete for it to be carried out by the person skilled in the art' by merely stating how to administer it. As observed by the UK Supreme Court in the context of second medical use patents,

> The skilled person already knows how to make the product from the prior art....[A]ll that needs to be disclosed is the new purpose, which is enough to enable it to be administered to a patient suffering from the relevant condition. The skilled person does not need to know how or why the invention

---

14 T 0116/18 *SUMITOMO* (n 8). This case concerned the technical contribution made by the synergy of a combination of known insecticides which was only evidenced in a post-filed data. This chapter has been submitted for publication prior to the decision of the Enlarged board of Appeal.
15 Referral to the Enlarged Board of Appeal – G 2/21 (21 October 2021).
16 Bad patents have been held to include ridiculous ideas, impossible concepts, and those that overreach in their technical field. Mark Lemley, Doug Lichtman and Bhaven Sampat, 'What to do About Bad Patents?' (2005–2006) 28 Regulation 10,10.
17 T 488/16 *BRISTOL-MYERS SQUIBB* (n 5) [5.7].

works in order to replicate it. The result would be that the knowledge which made the identification of the new purpose inventive need not be disclosed at all.[18]

On a strict reading of the law, therefore, there is no express requirement to provide evidence that the claimed use is achievable.[19] Plausibility avoids this problem by requiring that the description not only make the product itself reproducible but demonstrate that the (therapeutic) effect is also realisable.[20]

4.3 Filling the legislative lacuna

Although lacking any use of the words *plausible* or *plausibility*, the origins of the test can be traced back to the 1996 decision in T939/92 *AGREVO/Triazole sulphonamides*.[21] In this decision, the TBA held that the claimed invention was unpatentable for failing to provide enough evidence to make it *credible* that the technical problem was being solved across the scope of the claim. Without this evidence there was no inventive contribution that could justify the grant of a patent. This case was decided under Article 56 for lack of an inventive step. Based on application of the problem-solution approach, a claim to a selection of chemical compounds, said to have herbicidal activity, was obvious as there was no evidence that, as a group, they had such activity. Without such evidence the selection was arbitrary, being indistinguishable from other chemicals existing in the prior art and thus devoid of any technical contribution. This line of reasoning was repeated in T 1329/04 *JOHN HOPKINS/FACTOR-9* where a new polypeptide was held to be obvious because 'there is not enough evidence in the application to make it at least *plausible* that a solution was found to the problem which was purportedly solved.'[22] It is in this case that we first see the emergence of the term *plausible* as a designation for the wider test.

Post *AgrEvo*, the plausibility test has also arisen in the context of sufficient disclosure and industrial application. In T 609/02 *SALK INSTITUTE FOR BIOLOGICAL STUDIES/AP-I complex* the TBA held that,

> [A] simple verbal statement in a patent specification that compound X may be used to treat disease Y is [not] enough to ensure sufficiency of disclosure in relation to a claim to a pharmaceutical. It is required that the patent provides some information in the form of, for example, experimental tests, to the avail that the claimed compound has a direct effect on a metabolic mechanism specifically involved in the disease.[23]

---

18 *Warner-Lambert v Generics* (n 2) [19].
19 For a more detailed consideration of problematic alignment of plausibility with the statutory language of insufficiency see Jacob (n 6) 224.
20 See for example, T 609/02 *SALK* (n 11); T 488/16 *BRISTOL-MYERS SQUIBB* (n 5).
21 T 939/92 *AGREVO* (n 3).
22 T 1329/04 *JOHN HOPKINS* (n 10) [11] (Emphasis added).
23 T 609/02 *SALK* (n 11) [9].

In the context of industrial application, the use of the plausibility test has been far more limited, being mostly confined to biotechnology inventions[24] and perpetual motion machines and other inventions that defy laws of nature.[25] This is somewhat surprising given that 'an invention which lacks a technical contribution must necessarily lack industrial application.'[26] Yet, the EPO have a clear preference for utilising Articles 56 and 83 to ensure that the technical contribution made by the invention justifies the grant of a patent monopoly, and have subjugated the requirement for industrial application to very specific circumstances.

From the case law of the EPO, it is possible to identify some key principles that appear common to its application in the context of inventive step, sufficiency and industrial application. Plausibility is to be assessed at the date of filing and the assessment will be based upon the teaching in the application as filed and/or common general knowledge of the person skilled in the art.[27] It will not always be necessary for the applicant to provide experimental data when a theoretical based justification would be sufficiently understood by the skilled addressee.[28] However, where a technical effect is neither self-evident, predictable or based on sound theoretical concepts, further verifiable evidence will be required.[29] This need not be in the form of *in vivo* or clinical data, as absolute proof is not required. The results of *in vitro* tests will often be sufficient to demonstrate directly and unambiguously the technical effect.[30] Finally, where an application is deemed to meet the plausibility threshold at the date of filing, post-published documentation may later be submitted to refute an allegation of a lack of reproducibility.[31] However, where the technical effect is not deemed plausible at filing, post-published evidence cannot later be relied upon to support an application.[32]

---

24 See for example, T 898/05 ZYMOGENETICS (n 12).
25 However, as noted in the EPO Guidelines for Examination, in the case of inventions that appear to violate physical laws, such as perpetual motion machines, '[A]n objection could arise under Art 57 only in so far as the claim specifies the intended function or purpose of the invention, but if, say, a perpetual motion machine is claimed merely as an article having a particular specified construction, then an objection is made under Art. 83'. EPO, 'Guidelines for Examination' (March 2022) Part G, Chapter III [1].
26 Alison Slade, 'Plausibility: A *conditio sine qua non* of Patent Law' (2020) 3 IPQ 180, 186. In this article, I explain in more detail the reasoning for the limited application of plausibility in the context of industrial application.
27 T 1329/04 *JOHN HOPKINS* (n 10) [12]; T1043/10 *NOVO NORDISK/Diabetic late complications* (21 October 2014) [12]; T488/16 *BRISTOL MYERS SQUIBB* (n 5) [4.2]; T950/13 *BRISTOL MYERS SQUIBB/Dasatinib* (3 February 2017) [3.2]
28 T 488/16 *BRISTOL MYERS SQUIBB* (n 5) [4.15].
29 ibid [4.6.2] & [4.9].
30 T 578/06 *IPSEN/Pancreatic cells* (29 June 2011); T 488/16 *BRISTOL MYERS SQUIBB* (n 5) [4.9]; T 950/13 *BRISTOL MYERS SQUIBB* (n 27) [3.10.3].
31 T 1329/04 *JOHN HOPKINS* (n 10) [12]; T1043/10 *NOVO NORDISK* (n 27) [12]; T488/16 *BRISTOL MYERS SQUIBB* (n 5) [4.2]; T 950/13 *BRISTOL MYERS SQUIBB* (n 27) [3.10.4].
32 T 1329/04 *JOHN HOPKINS* (n 10) [12]; T1043/10 *NOVO NORDISK* (n 27) [12]; T488/16 *BRISTOL MYERS SQUIBB* (n 5) [4.2]; T950/13 *BRISTOL MYERS SQUIBB* (n 27) [3.2].

Despite a long line of case law apply the above principles, some inconsistency has emerged between various Boards of Appeal decisions. In a long-awaited referral, the Enlarged Board of Appeal has at last been given the opportunity to define the relevance, if any, of the plausibility test and to set out how the test is to be applied.

4.4 Defining the plausibility standard

Plausibility has been described by the TBA as a *conditio sine qua non* of the problem and solution approach to inventive step.[33] Yet, divergence has been identified as to the standard of disclosure an application must meet in order to pass the plausibility test and, thus, the circumstances in which post-published documentation can be used as supporting evidence.

In its referral to the EBA in October 2021, the TBA identified two distinct lines of case law. The first applied the '*ab initio* plausibility standard.'[34] This standard requires the application to include experimental data or a scientific explanation that provides the skilled person with sufficient information to 'assume the purported technical effect to be achieved.'[35] It is only once this standard is satisfied that supporting evidence not submitted with the application as filed, i.e. post-published or post-filed evidence, can be considered. The second line of case law applied the '*ab initio* implausibility standard'. In contrast to the above, the consideration of post-published evidence is prevented only when the skilled person has reason to doubt that the technical effect in the application was achievable. In other words, 'post-published evidence must always be taken into account if the purported technical effect is not **im**plausible' at the date of filing.[36]

In light of this apparent discrepancy the following questions have been referred to the EBA in Referral G 2/21,

1. Should an exception to the principle of free evaluation of evidence be accepted in that post-published evidence must be disregarded on the ground that the proof of the effect rests **exclusively** on the post-published evidence?
2. If the answer is yes, can the post-published evidence be taken into consideration if, based on the information in the patent application in suit or the common general knowledge, the skilled person at the filing date of the patent application in suit would have considered the effect plausible (*ab initio* plausibility)?
3. If the answer to the first question is yes, can the post-published evidence be taken into consideration if, based on the information in the patent application in suit or the common general knowledge, the skilled person at the filing date of the patent

---

33 T 488/16 *BRISTOL MYERS SQUIBB* (n 5) [4.9].
34 Cases referred to by the Board include T 1329/04 *JOHN HOPKINS* (n 10); T 609/02 *SALK* (n 11); and T 488/16 *BRISTOL MYERS SQUIBB* (n 5).
35 T 0116/18 *SUMITOMO* (n 8) [13.4].
36 T 0116/18 *SUMITOMO* (n 8) [13.5].

application in suit would have seen no reason to consider the effect implausible (*ab initio* implausibility)?[37]

Before considering the implications and policy behind the *ab initio* plausibility and implausibility tests set out in questions 2 and 3, it is important to first address question 1. This asks the EBA to consider whether plausibility is an exception to the principle of free evaluation of evidence, given that its application prevents the consideration of evidence submitted after the filing date. If answered 'no', this could mark the end of plausibility within EPO jurisprudence and a weakening of the objectives it seeks to uphold.

The principle of free evaluation of evidence operates to preserve procedural integrity in accordance with Article 117 EPC, on the 'means and taking of evidence', and the right to be heard enshrined in Article 113 EPC.[38] Together these provisions establish that there are no firm rules according to which certain types of evidence are, or are not, convincing for the deciding body.[39] Thus, all relevant evidence must be considered before reaching a decision. This doctrine is well established within EPO jurisprudence and, in light of the following, raises questions about plausibility's compatibility with the EPC.

In applying the problem-solution approach to inventive step, it is common practice for the EPO to reformulate the objective technical problem where a new closest prior art is identified.[40] In such instances the applicant may find their invention solving a different problem to the one they identified in the application as filed, and which they had submitted initial evidence for. Under the principle of free evaluation of evidence, the applicant can submit post-filed evidence in support of the reformulated problem. However, adopting a rigid application of the plausibility could deprive the applicant of the ability to support their, now reformulated, technical contribution by relying on post-filed evidence. This risks the rejection or curtailment of technologically viable inventions on the basis that the applicant overlooked or failed to recognise the significance of a piece of existing prior art, and not on the basis that the invention lacked a technical contribution.

In fact, several Technical Boards of Appeal have advanced this argument to deny the applicability of a plausibility test and to express the incompatibility of such a test with the problem-solution approach to inventive step altogether. As summarised by the TBA in T 2371/13,

> A lack of plausibility of an effect based on the absence of proof in the patent application is not a sufficient reason to disregard comparative tests filed subsequently and aimed at proving this effect. Dismissing them for this reason is incompatible with the problem/solution approach which requires

---

[37] G 2/21 (n 15).
[38] Article 113 EPC states that 'decisions of the European Patent Office may only be based on grounds or evidence on which the parties concerned have had an opportunity to present their comments.'
[39] T 474/04 *ALTHIN MEDICAL/ Declaration in lieu of an oath* [2005] EPOR 47 [8], citing G 3/97 *INDUPACK/ Third party opposition* [2000] EPOR 81 [5].
[40] EPO, 'Guidelines for Examination' (March 2022) Part G, Chapter VII [5.2].

defining a technical problem from the closest prior art document, which is not necessarily the one cited in the patent application.[41]

The EBA has recently communicated a non-binding preliminary opinion on the key issues to be resolved in Referral G 2/21.[42] After confirming the admissibility of the referral, the Board offered some early insight into the relationship between the principle of free evaluation of evidence, plausibility and the impact on post-published evidence. It noted that disregarding evidence *per se* or as a 'matter of principle' is contrary to a basic procedural right.[43] Yet, the Board does not dismiss the relevance of plausibility for the application of inventive step, and its compatibility with this basic right. Instead, it noted that, 'The technical effect relied upon, even at a later stage, needs to be encompassed by that technical teaching [in the application as filed] and to embody the same invention.'[44] This appears to introduce a two-stage analysis in situations that involve reformulation of the objective technical problem under the problem-solution approach. First, establish that the technical effect, after reformulation, relates to the 'same invention'. This is a legal concept well established in EPO jurisprudence, requiring that alleged or new effects must be deduced or implied from the original disclosure.[45] Thus, the applicant can only rely on a technical effect that is derivable from the application as filed. The second step is to ask whether the technical effect is plausible.

Ab initio plausibility & ab initio implausibility in practice

Ab initio plausibility results in a positive obligation for the applicant to provide supporting data or theoretical reasoning within the application, even when the skilled person, in light of common general knowledge, has no reason to be sceptical that the technical contribution is achievable. Post-published evidence can only be considered once this positive obligation has been satisfactorily discharged. It has been succinctly described as the "allowable only if plausible test".[46] This approach finds support in the majority decision of the UK Supreme Court in *Warner-Lambert v Generics*, where Lord Sumption held that, 'it is not enough that the patentee can prove that the product can reasonably be ex-

---

[41] T 2371/13 *L'OREAL/Combination of two cationic dyes* (4 July 2017) see the 'Exergue'. An English translation of the relevant sections of the decision is provided in T 0116/18 *SUMITOMO* (n 8) [13.6.2.].
[42] 'Communication from the Enlarged Board of Appeal pursuant to Articles 13 and 14(2) of the Rules of Procedure of the Enlarged Board of Appeal (RPEBA)' (13 October 2022).
[43] Ibid [12].
[44] Ibid [15].
[45] EPO, 'Guidelines for Examination' Part G, Chapter VII, [5.2].
[46] Chris Milton, 'EPO Enlarged Board of Appeal Issues Preliminary Opinion in Plausibility Referral G2/21' (20 October 2022) https://jakemp.com/en/news/epo-enlarged-board-of-appeal-issues-preliminary-opinion-in-plausibility-referral-g2-21/ accessed 26 October 2022.

pected to work in the designated use, if the skilled person would not derive this from the teaching of the patent.'[47] The policy behind this approach is clear,

> [It is] to ensure that the patent applicant was actually in possession of the invention at the time of filing to prevent purely speculative claiming and thus to safeguard a balance between the actual technical contribution and the patent monopoly defined by the claims.[48]

In contrast, *ab Initio* implausibility creates a presumption in favour of the applicant that can only be rebutted by substantiated doubts to the contrary, i.e. because the common general knowledge or the application as filed 'give an indication that the purported technical effect cannot be achieved.'[49] The minority opinion of the Supreme Court in *Warner-Lambert v Generics* adopted this reasoning, holding that 'Only if a person skilled in the art would have significant doubts about the workability of the invention would it, in such a case, fail…'[50]

On a practical level *Ab initio* plausibility creates a stronger obligation on the applicant to provide supporting data or cogent scientific explanation as to the achievability of the purported technical contribution of the invention. Without this information the person skilled in the art is entitled to presume that the stated technical effect is not achievable. The result is that,

> [P]atent applicants receive a patent only for embodiments for which experimental data or other substantiation is contained in the application as filed that makes the effect invoked for inventive step plausible for these embodiments. Hence, any extension of the claimed scope over what has been experimentally shown or otherwise substantiated in the application as filed would lead to refusal of the application.[51]

Ab initio **im**plausibility appears more favourable to the patentee. The application is presumed to be producing a technical effect unless evidence or contemporary knowledge suggests otherwise. It does not excuse the applicant who speculates rather than invents, but it does fall short of requiring that the applicant is in possession of the invention at the time of filing.

It is interesting to note that of the six *ab initio* plausibility cases cited by the TBA in its referral, plausibility was denied by the Boards of Appeal in all of them.[52] This contrasts with the eight *ab initio* implausibility cases in which plausibility of the purported technical effect was acknowledged by all Boards.[53] While there may be a certain element of strategic selection by the TBA to support its reasoning, it is a notable statistic that

---

47 *Warner-Lambert v Generics* (n 2) [37].
48 T 0116/18 *SUMITOMO* (n 8) [13.4.1].
49 Ibid [13.5].
50 *Warner-Lambert. v Generics* (n 2) [195].
51 T 0116/18 *SUMITOMO* (n 8) [13.7.1].
52 Ibid [13.4.4].
53 Ibid [13.5.3].

hints at the practical consequences of each incarnation of the plausibility test and an indication that different results may arise depending on which plausibility test is adopted.

4.5 Which approach would secure stronger and more robust patents?

Answering this question very much depends on the defining theories and particular attributes we understand to be encapsulated in our modern patent system. Plausibility finds its normative foundations in the disclosure requirement of the patent system. The EPO and the UK courts have consistency held that the patentability criteria resolve to a requirement for full disclosure. As stated by the TBA,

> Article 56 (the need to provide a non-obvious solution to a technical problem), 57 (the need to indicate how to exploit the invention), and 83 EPC (the need to provide a sufficient disclosure of the claimed invention)…reflect the basic principle of the patent system that exclusive rights can only be granted in exchange for a full disclosure of the invention.[54]

Accordingly, the assessment of patentability and sufficient disclosure can only be made in light of the specification's technical teaching. Plausibility's role, therefore, is in upholding the disclosure and knowledge dissemination function of the system. However, to assume that 'full disclosure' means demonstrating possession of a complete and fully functioning embodiment overlooks important matters that must be considered when deciding on which emanation of the test, *ab initio* plausibility or implausibility, is best suited to this disclosure role.

Consider, therefore, the purpose of the patent system, which is to incentivise innovation, thus, adding to the stock of technical knowledge. How much weight should be given to the original disclosure when evaluating whether the applicant has met their side of the notional patent bargain? Several factors should be considered. First, is the impact of the first-to-file system, which inevitably requires less than full disclosure in many instances. As observed by the TBA,

> The patent system takes account of the intrinsic difficulties for a compound to be officially certified as a drug by not requiring an absolute proof that the compound is approved as a drug before it may be claimed as such. The Boards of Appeal have accepted that for a sufficient disclosure of a therapeutic application, it is not always necessary that results of applying the claimed composition in clinical trials, or at least to animals are reported.[55]

---

54 T 898/05 *ZYMOGENETICS*(n 12) [6]; T 18/09 *HUMAN GENOME SCIENCES/Neutrokine* (21 October 2009) [16]. In the UK court decisions see *Human Genome Sciences Inc v Eli Lilly & Co* [2011] UKSC 51 [134]; *Warner-Lambert* (n 2) [17]; and Lord Hodge in *Actavis Group v ICOS Corp* [2019] UKSC 15 [53]-[54].
55 T 609/02 *SALK* (n 11) [9].

Second, given that patent system speaks to a more limited disclosure at the filing date, it may be necessary to rethink at what point the patent bargain is deemed to be fulfilled. Disclosure can be said to occur at two key stages – on publication of the application and on expiry of the patent.[56] Commentators and judges have questioned whether assessing fulfilment of the patent bargain only at the application stage is appropriate.[57] As observed by Graham J,

> In my judgement, it is what the patentee has actually achieved and not what he has promised (provided of course his promise is not false) which matters from the point of view of consideration and subject-matter in the sense of inventive merit.[58]

In this case, the validity of the patent was upheld, and the patent bargain fulfilled, based on post-filed evidence which established that the claimed technical effect was achievable across the full scope of the claim. It was irrelevant that the evidence was not submitted with the application, as long as the original promise made on filing was not false.[59]

Third, onerous disclosure requirements can operate as a disincentive to innovate and thus undermine the whole basis of the patent system. While disclosure and incentive are regularly advanced as complementary objectives of a well function patent system, 'the normative implications of disclosure and incentive-to-invent principles point in opposite directions.'[60] According to Alan Devlin, 'Disclosure is in fact *a cost* that inventors pay only because they need patent protection to derive a sufficient financial return from their discoveries'. If the disclosure requirement is set to high the incentive to utilise the patent system may be reduced in favour of secrecy laws that can operate to deny disclosure completely.[61] Alternatively, a lack of patent protection over yet to be tested ideas, may disincentivise important, yet costly, trials. This is particularly so in sectors such as pharmaceuticals, applied chemistry and biotechnology, where, as noted above, verifiable evidence can involve lengthy and potentially novelty destroying experiments.

Fourth, the characteristics of patent law's objective measure – the person skilled in the art – also raises questions over the standard to adopt. While knowledgeable in the

---

[56] This can occur at the end of the full 20-year term or if patent protection is not renewed and allowed to lapse.
[57] Jacob (n 6) 232.
[58] *Olin Mathieson Chemical Corp. v Biorex Laboratories Ltd* [1970] RPC 157 – as noted by Jacob (n 6) 232. This case predates the UK Patents Act 1977. However, as an indicator of policy direction, the comment is relevant for today's patent system.
[59] This case was decided under the 1949 Patents Act which included provisions allowing for the rejection or revocation of patents on the basis of 'inutility', 'lack of fair basis' and 'false suggestion'. As has been argued elsewhere, these provisions, together with the requirement for sufficiency of description, covered most if not all the objections now addressed by plausibility. See Slade (n 26) 189–190.
[60] Alan Devlin, 'The Misunderstood Function of disclosure in Patent Law' [2010] 23 Harv J L & Tech 410, 425.
[61] Of course, much will depend upon the nature of the invention in question.

field of the inventor, the skilled addressee lacks the capacity for creative or inventive activity and thus may not always appreciate the full implications of the disclosure. In the context of inventive step, this lack of understanding may simultaneously indicate a non-obvious technical development but also an implausible technical effect.[62] For example, a patent application over a class of chemicals which are said to have a specific therapeutic activity may be non-obvious to the person skilled in the art, because the activity is not expected based on the common general knowledge of the time. However, this same lack of knowledge or understanding may also give rise to doubts over the plausibility of stated technical effect if no experimental data or cogent theoretical reasoning are presented to support the therapeutic activity across the whole class. The implications of this paradox for plausibility are far from clear. A stricter disclosure requirement may remove this anomaly. However, this must be balanced against the need to ensure that the standard of disclosure does not exclude unpredictable or ground-breaking inventions where the nature of the invention may be beyond the sensible comprehension of the skilled addressee.[63]

Finally, it is important to remember that plausibility has no legislative basis. It operates as a substantive principle which bars entry to the statutory questions of inventive step or sufficient disclosure. Consequently, it is a judge-made rule that must be satisfied before consideration can be given to express provisions of the EPC that reflect the agreed text. While appreciating its objectives, it is right to be circumspect about the rigour of, what is essentially, a judge-made substantive legal rule on patent validity.

The considerations outlined above emphasise the difficult task faced by the EBA in trying to balance the competing objectives and practicalities of the current patent system. On the one hand a robust application of plausibility clearly avoids 'speculative' claiming, which would 'allow the armchair inventor a monopoly over a field of endeavour to which he has made no contribution.'[64] Such forms of patenting risk the monopolisation of fields of important scientific information in which a practical application has yet to be found. On the other hand, setting a high bar by requiring evidence that the applicant is in possession of the invention at the time of filing risks overburdening the applicant in a first-to-file system. If applications are only filed once the research is complete the financial viability of certain fields of research become questionable.[65] The costs in producing detailed verifiable evidence together with the risk of being 'pipped to the post' by a competitor significantly diminishes the incentive effect of the patent sys-

---

62 Friederike Stolzenburg, Barbara A Ruskin and Hans-Rainer Jaenichen, 'Of Incomplete Inventions: T1329/04' (2006) 1 epi Information 15, 24.
63 Ibid.
64 *Warner-Lambert Co v Generics (UK) Ltd t/a Mylan* [2016] EWCA Civ 1006 [46].
65 This is an argument advanced strongly by the UK BioIndustry Association in its amicus curiae submissions in G 2/21 (29 April 2022) https://www.epo.org/law-practice/case-law-appeals/eba/pending.html accessed 10 October 2022.

tem. The chances of securing the benefits of patent protection may, in such instances, be outweighed by the risks involved in assembling a *plausible* application.

That being said, the fact-based nature of the plausibility assessment will, in practice, often make it difficult to define any clear difference between the *ab initio* plausibility and *ab initio* implausibility standards. For example, the greater the likely suspicion of the skilled reader as to the workability of the invention the greater the evidence required to support the application. As observed above, where the technology in question is in a new or emerging field, or the invention is unexpected, there will be a greater obligation on the applicant to provide supporting evidence in the application itself to, at the very least, avoid giving rise to any substantiated doubts.

4.6 Implications for the UPC: a lack of legal coherency

In its recent communication, the EBA appears to favour the *ab initio* implausibility standard. As explained in its preliminary comments released ahead of the oral proceedings on 24 November 2022,

> [A] purported technical effect relied upon for inventive step is to be assessed as to whether the skilled person, having the common general knowledge in mind, would have any significant reason to doubt it.
>
> In the absence of any such doubts, the reliance on post-published evidence, such as experimental data, for the purported technical effect would seem to serve as a potential source for a deciding body to conclude whether or not it is convinced of said technical effect when deciding on the inventiveness of the claimed subject-matter.

The opinion does not bind the Board. However, it does signal its intent to set the plausibility standard at the lower hurdle. It must be remembered that if satisfied, plausibility does not prevent a challenge via opposition or invalidity proceedings should later evidence arise questioning the technical effect.[66] The low threshold does not excuse applicants who speculate about the nature of their purported invention or who submit substandard and unsupported applications. However, it does safeguard the applicant who has an invention but who has yet to definitively establish its use.

Unfortunately, the referral is unlikely to address many of the other questions and uncertainties that surround the plausibility test. The EBA has specified that it will only consider the issue in the context of inventive step and not insufficiency. This leaves many of the conceptual problems touched upon above unresolved. A key problem for the plausibility test is that nowhere in the EPC does it state that plausibility, in whatever form, is a precondition for grant of a patent. In the context of obviousness, it is perhaps understandable that an application that does not support the purported technical effect

---

[66] See, for example, *Eli Lilly & Co v Janssen Alzheimer Immunotherapy* [2013] EWHC 1737 (Pat) [258].

cannot advance the art and thus cannot give rise to an inventive step. However, it is hard to find support for this approach and extrapolate the plausibility test from the wording of Article 56 of the EPC.[67] The provision on inventive step requires the examining institution to establish the existence of an inventive step by evaluating its obviousness over the prior art. It does not require an assessment of the capacity of the claimed invention to solve a technical problem. As discussed above, a speculative effect may none-the-less satisfy a formal and rigid interpretation of the non-obviousness criterion.

Nonetheless, the EPO's adoption of the pragmatic *effects-centred* problem-solution approach to inventive step forces attention on whether the invention provides a solution to the underlying technical problem and in doing so avoids the patenting of 'odd, useless structures (for example abstract sculptures or effectless chemical compounds) which are then the more inventive, the odder.'[68] However, plausibility is not directed at establishing inventive step, and even sufficiency, as the EPC formally defines those terms. It is about establishing the viability of purported technical contribution to the art. In this regard, it defines the inherent characteristics of a patentable invention and, therefore, more appropriately aligns with patent law's conception of the 'invention'.

Plausibility: a characteristic of inherent patentability?

According to article 52(1) EPC, a patentable invention is one that satisfies both the initial requirement of being an 'invention' and the secondary criteria of novelty, inventive step and industrial application. However, as discussed above, incorporating plausibility into the secondary requirements to patentability, in particular inventive step, raises questions regarding its legitimacy. As argued in more detail elsewhere, greater coherency could be achieved if plausibility was linked to patent law's requirement for an invention.[69] Without any plausible technical contribution there is surely no invention in the first place, and thus nothing to advance to the secondary criteria of novelty, inventive step and industrial application. As observed by the TBA,

> The verification that claimed subject-matter is an invention within the meaning of Article 52(1) EPC is in principle a prerequisite for the examination with respect to novelty, inventive step and industrial application since these latter requirements are defined only for inventions.[70]

---

67 EPC, Article 56 states 'An invention shall be considered as involving an inventive step if, having regard to the state of the art, it is not obvious to a person skilled in the art.'
68 George S.A. Szabo, 'Letter re Paul Cole's Article' (1999) 21 EIPR 42, 43. In his article, George Szabo, former Chairman of the Boards of Appeal and Member of the Enlarged Board of Appeal, see the EPO's problem-solution approach to address limitations in other approaches, such as the UK's *structure centred* approach which could, in principle, allow for the patenting of such truly unworkable inventions.
69 Slade (n 26) 200–202.
70 T 258/03 *HITACHI/Auction Method* [2004] EPOR 55 [3.1].

Such an approach would acknowledge that the objectives that the plausibility test seeks to achieve are fundamentally linked to the current conception of an invention as being one that makes a contribution to the art. An application that fails to make such a contribution is one that is inherently unpatentable. It seems illogical to distort the language of the inventive step criteria to achieve these ends, when a perfectly viable option already exists.

That being said, the EPO's approach to the requirement for an invention is currently not capable of being used in this way. Historically, the EPO has endorsed the 'technical contribution approach' to inherent patentability. This approach defined an 'invention' as one that makes a technical contribution to the art and is not excluded as a 'non-invention' under Article 52(2).[71] However, more recent case law has characterised the 'invention' very narrowly. The requirement for an invention under article 52(1) is now satisfied when at least one *technical feature* is identified in the claim, irrespective of the invention's technical contribution to the field in question.[72] Therefore, without a significant shift in approach, it seems that plausibility will remain aligned with the secondary patentability criteria, in particular inventive step, and legal incoherency will remain.

4.7 Conclusion

There is little doubt that the objectives plausibility seeks to uphold should be reflected in any well-functioning patent system. Even 'prospecting' theories that encourage early patenting do not go so far as to support the patenting of completely unsubstantiated ideas. Prospecting, by its very nature, assumes some reason already exists to indicate future success. Edmund Kitch, the seminal advocate of the prospect function of patent rights, defined a prospect as 'a particular opportunity to develop a *known* technological possibility.'[73] To adopt anything less risks undermining the incentive and disclosure rationales which underpins the patent system. However, plausibility has long suffered from several conceptual, legal and practical difficulties that have created uncertainty and undermined its application.

The EPO's Enlarged Board of Appeal is set to address some of these issues, in particular, the question of what standard is to be used when applying the test. It currently favours the *ab initio* implausibility approach, which appears to encapsulate the character-

---

71 T 208/84 *VICOM/Computer-related invention* [1987] EPOR 74.
72 A technical feature can be 'implied by the physical features of an entity or the nature of an activity, or may be conferred to a non-technical activity by the use of technical means.' T 258/03 *HITACHI* (n 70) [4.5].
73 Edmund W Kitch, 'The Nature and Function of the Patent system' (1977) 20 Journal of Law and Economics 265, 266. Kitch draws analogies with mineral claims in the American West in the last half of the nineteenth century. In that system, mineral claims could only be established once the claimant had shown 'surface mineralisation'. There was no need for the claimant to go so far as to show that the mineralisation was of commercial significance.' 271.

istics of the modern European patent system and the nature of technological innovation is many fields. It certainly appears more favourable to the patentee than the *ab initio* plausibility standard. However, it must be noted that the fact-based nature of the plausibility assessment means that where the technology in question is in a new or emerging field, or the invention is unexpected, there will always be a greater obligation on the applicant to provide supporting evidence and to avoid the emergence of 'substantiated doubts'. In adopting the lower standard for plausibility, the EBA will certainly not be removing the obligation for patentees to demonstrate that their invention makes a technical contribution to the art in return for the award of a patent, but they are ensuring that plausibility does not usurp the statutorily defined criteria for patentability and sufficient disclosure. The rationale that justifies the plausibility test also provides foundational support for these other statutory provisions. There are certainly some inherent weaknesses in their application but placing too much emphasis on plausibility risks usurping the role of the agreed text of the EPC.

Plausibility's relationship with various provisions of the EPC, however, looks set to remain unresolved. Despite acknowledgement by the referring Board that the same plausibility standard has been applied in the context of both inventive step and sufficiency, the EBA have confined its response to plausibility in the assessment of inventive step. Uncertainty will therefore remain as to whether the same test is applicable in the assessment of sufficiency, and even industrial application. Furthermore, plausibility is not about ascertaining obviousness, as we formally understand the term. It is about establishing the viability of the purported technical contribution to the art. Plausibility's objective, therefore, finds a more natural home as a constituent part of the requirement for an invention. In this context, a more coherent acceptance of plausibility's role across various patent criteria could and should be developed.

Amandine Léonard

5 Wrongful preliminary injunctions and EU procedural law

5.1 Introduction

On 12 September 2019, in *Bayer Pharma AG v Richter* (C-688/17)[1], the Court of Justice of the European Union (CJEU or the court) provided some guidance on the consequences of enforcing preliminary injunctions (PIs) when the intellectual property right (IPR) justifying the measure is subsequently revoked, when it is demonstrated that there was no (risk of) infringement, or when the right holder wrongfully enforced a PI. In essence, the court's guidance was solicited in order to determine whether article 9(7) of the Enforcement Directive[2] (IPRED or the Directive), which provides that compensation can take place when such a measure causes an injury to a defendant, allows for a regime of liability *with fault* or if it supports a regime of liability *without fault*.

This decision highlights the fact that, currently, and despite the existence of article 50(7) of the TRIPs Agreement[3] and article 9(7) IPRED, there is no harmonized practice between EU member states vis-à-vis this regime of liability.[4] While some jurisdictions (such as Germany, France[5], Finland[6], Spain[7] or the Netherlands[8]) provide for a relative

---

1 Case C-688/17 *Bayer Pharma AG* [2019] EU:C:2019:722.
2 Directive 2004/48/EC on the enforcement of intellectual property rights (Enforcement Directive) [2004] OJ L 195, p. 16–25.
3 Agreement on Trade-Related Aspects of Intellectual Property Rights (TRIPs Agreement) 1994.
4 Christopher Heath, 'Wrongful Patent Enforcement – Threats and Post- Infringement Invalidity in Comparative Perspective' [2008] 39(3) International Review of Intellectual Property and Competition Law (IIC) 307–322, 308; Winfried Tilmann, 'Consequences of the CJEU's *Bayer v Richter* decision' [2022] 17(6) Journal of Intellectual Property Law & Practice (JIPLP) 526–532.
5 Article L 111-10 French Code of Civil Execution Procedures. This provision stipulates that the enforcement of a temporary order is at the risk of the plaintiff. Additionally, it is prescribed that the plaintiff restores the debtor's rights in kind or by equivalent if the title is subsequently amended. Isabelle Romet, Amandine Metier and Dora Talvard, 'Patent Enforcement in France' in Christopher Heath (ed) *Patent Enforcement Worldwide: Writings in Honour of Dieter Stauder*, (Oxford Bloomsbury Collection 2015) 145–180, 162.
6 Paragraph 11 of Chapter 7 of the Finnish Code of Judicial Procedure.
7 Article 742 of the Spanish Civil Procedure Act.
8 To enforce a PI which is overturned after proceedings on the merits is considered a wrongful enforcement and will lead to damages. Willem Hoyng and Leon Dijkman, 'Netherlands' in Jorge Contreras and M. Husovec (eds) *Injunction in patent law* (CUP 2022) 218, 225 and references. See also Jan Brinkhof and

---

Amandine Léonard, is Early Career Fellow in Intellectual Property Law, The University of Edinburgh, Edinburgh Law School.

automatic compensation in case of wrongfully granted or enforced PIs, others (such as Belgium[9] or Hungary) require that the right holder be at fault before ordering compensation to the debtor of a PI. In almost all jurisdictions, the source of such liability is also found in civil procedural law and not in specific IP laws.

Despite being brief, the court's decision provides some general food for thoughts. This chapter investigates various legal implications of the decision. First, it explores the distinction between liability with or without fault (also referred to as strict liability) for wrongful PI under IPRED and different national approaches. Second, it elaborates on two key aspects of the case: the adoption of a uniform interpretation of the notion of 'appropriate compensation' and the question of 'abuse' under the general obligation of article 3 of the Directive. Finally, the decision also opens the door for discussion on the role of EU procedural law in patent litigation. This chapter explores the relationship between EU procedural law, the Enforcement Directive and national procedural autonomy in the context of patent litigation.

5.2 Wrongful preliminary injunctions – liability with or without fault?

Article 9(7) IPRED stipulates that, *'where [] provisional measures are revoked or where they lapse due to any act or omission by the applicant, or where it is subsequently found that there has been no infringement or threat of infringement of an intellectual property right, the judicial authorities shall have the authority to order the applicant, upon request of the defendant, to provide the defendant appropriate compensation for any injury caused by those measures'*.

This provision envisages three alternative scenarios which may lead to compensation for a defendant who unduly suffers the consequences of provisional measures such as PIs. First, the revocation of the measure. Second, the action or inaction of the applicant. Third, the absence of infringement or threat thereof. This third scenario also implicitly includes the revocation of the right justifying the measure. This is because there

---

Anselm Kamperman Sanders, 'Patent Enforcement in the Netherlands' in Christopher Heath (ed.) *Patent Enforcement Worldwide: Writings in Honour of Dieter Stauder* (Oxford Bloomsbury Collection 2015) 181–203, 200. And reference to the Dutch Supreme Court decision in *Ciba Geigy v. Voorbraak*, 16 Nov. 1984, NJ 1985, 547.

9 Stefan Cattoor and Margot Van Meerbeeck, 'Compensation to the alleged infringer of an IP right for harm caused by provisional measures in case of a different outcome on appeal or on the merits; in Francois Pétillion (ed) *Handhaving van intellectuele rechten in Belgie/Respect des droits intellectuels en Belgique* (Gent: Uitgeverij Larcier 2017) 127–146. For an application of the liability regime to measures for preserving evidence, see also: *Snowfall*, Brussels Court of Appeal, 8th Div. 28 February 2018 [2018] ICIP Ing.-Cons. 325.

can be no infringement of an exclusive right if that right is deemed invalid. This is particularly relevant in patent litigation as invalidity is the most common counterclaim to infringement. If a right holder obtains a PI but sees his patent invalidated on the merits, the claim of infringement cannot be sustained. In this case, invalidity triggers the absence of infringement and the conditions of the third scenario under article 9(7) IPRED are met.

What this provision does not specify is whether the compensation for any injury suffered by a defendant should come automatically upon the realization of these scenarios or if other conditions must exist. Article 9(7) only stipulates that national courts shall have the authority to order compensation. At national level, there are different practices. For example, in Germany, right holders who request PIs[10] will be asked to provide a security (generally a monetary bank guarantee) conditioning the grant of the measures.[11] If it is later found that the patent involved in the dispute is either not infringed or invalid, there will be compensation.[12] The amount of the security is, generally, calculated to cover the costs and damages incurred by the defendant. This is due to the obligation contained in Section 945 of the German Code of Civil Procedure (*Zivilprozessordnung* – ZPO) which provides compensation for damages suffered as a result of the enforcement of an injunction.[13] There is no consideration of fault or negligence on behalf of the applicant. The security (or part thereof – as discussed hereafter) will be transferred to the defendant in order to repair the injury caused during the time of existence of the measure. This can be considered a regime of liability without fault, or strict liability, as compensation takes place upon the realization of (one of) the scenarios mentioned supra. A similar approach is followed by the courts of England and Wales where

---

[10] Under sections 935 and 940 ZPO.
[11] Peter Georg Picht and Anna-Lena Karczewiski, 'Germany' in Jorge Contreras and Martin Husovec (eds) *Injunctions in Patent Law* (CUP 2022) 142–170, 149 and reference. For the Netherlands see Hoyng and Dijkman (n 8) at 228 and reference to article 233(3) of the Dutch Code of Civil Procedure. Contrary to Germany, in the Netherlands, the security deposit is not mandatory.
[12] The defendant must nonetheless file an action for recovery under section 767 ZPO. As provided under article 9(7) IPRED compensation takes place at the initiative of the defendant. Additionally, compensation will take place unless the right holder declares that he is not going enforce the order. Christian Osterrieth, 'Patent Enforcement in Germany' in Christopher Heath (ed) *Patent Enforcement Worldwide: Writings in Honour of Dieter Stauder* (Oxford Bloomsbury Collection 2015) 111–144, 140.
[13] Section 945 ZPO: 'Obligation to compensate for damages. Should the order of a seizure or an injunction prove to have been unfounded from the start, or should the measure directed be repealed pursuant to section 926 subsection (2) or section 942 (3), the party that has obtained the order is under obligation to compensate the opponent for the damages that he has suffered as a result of the measure directed having been enforced, or as a result of the opponent having provided security in order to avert the enforcement or to obtain the repeal of the measure'. Translated from: https://www.gesetze-im-internet.de/englisch_zpo/englisch_zpo.html#p2417. See also section 717(2) ZPO providing that: '(2) If a judgment declared provisionally enforceable is reversed or modified, the plaintiff shall be obligated to compensate the defendant for the damages he has suffered by the judgment being enforced, or by the payments he had to make, or any other actions he had to take in order to avert enforcement'.

it is generally required that right holders provide a cross-undertaking for a PI. The cross-undertaking serves to compensate defendants in the event of a wrongfully granted PI. Arguably, these regimes of strict liability may 'internalize positive benefits and deter wrong behaviour as well as remove improper motives to engage in an overall socially desirable behaviour'[14]. Compensation to the debtor of the preliminary measure is justified on the fact that, without a final decision on the merits, the enforcement of such order comprises some risks for right holders.[15]

A contrario, in Belgium (or in Hungary – as discussed hereafter), compensation will only take place if a defendant can prove that a right holder acted negligently when requesting (and enforcing) the provisional measure.[16] Under this approach, we have a regime of liability with fault, where a right holder will only be ordered to compensate a defendant if it is found that the request was 'faulty'.[17]

---

[14] Ofer Grosskopf and Barak Medina, 'Remedies for Wrongfully-Issued Preliminary Injunctions: The Case for Disgorgement of Profits' [2009] 32 Seattle Univ. L. Rev. 903–941, 941. Arguing that right holders should disgorge the benefits obtained during the wrongfully enforced preliminary injunction and not necessarily compensate the defendants based on the loss suffered.

[15] Xavier Seuba, *The Global Regime for the Enforcement of Intellectual Property Rights* (CUP 2017) 226 and 2334: 'compensation will follow if an injunction wrongly granted causes injury, regardless of the existence of any mistake on the part of the right holder'. '[] compensation would follow even where the plaintiff did not act maliciously because, 'after all, the plaintiff entertains a calculated risk when requesting a provisional measure" (reference omitted).

[16] Under Belgian Law, article 1369ter para. 3 of the Judicial Code provides that courts may grant appropriate compensation. Liability for compensation will be assessed under article 1382 of the Belgian Civil Code and the regime of extracontractual liability. See also Cattoor and Van Meerbeeck (n 9); Tanguy de Haan and Christel Brion, 'Pas de responsabilité objective en matière de saisie-contrefaçon' [2018] 2 ICIP Ing.Cons., 334; Damien Dessard, 'Les abus de la saisie-description' [2005] ICIP Ing.-Cons., 304; Fernand de Visscher, 'Note sous Cass., 11 mars 2005', [2005] Auteurs & Media, 400; Brussels Court of Appeal 28 Feb. 2018 (2016/AR/4) [2018] 2 ICIP-Ing.Cons., 316.

[17] The Enforcement Directive does not distinguish between different types of provisional measures. A distinction between preliminary injunctions and seizure measures may nonetheless be important to make when it comes to liability regimes. Arguably, a regime of strict liability may be more adequate to repair the harm caused by the enforcement of a preliminary injunction than for the enforcement of a seizure. This is due to the object of the measures. The object of a seizure is to preserve evidence while a preliminary injunction aims at putting an end to infringement. The execution of the later may, therefore, per se, be particularly harmful to the interests of a debtor. On the other hand, the execution of a seizure is less likely, but not immune, to have the same effects. Therefore, a regime of liability with fault may seem more appropriate. Additionally, it should be noted that, due to the potential invasiveness of a seizure, national judges thoroughly assess all the circumstances of a particular case before ordering such measure. In light of these elements, a regime of strict liability for the enforcement of seizure measures, when it is later established that there was no infringement, may be criticised. See Sam Granata and Amandine Leonard, 'Restrictions on IP rights holders to bring legal proceedings – Belgium' in Pierre Kobel et al (eds) *Competition Law Analysis of Price and Non-price Discrimination & Abusive IP Based Legal Proceedings* [Springer 2021] 349–380.

5.2.1 The case

The CJEU was asked to ponder on this question of liability. To provide some contextual background to the case, in 2000 Bayer Pharma (the right holder) applied for a patent at the Hungarian patent office. The patent application was published in 2002. In late 2009 and 2010 Richter and Exeltis (the defendants) started marketing allegedly infringing products. In October 2010, the patent office granted the disputed patent. A month later, the defendants filed an application for a declaration of non-infringement. At the same time, the right holder applied to the Budapest High Court for a PI to prohibit the commercialisation of the allegedly infringing products. This first application was denied. The defendants then applied for a declaration of invalidity to the Hungarian patent office. Hungary having a bifurcated system of patent litigation, the questions of validity and infringement are dealt with separately. In May 2011, the right holder applied again for provisional measures. This time, the Budapest High Court granted a PI prohibiting the defendants from further commercialisation. Shortly after, Bayer initiated proceedings on the merits for infringement. In 2012, the Budapest Regional Court of Appeal upheld the provisional measures, however, shortly after, the patent office revoked the patent. By mid-2017, the Budapest High Court had definitively dismissed the claim for infringement on the grounds of invalidity.

In light of the findings of invalidity and article 9(7) IPRED, the defendants requested that the right holder be ordered to compensate the losses[18] suffered as a result of the PI granted in May 2011. On the other hand, Bayer claimed that such compensation should not take place as article 339(1) of the Hungarian Civil Code[19] stipulates that: *'any person who unlawfully causes harm to another must provide a remedy for that harm'* but that *'a person is relieved of that obligation if it is demonstrated that the person concerned acted as would generally be expected in the circumstances in question.'* Additionally, article 340(1) provides: *'The injured party is under an obligation to act as would generally be expected in the circumstances in question in order to avoid or to mitigate the loss. A party shall not be compensated for loss resulting from the injured party's failure to comply with that obligation.'* Therefore, under Hungarian civil law, compensation depends on the conduct of the applicant as well as on the conduct of the defendant.[20] According to Bayer, the defendants were responsible for their own losses because they intentionally and unlawfully placed products on the market while knowing that a patent application was pending.[21] As they decided to launch their products 'at risk' they did not act 'as would generally be expected in the circumstances in question in order to avoid or mitigate the loss' and therefore, could not claim the application of article 339(1) first sen-

---

18 The defendants argued that compensation for loss of sales due to the PI, loss of promotional costs related to the marketing of products and moral prejudice.
19 Article 339(1) of the Hungarian Civil Code.
20 Tilmann (n 4) 527.
21 C-688/17 (n 1) 31.

tence[22]. The defendants nonetheless argued that article 9(7) IPRED provides for a regime of liability without fault, or strict liability, and that it was not necessary to dive into the rules of civil liability.

Faced with this apparent contradiction, the Budapest High Court referred two questions to the CJEU, essentially questioning the compatibility of such regime of civil liability with article 9(7) IPRED. After reformulating the two questions, the CJEU considered that 'the referring court asks, in essence, whether article 9(7) of the Directive 2004/48, and in particular the concept of 'appropriate compensation' referred to in that provision, must be interpreted as precluding national legislation which provides that *a party shall not be compensated* for losses which he has suffered *due to his not having acted as may generally be expected* in order to avoid or mitigate his loss and which, in circumstances such as those in the main proceedings, results in the court not making an order for provisional measures against the applicant obliging him to provide compensation for losses caused by those measures *even though* the patent on the basis of which these were requested and granted has subsequently been found to be invalid'[23] (emphasis added).

5.2.2 Analysis

Under the reformulated question, the CJEU puts the emphasis on the meaning of 'appropriate compensation'. By doing so, the court arguably evades answering the fundamental question of which liability regime is provided by article 9(7) IPRED.[24] It nonetheless enquires whether compensation can be dependent on the behaviour of litigants (defendant as well as right holder) or if the realisation of one of the three scenarios envisaged under article 9(7) may be enough to trigger compensation. On its face, a simple analysis of this would lead to the conclusion that, if appropriate compensation depends on the behaviour of litigants, then, article 9(7) provides for a regime of liability *with* fault. While, if the scenarios envisaged in the provision are sufficient to justify compensation, then article 9(7) is arguably leaning towards a regime of liability *without* fault.

In his Opinion, Advocate General (AG) Pittruzella, argued that article 9(7) does not actually weigh in on the issue and that it is for each member state to decide on the rules which apply to determine the causal link between the measures adopted and the harm

---

[22] The question of launch at risk, as well as the practice of 'clearing the way' in the pharmaceutical sector is too specific to be discussed at length in this contribution. It is nonetheless one of specificities of patent litigation in the pharmaceutical sector and cannot be disregarded as a key element in this case.
[23] C-688/17 (n 1) 34.
[24] Others have nonetheless concluded that the court has excluded a regime of strict liability. See e.g. Tanguy de Haan, 'The CJEU sides with IP right holders: the Bayer Pharma judgment (C-688/17) and the consequences of the Europeanisation of provisional and precautionary measures relating to IP rights' [2020] 42 (11) EIPR, 767–773. Tilmann (n 4). The latter considers that the decision 'gives reason to reconsider' the German practice of strict liability.

caused as well as whether compensation should take place. He nonetheless points at one possibility which would contradict the wording as well as the spirit of article 9(7). This would be a regime which automatically prohibits compensation when the defendant entered the market without waiting for the revocation of a patent. To launch a product 'at risk' cannot automatically disqualify the defendant from compensation. This would, among other things, encourage abusive recourse to preliminary proceedings by right holders.[25] A point discussed hereafter.

In its decision, the court did not explicitly rule out that a regime of liability without fault (or a strict liability regime) would be contrary to the Directive as this was not the question referred to the court.[26] The question focused on a regime of liability with fault which, once applied to the facts of the case, would have led to the denial of compensatory damages due to the behaviour of the applicants. In other words, the question was related to the possibility for national courts to embrace a regime of liability with fault which would require to consider the behaviour of both parties before granting a compensation. On that question, the court ruled that article 9(7) and the specific reference to 'appropriate compensation' does not preclude a national rule which provides that there will not be any compensation when the applicant did not behave in a way which could have been expected by any person in order to avoid or mitigate the harm caused by the ordered measure. This, as long as national courts can consider every objective circumstance of the case, including the behaviour of all parties involved, in order to verify whether the right holder did not abuse of the measures.

Regarding the three scenarios envisaged under article 9(7), the court observes that[27] 'appropriate compensation' is strictly subject to the precondition that measures have either been repealed, or ceased to be in application due to the action or omission of the right holder, or because it has subsequently been found that there was no (threat of) infringement. The court therefore sees the three scenarios as alternative mandatory preconditions for appropriate compensation but not sufficient conditions in themselves. The court takes the position that, 'the fact that those conditions are satisfied in a specific case does not mean that the competent national courts will automatically and in any event be obliged to order the applicant to provide compensation for any losses suffered by the defendant as a result of those measures'.[28]

---

25 Opinion of Advocate General Pitruzzella in C-688/17 (AG Opinion), EU:C:2019:324, 56.
26 See a contrario, de Haan (n 24) at 769 arguing that: 'the court could not have been clearer on this point: there is no strict liability on the part of the applicant when the measures provisionally requested to protect its intellectual property right cease to be applicable in the situations at issues. The right to compensation will depend on the specific circumstances of each case and not on the mere fact that the measures were invalidated or lapsed'. As this was not the question before the court, it is difficult to fully support the claim that the court rejected, once and for all, strict liability regimes. This is also difficult to reconcile with the actual regimes of strict liability as they exist and are interpreted under national laws (such as Germany, the UK or Finland).
27 C-688/17 (n 1) 52.
28 Ibid.

While this does not form part of the operative part of the decision, this interpretation of article 9(7) seems to refute the compatibility of a regime of strict liability with the EU provision and the interpretation of 'appropriate compensation'. However, due to the lack of legal authority of this part of the judgment, it also cannot be ruled out that such a national regime might be compatible with the Directive.

This can be demonstrated by looking at the German regime of liability. Under this regime, while right holders are entitled to obtain a PI, it is also envisaged that they should put a security (or a bound) in place. In case of wrongful PI, the security will serve to repair the injury which may have been caused to the defendant for the period of existence of the measure.[29] It is however not excluded that the behaviour of the parties will be considered in the evaluation of the sum of damages which should be attributed to the defendant.[30] Therefore, if the defendant is responsible for part of the harm, or has been negligent, or did not act 'as may generally be expected in order to avoid or mitigate [] loss'[31], the defendant will not be entitled to (part of) the security. This can lead to a partial or total disqualification for compensation. This shows that even a regime of so-called strict liability can comply with the interpretation of article 9(7) and the autonomous concept of 'appropriate compensation' as provided by the court in this case.

The conclusion, that both regimes of liability with and without fault may be compliant with article 9(7) IPRED as well as the decision of the court in the Bayer case, opens the door to the issue of harmonisation (or lack thereof) of EU procedural law in patent litigation. While it is clear that the Enforcement Directive only provides for minimum harmonisation and that national courts must ensure that national provisions are interpreted in conformity with the CJEU case law, the question remains as to what has been truly achieved in terms of harmonisation? This chapter explores two elements discussed in this case: the concept of 'appropriate compensation' and the meaning of 'abuse' under the Enforcement Directive.

---

29 E.g. Heath (n 4) 321.
30 The same appears to apply in Finland where it is settled case law that, under the general principles of the law of compensation, the level of liability may be reduced considering the behaviour of the parties. See on this the request for preliminary ruling C-473/22 *Mylan AB v. Gilead Sciences Finland Oy*. In July 2022, the Finnish Market Court referred a question to the CJEU on the compatibility of a strict liability regime with article 9(7) IPRED. The decision of the court is awaited but, if anything, this shows that the 2019 decision did not provide sufficient clarity to member state courts.
31 As stipulated in the operative part of the decision. C-688/17 (n 1) 71.

5.3 'Appropriate compensation' and the meaning of 'abuse' under IPRED

5.3.1 A uniform interpretation of 'appropriate compensation'

Contrary to the Opinion of the AG, the court favoured an independent and uniform interpretation of 'appropriate compensation' as an autonomous concept of EU law[32]. For the court, article 9(7) IPRED not only provides defendants with a right to compensation, but it also defines the content of this right. As such, national rules concerning liability, which may or may not be found in IP-specific legislation, must be overridden. The court rests the adoption of a uniform interpretation on two objectives of the Directive. More specifically, on the objective of harmonisation and the objective expressed at Recital 10, namely 'to ensure a high, equivalent and homogeneous level of protection [of IP rights] in the internal market'.[33] According to the court if member states remained free to determine the content, the scope and methods to apply the concept of appropriate compensation, this would fail the objective of equivalence and homogeneity in the high level of protection of IP.[34] A uniform interpretation would not contradict the TRIPs Agreement as it allows for a decision of participating states, and that the EU member states, by participating in the Enforcement Directive, have agreed on this higher level of harmonisation.[35] In other words, by adopting the Directive, EU member states have decided to go one step further than the general standards of TRIPs.[36]

As previously mentioned, AG Pitruzzella was of the opinion that more harmonisation than what was provided under the TRIPs Agreement (especially under Part III – Enforcement) was not the objective of the Directive and that member states should remain free, via the TRIPs flexibilities, to determine what appropriate compensation mean un-

---

[32] C-688/17 (n 1) 40. The court therefore went one step further than in its decision in C-681/13 *Diageo* [2015] EU:C:2015:471, which left the conditions for appropriate compensation, or the type of liability, unspecified.
[33] C-688/17 (n 1) 42; 48. The court has regularly cited this recital as embodying the main objective of the Directive. See e.g.: C-264/19 *Constantin Film* [2020] EU:C:2020:542, 35; C-324/09, *L'Oreal v eBay* [2011] EU:C:2011:474, 144; C-494/15 *Tommy Hilfiger* [2016] EU:C:2016:528; C-681/13 *Diageo* [2015] EU:C:2015:471, 77; C-57/15 *United Video Properties v Telenet* [2016] EU:C:2016:611, 27; C-44-21 *Phoenix Contact* [2022] EU:C:2022:309, 37.
[34] C-688/17 (n 1) 44.
[35] *Ibid* 42.
[36] Article 50(7) TRIPs stipulates that: 'Where provisional measures are revoked or lapse by reason of an act or omission of the claimant or where it is subsequently found that there has been no infringement or threatened infringement of an IP right, the courts shall have the power to order the claimant, at the request of the defendant, to pay to the defendant appropriate compensation for any prejudice caused by such measures'. See also Matthias Leistner and Viola Pless, 'European Union' in Jorge Contreras and Martin Husovec (eds) *Injunctions in patent law* (CUP 2022) 26–64, 27.

der national laws. Each member state should be free 'to determine the substantive rules governing the defendant's right to compensation' by either providing specific IP-related provisions or relying on existing normative frameworks.[37]

Despite this divergence, the court and the AG agreed on few key points when it comes to the determination of appropriate compensation. First, appropriate compensation should be accessible to defendants and a blanket denial of compensation on the basis of a situation of 'launch at risk', would be contrary to the Directive. Second, the regime of appropriate compensation should not dissuade right holders from applying for provisional measures. By doing so, the court does not provide specific guidance on what appropriate compensation actually *is* but only what is *ought not to be*. The court leaves it to national courts to consider the specific circumstances of each case before determining what will be appropriate compensation.

From a harmonisation standpoint, this approach might have some shortcomings. First, even though the court states that 'appropriate compensation' must benefit from a uniform interpretation, the guidelines as to what this interpretation should be are vague. As mentioned, the court considers that it is for national courts to assess the specific circumstances of a case to decide whether it is appropriate to order an 'compensation' or not. How different national courts will interpret this remains to be seen. Second, in the specific context of article 9(7) and the consequential regimes of liability of a PI, it must be noted that many member states do not have specific rules in their IP laws and therefore rely extensively on civil law, tort law, or procedural law principles in order to determine whether there should be any compensation. The decision of the court to foster a uniform interpretation within the framework of IP litigation may present some challenges for these other bodies of law, in particular when it might not be possible to interpret applicable national rules in conformity with the decision.

The decision makes clear that appropriate compensation should not dissuade right holders from requesting provisional measures such as PIs. Understandably, such measures are primordial for right holders to protect their exclusive rights. However, if appropriate compensation was not envisaged, right holders may be prone to request measures without either a clear intention to pursue an action on the merits or simply without having sufficient ground for a claim of infringement. The absence of compensation could leave these requests unchecked and abusive or unjustified requests could flourish. Despite the existence of balancing mechanisms embedded in the conditions to obtain provisional measures[38],

---

37 AG Opinion (n 25) 36–41.
38 Article 9(1)(a) stipulates that a request for a PI must prevent an 'imminent' infringement of an IP right or forbid the continuation of alleged infringements of that right. National courts must therefore verify that these conditions are met. In the event of on-going acts of infringement, the Directive also envisages that a recurring penalty payment may be put in place 'where appropriate' or that guarantees intended to ensure compensation of the right holder be envisaged. There again, national courts have some flexibility to consider all the circumstances of a case and therefore the interests and behaviour of both parties. Article 9(3) also requires that national courts have the authority to require the applicant (i.e. the right holder)

the presence of a compensation scheme may also dissuade right holders from making frivolous claims.

In its decision, the court may have weakened this effect. The court considers that appropriate compensation should take place when a provisional measure has been unjustifiably applied for. The interpretation of 'unjustified application' is rather strict as the court concludes that the 'unjustified nature of a claim presupposes the absence of risk of irreparable harm to the IP right holder in the event of delay in the adoption of the requested measure'.[39] To determine if a request is unjustified, it is necessary to refer to the time of application and not to a time, *a posteriori*, when it has been established that the measures have lapsed or that there is no infringement. For the court, what may be indicative of a risk of irreparable harm is a situation where a defendant has started to commercialise a potentially infringing product or service despite the existence of a registered patent or patent application.[40]

This strict interpretation of unjustified requests raises two further queries. First, if, at the time of the request, there is no risk of irreparable harm, it may be questioned why a national court would grant a preliminary injunction. The risk of irreparable harm may condition the grant of a PI.[41] The purpose of a PI is to put a temporary end to infringement (or threat thereof) which may cause irreparable harm. However, it is not clear why appropriate compensation should also be dependent on this condition of irreparable harm.[42] In practice, this approach may effectively exclude compensation in a certain number of cases as it will become more difficult for defendants to demonstrate that right holders requested unjustified measures.[43]

---

to provide any reasonable available evidence to satisfy themselves with a sufficient degree of certainty that the applicant is the right holder, and that the applicant's right is being infringed, or that such infringement is imminent. Overall, request for PIs and other interim measures, require that national authorities examine the specific features of each case and engage with an 'overall objective assessment' of the facts before granting the requested measures. The conditions to obtain a PI are demanding. See for France, article L. 615-3 IPC and Thibault Gisclard and Emmanuel Py, 'France' in Jorge Contreras and Martin Husovec (eds) *Injunctions in patent law* (CUP 2022) 124, 129. For the Netherlands, see Hoyng and Dijkman (n 8) 219, 221.

39 C-688/17 (n 1) 62. Referring to Recital 22 IPRED. See also de Haan (n 24) 769.
40 C-688/17 (n 1) 63.
41 For example, the requirement of 'risk' is a condition under Finnish law. See request for preliminary ruling C-473/22 *Mylan AB v. Gilead Sciences Finland Oy*.
42 For Tilmann (n 4) national courts will have to consider this aspect once at the stage of granting an injunction and again when deciding on (the amount of) damages (at 532).
43 On the relationship between procedural rules and substantive rules protecting defendants and the risk of 'one-sided view' see Matthias Storme, 'Harmonisation of Civil Procedure and the Interaction with Substantive Private Law' in Xandra E. Kramer and C.H. (Remco) van Rhee *Civil Litigation in a Globalising World* (Springer 2012) 141–156, 152; 153. Observing that: 'where rules of substantive law are too harsh or of punitive nature, even defendants who are quite convinced of their innocence will prefer a bad settlement over the small risk of incurring such a sanction' and that 'procedural law also plays a role in limiting legal harassment and more generally in limiting the procedural burden of 'innocent' defendants'.

Second, article 9(7) IPRED does not refer to the terms 'justified' or 'unjustified'. This wording is only to be found in Recital 22. Additionally, even in Recital 22, there is some uncertainty as to the relevance of an irreparable harm for the determination of appropriate compensation. It is stipulated that 'guarantees need [] to cover the costs and the injury caused to the defendant by an unjustified request'. However, in its English version, the Directive only refers to the risk of irreparable harm as an example of a situation which would 'particularly' justify that measures be provided. In French, it is equally considered that such measures would be justified, 'including'[44] in case of irreparable harm. Recital 22 therefore leaves the door open to other scenarios which may qualify as justified or unjustified.

Interestingly, in a subsequent decision from the CJEU, the court notes that provisional measures are, indeed, '*particularly justified* where any delay would cause irreparable harm to right holders' (emphasis added).[45] This might attenuate some of the effects of the Bayer decision. However, the analysis hereabove regarding the role and place of the terms 'justified' would still stand.

5.3.2 The question of 'abuse' under article 3(2) IPRED

The court makes two important points regarding the principle of abuse. First, it recognises that article 3(2) is a general obligation which applies to the whole chapter II of the Directive[46]. This means that, for the circumstances of each case, article 9(7) should be read in combination with article 3. This also means that, in interpreting every provision of chapter II, a similar approach must be followed. Therefore, article 11 'Injunction' must also be read in combination with article 3. If the court focuses on the question of abuse in this case, it does not exclude that the other fundamental principles consecrated in this provision should not also govern the appreciation of measures, procedures and remedies. The grant and/or enforcement of an injunction should therefore comply with these principles of effectiveness, dissuasiveness, and proportionality.[47] The latter principle being at the heart of current debates as to whether it should influence the practice of national courts (in particular German courts) that grant automatic injunctions.[48]

---

44 The original text in French uses the word '*notamment*'.
45 Martin Stierle, 'Provisional measures and the risk of patent invalidity – *Phoenix Contact* and the German approach to interlocutory injunctions' [2022] 17(11) JIPLP 962–971, 966. C-44-21 *Phoenix Contact* [2022] EU:C:2022:309, 32.
46 C-688/17 (n 1) 66 et seq. See also C-367/15 *Stowarzyszenie* [2017] EU:C:2017:36, 21; C-597/19 *Mircom* [2021] EU:C:2021:492, 94.
47 Ansgar Ohly, 'Three Principles of European IP Enforcement Law: Effectiveness, Proportionality, Dissuasiveness' in Josef Drexl (ed), *Technology and Competition, Contributions in Honous of Hanns Ullrich* (Larcier 2009) 257–274.
48 See in general Jorge Contreras and Martin Husovec (eds) *Injunctions in patent law* (CUP 2022). Most, if not all, contributors argue in favour of more proportionality in the assessment of injunctive relief. In par-

The second important point made by the court vis-à-vis the principle of abuse is that it provides that an abusive PI should be assessed in light of all the *objective* circumstances of a case[49] and that it is for the national courts to determine such abuse.[50] Under many national interpretations of the principle of abuse, the meaning of abuse is dependent on *subjective* circumstances. The bad faith[51] of the right holder, its intention to harm[52] or his specific knowledge of essential elements of a case[53] have led national courts to consider some enforcement actions to be abusive. However, other objective elements may also lead to the conclusion that there is an abuse. The interpretation of article 3(2) IPRED provided by the court may mitigate some of the effects discussed above and the fact that right holders will have to provide appropriate compensation when the measures was unjustified. By recognising that appropriate compensation requires that courts consider all the objective circumstances of a case, it may be found that to request a PI is abusive and therefore unjustifiable. On the other hand, the fact that defendants will have to demonstrate that right holders have 'abusively' requested provisional measures, makes it particularly difficult to obtain appropriate compensation. Defendants are burdened with a great duty of care as well as a great burden of proof. Right holders however, who enforce probabilistic rights[54] and request provisional measures without having to demonstrate, on the merits, that there is an infringement or that their right is valid, are in an advantageous position.[55] It is unclear why the risk taken by right holders when initiating preliminary proceedings benefits from the safety valves elaborated by the CJEU. While defendants are left in a weakened position. Arguably, in this scenario,

---

ticular for permanent injunctions. See also Hoyng and Dijkman (n 8) 231 considering that 'the CJEU has revolutionized European IP through a series of decisions in which it interprets and weaponizes the proportionality requirement in article 3(2) Enforcement Directive []'.

49 C-688/17 (n 1) 69; 70.

50 This point has also been reiterated in *Phoenix Contact* (n 33) at 42–44. The CJEU considers that article 3 (2) IPRED represents a 'mechanism for national courts to mitigate the risk that defendants may suffer harm as a result of the adoption of interim measures'.

51 See in Germany where the principle of abuse of rights is grounded in section 242 BGB and the duty to perform in good faith.

52 See for example in France, where the principle of abuse is connected to negligence and malicious intent. Gisclard and Py (n 38) 132 and reference.

53 The court points to the fact that there may be an abuse if the applicant files an application for a PI knowing of the grounds for invalidity which lead to the revocation of the patent.

54 Meaning that despite being granted by patent office, it can never be certain that patents are valid. In *Phoenix Contact* (n 33), the CJEU refers to another decision (*Generics*) in which the court stated that the presumption of validity sheds no light on the outcome of any dispute in relation to the validity of that patent. See also Heath (n 4) at 319 asking: '[] to what extent a system that inherently (and perhaps inevitably) grants faulty patents should provide for appropriate balancing mechanisms for their invalidation'.

55 See also de Haan (n 24) 771: 'The advantages given by the Court of Justice to right holders should prompt third parties which run the risk of facing claims for the infringement of intellectual property rights owing to their activities to exercise greater caution'.

the substantial impact that a PI may have on the business of defendants is only partially accounted for.[56]

5.4 EU procedural law and patent litigation

It has been argued that the case confirms that 'as far as civil law liability is applied to intellectual property, national courts in the EU can only apply their national law provided that the latter is in line with EU law'[57] and that the 'Bayer Pharma judgment confirms the advanced Europeanisation of provisional and precautionary measures relating to intellectual property rights'.[58] While the first conclusion is certainly true, this issue lies in the assessment of such compatibility between national law and EU law. As for the question of Europeanisation of IP litigation principles (and patent litigation in particular), it may be difficult to argue that the decision represents such a clear step forward. The court takes from Recital 7 and 8 of the Enforcement Directive that there are discrepancies between member states in terms of enforcement and that these affect the proper functioning of the internal market and prevent IP rights from being equally protected throughout the Union.[59] The decision nonetheless does not redress these discrepancies in the case of wrongful preliminary injunction. As shown supra, there are ways to conclude that both, a fault-based regime and a strict liability regime for wrongful PI, are compatible with the Enforcement Directive.[60] More generally, this conclusion opens the door for discussion on the role and effect of harmonisation of IP litigation in Europe and the specific place of patent litigation.

5.4.1 IP Enforcement and vertical harmonisation

The regulatory framework for the enforcement of IPRs within the EU is represented by the traditional 'multi-layered EU law system of primary EU law, secondary EU law, i.e. unification and harmonisation of member states' law by way of regulations and directives, and member states' laws which in particular implement the EU directives into na-

---

56 In jurisdictions with a bifurcated system this might lead to more detailed considerations going beyond the scope of this chapter.
57 de Haan (n 24) 767.
58 Ibid, 770.
59 Tilmann (n 4) 528.
60 This is not the only decision which has led commentators to conclude that different practices can be interpreted in compatibility with the Enforcement Directive. See for example the recent decision *Phoenix Contact* (n 33). Stierle (n 45) observed that: 'prominent judges have already declared that they will not change the existing practice' (at 967 and references).

tional law'[61]. The Enforcement Directive is clearly intended to create uniform protection of IP rights and member states must respect the principle of primacy of EU law. Nevertheless, the directive only establishes minimum standards for enforcement and member states are given certain leeway for implementation. This notwithstanding the creation of 'autonomous concept of EU law'.

Contrary to other harmonisation efforts in the field of civil procedural law which are based on article 81 TFEU[62], the Enforcement Directive is based on article 114 TFEU. Under this provision, the EU adopts legislative measures for the approximation of the laws of the member states 'which have as their object the establishment and functioning of the internal market'. Under article 81 TFEU, the competence of the EU is limited to develop cooperation in civil matters with cross-border implications.[63] This limitation does not apply to article 114 TFEU where the EU can adopt legislative measures which will be applicable to domestic disputes only. It is this limitation of article 81 TFEU which has led to the development of additional bases for European legislation in the area of civil procedure[64] and to considering article 114 TFEU as the proper legal basis of the Enforcement Directive. This development has been referred to as a 'new approach' to procedural harmonisation, 'vertical harmonisation' or the 'invisible pillar of Europeanisation of procedural law'.[65] The Enforcement Directive is sector-specific and does apply to exclusively domestic disputes. It is therefore part of this vertical harmonisation effort and the invisible pillar of Europeanisation of procedural law.[66]

---

[61] Leistner and Pless (n 36) 26.
[62] C.H. (Remco) van Rhee, 'Harmonisation of Civil Procedure: An Historical and Comparative Perspective' in Xandra E. Kramer and C.H. (Remco) van Rhee *Civil Litigation in a Globalising World* (Springer 2012) 39–63, 54.
[63] Such as the Council Regulation (EU) 1215/2012 on jurisdiction and the recognition and enforcement of judgments in civil and commercial matters (recast) (Brussels I Regulation) [2012] OJ L 351, 1–32 or the Council Regulation (EC) 593/2008 on the law applicable to contractual obligations (Rome I Regulation) [2008] OJ L 177, 6–16. On the distinction between instruments based on article 81 TFEU and article 114 TFEU see more generally Eva Storskrubb, 'EU Civil Justice at the Harmonisation Crossroads?' in Anna Nylund (ed) *Civil Procedure and Harmonisation of Law* (Intersentia 2019) 11–34; Gerhard Wagner, 'Harmonisation of Civil Procedure: Policy Perspectives' in Xandra E. Kramer and C.H. (Remco) van Rhee *Civil Litigation in a Globalising World* (Springer 2012) 93–119, 95; 97.
[64] Wagner (n 63) 101; Burkhard Hess, 'Procedural Harmonisation in a European Context' in Xandra E. Kramer and C.H. (Remco) van Rhee *Civil Litigation in a Globalising World* (Springer 2012) 159–173, 162.
[65] Storksrubb (n 63) 17 and references.
[66] *Ibid.*, 18 observing that: 'With [the adoption of] sector specific procedural rules, it shows that Member States are willing to proceed with harmonisation in some instance under the guise of effective enforcement of substantive EU civil law'.

5.4.2 Reflections for patent litigation and civil procedural law

Much of the literature on EU procedural law sees the Enforcement Directive as a particularly successful example of harmonisation.[67] Under EU law, it is generally[68] considered that procedural tools (such as the Enforcement Directive) are meant to complement or support the exercise of EU substantive rights.[69] Procedural rules are there to, ultimately, help the harmonisation of substantive law which could be prevented by 'extensive differences in the court procedure'.[70] There is therefore a strong path dependency between substantive and procedural rules.[71] This is particularly the case for procedural tools which are adopted on the basis of article 114 TFEU, such as the Enforcement Directive.[72] This understanding of the place of EU procedural law raises two issues when we consider patent litigation as well as civil procedural law.

First, it is clear that this rationale of complementary and support works to some extent for copyright and trademark law because substantive EU law rules exist for these two fields of IP law. On the other hand, this rationale cannot fully work for patent law as there is no EU substantive patent law.[73] The Enforcement Directive is however meant to

---

67 See for example Xandra E. Kramer and C.H. (Remco) van Rhee *Civil Litigation in a Globalising World* (Springer 2012) 7; and reference to Wagner's chapter (n 63) arguing that vertical harmonisation realised, for example, by the Enforcement Directive is 'fruitful since it offers a valuable tool for experimenting with harmonisation []'. See also Hess (n 64) 165; observing that 'existing (successful) instruments are used as models for additional legislation'. The model referred to is the Enforcement Directive which has subsequently been used by the European Commission in other projects such as collective redress in cartel and consumer protection law.
68 See however Storme (n 43) 142: '[] the function of procedural law should not be reduced to merely making effective the legal effects stated by substantive law, i.e. mainly protecting and enforcing subjective rights; its role is also to make the effects of substantive law in a concrete case acceptable, to legitimise them to a certain extent'.
69 Storksrubb (n 63) 14–15, arguing that special procedural rules enacted for specific types of disputes, such as IP, are ancillary to the harmonisation of substantive rules. Wagner (n 63) 101, noting that legislation in the area of civil procedure is concerned with 'substantive' policy areas and 'substantive rights created or protected by European law'. Hess (n 64) 159: 'The principles of effectiveness and equivalence regarding the enforcement of EU law also have an impact on civil procedure, including the new competence to harmonise procedural laws if these do not sufficiently implement substantive EU law, laid down in article 114 TFEU'. Hess (n 64) 161: 'According to the case law of the [CJEU], the judiciaries of the Member States must efficiently enforce EU law on the basis of their respective domestic procedures. In this field [] a genuine harmonisation of procedural laws takes place which shall reinforce the proper implementation of EU law'.
70 Kramer and van Rhee (n 67) 2.
71 *Ibid.*, 5. See also Louis Visscher, 'A Law and Economics View on Harmonisation of Procedural Law' in Xandra E. Kramer and C.H. (Remco) van Rhee *Civil Litigation in a Globalising World* (Springer 2012) 65–91.
72 Hess (n 64) 167; Article 114 includes 'the power of harmonising national procedural laws if the latter do not sufficiently implement substantive EU law'.
73 With the exception of the Biotechnology Directive.

be applied equally to copyright, trademark, and patent law.[74] Moreover, due to the nature of patent rights as negative rights, or rights to oppose to infringement, we can also easily understand that enforcement rules are of great importance, and may even delineate the actual scope of patent rights.[75]

Second, as we saw from the *Bayer Pharma* case, the applicable procedural rules in IP disputes are to be found mostly in civil procedural law and not in specific IP instruments. The Enforcement Directive is not meant to harmonise certain aspects of civil procedure, but to improve the enforcement of intellectual property rights, by providing tools to obtain 'compensation for the harm caused by infringements of intellectual property rights, as well as, for enjoining future infringements'.[76] It remains however that the Directive touches upon 'topics which lie close to the heart of any system of civil procedure'[77] and despite being technically confined to the enforcement and protection of IP rights, the Directive may have far reaching consequences.[78] As observed by T. de Haan, 'through its interpretation of Directive 2004/48 [], the Court of Justice is intruding, concretely and tangibly, into the area of civil liability law. As this law comes into play in the protection of intellectual property rights, it must be applied and understood in accordance with EU law, as interpreted by the Court of Justice'.[79] This is not new as 'there has been considerable interaction between EU law and domestic procedural law over the decades and the impact of EU law, both on domestic procedural law in general and in domestic courts, can be considered significant'.[80] However, the court as well as EU institutions in general, have limited competence to define civil liability rules or substantive rules of patent law[81]. These remain within the privy of national legislators. Instances such as the one discussed in this chapter raise concerns in terms of national procedural autonomy[82] and delineation of legislative powers.

---

[74] Leistner and Pless (n 36) 27.
[75] R. Hilty, 'The Role of Enforcement in Delineating the Scope of IP Rights', Max Planck Institute for Innovation & Competition Research Paper No. 15-03 (2015). Available at SSRN:https://ssrn.com/abstract=2602221
[76] Wagner (n 63) 102.
[77] *Ibid.*, 103.
[78] *Ibid.*, 93.
[79] de Haan (n 24) 772.
[80] Storskrubb (n 63) 12.
[81] See e.g. Jan Brinkhof and Ansgar Ohly, 'Towards a Unified Patent Court in Europe' in Ansgar Ohly and Justine Pila (eds) *The Europeanization of Intellectual Property Law* (OUP 2013) 199–216, 215: 'the CJEU should decide issues of broader relevance which relate to basic principles or other areas of EU law, but it should not get involved in technicalities of patentability or of patent scope'.
[82] Storskrubb, (n 63) 12. Observing that there is an 'awareness that the MS' procedural autonomy is *de facto* limited'.

5.5 Conclusion

On its face, the decision of the court and the narrow question of wrongful preliminary injunctions may seem rather trivial. It nonetheless proved to open a Pandora box on the question of the (in-)visible hand of EU procedural law in IP litigation. This includes to, not only look at the existence and effect of the Enforcement Directive in IP litigation (i.e. the visible part of EU procedural law) but also at the implications, sometimes unintended, of such instrument of harmonisation on patent litigation, as a sub-set of IP litigation, and other fields of civil procedural law (i.e. the less, if not in-visible part of EU procedural law). It might be worth considering the actual impact of the case law of the CJEU in terms of achieving its objective of harmonisation[83] and Europeanisation of IP. Bearing in mind the potential consequences for patent litigation, this seems particularly time sensitive considering the Unified Patent Court.

5.6 References

5.6.1 Legislation

Agreement on Trade-Related Aspects of Intellectual Property Rights (TRIPs Agreement) 1994.
Directive 2004/48/EC on the enforcement of intellectual property rights (Enforcement Directive) [2004] OJ L 195, p. 16–25.

5.6.2 Case law

Request for preliminary ruling C-473/22 *Mylan AB v. Gilead Sciences Finland Oy*.
C-44-21 *Phoenix Contact* [2022] EU:C:2022:309.
C-597/19 *Mircom* [2021] EU:C:2021:492.
C-264/19 *Constantin Film* [2020] EU:C:2020:542.
Case C-688/17 *Bayer Pharma AG* [2019] EU:C:2019:722.
Opinion of Advocate General Pitruzzella in C-688/17, EU:C:2019:324.
C-367/15 *Stowarzyszenie* [2017] EU:C:2017:36.
C-494/15 *Tommy Hilfiger* [2016] EU:C:2016:528.
C-57/15 *United Video Properties v Telenet* [2016] EU:C:2016:611.
C-681/13 *Diageo* [2015] EU:C:2015:471.
C-324/09, *L'Oreal v eBay* [2011] EU:C:2011:474.

---

83 As previously mentioned, one of the objectives of the Directive is to approximate the previously divergent national legal systems of IP enforcement. See Leistner and Pless (n 36) 28.

5.6.3 Secondary sources

Brinkhof J. and Kamperman Sanders A., 'Patent Enforcement in the Netherlands' in Christopher Heath (ed.) *Patent Enforcement Worldwide: Writings in Honour of Dieter Stauder* (Oxford Bloomsbury Collection 2015) 181–203.

Brinkhof J. and Ohly A., 'Towards a Unified Patent Court in Europe' in Ansgar Ohly and Justine Pila (eds) *The Europeanization of Intellectual Property Law* (OUP 2013) 199–216.

Cattoor S. and Van Meerbeeck M., 'Compensation to the alleged infringer of an IP right for harm caused by provisional measures in case of a different outcome on appeal or on the merits; in Francois Pétillion (ed) *Handhaving van intellectuele rechten in Belgie/Respect des droits intellectuels en Belgique* (Gent: Uitgeverij Larcier 2017) 127–146.

de Haan T., 'The CJEU sides with IP right holders: the Bayer Pharma judgment (C-688/17) and the consequences of the Europeanisation of provisional and precautionary measures relating to IP rights' [2020] 42(11) EIPR, 767–773.

de Haan T. and Brion C., 'Pas de responsabilité objective en matière de saisie-contrefaçon' [2018] 2 ICIP Ing. Cons., 334.

de Visscher F., 'Note sous Cass., 11 mars 2005', [2005] Auteurs & Media, 400.

Dessard D., 'Les abus de la saisie-description' [2005] ICIP Ing.-Cons., 304.

Gisclard T. and Py E., 'France' in Jorge Contreras and Martin Husovec (eds) *Injunctions in patent law* (CUP 2022) 124–141.

Granata S. and Leonard A., 'Restrictions on IP rights holders to bring legal proceedings – Belgium' in Pierre Kobel et al (eds) *Competition Law Analysis of Price and Non-price Discrimination & Abusive IP Based Legal Proceedings* [Springer 2021] 349–380.

Grosskopf O. and Medina B., 'Remedies for Wrongfully-Issued Preliminary Injunctions: The Case for Disgorgement of Profits' [2009] 32 Seattle Univ. L. Rev. 903–941.

Heath C., 'Wrongful Patent Enforcement – Threats and Post- Infringement Invalidity in Comparative Perspective' [2008] 39(3) International Review of Intellectual Property and Competition Law (IIC) 307–322.

Hess B., 'Procedural Harmonisation in a European Context' in Xandra E. Kramer and C.H. (Remco) van Rhee *Civil Litigation in a Globalising World* (Springer 2012) 159–173.

Hilty R., 'The Role of Enforcement in Delineating the Scope of IP Rights', Max Planck Institute for Innovation & Competition Research Paper No. 15-03 (2015). Available at SSRN: https://ssrn.com/abstract=2602221

Hoyng W. and Dijkman L., 'Netherlands' in Jorge Contreras and M. Husovec (eds) *Injunction in patent law* (CUP 2022) 218–236.

Leistner M. and Pless V., 'European Union' in Jorge Contreras and Martin Husovec (eds) *Injunctions in patent law* (CUP 2022) 26–64.

Ohly A., 'Three Principles of European IP Enforcement Law: Effectiveness, Proportionality, Dissuasiveness' in Josef Drexl (ed), *Technology and Competition, Contributions in Honous of Hanns Ullrich* (Larcier 2009) 257–274.

Osterrieth C., 'Patent Enforcement in Germany' in Christopher Heath (ed) *Patent Enforcement Worldwide: Writings in Honour of Dieter Stauder* (Oxford Bloomsbury Collection 2015) 111–144.

Picht P. and Karczewiski A-L., 'Germany' in Jorge Contreras and Martin Husovec (eds) *Injunctions in Patent Law* (CUP 2022) 142–170.

Romet I., Metier A. and Talvard D., 'Patent Enforcement in France' in Christopher Heath (ed) *Patent Enforcement Worldwide: Writings in Honour of Dieter Stauder*, (Oxford Bloomsbury Collection 2015) 145–180.

Seuba X., *The Global Regime for the Enforcement of Intellectual Property Rights* (CUP 2017).

Stierle M., 'Provisional measures and the risk of patent invalidity – *Phoenix Contact* and the German approach to interlocutory injunctions' [2022] 17(11) JIPLP 962–971.

Storme M., 'Harmonisation of Civil Procedure and the Interaction with Substantive Private Law' in Xandra E. Kramer and C.H. (Remco) van Rhee *Civil Litigation in a Globalising World* (Springer 2012) 141–156.

Storskrubb E., 'EU Civil Justice at the Harmonisation Crossroads?' in Anna Nylund (ed) *Civil Procedure and Harmonisation of Law* (Intersentia 2019) 11–34.

Tilmann W., 'Consequences of the CJEU's *Bayer v Richter* decision' [2022] 17(6) Journal of Intellectual Property Law & Practice (JIPLP) 526–532.

van Rhee C.H., 'Harmonisation of Civil Procedure: An Historical and Comparative Perspective' in Xandra E. Kramer and C.H. (Remco) van Rhee *Civil Litigation in a Globalising World* (Springer 2012) 39–63.

Visscher L., 'A Law and Economics View on Harmonisation of Procedural Law' in Xandra E. Kramer and C.H. (Remco) van Rhee *Civil Litigation in a Globalising World* (Springer 2012) 65–91.

Wagner G., 'Harmonisation of Civil Procedure: Policy Perspectives' in Xandra E. Kramer and C.H. (Remco) van Rhee *Civil Litigation in a Globalising World* (Springer 2012) 93–119.

Maciej Padamczyk, Duncan Matthews
6 Proportionality and patent injunctions

6.1 Introduction: proportionality and enforcement of patent rights

A large part of the current debate surrounding the patent system is concerned with the perceived excessiveness of patent protection. Such arguments pertain to the scope and duration of patent protection, but also to enforcement of patent rights. The exponential technological and economic development and the emergence of multiple disturbing market practices led the literature and jurisprudence to identify certain factual patterns in which patent enforcement, in particular the issuance of final,[1] and preliminary injunctions,[2] may lead to results undesirable from the standpoint of the purposes of the patent system. Thus, a need emerged to provide for theoretical and legal tools which would ensure that all relevant policy factors are taken into account when deciding on the grant of injunctions. Amongst the principles that seem to be the most likely candidates to guide courts' discretion in this respect is the principle of proportionality, which can be found in the basic international documents in the area, the World Trade Organisation (WTO) Agreement on Trade-Related Aspects of Intellectual Property Rights (the TRIPS Agreement)[3] and the European Union (EU) Enforcement Directive.[4] But what the principle of proportionality actually means and how it should be applied in practice is not clearly defined. Instead, scholars and courts have developed a variety of possible interpretations and applications which are concentrated around the following questions. Is the right to obtain an injunction absolute? Is complexity of the product a relevant factor? Should only practicing entities be entitled to receive an injunction? What role should the proportionality principle play in courts' decisions, namely is it simply a safety valve to prevent cases of gross abuse of patent rights, or is it an overarching principle applicable to all cases; and if the latter, how can the courts ensure an appropriate structure of argumentation and legal certainty? Finally, to what extent should these considerations apply to preliminary in-

---

1 Note that final injunctions are also referred to as 'permanent' injunctions. For the sake of consistency, this chapter will apply the former term, unless when quoting from another source.
2 Note that preliminary injunctions are also referred to as 'interim' or 'interlocutory' injunctions. For the sake of consistency, this chapter will apply the former term, unless when quoting from another source.
3 Art. 41 and 44 of The Agreement on Trade-Related Aspects of Intellectual Property Rights ('TRIPS' or 'TRIPS Agreement').
4 Directive 2004/48/EC of the European Parliament and of the Council of 29 April 2004 on the enforcement of intellectual property rights (OJ L 157, 30.4.2004).

Maciej Padamczyk, is Research Associate and PhD Candidate, Queen Mary University of London.
Duncan Matthews, is Professor of Intellectual Property Law, Queen Mary University of London.

https://doi.org/10.1515/9783110781687-006

junctions, given their specificity as provisionary measures? The way in which the public decision makers will answer these questions is likely to shape the way patent rights are enforced, and will likely affect, for the good or the bad, the attractiveness of patent protection and thus investment in innovation. All these issues will be of even greater importance with the advent of the Unified Patent Court (UPC), which will be issuing injunctions covering the territories of all contracting member states of the EU.

The purpose of this chapter is to address these issues by presenting the current landscape of the enforcement of patent rights through injunctions, identifying the most important tendencies that might shape the future European patent system, particularly the UPC. First, the chapter will outline the technological and economic developments that led to the identification of a set of policy considerations which in turn led commentators to call for greater inclusion of proportionality when deciding on the grant of injunctions. Second, it will describe how the subject matter literature tries to conceptualise the principle of proportionality. Third, an analysis of the current legal frameworks for the grant of injunctions will follow, with an explanation of the applicable provisions of the US, UK and German patent systems in comparative analysis. The chapter will also take into account the impact that policy considerations can have on preliminary injunctions, particularly with regard to provisional measures. Finally, the chapter will suggest how the proportionality principle can be better conceptualized in a manner capable of ensuring that the policy factors we have identified are properly addressed and, ultimately, reflected in judicial practice.

6.2 Injunctions: policy considerations

One possible approach for addressing policy considerations is to view injunctive relief as an essential component of patent protection.[5] In this regard, in civil law jurisdictions, such as Germany or France, the courts' predilection for granting permanent injunctions seems to follow from the exclusionary nature of patent rights as property rights.[6] Weakening patent protection by refusing to grant final injunctions could hinder the purpose of the patent, namely the protection of the invention. In the US, prior to the *Ebay* ruling, similar types of argumentation were traditionally presented within the framework of 'entitlement theory', which considered damages as an insufficient remedy in case of patent infringement.[7]

---

5 Bundesrat Drucksache 683/20, 56; see also, for example, the opinion of Advocate General Wathelet in Huawei v ZTE Case C-171/12 [34], as cited in Jorge Contreras, Martin Husovec, *Introduction*, [in] *Injunctions in Patent Law: A Trans-Atlantic Dialogue on Flexibility and Tailoring*, Contreras, Husovec (eds.), Cambridge University Press 2022, 334.
6 Germany: Bundesrat Drucksache 683/20; France: Thibault Gisclard, Emmanuel Py, 'France' [in] Contreras, Husovec (eds.), *Injunctions...* (n 5).
7 James Fischer, 'What hath the *eBay v. MercExchange* wrought', 14 Lewis and Clark Law Review (2010), 559.

These traditional views subsequently came under pressure due to situations where, as Justice Kennedy put it, the nature of the patent being enforced and the economic function of the patent holder present considerations unlike earlier cases.[8] Scholars identified several types of cases where such tensions are most likely to arise. First, there is a general problem of anticommons in patent law, and the related existence of patent thickets.[9] The problem of anticommons in the context of patent law occurs where numerous entities possess patent rights over the same product, leading to a problem of patent thickets. A patent thicket arises when the patent rights of different entities in relation to one product coincide. The existence of anticommons and patent thickets require interested parties to enter into complex licensing arrangement, which makes market access more difficult and costly. This is exacerbated by the increasing complexity of products,[10] especially in information and communication technology,[11] and also in the vehicle manufacturing sector.[12] The practical consequence is that entities owning a patent, even on an insignificant component of a complex product, may prevent manufacturing and distribution of an entire product.[13] What is more, the order granting a final injunction may come at a time when production has commenced, or the product has already been distributed. In this way, a relatively small patent can have a disproportionate significance.

Another facet of the anticommons problem is the emergence of 'patent hold-up' and royalty stacking,[14] which are not caused inasmuch by the grant of injunctions as such, but rather by the mere possibility of them being granted. The potential market significance of receiving a final injunction enhances a patentee's bargaining power, allowing him to overcharge for licensing. This problem is magnified by the practice of royalty stacking, that is to say the situation whereby numerous patents cover the same product. Thus, judicial reliance on permanent injunctions as a matter of course may provide un-

---

8 *eBay v MercExchange* (2006) 547 U.S. 388.
9 Generally on anticommons see: Michael Heller, 'The Tragedy of Anticommons: A Concise Introduction and Lexicon' (2013) 76(1) MLR 6–25 and the literature cited therein; in the context of patent law see: Dan L. Burk, Mark A. Lemley, 'Tailoring Patents to Different Industries' [in:] *Biotechnology and Software Patent Law*, Emanuela Arezzo and Gustavo Ghidini (ed.), Edward Elgar 2011, 21.
10 Anton Frey, *Die Aufbrauchfrist im Patentverletzungsprozess*, Tectum Verlag 2021, 2.
11 Rafał Sikorski, 'Towards a More Orderly Application of Proportionality to Patent Injunctions in the European Union', IIC 53, 31–61 (2022), 33.
12 Position paper of the VDA (*Verband der Automobilindustrie*) of 27 October 2020, available at https://www.vda.de/de/presse/Pressemeldungen/201028-Patentrechtsreform—Verh-ltnism–igkeitspr-fung-sorgt-f-r-Schutz-der-Industrieproduktion, accessed 19 May 2023.
13 Zhu/Kouskoutis, *Der patentrechtliche Unterlassungsanspruch und die Verhältnismäßigkeit*, GRUR 2019, 886.
14 Mark A. Lemley & Carl Shapiro, 'Patent Holdup and Royalty Stacking', 85 TEX. L. REV. 1991, 1992–93 (2007).

due market advantages. In addition, there is a problem of excessive patent litigation in general, which amplifies all the foregoing factors.[15]

The problems associated with excessive patent litigation are exacerbated by the activities of non-practicing entities (NPEs), patent trolls and patent assertion entities (PAEs).[16] Excessive enforcement of patent rights by such entities is considered to be in itself inconsistent with the purpose of the patent system, because it forces implementers to conclude disadvantageous settlements.[17] At the same time, some NPEs, with the most notable example being universities, may be justified in not wanting to practice the invention and having legitimate interests in enforcing their rights through injunctions.[18] Thus, the problem of patent trolls is usually context-sensitive.

The issuance of injunctive relief in patent rights can also unduly affect not only the defendant, its employees, suppliers and customers, but also unrelated third parties and the general public. Injunctive relief can potentially infringe fundamental human rights that come into frequent conflict with patent protection, such as the right to health.[19] The recent COVID-19 pandemic led to several instances in which public health constituted the core policy factor for the courts when deciding on the grant of an injunction. In Germany, a dispute arose between Fisher & Pykel, a producer of respirators, essential medical devices for COVID-19 patients, and the unauthorized distributor of the patented product, Flexicare.[20] In the course of proceedings between the Regional Court in Düsseldorf, the defendant invoked the general health crisis and distribution bottlenecks as the grounds on which injunctions should be refused and the 'use-by' period (*Aufbrauchfrist*)

---

[15] For the discussion in the US, see James Bessen, Michael J. Meurer, 'The Patent Litigation Explosion', 45 Loyola University Chicago Law Journal 401 (2013).

[16] Jacques de Werra, 'La mise en œuvre judiciaire de la protection des droits de propriété intellectuelle : réflexions prospectives sur les conditions des actions défensives en interdiction et en cassation', Sic!, 2008, n° spécial pour ses 10 ans, 5–21, 15; Annsley Merelle Ward 'Has Europe turned into the Eastern District of Texas? New study shows NPE activity has risen 19% year-on-year', https://ipkitten.blogspot.com/2018/02/has-europe-turned-into-eastern-district.html, accessed on 19 May 2023.

[17] de Werra (n 16) provides an example of the settlement between Research in Motion (the producer of Blueberry products) and NTP, where the threat of litigation by NTP, considered a patent troll, led the former to enter into a $612.5m settlement.

[18] Mark A. Lemley, 'Are Universities Patent Trolls?', 18 Fordham Intell. Prop. Media & Ent. L.J. 611 (2008). Available at: https://ir.lawnet.fordham.edu/iplj/vol18/iss3/2.

[19] See Graeme B. Dinwoodie and Rochelle C. Dreyfuss, 'Injunctive Relief in Patent Law under TRIPS Agreement', [in:] Contreras, Husovec (eds.), *Injunctions...* (n 5) 18–19. For the discussion on the relation between human rights and patent law, see Matthews, Duncan, 'Intellectual Property Rights, Human Rights and the Right to Health' [in:] *Intelltecual Property Rights and Human Rights: A Paradox*, W. Grosheide, ed., Edward Elgar November 2009.

[20] Frey (n 10) 3. See also Konstanze Richter, 'Despite COVID-19 no exemption for Flexicare against Fisher Paykel', juve-patent, 27 August 2020, available at https://www.juve-patent.com/news-and-stories/cases/despite-COVID-19-no-exemption-for-flexicare-against-fisher-paykel/, accessed on 19 May 2023.

granted.[21] The court rejected the defendants demands, indicating that no evidence has been presented that there were no alternatives available on the market that would not infringe the patent in suit. According to the court, the defendant's assertion pertained to the general pandemic situation, and could not justify the limitation of patent protection in this case. At the same time, the court acknowledged the interest of patients in receiving medical care with the use of all available medical equipment. In a similar fashion, the English High Court considered the right to health in the context of final injunction in *Evalve*.[22] The defendant in this case, argued that its product, which had been found to infringe the patent in suit, is considered by at least some doctors in the UK as the best solution for some patients. Consequently, preventing patients from receiving the product would, the defendant argued, give rise to a situation that would undermine their right to receive the best available treatment. The court considered the evidence presented by the defendant as insufficient and granted the injunction, with a carve out for the patients in instances where therapy with the patented product has been unsuccessful. While both sets of public health arguments were ultimately unsuccessful, both of these cases provide an illustration of the possible negative impact of the grant of a final injunction on the right to health. It also demonstrates that the courts are, at least as a matter of principle, inclined to entertain the arguments of defendants invoking health as a public policy defense.

6.3 Injunctions and proportionality: an outline of the debate

The foregoing analysis presents a wide spectrum of policy factors putting the idea of an automatic final injunctions under pressure. At this point, the notion of proportionality enters the picture. As we shall see, the proportionality principle, which can be derived from the main international law documents in the field, has been used by legal scholars and courts as a strategy to invoke when policy reasons speak against the grant of injunctions.

Proportionality is a legal concept of wide scope, present in common law for centuries.[23] Today, it is mostly associated with constitutional law, both at the national and European level. In this context, the principle of proportionality invites the judges to en-

---

21 Regional Court in Düsseldorf, decision of 4 August 2020, 4c O 43/19, available at https://openjur.de/u/2374373.html.
22 *Evalve Inc, Abbott Cardiovascular Systems Inc., Abbott Medical U.K. Limited v. Edwards Lifesciences Limited* [2020] EWHC 513 (Pat).
23 Thomas J. McSweeney, 'Magna Carta, Civil Law, and Canon Law' (2014) *Faculty Publications*, 1854. https://scholarship.law.wm.edu/facpubs/1854, 284.

gage in a 'structured discretion' to assess whether any limitations of rights serve a 'proper purpose'.[24] A balancing exercise is therefore implied.

In the context of patent law, Siebrasse *et al.* suggested that the concept of proportionality should be used as a limiting principle for injunctive relief.[25] An injunction would be disproportionate where 'the expected negative effects of an injunction substantially outweigh, rather than merely incrementally outweigh, the expected noncompensable harm to the patentee if an injunction is denied'.[26] While the authors refrain from adopting a very far-reaching, equipoise style of proportionality analysis, in their opinion disproportinality should always preclude the grant of the measure, regardless of the size of damage incurred by the patentee.[27] Martin Husovec describes this notion of proportionality as establishing a 'prescriptive policy tool'.[28] At the same time, he warns not to conflate proportionality as constitutionality with proportionality as equity, with the latter being the proper one for patent law purposes. Proportionality would be 'a test of equity for individual circumstances given the goals and accepted costs of the patent system'.[29]

One possible downside of proportionality is legal uncertainty resulting from the judicial discretion. This is especially true where the exercise of discretion lacks adequate structure.[30] In addition, efficient infringement may occur where there is a deliberate strategy of optimising infringing acts so as to make the benefits of infringement outweigh the costs of litigation and remedies awarded to the patentee.[31] Efficient infringement weakens patentees' control over their statutory monopoly and undermines the attractiveness of the patent system. Because of these factors, it has been suggested that any discretional intervention by the court should be conducted in a structured manner, with due account of the traditional presumptions stemming from case law.[32]

---

24 Aharon Barak, *Proportionality. Constitutional Rights and their Limitations.* Cambridge University Press, 2012, 460–461.
25 Norman V. Siebrasse, Rafal Sikorski, Jorge L. Contreras, Thomas F. Cotter, John Golden, Sang Jo Jong, Brian J. Love, and David O. Taylor, 'Injunctive Relief', *forthcoming* [in:] *Patent Remedies and Complex Products: Toward a Global Consensus*, C. Bradford Biddle, Jorge Contreras, Brian Love, Norman V. Siebrasse (eds.), Cambridge University Press, SMU Dedman School of Law Legal Studies Research Paper No. 406, Available at SSRN: https://ssrn.com/abstract=3249058, 145.
26 Ibid, 152.
27 Ibid, 153.
28 Martin Husovec, 'How Will the European Patent Judges Understand Proportionality?', 60 JURIMETRICS, (4) 383–387 (2020).
29 Ibid.
30 Mark P. Gergen, John M. Golden, Henry E. Smith, 'The Supreme Court's Accidental Revolution? The Test for Permanent Injunctions', Columbia Law Review, March 2012, Vol. 112, No. 2, 242, where the authors indicate the risks of 'destabilizing and chilling effect' of the application of the *eBay* four factors test.
31 Adam Mossoff, Bhamati Viswanathan, 'Explaining Efficient Infringement', *Center for Intellectual Property x Innovation Policy*, 11 May 2017, available at https://cip2.gmu.edu/2017/05/11/explaining-efficient-infringement/.
32 Gergen et al. (n. 30) 249.

As one can appreciate, several possible interpretations of what proportionality should look like and how it should be exercised can be identified. Proportionality can mean the analysis of harm/benefit elements of the case at hand; it can pertain to equity and fairness; or it can be understood as a structured exercise of equitable presumptions.

6.4 Injunctions and proportionality in national and international law

The recent US experience with injunctions is particularly informative when we consider the cases where the grant of a final injunction may be denied on the grounds of equity or proportionality. In the watershed judgment in eBay, the principle of 'proportionality', even though not a legal term in the US had immense influence on the scholarly debate about the EU Enforcement Directive.[33] In the UK, a consistent thread of case law has been built up to include equitable considerations when granting final injunctions. Equally, Germany has introduced specific legislative provision dealing with the problem of proportionality, and the guidance provided by the provision itself, the accompanying legislative documents, as well as the jurisprudential response (or lack thereof) offers a helpful insight into how law on patent injunctions in Europe may develop in the future. Against this background, the chapter will then consider how the injunctions framework in the new UPC system may evolve.

6.4.1 International law

The main international documents covering injunctions in patent cases are the TRIPS Agreement and the EU Enforcement Directive. The TRIPS Agreement binds all members of the WTO and provides for a basic uniform framework for minimum standards of patent protection. If a WTO member does not comply with the provisions of TRIPS, it may face complaint proceedings in accordance with the Agreement.

The Part III of the TRIPS Agreement is dedicated in its entirety to the enforcement of IP rights. Article 41 provides a set of requirements for the enforcement provisions in the WTO member states. Under the provision, each WTO member must ensure that enforcement procedures enable 'effective action' against infringement of IP rights, including expeditious remedies to prevent infringement, and remedies which constitute a deterrent to further infringements. All such procedures should be applied in such a manner as to avoid the creation of barriers to legitimate trade and to provide for safeguards against

---

33 See Lisa von Dongen, 'The Enforcment Directive: Judicial Discretion on a leash?', Tilburg University, 2 February 2018, available at http://arno.uvt.nl/show.cgi?fid=145202., 2.

abuse. In addition, such procedures should be 'fair and equitable', and not be unnecessarily complicated or costly, entail unreasonable time-limits or unwarranted delays.[34] Article 44 of the TRIPS Agreement deals directly with injunctions, requiring each member to grant its judicial authorities with the authority to order a party to desist from an infringing act. The provision, in itself, does not indicate that the TRIPS Agreement requires automatic grant of final injunctions. Thus, the TRIPS Agreement creates a twofold standard for WTO members: on the one hand, injunctions should be effective but, at the same time, fair and equitable and should not amount to abuse, what constitutes a basic form of the standard of proportionality.[35] Indeed, arguments have been made that it is an actual obligation of the members to ensure that such a standard is included within their national laws and, therefore, that excessive enforcement would constitute a breach of the TRIPS Agreement.[36]

In a similar fashion, the EU Enforcement Directive permits, and arguably requires, EU member states to allow for judicial discretion when granting an injunction. Article 3 of the Directive stipulates that measures and remedies necessary to ensure the enforcement of IP rights are fair and equitable, not unnecessarily complicated or costly, and do not entail unreasonable time-limits or unwarranted delays. They should be also effective, proportionate and dissuasive, and be applied in such a manner so as to avoid the creation of a barrier to legitimate trade and to provide for safeguards against abuse. The latter obligation implies that, in some cases, a claim for a final injunction may be disproportionate under the Directive.[37] Article 11 of the Directive imposes on member states an obligation to ensure that, in case of infringement, judicial authorities may issue a final injunction. The way this provision is formulated seems to imply that the European legislator required judicial discretion in the grant of injunctions, but the extent of such discretion is not specified. It can be argued that even minimal discretion would satisfy the Directive's requirements, as long it appropriately addresses the values outlined above. The Directive provides an option for member states to grant their judicial authorities the discretion to impose, on the request of the defendant and in appropriate cases, that, instead of an injunction, a pecuniary compensation be available if the infringer acted unintentionally and without negligence, where the execution of the injunction would cause him disproportionate harm, and if the pecuniary compensation seems satisfactory to the other party. The literature in the field has identified several issues with the application of the Directive:[38] While motivated by the desire to prioritise the public interest when preventing 'unfair litigation', the measure may only be applied on the application of the defendant. Furthermore, the imposition of damages where the defendant's conduct was unintentional and not negligent is problematic in many civil law jurisdictions.

---

34 Art. 41(2) TRIPS.
35 See Dinwoodie, Dreyfuss (n 19) 10.
36 Ibid. 7.
37 Bundesrat Drucksache 683/20, 30.
38 See von Dongen (n 33) 7ff and the sources cited therein.

Thus, both the TRIPS Agreement and the EU Enforcement Directive provide a basis for the inclusion of proportionality in injunction proceedings, but give only a limited guidance as how proportionality should be understood. A wide variety of possible interpretations can be acceptable, as is evidenced by the fact that considerable differences still exist between the members states in this regard.

6.4.2 United States

In the US, final injunctions constitute an equitable remedy, subject to a judge's discretion.[39] Despite being statutorily authorized to do so, US trial courts were traditionally reluctant to refuse a final injunction, which could only take place in exceptional circumstances, for instance when the non-use of the invention by the patentee would frustrate an important public need such as the protection of public health.[40] This practice has traditionally been rooted in the belief that infringement of patent rights could not be adequately compensated by damages. In the face of strategic litigation by some patent owners and faced with an increasing complexity of products,[41] in 2006 the US Supreme Court in *eBay v Merchexchange* decided that the four-factor test applicable when deciding on the grant of permanent injunctions should apply to such measures sought under the Patent Act.[42] Under the equitable remedy test in the US, the claimant needs to prove: (1) that it has suffered an irreparable injury; (2) that remedies available at law are inadequate to compensate for that injury; (3) that considering the balance of hardships between the plaintiff and defendant, a remedy in equity is warranted; and (4) that the public interest would not be disserved by a permanent injunction. While the Supreme Court clearly contested the principle, relied on by the Court of Appeals, that the injunction should granted in case of infringement as a matter of course,[43] it also cautioned against applying the four factors too 'expansively', as had been the case in the District Court which decided not to grant an injunction at first instance.

The eBay ruling incited controversies, with its effects being described as cataclysmic.[44] Gegner *at al.* suggest that the judgment undermines a set of valuable presumptions, traditionally present in equity.[45] The presumption of irreparable harm, the only element of the test that has provided a ground for a consistent post-*eBay* jurispru-

---

[39] 35 US § 283:
[40] *Richardson v. Suzuki Motor Co.*, 868 F.2d 1226, 1246–47 (Fed. Cir. 1989); *Rite-Hite Corp.*, 56 F.3d at 1547.
[41] Stephen Bennett, Stanislas Roux-Vaillard, Christian Mammen, 'Shifting Attitudes to Injunctions in Patent Cases', 246 Managing Intellectual Property 22 (2015), 25.
[42] *Ebay Inc. v. Mercexchange, L. L. C.* 547 U. S. 388 (2006).
[43] eBay 4: 'this Court has consistently rejected invitations to replace traditional equitable considerations with a rule that an injunction automatically follows a determination that a copyright has been infringed'.
[44] Gergen et al. (n 30) 205.
[45] Ibid 220ff.

dence,[46] which had been applied in situations of continuous or threatened infringement of patent rights, has been effectively undermined in *eBay*.[47] As a result, it is now harder for NPEs to obtain an injunction.[48] What may disproportionately affect patentees is that lack the recourse to use the invention themselves undermines innovation.[49] In addition, the good faith exception, which has been traditionally applied in equity to ensure that market participants are not restrained by excessive fear of infringement, has also not been accounted for by the Supreme Court in *eBay*. Thus, *eBay* fails to consider traditional factual patterns that used to guide courts' discretion in equity.

Other scholars note a significant drop of injunction grants in what has been described as a 'broad abuse' and a corresponding change in the number of motions filed.[50] According to a study published in 2016, from 2000 to 2012, while the number of patent cases in District Courts rose by approximately 38 %, the number of motions for injunctions fell by approximately 29 %.[51] At the same time, the number of granted injunctions between 2000 and 2006 (pre-*eBay*) was 191 for operating entities and 20 for NPEs, and for the corresponding 6-year period 2006–2012, the numbers were 101 and 9 for operating entities and NPEs respectively. What is more, the ruling has disproportionately affected smaller businesses that find it more difficult to enforce their rights on great corporations, and who thus obtain a licence to 'wilfully steal patented technology.[52] Sir Robin Jacob describes the eBay judgment as 'irrelevant and wrong'.[53] The ruling was intended to address the flood of patent litigation, but instead of solving the real issues that caused it, including lack of compensation of the winner by the loser for the costs of litigation, it in fact undermined patents themselves.[54]

The impact of the *eBay* ruling seems to be industry-specific. Life sciences firms, for instance, find it relatively easy to prove irreparable harm, as market exclusivity is con-

---

46 Fischer, (n 7) 574.
47 Gergen et al. (n 30) 220.
48 *Voda v Cordis Corp.* 536 F.3d 1311 (Fed. Cir. 2008).
49 Gergen et al. (n 30) 245.
50 Ryan Holte, 'The *Misinterpretation of eBay v MercExchange*' 18 Chapman Law Review 677 (2015), Available at SSRN: https://ssrn.com/abstract=2570944, 733.
51 Kirti Gupta, Jay P. Kesan, 'Studying the Impact of eBay on Injunctive Relief in Patent Cases', University of Illinois College of Law Legal Studies Research Paper No. 17-03, available at SSRN: https://ssrn.com/abstract=2816701 or http://dx.doi.org/10.2139/ssrn.2816701, 10.
52 William R. Everding, '*Heads-I-Win, Tails-You-Lose*: The Predicament Legitimate Small Entities Face post eBay and the Essential Role of Willful Entities Face post eBay and the Essential Role of Willful Infringement in the Four-Factor Permanent Injunction Analysis', Infringement in the Four-Factor Permanent Injunction Analysis', 41 J. Marshall L. Rev. 189 (2007) J. Marshall L. Rev. 189 (2007), 205.
53 Sir Robin Jacob, 'Injunctions in Patent Cases', talk delivered during the Munich IP days, available at https://discovery.ucl.ac.uk/id/eprint/10093090/6/Jacob_Injunctions%20in%20Patent%20Cases_AAM.pdf, question 4.
54 Ibid., question 4.

sidered to be of paramount importance in life sciences sector, but sometimes struggle under the public interest factor.[55]

6.4.3 United Kingdom

In the United Kingdom, once infringement and validty of the patent have been successfully established, a final injunction will generally be granted. However, as injunction is a discretionary measure, the grant is not available as a matter of course.[56] Case law has identified several types of situation where injunctions are most likely to be denied. The first scenario is when there is no intention of further infringement, given that the main purpose of an injunction is the prevention of further infringing acts.[57] Secondly, an injunction will not be granted where the grant would be 'grossly disproportionate'.[58]

6.4.4 Germany

While German law did not address the proportionality of injunctions directly until the recent amendment to the German Patent Act, the jurisprudence of the German courts, particularly of the Federal Court of Justice, has provided some guidance in this respect. In the *Wärmetauscher* judgment, the court acknowledged that the right to immediate injunctive relief in the case of patent infringement may be limited if, considering special circumstances of the case, the enforcement of proprietary rights over the invention would constitute disproportionate, unjustified in view of regular effects of enforcement, hardships for the defendant and thus be inconsistent with good faith.[59] The case concerned a patent over a vehicle heating system which the defendants were incorporating into the seats of the vehicles they produced. The defendants argued that, in case of the court finding infringement, instead of granting immediate injunctive relief, additional time should be given to allow them to sell the vehicles to deliver the vehicles that have already been manufactured. The court acknowledged, referring to related judgments of the English courts, that injunctive relief may be refused in the case of infringement but only if its effect would be grossly disproportionate to the benefit of the right holder. As the court stated, this was not the case in this instance. The prohibition of further use of the patented heating system did not affect the general usability of the produced vehicles,

---

55 Aaron Stiefel, '10 Years Later—Impact of eBay on Patent Injunctions in the Life Sciences', available at https://www.arnoldporter.com/en/perspectives/publications/2016/06/2016_06_21_10_years_later_impact_of_ebay_13037.
56 *Coflexip SA v. Stolt Comex Seaway MS Ltd* [2001] RPC 182, 186.
57 Lionel Bently, Richard Arnold, *United Kingdom* [in:] Contreras, Husovec (eds.) (n 5) 270–271.
58 *Virgin Atlantic Airways Ltd v Premium Aircraft Interiors UK Ltd* [2009] EWCA Civ 1513.
59 Federal Court of Justice, judgment of 10.05.2016, X ZR 114/13.

and given the imminent expiry of the patent in question, the inability to sell the vehicles did not affect the entire business of the defendants disproportionately.

In 2020 the German legislator introduced an amendment to § 139 of the German Patent Act, which introduces the right to injunctive relief. Under the new provision, an application for an injunction is not to be allowed if, due to special circumstances of the case and the requirements of good faith, enforcement would lead to disproportionate hardships for the defendant, which hardships cannot be justified by the exclusionary nature of patent rights. In such a case, the defendant should pay equivalent damages, without prejudice to the main claim for damages. The amendment constitutes a 'legislative clarification'.[60] It is based on the rationale that the proportionality principle is consistent with general principles of Article 14 of the German Constitution and the civil law (§§ 242 and 275(2) of the German Civil Code), and is reflected in the jurisprudence of the German courts. While the legislative bill acknowledged that the necessity to apply proportionality when deciding on injunctions is required by the EU Enforcement Directive and recommended by literature, it also emphasized that any limitation in this respect encroaches on the essence of IP rights, and hinders effectiveness and deterrence also required by the Directive. Thus, the new regulation should be only used in exceptional circumstances.

Some commentators view the amendment as being of moderate, yet useful, significance. Indeed, while not going as far as the US Supreme Court in *eBay*, it opens a 'small door' to allow the courts to be more flexible when deciding on the grant of injunctions and determining their scope, and thus to better address the technological and economic changes.[61] So far, the impact of the amendment on the jurisprudence of German trial courts therefore appears insubstantial.[62]

6.4.5 Final injunctions in the UPC

The UPC Agreement (UPCA) appears to confirm the trend towards a more flexible approach towards the granting of injunctive relief. Article 63 of the UPCA states that, upon finding infringement, the UPC *may* grant an injunction against the infringer or an intermediary, subject to, where appropriate, a recurring penalty in case of non-compliance. Unfortunately, however, no further clarification of the grounds on which a final injunction could be granted or refused has been provided in the UPC Rules of Procedure. In the course of public consultations, numerous suggestions have been made about providing

---

60 Bundesrat Drucksache 683/20, 55.
61 Julia Schönbohm, Natalie Ackermann-Blome, 'Products, Patents, Proportionality – How German Patent Law Responds to 21st Century Challenges', GRUR International, Volume 69, Issue 6, June 2020, 583.
62 Mathieu Klos, 'One year since the new German patent law, the injunction remains the same', juve.patent.com, 17 August 2022, https://www.juve-patent.com/news-and-stories/legal-commentary/one-year-since-the-new-german-patent-law-the-injunction-remains-the-same/, accessed 19 May 2023.

for more specific grounds under which the injunction could be denied by the UPC.[63] In response to this suggestion, it has been stated that Article 63 provides for a 'general discretion' to grant a final injunction. Thus, it appears that the UPCA drafters deliberately left the matter for the judges of the UPC to develop. In this way, the UPC system has a potential for a wide inclusion of proportionality in their jurisprudence. However, whether the potential will be realised remains to be seen and it is hard to imagine the UPC would go much further than the English or German courts.

Injunctions issued by the UPC will cover the territories of all UPCA contracting states. Concern has been expressed that the wide territorial scope of the injunction will provide fertile ground for patent trolls' activities. In response to such claims, it has been argued that the combination of the opposition procedure before the UPC, the strong power of discretion of the UPC judges and some patent abuse prevention mechanism already put forward by the Court of Justice of the European Union (CJEU), constitutes a sufficient safeguard for the system.[64] While the relatively high quality of European patents certainly helps, as has been previously mentioned, it remains to be seen to what extent the judges will consider proportionality in their decisions, and how will it affect patent trolls's activity in the new system.

6.5 Preliminary injunctions

All the foregoing policy factors apply also to preliminary injunctions, but these call for some additional remarks. In the case of preliminary measures injunctions, infringement is only alleged, and not proven, until the issuance of the final judgment after trial. At the early stage of legal proceedings, or even before the main proceedings have even commenced, the court can only consider the prima facie evidence submitted by the claimant. Moreover, in case of ex parte applications, the respondent will not be able to address the applicant's allegations. Thus, the courts have remained cautious, requiring the applicant to show likelihood of infringement and at least some degree of urgency.[65] In addition, most jurisdictions envisage some form of legal protection of the respondent in case the preliminary measure process prove to have been unfounded. In the UK, for instance, the applicant may be required to provide an adequate undertaking, and in civil law jurisdic-

---

[63] Responses to the Public Consultation on the Rules of Procedure of the UPC – Digest of Comments Received, 93ff.
[64] See the opinion of Andrus Ansip, Vice President for the European Digital Single Market, cited in Emmanuel Gougé, Valicha Torrecilla, 'SMEs and Patent Litigation: A European Perspective', les Nouvelles – Journal of the Licensing Executives Society, Volume LII No. 4, September 2017, available at SSRN: https://ssrn.com/abstract=3009023, 165.
[65] Noam Shemtov, Olga Gurgula, Maciej Padamczyk, Alina Trapova, Anna Shtefan, *Ukraine DFID/FCO IP Court Project: The Final Report* (February 21, 2021), Queen Mary Law Research Paper No. 353/2021, Bocconi Legal Studies Research Paper No. 3789913, available at SSRN: https://ssrn.com/abstract=3789913, 46–47.

tions the respondent will be subject to civil liability and may be demanded to provide adequate security.[66]

However, in many jurisdictions, especially in civil law countries, the grounds for the issuance of injunctions refer mostly to the timeframes of the proceedings and the likely outcome of the case rather than to the interests of the parties. In civil law countries like Poland,[67] Italy,[68] France[69] and the Netherlands,[70] if sufficiently convincing prima facie evidence of validity of the patent and likelihood of infringement is presented and urgency substantiated, a preliminary injunction will usually be granted. Nevertheless, even in these legal systems, some limited consideration is given to the possible negative effects of the injunction on the respondent, especially if the claimant is not practicing the invention.[71] In other jurisdictions, especially common law jurisdictions,[72] and also to a certain extent in Germany,[73] the interest of the parties will be taken into account, and this may include scope for argumentation relying on the policy factors presented above.

Thus, the grant of preliminary injunctions faces similar problems with the inclusion of the policy factors described above. To some extent these are addressed indirectly, as the grant of preliminary injunctions requires some degree of urgency, which may in itself preclude NPEs from obtaining the provisional measure. Nevertheless, many civil

---

66 Ibid.
67 Art. 730¹(1) of the Polish Civil Procedure Code (*Kodeks Postępowania cywilnego*); Tomasz Targosz, 'Zabezpieczenie roszczeń w prawie własności intelektualnej – przesłanki udzielenia i specyfika postępowania', Transformacje Prawa Prywatnego, 1/2019, SSN 1641–1609.
68 See *Pharmaceutical, Biotechnology and Chemical Inventions*, Duncan Bucknell, Theo Bodewig (eds.) Oxford University Press, 195.
69 Art. 615-3 of the Code of Intellectual Property (*code de la propriété intellectuelle*).
70 Article 254 of the Dutch Civil Procedure Code, in the jurisprudence of Hoge Raad 15.04.2016, (ECLI:NL: HR:2016:666).
71 France: The Paris Court of High Instance held that if an owner of a patent portfolio is unable to prove that absent preliminary injunctive relief it would suffer harm resulting from the annihilation of the value of the portfolio which it would not be compensated by the final judgment of the court, the measure would not be proportionate (Tribunal de grande instance de Paris, 20 janvier 2020, 19/60318). Poland: Under art. 730¹(2) of the Polish Civil Procedure Code, a legal interest exists when refusing to grant preliminary injunctive relief will make it impossible or significantly more difficult to perform the final judgment, or will make it impossible or significantly more difficult to achieve any other objective of the legal proceedings in the case.
72 Shemtov et al (n 65), Parts I and II, s. 2.4.1. about US and UK.
73 In patent cases in Germany, preliminary injunctive relief is governed by the provisions of the Civil Procedure Rules (*Zivilprozessordnung*) and of the German Patents Act (*Patentgesetz*). An applicant has to demonstrate and substantiate two elements: 1) entitlement (*Verfügungsanspruch*), i.e. that the applicant is entitled to file for injunction and that the infringement has likely occurred or will occur in the future, and 2) urgency (*Verfügungsgrund*), which covers not only the question as to whether the applicant filed for relief without undue delay but also involves the balance of interests (Abwägung der Interesse', Rüdiger Rogge, Klaus Grabinski in Benkard, *Patentgesetz*, 10th ed., 2006, 1474.

jurisdictions still do not incorporate sufficient legal tools to allow for the full considerations of proportionality considerations in practice.

6.6 Concluding remarks

As has been established above, the traditional policy of granting final injunctions almost automatically has been challenged by the identification of numerous vital policy factors, such as the existence of patent thickets, growing complexity of products, increasing role of NPEs and PAEs, booming patent litigation, and concerns surrounding the rights of third parties and fundamental rights. In order to provide a conceptual framework for the inclusion of these considerations into patent law, commentators and courts referred to the principle of proportionality, the meaning of which is still not entirely clear. While further empirical studies would be of paramount importance as a means of providing clarification in this respect, one may point out several issues on which the solution to the problem turns.

The main issue from which all others will follow is whether we consider injunctions to be an essential and necessary component of patent protection. This had been the prevalent approach both in Europe and was the case in the US before the *eBay* decision. The right to an injunction gives patentees market control and allows them to build up optimal market structures. The weakening of the power to exclude others undermines the statutory monopoly over the claimed invention and may facilitate infringement, or even allow for the existence of efficient infringement. Thus, patent protection is compromised and innovation hindered. At the same time, however, the policy factors presented above indicate that such a rigid view may lead to obviously unfair and inequitable results. If, on the other hand, one believes that proportionality should govern the grant of injunctions, one takes control over the patent monopoly from the patentees and gives it to the courts. If a court considers the exploitation of a patent to be excessive (disproportionate) in an individual case, it can deny the patentee the exclusionary right of use and make the invention available not only to the defendant in question, but also to the group of similar defendants in the future. One might argue that patent protection remains attractive, as it gives the patentee the right to demand damages or even pecuniary compensation for unintentional or not negligent use, but to do so ultimately affects the patentee's ability to take full advantage of the patent monopoly. Conversely, it can be claimed that the lack of strong injunctive relief may adversely affect weaker market participants, such as SMEs[74], and enable effective infringement by big corporations.

In our view as the authors of this chapter, these points illustrate that the question of injunctions cuts to the heart of the debate concerning the utility of the patent system. Depending on the answer to the question of what should be the degree of patent monopoly,

---

74 Everding (n 52) 217–218.

and how it should be kept in check, one may come up with a corresponding notion of proportionality. Some suggest this should be understood as a general principle that negative consequences of the injunction should not outweigh the positive. Others emphasize the close link between proportionality and equity and fairness. Finally, as is the case in Germany and the UK, proportionality may be limited only to exceptional circumstances, a kind of safety valve intended to prevent cases of blatant abuse.

Thus, the question of proportionality of injunctions is closely linked with the core issues concerning the utility of the patent system as an innovation incentivising mechanism. At the same time, as Sir Robin Jacob has suggested, solving the problem of unfair injunctions should not be considered as a solution for a systemic reform of patent law which would eliminate patent thickets, patent trolls or remedy the lack of sufficient compulsory licences mechanisms.[75] Injunctions are only a part of the problem which can only be solved by a variety of measures, for example by improving the quality of patents, enhancing the system of compulsory licences and by implementing other access-improving mechanisms.

To sum up, how proportionality should be defined depends on our general understanding of the role of the patent system and our convictions as regards its utility. In addition, the grant of injunctions is just one of the instruments of patent law and any changes in this respect should be considered alongside the other policy options available.

Regardless of the concept of proportionality ultimately adopted by the courts, the analysis of the literature and the judicial and legislative developments in the US, the UK and Germany allows us to identify some practical advice that can make the exercise of the principle more structured and focused.

---

75 Sir Robin Jacob (n 53).

Part 2: **The European Patent with unitary effect and the Unified Patent Court**

Frantzeska Papadopoulou
7 The novelty and inventive step requirement in Europe and under the UPP

7.1 Background

The harmonisation of substantive patent law in the European Union has proven to be a lengthy, cumbersome, and controversial matter. Early initiatives towards a uniform application of patent law in Europe were initially entrusted to the Council of Europe by means of its adoption of the Strasbourg Convention in 1962.[1] It was in fact the Strasbourg Convention that introduced the three substantive requirements of patentability, novelty, inventive step and industrial application, requirements that came to be central for European patent law, the 'common' system of patent law criteria under the EPC.[2]

Novelty and inventive steps are two requirements that provide for a two-tier system of control of the invention, securing a qualitative and quantitative examination.[3] The novelty requirement constitutes a form of 'quantitative' control, securing that the technical solution provided by the patent has not been available to the public prior to the submission of the patent application. The inventive step requirement on the other hand introduces a "qualitative" control, the technical contribution must be non-obvious to the person skilled in the art in order to justify the grant of an exclusive right for a period of 20 years. Thus, a rigorous examination of the novelty and inventive step requirements

---

1 In Article 1 of the Strasbourg Convention it is provided that in the Contracting States, patents shall be granted for any inventions which are susceptible of industrial application, which are new and which involve an inventive step. An invention which does not comply with these conditions shall not be the subject of a valid patent. A patent declared invalid because the invention does not comply with these conditions shall be considered invalid ab initio. In terms of previous harmonisation attempts, see also, Convention for the European patent for the common market (Community Patent Convention) 1976 O.J. L 17/1, 26/01/1976. For an overview of the origins of the European patent harmonisation see, C. Wadlow, 'Strasbourg, the Forgotten Patent Convention, and the Origins of the European Patent Jurisdiction' (2010) 41 IIC- International Review of Intellectual Property and Competition Law, 123–149.
2 Resolution (1952) 49 on the examination of patent applications for novelty and resolution (1952) 50 on a uniform system of patent classification and (52) 51 on the plan of future work for the CEP. *Supplementary report of the Third Report of the Committee of Ministers* (Doc. 42 (1952) Part I, chapter I (c)). See also in this respect, T. Mylly, 'Hovering between Intergovernmentalism and Unionization: The Shape of Unitary Patents' (2017) 54 Common Market Law Review, 1381–1425.
3 J. Pila, 'On the European Requirement for an Invention' (July 1, 2010). International Review of Intellectual Property and Competition Law, Vol. 42, Oxford Legal Studies Research Paper No. 77/2010.

Frantzeska Papadopoulou, is Professor of private law, Intellectual Property Law, Law Faculty, Stockholm University.

becomes a sine qua non for strong patent rights.[4] However, despite the important role they play for the well-functioning of the patent system, and the attempt to provide a harmonized view already in the early 1960s, their interpretation remains an issue for the national courts. This contributes to a further fragmentation of the system.[5]

The Unitary Patent Package (UPP)[6] provided a unique opportunity to proceed with a project that was envisioned already in 1949 as one of the three top priorities for the reconstruction of Europe after WWII, namely a unitary patent right.[7] Although the interest in introducing a unitary patent right and thus also providing for a substantive harmonisation of patent law has been present throughout the years, member states' reluctance to submerse their national patent laws and thus also eventually their national economic and innovation policies to the EU has undoubtedly prevailed.[8]

It is this same reluctance that has stalled negotiations on a unitary patent right for seventy years that now comes to shape the UPP. The objective of Regulation No 1257/2012 has been the creation of unitary patent protection and thus also of a uniform patent protection in the participating member states.[9] Its legal basis originates in the first paragraph of Article 118 TFEU a provision that enables the EU legislature to establish measures for the creation of European intellectual property rights and to provide uniform protection of intellectual property rights 'throughout the Union', as part of the establishment and functioning of the internal market. According to the CJEU, the term used in Article 118, 'throughout the Union' does not require that the European intellectual property right is introduced is valid in the Union in its entirety, but could be limited to the territory of the participating Member States.[10]

As encouraging as the confirmation of the legality of the UPP and in particular of the Regulation No 1257/2012 may be, the CJEU rulings signal also what seems to be the lost momentum to provide for a harmonisation of the substantive patentability require-

---

4 In terms of patent rights that should be granted, contributions to the technological field that in fact deserve the grant of an exclusive right.
5 J. Pila, "An Historical Perspective I: The Unitary Patent Package" in Justine Pila and Christopher Wadlow (eds), The Unitary EU Patent System (Oxford: Hart Publishing, 2014); and Christopher Wadlow, "An Historical Perspective II: The Unified Patent Court" in The Unitary EU Patent System (2014).
6 Regulation 1257/2012 implementing enhanced cooperation in the area of the creation of unitary patent protection [2012] OJ L361/1 (Regulation 1257); Regulation 1260/2012 implementing enhanced cooperation in the area of the creation of unitary patent protection with regard to the applicable translation arrangements [2012] OJ L361/89 (Regulation 1260); Agreement 2013/C on a Unified Patent Court [2013] OJ L175/01 (UPCA).
7 A. Plomer, 'A Unitary Patent for a (Dis)United Europe: The Long Shadow of History' (August 1, 2015). IIC – International Review of Intellectual Property and Competition Law: Volume 46, Issue 5 (2015), Page 508–533.
8 Ibidem.
9 Regulation 1257/2012.
10 Spain v Council of the European Union (C-274/11) EU:C:2013:240; [2013] 3 C.M.L.R. 24. Spain v European Parliament (C-146/13) EU:C:2015:298, [2015] All E.R. (EC) 1162; and Spain v Council of the European Union (C-147/13) EU:C:2015:299.

ments.[11] The question is of course whether there actually is a need for substantive patent law harmonisation, or whether this has been achieved indirectly by means of the European Patent Convention (EPC) and the European Patent Office (EPO) case law.[12]

7.2 Novelty and inventive step requirement in Europe a fragmentised view?

7.2.1 Novelty requirement under the EPC

Article 54(1) EPC provides that for an invention to be patentable it has to be new, while an invention is in its turn new if it does not form part of the state of the art. The examination of the novelty requirement takes place primarily pre-grant, as one of the central patentability criteria, but also post-grant related the validity of the patent right.[13]

Ascertaining novelty presupposes the determination of certain steps that are of decisive importance. Firstly, one must define the core of the invention, and based on that specify what is included under the state of the art. The approach adopted by national courts in Germany, UK, France, has as a starting point in Article 54 EPC.[14] Difficulties in the examination of the novelty requirement, such as in the field of selection inventions or second medical indications, have been clarified in rulings of the EPO boards of appeal.[15] While this seems reassuring from a harmonisation perspective, there is no doubt that there are still considerable differences in the interpretation among the EPC member states. In particular with regards to the application of claim construction methods applicable in infringement cases and the role these might play for the purpose of assessing novelty. The UK applies the same claim construction for both novelty and infringement. Thus, a claim construction used by a patentee for purposes of infringement should also be used against them for matters of validity. On the other hand, in Germany it is not possible to make this 'double evaluation' of claims both for infringement and validity, due to the bifurcation of the system. The question thus remains what the role of the Pro-

---

[11] T. Jaeger, 'Reset and Go: The Unitary Patent System Post-Brexit' (2017) 48 IIC-International Review of Intellectual Property and Competition Law, 254–285. T. Mylly (2017).
[12] Convention on the Grant of European Patents (European Patent Convention) of 5 October 1973 as revised by the Act revising Article 63 EPC of 17 December 1991 and the Act revising the EPC of 29 November 2000.
[13] EPO Guidelines of examination, Chapter VI Novelty (March 2022), for the examination of novelty requirement pre-grant. Post-grant is a matter for national legislation. With regards to the examination of novelty in the case law of the EPO see, T305/87 or T717/98, G2/98, 31 May 2001, OJ EPO 2001/413.
[14] Societé Apotex France and Societé Apotex Inc v Wellcome Foundation Ltd 15 September 2000 PIBD, 2001, III 429. BGH Elektrische Steckverbindung GRUR 95, 330.
[15] G2/98, 31 May 2001, OJ EPO 2001/413.

tocol on the interpretation of Article 69 EPC could be in validity cases when these are to be ruled under the UPC.[16]

Apart from the issues that concern the differences in the interpretation and application on a national level, the way the novelty requirement is examined in the EPO seems far from being a settled case. One central issue that has been considered is whether patent applicants in Europe should enjoy a grace period, as their counterparts in the US and Japan. The latest survey of the EPO in the matter, reveals that while it seems that only a limited amount of the total users of the European patent system would actually make use of a grace period, it is actually that exact category of users that the European patent system should boost, namely, universities, start-ups and SMEs. The lack of a grace period in Europe leads, according to the same survey, to a number of potentially very lucrative inventions being lost. Providing for a grace period would allow inventors to publish research results and test inventions prior to patent applications without the risk of destroying novelty.[17]

7.2.2 Inventive step under the EPC

According to Article 56 of the European Patent Convention (EPC),

An invention shall be considered as involving an inventive step if, having regard to the state of the art, it is not obvious to a person skilled in the art.

Although this seems to be a straightforward requirement, its practical application is often very complicated. Answering the question of whether an invention is obvious or not is highly dependent on the nature of the invention, the character of the technological field and how well-populated this is. To avoid subjectivity in the examination of inventive step and provide a transparent structure of the parameters that are taken into account, the EPO, but also national courts have developed a structured model models of examination.

The EPO employs the problem-and-solution approach, under which the court is to determine the 'closest prior art', establish the 'objective technical problem' that is to be solved, and consider whether the claimed invention would have been obvious to the skilled person, taking into consideration the closest prior art and the objective technical problem to be solved. Furthermore, the EPO uses the 'could-would' approach which in principle means that the EPO would base its examination on whether there are any technical teachings that would (and not only could) prompt the skilled person to arrive to the same solution as the patent applicant.[18]

---

16 See also P. England, 'Novelty of patents in Europe and the UPC', Journal of Intellectual Property Law & Practice, Volume 12, Issue 9, September 2017, Pages 739–746.
17 'The European Patent System and the Grace Period; An impact analysis', June 2022 p. 16.
18 Guidelines G-VII, 4.

Due to the fact that the EPO case law bases its evaluation of the inventive step requirement on the question of whether the invention actually constitutes a solution to the technical problem, it has provided for an additional definition of obviousness, elaborated in two cases, the AgrEvo case[19] and the John Hopkins case.[20] In these cases, the EPO concluded that in order for an invention to be patentable, its technical contribution should at least be *plausible*.

The EPO problem-solution approach is of course not a panacea, there are inventions in which its application is inappropriate and could lead to inaccurate outcomes. A characteristic example of this is when the invention constitutes a ground-breaking technological advancement, the test becomes very difficult to apply since there is no actual closest prior art to build the definition of the 'problem' on. In fact, the problem-solution approach is based on the prior art search that is performed with the prior knowledge of the invention as a necessary starting point. This becomes problematic when part of the invention is actually perceiving that there is a technical problem to begin with.

France uses a method of evaluating inventive step, similar to that of the EPO, with some characteristic deviations that could in fact make a difference in the outcome of the inventive step examination. French courts use a three-step test that includes, identifying the closest prior art document to the invention that performs the same function, together with other evidence that the skilled person would take into consideration (step 1),[21] identifying the differences between the patent and the closest prior art document (step 2), and finally having as a starting point the closest prior art (step 1), assess whether a person skilled who is willing to solve the problem would solve it in the same way as described in the patent. Thus, in this case, an objective technical problem does not have to be defined, while the core aspect of this method is instead whether the skilled person would be prompted by the prior art, and in the expectation of achieving the advantages of that invention, to proceed in the same way as the inventor.[22]

Germany has adopted a more liberal approach in testing non-obviousness than the EPO problem-solution approach, mainly in order to address the risks of basing the inventive step test on hindsight. The German approach will instead take into consideration several pieces of prior art, rather than being limited to just one closest document. These different prior art elements may be combined and mosaiced, under the precondition that the skilled person in the art would be aware of their existence and would combine them. The German test includes two steps that are primarily based on the intention

---

19 T 0939/92.
20 T 1329/04 (Factor-9/JOHN HOPKINS) of 28.6.2005.
21 Taking into consideration the problem that is to be solved and the knowledge that this person skilled in the art is expected to possess.
22 Concerning the French courts' examination of the inventive step requirement see, Sté EFSA v Gérard CECCHI, Cour d'Appel, Paris, 14 April 1995, PIBD 1995, III, 320. Cour d'Appel, Paris, SAS Sandoz v Eli Lilly and Company, 13 January 2012, Case no. 10/17727. Tribunal de Grande Instance, Paris, Hutchison/Gomma Barre Thomas, 10 March 2009.

of the person skilled in the art and more specifically, whether the person skilled in the art would have cause to direct their evaluation towards the direction adopted by the patent applicant. Finally, the last step consists of an evaluation as to whether the person skilled in the art would in fact carry out these considerations and arrive at the solution claimed in the application or in the patented invention.[23]

The UK approach to the inventive step requirement, introduced in the Windsurfing/Pozzoli case includes four steps.[24] The first step concerns the identification of the person skilled in the art and the common general knowledge this would possess. Step two consists of specifying the inventive concept of the claim, while the third step focuses on identifying the differences between the matter cited as "state of the art" and the inventive concept of the claim. The final step concerns assessing whether, without having any knowledge of the alleged invention as claimed, those differences would constitute steps which would have been obvious to the person skilled in the art or whether they require a degree of invention?[25]

The EPO approach in assessing inventive step does not seem to have been persuasive enough for national courts. There is without a doubt a serious concern with the problem-and-solution approach mainly because it presupposes the definition of an objective technical problem a priori. In fact, this post-application determination of the 'objective technical problem' may not have been the actual technical problem considered by the inventor. This ex post de facto approach on inventive activity, something that actually creates its own set of problems and could distort the examination of the inventive step requirement.[26]

Certain jurisdictions allow for evidence to influence the evaluation of inventive step, such as long-felt want, commercial success, prejudice against the invention at the priority date, the elapse of time between the identification of a technical problem and providing for a solution.[27]

---

[23] For German case law, see BGH GRUR 2009, 382—Olanzapine. 20 BGH, Stobwellen—Lithotripter, XZR 115/96. 21 Pagenberg, 'Beweisanzeichen auf dem Prüfstand – Für eine objective Prüfung auf erfinderische Tägigkeit', GRUR Int. 1986, 83 ff. 22 BGH, Ziehmaschinenzugeinheit II, X ZR 49/09, 29 June 2010.

[24] Windsurfing [1985] RPC 59 (CA), Pozzoli [2007] EWCA Civ 588, The Windsurfing/Pozzoli four-step test has not escaped criticism, it has been considered to be inadequate and confusing. In fact, in Bristol-Myers 2017 FCA 76[64] Pelletier JA remarked that "It is true that the Windsurfing / Pozzoli framework does provide structure but it is not obvious that it has been useful."

[25] There are also other tests that are applied in assessing inventive step employed in the UK, such as the 'obvious-to-try' in the expectation of some success, the 'lying in the road' test, the 'workshop variation' approach, or the 'lion in the path', a perceived problem that would deter the skilled person from taking the path the inventor took to arrive at the invention.

[26] Guidelines Chapter VII-3, 5, 2 (March 2022).

[27] Sweden, Netherlands, France are examples of such jurisdictions.

7.3 Unitary patent but disharmonised European patent law?

7.3.1 The role of the EPO towards a European substantive patent law

A study looking into 9000 patent suits during the years 2000–2010 from the seven most important patent jurisdictions in Europe is illustrative of the divergent ways patentability requirements are interpreted by national courts. Invalidity challenges to a European patent, led to a valid patent in 50 % of the cases in total, 38 % in the UK while in Germany 42 % and in France 56 %. At the same time, in patent litigation concerning in particular lack of inventive step, the validity of the patent was preserved in 36 % of the cases in the Netherlands and 62 % in France. It seems thus clear that the post-grant fate of European patents is very much dependent on a divergent national landscape.[28]

National courts are not formally bound by the case law of the EPO with regards to the interpretation and application of the novelty and inventive step requirement. EPO Member states have however, agreed to adhere to an EPC 'common' system of law, and that means also that they are guided by the EPO's interpretation of the patentability requirements. National courts have the formal institutional independence and the full discretion to revisit the fulfilment of requirements of patentability in invalidity or infringement proceedings concerning European patents. The fragmentation of the post-grant patent litigation of European patents, gives rise to legal uncertainty, that constitutes in its turn an impediment to the overarching goal of the internal market.[29]

That being said, the EPO cannot be accused of being modest in the execution of its mandate. To the contrary, in absence of another source of patent law in Europe, the EPO has without a doubt taken the role of an informal patent lawmaker. This strikes as a paradox taking into consideration that its main role is primarily that of an administrative body with the main mandate of applying the regulatory framework provided for by the EPC, in the examination and grant of patents. The administrative character of the EPO as an organization, becomes obvious when we look into the composition of the EPO boards. The examining division, that constitutes the first layer of examination, includes solely technically qualified officials while the Opposition Division includes three quali-

---

[28] S. Graham, and N. van Zeebroeck, 'Comparing Patent Litigation Across Europe: A First Look' (May 23, 2014). Stanford Technology Law Review, vol. 17, pp. 655–708.
[29] The EPC does not have the role of harmonising European patent law, nor is it an instrument expected to enhance the internal market, since it is not part of EU law to begin with. See also, H. Ullrich, 'Patent Protection in Europe: Integrating Europe into the Community or the Community into Europe?' (2002) 4 European Law Journal, 433–491. On the history of the creation of the EPO and the EU's ambition to create a single patent court in the EU, see A. Plomer, 'A Unitary Patent for a (Dis)United Europe: The Long Shadow of History' (2015) 46 IIC-International Review of Intellectual Property and Competition Law, 508–533.

fied officials with the possibility to co-opt a legally qualified member. The Technical Board of Appeal includes two technically qualified members and one legally qualified official. However, and while there is a clear majority of technical experts in the Boards, all members of the Boards are called "judges". In a very interesting empirical study investigating the status and character of the judges, it was shown that the culture of the Boards of Appeal has historically been an 'administrative and examination-led' one.[30] In the same study, it is provided that Boards judges apply a methodology that is documentation-driven and that is made by officials with background in patent examination and patent skills, rather than judicial skills.[31]

What makes things even more interesting and complicated is the fact that although the EPO is characterised predominantly by an administrative internal culture, it has at the same time been applying and interpreting the EPC provisions in the same way as a national court would do with national legislation. The EPO enjoys considerable freedom and autonomy as an agent with delegated powers to act on behalf of the contracting states. The rulings of the Boards of Appeal may not be appealed to other courts, regional or national. That means in effect that the rulings of the Boards of Appeal are 'safe' from any interference by other courts. At the same time, the boards are not expected to apply or interpret any rules found outside the scope of the EPC.[32]

The examination of novelty and inventive step includes two sides, both the examination of a technical aspect, concerning the technical elements of the claims as well as the application of the legal threshold to be met for the patent to be considered 'non-obvious'. When this examination is made by national patent offices, the patent office may proceed with its examination while that could later on be appealed and overturned by the national court. This is not the case with EPO rulings.

It could be claimed that the EPO has a status comparable to the European Union Intellectual Property Office (EUIPO); and yet not. The decisions of the boards of appeal of the EUIPO may be appealed to the CJEU, while the decisions of the EPO Boards' decisions may not be reviewed by the CJEU. Nevertheless, with the entry into force of the Unitary Patent Package, the European patent with unitary effect will be granted by the EPO under the exact same rules as all other European patents and in accordance with the requirements of the EPC. The unitary patent will thus be a legal object of the European Union, that is created by means of an EU Regulation, but will be granted and administered by an international organisation that is found outside the European Union partly in accordance with the terms of a Treaty, in which the EU is not a member.

What is interesting is of course that legal requirements for the European patent with unitary effect are in principle left undefined in European Union law, something

---

30 P. Leith, 'Judicial or Administrative Roles: The Patent Appellate System in the European Context' (2001) 1 Intellectual Property Quarterly, 50–99.
31 Ibid p. 76.
32 This was pinpointed by the CJEU in G 0002/06 (Use of embryos/WARF) of 25.11.2008. ECLI:EP:BA:2008: G000206.20081125.

that means in its turn that the role of the EPO will be enhanced. However, contrary to what has been the case until now, EPO decisions will be subject to the scrutiny of the UPC as a new layer of judicial review. It will be interesting to see how this will frame the mandate of the EPO, and how it will influence the further development of its case-law.

7.3.2 The Unitary Package, the Unitary Patent Court and the CJEU

The UPC is the court with the exclusive competence to rule in actions for revocation of unitary patents and SPCs as well as counterclaims for revocation of unitary patents and SPCs. The patents that are included under the competence of the UPC are European patents as well as European patents with unitary effect. During a transitional period of seven years after the UPCA enters into force, a revocation action of a European patent or an SPC based on a European patent may still be brought before national courts or other competent national authorities.

The Unified Patent Court Agreement (UPCA) is without a doubt a complex international agreement. It creates a court that will base its decisions on Union law, international law and national law, but at the same time a court that will also be 'a common court of the Member States'.[33] This is also a court that will operate under the obligation to apply Union law in its entirety[34] while it is granted exclusive jurisdiction for the enforcement of "European patents with Unitary Effect", an exclusive right that has been created by means of EU legislation, but at the same time, granted and administered by the European Patent Office (EPO), an independent, international organisation.

Details on the negotiations preceding the unitary patent package have not reached the public. However, what has been clear is that there was a certain reluctance expressed in particular by certain member states with regards to granting the CJEU a predominant role in forming future substantive patent law.[35]

As mentioned previously according to Article 20 of the Agreement, the Court shall apply Union law in its entirety and shall respect its primacy. Furthermore, when hearing a case brought before it under this Agreement, the Court shall base its decisions on: (a) Union law, including Regulation (EU) No 1257/2012 and Regulation (EU) No 1260/2012 (1); (b) this Agreement; (c) the EPC; (d) other international agreements applicable to patents and binding on all the Contracting Member States; and (e) national law.[36]

---

33 Article 1 UPCA.
34 Article 24 (1)(a).
35 Case C-428/08, Monsanto Technology LLC v. Cefetra BV, EU:C:2010:402 and Case C-34/10, Oliver Brüstle v. Greenpeace eV, EU:C:2011:669. See for a critique of Monsanto ruling G.R.L. Van Overwalle, "The ECJ's Monsanto Soybean Decision and Patent Scope—As Clear as Mud", International Review of Intellectual Property and Competition Law (2011), 1–3.
36 Article 24 UPCA.

In turn, Art. 21 of the UPCA states that:

"As a court common to the Contracting Member States and as part of their judicial system, the Court shall cooperate with the Court of Justice of the European Union to ensure the correct application and uniform interpretation of Union law, as any national court, in accordance with Article 267 TFEU in particular. Decisions of the Court of Justice of the European Union shall be binding on the Court."

The UPC should thus rely on and respect the primacy of the CJEU case-law by requesting preliminary rulings on matters of EU law. However, the fundamental patent law principles related to validity and infringement are not derived from EU legislation but other sources, in particular the UPC Agreement itself and the European Patent Convention. The UPC will also have regard to other international agreements and national laws where applicable. The question as to the role the CJEU will have in interpreting material patent law, is rather unclear.

In its original version, Regulation 1257/2012 included a number of substantive law provisions such as provisions on prohibitive use, injunctions following a finding of validity and infringement and provisions on limitations (articles 6–8). Including these provisions in the text of the Regulation granted the CJEU a central role in the development of substantive patent law. It is exact this fear of allowing CJEU to hold a central role in the future development of patent law, that stalled negotiations. A necessary compromise in order to proceed was to remove these provisions from Regulation 1257/2012 and transfer them to the UPCA.

Naturally this was not a mere technical move. By transferring the provisions from an EU Regulation to the UPCA the ambition was to place them outside the jurisdiction of the CJEU. While this 'transfer' was deemed the best way of actually dealing with a potential new obstruction to negotiations, it is a solution with no real precedent in EU law, and thus one with unpredictable results.

The final structure of the unitary patent package seems to entail that unitary patents will not be really unitary since they will lack "uniform protection" and "equal effect", despite of what is stated in Article 3.2 of the Regulation 1257/2012. National law will continue to play a predominant role on issues related to validity and infringement, and that means that despite the indirect harmonisation that has occured during the past five decades due to the the European Patent Convention and the EPO case-law, the protection enjoyed by unitary patents could still be divergent.

7.4 Concluding remarks

A unitary patent right operating under an EU harmonised patent law would presuppose also harmonising post-grant evaluation of the novelty and inventive step requirement in validity cases. It is obvious that this is not the case now, and it remains somehow unclear whether this would change with the entry into force of the UPP, taking into consideration the choices that have been made in the structure, content, and character of the legal acts included in the UPP. An important component in this respect is the marginalisation of the CJEU.

The relunctancy to give the CJEU a central role in shaping future EU patent law, originates primarily in what have been considered to be less fortunate rulings in the interpretation of the Biotech Directive.[37] In this respect, the CJEU has been accused of being unable to understand the nature and role of patent rights, proceeding to stricter limitations in the scope of the patentable subject-matter than was actually necessary.[38] To its defence, the CJEU has had too few opportunities to rule in patent law cases and has thus yet to develop the necessary expertise. At the same time, one could also question whether patent law expertise is necessary or whether the role of the generalist court would be a necessary complement to the utterly specialised character of the UPC.

The UPC will base its decisions on Union law, the UPCA, the EPC, other international agreements applicable to patents and binding on all Contracting Member States and national law. The substantive law providing grounds for invalidity is therefore mainly to be found in the EPC. With regards to patentability requirements such as novelty and inventive step, the Court will follow the EPO rulings, and hopefully interpret in a manner uniform across all participating Member States.[39] The effects the new system has on infringement cases is more complicated since, acts of infringement are to be judged, in a manner uniform across all participating Member States, according to the national law of the EU country where the applicant for the patent was resident or had its principal place of business, or otherwise had any place of business, at the date of application.[40] However, as has been previously shown, infringement and validity cases are very often intertwined and these have been previously treated differently by national courts. It is also characteristic of the new system that not all EU countries are actually participating in the UPP.

Taking into consideration the divergences on the national level, the UPC's tight timeplan on invalidity and infringement proceedings arguing around novelty and inventive step under the new system might prove challenging for both future parties in such proceedings and the UPC itself. In addition, it remains to be seen how the UPC will interpret the grounds for invalidity of the EPC, to what extent it will follow the standards of the EPO and what significance the fact will have that judges from the entire UPCA territory from different jurisdictions and with a correspondingly different understanding of the patentability criteria will have to create a uniform case law.

---

37 See Brüstle v Greenpeace eV (C-34/10) EU:C:2011:669; [2011] E.C.R. I-9821; [2011] 10 WLUK 429 (ECJ (Grand Chamber)); International Stem Cell Corp v Comptroller General of Patents, Designs and Trade Marks (C-364/13) EU:C:2014:2451; [2015] Bus. L.R. 98; [2014] 12 WLUK 658 (ECJ (Grand Chamber)).
38 M.I. Schuster, "The Court of Justice of the European Union's Ruling on the Patentability of Human Embryonic Stem-Cell-Related Inventions (Case C-34/10)", International Review of Intellectual Property and Competition Law (2012), 626–640.
39 Although there are diverging national traditions, in particular in the field of inventive step.
40 For disputes involving entirely non-EU based applicants with no other jurisdictional basis, as a fallback position, the Court will apply German law.

Expectations on the case law to be developed by the UPC on validity and infringement issues are high and the hope is that this case law will constitute a source of substantive patent law harmonisation. It is however difficult to envision how this "uniform protection" and "equal effect" of the unitary patent objectives that constitute the background and at the same time the policy goals of the UPP, are to be achieved without the CJEU footprint.

Ana Nordberg
8 Exceptions and limitations (27 UPCA)

8.1 Introduction: historical origin of UPCA limitations

The UPCA for the first time establishes harmonized exceptions and limitations to the effects of granted patent rights. Previously these were the sole province of national law. However, any brief historical comparison of national law will show that a degree of similarity was already achieved, long before the UPCA.

Article 27 UPCA incorporates nearly literally all six general limitations to patent rights contained in Article 27 of the Community Patent Convention (CPC)[1] signed on 15 December 1975, by the then nine member states of the European Economic Community. These limitations correspond to acts done privately (Article 27(a) UPCA), acts done for experimental purposes (article 27(b) UPCA), extemporaneous preparation of medicines (article 27(c) UPCA); and three classical international law limitations concerning vessels, aircrafts and land vehicles (Article 27(f),(g) and (h) UPCA), which in turn originated respectively in the Paris Convention[2] and in the Convention on International Civil Aviation[3].

The CPC never entered into force, due to an insufficient number of ratifications.[4] In 1989, there was an attempt to revive the CPC with the Agreement relating to Community patents (Luxemburg Agreement),[5] which ultimately had a similar fate, also failing to gather sufficient ratifications.[6] The text of Article 27 CPC relating to limitations of the effect of patent rights was recuperated, becoming Article 31 of the Luxemburg Agreement. Despite never entering into force, over the past 50 years these limitations to patent

---

[1] Agreement on a Unified Patent Court OJ C 175, 20.6.2013, p. 1–40 (UPCA; 76/76/EEC, Convention for the European patent for the common market signed in Luxembourg on 15 December 1975 (Community Patent Convention) Official Journal L 017, 26/01/1976 P. 0001–0028.
[2] Article 5ter of the Paris Convention for the Protection of Industrial Property, adopted in 1883 (as amended on September 28, 1979).
[3] Article 27 of the International Civil Aviation Organization (ICAO), Convention on International Civil Aviation of 7 December 1944, (Document 7300/9, 9th edition, 2006) (Chicago Convention).
[4] Justine Pila, Christopher Wadlow, The Unitary EU Patent System (Bloomsbury Publishing 2015), 33–35.
[5] Agreement on Community patents 89/695/EEC: Agreement relating to Community patents, done in Luxembourg on 15 December 1989, Official Journal L 401, 30/12/1989 P. 0001–0027.
[6] This Agreement consisted of an amended version of the original Community Patent Convention. Twelve states signed the Agreement: Belgium, Denmark, France, Germany, Greece, Ireland, Italy, Luxembourg, the Netherlands, Portugal, Spain, and the United Kingdom. All of those states would need to have ratified the Agreement to cause it to enter into force, but only seven did so: Denmark, France, Germany, Greece, Luxembourg, the Netherlands, and the United Kingdom.

Ana Nordberg, is Associate professor and Senior lecturer, Faculty of Law, Lund University.

https://doi.org/10.1515/9783110781687-008

rights have influenced legislative bodies and found their way into the national law of both several EU MS and other EPO signatory parties.[7]

Additionally, the UPCA codifies by direct referral a third group of limitations previously harmonized by various EU legislation. These limitations can be organized by subject-matter into three distinct subcategories:

i) The so-called *Bolar exception* (Article 27(d) UPCA), a limitation to the effects of a patent supporting early market entry of generics and biosimilars, by allowing manufacturers to prepare pharmaceutical products anticipating the expiration of the patent. A limitation was previously introduced in EU Law by the Community Code relating to medicinal products for human use[8] and the Community Code relating to veterinary medicinal products[9];

ii) Limitations related to *plant* patents and their interface with plant varieties rights, that have their origin in patent effects limitations and exceptions imposed by the Biotechnology Directive[10] (Article 27(l) UPCA) and the Plant Variety Regulation (PVR)[11] (Article 27(c),(i) and (j) UPCA);

iii) Limitations to computer-implemented inventions relating to the acts of decompilation and interoperability allowed under the computer programs directive[12] and seeking to align patent right on computer-implemented inventions and EU harmonised copyright protection for computer programs.

In this sense, the limitations on the effects of patent rights imposed by the UPCA are not new to the contracting MS patent law. However, since national law provisions have over

---

7 See WIPO, *Certain Aspects of National/Reginal Patents Laws*, Revised Annex II of document SCP/12/3 Rev.2: Report on the International Patent System, exceptions and Limitations of the Rights (status as of June 2022) <https://www.wipo.int/scp/en/annex_ii.html> accessed 29 January 2023.
8 Article 10(6) of Directive 2001/83/EC of the European Parliament and of the Council of 6 November 2001 on the Community code relating to medicinal products for human use, OJ L 311, 28.11.2001, p. 67–128, (last amended by Directive (EU) 2022/642 of the European Parliament and of the Council of 12 April 2022, OJ L 118, 20.4.2022, p. 4–13) (Human medicinal products Code) (consolidated text ELI: http://data.europa.eu/eli/dir/2001/83/2022-01-01).
9 Article 13(6) of Directive 2001/82/EC of the European Parliament and of the Council of 6 November 2001 on the Community code relating to veterinary medicinal products OJ L 311, 28.11.2001, p. 1–66 (last amended by Regulation (EU) 2019/6 of the European Parliament and of the Council of 11 December 2018 on veterinary medicinal products and repealing Directive 2001/82/EC OJ L 4, 7.1.2019, p. 43–167) (Veterinary products Code).
10 Article 10 of Directive 98/44/EC of the European Parliament and of the Council of 6 July 1998 on the legal protection of biotechnological inventions (OJ L 213, 30.7.1998, p. 13) ELI: http://data.europa.eu/eli/dir/1998/44/oj (Biotechnology Directive).
11 Articles 14 and 15 of Council Regulation (EC) No 2100/94 of 27 July 1994 on Community plant variety rights (OJ L 227, 1.9.1994, p. 1) Consolidated version ELI: http://data.europa.eu/eli/reg/1994/2100/2008-01-31 (Plant Variety Regulation).
12 Articles 5 and 6 of Directive 2009/24/EC of the European Parliament and of the Council of 23 April 2009 on the legal protection of computer programs (OJ L 111, 5.5.2009, p. 16) ELI: http://data.europa.eu/eli/dir/2009/24/oj (Computer Programs Directive).

the years been legislated and adjudicated with some degree of variation, the UPCA will imply harmonization concerning limitations of patent rights effects under the jurisdiction of the UPCA. Those wishing to avail themselves of such limitations and respective patent holders may find themselves in a different legal position depending on whether the discussion concerns a national, European (EP) or unitary patent (UP) and whether the eventual dispute falls under the jurisdiction of the Unified Patent Court (UPC).

This chapter briefly analyses the historical origin, legal nature and scope of Article 27 UPCA, the future harmonizing effect of UPCA patent limitations, followed by a discussion on each limitation's respective requirements. For this effect, limitations are organized and presented according to their historical origin and applicable sources of law.

8.2 Legal nature and scope of Article 27 UPC

8.2.1 Legal nature of limitations

Article 27 UPCA contains a list of twelve 'limitations to the effects of a patent'. In the context of this provision 'limitations to the effects of a patent', means limitations to the enforcement of the rights conferred by a patent, as described under the preceding Articles 25 and 26 UPCA.

The UPCA limitations are context-specific privileged acts of use of patented inventions. Uses covered by the limitations are exempted from infringement actions and constitute possible procedural defences. In this sense, and pursuant to Article 26 UPCA, limitations on the effects of a patent do not create a right to use patented inventions. Neither are these to be understood as akin to statutory compulsory licences, which would generate an obligation of adequate compensation. Article 27 UPCA describes privileged acts, that can constitute the basis for defences against infringement, and non-infringement declarative actions. In such cases, patent rights remain valid with their original scope of protection unchanged but are unenforceable concerning the typified statutory uses and insofar as the conduct of the agent can be subsumed to the specific requisites of the invoked limitation.

The provision only provides for post-grant limitations to the legal effects of a patent. In other words, it explicitly exempts a list of acts from restricting the patent owner's ability to enforce the rights conferred by the patent, without limiting the patentability of inventions. In this sense limitations differ from pre-grant exclusions and exceptions to patentability. These restrict the object and subject-matter of patent rights and remain regulated by the European Patent Convention (EPC),[13] the Biotechnology Directive,[14] and applicable national law.

---

13 Article 52 and 53 of Convention on the Grant of European Patents of 5 October 1973, as revised by the Act revising Article 63 EPC of 17 December 1991 and the Act revising the EPC of 29 November 2000 OJ EPO 2001, Special edition No. 4, p. 55 (EPC).
14 Biotechnology Directive (n. 10).

8.2.2 A closed list or does the provision allow for further limitations?

Article 27 UPCA does not mention all existing limitations to the effects of a patent. A point of interpretation that may arise is whether the UPCA contains a closed list of limitations or whether the provision allows for further limitations to be considered, and applicable to the patents under its jurisdiction.

The language used in the provision points to a closed list, meaning that under the UPCA a valid unitary patent is subject to this list of harmonized limitations to the rights conferred under Articles 25 and 26 UPCA – the Right to prevent the direct and indirect use of the invention. This understanding is reinforced by the adopted legislative technique of direct reference to international instruments and EU secondary legislation.

Speaking against this line of argumentation, is the notable absence of an overall open provision to incorporate additional limitations allowed under TRIPS or EU Law

Since, not all TRIPS agreement provisions that allow limitations to patent rights are harmonized under the UPCA, the listing of limitations allowed under the UPCA should not preclude the application of norms collectively known as TRIPS flexibilities. Notable examples left untouched by the UPCA are compulsory licenses, waivers and the requirement of obligation to work the patent. Several EU MS contain in national patent law provisions establishing obligations to work the patent in the country where protection is granted or in a less strict interpretation an obligation to exploit the patent (directly or indirectly).[15] Originating in the Paris Convention,[16] failure to work the patent under national law[17] can be considered either as a validity requirement and ground for revocation or forfeit; understood as a limitation to the exercise of patent rights and a legal basis for a compulsory license; or both.[18] The TRIPS agreement has incorporated Articles 1 through 12 and article 19 of the Paris Convention[19] and as such under TRIPS, any signa-

---

[15] For an historical perspective see: Marketta Trimble, (2016). 'Patent Working Requirements: Historical and Comparative Perspectives' [2016] 6 UC Irvine law Review, 483.
[16] Article 5 section A Paris Convention (n. 2).
[17] The rules on what exactly constitutes 'working' vary from country to country. Generally, requires availability to meet local demand. Nominal working, such as marketing of a patented product is not usually sufficient to establish working. The UK and some EU MS have a global WTO approach accepting manufacture in any WTO country (e.g. Denmark, Netherlands, Luxembourg, Portugal, Spain); but others mention manufacture in the EU (e.g. France). These rules leave many questions open that remain mostly untested by courts. WIPO, *Draft Reference Document on the Exception Regarding Compulsory Licensing* (SCP/30/3) https://www.wipo.int/edocs/mdocs/scp/en/scp_30/scp_30_3-main1.pdf accessed 29 January 2023.
[18] For example, in Austria, Italy and Spain, patents may become open to revocation if, two years after grant of a compulsory license, the invention is still not being sufficiently worked. WIPO, *Compilation of Various Legal Provisions on Compulsory Licenses and Government Use*, Appendix to document SCP/30/3. https://www.wipo.int/edocs/mdocs/scp/en/scp_30/scp_30_3-appendix1.pdf accessed 29 January 2023.
[19] Article 2(1) Agreement on Trade-Related Aspects of Intellectual Property Rights, Apr. 15, 1994, Marrakesh Agreement Establishing the World Trade Organization, Annex 1C, 1869 U.N.T.S. 299, 33 I.L.M. 1197 (1994) (TRIPS).

tory party may include provisions that limit or restrict granted patents, in accordance with the applicable provisions of both the TRIPS Agreement[20] and the Paris Convention. The UPCA is a regional Treaty, and as far as this matter is concerned, these limitations are *lex specialis* – a specification of limitations generally allowed under TRIPS. Therefore, in principle, any other limitations allowed under TRIPS, remain applicable to patents under the jurisdiction of the UPC.

The main goal of the UPCA and the establishing of the patent with unitary effect is to provide for further patent harmonization and thus eliminate barriers to the internal market. It does speak to reason that further, present or future, limitations created in line with such purposes would be applicable (for example under competition law rules of Article 102 TFEU and general abuse safeguard clause in Article 3(2) of the Enforcement Directive; and pharmaceutical legislation such as the SPC waiver).

In conclusion, Article 27 UPCA should be understood as providing a closed list of harmonized limitations within the internal context of the UPCA. These are complemented by additional limitations imposed by Article 28 UPCA (prior use or personal possession) and Article 29 UPCA (exhaustion of rights). Article 27 UPCA does not prevent the enforcement of other limitations in accordance with other sources of law. Indeed, the rules on hierarchy of legal sources speak strongly against any such arguments. Since due to the dynamics of legal interpretation, succession and interaction between sources of law, when adjudicating legal disputes, the UP Court can consider other limitations following the list of legal sources to be used by the UP Court as stipulated in Article 24 UPCA and rules concerning applicable law.

8.2.3 Analogy and extensive interpretation

The UPCA has the nature of a regional agreement and as such, legal interpretation of substantive provisions on limitations to patents rights is subject to the principles and rules of interpretation prescribed by the Vienna Convention on the Laws of Treaties (VCLT),[21] and under Article 38 of the statute of the International Court of justice[22] crystalizing consuetudinary rules of international law interpretation.[23]

---

20 See articles 2; and 30 through 31 bis TRIPS (n. 19).
21 Vienna Convention on the Law of Treaties, Done at Vienna on 23 May 1969. Entered into force on 27 January 1980.United Nations, Treaty Series, vol. 1155, p. 3311969 (VCLT).
22 Article 38 Statute of the International Court of Justice, annexed to the Charter of the United Nations, 18 April 1946 (ICJ Statute).
23 Under Article 36(2)(a) ICJ Statute (n. 22), The ICJ has competence to adjudicate on legal disputes concerning treaty interpretation.

Some authors suggest that Article 27 UPCA can be subject to legal analogy but within narrow limits.[24] Generally, EPO decisions have tended to interpret exceptions and limitations narrowly, while simultaneously clearly affirming that, as such, the EPC system does not contain a principle of narrow interpretation of exceptions and limitations.[25] Considering the nature of the UPCA as an international agreement and its 'long arm jurisdictional application', one would suggest that legitimacy concerns would speak in favour of a conservative approach favouring a narrow interpretation of all derogatory norms, such as exceptions and limitations. Article 27 UPCA will likely be subject to a teleological interpretation concerning the question of whether a given factual situation can be subsumed to the legal text of the limitation.[26] Teleological interpretation allows room for including contextual elements, however, it may not go as far as having the effect of including by analogy new items in the list of accepted limitations, nor may it expand the scope limitations beyond what is intended by the contracting parties.

8.3 Harmonization and uniformity of patent limitations

In some cases, limitations to the scope of protection and enforcement of patent rights have already been subject to various degrees of harmonization through international or EU law. In some instances, limitations have evolved in parallel with variations in the scopes of application. The UPCA and the Unitary Patent Regulation (UP Regulation)[27] seek to ensure uniformity in the scope and respective limitations of the European patent with unitary effect.[28] This goal of fostering more than harmonization, but rather 'uniformity' is stated in Article 5(1) of the UP Regulation which mentions that 'The scope of that right and its limitations shall be uniform in all participating Member States in which the patent has unitary effect.' This goal can also be inferred from Article 5(4) and Recital 11

---

[24] Winfried Tilmann, Clemens Plassmann (eds) Unified Patent Protection in Europe (Oxford University Press 2018) 530.
[25] See with further references Ana Nordberg, 'Legal method and interpretation in international IP law: Pluralism or systemic coherence' in Susy Frankel (ed), Is Intellectual Property Pluralism Functional? (Edward Elgar Publishing 2019) 96–127.
[26] Strictly following the general principles of treaty interpretation under the VCLT (n. 21).
[27] Regulation (EU) No 1257/2012 of the European Parliament and of the Council of 17 December 2012 implementing enhanced cooperation in the area of the creation of unitary patent protection, OJ L 361, 31.12.2012, p. 1–8. (Unitary Patent Regulation). ELI: http://data.europa.eu/eli/reg/2012/1257/oj.
[28] Article 5 (1) Unitary Patent Regulation (n. 27) 'The scope of that right and its limitations shall be uniform in all participating Member States in which the patent has unitary effect.'

of the UP Regulation, which opens the door for authentic interpretation in soft law instruments and further legislative intervention to achieve uniformity goals.[29]

Pursuant to Article 24 UPCA (sources of law) in conjunction with Article 5(3) of the UP Regulation,[30] the applicable national will be used in matters where the UPCA is silent or incomplete. The use of national law (including jurisprudence) is subsidiary, following the principle of primacy and respect for Union Law re-stated by Article 20 UPCA.[31] It is therefore expected that the interpretation and application of Article 27 UPCA limitations will be conducted under the assumption that these are to be understood as autonomous concepts of EU law, at least concerning patents with unitary effect[32] and limitations that are based on or directly defer to EU Law legislative instruments.

Insofar as European patents with unitary effect are concerned, to understand limitations as subject to national interpretative variation, would deny the purpose of the UPCA and the creation of a European patent with unitarian effect, clearly intended to provide uniform protection and have equal effect in all the participating MS, including uniform application of limitations.[33]

Likely the UPC will face the challenge of determining a unified autonomous meaning of limitations and their respective requirements, while confronted with diverse national statutory texts, and doctrinal and jurisprudential interpretations. A political approach would focus on determining the prevalence interpretation in participant EU MS and applying a rule of majority. A pragmatic approach, prevails in the EPO tradition of establishing or importing authentic interpretation in the implementing regulations and through the enactment of Administrative Council decisions. It brings the benefit of political consensus amount MS representatives, but that is vulnerable to legal philosophical critique based on justice and fairness, as well as challenges based on separation of powers and democratic legitimacy issues.

Unlike traditional international courts and tribunals, within its competence the UPC will adjudicate directly, determining the legal situation of private parties. Decisions will be final without further appeal or intervention of national courts. In this context, interpretative dilemmas will be better solved under a jurisprudential approach, using tools such as dynamic contextual legal interpretation to determine the normative content of Article 27 UPCA in accordance with its legislative intent and using literal, historical, systema-

---

29 Recital 11 UP Regulation (n. 27) 'In its report on the operation of this Regulation, the Commission should evaluate the functioning of the applicable limitations and, where necessary, make appropriate proposals, taking account of the contribution of the patent system to innovation and technological progress, the legitimate interests of third parties and overriding interests of society. The Agreement on a Unified Patent Court does not preclude the European Union from exercising its powers in this field.'
30 Article 5(2) UP Regulation (n. 27).
31 Article 20 UPCA (n. 1): 'The Court shall apply Union law in its entirety and shall respect its primacy.'
32 Article 5(2) Unitary Patent Regulation, supra n. 27 'The scope of that right and its limitations shall be uniform in all participating Member States in which the patent has unitary effect'.
33 Article 3(2) and Recital 7, Unitary Patent Regulation (n. 27).

tic and contextual elements, extracted from the various layers of sources of law available under Article 24 UPCA. to provide insight into such intent and to determine the interpretation that best serves the purpose of providing due consideration to the various conflicting legitimate societal interests and positive rights the norm was enacted to balance.

8.4 Article 27 Limitations to the effects of a patent

8.4.1 Limitations based on international law

Classical international law patent limitations are also codified under the UPCA: *use on board of vessels* (Article 27(f) UPCA); *Use in the construction or operation of aircraft or land vehicles* (Article 27(g) UPCA); and *the civil aviation convention privilege* (Article 27(h) UPCA). These limitations cater to the needs of international transport and commerce, as well as in the specific UPCA context realization of the internal market characterized by the free movement of goods and persons.

The limitation in Article 27(f) UPCA – Use on board of vessels, exempts from infringement the use of a patented invention on board of vessels (in the body of such vessel, in the machinery, tackle, gear and other accessories). The limitation applies both to ocean and in-land water vessels, and requires several cumulative conditions the vessel has to be registered to a country of the International Union for the Protection of Industrial Property (Paris Union) or members of the World Trade Organisation (WTO), the invention is not object to a patent in the flag country; and that the vessel temporarily or accidentally enters the waters of a UPCA Contracting MS in which that patent has effect; and finally the invention can only be used exclusively for the needs of the vessel.

Also exempted is the use of patented inventions in the construction or operation of aircraft or land vehicles (Article 27(g) UPCA). The provision does not distinguish between types of aircraft and vehicles; thus, it is irrelevant how the vehicle operates and what kind of propulsion it uses. The limitation applicability to drones and other autonomous, automated or distant-operated mechanical items will depend on whether these can be characterised as 'aircrafts', 'land vehicles' or 'other means of transport' as opposed to a generic piece of machinery. Since the limitation is intended to protect freedom of movement, serving to transport persons or things is in this context the distinctive operative concept. The use of the invention is only exempt when the aircraft or vehicle temporarily or accidentally enters the territory of a UPCA Contracting MS in which the invention is object of a patent, provided that the vehicle originated in a country of the Paris Union or WTO in which the invention is not object to a patent.

Finally, Article 27(h) UPCA includes the international civil aviation limitation introduced by the Chicago Convention.[34] The policy objective of the original provision is to

---

34 Article 27 Chicago Convention (n. 3).

protect and ensure international air transportation and thus the Chicago Convention (and thus the UPCA) only exempts aircrafts and companies operating them, while engaged in international transit. The limitation exempts aircrafts of a country party to that convention other than a UPCA contracting MSA in which the patent has effect, from seizure or detention, as well as any related deposit of security, or any claim against the owner or operator and any other interference, based on execution of patent infringement enforcement measures. The provision is also extended to the storage of spare parts and spare equipment for the aircraft and the right to use and install the same in the repair of an aircraft while considered in transit and it does not apply to ordinary activities of construction or repair of foreign aircrafts.

8.4.2 Limitations based on EU policy (Community Patent Convention)

8.4.2.1 Acts done privately and for non-commercial purposes

The grant of a patent right creates an entitlement to prevent others from direct and indirect use of the patented invention. Article 27(a) UPCA excludes infringement acts done privately and for non-commercial purposes. Although this limitation is not new to most EU jurisdictions, exactly what activities are to be considered private non-commercial for the purposes of IP law enforcement will now be considered from the perspective of developing an autonomous concept of EU patent law.

Determining the scope of the patent right is prejudicial to determining the scope of a limitation. In this specific case, any activity that is not considered an industrial use to establish the patentability requirement of industrial application is necessary and by nature outside the scope of the granted patent right. Conversely, the understanding of 'private acts and for non-commercial purposes' will have to include at least activities that are not suitable to fulfil the substantive requirement of industrial application as defined by Article 56 EPC.[35]

A second important point of interpretation is whether these two elements – the private nature of the act, and the non-commercial nature are cumulative or alternative. Not all acts performed in the private sphere are non-commercial in nature and not all non-commercial acts are performed in the private sphere of individuals. Understanding these as alternative categories of exempt acts would broaden the scope of the provision considerably and beyond what is acceptable under TRIPS.

Acts done privately, are those that can be described as performed in activities included in the private sphere of a natural person. In this sense, acts performed by legal persons can never qualify, even if these entities are public institutions or non-profit or-

---

[35] Article 56 EPC (n. 13).

ganizations. However, a broader interpretation would include also acts performed during activities linked to cultural fruition, personal actualization, and self-expression, including among other learning, religious, and artistic activities.

The standard for qualifying an act as having a commercial purpose traditionally has been linked to whether the activity can be considered an act of commerce, as defined by commercial law (i.e. practised by a commercial entity or commercial in nature). However, the choice of the expression *commercial purpose* points to the nature of the conduct, rather than the qualification of the agent. In this sense, occasional and limited in scale second-hand sales, gifts and other exchanges between private parties can be generally seen as non-commercial regardless of the professional qualification of the intervenient and the financial element of the transaction.[36]

Regarding repair activities and because there is no general repair exemption,[37] only private and non-commercial repair activities might qualify as exempt. The possibilities afforded by new technologies, such as for example 3D printing and bio-printing, AI and automation, combined with situations of scarcity and public emergency,[38] will pose enforcement difficulties in distinguishing private acts and non-commercial activities from infringement.[39] The recent EU Parliament resolution concerning a 'right to repair' justified by the environmental need to reduce consumption and foster a circular economy,[40] may lead to EU legislation, specific IPR issues will likely be addressed clarifying whether a patent exemption for certain acts of repair is indeed intended by the EU Legislator.

Teaching activities are also not explicitly exempted in Article 27 UPCA, contrasting with the policy option regarding other IP rights (e.g. Copyright, Design). The use of the patented subject matter for teaching and studying purposes, including for example, use as research tools, will only be exempted insofar as the specific factual conduct can be justified as an act of use for private and for non-commercial purposes. Institutional organized teaching (schools, universities, etc) even if no tuition is charged, will not meet the private act requirement. Questions may arise as to the qualification of activities, developed as part of semi-private or loosely organized groups (Biohackers, Tinkering, DYI, etc). These will have to be evaluated depending on the specific facts on a case-by-case basis.[41]

---

[36] In some cases the principle of exhaustion would apply, but only provided that the object of such transactions was previously placed on the market with the right owner consent.

[37] Cf. Jorge L Contreras, [2020] 'Research and repair: expanding exceptions to patent infringement in response to a pandemic', 7(1) Journal of Law and the Biosciences, https://doi.org/10.1093/jlb/lsaa014.

[38] During the Covid19 pandemic there were numerous examples of impromptu use of 3D printers to create parts to repair medical equipment; See some examples and discussion see Contreras 2020, above n. 38, 5–6.

[39] Rosa Ballardini, Nari Lee, 'The Private and Non-commercial Use Defence Revisited: The Case of 3D Printing Technologies' in R. M. Ballardini, M. Norrgård, & J. Partanen (ed.), 3D Printing, Intellectual Property and Innovation: Insights from Law and Technology (Kluwer Law International 2017).

[40] European Parliament, Resolution of 7 April 2022 on the Right to Repair, 2022/2515(RSP).

[41] See section 4.2.2 infra discussion on teaching and learning activities under the research exemption.

8.4.2.2 Acts done for experimental purposes

Colloquially known as the *experimental use exception*, this is one of the most important and controversial patent limitations, having evolved separately in the various EU jurisdictions.[42] Generally, this limitation is a response to public policy objectives linked with promoting scientific research (understood both as basic and applied research), as well as fostering technological development and encouraging inventive activities in general.[43] Accordingly, this patent limitation allows third parties, without the patentee's permission, to: (i) examine the stated effects or reproducibility of the patented subject matter in order to, for example, acquire knowledge, facilitate licensing or challenge the validity of patents; and (ii) improve and further develop the patented invention.

The scope of national provisions, their respective interpretation and case law traditions evolved differently in EU MS.[44] The legislator must be presumed to have been aware of this and to have intended to refer only to '*acts done for experimental purposes*' without additional specifications. It is reasonable to infer that the legislator intended to establish an *experimental exemption* and not a *research exemption*. Functional equivalent statutory national law provisions relating to this limitation employ some linguistic variation, pointing to some diversity of understanding concerning the scope of activities considered exempt under this limitation. Some contracting MS restrict the limitation specifically to '*acts performed for experimental purposes*'.[45] While others either further qualify the scope of the limitation as applicable only to 'exclusively for trial or experimental purposes';[46] Some MS use the broader expressions of 'experimental or investigative activities'[47] and 'experimental purposes or for scientific research'.[48]

The fact that the UPCA focus on acts done for experimental purposes clearly detaches from an interpretation that only includes acts that qualify as scientific research, or that require the use of an accepted research methodology. The limitation is not a research exemption, but rather an experimental exemption or privilege.

---

[42] See section 1 supra on the origin of this limitation.

[43] WIPO Standing Committee on the Law of Patents, 'Exceptions and limitations to Patent Rights: Experimental use and/or Scientific Research', Twentieth Session, Geneva, January 27 to 31, 2014 (Document SCP/20/4), para. 6.

[44] See national responses in WIPO SCP/20/4 (n. 41) para 14.

[45] Section 3(3)(iii) of the Consolidated Patents Act of Denmark, of January 29, 2019; Article L613-5(b) of the Intellectual Property Code of France, Act n. 92-597 of 1 July 1992, last amended by Act n°2016-1087 of 8 August 2016; Section 11(2) of the Patent Act of Germany; Article 68(1)(a) of the Industrial Property Code of Italy.

[46] Article 103 (1) (c) Industrial Property Code of Portugal.

[47] Section 20(2) of the Patent Law of Latvia, of 15 February 2007, last amended 15 June 2021 (translation available at https://likumi.lv/ta/en/en/id/153574-patent-law).

[48] Article 35 (3) 2) of the Patent Law of Lithuania, of 18 January 1994, last amended 23 December 2010 (translation available https://vpb.lrv.lt/uploads/vpb/documents/files/Patent%20Law.pdf).

A point of discussion concerns whether the exemption covers both commercial and/or non-commercial experimental purposes.[49] In this regard, the fact that unlike in the preceding paragraph, the expression non-commercial was not added, points to the already prevailing understanding in some participating MS,[50] that the UPCA experimental privilege is not limited by the commercial goal or intention of the experimental acts, and may be invoked both regarding commercial and non-commercial experimental acts. Notably absent is also any restriction concerning entitlement, the qualification of the agent is irrelevant. Arguably, the experimental acts may be exempt, and the privilege invoked regardless of being performed by a commercial actor. However, it is contentious whether the exemption can apply to third parties' suppliers of products, and laboratories providing commissioned experimentation services, to be used in exempt experimental acts.[51] The matter remains unsettled, depending on the specific circumstances of the case[52] and subject to diverse national approaches.[53] Arguably, for the purposes of interpreting Article 27(b) UPCA each conduct and respective agent should be considered on its own merit and can only be exempted if all requirements are fulfilled and the specific conduct can be subsumed to the exemption.

As mentioned above, the UPCA does not contain a teaching or academic exemption. Teaching and academic research activities are not exempted, unless these can be constructed as experimental acts on the patented subject-matter, or another exemption applies. The provision's main qualifier resides in the second part of the text of the provision, restricting the scope of the exempted acts to experimental acts on the invention

---

49 Cf. Monsanto Co v Stauffer Chemical Co and another [1985] RPC 515; CoreValve v Edwards Lifesciences [2009] EWHC 6 Pat Ct.

50 See answers of Cyprus, Denmark, Finland, France, Germany, Netherlands and Portugal in WIPO SCP/20/4, supra n. 41, para 41; see also German Federal Court of Justice (FCJ) decisions of July 11, 1995 (Klinische Versuche I) (Clinical Trials) BGH NJW 1996, 782 and April 17, 1997 (Klinische Versuche II) (Clinical Trials II) BGH NJW 1997, 3092.

51 See with further references the analysis of several possible scenarios at Romandini, R., Slowinski, P., Wright, G., et al., Study on the legal aspects of supplementary protection certificates in the EU: final report (European Commission, Directorate-General for Internal Market, Industry, Entrepreneurship and SMEs, Publications Office, 2018) https://data.europa.eu/doi/10.2873/680006 accessed 29 January 2023 (MPI Study, 2018), 362–363.

52 Joseph Straus, 'The Bolar exemption and the supply of patented active pharmaceutical ingredients to generic drug producers: an attempt to interpret Article 10(6) of Directive 2004/27' [2014], 9(11) Journal of Intellectual Property Law & Practice, 895–908 analysis of decisions: District Court of Düsseldorf, Decision of 3 July 2012, 4a O 282/10 [2013] IIC 361; Court of Appeal of Düsseldorf, Marktzulassungsprivileg (Marketing Authorisation Privilege), I-2 U 68/12 [2014] GRUR-RR 100; Supreme Court of Poland, Astellas Pharma Inc v Polpharma SA, Decision of 23 October 2013, Case No IV CSK 92/13.

53 MPI 2018 (n. 52) 371; Trevor Cook, 'A European Perspective as to the Extent to which Experimental Use and Certain Other Defences to Patent Infringement Apply to Differing Types of Research', A Report for the Intellectual Property Institute, 2006, p. 45; Marco Stief, Tobias Matschke, 'Do the experimental use and bolar exemptions also apply in contributory patent infringement cases?' [2022] 17(8) Journal of Intellectual Property Law & Practice, 629–639.

and not any acts of research or experimentation performed with the invention. Acts are exempted if they are performed for experimental purposes, but only insofar as the experimentation is performed on the subject matter of the patented invention. Meaning that the use of inventions as research tools or general use in research is outside the scope of the limitation under the UPCA.

8.4.2.3 Extemporaneous preparation of medicines

Article 27(e) UPCA exempts 'the extemporaneous preparation by a pharmacy, for individual cases, of a medicine in accordance with a medical prescription or acts concerning the medicine so prepared' from the effects of a patent right. The scope of this exemption is limited to acts that simultaneously meet all the requirements of article 27(e) UPCA.

The qualification of the agent – pharmacy – is in this limitation a specific requirement. It is understood that this includes hospital dispensaries and both public and private pharmacies. The actions of pharmacists operating in other types of establishments and laboratories are not exempted.

The acts in question must be extemporaneous, meaning that only acts that are unpremeditated, necessary and urgent under the factual circumstances are exempted. Infringement will occur if the prescribed medicine is readily available and accessible to the individual patient, or if a license could be obtained without danger to the patient. These acts also must follow from an individual medical prescription to an individual patient and not to a category of patients. If the prescription covers prolonged treatment of a patient, the exemption only covers its extemporaneous preparation and not the complete course of treatment.

The exemption only covers prescribed medicines, but it is not restricted to medicines that require a medical prescription to be sold to the public. The text does not restrict the exemption to human medicines.[54] The expression *'medical prescription'*, can be interpreted as a broad category including also medical prescriptions issued by a veterinarian relating to veterinary medicinal products.[55]

---

54 See definition in Article 1(2) Directive 2001/83/EC (n. 8).
55 See definition in Article 1(2) Directive 2001/82/EC (n. 9).

8.4.3 Limitations based on EU Law

8.4.3.1 Use in the context of regulatory approval procedures: 'Bolar exemption'

Certain acts necessary for obtaining regulatory approval of medicines are specifically exempted under Article 27(d) UPCA. This limitation, colloquially known as the *Bolar exemption*, is to be understood as a specification of the general e*xperimental exemption* (Article 27(b) UPCA). As such, Bolar type provisions can be found in the patent law of some EU MS as a specific type of exemption,[56] while in other MS it is either textually included in the text of the experimental exemption or interpreted as such[57]

Under the UPCA, this limitation originates directly in the rules prescribed in Article 13(6) of Directive 2001/82/EC[58] and Article 10(6) of Directive 2001/83/EC[59]. Article 27(d) UPC, defers directly to these provisions, leading some authors to conclude that such should be understood as a dynamic reference requiring a narrow interpretation, by which only acts covered by the wording of the Directives are exempted.[60] However, this legislative technique also entails that its interpretation will necessarily need to incorporate any future amendments made to such provisions and related sources of law with interpretative value, which would include any further EU legislative interventions to clarify or broaden the scope of the said exemption in line with what has been argued in policy documents and doctrinal sources.[61]

Conversely, some authors interpret Articles 5 and 7 of the Unitary Patent Regulation[62], as establishing that the UPC will have to resort to national law provisions implementing these directives.[63] As far as the Unified patent is concerned, this understanding is inconsistent with Article 5(1) UP Regulation which states that '[…] limitations shall be uniform in all participating Member States in which the patent has unitary effect sets',[64] setting a clear goal of interpretative uniformity of the patent with unitary effect.[65]

---

56 Austria, Bulgaria, Denmark, Finland, France, Germany, Ireland, Italy, Latvia, Malta, Netherlands and Sweden. WIPO Standing Committee on the Law of Patents Twenty-Seventh Session, Geneva, December 11 to 15, 2017, 'Draft Reference Document on Exception Regarding Acts for obtaining Regulatory Approval from Authorities' (SCP/27/3, November 20, 2017), Box 3, p. 10.
57 For example: Czech Republic, Hungary, Portugal, Slovakia, Slovenia. Ibid (n. 57).
58 Directive 2001/82/EC (n. 9).
59 Directive 2001/83/EC (n. 8).
60 MPI Study 2018 (n. 52) 354.
61 Ibid, 356–360.
62 UP Regulation (n. 27).
63 Liz Cohen, Laura Peirson, 'The UK research and 'Bolar' exemptions: broadening the scope for innovation?' [2013] 8(11), Journal of Intellectual Property Law & Practice, 837–845.
64 Article 5(1) UP Regulation (n. 27).
65 In this sense see: MPI 2018 (n. 52) 354; Concerning interpretation of Article 5(3) UP Regulation, supra n. 27; see also Tilman Müller-Stoy, Florian Paschold, 'European patent with unitary effect as a property right' [2014] 9(10) Journal of Intellectual Property Law & Practice, 848–860.

Following the wording of the directive,[66] to be exempted the relevant acts must satisfy three requirements: (a) the acts concerned are undertaken for trials and studies to generate data for a Marketing approval (MA) procedure in an EU or EEA country; (b) the MA procedure concerned is abridged, meaning the grant of an MA for a generic product or biological equivalent; (c) the studies and trials concerned are 'necessary' for instructing the product MA application.

Crucial issues of interpretation regarding the scope of this exemption under the Dir. 2001/83/EC remain unsettled,[67] waiting for clarification by the Court of Justice of the European Union (CJEU).[68] Namely, the question of how to deal with situations in which third-party manufacture and or supply of active pharmaceutical ingredients (APIs) is necessary for conducting the trials, and whether such third-party activities can also rely on the exemption.

Moreover, while all member states have transposed at least the minimum standards of the exemption as laid down in these Directives,[69] a variety of approaches and legislative models has been observed.[70] A 2018 study commissioned by the European Parliament and conducted by the MPI concluded that the majority of EU MS(s) legislation provides for an exemption 'that is at least in one aspect broader than the minimum standard'.[71] Notably, MS(s) have different approaches concerning the products covered under the exception. Specifically, while in some MS(s), the exception is limited to activities relating to marketing approval of generic medicines, in others it is applied to acts relating to innovative medicines.[72] Because the directives were not meant for direct application and leave room for MS to make policy choices, some MS(s) have expanded the exemption scope to also apply to studies and trials that are useful, but not strictly necessary, to obtain a MA under Article 10(6) Dir. 2001/83/EC; for studies and trials related to a MA application conducted outside the EU/EEA; and/or for studies and trials not pertaining to an abridged MA procedure, but also to those pertaining to an MA application under Article 8 Dir. 2001/83/EC;[73] MS also remain free to expand the scope of the exemption to activities directed to gathering data necessary for health technology assessments.[74]

---

66 As described under Article 10(1) to (4) of Dir. 2001/83/EC (n. 8).
67 See Strauss 2014 (n. 53), 896–897.
68 In 2013 the Higher Court of Düsseldorf submitted a referral to the CJEU, but the case was settled before a decision could be issued (referral decision dated 5 December 2013; case n. 2 U 68/12.
69 Straus 2014 (n. 53).
70 See table of national legislation, MPI Study, 2018 (n. 52) 340–353.
71 Ibid, 339.
72 WIPO Standing Committee on the Law of Patents Twenty-Seventh Session, Geneva, December 11 to 15, 2017, 'Draft Reference Document on Exception Regarding Acts for obtaining Regulatory Approval from Authorities' (SCP/27/3, November 20, 2017).
73 E.g. France, Germany, Italy, Ireland.
74 MPI Study 2018 (n. 52) 339.

The exemption is Article 10(6) Dir. 2001/83/EC applies both to patents and patented active ingredients covered by a Supplementary Protection Certificate (SPC).[75] Further interpretative issues arise, concerning the interface of the exemption with the rules concerning the SPC waiver. Effectively available since 2 July 2022[76] the SPC waiver creates an exemption from the rights conferred by the SPC, permitting the manufacturing in the MS territory of generic and biosimilar products, as well as related activities, for exportation to third countries.[77] Under Article 30 UPCA SPCs confer the same rights and are subject to the same limitations and obligations as the patent.[78] However, nothing is mentioned concerning the SPC waiver as a limitation to the extension of patent term for the active ingredient provided by SPCs and its interface with the bolar exemption.

As mentioned above, the reference in Article 27(d) UPCA, has to be considered to include any subsequent amendments. In 2020, the EU commission announced work on 'targeted policies that support greater generic and biosimilar competition'.[79] One of the presented 'Flagship initiatives on access to medicines'[80] concerns legislation to 'further clarifying the provisions for the conduct of trials on patented products to support generic and biosimilar marketing authorisation applications (the so-called 'Bolar' provision).'[81] In 2021, the European Parliament adopted a resolution on a pharmaceutical strategy for Europe,[82] calling on the Commission, inter alia, to 'harmonise at EU level the interpretation of the Bolar provision concerning possible exemptions from the legal framework for the Unitary Patent system for generic drug manufacturers.'[83] More recently, in April 2023, the Commission proposed a pharmaceutical legislative package, including a new medicine products directive.[84] Under this proposal '[t]he 'Bolar exemption' [...], will be broadened in scope and its harmonised application in all Member States ensured.'[85]

---

75 Regulation (EC) No 469/2009 of the European Parliament and of the Council of 6 May 2009 concerning the supplementary protection certificate for medicinal products (Codified version) ELI: http://data.europa.eu/eli/reg/2009/469/2019-07-01) (SPC Regulation).
76 Article 5 (10) SPC regulation (n. 78).
77 Article 5 (2) SPC regulation (n. 78).
78 Article 30 UPCA (n. 1).
79 Communication from the Commission to the European Parliament, the Council, the European Economic and Social Committee and the Committee of the Regions, Pharmaceutical Strategy for Europe, COM(2020) 761 final.
80 Ibid, page 8.
81 Ibid, page 7.
82 European Parliament resolution of 24 November 2021 on a pharmaceutical strategy for Europe (2021/2013(INI)).
83 Ibid, para 45.
84 Proposal for a Directive of the European Parliament and of the Council on the Union code relating to medicinal products for human use, and repealing Directive 2001/83/EC and Directive 2009/35/EC COM/2023/192 final.
85 Com(2023)192 final, Explanatory Memorandum para5; see also Article 85 and recitals 63 and 64.

8.4.3.2 Plant and animal related patent limitations

Plant varieties as such are not patentable, pursuant to Article 52(b) EPC. IP protection for plant varieties can be obtained under the framework for EU-wide plant variety rights,[86] also known internationally as plant breeders' rights.[87] The UPCA imports and re-states a limitation to the effect of patents concerning the 'use of biological material for the purpose of breeding, or discovering and developing other plant varieties'.[88]

The UPCA establishes jurisdiction over patent law issues and this limitation only applies to the infringement of patent rights. The competence of the Unified Patent Court, as detailed in Article 32 UPCA, does not include decisions on infringement of a plant variety right. National plant variety rights remain subject to the respective national law and jurisdiction. Likewise, infringement actions relating to a community plant variety are to be adjudicated under the competent national law and national jurisdiction to be determined by the rules of Article 101 CPVR.[89] Therefore, Article 27(c) UPCA cannot be interpreted in the sense of creating a new exception or limitation applicable to the infringement of plant variety rights.

Inventions relating to plants may result in patents over subject-matter that is simultaneously protected by a plant variety right. In such cases, the provision on Article 27(c) UPCA can be interpreted as a specific extension of the limitation or exception relating to experimental purposes to patented biological material, where the experimental purpose is related to breeding other plant varieties or discovering and developing additional plant varieties. The word breeding, in this context, has to be interpreted narrowly, since other acts are the object of specific limitations under Article 27 UPCA.[90]

One of these other limitations refers to the *farmer's saved seed exemption* (Article 27(i) UPCA), which seeks to align patent law under the UPCA with the exemption applicable to plant variety.[91] Its policy objective is to be understood as balancing the interest of IP rights holders and society's interest in innovation, with safeguarding agricultural production[92] understood as ensuring access to food, and the social cultural and economic interest of rural communities. The *farmer's privilege* exempts from patent enforcement the use by a farmer of the product of his harvest for propagation (sexual plant reproduction) or multiplication (asexual plant reproduction). Such use is limited to acts by the farmer themselves (arguably including employees) in their own holding and provided that original plant propagating material was subject to exhaustion by

---

86 Plant Variety Regulation (n. 11).
87 International Convention for the Protection of New Varieties of Plants, adopted in Paris, on December 2, 1961 (UPOV Convention).
88 Article 27(c) UPCA (n. 1).
89 Article 101, Plant Variety Regulation (n. 11).
90 Article 27(i), and (l) UPCA (n. 1).
91 Article 14, Plant variety Regulation (n. 11).
92 Recitals, Plant Variety Regulation (n. 11).

being previously sold or otherwise commercialised to the farmer by or with the consent of the patent proprietor for agricultural use. This limitation does not apply to all harvested products, but only to those usually seen as basic products specifically listed in Article 14(2) Plant Variety Regulation: fodder plants, cereals, potatoes, as well as oil and fibre plants.

A corresponding limitation is extended to *livestock breeding* (Article 27(j) UPCA). Its policy purpose is by analogy linked with the protection of agricultural production and originates in the Biotechnology Directive[93] Animal varieties are equally excluded from patentability under Article 53(b) EPC. The limitation will, thus only apply to the effects of patents regarding livestock animals.[94] The limitation requires the use by a farmer of livestock for an agricultural purpose and only insofar as the breeding stock or other animal reproductive material were previously sold or otherwise commercialised to the farmer by or with the consent of the patent proprietor (with the exclusion of commercial reproductive activities or services).

Finally, Article 27 UPCA also exempts the acts of *reproduction of biological material*. deferring directly to Article 10 of the Biotechnology Directive, its interpretation has to be made accordingly by reference to the content of this directive and respective recitals. This limitation corresponded to a specific exhaustion rule for biological material. Accordingly excluding from the scope of protection, 'biological material obtained from the propagation or multiplication of biological material placed on the market in the territory of a Member State by the holder of the patent or with his consent, where the multiplication or propagation necessarily results from the application for which the biological material was marketed, provided that the material obtained is not subsequently used for other propagation or multiplication.'[95]

8.4.3.3 Computer-implemented inventions decompilation and interoperability

Computer programs as such cannot be object of a patent[96], but computer-implemented inventions can obtain patent protection. Articles 5 and 6 of the Computer Programs Directive[97] ensure that certain acts are exempted from enforcement of copyright concerning computer programs. Article 27(k) UPCA extends the exemption also to computer-implemented inventions. The objective is to align patent and copyright exemptions.

---

93 See recitals 50 and 51 and Article 11(2) Biotechnology Directive (n. 10).
94 Livestock animals are defined in EU law in Article 2 (1), Council Directive 98/58/EC of 20 July 1998 concerning the protection of animals kept for farming purposes, OJ L 221, 8.8.1998, p. 23–27, consolidated version ELI: http://data.europa.eu/eli/dir/1998/58/2019-12-14.
95 Article 10, Biotechnology Directive (n. 10).
96 Article 52(2)(c) and (3) EPC (n. 13).
97 Computer Programs Directive (n. 11).

Divergences in subject-matter and scope of protection between patent and copyright make the resource to direct referral an objectionable legal technique.

The limitation is restricted to the use of the obtained information through one of the acts mentioned in the Computer Programs Directive. It thus follows that the requirements for the copyright exemption are applicable *mutatis mutandi* to the patent limitation. The limitation covers acts of decompilation to ensure the interoperability of various independently computer programs, following the specifications of Article 6 Computer Program Directive. It is a requirement that those acts are performed by or on behalf of the licensee (or otherwise authorised user);[98] that the acts are necessary, in the sense that the information necessary to achieve interoperability has not previously been readily available to the authorised user;[99] and that those acts are restricted to the parts of the original program necessary to achieve interoperability.[100] Article 6(2) Computer Programs Directive restricts the allowed use of information obtained through decompilation, and thus the exemption does not cover the use of the said information for the development, production or marketing of a computer program substantially similar. Applying this rule in patent law requires a restrictive approach since a patent scope of protection does not extend to the inventors' expression of the inventive concept.

Other acts exempted are those necessary for using the program in accordance with its intended purpose, including correcting errors (including storing and using a corrected version of the computer program);[101] making a back-up copy[102] and conducting test runs (acts related to observing, studying or testing the functioning of the program, to determine the ideas and principles which underlie a program element), provided that these acts are performed during authorized loading, displaying, running, transmitting or saving the program.[103]

8.5 Conclusion

UPCA limitations on the effects of patent rights are for the most part rooted in international and EU legal traditions but have evolved following the plurality of national MS jurisdictional traditions. The UPCA legislator chose to use in Article 27 UPCA a legislative technique of directly incorporating existing international and EU law limitations by referral to the original legislative source of the provisions. It does so, without further clarifying requisites and elements known to be controversial or subject to a variety of established national interpretations and policy options. The result is twofold, first, the

---

98 Article 6(a) Computer Programs Directive (n. 11).
99 Article 6(b) Computer Programs Directive (n. 11).
100 Article 6(c) Computer Programs Directive (n. 11).
101 Article 5(1) Computer Programs Directive (n. 11).
102 Article 5(2) Computer Programs Directive (n. 11).
103 Article 5(3) Computer Programs Directive (n. 11).

technique leaves unsolved the possibility for divergences and variations concerning applicable limitations depending on the type of patent and whether these are to be litigated under the jurisdiction of the UPC; and second, it also entails that the effects of patent limitations harmonization via the UPCA are in some cases likely to be less striking than many hoped for and in some areas difficult to fully predict.

Moreover, Article 27 UPCA is intended to harmonise the patent limitations it describes, but it does not preclude the application to the patents under its jurisdiction of additional limits to the effects of a patent under TRIPS or via other EU law instruments.

Jacques de Werra
9 Patent arbitration under the Agreement on a Unified Patent Court

9.1 Introduction

The complexities and risks of intellectual property litigation before national courts can be particularly burdensome in cross-border intellectual property transactions[1] and the advantages of alternative methods of dispute resolution[2] contribute to explain why arbitration is growingly considered as an adequate method for solving global intellectual property disputes[3].

While the expanding importance of arbitration for solving international intellectual property disputes is a global phenomenon (which is reflected in the ever growing legal literature published on this topic[4]), this trend is also visible in the new European patent court system that is emerging from the Agreement on a Unified Patent Court ("UPCA")[5]. The UPCA indeed provides for the setting up of a new Patent Mediation and Arbitration

---

1 Which include the high costs and length of – parallel – state court litigation, the unpredictability of the outcome, the risk of conflicting and inconsistent decisions, the uncertainties about the courts having jurisdiction, the definition of the governing law, and the risks of unenforceability of foreign court judgments.
2 Particularly confidentiality and expertise.
3 Even if arbitration proceedings are generally confidential (which can be one of their key advantages) so that statistical data remains uncertain (particularly with respect to ad hoc arbitration proceedings); see in any event the ICC Intellectual Property Roadmap, 2020, p. 88 (https://iccwbo.org/publication/icc-intellectual-property-roadmap-current-emerging-issues-business-policymakers/) (holding that "several arbitral institutions, including the global ICC International Court of Arbitration administer a large number of arbitration proceedings in IP disputes every year").
4 See in particular the books of Trevor Cook/Alejandro I. Garcia, International Intellectual Property Arbitration, Wolters Kluwer, 2010 and of Thomas D. Halket (ed.), Arbitration of International Intellectual Property Disputes, Juris Publishing, 2nd ed. 2021; Peter Chroczziel/Boris Kasolowsky/Robert Whitener/Wolrad Prinz zu Waldeck und Pyrmont, International Arbitration of Intellectual Property Disputes – A Practitioner's Guide, Munich 2017; see also the Global Arbitration Review (GAR)'s Guide to IP Arbitration, 2021 (John V. H. Pierce/Pierre-Yves Gunter eds), available online at: https://www.iam-media.com/global-guide/the-guide-ip-arbitration/1st-edition.
5 This chapter will focus on the specific issue of patent arbitration (Art. 35 UPCA) and will not generally present the UPCA.

Jacques de Werra, is Professor of intellectual property law and contract law, Director of the Digital Law Centre (www.digitallawcenter.ch), University of Geneva; member of the Committee of the Geneva Master in International Dispute Settlement (www.mids.ch).

Centre, whereby this paper will focus on patent arbitration[6], knowing that another chapter of this book addresses the topic of patent mediation[7].

One should note from the outset that this trend for integrating ADR mechanisms in IP regulations and for IP institutions to offer ADR services (which is what is done in the UPCA with respect to the Centre) is reflected in other European regulations. By way of illustration, the EUIPO offers mediation services for certain types of trademark and design disputes[8]. Beyond the European Union, one can further note that the trend promoting the use of arbitration for solving international intellectual property disputes is observable[9].

---

[6] There is only limited legal literature on patent arbitration & the UPC/the Centre, see the doctoral thesis of Daniel Kenji Kaneko, EU-Einheitspatent und Schiedsverfahren. Zugleich ein Beitrag zur objektiven Schiedsfähigkeitsklage der Patentnichtigkeitsklage, 2018 Nomos; see also Peter Picht, Einheitspatentsystem: Die Kompetenzreichweite des Mediations – und Schiedszentrums, [2018] GRUR Int 1; Peter Picht, Arbitration Through the Unified Patent Court's Arbitration Centre, to be published in Klopschinski/McGuire (ed.), Research Handbook on Intellectual Property Rights and Arbitration, Edward Elgar Publishing, Forthcoming 2023, available at: https://ssrn.com/abstract=4305883 (that unfortunately could not be cited further in this chapter); Sam Granata, The Patent Mediation and Arbitration Centre: a centre of opportunities, in: Christophe Geiger/A. Craig Nard/Xavier Seuba (eds), Intellectual Property and the Judiciary (Edward Elgar Publishing, 2018), 255; Alba Betancourt, A., 2016. Cross-Border Patent Disputes: Unified Patent Court or International Commercial Arbitration?, Utrecht Journal of International and European Law, 32(82), 44; Winfried Tilmann/Clemens Plassmann, Patent Mediation and Arbitration, in Winfried Tilmann/Clemens Plassmann (eds), Unified Patent Protection in Europe: A Commentary, Oxford 2018; this paper is partly based on a previous paper that the author wrote in 2013, see Jacques de Werra, New Developments of IP Arbitration and Mediation in Europe: The Patent Mediation and Arbitration Centre Instituted by the Agreement on a Unified Patent Court, Revista brasileira de arbitragem 2014, 17, available at: https://archive-ouverte.unige.ch/unige:39878.

[7] This paper will not discuss all the facets of the Centre, in particular those relating to the governance and organization of the Centre.

[8] See https://euipo.europa.eu/ohimportal/en/mediation.

[9] By way of example, Switzerland has a long-standing reputation and tradition for offering an arbitration-friendly environment, which also applies as far as intellectual property arbitration is concerned; this position results from old case law (decision of the Swiss Supreme Court published in ATF 71 III 198) and from an official statement of the Swiss intellectual property office on the basis of which the arbitrability of intellectual property disputes was duly admitted (so that a final and enforceable award rendered by an arbitral tribunal seating in Switzerland finding the invalidity of a Swiss patent shall constitute a valid basis for cancelling the patent from the Swiss patent registry), this official statement was published in the Swiss review of intellectual property law in 1976, RSPI 1976, 36 seq.

9.2 The Patent Mediation and Arbitration Centre instituted by the UPCA

9.2.1 Introduction

With Regulation (EU) No. 1257/2012 of the European Parliament and of the Council of December 17, 2012 implementing enhanced cooperation in the area of the creation of unitary patent protection[10] and the Council regulation (EU) No. 1260/2012 of December 17, 2012 implementing enhanced cooperation in the area of the creation of unitary patent protection with regard to the applicable translation arrangements,[11] the European Union has adopted a new regulatory framework that facilitates the protection of patents within the European Union. This system creates a "European patent with unitary effect", i.e., a patent which shall benefit from a unitary effect in the participating Member States of the European Union. The practical implementation of a European patent with unitary effect calls for the creation of a new judicial body which shall be in charge of solving the disputes which relate to these patents which is the mission of the Unified Patent Court (hereinafter: "the Court")[12], as instituted by the UPCA.

Despite its (narrow) title, the UPCA is not limited to the creation of a "Unified Patent Court". The UPCA indeed provides (Article 35) for the creation of a Patent Mediation and Arbitration Centre (hereinafter: "the Centre") in the following terms:

"(1) A patent mediation and arbitration centre ('the Centre') is hereby established. It shall have its seats in Ljubljana and Lisbon.
(2) The Centre shall provide facilities for mediation and arbitration of patent disputes falling within the scope of this Agreement. Article 82 shall apply mutatis mutandis to any settlement reached through the use of the facilities of the Centre, including through mediation. However, a patent may not be revoked or limited in mediation or arbitration proceedings.
(3) The Centre shall establish Mediation and Arbitration Rules.
(4) The Centre shall draw up a list of mediators and arbitrators to assist the parties in the settlement of their dispute".

Art. 35 UPCA is of particular significance because it constitutes the first official legal provision adopted in the European Union which provides for the submission to arbitration of certain intellectual property disputes (in this case patent disputes). By its integration in the UPC, this provision is somewhat unusual because it intrinsically connects the Centre with the UPC.

---

[10] See http://eur-lex.europa.eu/LexUriServ/LexUriServ.do?uri=OJ:L:2012:361:0001:0008:EN:PDF.
[11] See http://eur-lex.europa.eu/LexUriServ/LexUriServ.do?uri=OJ:L:2012:361:0089:0092:EN:PDF.
[12] See recitals 24 and 25 of Regulation 1257/2012.

As put by Sam Granata[13], the ambition is that the UPC shall be "a one-stop shop dispute resolution system"[14]. The Member States participating in the Period of Provisional Application of the Agreement on a Unified Patent Court (UPC) have adopted the Organisational Rules[15] of the Patent Mediation and Arbitration Centre (PMAC) during the Administrative Committee's 2nd meeting, which took place on July 8, 2022 in Luxembourg[16] and that have come into force on August 1, 2022. The PAMC Rules provide in this respect that (Rule 2) "1. The Centre forms part of the Unified Patent Court (UPC)" and that "2. It operates independently, but carries out its tasks in close contact and cooperation with the committees / bodies of the UPC which will have to take decisions in relation to the operation of the Centre". From a financial perspective, the Centre is dependent on the Court (Art. 39 UPCA provides in this respect that "the operating costs of the Centre shall be financed by the budget of the Court"[17]). This integration of the Centre in the UPC – in spite of its operational independence – stands in clear contrast to the complete independence of other providers of alternative dispute resolution mechanisms (particularly those managing arbitration proceedings) which are not affiliated with public courts and offer *alternative* solutions to court proceedings: arbitration is not usually a part of court proceedings, whereby mediation can by contrast perfectly be integrated in court proceedings. In this respect, one can consider that mediation constituted the *Leitbild* that was envisioned by the drafters of the UPCA and that arbitration was most certainly not the focus of their attention[18]. Based on this *Leitbild*, the structural design is that mediation proceedings should be made available as an optional feature in the course of court proceedings taking place before the UPC. This clearly results from Art. 52 para. 2 UPCA which provides that the judge acting as Rapporteur (in the course of court proceedings

---

[13] Who was a member of the Legal Framework Group Unified Patent Court (Subgroup 1: Rules of Procedures of the Court and Subgroup 6: Rules on Mediation and Arbitration) and has extensively written and commented about the Centre, see e.g. http://patentblog.kluweriplaw.com/2015/10/11/judge-sam-granata-success-mediation-and-arbitration-centre-of-unified-patent-court-will-depend-largely-on-performance-court/; Sam Granata has been appointed to the Court of First Instance for the Local division in Brussels: https://www.unified-patent-court.org/news/unified-patent-court-judicial-appointments-and-presidi um-elections.

[14] Sam Granata, The Patent Mediation and Arbitration Centre: a centre of opportunities, in: Christophe Geiger/A. Craig Nard/Xavier Seuba (eds), Intellectual Property and the Judiciary (Edward Elgar Publishing, 2018), at 256.

[15] Doc "AC/06/08072022_E" (in the English version) available at: https://www.unified-patent-court.org/sites/default/files/ac_06_08072022_rules_of_operation_mediation_arbitration_centre_en_final_for_publica tion.pdf, entitled "Rules of Operation of the Mediation and Arbitration Centre" (with reference to the abbreviation "PMAC Rules" that will be used here).

[16] See https://www.unified-patent-court.org/content/official-documents-2nd-meeting-upc-administrati ve-committee-8-july-2022.

[17] See also the PAMC Rules which similarly state that (Rule 7 para. 2) "[t]he Centre shall be financed by the budget of the UPC".

[18] The view was expressed that the UPCA could have ambitioned to create only a patent mediation center and not a patent mediation and arbitration center, see A. Walz, at 149.

conducted before the UPC) shall "explore with the parties the possibility for a settlement, including through mediation, and/or arbitration, by using the facilities of the Centre referred to in Article 35" (Art. 52 para. 2 UPCA)[19]. This *Leitbild* – which is also reflected in the Rules of Procedure[20] – consequently conceives ADR proceedings as an optional feature of court proceedings (in the form of a time window for finding an amicable settlement).

The wording of Art. 52 para. 2 UPCA further evidences the lack of clear distinction between mediation and arbitration to the extent that arbitration does not intrinsically lead to a "settlement" (within the meaning of Art. 52 para. 2 UPCA)[21] but rather to an arbitral award (which is a unilateral decision made by the arbitral tribunal)[22]. More generally, one can note that the UPCA does not sufficiently distinguish between mediation and arbitration which may cause confusion[23].

These provisions convey the impression that the reference to mediation and arbitration made in the UPCA was conceived by its drafters as a tool for the parties to solve their dispute once their dispute had already been submitted to the Court[24]. This scenar-

---

19 Art. 52 para. 2 UPCA: "In the interim procedure, after the written procedure and if appropriate, the judge acting as Rapporteur, subject to a mandate of the full panel, shall be responsible for convening an interim hearing. That judge shall in particular explore with the parties the possibility for a settlement, including through mediation, and/or arbitration, by using the facilities of the Centre referred to in Article 35".
20 The Rules of Procedure of the Unified Patent Court ("the Rules of Procedure") as adopted by decision of the Administrative Committee on 8 July 2022 which entered into force on September 1, 2022 (available at: https://www.unified-patent-court.org/sites/default/files/rop_en_25_july_2022_final_consolidated_published_on_website_0.pdf provide that (art. 11 para. 1): "At any stage of the proceedings, if the Court is of the opinion that the dispute is suitable for a settlement, it may propose that the parties make use of the facilities of the Patent Mediation and Arbitration Centre ("the Centre") in order to settle or to explore a settlement of the dispute. In particular, the judge-rapporteur shall during the interim procedure, especially at an interim conference in accordance with Rule 104(d), explore with the parties the possibility of a settlement, including through mediation and/or arbitration, using the facilities of the Centre".
21 In the German version of the UPCA "die Möglichkeit eines Vergleichs"; in the French version of the UPCA "les possibilités de parvenir à un règlement".
22 See Kaneko, at 93 (holding that the reference to arbitration in Art. 52 para. 2 UPCA and in Art. 11 para. 1 of the Rules of Procedure is "systemfremd").
23 See Kaneko, at 94 and 97; by way of illustration, Art. 35 para. 4 UPCA provides that "[t]he Centre shall draw up a list of mediators and arbitrators to assist the parties in the settlement of their dispute", whereby this wording does not adequately reflect the difference between mediation in the course of which mediators do indeed "assist the parties in the settlement of their disputes" and arbitration in which the arbitrators decide the dispute (Kaneko, at 97).
24 See the Communication from the Commission to the European Parliament, the Council and the European Economic and Social Committee, An Industrial Property Rights Strategy for Europe COM(2008) 465 final, of July 16, 2008 (available at: http://eur-lex.europa.eu/LexUriServ/LexUriServ.do?uri=COM:2008:0465:FIN:en:PDF), p. 12: "Although ADR would not be mandatory, a judge of the integrated patent jurisdiction would investigate with the parties the possibilities for settlement of the dispute by the arbitration and mediation centre".

io, even if it is not unrealistic, does not cover the quite frequent cases in which the parties select ADR mechanisms before a dispute arises. Contracting parties in business transactions and specifically in intellectual property transactions (including patent transactions) generally anticipate the potential occurrence of future disputes and consequently choose in advance the types of alternative dispute resolution mechanisms that they shall use if a dispute arises. As a result, there is no doubt that parties should be in a position to agree to submit their dispute to arbitration proceedings managed by the Centre even before a dispute arises[25].

On this basis, the *Leitbild* envisioned by the UPC does not reflect the nature of arbitration proceedings which as a matter of principle exclude court proceedings and constitute an *alternative* way to solve the dispute between the parties. The reference that is made to arbitration in Art. 52 para. 2 UPCA is consequently somewhat ill-guided to the extent that it is unlikely that parties will agree to move from court litigation (before the Court) to arbitration at the stage of the interim procedure which takes place after the written procedure (in view of the investments already made for the proceedings before the UPC)[26].

9.2.2 Substantive scope of the arbitration services offered by the Centre

Art. 35 para. 2 first sentence UPCA states that "the Centre shall provide facilities for mediation and arbitration of patent disputes *falling within the scope of this Agreement*" (emphasis added). The scope of application of the UPCA is defined in Art. 3 which provides that the UPCA "shall apply to any: (a) European patent with unitary effect; (b) supplementary protection certificate issued for a product protected by a patent; (c) European patent which has not yet lapsed at the date of entry into force of this Agreement or was granted after that date, without prejudice to Article 83; and (d) European patent application which is pending at the date of entry into force of this Agreement or which is filed after that date, without prejudice to Article 83". Art. 32 para. 1 UPCA further defines the disputes for which the Court has exclusive competence, which include "actions for actual or threatened infringements of patents and supplementary protection certificates and related defences, including counterclaims concerning licences" (Art. 32 para. 1 (a) UPCA)[27].

From the wording of Art. 35 para. 2 first sentence UPCA, it seems that the mediation and arbitration services of the Centre would only be available for patent disputes relat-

---

25 Kaneko, at 91; Picht, at 10; this is what was done in the Samsung Commitments (see below text at footnotes 82–86).
26 Kaneko, at 93–94.
27 Whereby "patent" means "a European patent and/or a European patent with unitary effect" (art. 2 (g) UPCA).

ing to a European patent or a European patent with unitary effect (as defined above). *A contrario*, the Centre would not be in a position to offer its mediation or arbitration services for other types of disputes relating to other patents or even other types of intellectual property rights. This substantive limit to the scope of services to be rendered by the Centre is difficult to reconcile with the standard expectations of parties to a business dispute that generally have an interest to solve their dispute in one single proceeding (and not in multiple parallel proceedings). This can particularly be the case of contracting parties to a global patent transaction (e.g. a patent license agreement) which would not be limited to European patents and/or European patents with unitary effect (but would also cover – for instance – US patents, Japanese patents, or even trademarks or know-how)[28]. These parties will have an interest in submitting their dispute to the arbitration rules of the Centre only if this can ensure the global settlement of their dispute. Otherwise, such parties are likely to select another arbitration system that would not be submitted to such limited jurisdictional power[29].

In this respect, one should not expect the Centre to have substantive expertise in all the areas of the arbitration disputes that could be submitted to it. One important reason is that it is likely that in many disputes, contractual issues will arise (e.g. what is the scope of a license granted to a given patent or has the license agreement been validly terminated?) which will be governed by the law applicable to the contract at issue, which will not necessarily be the law of any EU Member State (which are parties to the UPCA)[30] and on which the arbitral tribunal should be in a position to decide[31]. On this basis, requiring such expertise from the Centre should not be a factor justifying the limited scope of the Centre's activities (in line with the wording of Art. 35 para. 2 UPCA)[32]. The reason is that arbitration centers do not need to (and actually cannot) have substantive law expertise in all legal areas that are at stake in the disputes that are submitted to those centers. For instance, the International Court of Arbitration of the International Chamber of Commerce (ICC) is not expected to have substantive knowledge of all the legal areas that may be at issue in any given dispute submitted to ICC arbitration. This is however not determinative given that arbitration centers do not decide on the disputes (only the arbitral tribunals do so), but merely manage them. What will consequently be

---

28 Which is quite frequent in practice given that license agreements can cover different types of intellectual property rights and different countries / regions of the world.
29 Picht, p. 10–11.
30 Art. 24 para. 1 UPC e) provides for the possibility for the Court to base its decisions on "national law" which can be the national law of non-contracting States and Art. 24 para. 2 defines how to identify the applicable national law.
31 Picht, at 10 (noting that the Centre should have the capacity to decide on licensing issues connected to the invalidity of a patent).
32 See however Picht, at 10, mentioning that the Centre will develop its expertise about patent disputes falling within the exclusive competence of the Court and that the Centre will not have the same level of expertise for other legal matters so that the Centre should focus its activities on the patent disputes falling within the exclusive competence of the Court.

impactful is to ensure that the arbitrators shall have the relevant expertise. In this respect, it will be interesting to see what review mechanism (if any) the Centre will put into place in order to scrutinize the draft awards to be rendered by arbitral tribunals in proceedings managed by the Centre as it is done in ICC arbitration proceedings[33].

The question of the scope of the Centre's activities particularly arises with respect to the European patents for which their holder would have "opted out" of the exclusive jurisdiction of the UPC (pursuant to Art. 85 para. 3 UPCA)[34]. If the parties to a dispute relating to such patents want to submit their dispute to arbitration under Art. 35 UPCA, this should prevail and could be considered as an opt-in (for arbitration)[35].

From this perspective, the Centre should ideally have the power to handle a dispute arising out of these patents or other intellectual property rights which would fall outside the scope of the UPCA even if this is not supported by the wording of Art. 35 para. 2 first sentence[36]. The interests of the parties as well as the need to foster efficient dispute resolution mechanisms should make it possible for the parties to submit their dispute to arbitration by using the facilities of the Centre even if their dispute is not limited to patents falling within the exclusive competence of the Court. In other words, the power of the Centre to manage arbitration proceedings does not necessarily need to mirror the jurisdictional power of the Court to handle patent disputes falling within its (exclusive) competence. One can note in this respect that the Mediation Rules[37] make it possible to include in the mediation proceedings legal issues that are "factually or legally linked to the dispute falling within the exclusive competence of the UPC"[38]. Similarly, the PMAC Rules provide (Rule 5 para. 1) that "[t]he objective of the Centre is

---

[33] See ICC Arbitration Rules (2021), Art. 34: "Before signing any award, the arbitral tribunal shall submit it in draft form to the Court. The Court may lay down modifications as to the form of the award and, without affecting the arbitral tribunal's liberty of decision, may also draw its attention to points of substance. No award shall be rendered by the arbitral tribunal until it has been approved by the Court as to its form".

[34] "(3) Unless an action has already been brought before the Court, a proprietor of or an applicant for a European patent granted or applied for prior to the end of the transitional period under paragraph 1 and, where applicable, paragraph 5, as well as a holder of a supplementary protection certificate issued for a product protected by a European patent, shall have the possibility to opt out from the exclusive competence of the Court".

[35] See Kaneko, at 90.

[36] For an intermediate view (admitting the jurisdiction to the extent that the patent dispute at issue covers at least a patent falling within the scope of the UPCA along with another patent), see Picht, at 10; for a more restrictive view (supporting the narrow jurisdictional power as reflected in Art. 35 para. 1), see Kaneko, at 89.

[37] This paper is based on Version 5 dated November 27, 2015 of the Mediation Rules (the rules were available at: https://www.unified-patent-court.org/sites/default/files/upc_mediation_rules.pdf but have subsequently been removed from the UPC website).

[38] See Mediation Rules, Art. 2 para. 3: "The parties may decide on any other disposable right or obligation factually or legally linked to the dispute falling within the exclusive competence of the UPC to be included into mediation".

to promote mediation and arbitration in cases which fall wholly or in part within the competence of the UPC".

This must be understood to mean that mediation or arbitration proceedings could cover factual and legal issues that would relate to a license agreement on patents covered by the UPCA because such issues would be legally linked to the dispute about the validity or infringement of such patents. In the same vein, it should be possible to submit to arbitration disputes that are linked to patents covered by the UPCA[39]. In this respect, it would make sense to adopt a uniform scope of competence of the Centre in both mediation and in arbitration proceedings because parties may be willing to adopt med-arb clauses by which the parties would first submit their dispute to mediation and then to arbitration in case the mediation would not succeed. In such a case, it would be critical to ensure that the jurisdictional power of the arbitral tribunal shall be at least as broad as the (non-jurisdictional) power of the mediator. On this basis, one should admit that the Centre shall have the power to manage broadly patent disputes in spite of the narrower wording of Art. 35 para. 2 UPCA.

9.2.3 No exclusivity for arbitration instituted by the Centre

The question arises whether parties wishing to submit to arbitration a dispute that would fall within the exclusive competence of the UPC (and thus could be managed by the Centre) could select another arbitration service provider that could be located either in the European Union (potentially the International Chamber of Commerce in Paris), or somewhere else in Europe (including the WIPO Arbitration and Mediation Centre having its seat in Geneva) or even in other parts of the world, instead of selecting the Centre[40]. Given that arbitration is based on the consent of the parties, the parties should be free to decide how the arbitration proceedings shall be organized (including by choosing ad hoc arbitration) and shall also be free to choose the arbitration institutions and the arbitration rules that they shall see fit even if the dispute is about a European patent with unitary effect or a European patent[41]. In other words, the Centre should not have any exclusivity to manage arbitration proceedings relating to European patents with

---

[39] See Sam Granata, The Patent Mediation and Arbitration Centre: a centre of opportunities, in: Christophe Geiger/A. Craig Nard/Xavier Seuba (eds), Intellectual Property and the Judiciary (Edward Elgar Publishing, 2018), at 259 (holding that "the objective of the Centre is to promote arbitration and mediation in cases falling, wholly or in part, within the competence of the Unified Patent Court").

[40] It being noted that the submission of a dispute to institutional mediation or arbitration rules does not necessarily means that mediation or arbitration proceedings will necessarily be geographically or legally connected to the country or city of location of the relevant institution providing mediation and arbitration services (e.g. a WIPO arbitration does not necessarily have its seat in Switzerland/in Geneva).

[41] See Kaneko, at 91; approved by Axel Walz, EU-Einheitspatent und Schiedsverfahren. Zugleich ein Beitrag zur objektiven Schiedsfähigkeit der Patentnichtigkeitsklage (book review of the thesis of Daniel Kenji Kaneko), SchiedsV 2019, 148 at 149.

unitary effect or a European patent. The wording of Art. 35 para. 2 first sentence UPCA does not specify that the Centre shall have any exclusivity: it merely provides that "the Centre shall provide facilities for mediation and arbitration of patent disputes falling within the scope of this Agreement" without expressing in any manner that the Centre should benefit from any exclusivity for this purpose (contrary to the exclusive competence granted to the Court by Art. 32 para. 1 UPCA).

This consequently means that the parties should not be constrained to use the facilities of the Centre and should not be bound to apply its arbitration rules (that shall be adopted, as provided under Article 35 para. 3 UPCA) even if the arbitration proceedings relate to a European patent with unitary effect or a European patent. However, the arbitral tribunal shall comply with the limits of its powers as resulting from Art. 35 para. 2 UPCA which provide that "patents may not be revoked or limited in mediation or arbitration proceedings"[42]. This would mean that arbitral awards rendered by an arbitral tribunal that would not have been instituted by the Centre should not conflict with the limits of the powers as resulting from Art. 35 para. 2 UPCA (e.g. an arbitral award that would conflict would not be enforced).

9.2.4 Interactions between arbitration proceedings and court proceedings before the Court

If the parties have validly opted for arbitration instituted by the Centre to solve their dispute, the Court should decline its jurisdiction to decide this dispute *on the merits* even if it would fall under the exclusive jurisdictional power of the Court under Art. 32 UPCA[43]. On this basis, the arbitral tribunal that would have been instituted in order to decide on an infringement claim raised by the patent holder shall not suspend its proceedings in case the defendant would raise a counterclaim for revocation of the patent (by application by analogy of Art. 33 para. 4 second sentence UPCA) because such counterclaim should also be decided by the arbitral tribunal[44].

---

[42] On this issue, see below 9.2.5 (and text ad footnotes 51–53); this seems to be confirmed by Rule 11 (2) of the Rules of Procedure which provides that "[p]ursuant to Rule 365 the Court shall, if requested by the parties, by decision confirm the terms of any settlement or arbitral award by consent (*irrespective of whether it was reached using the facilities of the Centre or otherwise*), including a term which obliges the patent owner to limit, surrender or agree to the revocation of a patent or not to assert it against the other party and/or third parties" (emphasis added).
[43] See Kaneko, at 324 (provided that the parties have not limited the jurisdictional power of the arbitral tribunal with respect to selected issues, e.g. the validity of the patents that could then be submitted to the Court).
[44] See Kaneko, at 324; this author raises the question whether the arbitral tribunal must not suspend its proceedings when the arbitral tribunal consists only of lawyers (and not of technical experts, whereby the UPC is composed of technical judges); this should not be the case also because it is usual in arbitration proceedings that experts shall be appointed to clarify selected issues of relevance for deciding the dispute

However, the Court would as a matter of principle keep its jurisdictional power to grant provisional and protective measures. Article 32 para. (c) UPCA states indeed that the UPC has exclusive competence in respect of actions for provisional and protective measures and injunctions and art. 62 UPC defines the conditions under which provisional measures can be granted by the UPC. This could be relevant if a patent licensee allegedly uses the licensed patent outside of the scope of the license which could thus trigger patent infringement remedies (including provisional measures). In this case, the exclusive jurisdiction of an arbitral tribunal to decide on the merits of the dispute does not bar the jurisdictional power of the UPC to grant provisional measures (on the basis of Art. 32 and 62 UPC). This remaining power of the UPC could be specified in the arbitration rules to be established by the Centre (see by comparison Art. 48 (d) of the WIPO Arbitration Rules[45]).

Another question is whether an arbitral tribunal instituted by the Centre can grant provisional measures? At first, one could consider that the power to grant provisional measures would be within the exclusive power of the UPC because Art. 32 para. 1 (c) confers exclusive jurisdiction to the Court. However, the exclusivity granted to the Court only excludes the jurisdiction of other courts and should consequently not exclude the jurisdiction of arbitral tribunals. On this basis, an arbitral tribunal instituted by the Centre should have the jurisdiction to grant provisional measures. One can note in this respect that the Mediation Rules (Art. 14 para. 3) contain a rule that addresses the availability of provisional remedies during the conduct of mediation proceedings by providing that "[t]he parties undertake not to bring or actively continue any judicial, arbitral or similar proceedings to a dispute which is subject to pending mediation at the Centre. The parties are not precluded from applying to the competent court or arbitral Tribunal for interim measures of protection". This provision consequently indicates that the parties remain in a position to obtain provisional measures from "the competent court or arbitral Tribunal" even during mediation proceedings. This must be understood to mean that arbitral tribunals instituted by the Centre (and also other arbitral tribunals) have the jurisdictional power to grant provisional measures even during mediation proceedings. This scenario does not however appear very likely given that in most cases in which the parties have agreed to submit to mediation and arbitration (in med-arb proceedings), when a mediation is conducted, the arbitral tribunal is not constituted yet. This means that parties cannot request provisional measures during the mediation unless they can request them from an emergency arbitrator that would be appointed by

---

between the parties; the limited jurisdictional power of arbitral tribunals as resulting from Art. 35 para. 1 in fine UPCA should not constitute either a ground for suspending the arbitral proceedings, see Kaneko, at 326–327.

45 Available at: https://www.wipo.int/amc/en/arbitration/rules/index.html: "A request addressed by a party to a judicial authority for interim measures or for security for the claim or counter-claim, or for the implementation of any such measures or orders granted by the Tribunal, shall not be deemed incompatible with the Arbitration Agreement, or deemed to be a waiver of that Agreement".

the Centre. The creation of an emergency arbitration mechanism is not contemplated in the UPCA and in the other documents relating to the Centre that have been published at this stage. It could however make sense to provide for the availability of emergency arbitration proceedings, because this corresponds to the best practices of international commercial arbitration (and is consequently reflected in the arbitration rules of all major arbitration institutions). Emergency remedies and thus emergency arbitration further play a particularly important role in many IP-related arbitration cases. It remains to be seen whether and in the affirmative how this might be implemented in the Centre's arbitration rules (by comparison, Art. 49 of the WIPO Arbitration Rules provides for detailed rules relating to "Emergency Relief Proceedings"[46]).

If the parties to a patent transaction covering a European patent with unitary effect or a European patent (that would fall within the exclusive competence of the Court) are bound by an arbitration agreement providing for the submission of their disputes to another arbitration institution or to ad hoc arbitration, this choice made by the parties should be binding on the Court. The Court should consequently defer to such choice for arbitration made by the parties which reflects a fundamental principle of international arbitration[47]. The exclusive competence granted to the Court by Art. 32 UPCA for disputes relating to a European patent with unitary effect or a European patent should consequently not prevent such finding because the exclusivity granted to the Court by this provision for deciding patent disputes only means that national state courts shall have no power to decide on the relevant disputes (because of such exclusivity). This is supported by Art. 32 para. 2 UPCA which provides for a residual competence of the national courts for disputes which do not fall within the exclusive competence of the Court ("[t]he national courts of the Contracting Member States shall remain competent for actions relating to patents and supplementary protection certificates which do not come within the exclusive competence of the Court").

A final point of practical relevance from a EU law perspective relating to the interactions and differences between arbitral tribunals instituted by the Centre and courts is that arbitral tribunals do not have the power (and even less the obligation) to submit directly to the CJEU questions for preliminary ruling under Art. 267 of the Treaty on the Functioning of the European Union (even if they might do it indirectly via the UPC)[48].

---

46 See Art. 49 (b) providing (among others) that "[a] party seeking urgent interim relief prior to the establishment of the Tribunal may submit a request for such emergency relief to the Centre. [...]".
47 Art. 2 para. 3 of the New York Convention on the Recognition and Enforcement of Foreign Arbitral Awards (of June 10, 1958): "The court of a Contracting State, when seized of an action in a matter in respect of which the parties have made an agreement within the meaning of this article, shall, at the request of one of the parties, refer the parties to arbitration, unless it finds that the said agreement is null and void, inoperative or incapable of being performed"; the issue however remains open if and to what extent the Court instituted by the UPCA would be bound by such obligation and whether it can be assimilated to "the court of a Contracting State".
48 Kaneko, at 327 – 331.

9.2.5 No right to revoke or limit patents in arbitration proceedings

Article 35 para. 2 in fine UPCA provides that "a patent may not be revoked or limited in mediation or arbitration proceedings"[49]. This provision limits the use of ADR for solving patent disputes given that neither the validity nor the scope of a patent shall be affected by mediation or arbitration proceedings. It, however, remains somewhat unclear how this provision must be interpreted with respect to arbitration proceedings. It is generally admitted that arbitral tribunals may not decide on the validity of a patent with effect *erga omnes* and thus decide that a patent would be partly or totally invalid[50] because the Court has exclusive jurisdiction to decide on the revocation of the patents at issue (Art. 32 para. 1 let. d and e UPCA). This provision should apply to all arbitral tribunals irrespective of whether they have been instituted by the Centre and should also apply irrespective of the seat of the arbitration[51]. However, should the seat of the arbitration be outside of the countries that are contracting parties to the UPCA (in particular Switzerland), it is uncertain on what basis arbitral tribunals would have to take this into account[52]. Should foreign-based arbitral tribunals not comply with the limits resulting from Art. 35 UPCA, this could in any event raise difficulties at the time of enforcement of the arbitral awards in contracting States of the UPCA. An award rendered by a foreign-based arbitral tribunal deciding on the invalidity of a European patent would most likely not be enforced in the contracting States of the UPCA[53].

Does this provision mean that the arbitral tribunal shall have no power at all to decide on the issue of the patent validity or the patent scope in any circumstances or shall the arbitral tribunal have the power to decide on these issues but only with inter partes effect (so that this shall not affect the registration of the patent as such and its effect on third parties)? It is adequate to consider that arbitral tribunals should have the power to decide on these issues at least with effect between the parties (inter partes) because it is most common that the issue of partial or total invalidity of a patent can arise in disputes relating to the contractual use of such patent[54]. This is particularly the case in patent li-

---

[49] Article 79 UPCA similarly provides that "[t]he parties may, at any time in the course of proceedings, conclude their case by way of settlement, which shall be confirmed by a decision of the Court. *A patent may not be revoked or limited by way of settlement.*" (emphasis added).
[50] Sam Granata, The Patent Mediation and Arbitration Centre: a centre of opportunities, in: Christophe Geiger/A. Craig Nard/Xavier Seuba (eds), Intellectual Property and the Judiciary (Edward Elgar Publishing, 2018), at 256 (who understands that Art. 35 para. 2 prohibits decisions with erga omnes effect); see also Picht, at 6.
[51] See Kaneko, at 102–103 (giving a concrete example of an hypothetical ICC arbitration case with the seat of the arbitration in Zurich).
[52] For a discussion, see Kaneko, at 105–106 (discussing the issue for Switzerland-based arbitral tribunals).
[53] See Kaneko, at 315 footnote 1391.
[54] For a general discussion, see Kaneko, at 235 et seq. and at 315–316, and Picht, at 6–9; the view was expressed by the Commission that the Centre should deal with cases "where validity is not at stake", see the

cense agreements on the basis of which the licensee may raise the argument that it shall not be bound to pay royalties because the licensed patent would allegedly not be valid.

This can be supported by the rationale that the exclusive jurisdictional power of the Court with respect to decisions on revocation or scope of patents (Art. 65 UPCA) is justified essentially to the extent that such decisions have an effect against third parties, i.e., that a decision of the Court revoking entirely or partly a patent shall be reflected in the relevant patent registry (Art. 65 para. 5 UPCA): for European patents with unitary effect, the relevant registry will be the "register for unitary patent protection"[55]. Consequently, if there is no effect on third parties, the exclusive jurisdictional power of the Court is not justified so that arbitral tribunals may also decide on the validity of a patent with effect inter partes[56].

The question also arises whether arbitral tribunals would have the power to decide indirectly on the validity of the patents so that they would have the power to order a party to cancel or to limit its patent by submitting the adequate request to the relevant patent office ("mittelbare erga-omnes Wirkung")[57].

Rule 11 para. 2 of the Rules of Procedure provides in this respect that "[p]ursuant to Rule 365 the Court shall, if requested by the parties, by decision confirm the terms of any settlement or arbitral award by consent (irrespective of whether it was reached using the facilities of the Centre or otherwise), including a term which obliges the patent owner to limit, surrender or agree to the revocation of a patent or not to assert it against the other party and/or third parties [...]". Rule 365 para. 1 states that "[w]here the parties have concluded their action by way of settlement, they shall inform the judge-rapporteur. The Court shall confirm the settlement by decision of the Court [Rule 11.2], if requested by the parties, and the decision may be enforced as a final decision of the Court"[58].

Communication from the Commission to the European Parliament, the Council and the European Economic and Social Committee, An Industrial Property Rights Strategy for Europe COM(2008) 465 final, of July 16, 2008, p. 12: "In the context of work on the Community patent and an integrated patent jurisdiction system, the creation of a patent arbitration and mediation centre at Community level is being explored to deal with cases *where validity is not at stake*" (emphasis added).

55 As defined in Art. 2 (e) of Regulation 1257/2012, "Register for unitary patent protection" means "the register constituting part of the European Patent Register in which the unitary effect and any limitation, licence, transfer, revocation or lapse of a European patent with unitary effect are registered".

56 Sam Granata, The Patent Mediation and Arbitration Centre: a centre of opportunities, in: Christophe Geiger/A. Craig Nard/Xavier Seuba (eds), Intellectual Property and the Judiciary (Edward Elgar Publishing, 2018), at 256 (who understands that Art. 35 para. 2 prohibits decisions with erga omnes effect).

57 For a discussion, see Picht, at 7.

58 Rule 365 further provides (para. 2) that "[a]t the request of the parties the Court may order that details of the settlement are confidential".

Rule 11 para. 2 refers to "arbitral award by consent" which must be understood to refer only to a so-called "consent award"[59], i.e. an arbitral award that results from the settlement of the dispute between the parties and thus reflects an agreement that was entered into by the parties and for which the parties want to ensure the enforceability of their respective obligations resulting from the settlement by structuring the settlement in the form of an arbitral award (that is enforceable under the New York Convention). The question arises whether this provision also applies to ordinary arbitral awards (i.e. not consent awards) so that these arbitral awards could be confirmed by the Court and could be enforced as final decisions of the Court. Neither the wording of Rule 11 para. 2 (in German and in French), nor other provisions of the UPCA (in particular Art. 35 para. 2) make it possible to consider that arbitral awards should be treated like settlements and thus be enforced as final decisions of the Court[60]. The legal distinction remains between what parties can voluntary do (i.e. a patent holder can voluntary accept to limit or cancel its patent) and what a private dispute resolution body (i.e. an arbitral tribunal) can validly decide. Under the UPCA (Art. 35 para. 2), the decision was made that an arbitral tribunal shall not have the power to decide on the partial or total invalidity of the relevant patents with effect *erga omnes*, which means that the arbitral tribunal shall not have the power to take decisions relating to the invalidity of the patents that would materialize in the cancellation of the patents from the relevant patent registries with effect erga omnes[61]. This is ultimately what arbitral tribunals would do if they could render decisions with an indirect erga omnes effect which would take the form of orders made by the arbitral tribunal to the patent owner to cancel partly or totally its patents from the relevant patent registries (irrespective of whether this would be formulated in terms of withdrawal or in terms of cancellation that may have a retroactive effect).

In order to ensure a unified definition of the power of arbitral tribunals to decide on the validity of patents covered by the UPCA within all the countries that are concerned (including those that are parties to the European Patent Convention and most particularly Switzerland, which has a very liberal system admitting the arbitrability of the validity of patents with effect erga omnes)[62], the proposal was made to clarify the scope of Art. 35 para. 2 in fine UPCA in the sense that the lack of power of arbitral tribunals to de-

---

[59] This results from a comparison with the French and German versions of Rule 11 para. 2 which respectively refer to "toute sentence arbitrale par accord des parties" and to "einvernehmliche Schiedssprüche".
[60] See however Kaneko, at 317 (holding that this indirect erga omnes effect does not circumvent Art. 35 para. 2 in fine UPCA) and Picht, at 7–8.
[61] See Art. 65 para. 5 UPCA: "Where the Court, in a final decision, revokes a patent, either entirely or partly, it shall send a copy of the decision to the European Patent Office and, with respect to a European patent, to the national patent office of any Contracting Member State concerned".
[62] See Kaneko, at 319, noting that it would not be adequate to have an arbitration system under which an arbitral tribunal could validly decide on the invalidity of the Swiss part of a European patent (because Swiss arbitration law grants this power to arbitral tribunals, see above footnote 9) but could not decide on other national parts of the same European patent (because Art. 35 para. 2 in fine would not authorize this) in the same arbitration proceedings.

cide on the validity of patent with effect erga omnes shall not be limited to arbitral tribunal instituted by the Centre but shall apply to all arbitral tribunals[63].

In any event, there does not seem to be any practical advantage in obtaining a decision of the Court in order to enforce an arbitral award as a final decision of the Court (Rule 365), because the enforcement of arbitral awards can already be ensured quite effectively and globally on the basis of the 1958 New York Convention.

9.2.6 Improved enforceability of settlements reached through the use of the facilities of the Centre

Article 35 para. 2 UPCA states that "[a]rticle 82 shall apply mutatis mutandis to any settlement reached through the use of the facilities of the Centre, including through mediation". Article 82 UPCA addresses the enforceability of the decisions to be rendered by the Court by stating that such decisions shall be enforceable in all contracting Member States.[64] Art. 35 para. 2 UPCA confirms the EU policy promoting the enforceability of settlements resulting from mediation which is anchored in the Mediation Directive[65].

Pursuant to Article 35 para. 2 UPCA, the application by analogy of Art. 82 covers "any settlement", whereby "settlement" refers to an agreement between the parties in dispute which is entered into in order to settle a dispute[66]. This is reflected in Art. 79

---

[63] See the proposal drafted by Kaneko, at 341, for a new Art. 35a UPCA that shall replace the last sentence of Art. 35 para. 2 last sentence (in the German text as drafted by Kaneko): "ARTIKEL 35a Bestandsklagen "Die Bestimmungen dieses Übereinkommens berühren nicht die Anwendung nationaler Vorschriften der Vertragsmitgliedsstaaten über die Schiedsgerichtsbarkeit. In Schiedsverfahren darf ein Patent allerdings weder für nichtig erklärt noch beschränkt werden. Vorbehaltlich Satz 1 steht dem Schiedsgericht jedoch die in Regel 11.2 Satz 1 Hs. 2 der Verfahrensordnung bestimmte Gestaltungsmacht zu'"; in English: "The provisions of this Convention shall not affect the application of national rules of arbitration of the Contracting Member States. In arbitration proceedings, however, a patent may neither be declared invalid nor limited. Subject to the first sentence, the arbitral tribunal shall, however, have the decisional power provided for in Rule 11.2, first sentence, second section, of the Rules of Procedure"; as noted above (see text ad footnotes 59–60) Rule 11 para. 2 of the Rules of Procedure do not apply to all arbitral awards, but only to consent awards and thus should not be relied upon as a tool that could empower arbitral tribunals to decide even indirectly on the invalidity of patents with effect erga omnes.

[64] Article 82 para. 1 UPCA: "Decisions and orders of the Court shall be enforceable in any Contracting Member State. An order for the enforcement of a decision shall be appended to the decision by the Court".

[65] Article 6 (Enforceability of agreements resulting from mediation) of the EU Mediation Directive 2008/52/EC provides that "1. Member States shall ensure that it is possible for the parties, or for one of them with the explicit consent of the others, to request that the content of a written agreement resulting from mediation be made enforceable. The content of such an agreement shall be made enforceable unless, in the case in question, either the content of that agreement is contrary to the law of the Member State where the request is made or the law of that Member State does not provide for its enforceability".

[66] This is confirmed by the German version of Art. 35 para. 2 which provides that "Artikel 82 gilt *für jeden Vergleich*, der durch die Inanspruchnahme der Dienste des Zentrums, auch im Wege der Mediation, erreicht worden ist, entsprechend" (emphasis added); the French version is not as clear given that it

UPCA (which bears the title: "Settlement") and provides that "[t]he parties may, at any time in the course of proceedings, conclude their case by way of settlement, which shall be confirmed by a decision of the Court. A patent may not be revoked or limited by way of settlement". As a result, arbitral awards, even if they would be issued at the end of arbitration proceedings conducted under the rules of the Centre (to be adopted under Art. 35 para. 3 UPCA), will not fall under the concept of "settlement" referred to in Article 35 para. 2 UPCA[67].

Article 35 para. 2 UPCA provides that the improved enforceability will apply to "any settlement reached through the use of the facilities of the Centre, *including through mediation*" (emphasis added) thereby implying that a settlement can be reached outside of a mediation. This is not surprising because a settlement could also be reached "through the use of the facilities of the Centre" without being limited to mediation, i.e. a settlement could also be reached in the course of an arbitration proceeding. It is indeed not uncommon that a settlement is reached once arbitration proceedings have been initiated. This can particularly be the case if the arbitral proceedings are split into two phases, the first one focusing on the issue of validity/infringement of the patents/IP rights in dispute, and the second one (in the case of a finding of infringement) covering the quantification (quantum) of the financial claims of the patents/IP rights owner (claims for damages). This is confirmed by the experience made by other providers of IP arbitration services[68].

Article 35 para. 2 UPCA means that a settlement "reached through the use of the facilities of the Centre" will be enforced in the same way as formal decisions rendered by the Court. While such improved enforceability of settlement transactions is good news as such, it can be wondered why this feature shall only apply to settlements "reached through the use of the facilities of the Centre" (as provided by Article 35 para. 2 UPCA). This seems to imply that there would be a legal incentive to use the facilities of the Centre because only such use would trigger the improved enforceability of settlement transactions. This does not appear as a legitimate solution because Article 35 para. 2 UPCA could thus be perceived as privileging the services offered by the Centre by comparison to other providers of ADR services[69]. This approach also conflicts with the basic freedom of the parties to select the ADR service providers that they consider as being the most

---

broadly indicates that "L'article 82 s'applique mutatis mutandis à *tout règlement d'un différend* par le biais des services fournis par le centre, y compris la médiation" (emphasis added), whereby the reference to "tout règlement d'un différend" is broader to the extent that it could potentially cover arbitral awards.
67 Arbitral awards will be enforceable under the rules of the 1958 New York Convention.
68 According to the statistics of the WIPO Arbitration and Mediation Centre, the settlement rate in arbitration proceedings is 33 %: http://www.wipo.int/amc/en/center/caseload.html.
69 A more neutral approach is reflected in Rule 11 para. 2 of the Rules of Procedure which provide that "[p]ursuant to Rule 365 the Court shall, if requested by the parties, by decision confirm the terms of any settlement or arbitral award (*irrespective of whether it was reached using the facilities of the Centre or otherwise*), [...]" (emphasis added).

adequate for helping them to solve their dispute. It is therefore difficult to conceive why settlements "reached through the use of the facilities of the Centre" should benefit from a privileged treatment by comparison to settlements reached through other means. The "use of the facilities of the Centre" cannot imply that a settlement reached through such use would have a higher quality, reliability or fairness from a substantive perspective because settlements ultimately reflect the mutual intentions of the parties in dispute (even if settlements can be reached thanks to the assistance and guidance of third parties, and particularly of mediators, instituted by the Centre). The use of the facilities of the Centre further does not necessarily imply that the parties to the settlement have any geographic connection with the territory of the European Union. One may therefore also consider that settlements reached through the use of the facilities of other EU-based (or even non-EU based) IP mediation dispute resolution providers should also benefit from the mutatis mutandis application of Art. 82 UPCA.

There is consequently no justification why the improved enforceability (as provided by Article 35 para. 2 UPCA) shall not be available if the parties to a dispute reach a settlement without using the facilities of the Centre.

9.2.7 Double seat of the Centre and provision of "facilities" by the Centre

Article 35 para. 1 UPCA provides that the Centre will have two seats – in Ljubljana (Slovenia) and in Lisbon (Portugal) respectively.[70] Based on the PMAC Rules (art. 4), "Mediation and arbitration proceedings can be held either at the seats or elsewhere. For this purpose appropriate facilities shall be provided for at the seats of the Centre, in Ljubljana and Lisbon". This provision consequently refers to the physical facilities at which the proceedings shall take place. It can be noted that the PMAC Rules do not address and consequently do not regulate virtual hearings, even though virtual hearings have been massively used in arbitration proceedings (as well as court proceedings) during the COVID-19 pandemic and have been regulated by other major arbitration service providers[71] (this may be addressed in the future arbitration rules of the Centre).

Pursuant to Art. 35 para. 2 UPCA, "[t]he Centre shall provide facilities for mediation and arbitration of patent disputes falling within the scope of this Agreement", whereby "facilities" are defined as "services" in the version French of the UPCA and as "Dienste"

---

[70] This rather unusual solution appears to be the result of a political decision, rather than being dictated by an established pre-existing expertise and tradition of the relevant cities / countries for offering ADR services for intellectual property disputes.

[71] See e.g. the ICC Checklist for a Protocol on Virtual Hearings and Suggested Clauses for Cyber-Protocols and Procedural Orders Dealing with the Organisation of Virtual Hearings, available at: https://iccwbo.org/publication/icc-checklist-for-a-protocol-on-virtual-hearings-and-suggested-clauses-for-cyber-protocols-and-procedural-orders-dealing-with-the-organisation-of-virtual-hearings/.

in the German version of the UPCA. One can note that other provisions of the UPCA which use the term "facilities" use it in order to designate *physical* facilities (i.e. "infrastructures"). By way of example, Art. 37 para. 1 2nd subparagraph UPC provides that "Contracting Member States setting up a local division shall provide the facilities necessary for that purpose"[72].

In any event, the parties shall be free to choose the seat of the arbitration under the patent arbitration system enabled by Article 35 UPCA[73]. This freedom is indeed of key importance for the parties in making the choice to submit their disputes to arbitration: the choice of the seat of the arbitration has an impact on many fundamental issues, including the conditions of a challenge against the award before the national courts of the country of the seat (e.g. annulment proceedings against arbitral awards) as well as the nationality of the award, which is of relevance for the purpose of the future enforceability of the award in foreign countries (under the New York Convention).

In this respect, even though the double seats of the Centre in Portugal and in Slovenia can be explained and understood from a political perspective[74], this localization should not prevent the parties to localize the seat of the arbitration in other countries to the extent that the parties feel it necessary in view of their respective interests. While Portugal and Slovenia are both parties to the 1958 New York Convention on the Recognition and Enforcement of Foreign Arbitral Awards[75] so that the parties' choice of Lisbon or Ljubljana as the seat of the arbitration will not prevent them from benefiting from the advantages of the New York Convention in terms of global enforceability of the arbitral award, the parties may still want to submit an arbitration relating to a European patent with unitary effect or to a European patent to another arbitration service provider and to choose a seat in other countries than Portugal or Slovenia (and potentially in non EU-countries) for various reasons (including the neutrality of the country where the arbitration shall have its seat and of the law that shall govern the arbitration).

It should in any case be avoided that the parties shall insufficiently identify the seat of the arbitration, which might particularly result from an inadequate contractual wording which would, by way of example, submit disputes to the "mediation and arbitration Centre instituted under Article 35 UPCA": in such a case, the difficultly would result from the double seat of the Centre (in Lisbon and Ljubljana). It can be expected that this risk can be significantly reduced or even eliminated by the standard contractual arbitration clauses that will be made available by the Centre, as done by other (IP) ADR institutions, and that this issue will be addressed in the future arbitration rules of the Cen-

---

72 In French: "Les Etats membres contractants qui créent une division locale fournissent les infrastructures nécessaires à cette fin" / in German: "Vertragsmitgliedstaaten, die eine Lokalkammer errichten, stellen die hierfür erforderlichen Einrichtungen zur Verfügung".
73 Kaneko, at 96.
74 See Tilmann/Plassmann (eds), N 6 ad Art. 35.
75 See the list of contracting parties at: http://www.uncitral.org/uncitral/fr/uncitral_texts/arbitration/NYConvention_status.html.

tre (which could provide that the Centre shall decide on the seat of the arbitration in the absence of the decision made by the parties, as done in other arbitration rules, see e.g. Art. 38 (a) of the WIPO Arbitration Rules which provide "(a) Unless otherwise agreed by the parties, the place of arbitration shall be decided by the Center, taking into consideration any observations of the parties and the circumstances of the arbitration").

9.2.8 List of arbitrators

One must also note the somewhat unclear wording of Article 35 para. 4 UPCA which provides that "[t]he Centre shall draw up a list of mediators and arbitrators to assist the parties in the settlement of their dispute"[76], given that it is not the function of arbitrators to "assist the parties in the settlement of their dispute" but rather to decide the dispute (in a way comparable to what state courts would do), and that the parties should as a matter of principle have the power to choose who shall decide their dispute (arbitration) or help them to solve it (mediation) without being unduly constrained in their choice. In any event, one can note that the PMCA (Art. 14 para. 1) provides that "[t]he Centre shall establish and maintain a list of mediators and arbitrators in the field of patent law. The Centre will strive to enlist mediators and arbitrators of each contracting Member State on the list".

9.3 Concluding remarks

Article 35 UPCA is of high legal as well as symbolic importance in the European intellectual property regulatory landscape because it confirms in an international European agreement that patent disputes (subject to the limits resulting from Article 35 para. 2 UPCA) can be subject to arbitration. By doing so, it somehow puts aside the diverging solutions that exist under the respective national arbitration laws in the various Member States relating to the issue of arbitrability of patent (and more generally of intellectual property) disputes. As a result, it appears unlikely that an arbitral award rendered by an arbitral tribunal instituted under the arbitration rules of the Centre (on the basis of Article 35 UPCA) might not be enforced in a Member State of the European Union on the ground that under the national laws applicable in such country a patent dispute would not be arbitrable at all. From this perspective, Article 35 paves the way for a broader arbitrability of patent disputes within the European Union.

---

[76] This wording was already reflected in the Communication from the Commission to the European Parliament, the Council and the European Economic and Social Committee, an Industrial Property Rights Strategy for Europe COM (2008) 465 final, of July 16, 2008, p. 12: "The centre would establish a Community list of mediators and arbitrators who could assist the parties in settlement of their dispute".

Article 35 UPCA further confirms the global trend promoting the use of ADR for resolving intellectual property disputes, as a favorable alternative to complex and costly patent litigation proceedings[77], particularly for small and medium enterprises[78]. While this trend constitutes goods news for all stakeholders given that ADR can offer tailored mechanisms and solutions which can adequately accommodate the interests and needs of the parties, certain issues will still need to be carefully reflected upon[79] and shall continue to be closely monitored in an international and comparative perspective[80]. It will be particularly important to ensure that the mediation and arbitration rules that shall be adopted by the Centre shall reflect best practices of international arbitration which are characterized by the autonomy of the parties to adopt dispute resolution mechanisms which shall be adapted to their needs and interests. On this basis, parties should particularly be free to select the law that shall apply to their dispute (for arbitration) and the language that shall be used. In this respect, the Centre may potentially develop its arbitration activities for solving FRAND patent disputes, for which arbitration is frequently perceived as a very adequate dispute resolution mechanism[81]. The attractiveness of the Centre was already reflected a few years ago in commitments made by Sam-

---

[77] This view was officially expressed in the process of adoption of the UPCA by the Committee on Industry, Research and Energy in its opinion for the Committee of Legal Affairs on jurisdictional system for patent disputes (2011/2176(INI)) of November 24, 2011 in which the Committee stated that it "welcomes the establishment of a mediation and arbitration centre as part of the agreement, and stresses that one of its main aims must be to reduce red tape and keep litigation costs down for the parties involved" (available at: http://www.europarl.europa.eu/sides/getDoc.do?type=REPORT&mode=XML&reference=A7-2012-9&language=EN).

[78] See the Communication from the Commission to the European Parliament, the Council and the European Economic and Social Committee, An Industrial Property Rights Strategy for Europe COM (2008) 465 final, of July 16, 2008, p. 12 ("Complementing ADR facilities for patents outside the Community framework, this centre [i.e. the Centre] could ensure proximity and better accessibility to patent disputes by SMEs").

[79] Some issues can be adequately addressed in the Mediation and Arbitration Rules that shall be established by the Centre (on the basis of Article 35 para. 3 UPCA) as well as in the standard arbitration and mediation clauses that will be made available for use by the parties (as done by all major arbitration and mediation service providers); the PMAC Rules provide in this respect (Art. 5 para. 2) that the objectives of the Centre include to "provide mediation and arbitration rules, fee schedules, *model clauses for use in mediation and arbitration and other regulations*" (emphasis added).

[80] This is why several global intellectual property institutions are monitoring the on-going developments of IPR ADR; this is particularly the case of AIPPI which has set up a Special Committee on this topic (Q225) that the author of this paper had the privilege to chair (https://www.aippi.org/?sel=questions&sub=listingcommittees&viewQ=225#225).

[81] See e.g. the recent statements made by Justice Arnold in the very recent judgment (dated October 27, 2022) in the case Optis Cellular Technology LLC & Ors v Apple Retail UK Ltd & Ors, [2022] EWCA Civ 1411, holding (in a post script to the judgment, para. 115) that the "only way to put a stop to such behavior is for [Standard Setting organizations, SSOs] like ETSI to make legally-enforceable arbitration of such disputes part of their IPR policies"; see also his scientific paper: Richard Arnold, SEPs, FRAND and Mandatory Global Arbitration, (2021) GRUR 123.

sung on April 29, 2014 in the course of the EU competition investigations which have been declared legally binding by the European Commission[82]. According to these commitments, Samsung committed not to seek injunctions in the European Economic Area (EEA) on the basis of its standard essential patents (SEPs) for smartphones and tablets against licensees who sign up to a specified licensing framework. Under this framework, any dispute over what are fair, reasonable and non-discriminatory (so-called "FRAND") terms for the SEPs in question will be determined by a court, or if both parties agree, by an arbitral tribunal. The commitments therefore provide a "safe harbour" for all potential licensees of the relevant Samsung SEPs. What is of particular interest in these commitments is that the dispute over FRAND can be settled at the choice of the parties "under the rules of arbitration of the ICC, unless the Parties mutually agree that the arbitration tribunal will be the patent mediation and arbitration Centre as established under Article 35(1) of the Agreement on a Unified Patent Court"[83]. The Centre was consequently identified as a potential provider of arbitration services for solving the FRAND disputes[84]. Interestingly, the arbitration proceedings which are contemplated in the Samsung Commitments provide for an appeal against the arbitral award that shall be rendered by a first arbitral tribunal before a second arbitral tribunal[85]. The commitments further provided that the arbitration must be conducted in English, that it is governed by the laws of England and Wales and that the "seat of the arbitration will be in an EEA jurisdiction in which national laws permit Parties to agree to make an arbitration decision subject to appeal to a second arbitration tribunal"[86]. This mechanism consequently confirms the parties' interests in adopting tailor made dispute resolution mechanisms.

As a final word, it is essential that the Centre's arbitration practice and the proceedings that shall be conducted under its aegis shall ensure that all parties involved in a dispute (and particularly intellectual property owners) will benefit from a dispute settlement system that shall meet their legitimate expectations and that shall efficiently address the challenges of intellectual property ADR mechanisms. In this respect, the view was expressed that the future success of the Centre will highly depend on the success of the Court itself[87]. One could however also claim the opposite to the extent that the

---

[82] Case 39939 Samsung – Enforcement of UMTS standard essential patents; see the dedicated webpage of the case at: http://ec.europa.eu/competition/elojade/isef/case_details.cfm?proc_code=1_39939.
[83] Art. 9(a) of Samsung's commitments (hereinafter: "the Commitments"), which are available at http://ec.europa.eu/competition/antitrust/cases/dec_docs/39939/39939_1502_5.pdf; the wording of the commitments is not necessarily optimal given that the arbitral tribunal should not be confused with the Centre itself (the arbitral tribunal is independent from the institution managing the arbitration proceedings).
[84] It being noted that the WIPO arbitration and mediation center has also launched specific services for FRAND disputes, see http://www.wipo.int/amc/en/center/specific-sectors/ict/frand/.
[85] See art. 9(f) of the Commitments.
[86] See art. 9(c) and (d) of the Commitments.
[87] Kaneko, at 107 referring to Sam Granata, Success mediation and Arbitration centre of Unified Patent Court will depend largely on performance Court, available at: http://kluwerpatentblog.com/2015/10/11/

success of arbitration may sometimes result from the absence of performance of the court system so that arbitration and courts can be considered to be in a competitive relationship. On this basis, the success of the patent arbitration system instituted and managed by the Centre may constitute an attractive *alternative* to court proceedings before the Court depending on how parties will perceive and experience litigating before the Court. In any event, as for any other provider of dispute resolution services, the market and thus the users will ultimately decide of the success of the Centre.

---

judge-sam-granata-success-mediation-and-Arbitration-centre-of-unified-patent-court-will-depend-largely-on-performance-court.

Justyna Ożegalska-Trybalska
10 Supplementary Protection Certificates (Article 30)

10.1 Introduction

A new unitary patent system not only revolutionises patent protection in the EU but also impacts the regime of Supplementary Protection Certificates ("SPCs"). An SPC, as the EU *sui generis* patent-linked IP right, allows for the extension of the monopoly period for patented medicinal products and plant protection products which are subject to additional regulatory requirements, which reduce the effective time of the exploitation of a patented product. The aim of an SPC is to compensate a patent holder for a maximum of five years period between the patent grant and the marketing authorisation when a patented product cannot be exploited. As a tool for market exclusivity, SPC protection, similarly to patents, is of essential strategic importance for the European pharma sector.

Although Article 5 (2) of the European Parliament and of the Council Regulation (EU) 1257/2012 implementing enhanced cooperation in the area of the creation of unitary patent protection[1] (hereinafter referred as "UPR") ensures the uniform scope of protection and limitations in all participating Member States only for unitary patents, the unitary "patent package" provides further rules in this regard for SPCs granted for unitary and European patents as basis patents. As Article 30 Agreement on Unified Patent Court[2] (hereinafter referred as "UPCA") on the effects of SPC provides:

> supplementary protection certificate shall confer the same rights as conferred by the patent and shall be subject to the same limitations and obligations.

The explicit wording of Article 3 (b) expresses the UPCA's applicability to SPCs issued for a product protected by a patent, with the latter understood as both a unitary and a European patent.[3] Additionally, 2 (h) UPCA clarifies the meaning of "supplementary protection certificate" by reference to the European Parliament and of the Council Regulation (EC) 469/2009 concerning the supplementary protection certificate for medicinal pro-

---

[1] [2012] OJ L 361/1.
[2] Agreement on a Unified Patent Court, OJ C 175, 20.6.2013, p. 1–40
[3] As in Article 3 (c) (d) in conjunction with Article 83 ACPA, European patents to which the opt-out procedure described later has been applied, excluding this type of patent from the jurisdiction of the JSP, do not fall within the scope of this regulation.

Justyna Ożegalska-Trybalska, is Assistant Professor, Intellectual Property Law Chair, Jagiellonian University in Kraków

ducts[4] and the European Parliament and of the Council Regulation (EC) 1610/96 concerning the creation of a supplementary protection certificate for plant protection products[5] (hereinafter referred as "SPC Regulations").

Furthermore, under Article 32 (1) UPCA, equally to unitary patents and European patents, the UPC has exclusive jurisdiction in respect of SPCs, including:
(a) actions for actual or threatened infringements of SPCs and related defences, including counterclaims concerning licences;
(b) actions for declarations of non-infringement of patents and SPCs;
(c) counterclaims for revocation of patents and for declaration of invalidity of SPCs; and
(d) actions for the revocation of patents and for declaration of invalidity of an SPC.

As the above confirms, the UPCA foresees SPC protection recently granted in the national procedure for unitary patents and European patents governed by UPCA, but neither contains material law rules regarding SPCs[6] nor creates delegation for an autonomous regime of granting a unitary SPC linked with a grant of a new type of patents with the EU dimension.

On one hand, the EU legislator offers a legal framework for a centralised UPC system applicable to an SPC linked with unitary patents but this conflicts with the essential nature of SPCs as *sui generis* national rights dependent upon both basic patent and national marketing authorisation. On the other hand, decentralised national systems of granting and enforcing SPCs collides with the idea of a centralised system of unitary SPCs with an extended territorial scope. This creates concerns which are the subject of discussion among academics, EU policymakers[7], and stakeholders – mainly pharmaceutical companies[8]. With the launch of the new unitary patent system after many years and obstacles, the situation also raises concerns about its effectiveness, attractiveness, and availability for current and future SPC holders.

---

4 [2009] OJ L 152/1, hereinafter referred as Regulation (EC) 469/2009.
5 [1996] OJ L 198/30, hereinafter referred as Regulation (EC) 1610/96.
6 Winfried Tilmann, Clemens Plassmann, Unified Patent Protection in Europe. A Commentary (OUP, 2018), 554–570.
7 EC communication *"Upgrading the Single Market: more opportunities for people and business,"* COM (2015) 550, followed by the study *"Assessing the economic impacts of changing exemption provision during patent and SPC protection in Europe"*, <https://publications.europa.eu/en/publication-detail/-/publication/6e4ce9f8-aa41-11e7-837e-01aa75ed71a1/language-en> accessed 20 September, 2022, Study *"Impact Assessment to evaluate options for optimising the legal framework concerning SPCs and patent research exemptions for sectors whose products are subject to regulated market authorisations,"* followed by public consultations. <https://ec.europa.eu/smart-egulation/roadmaps/docs/2017_grow_051_supplementary_protection_certificates_en.pdf> accessed 24 September 2022.
8 ECPA, EFPIA and IFAH-Europe Joint Position Paper Proposal for a Unitary SPC, https://www.efpia.eu/media/15414/ecpa-efpia-and-ifah-europe-joint-position-paper-proposal-for-a-unitary-spc-july-2015.pdf.

The chapter focuses on discussing a normative (imperfect) overlap or (factual) gap between unitary patents and SPC regimes and possible scenarios for resolving this problem. As the general standards and problems related to the rights conferred by SPCs are widely addressed in SPC-focused publications, the main attention will be given to the challenges, risks, and benefits of the establishment of a unitary SPC as a part of the UPCA framework, and recent proposals of both upgrading the latter and reforming the SPC system.

10.2 General overview of the SPC system in the EU – in fitting with or conflicting with unitary protection concept?

SPC protection in the EU is governed by Regulation (EC) 469/2009 and Regulation (EC) 1610/96. Under the SPC Regulations, SPCs are granted by national patent offices, based on: (a) national regulations for medicinal products (both for humans and animals); and (b) plant protection products protected by national patents (including European patents in force in the territory).

The conditions for granting an SPC for medicinal products are set forth in Article 3 of Regulation 469/2009, under which, a supplementary certificate may be issued if, in the country in which the application is filed, on the date of its filing[9]:
(a) the product is protected by a basic patent still in force;
(b) the product has not previously been the subject of a certificate;
(c) a valid marketing authorisation has been issued for the product; and
(d) the authorisation is the first authorisation to market the product in question as a medicinal product.

The subject of an SPC in the meaning of Article 3 of the SPC Regulations may be a basic national or European patent. 'Basic patent' means a patent which protects a product as such, a process to obtain a product or an application of a product, and which is designated by its holder for the purpose of the procedure for grant of a certificate[10].

According to Article 4 of Regulation (EC) 469/2009, within the limits of the protection conferred by the basic patent, the protection conferred by an SPC extends only to the product covered by the authorisation to place the corresponding medicinal product on the market. An SPC provides the same rights as conferred by the basic patent and is subject to the same limitations and the same obligations (Article 4).

As the duration of the protection granted by the certificate should provide adequate effective protection, an SPC duration is calculate in order to provide the holder of both a

---

[9] Similar requirements are provided by Regulation (EC) 1610/96.
[10] Article 1 (c) Regulation (EC) 469/2009.

patent and a certificate an overall maximum of 15 years of exclusivity from the time the medicinal product in question first obtains authorisation to be placed on the market.

The essential requirement for getting an SPC is the first and valid procedure to place protected product on the market. The required marketing authorisation is available in different procedures. First, national authorisation can be issued by the competent national authority; this covers a national market. The other two types of national authorisation allow applicants to extend the authorisation to multiple territories. The mutual recognition procedure allows for the recognition of the market authorisation issued in one EU country in another country if a medicinal product has already received authorisation in one Member State[11]. The decentralised procedure helps with simultaneous authorisation in multiple EU countries by filling an application to the competent authorities of the reference country and the concerned Member State, where the latter can base the authorisation on the draft report from the reference country[12]. From the point of view of the territorial scope, the most relevant is the Union authorisation in the centralised procedure[13]. This allows a market authorisation centrally with an EU-wide effect to be obtained[14]. This procedure is mandatory for some medicinal products[15] but is not available for some medicinal products and plant protection products. Irrespective of the applicable procedure, the territory of the SPC protection and the territory of marketing authorisation issued in any of the procedures should be the same.

As the brief overview shows, the "triple" territorial nature of an SPC with respect to a grant of the right, the scope of an SPC monopoly, and a regulatory requirement, are indeed the elements not "matching" the concept of the unitary protection, not to say colliding with it. This influences the scenarios for establishing the centralised system for granting unitary SPC protection.

10.3 The SPC under UPCA – the present

Central to evaluating the SPC framework in the new unitary patent system is Article 30 UPCA. This provision provides "the mirror" scope of rights (the same rights) conferred

---

[11] Provided by the European Parliament and of the Council Directive 2001/83/EC on the Community code relating to medicinal products for human use [2001] OJ L 311/ 67.
[12] Provided by the of the European Parliament and of the Council Directive 2004/27/EC amending Directive 2001/83/EC on the Community code relating to medicinal products for human use [2004] OJ L 136/34.
[13] The centralised procedure is governed by Regulation (EC) 726/2004 of the European Parliament and of the Council of 31 March 2004 laying down Community procedures for the authorisation and supervision of medicinal for human and veterinary use and establishing a European Medicines Agency [2004] OJ L 136/1.
[14] Sabrina Röttger-Wirtz, Mariolina Eliantonio, 'From Integration to Exclusion: EU Composite Administration and Gaps in Judicial Accountability in the Authorisation of Pharmaceuticals', European Journal of Risk Regulation, 10(2), 393–411.
[15] Art 3 (1) of Regulation (EC) 726/2004.

by an SPC and a patent, and the same limitations and obligations. The interpretation of the provision raises several issues for further consideration and clarification.

10.3.1 The subject matter application of Article 30

The first issue, as a matter of more detailed commentary on the subject matter of the effect provided by Article 30, is the types of SPCs to which the provision applies. This requires consideration of Article 3 (b), UPCA's definition of a patent, and the opt-out mechanism provided by Article 83 UPCA. In addition to the key category of a new European patent with unitary effect, Article 30 applies to European patents for which an SPC is granted. For further comments, it is thus important to distinguish between two situations, i.e.: (a) SPCs based on existing and future European patents, and (b) SPCs based on unitary patents.

As regards the first category of patents, all classical European patents designated for Member States that have ratified the UPC Agreement will become subject to the exclusive competence of the UPC after a 7-year transitional period (which can be extended to a maximum of 14 years) unless they opt-out. European patent holders and holders of a granted SPC may decide to waive the exclusive jurisdiction of the SPC (opt-out) or withdraw from it. An opt-out request for a patent or SPC with respect to which a case is pending before either the UPC or a national court before the end of the transition period should be considered ineffective, regardless of whether the case is pending or has been completed. Opting out from the UPC's jurisdiction is impossible regarding the unitary patent and the SPC granted for it.

The Rules of Procedure of the Unified Patent Court[16] govern the detailed procedure for exercising the opt-out option under APCA. The Rules contain a special provision for SPCs stating that both the opt-out from the UPC's jurisdiction and the withdrawal of the opt-out also has effects for SPCs granted for European patents (Rule 5.2). This effect is automatic for SPCs granted after the filing of an opt-out application. In contrast, for certificates granted on the date of the application, if the holder of the SPC is an entity other than the patent holder, they should file such an application simultaneously with the holder of the "underlying" patent. The opt-out must take place with respect to all countries for which a European patent has been granted or applied.

---

16 Adopted by decision of the Administrative Committee on 8 July 2022 and entered into the force on 1 September 2022.

10.3.2 The scope of Article 30

The second concerns the effects of an SPC in relation to the rights and obligations it confers. Article 30 UCPA confirms "the same rights" for an SPC as for a patent which should be determined with consideration to Article 5 of the SPC Regulations under Article 5 (1) UPR[17] and Articles 25 and 26 UPCA. Article 25 UPCA specifies the following rights which, if performed by an authorised party, constitute a direct infringement, i.e. making, offering, placing on the market, or using a patented product (a product obtained directly by a patented process and process), or importing or storing a patented product for those purposes. The protection conferred by an SPC extends to a right to prevent acts of indirect patent infringement. Defined by Article 26 UPCA as supplying or offering to supply to third parties, this relates to an essential element of that invention for putting the invention into effect if the infringer knows or should have known that those means are suitable and intended for putting that invention into effect.

In the meaning of Article 30 UPCA, "limitations" should be interpreted broadly as limitations of a substantial, temporal, and territorial scope of an exclusive right, and the limitation to its substance (defining acts conferred by a patent (SPC) monopoly). Unfortunately, and this is a detrimental shortcoming for the concept of unitary protection, neither the UPR nor UPCA has provided provisions defining the scope of the subject matter of a patent or an SPC. Admittedly, the rationale in this regard is the existence of Article 69 EPC which applies to unitary patents; however, the rules for determining the patent scope and the guidance provided by the Interpretation Protocol to Article 69 EPC have, for years, resulted in the absence of harmonised provisions and have been the subject of divergent interpretation in case law and doctrine. This problem will remain unresolved for unitary patents and SPCs granted for them at least until the UPCA develops uniform rules in this regard.

Also, the uniform application of limitations covered by Article 30 UPCA is not devoid of problems. The unitary effect referred to in Article 5 (2) UPR, at most, should be considered in relation to an autonomously regulated form of limitation; namely, the exhaustion of a unitary patent.

In light of Article 6 UPR (read for SPC respectively), the rights conferred by an SPC issued for a European patent with unitary effect as a basic patent should not extend to acts concerning a product covered by that patent which is carried out within the participating Member States in which that patent has unitary effect after that product covered by SPC has "been placed on the market in the Union by, or with the consent of, the patent proprietor, unless there are legitimate grounds for the patent proprietor to oppose further commercialization of the product".

---

17 As it states, the European patent with unitary effect confers, on its proprietor, the right to prevent any third party from committing acts against which that patent provides protection throughout the territories of the participating Member States in which it has unitary effect, subject to applicable limitations.

The same exhaustion conditions are repeated, independently, in Article 29 UCPA for European patents which, as a patent granted under the EPC's provisions, does not benefit from unitary effect by virtue of the UPR. The provision applies to SPCs issued for European patents respectively. Although both regimes provide for EU exhaustion, different interpretative standards may apply to them as different statutory bases governed by CJEU and UCPA case law. This dual regulation for different types of patents under UPC jurisdiction may surely be confusing and negatively impact the idea of creating unitary standards for enforcing unitary patents like an SPC before the UPC.

The lack of uniformity in the applicability of limitations is also the case for another separately regulated limitation applicable to SPCs, i.e. prior-user rights. This defence against an allegation of patent infringement, provided by Article 28 UCPA, limits a unitary patent only to those who have acquired a prior use status following national regulations. With consideration of national differences, this provision may not ensure uniform application by all the holders of a uniform patent and SPCs.[18]

For the limitations mentioned in Article 30 UPCA, the central reference is under Article 27 with the list of statutory exemptions which, to a large extent, are known but not fully harmonised by national patent regulations. These include, i.e. acts done privately, for non-commercial purposes, experimental purposes relating to the subject matter of the patented invention, and pharmacists' exceptions are provided. Among the exemptions provided for the unitary system, not all are relevant for an SPC; conversely, others are of essential importance for an SPC for medicinal products, such as the regulatory exemption[19] but are not fully harmonised in the EU. For plant protection, breeders' and farmers' exceptions reserve special attention. Locating the exemptions under the UPCA and the reference to national law as regards limitation included in Article 3 UPR (after the provision dealing with the exemptions was removed from the initial draft of the UPR), negatively impacts the creation of uniform norms on exceptions for patents in the EU.

The reference to "obligations" mentioned in Article 30 UPCA has no equivalent provisions in unitary package regulations (Article 5 (3) UPR or Article 27 UPCA) or national provisions defining the rights conferred by a patent and its limitations. As correctly noted, it seems to be taken from the wording of Article 5 of the SPC Regulations and may refer to obligations of an administrative nature.

10.3.3 Effects of SPC – unitary or not?

The third and most essential issue is the controversy over the unitary effects provided by Article 30 UPCA. On one hand, one can point to the argument about the lack of a clear

---

[18] Nari Lee, Adding Fuel to Fire: A Complex Case of Unifying Patent Limitations and Exceptions Through the EU Patent Package [2015] <https://papers.ssrn.com/sol3/papers.cfm?abstract_id=2619113>
[19] Article 27 (d) UPCA covers tests and trials performed for marketing authorisation procedures allowed under Article 13(6) of Directive 2001/82/EC or Article 10(6) of Directive 2001/83/EC.

basis for such a uniform effect in the UPR where such an effect is provided for patents only. Assuming that the UPR is the pillar of the system, some commentators argue that an SPC with a unitary effect does not yet exist and it can be established further to amendment of the UPR provisions. On the other hand, the argument that the UPR already offers the normative basis for the unitary effects of an SPC is convincing. As argued, it is a logical assumption that, as far as an SPC provides for the same rights as a basic patent having a unitary effect on the territories of the participating Member States, in principle, the same unitary effect should apply to an SPC.[20]

10.4 The SPC under UPCA – the future

The assumption that there is a normative basis for unitary effect, and the UPC has jurisdiction in SPC cases, does not mean that unitary protection under the SPC will be available once the unitary patent system is operational. Indeed, the commented provisions do not end the basis for granting such a unitary right. In contrast to a unitary patent granted by an existing body (EPO) to which an existing procedure governed by the EPC applies, no similar mechanism is available for the unitary SPC. The "unitary patent package" provides a legal framework for unitary patent protection and ensures the application of UPCA and the jurisdiction of the UPC to SPCs. However, it does not explicitly create an interconnected system for granting a unitary SPC. This results in a gap between the existing applicability of UPCA to SPCs and the jurisdiction of the UPC over actions for an infringement and validation of an SPC granted for unitary patents on one hand, and the non-existing unitary SPC procedure of grating a unitary SPC being subject of such an infringement on the other hand.

Under current SPC legislation, only national and European patents can enjoy SPC protection. As argued, SPC may also cover unitary patents as having the legal nature of European patents with extended unitary territorial effect. Still, such SPC granted nationally cannot easily convert to unitary protection. Unlike national systems, the existing unitary patent regulations make unitary protection for medicinal and plant protection products unavailable for the maximum period of the unitary patent and unitary SPC protection (as the latter does not exist). The situation discriminates against the holders of patents for these types of products and may discourage them from using a new centralised system. The existing SPC regime based on national rights, granted for products covered by basis patents by the national patent office in the national procedure, linked with the regulatory authorisation covering the national market, by its nature conflicts with the EU-wide approach of unitary patent protection and the centralised enforcement of basic patents. The entry of the unitary system into the force compels the EU leg-

---

[20] Dorothea von Renesse, Bettina Wanner, Madeleine Seym, Jörg Thomaier, 'Supplementary Protection Certificates with Unitary Effect ("U-SPC")' – a Proposal [2016] GRUR Int. 1130.

islator to recalibrate the existing SPC legal framework provided by Regulation 469/2009 or create a new one, in order to linking the two elements of non-existing unitary SPC protection and the existing centralised enforcement of an SPC.

10.4.1 Towards a unitary SPC

The logical step to fill the gap between a unitary patent and SPC systems is to create an SPC mechanism complementing a unitary patent, i.e. "a unitary SPC". To keep consistency with the unitary patent, a unitary SPC is to be understood as one SPC having unitary effect in all Contracting States or a bundle of national SPCs based on a single unitary patent.

That concept, which the EC has been investigating for some time, is in line with the most recent EU policy objectives to eliminate the existing fragmentation of the SPC system identified as its main shortcoming and a barrier to the functioning of the internal market.[21] It results from high costs, administrative burdens on applicants and legal uncertainty, as the scope of protection can differ across the EU.

To meet the goal, the EC 2022 call for evidence for an impact assessment of the initiative "Medicinal and plant protection products – single procedure for the granting of SPCs", and proposes a centralised SPC system as a mechanism for ensuring better transparency and uniformity of standards for granting and enforcing SPCs in the EU. An impact assessment that received a positive opinion on 16 December 2022 identified, among others, the following advanced scenarios for establishing the centralised SPC system[22]:
(i) introducing a 'unitary SPC' right, complementing the unitary patent granted by a central authority to applicants with a European patent with unitary effect;
(ii) launching a centralised procedure of filing and examination of SPC applications, resulting in a binding opinion;

Among the proposed options, the centralised system based on a centralised procedure linked with a new unitary SPC draws the attention of commentators and gets support from the European pharmaceutical industry, demanding better legal certainty, business predictability, and cost efficiency for business strategies based on an SPC.[23]

---

[21] Brussels, 25.11.2020 COM(2020) 760 final, Making the most of the EU's innovative potential – An intellectual property action plan to support the EU's recovery and resilience, Call for the evidence for the impact assessment – Medicinal & plant protection products – single procedure for granting SPCs.
[22] The other considered options included 1) no policy change, and 2) common guidelines/recommendations to national patent offices on the application of the SPC Regulation, 3) launching a centralised procedure of filing and examination of SPC applications resulting in a nonbinding opinion.
[23] See the ECPA, EFPIA, and IFAH-Europe Joint Position Paper. SPCs in the Unitary Patent System, https://www.efpia.eu/media/15414/ecpa-efpia-and-ifah-europe-joint-position-paper-proposal-for-a-unitary-spc-july-2015.pdf.

The package includes: 1) new Regulations creating a new "unitary certificate" ("unitary SPC") with the same centralised examination procedure for medicinal products[24] and plant protection products[25], and 2) Regulations introducing a centralised procedure for the grant of national SPCs for medicinal products[26] and plant protection products[27], recasting and repealing the existing EU Regulations[28].

As a part of a proposed reform of the SPC system set by these Regulations, the unitary certificate should become available both for medicinal products and for plant protection products under a centralised application and granting procedure on the basis of unitary patents. The unitary certificate will be available only on the basis of a European patent with unitary effect as a basic patent under conditions provided in Article 3 Proposal COM(2023)222, and will have its effects uniformly in all the Member States in which the basic patent has a unitary effect.

As for the other EU unitary IP rights, a legal basis to introduce unitary SPC protection is Article 118 TFEU. This empowers the EU legislator to establish measures to create IP rights that ensure protection in the internal market, including setting up centralised Union-wide authorisation, coordination, and supervision arrangements. The delegation involves adopting relevant regulations for granting a unitary SPC, appointing a centralised body responsible for granting, and providing special authorisation procedures for products seeking EU-wide SPC protection. These steps require critical analysis.

10.4.4.1 Centralised granting procedure

First, a centralised procedure of granting an SPC involves asking an important question regarding the authority responsible for a new unitary right. Under Article 9 (1) of Regulation No. 469/2009, the competent body to file the SPC application is the patent office of the Member State in which the basic patent was granted or (on whose behalf) and in

---

[24] Proposal for a regulation of the European Parliament and of the Council on the unitary supplementary certificate for medicinal products, and amending Regulation (EU) 2017/1001, Regulation (EC) No 1901/2006 as well as Regulation (EU) No 608/2013, COM(2023)222 (hereinafter referred to as "Proposal COM(2023)222").

[25] Proposal for a regulation of the European Parliament and of the Council on the unitary supplementary protection certificate for plant protection products, COM(2023)221.

[26] Proposal for a regulation of the European Parliament and of the Council on the supplementary protection certificate for medicinal products (recast), COM(2023)231, (hereinafter referred to as "Proposal COM (2023)231").

[27] Proposal for a regulation of the European Parliament and of the Council on the supplementary protection certificate for plant protection products (recast), COM(2023)223.

[28] For a summary of the proposed regulations see Oswin Ridderbusch, Alexa von Uexküll, Breaking news: Draft EU legislation on unitary SP and new centralized SPC examination procedure unveiled, Kluwer Patent Blog, April 27, 2023, https://patentblog.kluweriplaw.com/2023/04/27/breaking-news-draft-eu-legislation-on-unitary-spcs-and-new-centralized-spc-examination-procedure-unveiled/

which the marketing authorisation was issued. This provision provides the basis for the country in question to designate an "other responsible entity" for this purpose. Under a broad interpretation, the delegation may apply not only to the other national authority but to another entity to be entrusted with the competence of granting an SPC.

As the UPCA implies, the first choice could be the EPO as the office competent to grant unitary patents as basis patents for a unitary SPC. Although entrusting the EPO with a new competence seems to be an intuitive solution, its faces limitations. As a body of the European Patent Organisation operating under the EPC, the EPO is not an EU authority. It grants European patents with extended territorial scope (unitary effect) based on a regional, not EU, regulations. While appointing the EPO as a body to grant the bundle of SPCs for European patents seems more straightforward, granting EU-wide SPCs that protect unitary patents would be difficult. Expanding the EPO's functions would also not be possible without further arrangements between the members of the EPO which, formally speaking, would be a long-term task despite some flexibilities provided in the EPC for special arrangements related to European patents.[29]

Thus, the option for governing the centralised procedure to grant a unitary SPC provided in the European Commission proposals is the EUIPO as the central examinantion authority responsible for granting other EU unitary IP rights[30]. Undoubtedly, this is the right choice in the case of a complex reform aimed at centralising the management of all EU unitary rights, especially in in the most welcome future scenario of upgrading the current semi-unitary patent system to one which is truly unitary; therefore, covering the territory of all Member States.

As proposed, after assessing the formal admissibility of the unitary SPC application (after a positive examination opinion), the EUIPO would entrust the substantive examination of the application to a panel made up of a member of that Office and two qualified examiners experienced in SPC matters, from two different national patent offices that agreed to participate in this centralised examination system[31]. On the basis of the examination opinion, the EUIPO will either grant a unitary SPC, or reject the application.

---

[29] Entrusting the EPO with a new competence would face limitations. As a body of the European Patent Organisation operating under the EPC, the EPO is not an EU authority. It grants European patents with extended territorial scope (unitary effect) based on a regional, not EU, regulations, thus granting EU-wide SPCs that protect unitary patents would be difficult. Expanding the EPO's functions would not be possible without further arrangements between the members of the EPO under Article 149 EPC allowing for other agreements between the Contracting States.

[30] To ensure that the Office will be able to implement the procedures envisaged in the context of the present reform of the SPC regime, the EU proposal would amend Regulation (EU) 2017/1001, that lays down the tasks carried out by the Office

[31] To some extent, a concept addresses the proposal from the pharmaceutical industry to involve experts from national patent offices, specialising in SPCs – see The ECPA, EFPIA, and IFAH-Europe Joint Position Paper. SPCs in the Unitary Patent System [2015], https://www.efpia.eu/media/15414/ecpa-efpia-and-ifah-europe-joint-position-paper-proposal-for-a-unitary-spc-july-2015.pdf, accessed 11 September 2022. The original proposal involved a "virtual granting body" to eliminate disputes over the possible location of a

Invalidity proceedings (actions for a declaration of invalidity) will also be carried out before the Office. The experience of national experts can help develop uniform standards to interpret requirements for granting an SPC to determine the scope of SPC protection, and thus contributes to the better harmonisation of standards both for unitary and national SPCs and ensures legal certainty as SPC reform aims to do in the EU.

Under the proposals, the EUIPO will be entrusted with the examination of both unitary SPC applications and centralised SPC applications (for bundles of national SPCs). Thus, the reform aims at creating a centralised procedure for the filing and examination of 'centralised SPC applications', able to result in both 1) grant of unitary SPCs by the EUIPO for the for the Member States covered by the basic patent; 2) the grant at a national level of national SPCs in the Member States designated in that application based on a positive binding opinion of a central examination authority (a single "centralised SPC application" would allow to end up with a bundle of national SPCs).

The procedure for filing and examining unitary SPC applications would be the same as the centralised procedure for granting 'traditional" SPC. This allows for a 'combined' SPC application that possibly includes both a request for the grant of a unitary SPC (covering all states in which the underlying unitary patent has an effect) and a smaller bundle of national SPCs (in the other designated EU member states not covered by the unitary patent)[32]. To ensure that unitary SPC applicants/holders can apply before the central examination authority for extensions of unitary SPCs for paediatric medicinal products, the EC plans to adjust Regulation (EC) No 1901/2006, to apply to unitary SPCs in addition to national SPC.

10.4.4.2 Marketing authorisation for a unitary SPC

A future unitary SPC system needs to deal with the marketing authorisation requirement provided by Article 3(b) of Regulation (EC) 469/2009 and Article 2 of Regulation (EC) 1610/96.

Thus, establishing a new system of a unified SPC would have to involve a decision on whether a central marketing authorisation or other marketing authorisation procedures entitle an applicant to obtain a unitary SPC right based on a bundle of national authori-

---

„physical" office, ensure the reduction of the cost of operating in a traditional physical location with the impact of lower fees charged by the office and the reduced cost of obtaining a unified SPC.

32 The proposal addresses one of the scenarios, namely the centralised procedure for granting unitary SPCs based on European patents with unitary effect and the concept of PCT model for national SPCs, proposed in Roberto Romandini, Study on the Options for a Unified Supplementary Protection Certificate (SPC) System in Europe (September 8, 2022). Romandini, Roberto: European Commission, Directorate-General for Internal Market, Industry, Entrepreneurship and SMEs: Study on the options for a unified supplementary protection certificates (SPCs) system in Europe, 2022, Max Planck Institute for Innovation & Competition Research Paper No. 23–09, Available at SSRN: https://ssrn.com/abstract=4422200.

sations. The EU proposes that only a centralised marketing authorisation provided in Regulation (EC) No 726/2004 can serve as a basis for an application for a unitary SPC for a medicinal product, as most medicinal products are authorised under that procedure.

Although a marketing authorisation issued in a centralised EU-wide procedure, most often used by the applicants appears to be the best choice for a unitary SPC, it is not without its downsides. As the territorial scope of the authorisation does not coincide with the territorial scope of the underlying patent, a unitary SPC would not be the same territorially as a unitary patent. Consequently, this would lead to a situation when, for administrative reasons, a uniform SPC can only be "partially" exercised on the territory of protection. Which may rise concerns.[33] Moreover, the requirement of the centralised authorisation to grant a unitary SPC would discriminate against those products for which this procedure is unavailable. This is a case for plant protection and veterinary products covered by Regulation (EC) 1610/96. The proposal allows for plant protection products filing of centralized SPC on the basis of a European patent (with or without unitary effect) and at least one granted national marketing authorization. Such limitations may affect the concept of uniform protection, understood as being available on a uniform basis to all interested patent holders in a single market.

It is worth to mention, that for such products the less efficient system based on granting a bundle of patents with a dynamic effect was proposed as an option.[34] As the MPI study for the EC proposed, national marketing authorisations may be a basis for a unitary SPC based on a bundle of national marketing authorisations with the territorial scope defined statically or dynamically.[35] The first option refers to the limited territory of Member States covered by the marketing authorisation when granting the unitary SPC. However, this scenario seems unattractive because it closes off the possibility of covering the territories of countries in which, according to a business strategy, market authorisations may be obtained in the future.[36] In the second option, the territorial scope dynamically extends to additional Member States covered by a unitary SPC where a marketing authorisation is granted before the patent expiration date.[37]

---

[33] See Nicolas Binctin, Romain Bourdon, Matthieu Dhenne, Lionel Vial, *Feedback on the Intellectual Property Action Plan Roadmap of the European Commission* (2020), 27. <https://papers.ssrn.com/sol3/papers.cfm?abstract_id=3710475> accessed 6 September 2022.

[34] Study on the Legal Aspects of Supplementary Protection Certificates in the EU, Final Report, ed. Reto Hilty, Max Planck Institute for Innovation and Competition [2019] <https://ec.europa.eu/docsroom/documents/29524> accessed 19 August 2021.

[35] ibidem.

[36] Dorothea von Renesse, Bettina Wanner, Madeleine Seym, Jörg Thomaier, 'Supplementary Protection Certificates with Unitary Effect ("U-SPC")' – a Proposal [2016] GRUR Int. 1129.

[37] Ibidem.

10.5 Final remarks

The entry into force of the unitary patent system, coinciding with the reform of SPC protection which has been ongoing for several years, rightly makes the discussion of the future of SPCs timely and necessary, not only in normative and dogmatic terms but, above all, from a market perspective. An SPC is not only a legal tool of market monopoly but a significant incentive to develop innovative medicines. Next, patents not only play an essential role in the business strategies of pharmaceutical companies but are a socially important element of health care policy and the EU's recovery and resilience plan.[38]

An analysis of the provisions of the unitary patent package indicates that the EU legislator was aware that SPC protection is "genetically" related and built on patent protection. However, it seems to have adopted the principle that an SPC, as an additional "overlay" to certain patents, could automatically become part of the unitary patent system by extending UCPA's provisions to the SPC, without explicitly mentioning unitary effect for SPC in the UPR. Fortunately, Article 87(2) of UPCA allows Administrative Committee to amend the Agreement in order to be compatible with an international treaty elating to patents or Union law, which allows for the future introduction of a "unitary SPC." The proposed SPC regulations explicitly refer to that Article as a legal basis for including a new unitary SPC within the competences of the UPC. However, the creation of a parallel operational system of unitary SPCs that may extend unitary patents is complicated by the already existing less-than-perfect overlap between the patent's subject matter and the SPC's subject matter. Another level is the differentiation of basic patents which can be unitary or European patents and the next – the requirement of marketing authorisations obtained in procedures covering different territories.

Given the specifics of SPC regulations linked to both the procedure of granting the basic patent and the requirement for marketing authorisation through separate administrative procedures to that of granting SPCs, the implementation of a centralised unitary SPC is a challenge. However, some recommended elements of the reform involve the following.

A new SPC regime proposed by the EC The meets the goal of solution investigated by EC should focus on creating an additional option in parallel to national procedures as it is provided for other European rights, with normative roots in a separate unitary SPC regulation or the targeted amendment of the existing legal framework for an SPC. The proposed reform should considers the option to create a legal substrate for SPC with unitary effect along the unitary patent, but not or to returns to the tradition of building an EU IP system based on EU rights (EU SPC), which. It would be is justified by the legal nature of an SPC as a sui generis UE right governed by a SPC Regulation as an act of the European Union. The disadvantage of such an approach is exclusion from unitary SPC sys-

---

[38] See European Parliament resolution of 11 November 2021 on an intellectual property action plan to support the EU's recovery and resilience (2021/2007(INI)).

tem the European patents for which unitary effect is opted-out and countries which do not participate in the UPCA. The proposal's advantage is that the possible introduction of a unified SPC does not replace national SPC systems in the EU. The new regime will not affect the competence of national IP Offices in granting national SPCs, following the binding opinion issued by the examination authority, run by the EUIPO. However, the national route will not be available for SPC applications that cover European patents, including unitary patents, in which case they must be filed under a centralised SPC application at EUIPO. It also does not limit companies that are not interested in uniform protection from obtaining national SPCs.

The grant of unitary SPC (EU SPC) by a new authority seems or appointing an independent body or a new division of EUIPO while leaving the possibility to grant national SPCs is the most welcome scenario. Designing a new unitary SPC system should respect the flexibility of choosing centralised marketing authorisation procedures or other procedures, ensuring a bundle of national authorisations corresponding to unitary patents.

A critical issue to remember is that creating unitary SPC will not solve all the problems. Above all, on top of the different layers of the procedure for obtaining SPC, another one concerns the uniform effects of unitary rights and their limitations, unclearly determined in unitary patent package.

The "unitary SPC package" involves the existing problems concerning the different effects on the various patents. The previously mentioned problems with the more national than unitary nature of the limitations will not be easily resolved for the SPC, at least until the UPC develops rules for applying the thicket of relevant sources of law to the exercise of rights under the unitary patent as the underlying law for the SPC. The proposed reform does not modify and – more importantly – harmonise the substantive conditions currently laid down in Regulation (EC) No 469/2009 for the existing national SPC regimes or the new centralised procedure applying to unitary SPCs. There are also no substantive provisions in the UPR for unitary patents and unitary SPCs and therefore, unitary protection may be, at least to some extent, executed uniformly only in theory. The proposed reform does not modify and – more importantly – not harmonise the substantive features currently laid down in Regulation (EC) No 469/2009 for the existing national SPC regimes or the new centralised procedure applying to unitary SPCs. There are also no substantive provisions in the UPR for unitary patents and unitary SPCs and therefore, unitary protection may be, at least to some extent, executed uniformly only in theory.

Phillip Johnson
11 Liability for infringement of EU law

11.1 Introduction

The history of the Unitary patent (and the Community patent before it) has been marred in ambiguity[1] with its mix between intergovernmental and supranationalism[2] and the conflicting aims to keep the patent system institutionally separate from the European Union but also functionally linked to it.[3] So it was not surprising that when the Court of Justice considered the project in Opinion 1/09 *Creation of a unified patent litigation system*[4] it concluded that the Unified Patent Court (UPC) has to be 'a court of a Member State' or a court common to member states to be consistent with EU law.[5] In common with domestic courts[6] in the EU, there is an express obligation on the UPC to cooperate with the Court of Justice of the European Union to ensure the correct application and uniform interpretation of EU law.[7] This means that the UPC is subject to the same obligations under EU law as any national court[8] and that in case of any conflict its rules must

---

[1] There were still doubts that the agreement would ever come into force as late as 2021: see Sara Fallah, Alexander Koller and Michael Stadler "The UPCA's Path to Entry into Force between Delayed and Withdrawn Ratifications – Dead-end Street or Bumps in the Road?" (2021) 70 GRUR Int 662.
[2] For a history see Justine Pila "The European Patent: An Old and Vexing Problem" (2013) 62 ICLQ 917 and *Roughton, Johnson and Cook on the Law of Patents* (5th Ed Butterworths 2022), [24.121]-[24.127].
[3] Tuomas Mylly "A Constitutional Perspective" in Justine Pila and Christopher Wadlow, *The Unitary EU Patent System* (Bloomsbury 2015), p 78 at 79; also see Matthias Eck "Europäisches Einheitspatent und Einheitspatentgericht – Grund zum Feiern?" (2014) GRUR Int 114 at 115 and 117.
[4] [2011] ECR I-1137.
[5] Opinion 1/09 *Creation of a unified patent litigation system* [2011] ECR I-1137, [82 and 89]; and see Art 71a (2) of Regulation (EU) No 1215/2012 on jurisdiction and the recognition and enforcements in civil and commercial matters [2012] L351/1 (Brussels Regulation (Recast) (Art 71a was inserted by Regulation (EU) No 542/2014 regarding the rules to be applied with respect to the Unified Patent Court and Benelux Court of Justice [2014] OJ L163/1); also see European Commission Legal Service, Creating a Unified Patent Litigation System – Orientation Debate, 23 May 2011, Doc PI 50 COUR 27, Annex.
[6] The obligation in the Treaty on the Functioning of the European Union, arts 4(3) is on the Member States, but as an authority of a Member State the court must likewise discharge this duty.
[7] UPCA, art 21 (and art 1); Treaty on the European Union, arts 4(3) and 19; Opinion 1/09 *Creation of a unified patent litigation system* [2011] ECR I-1137, [84]; C-379/98 *Preussen Elektra v Schleswag* [2001] ECR I-2099, [38]; C-35/ 99 *Arduino und Compagnia* [2002] ECR I-1529, [24]; C-379/98 *Rheinmühlen v Einfuhr- und Vorratsstelle Getreide* [2001] ECR I-2099, [38].
[8] UPCA, art 1.

Phillip Johnson, is Professor of Commercial Law, Cardiff University. I would like to thank Dr Sara Drake for her helpful comments on an earlier version of this chapter.

https://doi.org/10.1515/9783110781687-011

give way to the supremacy of EU law.[9] The opening question must be, therefore, with its competence limited to patents[10] how much EU law is there which the UPC must apply and interpret?

11.2 The extent of EU law before the UPC

The starting point for answering this question is straightforward.[11] The Unitary Patent Regulation,[12] the Translation Regulation,[13] the Enforcement Directive,[14] the Biotechnology Directive,[15] the SPC Regulations,[16] the relevant provisions of the Brussels (Recast) Regulation[17] and certain other instruments which are relevant to exceptions[18] are all EU law which must be applied by the court. From this point it becomes increasingly contentious and uncertain. The first uncertainty is whether the infringement provisions (which were moved from the draft Unitary Patent Regulation[19] to articles 25 to 27 of the UPCA) are incorporated by reference into the Unitary Patent Regulation[20] and thereby

---

9 UPCA, art 20 (called 'primacy' in the UPC).
10 UPCA, art 32.
11 Some have even suggested that patents fall entirely within EU law: Roberto Romandini and Alexander Klicznik "The territoriality principle and transnational use of patented inventions – the wider reach of a unitary patent and the role of the CJEU" (2013) 44 IIC 524 at 537-8.
12 Regulation (EU) No 1257/2012 implementing enhanced cooperation in the area of the creation of unitary patent protection [2012] OJ L361/1.
13 Regulation (EU) No 1260/2012 implementing enhanced cooperation in the area of the creation of unitary patent protection with regard to the applicable translation arrangements [2012] OJ L361/89.
14 Directive 2004/48/EC on the enforcement of intellectual property rights [2004] OJ L195/16.
15 Directive 98/44/EC on the legal protection of biotechnological inventions [1998] OJ L213/13.
16 Regulation (EC) No 469/2009 concerning the supplementary protection certificate for medicinal products [2009] OJ L152/1; Regulation (EC) No 1610/96 concerning the creation of a supplementary protection certificate for plant protection products [1996] OJ L198/30.
17 Regulation (EU) No 1215/2012 on jurisdiction and the recognition and enforcements in civil and commercial matters, art 71a to 71d.
18 The the following instruments are also relevant to UPCA, art 27: Directive 2001/82/EC on the Community code relating to veterinary medicinal products [2001] OJ L311/1; Directive 2001/83/EC on the Community code relating to medicinal products for human use [2001] OJ L311/67; Regulation (EC) No 2100/94 on Community plant variety rights [1994] OJ L 227/1; and Directive 2009/24/EC on the legal protection of computer programs [2009] OJ L111/16.
19 Proposal for a Regulation implementing enhanced cooperation in the area of the creation of unitary patent protection COM (2011) 215, art 6 to 8.
20 The following argue that the provisions are so incorporated: Jochen Pagenberg 'Unitary patent and Unified Court — What lies ahead?" (2013) 8 JIPLP 480 at 481; Winfried Tilmann 'The compromise on the uniform protection for EU patents' (2013) 8 JIPLP 78 at 80; Winfried Tilmann and Clemens Plassmann, *Unified Patent Protection in Europe: A Commentary* (Oxford 2018), pp 136–8, 455; also see Chris Wadlow "Hamlet without the prince': Can the Unitary Patent Regulation strut its stuff without Articles 6–8?' (2013) 8 JIPLP 207. Some take the view without comment that the aim to exclude infringement was successful: Luke McDonagh, *The European Patent: An Old and Vexing Problem* (Elgar 2016), p 88–9.

bringing patent infringement within EU law.[21] These provisions were removed from the Regulation ostensibly to keep infringement outside the scope of EU law and away from the Court of Justice.[22] But if the Court of Justice takes the view infringement is within its purview then how far does this go? It is unlikely that the Court of Justice determining an autonomous meaning for what amounts to the "making" of the patented product would be profound, but if the Court took the view that the scope of protection[23] was part of infringement then issues such as the approach to claim interpretation and the extent to which the patent extends to equivalents might be within EU law. And its approach to this question in the context of patents and supplementary protection certifications has not been a shining example of clarity.[24]

While it is usually said that patentability is outside the scope of EU law[25] the Biotechnology Directive provides rules on *ordre public*, morality and an exclusion for animal and plant varieties[26] and so these rules, rather than those in the EPC,[27] are within EU law. But the Directive also provides that "inventions which are new, which involve an inventive step and which are susceptible of industrial application shall be patentable even if they concern a product consisting of or containing biological material..."[28] So is the meaning of 'new', 'inventive step' and 'industrial application'[29] in this context a question involving the interpretation of EU law? And if the Court of Justice determines

---

[21] Any preliminary reference to the Court of Justice would be a reference under Regulation (EU) No 1257/2012 implementing enhanced cooperation in the area of the creation of unitary patent protection, art 5 rather than the UCPA itself: see Romandini and Klicznik "The territoriality principle and transnational use of patented inventions" at 537–8.
[22] See for instance, Tuomas Mylly "A Constitutional Perspective" at 77–8; Jans Smits and William Bull "The Europeanization of Patent Law: Towards a Competitive Model" and Jan Brinkof and Ansgar Ohly "Towards a Unified Patent Court in Europe" both in Ansgar Ohly and Justine Pila (Eds), *The Europeanization of Intellectual Property Law: Towards a European Legal Methodology* (Oxford 2013), respectively p 39 at 52 and p 199 at 201.
[23] EPC, art 69 and Protocol on Interpretation; also see Maximilian Haedicke "Rechtsfindung, Rechtsfortbildung und Rechtskontrolle im Einheitlichen Patentsystem" (2013) GRUR Int 609 at 610–11.
[24] See Sir Robin Jacob 'What single reform?" in Gustavo Ghidini and Valeria Falce (Ed), *Reforming Intellectual Property* (Elgar 2022), 141 at 146–150; by mid-2023 there have been 44 judgments following preliminary references in relation to the two supplementary protection regulations.
[25] Winfried Tilmann and Clemens Plassmann, *Unified Patent Protection in Europe: A Commentary*, p 455; McDonagh, *The European Patent: An Old and Vexing Problem*, p 88–9.
[26] Directive 98/44/EC on the legal protection of biotechnological inventions, art 4(1) and 6.
[27] EPC, r 26 to 34.
[28] While the suggestion that this could have such a profound effect seems implausible, it must be remembered that the extent of harmonisation by Directive 2001/29/EC on the harmonisation of certain aspects of copyright and related rights in the information society [2001] OJ L167/10, art 2 to 4 was likewise unforeseen: see discussion in Sheldon Halpern and Phillip Johnson, *Harmonising Copyright Law and Dealing with Dissonance: A Framework for Convergence of US and EU Law* (Elgar 2014), pp 115–9.
[29] The case is even stronger for industrial application: Directive 98/44/EC on the legal protection of biotechnological inventions, art 5(3); although very few cases are likely to turn on whether an invention is industrially applicable.

an EU meaning for inventive step in relation biotechnology it would be strange if the UPC adopted something different for other areas of technology. Going further, Article 13 of the Enforcement Directive requires the courts to order the "infringer" to pay the "injured party" for damages caused by an "infringing activity"; will an interpretation of "infringer" make the rules of joint liability for patent infringement[30] a matter of EU law; will it determine which "injured party" can obtain damages;[31] and, at an extreme, would the Court of Justice give a meaning to "infringing activity"?

In addition to EU instruments relating to patents there are also international agreements concerning patents which fall to be interpreted by the Court of Justice, rather than UPC or national courts. Some are clearly within its remit, such as the WTO Agreement on Trade Related Aspects of Intellectual Property (TRIPS).[32] But does it go further? There are obligations under the European Economic Area Agreement[33] requiring EU Member States[34] to be a party (and so comply) with various industrial property conventions including the Paris Convention on the Protection of Industrial Property and the Budapest Treaty on the International Recognition of the Deposit of Microorganisms for the Purposes of Patent Procedure, and there are Partnership/Free Trade Agreements[35] which also require adherence to the Patent Law Treaty and the European Patent Convention.[36] In *Commission v Ireland*,[37] the Court of Justice considered that Ireland's failure to adhere to the Berne Convention as required by the EEA Agreement was a breach of EU law. This related to ratification only. But it is possible that it might go further with it being a matter for the Court of Justice to consider whether domestic law (and so that of the UPC) complies with the rules under those Conventions. As can be seen the central scope of EU law which must be applied by the UPC is clear, but the edges are very fuzzy indeed. This scope whether bright or blurred presents a critical issue for this discussion.

---

30 The Court of Justice has declined determining rules for accessory liability for trade marks but has started to sketch them out for copyright infringement: see Richard Arnold "Intermediary Liability and Trade Mark Infringement: A Common Law Perspective" in Giancarlo Frosio (Ed), *Oxford Handbook of Online Intermediaries Liability* (Oxford 2020), p 404 at 410–11.
31 Particularly, in line with Directive 2004/48/EC on the enforcement of intellectual property rights, art 4.
32 C-414/11 *Daiichi Sankyo Co*, EU:C:2013:520, [60–62]; also see the argument that there is a very broad competence in relation to patents based on TRIPS by Angelos Dimopoulos and Petroula Vantsiouri "Of TRIPS and Traps: The Interpretative Jurisdiction of the Court of Justice of the European Union over Patent Law" (2014) 39 European LR 210.
33 EEA Agreement, Protocol 28, art 5.
34 And the other parties to the agreement, namely Norway, Iceland and Liechtenstein.
35 Eg Stabilisation and Association Agreement between the European Communities and the Republic of Albania [2009] OJ L 107/166, art 73 and Annex V(2) (Paris Convention, Budapest Convention, PCT, PLT and EPC); Economic Partnership Agreement between the CARIFORUM States and the European Community [2008] OJ L/289/I/3, art 147A(1) (Budapest Convention, PCT and PLT).
36 There is a risk of circulatory here if the Court of Justice has to apply the European Patent Convention along with the European Patent Office case law, and the EPO does the same.
37 C-13/00 *Commission v Ireland* [2002] ECR I-2955, [20].

It is critical because the UPC must apply all EU law and give it primacy;[38] a failure to do so would open the court to sanction. In Member States the requirements of supremacy means that EU law has to be applied in preference to conflicting domestic law,[39] but for the UPC there is no existing jurisprudence as it starts from a clean slate and so the issue is really whether it should apply (and the weight it should give) to the other prescribed sources of law.[40] These begin with EU law, then there is the UPCA itself, followed by the European Patent Convention and other international agreements applicable to patents[41] and it ends with national law. Thus, the primacy of EU law will have effect if any of the subordinate sources of law are not compliant or there is new EU jurisprudence which conflicts with existing UPC law.

A corollary of the primacy obligation is that the UPC must refer to the Court of Justice any unresolved question of EU law.[42] In fact, while any division of the UPC will have a discretion to refer a question to the Court of Justice, only the Court of Appeal has a mandatory obligation to do so[43] as it is the court of last instance.[44] It *must* make a preliminary reference where any matter of EU law is unclear unless one of the three *Cilfit*[45] criteria apply, namely, first, the question is not relevant to the case before the UPC, secondly, the question is materially identical to a question which has already been the subject of a reference (*acte éclairé*), or, thirdly, the answer to the question is so obvious it leaves no room for doubt (*acte clair*).[46] If the court concludes one of these exceptions apply, the parties cannot compel a reference[47] as it is purely for the court to decide whether to refer or not[48] albeit

---

38 UPCA, art 20.
39 For a broad discussion: Karen Alter, *Establishing the Supremacy of European Law: The Making of an International Rule of Law in Europe* (Oxford 2001).
40 Set out in UPCA, art 24.
41 Subject of course to compliance not being an issue of EU law.
42 Opinion 1/09 *Creation of a unified patent litigation system* [2011] ECR I-1137, [83 and 84]. However, a possible issue for the UPC in that it is removed from the law of Member States and this might present a tension as to whether it is able to refer questions to the Court of Justice: see C-196/09 *Paul Miles v European Schools* [2011] ECR I-5105, [37–46] and Joachim Gruber "Das Einheitliche Patentgericht: vorlagebefugt kraft eines völkerrechtlichen Vertrags?" (2015) GRUR 323.
43 Under UPCA, art 21 by way of the application of TFEU, art 267(3).
44 Technically, the obligation falls on courts 'whose decisions there is no judicial remedy under national law': TFEU, art 267(3); C-99/00 *Lyckeskog* [2002] ECR I-4839, [16]; C-210/06 *Cartesio Oktató és Szolgáltató bt* [2008] ECR I-9641, [79].
45 Case 283/81 *Cilfit* [1982] ECR 3415.
46 Case 283/81 *Cilfit* [1982] ECR 3415, [10, 14 and 16]; also see C-561/19 *Consorzio Italian Management v Catania Multiservizi*, EU:2021:799, [66]
47 Case 93/78 *Lothar Mattheus v Deogo Fruchtimport und Tiefkühlkost* [1978] ECR 2203, [5]; The duty on the UPC of sincere cooperation (Art 4(3) TEU) does not oblige it to overturn a final decision of the Court of Appeal where a reference should have been made: C-234/04 *Kapferer v Schlank & Schick GmbH* [2006] ECR I-2585, [24]; C-2/08 *Amministrazione dell'Economia e delle Finanze v Fallimento Olimpiclub* [2009] ECR I-7501, [22–23].
48 C-317, 318, 319 and 320/08 *Rosalba Alassini v Telecom Italia SpA* [2010] ECR I-2213, [25]; Case 83/78 *Pigs Marketing Board v Redmond* [1978] ECR 2347, [25]; C-83/91 *Meilicke v ADV/ORGA* [1992] ECR I-4871, [23];

where a court refuses to refer a matter it must give reasons why one of the *Cilfit* conditions applies.[49] And once a reference has been made, the Court of Justice does not review whether the reference is necessary.[50] As can be seen the obligations on the UPC are well established in EU law as are the sanctions for not complying with those rules.

11.3 Compelling compliance

In Opinion 1/09 *Creation of a unified patent litigation system*[51] the Court of Justice made it clear that any court would have to comply with the duties usually imposed on national courts.[52] Thus making UPC judges 'agents of compliance'[53] in respect of EU law.[54] Accordingly, the Opinion made it clear that the UPC, like national courts, must be subject to the possibility of infraction[55]proceedings[56] for not complying with EU law.[57] Likewise, there has to be a mechanism for individuals to recover damages for any breach of EU law committed by the UPC in accordance with the *Köbler* decision.[58] This creates a 'dual vigilance' model with both individual and institutional redress.[59] This is why the UPCA in-

---

C-495/03 *Intermodal Transports v Staatssecretaris van Financiën* [2005] ECR I-8151, [37]; C-160/14 *Ferreira da Silva e Brito v Estado português*, EU:C:2015:565, [40].
49 C-561/19 *Consorzio Italian Management v Catania Multiservizi*, EU:2021:799, [51].
50 C-466/07 *Klarenberg v Ferrotron Technologies GmbH* [2009] ECR I-803, [26 to 28]; C-415/93 *Union Royale Belge des Sociétés de Football Association ASBL v Bosman* [1995] ECR I-4921, [59]; C-380/01 *Schneider v Bundesminister für Justiz* [2004] ECR I-1389, [21].
51 [2011] ECR I-1137.
52 Opinion 1/09 *Creation of a unified patent litigation system* [2011] ECR I-1137, [85].
53 Zsófia Varga, *The Effectiveness of the Köbler Liability in National Courts* (Hart 2020), p 6.
54 See C-2/88 *Zwartveld* [1990] ECR I-3367, [18] ("…the judicial authorities of the Member States, who are responsible for ensuring that Community Law is applied and respected in the national legal system"); Koen Lenaerts "The Rule of Law and the Coherence of the Judicial System of European Law" (2007) 44 CMLRev 1625 at 1659; André Nollkaemper "The Role of National Courts in Inducing Compliance with International and European Law – A Comparison" in Marise Cremona (ed), *Compliance and Enforcement of EU Law* (Oxford 2012), 157 at 157–8; John Temple Lang "The Duties of National Courts under Community Constitutional Law" (1997) 22 European LR 3 at 3.
55 These type of proceedings are commonly called infringement proceedings, but the lesser used name 'infraction' proceedings is used to avoid confusion with patent infringement.
56 TFEU, art 258 to 260; also see Melanie Smith, *Centralised Enforcement and Good Governance in the EU* (Routledge 2009).
57 Opinion 1/09 *Creation of a unified patent litigation system* [2011] ECR I-1137, [87]; C-129/00 *Commission v Italy* [2003] ECR I-14637, [29, 30 and 32].
58 C-224/01 *Köbler v Republik Österreich* [2003] ECR I-10239; Opinion 1/09 *Creation of a unified patent litigation system* [2011] ECR I-1137, [86].
59 Bernhard Hofstötter *Non-Compliance of National Courts: Remedies in European Community Law and Beyond* (Asser 2005), p 187.

cludes rules that subject Contracting Member States to infraction proceedings before the Court of Justice[60] and allow for *Köbler* damages claims.[61]

11.3.1 'Infraction' proceedings

There are two types of proceedings which can be brought in the Court of Justice against Member States where they have not complied with EU law (commonly called 'infraction' or 'infringement' proceedings[62]), which exist to maximise compliance with EU law.[63] The first, and most common, are infraction proceedings brought by the European Commission. These exist not only to ensure compliance with EU law, but also to iron out any differing interpretations of EU law, and to act as a warning to other Member States.[64] Secondly, infraction proceedings can be brought by other Member States all of whom 'are equally interested—just like the [EU] institutions—in ensuring sustained compliance with the Treaties by their peers'.[65] These two sorts of proceedings are equally available to address breaches of EU law by the UPC. So the Commission can bring infractions proceedings against all the Contracting States (jointly or individually) for any breach by the UPC.[66] Likewise, any Member State (and not just Contracting Member States) can bring infraction proceedings for any such breach.[67]

11.3.2 Köbler liability

The Court of Justice has recognised that any damage an individual suffers due to national courts of last resort not satisfying their EU obligations is recoverable: so called

---

60 UPCA, art 23.
61 UPCA, art 22. A claim should either be brought in the courts of the Contracting Member State where the claimant is established or domiciled or, if this does not apply, the courts of the seat of the Court of Justice: art 22(2).
62 These are also called enforcement actions or Commission supervision. To avoid any confusion, the term 'infraction' proceedings will be used here.
63 Stine Andersen, *The Enforcement of EU Law: The Role of the European Commission* (Oxford 2012), p 67.
64 Francis Snyder, "General Course in Constitutional Law of the European Union" (1995) VI (Bk 1) Collected Courses of the Academy of European Law 41 at 84.
65 Dimitry Kochenov, 'The Acquis and Its Principles: The Enforcement of the "Law" versus the Enforcement of "Values" in the EU' in András Jakab and Dimitry Kochenov (eds), *The Enforcement of EU Law and Values: Ensuring Member States' Compliance* (Oxford 2017), p 9 at 20; but member states are still not very interested as the small number of cases brought demonstrates. For a summary of the four cases up until 2017 see Graham Butler, "The Court of Justice as an inter-state court" (2017) 6 *Yearbook of European Law* 179 at 189–192 (there are currently further cases pending before the Court of Justice).
66 UPCA, art 23 and TFEU, art 258.
67 UPCA, art 23 and TFEU, art 259.

Köbler liability.[68] By way of background, in 1991, the Court of Justice held in *Francovich*[69] that where a Member State fails to implement or give effect to EU law[70] that state could be liable in damages. To establish such a claim the claimant needs to establish (1) the EU rule infringed was intended to confer rights on individuals; (2) the breach was sufficiently serious (or manifest);[71] and (3) there was a direct causal link between the breach of the obligation resting on the UPC and the damage sustained by the injured party. The judgment in *Köbler* made it clear that a *Francovich* claim could be made against a Member State where the decision or order of its highest national court is an infringement of EU law.[72] Such an assessment being based on more or less the same basis as other breaches by Member States.[73] In effect, the judgment acknowledged that the courts of Member States play a key role in giving effect to EU law.[74]

The *Köbler* doctrine raises many difficult issues, but for the purposes of this discussion these will be side-stepped and the examination will look only at the effect of this rule. Indeed, two of the three elements will usually be satisfied in relation to patent disputes before the court. This is because it would be difficult to see how a party to proceedings before the UPC would not be individually concerned in the outcome (as they either had to pay damages, did not receive a remedy or lost their patent wholly or in part), and the causation element may be relevant to the assessment of damages but in many cases this too will be straightforward.

---

68 The four cases dealing with principle are discussed in Varga, *The Effectiveness of the Köbler Liability in National Courts*, p 8–13.
69 C-479/93 *Francovich v Italian Republic* [1995] ECR I-3843; further developed in C-46/93 *Brasserie du pêcheur v Bundesrepublik Deutschland* [1996] ECR I-1029.
70 C-479/93 *Francovich v Italian Republic* [1995] ECR I-3843 (this applied only to Directives), but it was made of more general application in C-178/94 *Dillenkofer v Bundesrepublik* [1996] ECR I-4845..
71 This is often a difficult thing to establish, see for instance *Cooper v Attorney-General* [2010] EWCA Civ 464.
72 C-224/01 *Köbler v Republik Österreich* [2003] ECR I-10239, [50]; also see C-173/03 *Traghetti del Mediterraneo v Repubblica italiana* [2006] ECR I-5177, [44–45]; C-168/15 *Tomášová v Slovenská republika*, EU:C:2016:602, [22]; C-620/17 *Hochtief Solutions Magyarországi Fióktelepe v Törvényszék*, EU:C:2019:630, [35].
73 C-224/01 *Köbler v Republik Österreich* [2003] ECR I-10239, [51–52].
74 Varga, *The Effectiveness of the Köbler Liability in National Courts*, p 1 and 17; Michal Bobek "The Effect of EU Law in the National Legal System" in Catherine Barnard and Steve Peers (ed), *European Union Law* (3rd Ed OUP 2020), p 156 ("the courts...become de facto EU institutions when acting *within the scope of EU law*"); Maartje de Visser "The Concept of Concurrent Liability and its Relationship with the Principles of Effectiveness: A One Way Ticket into Oblivion" (2004) 11 Maastricht J of European and Comparative Law 47 at 61–2; John Temple Lang "The Duties of National Courts under Community Constitutional Law" at 3; Koen Lenaerts, Ignace Maselis and Kathleen Gutman, *EU Procedural Law* (Oxford 2014), 3 ("national courts are in effect the 'lynchpin' of the judicial system") and 13–4; Tobias Lock "Is Private Enforcement of EU Law Through State Liability a Myth? An Assessment 20 Years after Francovich" (2012) 49 CMLRev 1675 at 1675.

The difficult threshold is that the failure must be "manifest", a standard which was stricter for judicial acts from that of other failures of member states.[75] It requires an assessment of the degree of clarity and precision of the rule infringed, whether the infringement was intentional, whether the error of law was excusable or inexcusable, and the failure to make a preliminary reference to the Court of Justice.[76] So, for instance, where there is a clear decision of the Court of Justice which the UPC failed to follow, or it failed to seek further clarification, the breach is likely to be manifest.[77] There is one final imitation, namely that claims can only be made in relation to the court of last instance, for the UPC that is the Court of Appeal.[78]

11.4 Ways in which the UPC can breach EU law

There are a handful of instances when a court might infringe EU law and so face either infraction proceedings or a *Köbler* claim.[79] First, liability might attach if the court fails to apply an EU rule which has direct effect. Secondly, the court applies a rule in the UPCA (or other subordinate source of law[80]) which is incompatible with EU law. Thirdly, the court applies rules in a way which is contrary to EU law usually by misinterpreting the rule. Finally, the court fails to make a preliminary reference to the Court of Justice under Article 21 when it should have done so.[81] Each of these grounds will be now be sketched out.

---

75 Hofstötter *Non-Compliance of National Courts: Remedies in European Community Law and Beyond*, p 128 (the standard from C-46/93 and C-48/93 *Brasserie du Pêcheur v Germany* [1996] ECR I-1029 not being applied).
76 C-224/01 *Köbler v Republik Österreich* [2003] ECR I-10239, [53 to 56]; C-173/03 *Traghetti del Mediterraneo v Repubblica italiana* [2006] ECR I-5177, [43]
77 Varga, *The Effectiveness of the Köbler Liability in National Courts*, p 34 and 41; Takas Tridimas, "State Liability for Judicial Acts Remedies Unlimited?" (2005) in Paul Demaret, Inge Govaere and Dominik Hanf (eds), *European Legal Dynamics: Revised and Updated Edition of 30 Years of European Legal Studies at the College of Europe* (Lang 2007), p 146 at 155; Claus Classen "Case C-224/01 *Gerhard Köbler v Republik Österreich*, Judgment of 30 September 2003, Full Court" (2004) 41 CMLRev 813 at 820.
78 See UPCA, art 22(1); also see C-168/15 *Tomášová v Slovenská republika*, EU:C:2016:602, [20]
79 However, others suggest it can arise in more limited circumstances: 'if as a result of insufficiently clear national law either national courts adopt a universal interpretation of national law which is contrary to EU law or in a given Member State in the EU context differing judicial decisions emerge.': Maciej Taborowski "Infringement Proceedings and Non-Compliant National Courts" (2012) 49 CMLRev 1061 at 1086–7.
80 See UPCA, art 24.
81 See Tridimas, "State Liability for Judicial Acts Remedies Unlimited?" at 155 (as modified for UPC).

11.4.1 Failure to give direct effect to an EU law

A rule of EU law is only directly effective where it is clear, sufficiently precise and unconditional.[82] As the UPC is not a Member State, it is unclear what happens when a particular EU instrument is applicable to the dispute under the choice of law rules[83] but is not "implemented". For instance, in relation to EU Regulations, the Court might have to consider the TTBE[84] in a licensing/infringement dispute. This would be quite straightforward as the Regulation is directly applicable and so would be directly applied by the court (and it is presumed it will be applied in the language of the proceedings[85]). But what about Directives? The Biotechnology Directive is probably directly effective[86] and while one aspect is implemented in the UPC[87] the majority is not; it is possible that most of the remainder of the Directive would be applied by reference to the EPC.[88] But what about the rule in Article 9 of the Directive relating to products consisting of genetic information?[89] This rule is not in the EPC, but it still needs to be given effect. Will the UPC just treat the Directive like a Regulation? Or will it fail to give it direct effect? And if so, would litigants have a remedy?

11.4.2 Incompatible rules

Since at least the *Simmenthal* judgment[90] in 1978, it has been established that domestic courts should disapply their own national law where it conflicts with EU law. Thus, the UPC is obliged of its own motion to not apply any rule – whether in the UPCA, the EPC or any national law – which conflicts with EU law.[91] The room for the disapplication of in-

---

82 This originated in Case 26/62 *Van Gend en Loos v Administratie der Belastingen* [1963] ECR 3.
83 UPCA, art 24(2).
84 Commission Regulation (EU) No 316/2014 on the application of Article 101(3) of the Treaty on the Functioning of the European Union to categories of technology transfer agreements [2014] OJ L 93/17.
85 See UPCA, arts 49 and 50.
86 However, for the purpose of infraction or *Köbler* proceedings, it might need a positive decision from the Court of Justice to confirm this before the UPC could be criticised: Varga, *The Effectiveness of the Köbler Liability in National Courts,* p 26.
87 UPCA, art 27(1) gives effect to Directive 98/44/EC on the legal protection of biotechnological inventions, art 10.
88 EPC, rr 26 to 34.
89 See C-428/08 *Monsanto v Cefetra* [2010] ECR I-6765 and the diverging view of its effect in EU Commission, *Final Report of the Expert Group on the Development and Implications of Patent Law in the Field of Biotechnology and Genetic Engineering* (17 May 2016).
90 Case 106/77 *Amministrazione delle finanze dello Stato v Simmenthal* [1978] ECR 629, [21 and 24]; C-112/13 *A*, EU:C:2014:2195, [36]; C-617/10 *Akerberg Frannson*, EU:C:2013:105, [45]; C-258/98 *Carra* [2000] ECR I-4217, [16]; C-188/10 *Melki and Adbeli* [2010] ECR I-5667, [43].
91 Michael Dougan "Primacy and the Remedy of Disapplication" (2019) 56 CMLRev 1459 at 1460–71; Takis Tridimas "Black, White and Shades of Grey: Horizontality of Directives Revisited" (2001) 21 Yearbook of

compatible rules before the UPC itself is small as there are so few rules set out in the UCPA and Procedural rules. But the most likely point of tension would be between the Enforcement Directive[92] and the remedies and enforcement measure set out in the UCPA.[93] This is because the wording of the UPCA is in places slightly different from that in the Directive (such as in relation to damages[94]) and this may (following elucidative judgments from the Court of Justice) lead to incompatibility. Indeed, there are already some tensions. For instance, there is a rule in Article 14 of the Enforcement Directive for ensuring "that reasonable and proportionate legal costs and other expenses incurred by the successful party shall, as a general rule, be borne by the unsuccessful party, unless equity does not allow this." According to the Court of Justice in *United Video Properties*[95] scaled costs regime are permissible provided they reflect the real market prices of lawyers fees. If the fees scale in UPC[96] does not reflect market rates[97] then any costs award would be breaching an EU law and, it is possible, the balance of the fees could be collected in an action before the court of a Contracting Member State.

In addition to conflicts with Directives, there is the possibility that a decision, order or procedural rule is found to be contrary to the Charter of Fundamental Rights.[98] For instance, an injunctive order to prevent infringement may be too broad and so incompatible with articles 16 and 17 of the Charter. Likewise, Article 47 which governs the right to an effective remedy and to a fair trial may be engaged by a particular procedural rule.[99] A simple example would be if the proceedings before the court eventually becomes beset with long delays.[100]

European Law 327 at 350; C-188/10 *Melki and Adbeli* [2010] ECR I-5667, [43]; C-112/13 *A*, EU:C:2014:2195, [36]; there is some uncertainty as to whether the EU law must also be directly effective: Varga, *The Effectiveness of the Köbler Liability in National Courts*, p 26–7.
92 Directive 2004/48/EC on the enforcement of intellectual property rights.
93 UPCA, arts 59–63, 68 and 69.
94 Directive 2004/48/EC on the enforcement of intellectual property rights, art 13 cf UPCA, art 68.
95 C-57/15 *United Video Properties*, EU:C:2016:611; also see C-531/20 *NovaText GmbH v Ruprecht-Karls-Universität Heidelberg*, EU:C:2022:316.
96 UPCA, art 69(1) ("up to a ceiling set in accordance with the Rules of Procedure"); Rules of Procedure (adopted 8 July 2022), r 152.
97 See *Roughton, Johnson and Cook on Patents* (5th Ed, Butterworths 2022), [15.78–15.80]; Phillip Johnson "How High is My Costs Ceiling?" (2016) 11 JIPLP 885.
98 The Charter extends to "implementations" of EU law (Charter, art 51(1)) and from C-199/11 *Europese Gemeenschap v Otis NV*, EU:C:2012:684, [45 et seq] it appears that the Charter would apply to all the proceedings before the UPC (as remedies are harmonised); also see Mylly "A Constitutional Perspective", p 87–9.
99 Varga, *The Effectiveness of the Köbler Liability in National Courts*, p 80.
100 It will clearly be relevant if proceedings were unduly long: T-577/14 *EU v Gascogne e.a*, EU:T:2017:1, [78–81] (upheld on appeal C-138/17, EU:C:2018:1032, [30–32]); T-479/14 *Kendrion NV v EU*, EU:T:2017:48, [121–135] (upheld on appeal C-150/17, EU:C:2018:1014, [111–112]).

11.4.3 Failure to give conforming interpretation

Courts in Member States are obliged to interpret domestic law in accordance with EU law as far as is possible;[101] this is usually called indirect effect.[102] This 'interpretative obligation'[103] would apply to any provision of UPCA, EPC or domestic law in respect of which EU law might be relevant. Accordingly, if the UPC fails to interpret these laws in accordance with EU norms it may face infraction proceedings or be liable for damages for any harm caused.[104] For a damages claim, the breach must be manifest and so it is likely that only where there is clear jurisprudence from the Court of Justice setting out the meaning and then the UPC takes a different meaning would it be actionable. For instance, applying the Enlarged Board's decision in *WARF*[105] on the patentability of inventions involving embryonic stem cell without any reference to the decisions of the Court of Justice in *Brüstle*[106] and *International Stem Cell*.[107] Even this question is tricky as the answer may vary between Contracting State as some countries joined the European Patent Convention before joining the European Union and these may be able to argue that the earlier convention permits a derogation from EU law.[108]

11.4.4 Failure to request a preliminary reference

As has already been discussed, the Court of Appeal like 'any national court' of last instance has the same obligation to make a preliminary reference to the Court of Justice unless one of the *Cilfit* exceptions applies.[109] It had been suggested that a successful sanction being imposed for such a failure is impossible.[110] However, the Court of Justice in infraction proceedings against France (*Commission v France*[111]) concluded there was

---

101 Unless to do so would be *contra legem*: C-105/03 *Pupino* [2005] ECR I-5285, [47]; C-26/13 *Kásler v OTP Jelzálogbank Zrt*, EU:C:2014:282, [65].
102 The origins of this rule are Case 14/83 *Von Colson v Land Nordrhein-Westfalen* [1984] ECR 1891, [28]; C-106/89 *Marleasing v Comercial Internacional de Alimentación* [1990] ECR I-4135, [8]; for a full statement of the rule see C-441/14 *DI*, EU:C:2016:278, [35–37].
103 Sara Drake "Twenty Years after Von Colson: The Impact of 'Indirect Effect' on the Protection of the Individual's Community Rights" (2005) 30 European LR 329.
104 Tridimas, "State Liability for Judicial Acts Remedies Unlimited?", p 155.
105 G 2/06 *Use of embryos/WARF* [2009] OJ EPO 306.
106 C-34/10 *Oliver Brüstle v Greenpeace* [2011] ECR I-9821.
107 C-364/13 *International Stem Cell Corpn*, EU:C:2014:2451.
108 Mylly "A Constitutional Perspective" at 89; also see Hofstötter *Non-Compliance of National Courts: Remedies in European Community Law and Beyond* at 135–6.
109 UPCA, art 21.
110 Winfried Tilmann and Clemens Plassmann, *Unified Patent Protection in Europe: A Commentary* at 457.
111 C-416/17 *Commission v France*, EU:C:2018:811; also see C-160/14 *Ferrenia da Silva E Brito v Estado português*, EU:C:2015:565, [45].

an actionable failure to refer. It arose because the French court departed from a Court of Justice decision on the grounds the judgment had been based on a different scheme in another member state. The Court of Justice concluded that as the French Court was wrong on EU law it was reasonable to conclude that the answer to the question could not have been *acte clair* and so there should have been a reference. It may be a collateral challenge could also be made not because of the failure to make a reference but rather due to the failure to *explain* why no reference was made.[112]

In combination this might suggest a much stricter obligation to refer than really exists because in reality the *Cilfit* exceptions leave much discretion to the court.[113] The UPC may decide that the result of any preliminary reference would not be determinative for their judgment[114] negating the need for a reference.[115] Similarly the fact there are differing views between the UPC and the law of member states does not necessitate a referral,[116] and clearly only certain aspects of the provisions before the UPC could lead to differing views between it and domestic courts. In any event, if the law the UPC applies is manifestly incompatible with declared EU law then it does not matter whether a preliminary reference was made or not. That application is itself actionable if it is manifest. So it is only where the law applied out turns out to be wrong that the failure to refer the question to the Court of Justice turns into a serious breach.[117]

11.5 How real is the risk?

The picture painted so far is of a court facing a potential avalanche of challenges. However, unless sanctions against the UPC are approached very differently from sanctions imposed on existing domestic courts this will surely not be the case. It has been rare indeed for domestic courts in Member States to be sanctioned. So are there reasons to see difference? First, it is said that national courts and even the Court of Justice tend to avoid

---

112 C-561/19 *Consorzio Italian Management v Catania Multiservizi*, EU:2021:799, [66]; Classen 'Case C-224/01 *Gerhard Köbler v Republik Österreich*' at 820-1; however Varga, *The Effectiveness of the Köbler Liability in National Courts*, p 37 takes the view these are two distinct obligations.
113 Varga, *The Effectiveness of the Köbler Liability in National Courts* at 44.
114 As to this test see C-136/12 *Consiglio nazionale dei geologi v Autorità garante della concorrenza e del mercato*, EU:C:2013:489, [25]; C-160/14 *Ferrenia da Silva E Brito v Estado português*, EU:C:2015:565, [37 and 45]. It is also not possible to make a reference *after* a judgment has been handed down: Case 338/85 *Pardini v Ministero del commercio con l'estero* [1988] ECR 2041; C-159/90 *Society for the Protection of Unborn Children v Grogan* [1991] ECR I-4685; C-148/10 *DHL International* [2011] ECR I-9543, [29].
115 No reference was made in *Eli Lilly & Co v Human Genome Sciences Inc* [2011] UKSC 51, [2012] RPC 6 when industrial application was considered in a biotechnology case reaching the UK Supreme Court (albeit with a priority date before the coming into force of the Directive), but the court concluded the Directive was of little assistance (at [36]).
116 C-160/14 *Ferrenia da Silva E Brito v Estado português*, EU:C:2015:565, [41].
117 Varga, *The Effectiveness of the Köbler Liability in National Courts* at 44.

blaming the judiciary for breaches of EU law.[118] Even if this is true, it may not apply to the UPC as the politics are quite different. *Köbler* claims are usually started before courts of first instance who in turn are likely to be reticent about criticising let alone awarding damages against higher courts and, if it reaches the highest court, it would lead to criticising one's close peers. The Court of Justice wants to minimise criticism of national courts to retain their enthusiastic cooperation[119] whether in infraction or *Köbler* referrals. Yet the UPC is an 'other' and as cases could be brought in many different courts across the Contacting Member States. It may well be that some countries are more willing to find fault than others. Furthermore, the UPC is a close analogue to being an EU institution and the Court of Justice is always much more willing to criticise institutions of the EU than it is domestic institutions. This would suggest against any deference towards the UPC.

Secondly, Member States have been reluctant to bring infraction proceedings against their peers,[120] but things might be different in relation to breaches by the UPC. It is clear that the Spanish are unhappy with the UPC and they have challenged the legality of its creation twice[121] and other countries are still less than enthusiastic about the project.[122] So if a reasonable opportunity arose it may well be some Member States are inclined to challenge the approach of the UPC. Furthermore, infraction proceedings are rare between Member States because they have significant political ramifications going beyond the dispute itself thereby souring relations or encouraging possible tit-for-tat challenges. This does not apply to the UPC as any politics will be neatly confined and despite liability resting with Contracting Member States it is not the activities of those states being criticised. As has already been suggested, a challenge to the activities of the UPC is much closer to an action against the EU institutions; these are frequently[123] brought before the Court of Justice.[124]

---

118 Varga, *The Effectiveness of the Köbler Liability in National Courts* at 62–3; Georgios Anagnostraras "The Principles of State Liability for Judicial Breaches: The Impact of European Community Law" (2001) 7 European Public Law 281 at 298–299.
119 See Hofstötter, *Non-Compliance of National Courts: Remedies in European Community Law and Beyond*, p 187; Jan Komárek "Federal Elements in the Community Judicial System: Building Coherence in the Community Legal Order" (2005) 42 CMLRev 9 at 25 who explain this for the approach in C-129/00 *Commission v Italy* [2003] ECR I-14637.
120 Under TFEU, art 259.
121 C-274/11 and C-295/11 *Spain v European Council; Italy v European Council*, EU:C:2013:240; C-146/13 *Spain v Council of Europe*, EU:C:2015:298.
122 Anna Wszołek, "Still Unifying? The Future of the Unified Patent Court" (2021) 52 IIC 1143.
123 In 2022, there were 37 direct actions; in 2021, 30; in 2020, 37 and in 2019, 41 resolved by the Court of Justice: Court of Justice, The Year in Review (2020, 2021 and 2022): Annual Report (EU 2021, 2022, 2023), p 59, 73, 27 respectively.
124 Snyder, "General Course in Constitutional Law of the European Union" at 84 and Francis Snyder "The Effectiveness of European Community Law: Institutions, Processes, Tools and Techniques" (1993) 56 MLR 19 at 27–31.

Thirdly, *Köbler* claims were for a long time described are 'largely theoretical'[125] and the case itself suggests such claims would be 'exceptional'.[126] Even now there have been only five successful claims before domestic courts.[127] However, as Peter Wattel suggests "[i]f the pecuniary stakes are high enough, disappointed litigants will try to re-open their lost cases via the *Köbler* liability".[128] Patent litigation can involve disputes over millions of Euros and in a few cases even billions.[129] If when the "final judgment" is handed down the legal fees are already in the millions of Euros the parties are hardly lightly to hold back if some of the costs and losses can be recovered through a *Köbler* claim. Furthermore, the merging of legal cultures into a new court will inevitably lead to teething problems[130] and the Enforcement Directive and Charter of Fundamental Rights will be something to which parties may resort to try to restore what they see as the "right" outcome for the case.

11.6 Conclusion

The UPCA included various safety valves to ensure it was compatible with EU law. It is widely assumed that they will have little if any practical relevance. This may well be right. However, the moulds that have formed dealing with sanctions on errant domestic courts in Member States do not fit tightly to the UPC. Its supranational competence and jurisdiction makes it a much wider target and so more likely to face infraction and *Kö-*

---

125 Varga, *The Effectiveness of the Köbler Liability in National* Courts at 2; also see Björn Beutler "State Liability for Breaches of Community Law by National Courts: Is the Requirement of a Manifest Infringement of the Applicable an Insurmountable Obstacle" (2009) 46 CMLRev 773 at 804 ("Yet the requirement of a manifest infringement must neither in theory nor in practice be understood as an insurmountable obstacle"); Marc Loth "Who Has the Last Word? On Judicial Lawmaking in European Private Law" (2017) 25 European Review of Private Law 45 at 49 ("emergency provision…hardly meant to be used"); Dimitra Nassimpian "…And We Keep on Meeting: (De) Fragmenting State Liability" (2007) 32 European LR 819 at 826 ("if the conditions set by the Court were in reality so high as to make it virtually impossible to reach the threshold, is…*Köbler*… 'token jurisprudence'"); Morten Broberg "National Courts of Last Instance Failing to Make a Preliminary Reference: The (Possible) Consequences Flowing Therefrom" (2016) 22 European Public Law 243 at 250 ("it will probably be a rare occurrence"); Peter Wattel "Köbler, CILFIT and Welthgrove: We Can't Go on Meeting Like This" (2004) 41 CMLRev 177 at 182 (explaining why most errors should not lead to liability).
126 C-224/01 *Köbler v Republik Österreich* [2003] ECR I-10239, [53].
127 See Varga, *The Effectiveness of the Köbler Liability in National Courts* at 53.
128 Wattel "Köbler, CILFIT and Welthgrove: We Can't Go on Meeting Like This" at 182.
129 The highest value patents may well opt out of the system until it has stablished (at which point such claims are probably less likely); as to the opt out see: UPCA, art 83(3).
130 Many of the issues raised in Michal Bobek "The New European Judges and the Limits of the Possible" in A. Lazowski, *The Application of EU Law in the New Member States* (Asser 2010), p 127 and the role of EU law in new member states would equally to the UPC, particularly where cases are heard by judges with less national experience of patent matters.

bler proceedings. Yet even if this is true it is still a very small chance made slightly bigger. But everything about the UPC is new and maybe with novelty comes the reinvention of more robust sanctions on courts for not applying EU law.

Paul LC Torremans
12 Regulation 542/2014 on jurisdiction

12.1 Introduction

The question which arises logically is why a comprehensive agreement such as the UPC agreement that puts on the rails a fundamentally new and different court system in the area of patent law does not address the international jurisdiction of the new court in a systematic way. Instead, this chapter on the international jurisdiction of the UPC comes under the heading 'Regulation 542/2014'[1] and that Regulation in turn relies heavily on the Brussels I Regulation,[2] That situation becomes a lot less peculiar if one realizes that all countries signing up to the UPC are Member States of the European Union, and therefore bound by the Brussels I Regulation, which prohibits Member States from concluding any new conventions dealing with jurisdiction or recognition or enforcement in relation to particular matters (maybe unless they all sign or sign alongside the EU).[3] The UPC Agreement could therefore not deal with the international jurisdiction, but instead it had to refer on that point to the Brussels I Regulation.[4] And Regulation 542/2014 is then the tool that inserts the required additional provisions in the Brussels I Regulation.

And let us just remind ourselves why we need to deal with international jurisdiction. Every court needs to establish its international jurisdiction first. This is where it all starts and without international jurisdiction a court cannot hear the case. Before the Unified Patent Court can hear a case it has to establish that it has international jurisdiction to hear the case. Article 31 UPC Agreement imposes the Brussels I Regulation rules as the only rules by which the Unified Patent Court can establish its jurisdiction. That

---

[1] Regulation EU No 542/2014 of the European Parliament and of the Council of 15 May 2014 amending Regulation (EU) No 1215/2012 as regards the rules to be applied with respect to the Unified Patent Court and the Benelux Court of Justice OJ L 163/1 (29 May 2014).
[2] Regulation (EU) No 1215/2012 of the European Parliament and of the EU Council of 12 December 2012 on jurisdiction and the recognition and enforcement of judgments in civil and commercial matters OJ L 351 (20 December 2012) (Regulation 1215/2012).
[3] Article 71 Brussels I Regulation. See e.g the Cape Town Convention on international interests in mobile equipment and its Protocol relating to aircraft equipment [2009] OL L121/3 , Convention on civil liability for bunker oil pollution damage [2002] OJ L256/7 and A. Dickinson and E. Lein (eds), *The Brussels I Regulation Recast*, OUP (2015), para. 17.24, p. 572. If the Member States sign on their own they arguably sign as trustees of the EU interest and are acting on behalf of the Community. See M. Cremona, 'Member States as Trustees of the Community Interest: Participating in International Agreements on Behalf of the European Community', Working Paper, EUI LAW, 2009/17.
[4] Article 31 UPC Agreement.

Paul LC Torremans, is Professor of Intellectual Property Law, School of Law, University of Nottingham.

https://doi.org/10.1515/9783110781687-012

was also made clear by the change of the word 'jurisdiction' to the word 'competence' for the other elements contained in chapter VI. From Article 32 onwards one finds provisions on the internal distribution of labour inside the Unified Patent Court and its various local and regional divisions and aspects of subject matter jurisdiction. International jurisdiction is a separate matter and one that comes first. Only once international jurisdiction has been established can one turn to the competence of the court, which means on the one hand the subject matter jurisdiction of the court as a common patent court that will deal roughly speaking with the infringement and validity issues surrounding European Patents and European Patents with unitary effect and on the other hand the division of labour inside the Unitary Patent Court, its central, local and regional divisions.

With that in mind, let us turn to the new rules that Regulation 542/2014 did put in place.

12.2 The insertion of a common court: a mere clarification in Article 71(a)

The European Union is quite used to deal with the jurisdiction of courts in civil and commercial matters,[5] but in essence all that experience refers to national courts of single Member States. The Benelux Court[6] has been in existence for quite a number of years as a Court that is common to Belgium, the Netherlands and Luxembourg, but at least until now, it has never operated at first instance level.[7] That removed the need to include it into the jurisdiction rules. So even if that picture may change for the Benelux Court, the Unified Patent Court is the one that does not fit the mold. The Unified Patent Court will be a (first instance) court that is common to a large number of Member States. On top of that, the Unified Patent Court will have local and regional divisions, which again at least potentially raises issues of jurisdiction. That is the issue addressed in what has become

---

5 See the various versions of the Brussels Convention and the Brussels I Regulation that eventually resulted in Regulation (EU) No 1215/2012 of the European Parliament and of the EU Council of 12 December 2012 on jurisdiction and the recognition and enforcement of judgments in civil and commercial matters OJ L 351 (20 December 2012) (Regulation 1215/2012).
6 Verdrag betreffende de instelling en het statuut van een Benelux-gerechtshof (Treaty establishing a Benelux Court and its Statute) 31st March 1965, [1973] Belgisch Staatsblad – Moniteur belge 14062. The Court has been operational since 1974.
7 The Benelux Court issues preliminary rulings at the request of national courts, for example concerning the Benelux Trade Mark. Negotiations are ongoing to allow the public direct access to the court in trade mark matters. See the enabling Protocol 'Protocol tot wijziging van het Verdrag van 31 maart 1965 betreffende de instelling en het statuut van een Benelux-Gerechtshof, ondertekend te Luxemburg op 15 oktober 2012', Tractatenblad 2013, nr 12. Further changes to the relevant Benelux texts on intellectual property are still required before the system can be put into action.

Article 71(a) Brussels I Regulation. The solution it adopts is rather simple. The UPC is considered to be a court of a Member State and that means that its jurisdiction can be dealt with under the rules of the Brussels I Regulation.

A court common to several Member States does after all for each of the Member States concerned the work of a national court, so it makes sense to treat it as such for the purposes of the Brussels I Regulation.[8] It does however mean that in a system with national, regional and central divisions a defendant may de facto have to defend the case in a location that is not his domicile or the Member State designated by the Regulation on that basis or on the basis of the rule in Article 7(2), ie the place where the tort/infringement takes place.[9] The most obvious example is that of a defendant domiciled in a Member State where there is no national division of the UPC. Being sued in the court of its domicile will therefore in practice mean having the defend the case in a country where the regional division of the UPC that covers the Member State concerned is established. Article 71(a) and the clarification it provides then gives at least predictability to the defendant.[10] That may well be fair to a defendant of a Member State of the UPC Agreement, as it is a predictable allocation of a court and even inside a country the court dealing with the matter may be a fair distance away from the place of residence of the defendant, but one should not forget that the UPC may also take jurisdiction on the basis of Article 7 Brussels I Regulation, eg because the harmful event occurs in the territory covered by the UPC Agreement, even if the defendant is resident in an EU Member State that did not sign the UPC Agreement or in a State party to the Lugano Convention. Article 31 UPC does refer to the Lugano Convention, but that convention has not been amended in the same way as the Brussels I Regulation. This is regrettable as it seriously undermines the element of predictability and legal certainty, especially for citizens of Norway, Iceland and Switzerland. It is hard for them to realise that they may well be sued in the UPC.[11]

---

[8] P. Torremans, 'An International Perspective I: A View from Private International Law', in J. Pila and Ch. Wadlow (eds), *The Unitary EU Patent System*, Volume 19 Studies of Oxford Institute of European and Comparative Law, Hart/Bloomsbury (2014)161–178, at 165–166.
[9] P. De Miguel Asensio, 'Regulation 542/2014 and the International Jurisdiction of the Unified Patent Court', 45(8) (2014) IIC 868, at 873–874.
[10] A. Miglio, 'The Jurisdiction of the Unified Patent Court: A Model for the Application of the Brussels Ia Regulation?', in A. Trunk and N. Hatzimihail (eds), *EU Civil Procedure Law and Third Countries: Which Way Forward?*, Nomos (2021) 71–94.
[11] P. De Miguel Asensio, 'Regulation 542/2014 and the International Jurisdiction of the Unified Patent Court', 45(8) (2014) IIC 868, at 873–874.

12.3 The new rules on international jurisdiction: Article 71b

Paragraph 1

Paragraph 1 of the Article 71b that is inserted in the Brussels I Regulation contains the straightforward rule that flows from the application of the Brussels I system to the UPC. In a situation where the Brussels I Regulation gives jurisdiction to the courts of a Member State that is party to the UPC Agreement and where the subject matter of the case falls inside the scope of the subject matter covered by the UPC Agreement[12] that jurisdiction is transferred from the national court to the Unified Patent Court.

This works well if the Brussels I jurisdiction is based on the domicile of the defendant in the Member State concerned, in application of the basic rule found in Article 4 Brussels I Regulation. And persons so domiciled can also be sued in the courts of the place where the harmful event occurred or may occur, in application of Article 7(2) Brussels I Regulation.[13] Article 8(1) that allows the claimant to bring multiple defendants before a single court if certain circumstances are met can also be applied easily in principle, even if its exact interpretation may turn out to be problematic.[14] A domicile in a Member State remains the *conditio sine qua non*, unless the ground for exclusive jurisdiction in Article 24(4) applies, ie, in cases dealing with the validity of the patent. Article 24(4) does not create problems at this stage.

But is there a full transfer or does the UPC simply benefit from the same jurisdiction? By using the words 'a common court shall have jurisdiction', Article 71b seems to suggest that the UPC, as the common court will merely also have jurisdiction. This is not the intended conclusion though. The UPC Agreement clearly works on the basis that the jurisdiction of the national courts will be transferred to the Unified Patent Court and that the national courts lose their jurisdiction. It might have been better to spell this out *expressis verbis*. Now one should come to that conclusion from the use of the word 'would' later on, ie the national court would have had jurisdiction earlier on, but does no longer have it. Especially in relation to Article 24(4) there can only be one court with exclusive validity jurisdiction and the UPC Agreement clearly sees the Unified Patent Court

---

12 What the agreement calls the 'competence' of the court.
13 For a detailed analysis of the application to intellectual property cases of the jurisdiction rules of the Brussels I Regulation see JJ Fawcett & P Torremans, *Intellectual Property and Private International Law* (Oxford: OUP, 2nd edn 2011) ch 5.
14 Compare the evolution between Case C-539/03 Roche Nederland BV et al v Frederick Primus and Milton Goldenberg [2006] ECR I-6535, Case C-145/10 Eva-Maria Painer v Standard Verlags GmbH et al. [2011] ECDR 6 and Case C-616/10 Solvay SA/Honeywell et al (12 July 2012). And see P Torremans, Intellectual Property Puts Article 6(1) Brussels I Regulation to the Test, CREATe Working Paper No 8 <http://www.create.ac.uk/wp-content/uploads/2013/09/CREATe-Working-Paper-No-8-v1.0.pdf>.

in that role. But that can only happen if the Brussels I Regulation grants it exclusive jurisdiction. This is clearly intended, but it would have been clearer to spell it out at the level of the Brussels I Regulation.[15]

This lack of clarity is even more regrettable in as far as the seven year transition period is concerned. During that period Article 83(1) UPC Agreement accepts that parties will be able to bring cases before both the national courts and before the Unified Patent Court. This concurrent jurisdiction should ideally be spelled out in the Brussels I Regulation. Admittedly the current wording of Article 71b leaves this possibility open, but this is clearly not intended. The plan was not to leave it open and to again amend the Brussels I Regulation at the end of the seven year transition period. The UPC Agreement cannot allocate international jurisdiction and article 83 can therefore not change the international jurisdiction rules.[16] Any allocation of international jurisdiction has to be done at the level of the Brussels I Regulation. One has to accept therefore that it was the will of the legislature to leave the option of concurrent jurisdiction open in the Brussels I Regulation and that the language of article 71 merely adds an option in front of the UPC. Otherwise article 83(1) UPC makes no sense. But at the same time, article 83 (1) cannot close the concurrent jurisdiction door after 7 years. That has to be done at the level of the Brussels I Regulation. Unless one takes article 83(1) as an agreement between Brussels I member states that does not allocate jurisdiction, as that would not be possible, and treats it as an additional agreement that merely instructs member states to abandon the concurrent jurisdiction option after seven years. That would avoid the need for a modification of the text of the Brussels I Regulation, but such an interpretation stretches the wording of article 71 Brussels I Regulation and of article 8(1) UPC Agreement.

What makes the situation worse is that during the transition period there will be two courts with exclusive jurisdiction under Article 24(4) as a result of article 83(1) UPC agreement. Exclusive jurisdiction means that the jurisdiction of the court excludes the jurisdiction of any other court. But how is that supposed to work vis-à-vis another court with exclusive jurisdiction? Simply leaving Article 24(4) as it is does not lead to a solution, but this point will be discussed in more detail in the next chapter.

Far less controversial, but maybe unexpected, is the fact that Article 25 Brussels I Regulation may also apply. Parties to a licence agreement may agree that any infringement case amongst them will be brought before the Unified Patent Court.[17] This may be

---

[15] P. Torremans, 'An International Perspective I: A View from Private International Law', in J. Pila and Ch. Wadlow (eds), *The Unitary EU Patent System*, Volume 19 Studies of Oxford Institute of European and Comparative Law, Hart/Bloomsbury (2014)161–178, at 167–169.
[16] P. De Miguel Asensio, 'Regulation 542/2014 and the International Jurisdiction of the Unified Patent Court', 45(8) (2014) IIC 868, at 870–871.
[17] Parties are free not to treat the case as contractual for example when the licensee allegedly goes beyond what is allowed in the licence contract.

particularly useful during the seven year transition period, as it provides predictability and certainty.[18]

Paragraph 2

The logical conclusion is that Article 71b has now dealt with the international jurisdiction of the UPC over defendants that are domiciled in a Member State of the EU,[19] irrespective of whether they participate in the UPC, but in terms of substantive patent law that leaves open a large gap. Plenty of parties that are not domiciled in a member State, but in a third state, are involved in patent litigation in Europe. More importantly, their activities in the EU may give rise to legal disputes that need to be brought before a court. The Brussels I Regulation has traditionally left the issue of jurisdiction over a defendant that is not domiciled in a Member State to the national private international laws of each member State. During the 2012 recasting exercise of the Brussels I Regulation a proposal to extend the Brussels I harmonised jurisdiction rules to those defendants domiciled in a third state was rejected, That leaves us with the problem that a common court cannot derive its jurisdiction from (various) national laws on private international law. There was therefore a need for a harmonized rule if the court was to have jurisdiction over defendants domiciled in a third state and that was seen as desirable, if not essential, from a substantive patent law point of view.

Paragraph 2 of the new article 71b sets out therefore to deal with the situation where a defendant is domiciled in a third state and where the existing rules in the Brussels I Regulation do not grant the UPC jurisdiction over such a defendant The solution is simple. One is to disregard the domicile issue and apply the Brussels I jurisdiction rules regardless of domicile, The provision states that this is to be done 'as appropriate'.[20] What is intended here is probably the fact that article 4 simply cannot be applied in a sensible way, as it is based entirely on the domicile (in a Member State) of a defendant. Giving jurisdiction to a third state by disregarding the domicile in a Member State requirement.does not make sense and is therefore not appropriate. It is submitted that one should not try and look for a further discretion in applying the other jurisdiction

---

18 P. Torremans, 'An International Perspective I: A View from Private International Law', in J. Pila and Ch. Wadlow (eds), *The Unitary EU Patent System*, Volume 19 Studies of Oxford Institute of European and Comparative Law, Hart/Bloomsbury (2014)161–178, at 169.
19 Or a signatory state to the Lugano convention. P. De Miguel Asensio, 'Regulation 542/2014 and the International Jurisdiction of the Unified Patent Court', 45(8) (2014) IIC 868, at 875.
20 A. Miglio, 'The Jurisdiction of the Unified Patent Court: A Model for the Application of the Brussels Ia Regulation?', in A. Trunk and N. Hatzimihail (eds), *EU Civil Procedure Law and Third Countries: Which Way Forward?*, Nomos (2021) 71–94.

rules in these circumstances. The intended solution is simply to apply the exiting rules on jurisdiction regardless of domicile.[21]

The non-expert reader might find it very hard though to extract that simple message from the text. And applying Articles 7 and 8 Brussels I Regulation as mere subject matter jurisdiction is not without its risks. They have been designed to apply with the added safeguard that the defendant is domiciled in a Member State, which guaranteed a strong link between the case and the Brussels I territory. Removing that safeguard without replacing it can give the Unified Patent Court jurisdiction over defendants whose links with the Brussels I territory are extremely weak. Territorial patents are ideally suited to locate some damage in the jurisdiction and it is relatively easy to blame for example a foreign (parent) company for it. One may not succeed in substantive law, but harassing defendants by obliging them to defend the case becomes relatively easy.[22]

It would be far clearer for the user of the system and from a legal perspective much more elegant, clear and safe to provide Article 7 specific language. That could read as follows:

> In disputes concerned with the infringements of intellectual property rights over which a court common to several member states exercises subject matter jurisdiction, a person may be sued in the common court if the alleged infringement occurs or may occur in any of the member states concerned, unless the alleged infringer has not acted in any of the member states concerned and his or her activity cannot reasonably be seen as having been directed to that state.
>
> In disputes concerned with a contractual obligation that comes within the subject matter jurisdiction of a court common to several member states, a person may be sued in the common court if the obligation in question is to be performed in any of the member states concerned.[23]

Paragraph one clearly states what the mechanism is, ie place of infringement without domicile, but quite importantly it also builds in a safeguard mechanism to replace the one that was removed by dropping the domicile requirement. It is after all not desirable for the common court to have jurisdiction over a foreign defendant that did not act or direct action in or towards the jurisdiction, such as a manufacturer of a patented product based in a country where there is no patent protecting the product whose independent distributor imports the product in the member states (where a patent is in force). But as the safeguard applies cumulatively, any foreign parent company that di-

---

21 P. De Miguel Asensio, 'Regulation 542/2014 and the International Jurisdiction of the Unified Patent Court', 45(8) (2014) IIC 868, at 875..
22 P. Torremans, 'An International Perspective I: A View from Private International Law', in J. Pila and Ch. Wadlow (eds), *The Unitary EU Patent System*, Volume 19 Studies of Oxford Institute of European and Comparative Law, Hart/Bloomsbury (2014)161–178, at 169–172.
23 Based on Articles 2:201 and 2:202 of the CLIP Principles; see European Max Planck Group on Conflict of Laws in Intellectual Property (CLIP), *Conflict of Laws in Intellectual Property: The CLIP Principles and Commentary* (Oxford: OUP, 2013) ('CLIP Principles') 69–84. (The author is a member of CLIP).

rects the operations of subsidiaries, etc. will be caught without the need to rely on article 8(1).[24]

Article 8(1) Brussels I Regulation makes it possible to bring multiple defendants before a single court and it can, of course, also be extended to defendants that are not domiciled in a Member State, but its application in patent cases (and in intellectual property cases in general) is a mess.[25] *Roche Nederland*[26] was unduly strict and without saying so the CJEU has been backtracking ever since. There was the *Freeport* case and then the *Painer*[27] and *Solvay* cases.[28] These latter two are simply not compatible with the strict *Roche Nederland* approach.[29] One can leave it to the CJEU to sort out the mess and hope the court will continue with the de facto more flexible approach in *Solvay* and *Painer*. It is at least encouraging to see that Article 33(1)(b) UPC Agreement has very different language to offer:

> An action may be brought against multiple defendants only where the defendants have a commercial relationship and where the action relates to the same alleged infringement.

But before one gets excited and sees in here a new and more appropriate approach to the issue of multiple defendants one has to remind oneself that this provision cannot operate at international jurisdiction level, where Article 31 refers uniquely to the Brussels I Regulation, and its Article 8(1), as interpreted by the Court of Justice of the European Union. The new UPC Agreement provision therefore only operates at the competence level, i.e. once the Unified Patent Court already has jurisdiction over each of the defendants on the basis of one of more other Brussels I jurisdiction rules (not necessarily the same rule for each defendant though). That is clear for the private international law experts, but it may not be wise to leave both versions in existence side by side, without any clarification for the non-private international law expert as to which one applies when. Be that as it may, there will be little scope for Article 8(1) if the defendant is not domiciled in a Member State. There will very rarely be a defendant that one would want to join to the case before the Unified Patent Court, but that cannot be brought before the court on the basis of Article 7(2) if the domicile safeguard no longer applies. Any defendant against whom one has a realistic chance of success will at least contribute to the act causing the damage or be at least partially responsible for the damage. And once the jurisdiction point has been handled by Article 7(2) Brussels I Regulation the competence provision in

---

[24] For a complete explanation of the approach that is proposed and of the safeguard mechanism, see the CLIP Principles.
[25] A detailed analysis would lead too far here; see instead Torremans (n 21).
[26] Case C-539/03 *Roche Nederland BV et al v Frederick Primus and Milton Goldenberg* [2006] ECR I-6535.
[27] Case C-145/10 *Eva-Maria Painer v Standard Verlags GmbH et al* [2011] ECDR 6.
[28] Case C-616/10 *Solvay SA/Honeywell et al* ECLI:EU:C:2012:445.
[29] P. Torremans, 'Intellectual Property puts Art. 6(1) Brussels I Regulation to the Test' 2014(1) Intellectual Property Quarterly., 1–12.

Article 33(1)(b) will enable the claimant to centralize the claim against multiple defendants before a single division of the court.[30]

Finally, there is a sentence in paragraph 2 of article 71b Brussels I Regulation that deals in a very broad way with provisional and protective measures, Of course, the UPC will be able to issue such measures when it has jurisdiction to deal with the substance of the case, but this provision allows parties to make an application for such measures even if the courts of other Member States have jurisdiction as to the substance of the case. Article 35 Brussels I Regulation is extended to cover all these scenarios.[31] This gives the Unified Patent Court an appropriately wide power to issue provisional measures, to assist the foreign court and the parties. Jurisdiction is the issue here and hence the concept that one can make an application for provisional measures. The rules of substantive law will then apply to the question whether the court will in practice grant such measures and how far-reaching they will be.

Paragraph 3

Paragraph 3 was always intended to add to the basis on which jurisdiction can be taken, but what was proposed in the draft Regulation was very different from what made into the Regulation that was in the end adopted.[32] The starting point of the provision in the Regulation is now very clearly that this is not an independent ground of jurisdiction. The rule instead covers a scenario where the common court does already have jurisdiction on the basis of paragraph 2. The subject matter involved is the infringement of a European Patent, for the simple reason that such a patent may also be in existence (and can therefore also be infringed by the same activity) in a number of what are for paragraph 2 third states. In such a case damage inside the EU may be coupled with damage outside the EU in a third state. It may make sense for the common court to deal also with that latter damage and to avoid the need for there to be additional litigation in the third state. Article 7(2) Brussels I Regulation, even if applied without the domicile requirement as a result of paragraph 2, may not have covered damage in a third state and paragraph 3 serves a useful purpose on this point.[33]

---

30 Art 33(1) does not expressly extend the application of its paragraph (b) to defendants that are not domiciled in a Member State, but this is clearly intended. The paragraph on defendants that are not domiciled in a Member State merely adds the option to sue them before the central division, without excluding anything.
31 A. Dickinson and E. Lein (eds), *The Brussels I Regulation Recast*, OUP (2015), chapter 12,
32 P. Torremans, 'An International Perspective I: A View from Private International Law', in J. Pila and Ch. Wadlow (eds), *The Unitary EU Patent System*, Volume 19 Studies of Oxford Institute of European and Comparative Law, Hart/Bloomsbury (2014)161–178, at 173–174.
33 P. Véron, 'Extent of the long-arm jurisdiction conferred upon the unified patent court by Art. 71(b)(3) of the Brussels I Regulation as amended by Regulation 542/2014 of may 15, 2014: Turkish delight and a bit of Swiss chocolate for the unified patent Court', 27 (2015), issue 9, 588–596.

Useful as it may be for the claimant and in some cases no doubt for both parties to be able to bring the whole case in front of a single (common court), this remains a form of long-arm jurisdiction and involves therefore certain risks. One cannot predict whether foreign states will recognize and enforce these judgments, but it is interesting to see that a couple of safeguards have been put in place to weed out the cases with a very weak link with the UPC where the link with the jurisdiction would have been unduly weak. Jurisdiction may only be established if property belonging to the defendant is located in any Member State party to the instrument establishing the common court and the dispute has a sufficient connection with any such Member State. Recital 7 of the Regulation mentions that the judge who is deciding whether or not such a sufficient connection is present in a particular case can take into account the factor that the claimant has its domicile in the state concerned or the factor that evidence is available there. There is also a suggestion that one should look at the value of the property in that state. That may make sense if the system prefers to see the judgment enforced in that state, but the use of property as a basis for jurisdiction remains nevertheless questionable. The property involved does after all not have to be related to the allegedly infringing activity. It is then hard to see how such property links the case to the UPC and its contracting states.[34] This rule merely seems an attempt to offer a court with pan-European jurisdiction and to make the rules that are designed for a patent with unitary effect also fit in all scenarios for European patents. That is a laudable aim, but maybe one should have left the property basis for jurisdiction to one side and instead have required that the long arm subject matter was ancillary to damage resulting from the infringement inside the UPC zone.

12.4 Article 71c: *lis pendens*

For obvious reasons having two courts dealing with the same or a related issue between the same parties is not an ideal solution. Article 29 to 32 of the Brussels I Regulation address that issue, known in private international law as *lis pendens*. When the proceedings involve the same cause of action and the same parties the court first seized will hear the case and all the other courts will stay their proceedings (as the case is pending elsewhere, hence lis pendens).[35] If the actions are merely related, the obligation to stay is turned into an option to stay. Any court other than the court first seized may stay its proceedings in these circumstances.[36] And the first seized lis pendens rule is also applied to the scenario where several courts have exclusive jurisdiction.[37] Article 71c then merely expands that standard system to scenarios that involve the UPC.

---

34 P. De Miguel Asensio, 'Regulation 542/2014 and the International Jurisdiction of the Unified Patent Court', 45(8) (2014) IIC 868, at 879–883.
35 Article 29 Brussels I Regulation.
36 Article 30 Brussels I Regulation.
37 Article 31 Brussels I Regulation.

On a permanent basis there is the situation where proceedings are brought in the Unified Patent Court and in the national courts of an EU Member State that is not a party to the UPC Agreement.

On a temporary basis there is the situation where proceedings are brought in the Unified Patent Court and in the national courts of a Member State that is a party to the UPC Agreement during the transition period that is referred to in Article 83(1) of the Unified Court Agreement.

The latter solves the conflicting jurisdiction issues that were raised earlier, but it does so by treating article 83(1) UPC Agreement as a jurisdiction rule, which it arguably is not allowed to be.

And even if we leave that issue to one side and accept the 'practical' solution the fundamental question whether this solution is suitable remains. European patents with unitary effect are not really problematic, but issues arise in relation to standard European patents. Article 34 UPC Agreement stipulates that a decision of the UPC will in these cases cover the territory of all those Member States for which the European Patent has effect. It is not clear how that rule can be a private international law rule, but the clear intention seems to be to treat it as one, in the same way as Article 83(1). That means then that a first claim in a national court will trigger the *lis pendens* rule and stop the case from being dealt with by the UPC. That may well force the parties down the line of country by country litigation and rule out the single court solution in front of the UPC. Maybe that is not the best solution. Let us take an example that is entirely realistic and that involves the patent law complication that negative declarations and infringement actions are seen to involve the same cause of action. The potential defendant in a (common court) infringement case can after all bring a national negative declaration case by way of a first preemptive strike (potentially in combination with a validity claim, potentially in a torpedo jurisdiction). Article 29 Brussels I Regulation does then prevent the rightholder from bringing an infringement case in the common court, unless one wants to go down the wobbly route of arguing that the wider scope of the possible UPC case relegates this scenario to the related cases provision which then sees the UPC refuse to stay on the basis of its potential wider coverage whilst brushing the potential for a contradictory outcome in relation to one denomination of the European Patent (because of Article 34 UPC) under the carpet. That seems unlikely to happen, but does it then make sense to rely simply on the court first seized rule? Does one not, by paying lip service to Article 83(1) UPC Agreement, deny the rightholder the option to enforce its rights effectively by means of a single action? The defendant can effectively force the rightholder down the national country by country enforcement route as the holder of a supposedly valid right cannot sue on validity grounds. The question that needs to be asked here is whether a preference for the common court instead of the court first seised does not make more sense.[38]

---

[38] P. Torremans, 'An International Perspective I: A View from Private International Law', in J. Pila and Ch. Wadlow (eds), *The Unitary EU Patent System*, Volume 19 Studies of Oxford Institute of Eur-

12.5 Recognition and enforcement

Regulation 542/2014 leaves it to the provisions of the UPC Agreement to deal with the recognition and enforcement of a judgment given by the UPC in a Member State that is party to the agreement. But not all EU Member States will become parties to the UPC Agreement. There will therefore in practice be judgments from those Member States that did not join and judgments from the Unified Patent Court. Each of these may require recognition and enforcement in the other area. The Regulation then applies the standard Brussels I Regulation mechanism.[39] This does not give rise to major problems and is acceptable as a workable solution.

12.6 Conclusion

One could summarise matters by stating that Regulation 542/2014 simply expands the scope of the Brussels I Regulation to the UPC and patent litigation involving parties who are not domiciled in the EU. Things are unfortunately not that straightforward and especially in relation to standard European Patents and defendants that are not domiciled in the EU problems arise.

Both from a private international law and from a substantive patent law perspective one sees imperfections that may hinder the smooth operation of the system and that may render it more difficult for both the UPC and the national courts to do justice to the parties in this complex patent law area. This is clearly something that will need to be looked at again in the future.

And burying it all the way down in Article 71 of the Brussels I Regulation is also not the best way to draw the attention of the patent lawyers to the private international law aspects of the new system.

---

opean and Comparative Law, Hart/Bloomsbury (2014)161–178, at 174–177, where further examples can be found.
39 Article 71d regulation 542/2014.

Paul LC Torremans
13 Exclusive jurisdiction and competence

13.1 Introduction

We already touched upon the issue of exclusive jurisdiction in the previous chapter. The rules on exclusive jurisdiction apply to issues of registration and validity and play therefore in patent law a major role in revocation actions. In this chapter we will look at the exclusive jurisdiction of the UPC. Or maybe we should amend that statement and say straight away that we will look both at exclusive jurisdiction and exclusive competence. Such is after all the somewhat complex reality established by Chapter VI of the UPC Agreement.

13.2 The exclusive jurisdiction of the UPC: registration and validity

The first provision of Chapter VI UPC Agreement is Article 31, which is headed 'international jurisdiction'. We analysed that provision in detail in the previous chapter, so there is no need to repeat that exercise here. Suffice it to remind ourselves that the Brussels I Regulation[1] does, broadly speaking, not allow the Member States to enter into other treaties dealing with jurisdiction in areas covered by it. Hence, the reference in Article 31 UPC Agreement to the jurisdiction rules contained in the Brussels I Regulation and by extension in the Lugano Convention.[2]

13.2.1 Applying Article 24(4) Brussels I Regulation

In terms of exclusive jurisdiction that means a cross reference to Article 24(4) Brussels I Regulation. That article grants exclusive jurisdiction in the area of registration and validity to the courts of the Member State in which (or for which) the intellectual property

---

[1] Regulation (EU) No 1215/2012 of the European Parliament and of the EU Council of 12 December 2012 on jurisdiction and the recognition and enforcement of judgments in civil and commercial matters OJ L 351 (20 December 2012) (Regulation 1215/2012).
[2] [2007] OJ L339/3.

Paul LC Torremans, is Professor of Intellectual Property Law, School of Law, University of Nottingham.

https://doi.org/10.1515/9783110781687-013

right is registered[3], here of course the patent involved. Article 24(4) is highly problematical when it is applied to patents[4], but most of those complications can be left to one side when it comes to the UPC. After all, the UPC is a single common court for all contracting states that will deal with both infringement and revocation (invalidity) cases for both European Patents and European Patents with unitary effect. That simply means that the UPC will have international jurisdiction to hear any revocation/invalidity cases and that the issue of an invalidity issue arising in a different court with infringement jurisdiction will not arise, as the 'other' court will be the same UPC. The international jurisdiction of the UPC is therefore established easily and straightforwardly through the application of Article 24(4) Brussels I Regulation.

13.2.2 The transition period as a complicating factor

That latter statement needs to be qualified immediately though, as it applies only if one leaves the transition period to one side. We will not repeat the discussion whether or not Article 83(1)[5] should really be allowed to play a role when it comes to international jurisdiction.[6] That point was dealt with in the previous chapter. Let us simply accept that it does so in practice, as that is reflected in the *lis pendens* rules. That means that whilst nothing changes for European Patents with unitary effect during the transition period, the national courts regain concurrent international jurisdiction for infringement and revocation on the grounds invalidity of (any denomination of) a European Patent. The *lis pendens* rules in Article 71(d) Brussels I Regulation[7] then arbitrate that potential conflict between two courts with international exclusive invalidity jurisdiction in favour of the court first seized of the matter and instruct the other court to stay its proceedings. That is a rather blunt tool. Let us by way of example assume that the owner of a European Patent, rather sensibly, brings a single infringement action covering the 7 national denominations of its European Patent in the UPC during the transition period. The defendant can, of course, counterclaim for invalidity, but is not obliged to do that in the UPC proceedings. Instead, the defendant can bring an invalidity claim in the national courts of one of the denominations of the European Patent. That national court has (concur-

---

3 For a recent example in national courts, showing their creative struggle with the provision, see *GW Pharma Ltd v Otsuka Pharmaceutical Co Ltd* [2022] EWCA Civ 1462.
4 For a detailed analysis see JJ Fawcett & P Torremans, *Intellectual Property and Private International Law* (Oxford: OUP, 2nd edn 2011) ch 7.
5 Agreement on a Unified Patent Court [2013] OJ C 175/1.
6 See the previous chapter and P. Torremans, 'An International Perspective I: A View from Private International Law', in J. Pila and Ch. Wadlow (eds), *The Unitary EU Patent System*, Volume 19 Studies of Oxford Institute of European and Comparative Law, Hart/Bloomsbury (2014) 161–178, at 175.
7 As inserted by REGULATION (EU) No 542/2014 OF THE EUROPEAN PARLIAMENT AND OF THE COUNCIL of 15 May 2014 amending Regulation (EU) No 1215/2012 as regards the rules to be applied with respect to the Unified Patent Court and the Benelux Court of Justice [2014] OJ L163/1.

rent) exclusive jurisdiction and once the case is pending it will mean that on the basis of the *lis pendens* rule the UPC is estopped from dealing with the invalidity point. That does not stop the UPC from dealing with the infringement issue and, since its judgment necessarily covers all denominations of the European Patent, it may start from the presumption that a patent that has been granted is presumed to be valid until it is declared invalid and hold the patent to be infringed (all denominations). But the spanner gets into the wheels if the national court reaches a decision on the invalidity point before the UPC decides the infringement issue and one denomination of the patent is declared invalid. Does that mean that the presumption of validity no longer applies to the infringement proceedings in front of the UPC? If so, the UPC is estopped from finding the patent infringed, as there no longer is an exclusive right in one Member State and its decisions necessarily affect all denominations. That is, of course, if one accepts that the UPC is obliged to deal with the claim as filed originally, ie 7 denominations in existence and all infringed. Or can the UPC simply render a judgment covering the situation on the day of its own judgment, ie infringement of 6 denominations? Does that require the claimant to amend its claim and drop one jurisdiction? Article 34 UPC Agreement merely states that the territorial scope of the decision covers the territory of those Contracting States for which the European Patent has effect, but it does not say when that rule is put into effect, ie at the time the European patent is granted, at the time the claim is brought or at the time of the judgment. It seems to rule out the need for the claimant to amend a claim, but at the same time the most logical reading would mean that it applies at the time the claim is brought, as a claim cannot apply to denominations that have been revoked.[8]

There is a risk here that the single procedure in the UPC is undone and that one ends up with multiple national proceedings. And all turns on who is first to bring a case. That is not necessarily a safe route towards judicial efficiency and justice being done for all the parties. Would it not have been easier to give preference to the UPC as the court that can deal with the case in the most comprehensive way once it is seized of the litigation between the parties? The logic of article 34 UPC is after all to litigate the European Patent as a single entity. That solution would also still have allowed the parties to bring national proceedings during the transition period if they prefer to run a test case in one or two jurisdictions.

13.2.3 Other grounds of jurisdiction

Strange as it may sound, the Brussels I exclusive jurisdiction provision is not the only ground of international jurisdiction that is relevant in this context. If we leave the tran-

---

[8] See P. Torremans, 'An International Perspective I: A View from Private International Law', in J. Pila and Ch. Wadlow (eds), *The Unitary EU Patent System*, Volume 19 Studies of Oxford Institute of European and Comparative Law, Hart/Bloomsbury (2014) 161–178.

sition period issues behind it is clear that the UPC is to remain as the single forum for European Patents and European Patents with unitary effect. The international jurisdiction rules are then merely there to decide which parties are subject to the jurisdiction of the UPC and whether the location of the facts of the case can still bring cases involving parties located outside the UPC territory before the UPC. It does in that sense not matter whether we rely in this respect on the exclusive jurisdiction provision or on Articles 4 to 7 for example. The real impact of the fact that the case raises issues that are considered to raise exclusive jurisdiction concerns then moves to the level of the UPC and the division of labour inside the UPC. We therefore need to look next at the competence rules of the UPC Agreement.[9]

13.3 The Competence rules

13.3.1 An action for the revocation of a patent

It is first of all important to remind ourselves how we get to the competence rules and what their somewhat limited role is. The competence rules only become relevant once the international jurisdiction of the UPC has been established. The case will then be dealt with by the UPC and the question arises which division of the court will deal with the case. The competence rules deal in other words with the internal division of labour and competence inside the UPC.

Our main focus of attention here are Articles 32 and 33 UPC Agreement. If we look first of all at an action for the revocation of a patent that is brought in terms of international jurisdiction on the basis of the exclusive jurisdiction rule Article 32(1)(d) confirms first of all that the UPC will have exclusive competence for actions for the revocation of European Patents and European Patents with unitary effect (and for declaration of invalidity of supplementary protection certificates). Article 33(4) then specifies that such actions for revocations are to be brought before the central division of the UPC. That is entirely logical, as the new system considers both the European Patent and the European Patent with Unitary effect and article 34 UPC Agreement emphasizes that any UPC decision will cover all denominations of the patent involved. And as revocation and invalidity are linked to the patent as such, rather than to local facts or the defendant as a person it makes sense to have a single entity dealing with the issue and building up a consistent case law. A single European title's validity is therefore rightly dealt with by the central division of the UPC.

---

9 P. Torremans, 'An International Perspective I: A View from Private International Law', in J. Pila and Ch. Wadlow (eds), *The Unitary EU Patent System*, Volume 19 Studies of Oxford Institute of European and Comparative Law, Hart/Bloomsbury (2014) 161–178, at 178.

13.3.2 Infringement and other actions

But one should not forget that validity can surface as an issue in other cases. In terms of validity competence we may therefore be dealing with a case in which the international jurisdiction of the UPC was established on any of the grounds of jurisdiction. It does not have to be the provision on exclusive jurisdiction. Let us look in a bit more detail at the standard case, which is based on an infringement claim. In terms of international jurisdiction Articles 4, 7 and 8 Brussels I Regulation will bring the case to the UPC via Regulation 542/2014.[10] The question we are dealing with is where such a case ends up inside the UPC once the issue of invalidity is raised.

On this point we find in the UPC Agreement an approach that is radically different from the one proposed by the Court of Justice of the European Union in the context of Article 24(4) Brussels I Regulation. In *Gat v Luk*[11] the court broadly speaking suggested that the exclusive jurisdiction of the court of the country where the patent was granted (or for which it was supposed to be granted) kicked in as soon as the issue of invalidity was raised.[12] This had very unfortunate consequences. It could deprive eg the judge of the domicile of the defendant of the jurisdiction to deal in a single case with the infringement of identical denominations of a European Patent, simply because the defendant raised the point of validity. That then in turn became a simple trick to make the enforcement of a patent much more costly and difficult, especially as it is the alleged infringer who will become the claimant in the invalidity claims before the courts of the countries of registration. Such a party may not be motivated to speed up the case and to seek a speedy return to the court with infringement jurisdiction.

Article 33(3) UPC Agreement fortunately goes down a very different and, especially in the context of competence where the international jurisdiction of the UPC is no longer at issue, much more sensible and effective route. It gives the local or regional division in front of which the infringement claim is pending a discretion once it has heard the parties. That discretion essentially allows the court to decide on the one hand what is the core issue in front of the court, ie infringement or invalidity, and on the other hand how complex the validity issue is.

The local or regional division is first of all given the opportunity to proceed with the action for infringement and the counterclaim for revocation.[13] In that scenario it will request the assistance of a technically qualified judge with qualifications and experience

---

10 REGULATION (EU) No 542/2014 OF THE EUROPEAN PARLIAMENT AND OF THE COUNCIL of 15 May 2014 amending Regulation (EU) No 1215/2012 as regards the rules to be applied with respect to the Unified Patent Court and the Benelux Court of Justice [2014] OJ L163/1.
11 Case C-4/03 *Gesellschaft für Antriebstechnik mbH & Co. KG v Lamellen und Kupplungsbau Beteiligungs KG*. ECLI:EU:C:2004:539.
12 For a detailed analysis see JJ Fawcett & P Torremans, *Intellectual Property and Private International Law* (Oxford: OUP, 2nd edn 2011) ch 7.
13 Article 33(3)(a) UPC Agreement.

in the field of technology concerned. That builds in an additional safeguard on the point of invalidity and the understanding of the evidence in that regard. It is a sensible approach, but one cannot stress enough what a radical departure from the logic underpinning *Gat v Luk*.[14] it is. This approach will be particularly helpful in those cases where the court decides that the core issue that is in front of it is one of infringement

The court may of course also come to the conclusion that, despite the fact that an infringement claim was brought, maybe merely to secure the international jurisdiction of a certain local or regional division of the UPC, the real issue between the parties is that of the validity of the patent. That would be a case where it would be advisable for the local or regional division to refer the whole case to the central division.[15] The Agreement sees this as an exceptional decision that therefore requires the agreement of the parties.

Should the parties fail to agree or in case the scenario is not that extreme or clearcut, the local or regional division also has the option to refer the counterclaim, ie the invalidity and revocation issue, to the central division, which has more experience on this point. This solution may be advisable if the invalidity point is not only important, but also complex. It is therefore not restricted to the scenario where the parties do not agree. It therefore follows that such a referral does not affect the infringement case one way or another. The local or regional division remains in charge of the infringement claim, but it can decide whether it is desirable to either proceed with it or to suspend dealing with it until the central division has decided the invalidity point.[16] Here issues of timing will be crucial and one may understand that a local or regional division may well want to make progress with the examination of the infringement case so that a decision can follow swiftly once the central division gives its decision on the validity point, whilst it may not want to rush to a decision on infringement before the validity outcome is clear. Depending on the complexity of the infringement case a suspension or proceeding with the case may therefore turn out to be the best way forward. The UPC Agreement gives the local or regional division the autonomy and flexibility that they may need on this point, whilst putting in place sufficient safeguards to makes sure all points are heard fully in the best possible circumstances to do justice to the parties and their claims. And the solution also applies to the scenario where rather than as counterclaim the invalidity point is raised as a separate claim. Such a claim will need to be brought before the local or regional divisions that are already dealing with the infringement claim. The underpinning strategy is clearly to prefer a single case in a single court dealing both with the infringement and validity issues between the parties.[17]

That emphasis on and trust of the local and regional division becomes even clearer if one looks at the solution for the scenario in which the central division is already deal-

---

14 Case C-4/03 *Gesellschaft für Antriebstechnik mbH & Co. KG v Lamellen und Kupplungsbau Beteiligungs KG*. ECLI:EU:C:2004:539.
15 Article 33(3)(c) UPC Agreement.
16 Article 33(3)(b) UPC Agreement.
17 Article 33(4) UPC Agreement.

ing with the invalidity claim at the time when an infringement claim is brought. Such a claim can still be brought before the relevant local or regional division and that division will then have the same discretion to either hear the case (with or without a suspension) or to refer it on to the central division. No doubt with the issue of procedural efficiency in mind the Agreement also allows the claimant in the infringement claim to bring that claim before the central division, as the latter is already seized with the case from an invalidity point of view.[18]

13.4 *Lis pendens*

One can be very brief here. The new rules on *lis pendens* in article 71(c) Brussels I Regulation only deal with international jurisdiction and are strictly speaking irrelevant for the competence issue. But it is worth keeping in mind that the first seized *lis pendens* rule is also applied to the scenario where several courts have exclusive jurisdiction.[19]

On a permanent basis there is the situation where proceedings are brought in the Unified Patent Court and in the national courts of an EU Member State that is not a party to the UPC Agreement.

On a temporary basis there is the situation where proceedings are brought in the Unified Patent Court and in the national courts of a Member State that is a party to the UPC Agreement during the transition period that is referred to in Article 83(1) of the Unified Court Agreement.

The latter solves the conflicting jurisdiction issues that were raised earlier, but it does so by treating article 83(1) UPC Agreement as a jurisdiction rule, which it arguably is not allowed to be.

13.5 Conclusion

Exclusive jurisdiction, ie in the clear context of international jurisdiction, is far less of an issue when it comes to the UPC. It has been retained as a ground of jurisdiction in the Brussels I Regulation, as amended by Regulation 542/2014, but where in the past it has been used to reallocate cases to another court in the European system it will no longer have that function in the final UPC system. By that I mean the system as it will operate after the end of the transition period. Both for infringement and validity of European Patents and European Patents with a unitary effect there will then be only one court left and it will be the same, ie the UPC. The jurisdiction rules will then merely function as a

---

[18] Article 33(5) UPC Agreement.
[19] Article 31 Brussels I Regulation.

filter to decide which cases can be brought before the UPC and in that respect there is no difference in function between the different jurisdiction rules.

Once the UPC has jurisdiction the competence rules will take over and deal with the division of labour between the various divisions of the UPC. But in that context the more flexible and efficient solution that has been adopted leaves very little space for the concept of exclusivity and technically it does not deal with the issue of jurisdiction at all. It is fortunate that the legislature has left the legacy of *Gat v Luk*[20] behind.

---

[20] Case C-4/03 Gesellschaft für Antriebstechnik mbH & Co. KG v Lamellen und Kupplungsbau Beteiligungs KG. ECLI:EU:C:2004:539.

Fernand de Visscher

14 Constitutional aspects of the Unitary Patent Package (UPP) and the Unified Patent Court (UPC) – question marks remain

It is a difficult exercise to question the constitutional aspects of the *Unitary Patent Package* (UPP) and the *Unified Patent Court* (UPC). As we are not a specialist in questions of this nature, we will essentially limit ourselves to putting question marks. The *Unified Patent Court Agreement* (UPCA) being a classic international treaty, it does not call for much comment from this angle. It is obviously with regard to European Union (the Union) law (including the Charter) and the European Convention on Human Rights[1] that Regulations 1257/2012, 1260/2012 and 542/2014 (and in particular the first mentioned) as well as the UPCA and the UPC can be analysed from a "constitutionality" perspective.

The exercise of reflection may seem futile, at least in part, given the judgment of the Court of Justice of the European Union (CJEU) on 5 May 2015[2]. But, as we shall see, this judgment did not close the debate on the legality of Regulation 1257/2012, and even less on the legality of the UPCA and that of the court established, the UPC.

Prior to the adoption of the UPP, the field of patents in the European Union was regulated by national laws and the European Patent Convention (EPC). The European patent, once granted by the European Patent Office (EPO), "enters" the national sphere of each designated State and is subject to the same national rules as those applicable to the national patent except that, subject to an opposition procedure before the EPO, it may be revoked with effect in all designated states. From a jurisdictional point of view, in summary, infringement litigation follows the general rules of Regulation 1215/2012 (so-called Brussels 1a)[3] while validity litigation is reserved to the courts of the Member State concerned. It is the resulting fragmentation of patent litigation in Europe, and the desire to establish unified protection in the Member States, that gave rise to the Unitary Patent Package. The system includes Regulation 1257/2012 establishing a possible unitary effect for the European patent, Regulation 1260/2012 settling the question of translations of the European patent with unitary effect, the UPCA creating the UPC and containing the protection regime for this patent and the "standard" European patent, and finally

---

[1] Convention for the Protection of Human Rights and Fundamental Freedoms (European Convention on Human Rights, as amended) (ECHR).
[2] Case C-146/13 *Spain v Parliament and Council* EU:C:2015:298.
[3] Regulation (EU) 1215/2012 of the European Parliament and of the Council of 12 December 2012 on jurisdiction and the recognition and enforcement of judgments in civil and commercial matters [2012] OJ L351/1.

Fernand de Visscher, is partner, Simont Braun, Brussels, and Scientific associate CRIDES (UCLouvain).

https://doi.org/10.1515/9783110781687-014

Regulation 542/2014 adapting the above-mentioned Regulation 1215/2012 because of the court thus created. The UPP does not include measures for the harmonisation of national patent laws. The shortcomings and complications caused by this reform are the subject of numerous critical studies[4].

14.1 Regulation 1257/2012

1.1 Regulation 1257/2012 gives the possibility to confer a unitary effect to a European patent if this effect, upon request, is registered by the *EPO* and provided that this patent has the same claims for all participating Member States. This unitary *effect* means a unitary *character* and a *uniform protection*, the consequences of which are governed by this Regulation (and the UPCA).

Contrary to what is often written, it is not a unitary patent in the sense that it would be a title of Union law (as is, for example, the European Union trade mark), i.e. a legal title whose existence finds its source in the law of the Union itself or which, at the very least, would be integrated into that law. The European patent with unitary effect is first of all a European patent, a title under international law since it was created by an international treaty (the EPC) and granted by an international institution (EPO). Just as the European patent is not comparable to a national patent but constitutes a title under international law[5] whose effects are governed in each country by "incorporation by reference" of certain national legal provisions, the European patent with unitary effect, while remaining an international title, has uniform effects defined by Regulation 1257/2012 (Articles 5 and 7) and, by implicit and necessary reference, by the UPCA (Articles 25 to 29 and 62 to 72)[6]. Only these uniform effects, i.e. the "unitary effect" and certain[7] of its components, fall

---

4 See in particular the very long survey already carried out in 2014 by Vincenzo Di Cataldo, 'Competition (or confusion?) of models and coexistence of rules from different sources in the European patent with unitary effect. Is there a reasonable alternative?' in Costanza Honorati (ed), *Luci e ombre del nuovo Sistema UE di tutela brevettuale – The EU patent Protection – Lights and shades of the New System* (G. Giappichelli Editore 2014) 27 footnote 1; Nicolas Binctin, Romain David Bourdon, Matthieu Dhenne, Lionel Vial, 'Feedback on the Intellectual Property Action Plan Roadmap of the European Commission' (2020) Institut Stanislas De Boufflers <https://shs.hal.science/halshs-02970368/document> accessed 6 December 2022, 18; the studies cited in the November 2020 working paper of the CRIDES research centre (UCLouvain) (https://cdn.uclouvain.be/groups/cms-editors-crides/intellectual-rights/Prel%20%20Research%20Working%20Doc%20%28updated%207%20dec%2020%29.pdf); see also Alain Strowel, Fernand de Visscher, Vincent Cassiers and Luc Desaunettes (eds.), *The Unitary Patent Package and the Unified Patent Court – Problems, Possible Improvements and Alternatives* (Ledizioni 2023) (forthcoming).
5 Winfried Tilmann, 'Introduction to this Commentary' in Winfried Tilmann and Clemens Plassmann (eds), *Unified Patent Protection in Europe – A Commentary* (OUP 2018) 20–24, paras 74–88.
6 In this sense: Winfried Tilmann, 'The UPC Agreement and the Unitary Regulation – construction and application' (2016) Journal of Intellectual Property Law & Practice 545, 2.
7 And not all of them, since it is the UPCA alone which contains the concrete rules of protection attached to the unitary patent (Regulation (EU) 1257/2012 of the European Parliament and of the Council of 17 De-

under EU law. But its primary nature, that of being a legal title under international law, does not change: in addition to the title itself, various provisions of Regulation 1257/2012 confirm the "incidental" nature of the unitary effect "attributed after the grant of the European patent" (recital 7) on request[8] to the granted European patent, but which will be deemed not to have existed insofar as the European patent will have been revoked or limited (Art. 3 (3)). This reference to opposition and limitation procedures before the EPO clearly indicates that, like a European patent for a particular EPC State, the European patent with unitary effect in the UPCA States retains its original international nature. If the national court or the UPC can revoke the title for the national territory concerned or the UPCA territory, it is because Article 138 EPC authorises this[9] and within the limits of this authorisation. The mandatory retroactive nature of the recording of unitary effect (Articles 4 and 9(1)(g) of the Regulation) also indicates that the European patent is not intrinsically affected by this recording[10]: after having been given national effect for a few days in either country, it is now given unitary effect in the UPCA territory and will only be "deemed" not to have taken effect according to the national law[11].

1.2 The content of Regulation 1257/2012 then raises the question of whether this Regulation, which thus establishes a unitary effect for an intellectual property right of an international nature, complies with the Treaty on the Functioning of the European Union (TFEU) and in particular with Article 118 (1)[12], which it relies on[13].

This article reads as follows: *"In the context of the establishment and functioning of the internal market, the European Parliament and the Council, acting in accordance with*

---

cember 2012 implementing enhanced cooperation in the area of the creation of unitary patent protection [2012] OJ L361/1, arts 25 to 29).

8 Which may be subsequent to the grant of the European patent, but must be filed within one month of the publication of the mention of the grant (Reg (EU) 1257/2012 of the European Parliament and of the Council of 17 December 2012 implementing enhanced cooperation in the area of the creation of unitary patent protection [2012] OJ L361/1, art 9 (1) (g)).

9 Like a national law, Article 65 (2) of the *UPCA* regulates the revocation of the unitary (or "standard" European non-opted out) patent. But, as we know, the UPCA is not Union law.

10 In this sense: Winfried Tilmann, 'Art. 4 EPUE Reg' in Winfried Tilmann and Clemens Plassmann (eds), *Unified Patent Protection in Europe – A Commentary* (OUP 2018) 126–127, para 3. Defending the international nature of the European patent with unitary effect like that of the earlier European patent, and recalling in this respect the error of considering the European patent as a "bundle of national patents" in the strict sense, the author comes to consider Article 4 (2) as superfluous and criticises the wording "as a national patent" in this provision (127–128, paras 5 to 10).

11 To the extent incompatible with the provisions of the Regulation and the UPCA (ibid para 9).

12 Consolidated version of the Treaty on the Functioning of the European Union [2016] OJ C202/1 (TFEU). Art 118(2) on translations, which Regulation 1260/2012 intends to apply, is omitted here; this study does not deal with this aspect of the Unitary Patent Package.

13 It should be noted that in the language versions we understand, except for the German version, recital 2 of Regulation 1257/2012 incorrectly reflects the exact content of Article 118 (1) TFEU since it presents it as aiming at "the creation of uniform patent protection throughout the Union".

the ordinary legislative procedure, shall establish measures for the creation of European intellectual property rights to provide uniform protection of intellectual property rights throughout the Union and for the setting up of centralised Union-wide authorisation, coordination and supervision arrangements."

If words still have meaning and if a text of a constitutional nature in the European Union is to be interpreted without offending the common meaning of the terms in which it is approved by the parliamentarians of various countries, it is difficult to deny that "creation" refers to the act of bringing into existence, of drawing out of nothing, what did not previously exist or, at the very least, of bringing into existence or entering into a legal order different from the one in which it began to exist. Moreover, everything indicates that by "European titles" the authors of the TFEU meant titles *of Union law* such as were already known at the time (the best known being the then Community trade mark and the Community design).

Since Article 118(1) TFEU provides for uniform protection as the *result* to be achieved *by the creation of European* intellectual property *rights*, it is doubtful whether Regulation 1257/2012 complies with this provision of the Treaty[14] by establishing[15] uniform protection, but without *creating* a *European* title from which this protection derives.

Indeed, for a legal order such as Union law, to create a title of protection, a new subjective right appearing in this legal order, means at least, if not to draw this title "from nothing", to make it exist within said legal order, to appropriate it from another legal order, to take hold of it in order to define at least the object, the conditions of validity and the content of the prerogatives that derive from the title. It must itself define these rules, if necessary by copying or appropriating them – be it largely – from one or more other legal orders.

However, in this case, Union law does not do this: Regulation 1257/2012 merely gives unitary effect to a title of protection which will always be intrinsically governed by international law[16]. It certainly refers to national law (Art. 5(3) and 7) and thus to the UPCA to define the content *of the uniform protection*[17], but it does not define in its own text[18]

---

14 And/or the decision establishing enhanced cooperation, which "must establish measures for the creation of a European intellectual property rights to provide uniform protection of intellectual property rights" (Case C-274/11 and C-295/11 *Spain and Italy v Council* EU:C:2013:240, para 67; see also para 92).
15 Indirectly, moreover, through the reference to a national law and thus to the *UPCA*. But this aspect does not affect the core of the question itself.
16 See in the same sense, Manuel Desantes Real, 'Le "paquet européen des brevets", paradigme du chemin à rebours: De la logique institutionnelle à la logique intergouvernementale' (2013) Cahiers de droit européen 577, paras 72 and 78.
17 This was admitted by the Court of Justice in its judgment of 5 May 2015 (n2), but outside the specific question of the *creation of a* Union law *title*.
18 The reference to the UPCA in the recitals of the Regulation seems to us insufficient to constitute an endorsement of or even an "incorporation by reference" to that agreement as regards the conditions of validity, a matter which the Regulation nowhere contemplates *as such*. It only states that unitary character

the conditions of *validity* of this title, this question being governed exclusively by Article 65 of the UPCA, a text of international law. Can we say that a legal order creates a legal title within itself, for which it defines neither the conditions of validity nor the sanction for failure to comply with them?

Admittedly, Article 118 is a competence shared between the Union and the Member States (Article 4(2)(a) TFEU). However, when a particular provision of the Treaty specifies how the Union legislator is to act in the field in question and to achieve a certain result, is that legislator not required to act strictly in accordance with that provision? The question is permissible under Articles 5(1), 5(2) and 13(2) TEU (limited conferral of powers on the Union and on each of its institutions).

Wouldn't the regulation find its salvation in Article 114 TFEU as a measure for harmonising national legislation? However, on the one hand, the opinion of the Economic and Social Committee, required by Article 114 (1), has not been requested. On the other hand, in the TFEU chapter devoted to the approximation of legislation, Article 118 (1) appears as a *lex specialis*. While this article does not prevent recourse to Article 114 TFEU to "approximate" national laws on intellectual property[19], something else is to "provide uniform protection throughout the Union"[20], which goes further than an "approximation" of national laws when considering the territory covered and the required "uniform" nature of the protection. For this result, which is purportedly achieved by Articles 5(3) and 7 of Regulation 1257/2012, Article 118(1) requires the creation of a European IP right. Moreover, the content of the protection is not concretely defined by Regulation 1257/2012 itself but by the UPCA, while this international treaty thus concluded outside Union law can hardly be qualified as "measures adopted" by the European Parliament (and the Council) within the meaning of Article 114 TFEU.

1.3 However, it would have been possible for EU law to appropriate the European patent, once granted by the EPO, to make it a legal title under its own legal order (EU law). This is reflected in the 2009 draft.

---

means that, to the extent of a revocation or limitation, which certainly covers opposition and limitation before the EPO, the unitary effect is deemed not to have existed (Reg (EU) 1257/2012 of the European Parliament and of the Council of 17 December 2012 implementing enhanced cooperation in the area of the creation of unitary patent protection [2012] OJ L361/1, art 3(3)). But this is only a *consequence* of revocation or limitation, without regulating them, which is left to the EPC and UPCA as to the rules governing them; the substantive issue is governed by Article 65 UPCA.
19 Dominik Eisenhut and Daniel-Erasmus Khan, 'Article 118 TFEU', in Rudolf Geiger, Daniel-Erasmus Khan and Markuys Kotzur (eds), *European Union Treaties – A Commentary* (CH Beck Verlag-Hart 2015) 570, para 6.
20 TFEU, art 118(1).

In November 2009, the Council Presidency submitted a revised version[21] of the Commission's August 2000 proposal for a Regulation on the Community patent[22]. Adopting the terminology "European Union" under the Lisbon Treaty and referring to Article 118 TFEU introduced by that Treaty, this revised proposal provided[23] that the EU Patent is a European patent designating the European Union, granted by the EPO and that this patent has a unitary character, not just effect. This unitary character went very far. According to this text, the EU patent has an autonomous character in that it is only subject to the (draft) regulation and to the general principles of European Union law, the EPC only playing a complementary role on a subsidiary basis (Article 2 of the proposal). The EU patent thus proposed was indeed a title of EU law: the Regulation itself, and it alone, was to govern in particular the grounds for revocation[24] and the limitation of this patent.

It was, therefore, not because it was unlikely to introduce a new authority and procedure for issuing the title of protection when the EPO already fulfils this role, that it was permissible or obligatory to dispense with the inclusion of this title as such in Union law[25].

1.4 This abstention from creating a title of Union law ("the EU patent") is not the result of chance or an oversight. The aim was to limit the influence of Union law as much as possible, above all in order to exclude the intervention of the Union legislator, and thus of the Court of Justice[26], by placing the concrete rules of validity in international law (EPC and UPCA), as was done in the end for the concrete rules of protection (UPCA).

---

21 Council of the European Union, 'Addendum to the note. Proposal for a Council Regulation on the Community patent – General approach' (2009) 16113/09 ADD 1 (27 November 2009) (see in particular arts 7 to 13a, 28 and 29a).
22 Commission, 'Proposal for a Council Regulation on the Community patent' COM (2000) 412 final.
23 like in the previous revision contained in Council of the European Union, 'Working document. Revised proposal for a Council Regulation on the Community patent' (2009) 8588/09 PI 28 (submitted to the Court of Justice for Opinion 1/09 of 8 March 2011, discussed below) (arts 7 to 13, 28 and 29a).
24 The same was true of all previous texts: Council Convention for the European Patent for the Common Market (Community Patent Convention)(15 December 1975) [1976] OJ L17/1, art 57; Council Agreement relating to Community patents (15 December 1989) [1989] OJ L401/1, art 56; Commission, 'Proposal for a Council Regulation on the Community patent' COM (2000) 412 final, art 28.
25 *Contra*: Tilmann, 'Introduction to this Commentary' (n 5) 37, para 137.
26 See in particular Franklin Dehousse, *'The Unified Court on Patents: the New Oxymoron of European Law'* (2013) Egmont – The Royal Institute for International Relations Paper 60 <http://www.egmontinstitute.be/content/uploads/2013/10/ep60.pdf?type=pdf> accessed 7 December 2022; report of 13 November 2013 by M. Berthou to the Senate (No. 141, ordinary session 2013–2014) in France, p. 26.

Neither Regulation 1257/2012 nor the national laws governing the European patent change the international nature of this title of protection and it is therefore legitimate to object[27] that it has therefore not created the title of protection as provided for by Article 118 (1) TFEU[28].

1.5 This precise question does not seem to us to have been decided by the judgment of 5 May 2015 of the Court of Justice[29]. Spain's complaint under Article 118 (1) TFEU was essentially that Regulation 1257/2012 did not itself define either the acts against which the European patent with unitary effect provides uniform protection, and the applicable limitations, as these acts and limitations either are governed by national law (and, consequently, by the UPCA). The failure of the Regulation to *create* a *European title* was neither submitted nor discussed. The reasoning of the judgment[30] focuses on the uniform protection sought by the Regulation, which the Court considers to be satisfied by the reference to a national law (and to the UPCA[31]), but it does not address the question of the creation of a IP right under Union law in the light of Article 118 (1) TFEU, nor in particular the international (and therefore neither national nor Union law) nature of the rules governing the validity of the patent with unitary effect.

The Court notes that Regulation 1257/2012 *"is in no way intended to delimit, even partially, the conditions for granting European patents — which are exclusively governed by the EPC and not by EU law"* and that, therefore, *"it merely establishes"* the conditions for unitary effect and *"provides a definition"* of that effect[32]. It further observes that the Regulation thus also does not incorporate the procedure for granting the European patent into Union law. These reasons taken together confirm our analysis of the strictly international nature of the European patent with unitary effect as a protection title. However, in the absence of a complaint (which Spain could have raised) on this point,

---

27 As the Max Planck Institute had already pointed out (Reto M. Hilty, Thomas Jaeger, Matthias Lamping and Hanns Ullrich, 'The Unitary Patent Package: Twelve Reasons for Concern' [2012] Max Planck Institute for Intellectual Property and Competition Law Research Paper <https://ssrn.com/abstract=2169254> accessed 7 December 2022, points 9a and 10a).
28 A similar question has been raised about the requirement in Article 118(1) to establish authorisation, coordination and control regimes "centralised *at Union level*" (or more precisely: of the Member States participating in enhanced cooperation), which seems to imply that the application of these regimes should be controlled by a body or court belonging to the Union itself.
29 *Spain v Parliament and Council* (n 2).
30 *Spain v Parliament and Council* (n 2), paras 39 to 53.
31 Implicitly but definitely, in paragraph 50 of its judgment, the Court of Justice recognised that the uniformity of protection does not derive from the reference to national law alone (Reg (EU) 1257/2012 arts 5(3) and 7) but from the UPCA (see our study 'Unitary Patent Package & Unified Patent Court: a (fragile) progress of the European Union?' [2022] Revue de droit intellectuel – L'Ingénieur-Conseil – ICIP 2022, 523–541, 532–534).
32 *Spain v Parliament and Council* (n 2), paras 30 and 31.

no consequences are drawn from this finding with regard to the requirement of Article 118 (1) TFEU to create a European IP right.

It is also true that the CJEU has ruled that Article 118 "does *not necessarily require the EU legislature to harmonise completely and exhaustively all aspects of intellectual property law*"[33]. But this statement is part of the discussion of the uniform protection that the patent should provide. It does not concern either the issue of the patent belonging to the Union's own autonomous legal system and the conditions of validity and therefore of revocation of the title either, conditions whose complete absence in the Regulation is, in our opinion, an obstacle to a genuine integration into Union law. In this respect, it should be remembered that while this Regulation refers to national law (and hence to the UPCA) for the content of the uniform protection, it says nothing (not even by reference) about the *conditions* of validity and therefore the *grounds for* revocation. It is only in the UPCA (Art. 65), a text of international law, that the question is regulated.

The judgments of the CJEU have a *res judicata* limited to the grounds for annulment put forward by the applicant[34] and one cannot exclude the difficulty may come to the Court upon a preliminary question of validity[35].

1.6 A further question about Regulation 1257/2012 would certainly merit further consideration. By referring to national law and thus to the UPCA, the regulation intends to define the concrete content of the uniform protection[36].

On the one hand, however, at the time of the adoption of the Regulation in December 2012, the UPCA was still only a draft and the European Parliament was not called upon to examine it. It is therefore questionable whether the assent of the European Parliament itself, as required by Article 118 (1) TFEU to ensure "uniform protection" in the territory covered, was actually obtained.[37]

On the other hand, when, after the adoption of the regulation, the agreement was signed on 19 February 2013, the dominant discourse was to present its ratification to national parliaments as intimately linked to the already adopted regulations 1257/2012 and 1260/2012 and therefore without suggesting any debate either in principle or in detail[38],

---

[33] *Spain v Parliament and Council* (n 2), para 48.
[34] Melchior Wathelet and Jonathan Wildemeersch, *Contentieux européen* (2nd edn, Larcier 2014) 212–220, paras 189–195, 285, para 230, 464, para 378; Koen Lenaerts, Dirk Arts and Ignace Maselis, *Procedural Law of the European Union* (2nd edn, Sweet & Maxwell 2006) 323, paras 7–179.
[35] TFEU, art 267(1)(b).
[36] The Regulation is linked to the UPCA in other respects than the concrete protection attached to the patent, but our point here is limited to reminding of the economic and social consequences of the protection for questioning the absence of real parliamentary debates on them.
[37] However, the statement by the Court (n 33) could read as supporting the view to the contrary.
[38] See e.g. in France the above-mentioned report by Mr Berthou to the Senate(n26); in the Netherlands, document 34.411, No. 3 (*Tweede Kamer*, session 2015–2016), *Memorie van toelichting*, p. 6, *sub* 2.5, p. 22 *sub* 4 *in limine*, and pp. 34–35, *sub* 12). Recital 25 of the regulation could suggest such approach.

and even, according to some, as part of the participating Member States' obligation of sincere cooperation[39].

Can we then consider that democracy has been respected in practice in the sense of this value expressly enshrined in Article 2 of the Treaty on European Union (TEU)? The legal consequences of this singular course with regard to this value are, however, not easy to determine[40].

14.2 The UPCA

2.1 The legality of the UPCA was not examined by the judgment of 5 May 2015: Spain's two objections to the UPCA as such were held to be inadmissible since, in the frame of Article 263 TFEU, the Court has no jurisdiction to rule on the legality of an international agreement between Member States[41]. A debate therefore remains possible.

2.2 As is well known, certain features of the UPC are intended to respond to the criticisms of the CJEU in its Opinion 1/09 of 8 March 2011[42] against the Council's proposal for a European Patent Court and a European Union patent. Does the UPCA meet these criticisms?

We are among those who doubt a positive answer, especially in view of the Court's insistence on the exclusive role of the Court of Justice and the national courts in the Union's judicial system for the respect and autonomy of Union law, so that these national courts cannot be deprived of their right (or obligation) to refer for a preliminary ruling in respect of that law.

The response to these criticisms was to denominate the UPC as a court common to the States concerned and to lay down various rules recalling Article 267 TFEU and providing for the consequences of its violation. The precedent of the Benelux Court, mentioned by the Court in its opinion, was all the more timely as the Benelux Court, by an amending treaty of 15 October 2012, had just been reformed to give it jurisdiction to rule on appeals against decisions of the Benelux Office, in addition to the jurisdiction of interpretation that it has always held in respect of treaties and other texts common to the Benelux States. The identity of treatment seems to be self-evident and the above-men-

---

39 *Spain v Parliament and Council* (n 2), Opinion of AG Bot, paras 172–180. However, this statement was not repeated by the Court in its judgment (paras 104–107).
40 See recently and more generally on Article 2 TEU: Tom Boekestein, 'Making do with what we have: On the Interpretation and Enforcement of EU's Founding Values' [2022] German Law Journal (forthcoming) (ssrn 394795-3); Lucia Serena Rossi, 'La valeur juridique des valeurs. L'article 2 TUE: relations avec d'autres dispositions de droit primaire de l'UE et remèdes juridictionnels' (2020) 3 Rev. Trim. Dr. européen 639, 639, (ssrn 365-4069).
41 *Spain v Parliament and Council* (n 2), paras 100–103.
42 Opinion 1/09 (ECLI:EU:C:2011:123) [2011] ECR I-01137.

tioned Regulation 542/2014 puts the Benelux Court and the UPC on the same footing as 'common courts'.

But is it sufficient to name a court as common to the Member States for it to be regarded as, or to be assimilated to, a national court within the meaning of Article 19 (1) (2) TEU and Article 267 TFEU, whereas only the national courts and the Court of Justice are guarantors of the unity, coherence and autonomy of Union law? The obligation to apply Article 267 TFEU and the detailed consequences of non-compliance with it[43] certainly do not seem to be sufficient, as these are only *consequences* related to the *intended* nature of the court. It is not certain that these rules are sufficient to confer the nature of a national court (in the sense required by the above-mentioned provisions of the treaties) on a court which, intrinsically, is not one, being created by an international treaty. The draft agreement submitted to the CJEU included an Article 48 providing for preliminary rulings by the then envisaged Patent Court; the CJEU nevertheless rejected "an international court which lies outside the institutional and jurisdictional framework of the Union"[44].

It is true that the UPC can be considered common from a *functional point of view*, since it is entrusted by the States concerned with the performance of functions which, in its absence, would be carried out by them.[45] But is this common functional character sufficient?

In its *Miles* judgment, the Court of Justice made it clear that functional links are not sufficient if it is an international institution separate from the Union and the Member States.[46]

This is where the comparison with the Benelux Court and the assimilation of the UPC to it are no longer correct: at the *institutional level*, an essential difference must be noted which, to our knowledge, has been little noticed by the doctrine. The Benelux Court has always been composed exclusively of national judges: its judges "*are chosen from among the members of the Supreme Court of each of the three countries*" and, since the 2012 protocol, from among the members of the appeal courts of the three countries. And these judges have always been "*part of the Benelux Court as long as they are effectively in office in their country*".[47] The Benelux Court is therefore common to the three Benelux Member States not only because it performs judicial functions previously performed by each of these States (appeals against decisions of the Benelux Office) which

---

43 UPCA, arts 20–23.
44 Opinion 1/09 (n 42), paras 12, 71, 82 and 89.
45 Winfried Tilmann, 'Agreement on a Unified patent Court' in Winfried Tilmann and Clemens Plassmann (eds), Unified Patent Protection in Europe – A Commentary (OUP 2018) 335, para 45.
46 Case C-196-09 *Paul Miles and Others v Ecoles européennes* [2011] EU:C:2011:388, paras 40–42.
47 Treaty on the Establishment and Status of a Benelux Court of Justice, signed in Brussels on 25 October 1966 (*Moniteur belge* of 11 December 1973, p. 14.062), Articles 3.1 and 3.2. The last amending protocol to this treaty, signed on 15 October 2012 (*Moniteur belge* of 21 November 2016, p. 77.220), extending the competences of the Benelux Court, did not change the substance of these rules.

now entrust them to it, but also because it is composed of magistrates previously appointed as judges in each State in accordance with the applicable internal legal process and who remain in office in their respective States. It is thus truly this place where national judges exercise jurisdiction jointly, which makes it "common" in a way that is quite different from the merely functional attribution of jurisdiction by several States.

The UPCA makes no provision for the UPC to emanate from national courts in the same way as the Benelux Court. The judges of the UPC are appointed independently of any previous or concurrent judicial functions at national level. The international character of their function, like that of the UPCA itself which establishes them, is also marked by the process of their appointment, which is not made by 'ministers' as in the case of the Benelux Court (which underlines the latter's link with national institutions and political responsibilities) but by an administrative committee made up of representatives of the States concerned, a typically international formula.

2.3 The question therefore remains whether the UPC can indeed be regarded as a court or tribunal as referred to in Article 19 (1) (2) TEU and Article 267 TFEU. This is very doubtful, not only in the light of Opinion 1/09 but also of numerous previous and subsequent judgments and opinions of the Court of Justice[48], including the *Achmea* judgment[49]. The consequence, if the UPC does not meet the requirements of these treaty provisions, is not only that it is not entitled to refer questions to the CJEU for a preliminary ruling, but that the entire UPCA is unlawful as contrary to the Union's judicial system.

2.4 A second question that arises from the UPCA is whether the UPC can be described as a 'court established by law' and 'independent' in the sense required by Article 6 of the European Convention on Human Rights and Article 47 of the Charter of Fundamental Rights of the European Union. There are several question marks[50].

---

48 See the summary in Thomas Jaeger, 'Delayed Again? The Benelux Alternative to the UPC' [2021] GRUR Int. 1133, parts II and III.1. See also in this respect the judgement of 26 October 2021, Case C-109/20 *Republiken Polen v PL Holdings Sàrl* [2021] OJ C2/6, para 45 and the judgement of 27 February 2018, Case C-64/16 *Associação Sindical dos Juízes Portugueses v Tribunal de Contas* [2018] EU:C:2018:117, paras 29 and 32–34.
49 Case C-284/16 *Slowakische Republik v Achmea BV* [2018] EU:C:2018:158, paras 43–59, especially para 45 (which needs only be adapted *mutatis mutandis* in its second sentence to confirm our doubt that the UPC can constitute a jurisdictional element of the Member States) and paras 57–58. The exception discussed in favour of the Benelux Court (paras 47–48) does not yet take into account the new powers of this court since 2012, but this does impair neither the second consideration in para 48 (which remains relevant in view of the links of these new powers with the administrative procedures of the Benelux Office) nor the observation made above, in relation to the *Miles* judgment, on the requirement of an institutional link of the court with the legislation of a Member State (see also para 44 of the *Achmea* judgment in this respect). As is well known, the *Achmea* judgment has been largely upheld in subsequent cases.
50 See the contribution by Mathieu Leloup and Sébastien Van Drooghenbroeck, 'Unified Patent Court and the Right to a Fair Trial – Some Critical Remarks' in Alain Strowel, Fernand de Visscher, Vincent Cassiers and Luc Desaunettes (eds), *The Unitary Patent Package and the Unified Patent Court – Problems, Pos-*

UPC judges are appointed by the Administrative Committee, which is composed of one "representative" of each Contracting Member State (Art. 12.1. UPCA). But nothing is specified in this respect, and it is in any case not foreseen that this should be a minister or other person with political responsibility or democratic legitimacy. The difference with the Benelux Court, whose magistrates are appointed by the three ministers of the countries concerned, should be noted in this respect; it also underlines the distance, as mentioned above, between the UPC and the national institutions of the Member States.

Moreover, if the Administrative Committee appoints judges from a list presented by the Advisory Committee, it should be noted that the latter is appointed by the Administrative Committee itself (art. 5(2) of the UPC Statute). It is therefore questionable whether the process of appointing judges is sufficiently objective.

The power of the Administrative Committee to create and, above all, to abolish a local or regional division of the UPC is also questionable, since a court must be established by the legislator itself and cannot depend on an authority other than the legislator for its existence.

In general, the powers of the Administrative Committee are considerable: among them, we especially question the power to set the rules of procedure[51], which should, in our opinion, be the responsibility of the legislator itself (the UPCA agreement, and thus of national parliaments) rather than of a body of an administrative nature and which, in the absence of any further clarification of its composition and its links with national democratic institutions, has no democratic legitimacy or political responsibility.

When one also notes that the Administrative Committee sets the budget (supposed to be *self-sufficient*) and decides on the remuneration of the judges, there is complete doubt as to whether the requirement that a court be established by law and independent is respected.

14.3 What about the Court of Justice?

3.1 It is of course impossible to conclude the discussion on the "constitutional" aspects of the *Unitary Patent Package* without mentioning the role that the CJEU will play. The

---

sible Improvements and Alternatives (Ledizioni 2023) (forthcoming). The following reflections are largely inspired by this detailed study. We will only mention the main aspects that raise our questions among those raised by these authors. Article 47 of the Charter is linked to Article 19, paragraph 1er , subparagraph 2 TEU: Case C-896/19 *Repubblika v Il-Prim Ministru* OJ C228/7; Cases C-585/18, C-624/18, C-625/18 *A. K. And Others v Sąd Najwyższy, CP v Sąd Najwyższy and DO v Sąd Najwyższy* [2019] EU:C:2019:982.

51 It is true that many procedural rules can be taken from the UPCA, but some of them (e.g. third party intervention: rr 313–317) are not provided for in the UPCA and even appear to be contrary to it (e.g. Rule 317 prohibits appeal in this respect, whereas the UPCA provides for appeal without exception: UPCA, art 73(1)(b)(i)).

CJEU will have to tell us, upon preliminary questions on interpretation or validity to be raised by the UPC or by a national judge or even upon a possible action for failure to fulfil an obligation under the treaties brought by a Member State against another Member State[52], what we should think of the serious doubts that still seem to weigh on Regulation 1257/2012 and the UPCA. While the objective pursued by the UPP remains laudable overall, the construction seems no less fragile and its results, in any case, highly contested. If this construction should break down, there are alternative solutions already suggested by the doctrine[53], including a scheme fairly close to that of the European Union trade mark, and another which inserts the UPC as a specialised court in the Court of Justice of the European Union[54].

3.2 What will be the role of the Court of Justice if the *Unitary Patent Package* is immune from doubts of legality, and in particular from those we have seen remain?

Its competence to give preliminary rulings will extend to all primary and secondary law of the Union[55]: this general formula conceals some difficulties to be mentioned here with regard to patent law and in particular that of patents covered by the UPCA.

In the absence of harmonisation of national patent laws, one of the shortcomings of the *Unitary Patent Package*, the Court of Justice will obviously not play the same role of unifying interpreter as it does in the field of trade marks, design and plant varieties, in addition to its role as an administrative appeal body for the grant and revocation of these titles of protection by the specialised agencies of the Union (EUIPO, CPVO). As regards national patents, its power of unification by interpretation will be limited to general provisions of EU law (e.g. Directive 2004/48) or to certain specific regulations (Biotech Directive, supplementary protection certificates)[56].

While the competence to interpret obviously relates to Regulations 1257/2012[57], 1260/2012 and 542/2012 as such, what about the provisions of the EPC and UPCA, and thus the "classical" European patents (the "opted-out" and the "non-opted-out") and the European patents with unitary effect?

---

52 Art. 259 TFEU.
53 See the contributions of Thomas Jaeger, Vincent Cassiers, Fernand de Visscher and Annette Kur in in Alain Strowel, Fernand de Visscher, Vincent Cassiers and Luc Desaunettes (eds), *The Unitary Patent Package and the Unified Patent Court – Problems, Possible Improvements and Alternatives* (Ledizioni 2023) (forthcoming).
54 See our contribution in the above-mentioned forthcoming book and the commentary by Annette Kur.
55 Excluding national law: see in particular Case C-60/17 *Ángel Somoza Hermo and Ilunión Seguridad SA v Esabe Vigilancia SA and Fondo de Garantia Salarial (Fogasa)* [2018] EU:C:2018:559, para 44.
56 Hanns Ullrich, 'EuGH und EPG im europäischen Patentschutzsystem: Wer hat was zu sagen? – Versuch einer Standortbestimmung' [2016] Max Planck Institute for Innovation and Competition Discussion Paper No. 8 <https://ssrn.com/abstract=2942199> accessed 7 December 2022, 13–14 and 17–19.
57 In particular with regard to the individual decisions to be taken by the EPO to register or not the requested unitary effect.

The European Union is not a party to either the EPC or the UPCA. As a result, in our view, the Court of Justice has no power of *interpretation with* regard to these international treaties. Indeed, if an international treaty to which the European Union is a party becomes part of Union law with the consequence that the Court of Justice has jurisdiction to interpret it[58], its interpretative jurisdiction does not exist with regard to international agreements concluded by Member States only, even those concluded between them to cooperate in the implementation of a directive[59].

It is true that the Court's lack of jurisdiction ceases in the case of an agreement between Member States and third countries when the Union has assumed the competences previously exercised by the Member States in the field of application of that agreement and that, as a result, the agreement is binding on the Union[60]. However, this is not the case here. On the one hand, not all Member States[61] are bound by the UPCA, so that the Union itself does not appear to be bound by this agreement[62], at least initially. On the other hand, and more fundamentally, as the matter is one of shared competence and the Union has not exercised its shared competence in the matters specifically governed by the EPC and the UPCA, it can hardly be argued that the Union has assumed the competences of the Member States in respect of them, moreover while, under the terms of Regulation 1257/2012 itself, these two international agreements are provided for and recognised as subsisting on their own.[63]

It follows that the Court of Justice should decline jurisdiction to *interpret* the EPC and the UPCA.

Moreover, it seems excluded that the UPC would have the possibility to submit questions of interpretation of the EPC to the Court of Justice if one accepts that the validity of the European patent with unitary effect is in no way governed by Regulation 1257/2012

---

58 Case C-741/19 *Moldava v Komstroy LLC* [2021] OJ C431/21, para 23.
59 Case C-162/98 *Generalstaatsanwaltschaft and Others v Hartmann* [1998] ECR I-07083, paras 9–12. According to the *Hurd* judgment of 15 January 1986 (Case C-44/84 *Hurd v Jones* [1986] ECR I-00029), the links between an international agreement with the Community and the functioning of its institutions are not sufficient to consider it as part of Community law (paras 20, 31 and 37–38). This lack of *interpretative* jurisdiction does not, of course, prevent the Court from *reviewing compliance with* Union law by an agreement between Member States (Case C-370/12 *Thomas Pringle v Government of Ireland and Others* [2012] EU:C:2012:756 and Case C-44/84 *Hurd v Jones* [1986] ECR I-00029).
60 Case C-533/08 *TNT Express Nederland BV v AXA Versicherung AG* [2010] ECR I-04107, paras 59–62.
61 Not even all those who participate in the enhanced cooperation, for example Poland, which has not signed the UPCA and does not seem to be willing to do so.
62 Case C-135/10 *Società Consortile Fonografici (SCF) v Marco Del Corso* [2012] EU:C:2012:140, para 41.
63 Even if all Member States are parties to an international convention, this is not sufficient to bind the Union "in the absence of a full transfer of the powers previously exercised by the Member States to [the European Union]" (Case C-308/06 *The Queen, on the application of International Association of Independent Tanker Owners (Intertanko) and Others v Secretary of State for Transport* [2008] ECR I-04057, para 49). Such a transfer was neither expressed in Regulation 1257/2012 nor (certainly) intended by the Member States.

which clearly separates the granting of the patent from the granting of its unitary effect[64].

But this does not mean that the Court of Justice will have nothing to interpret or review in patent matters or in other matters to be applied in patent litigation.

In addition to the fairly obvious examples of primary law, Directives 2004/48 ("Enforcement"), "Biotech" (98/44)[65] and many other secondary legislation texts such as those governing supplementary protection certificates, the competence of the Court of Justice to *interpret* the TRIPs Agreement affirmed in the *Daiichi Sankyo* judgment (because this agreement falls within the exclusive external competence of the Union)[66], also opens up the prospect of a certain *control* over substantive patent law (because of the primacy of international agreements). But this control seems to have to remain marginal[67] as regards the European patent with unitary effect[68] as for the other European patents and national patents.

In the same vein, it may be thought that thanks to its competence to interpret the Charter of Fundamental Rights, the Court of Justice will have a certain control over the provisions of the UPCA because and insofar as it implements Regulation 1257/2012 and therefore Union law, and even over the provisions of the EPC if one considers that the latter is part of the Unitary Patent Package[69]. This requires further examination but it does not seem to us to be applicable where Union law is not at stake (in particular Regulation 1257/2012 which does not govern national patents of course, nor does it govern European *opted-out* and even *non-opted-out* patents, the latter being certainly subject to the UPCA but not to this Regulation).

In general, the Court of Justice will obviously have the task of monitoring UPCA's compliance with the Treaties[70].

---

64 In this sense: Ullrich, (n 56) 20–22 (in our opinion, the same should apply to European patents which the UPC will have to deal with, since their validity is governed exclusively by the EPC and the UPCA; the relevance in Union law of such a question to the Court of Justice is not apparent).
65 Even though, as far as European patents are concerned, the Biotech Directive is not applied as such by the EPO but only copied into the EPC as a norm of international law (rr 26 et seq.) (Ullrich, (n 55) 19–20).
66 Case C-414/11 *Daiichi Sankyo Co. Ltd and Sanofi-Aventis Deutschland Gmbh v DEMO Anonimos Viomikhaniki kai Emporiki Etairia Farmakon* [2013] EU:C:2013:520, paras 49–61.
67 This is due to both the nature of the TRIPS Agreement (lack of direct effect) and the rather limited concrete scope of the harmonisation it pursues. In the same sense: Tuomas Mylly, 'A Constitutional Perspective' in Justine Pila and Christopher Wadlow (eds), *The Unitary EU Patent System* (Hart Publishing 2015) 94–96.
68 Indeed, Regulation 1257/2012 itself says nothing about either the subject matter or the conditions of validity and as far as the protection is concerned, it refers to a national law and thus to the UPCA. The uniform character of the protection as set out in Article 5 of Regulation 1257/2012 does not allow to conclude that the CJEU has jurisdiction to interpret the UPCA itself: beyond this sole principle of uniformity of protection, which is Union law, the concrete rules of protection are contained only in the UPCA, an international text. The hypothesis appears even more theoretical for the EPC.
69 Mylly, (n 67) 85–91.
70 See *Thomas Pringle v Government of Ireland and Others* (n 59) and *Hurd v Jones* (n 59).

If one accepts that the UPC is to be assimilated to a national court, then, as H. Ullrich puts it, the relationship between the Court of Justice and the UPC can be compared to the judicial cooperation that is well known in the Union's judicial system. It should be a collaborative rather than a hierarchical relationship in which, while the UPC will say the law in its well-defined field of patent law, the Court of Justice will nevertheless have a very important role on general issues affecting that law, which the UPC will have to refer to it[71].

However much Union law may be involved in this dialogue, it will inevitably show the limited hold of Union law on patent matters. It will be necessary for the UPC, fully aware of its place in the Union's jurisdictional system, to ask the questions suggested not only by the express references to Union law in the UPCA but also by Union law in general. But it will also be necessary for the Union legislator to remain attentive to intervene by supplementing Union law[72] where developments of various orders will call for norms adjusting the exclusive rights attached to patents. On such initiatives targeting patent law in particular, we are not very optimistic. The *Unitary Patent Package*, by encapsulating this matter in the EPC and the UPCA respectively, suggests that Member States will be reluctant to diminish their powers (which have put the European Parliament out of the picture) over these two international treaties by agreeing, in the Council, to EU legislation when it will have the effect of amending them.

---

71 Ullrich, (n 56) 23–34.
72 Therefore, it should also be a matter of harmonising national laws in this area, which the Unitary Patent Package has not done at all.

Esther van Zimmeren

15 Trusting the Unified Patent Court: the importance of the institutional design of the UPC and its judges

15.1 Introduction

The institutional design of the European patent system will soon change significantly once the Unitary Patent Package (2012) will finally fully enter into force on 1 June 2023. The Unitary Patent Package was meant to solve some major deficits of the current European patent system, such as its complexity, its high costs (e.g. validation, translation, enforcement), legal uncertainty and the risk of forum shopping. In the new system, a new "type" of European patents will come into existence, the European patents with unitary effect (hereinafter "unitary patents"). More importantly for the current contribution, a new centralized, highly specialized patent court, the Unified Patent Court (hereinafter UPC or the court) is created.[1] The UPC is expected to improve the enforcement of patents by expeditious and high quality decisions (Art. 32(1)(i), 47(7) and 66 UPCA). According to the European Commission in particular Small- and Medium-sized Enterprises (SMEs) will presumably benefit from the Unitary Patent Package.

Despite a decade of delays towards the realization of the UPC for legal, political and technical reasons,[2] the entry into force of the UPC Agreement (UPCA) is at the moment of

---

[1] The Patent Package is a complex legal arrangement that consists of two EU regulations – one on implementing enhanced cooperation in the area of the creation of unitary patent protection (Reg. No. 1257/2012, [2012] OJEU L361/01) and another one implementing enhanced cooperation in the area of the creation of unitary patent protection with regard to the applicable translation arrangements (Reg. No. 1260/2012, [2012] OJEU L361/89) – and an international Agreement on a Unified Patent Court (UPCA) ([2013] OJEU C175/01).
[2] This chapter does not provide a detailed overview of all the different delays and the related challenges (i.e. language issues, institutional design of the UPC, seat of the court, position of the CJEU, procedures at the CJEU challenging the use of the enhanced cooperation procedure, the implications of Brexit, constitutional challenges before the German Bundesverfassungsgericht, technical issues with the CMS), as many

---

Esther van Zimmeren, is Professor in Intellectual Property Law & Governance University of Antwerp, Research Groups Government & Law and Business & Law, coordinator of the GOVTRUST Centre of Excellence of the University of Antwerp dedicated to research on dynamics, causes and effects of trust and distrust in multi-level governance, and partner in the TiGRE Horizon 2020 project on Trust in Governance and Regulation in Europe.
Acknowledgement: This paper has benefitted from interactions in the GOVTRUST consortium and the TiGRE consortium. TiGRE project has received funding from the European Union's Horizon 2020 research and innovation program under grant agreement No. 870722 (TiGRE).

https://doi.org/10.1515/9783110781687-015

finalization of this chapter foreseen for 1 June 2023.[3] Despite some technical challenges posed by the authentication for the Case Management System, all other preparatory work seems to be on track (e.g. adoption secondary legislation such as the Rules of Procedure, financial regulations, rules of operation, the appointment of judges).

The UPC will be a one-of-its-kind international court, a "legal UFO" according to some authors.[4] At many occasions it has been noted that the success of this unique court will largely depend on "public trust" or more specifically the "trust of the patent user community" in the UPC and its judges.[5] In this respect, in particular the exceptional institutional design of the UPC, but especially also the profile (i.e. expertise, experience, skills) of the UPC judges and their performance are considered very important. On 19 October 2022 the UPC confirmed the appointment of a total of 85 judges (34 legally qualified judges and 51 technically qualified judges) to take up their duties as of the entry into force of the UPCA.[6] The announcement has triggered generally quite positive and hopeful reactions from the European patent community on social media and in interviews in terms of the judges' expertise and experience.[7] This is highlighted by commentators as

---

authors have elaborated extensively on this in prior publications (see e.g. Thomas Jaeger, 'Reset and Go: The Unitary Patent System Post-Brexit' (2017), 48 *IIC*, 254–285; Matthias Lamping, 'Enhanced Cooperation in the Area of Unitary Patent Protection: Testing the Boundaries of the Rule of Law' (2013) 20 *Maastricht Journal of European and Comparative Law*, 589–600 and Hanns Ullrich, 'The European Patent and Its Courts: An Uncertain Prospect and an Unfinished Agenda' 46 *IIC*, 1–9) and in various chapters in this handbook.

3 The initial roadmap foresaw 1 January 2023 as the beginning of the so-called Sunrise Period with an entry into force of the UPCA on 1 April 2023. In December 2022 the start of the Sunrise Period was postponed for two months. The additional time was intended to allow future users to prepare themselves for the strong authentication which is required to access the Case Management System (CMS) and to sign documents. Users need to equip themselves with both a client authentication (hard device) and a qualified electronic signature.

4 See e.g. Mathieu Leloup and Sebastien Van Drooghenbroeck, 'Unified Patent Court and the Right to a Fair Trial Some Critical Remarks', in Luc Desaunettes-Barbero et al. (eds.). *The Unitary Patent Package & Unified Patent Court. Problems, Possible Improvements and Alternatives* (Ledizioni 2023) *287–306*.

5 See e.g. Clement S. Petersen & Jens Schovsbo, 'Decision-Making in the Unified Patent Court: Ensuring a Balanced Approach' in Christophe Geiger et al. (eds.), *Intellectual Property and the Judiciary* (Edward Elgar 2018); Esther van Zimmeren, 'Patent Reforms at Both Sides of the Atlantic: An Analysis of the Patent Package and the America Invents Act through the Lens of "Dynamic Patent Governance"' in Rosa M. Ballardini et al. (eds.), *Transitions in European Patent Law: Influences of the Unitary Patent Package* (Kluwer Law International 2015) 15–35; Petersen & Schovsbo, Schneider, 2014; Reto Hilty et al., 'Comments on the Preliminary Set of Provisions for the Rules of Procedure of the Unified Patent Court' (2013) Max Planck Institute for IP & Competition Law Research Paper No. 13–16.

6 The list of appointed judges is the result of an extensive selection process concluded by the adoption, by the Administrative Committee, of the list of most suitable candidate judges as proposed by the UPC's Advisory Committee. For the announcement of the news on 19 October 2022, see: https://www.unified-patent-court.org/en/news/unified-patent-court-judicial-appointments-and-presidium-elections (accessed 20 December 2022).

7 See e.g.: Amy Sandys, 'UPC divisions demonstrate clout with choice of experienced legal judges' (JUVE Patent Blog), https://www.juve-patent.com/news-and-stories/people-and-business/upc-divisions-demons

"a good move [which] creates trust".[8] Moreover, it seems that the UPC has managed to avoid the typical European political bartering among countries over proportional representation in filling the posts and prioritized quality, expertise and experience. At the same time, important concerns about the impartiality in particular of the technically qualified judges have been raised in view of their appointments on a part-time basis.[9] On the one hand, the choice for part-time appointments is understandable from a pragmatic perspective, as in the beginning it is uncertain how many cases will actually be received by the UPC and its various divisions. On the other hand, because most of them are patent attorneys in key patent firms or in industry, this has triggered major concerns about future conflicts of interest. There have been some rumors that these issues may be addressed in a Code of Conduct for UPC judges, but anyway the actual application in practice of the rules in the UPCA and the Statute will be determinant for the perception of the UPC. This controversy shows clearly how sensitive the role of the judges is in building trust in the UPC.

Interestingly, patent commentators who refer to the importance of "trust" in this context generally do not clarify what they mean by the concept of "trust", nor do they disentangle the form, causes and potential of trust with respect to such a new, unique, highly specialized international court system. One may wonder to what extent a complex psychological "interpersonal" notion such as trust can actually play a role in "interorganizational" settings (e.g. does company A (trustor; private organization) trust the UPC (trustee; judicial organization)? In addition, which factors explain whether a particular organization considers the other organization trustworthy or not and whether the trustor will actually trust the trustee? Therefore, the current chapter is aimed at exploring the complex concept of trust in the intricate institutional setting of the UPC. It identifies some common definitions, conceptualizations and models that seem helpful to better understand how assessments of trustworthiness are made and to pinpoint why UPC

---

trate-clout-with-choice-of-experienced-legal-judges/ accessed 20 December 2022 (giving a helpful overview of the affiliations and experience of many legally qualified judges). Thorsten Bausch, 'The UPC – Hopes and Headaches' (Kluwer Patent Blog, 21 October 2022), accessed 20 December 2022 (focusing on the experience and expertise of the judges, but also triggering the fundamental debate about the part-time nature of the appointments, which could especially be problematic for the technically qualified judges in view of the required impartiality). Sophie Corke, 'The UPC announces its judicial appointments and elections to the Praesidium' (The IP Kat Blog, 21 October 2022), https://ipkitten.blogspot.com/2022/10/the-upc-announces-its-judicial.html accessed 20 December 2022 (focusing in particular on the gender diversity regarding the legally qualified judges). Below I will elaborate more on the part-time nature of the appointments.
8 Mathieu Klos, 'The UPC will succeed if its part-time judges have space to grow' (JUVE Patent Blog, 31 October 2022), https://www.juve-patent.com/news-and-stories/legal-commentary/the-upc-will-succeed-if-its-part-time-judges-have-space-to-grow/ (accessed 20 December 2022).
9 Most of the 85 judges initially work part-time for the UPC, while five judges are full-time judges from the start, including Klaus Grabinski (Germany) as the President of the Court of Appeal and Florence Butin (France) as the President of the Court of First Instance, who are also members of the UPC Presidium.

judges appear to play such a predominant role in assessing the trustworthiness of the UPC as an organization.

The literature on trust within the context of European judicial governance is relatively limited.[10] Although some research exists on public trust (trust of ordinary citizens) in national and European courts and on trust between courts (e.g. CJEU and national courts), it is not so clear how trust amongst members of an expert community vis-à-vis a new highly specialized institutional setting might be build. The UPC is thus a very interesting setting to start exploring this topic. In the following sections, I start by explaining the unique structure and institutional design of the UPC. This is followed by an analysis of some key concepts, theoretical and empirical insights and an application of the so-called ABI-model from the trust literature, which I translate to the context of the UPC. This analysis is by far not-exhaustive and is limited to an overview of issues that appear relevant as a first exploration of this topic within the wider context of this handbook. This chapter concludes with some lessons learnt from the trust literature to better understand the potential trust dynamics in the UPC setting.

15.2 The one-of-its kind unique nature of the UPC

The earlier mentioned unique nature of the court has been a reason for some patent experts and others to challenge the very constitutional foundations of the court.[11] The court is unique in many different ways. First, it has a hybrid nature "floating somewhere in legal no man's land between the national and international dimensions".[12] The UPCA is an intergovernmental agreement negotiated, signed and – currently – ratified by 17 EU Member States on the basis of international law. The fact that some EU Member States are not participating for fundamental, legal, economic, political or strategic reasons or some are lagging behind due to national constitutional requirements (e.g. the need to organize a referendum) will make the already complex European patent system[13] even more multi-layered, fragmented and complex. As one of the original objectives of the Unitary Patent Package was to simplify the current system, it is clear that this objective has not been achieved.

The UPC will not be an EU institution but a court "common" to the Contracting EU Members States and thus part of their judicial systems. It will have exclusive competence with regard to unitary patents and European patents, unless proprietors or applicants of

---

10 For a literature review, see: Patricia Popelier et al., 'A research agenda for trust and distrust in a multi-level judicial system' (2022) 29 *Maastricht Journal of European and Comparative Law*, 351–374.
11 For more information, see Chapter 17.
12 Mathieu Leloup and Sebastien Van Drooghenbroeck, 'Unified Patent Court and the Right to a Fair Trial Some Critical Remarks' (2022), in Luc Desaunettes-Barbero et al. (eds.). *The Unitary Patent Package & Unified Patent Court. Problems, Possible Improvements and Alternatives* (Ledizioni 2023) *287–306.*
13 For more information, see Chapters 1, 3, 4 and 5.

European patents or holders of related supplementary protection certificates (SPCs) use the so-called opt-out option during the transitional period of seven years (Art. 83(3) UPCA).[14] In such cases, infringement actions or revocations may still be brought before the national courts. This distinctive flexibility offered by the system involves a risk for the sustainability of the institutional design; if stakeholders will make massive use of opt-outs this will likely mean that in the first years the UPC will only slowly get up to speed. At the moment of publication of this book, already more empirical information will be available on this point, but for now it is still quite uncertain and "UPC believers" and "non-believers" have widely divergent expectations as to the actual use of the opt-out mechanism which will be available from the start of the sunrise period.[15] This is quite important due to another exceptional feature of the UPC design, which is the self-financing nature of the court (Art. 36 UPCA).[16]

Second, the UPC is highly specialized, as it will only deal with patent law matters. A survey study shows that in many jurisdictions courts specialize in intellectual property law in general or their expertise is combined with other legal areas.[17] For such a highly specialized court, the risk of isolation of the paten case-law, a tunnel vision and a pro-patent bias are high.[18] The UPC Court of Appeal and to a certain extent also the CJEU will have an important supervision role to play in safeguarding the coherence, fairness, impartiality and balance of the case-law.

Third, the structure of the UPC, in particular at the first instance level is quite exceptional, hybrid and complex. The Court of First Instance will have local and regional divisions in the different Contracting Member States in line with their requests and the central division would normally have had its seat in Paris, with sections in London and Munich. The section in London has been abandoned due to the Brexit and will normally

---

14 For more information, see Chapter 4. It is noteworthy that unless an action has already been brought before a national court, proprietors of or applicants for European patents or holders of relate SPCs who made use of the opt-out in accordance with Art. 83(3) UPCA shall be entitled to withdraw their opt-out at any moment.
15 The possibility to file an opt-out will be available as of the start of the sunrise period which will begin after Germany has deposited its ratification instrument for the UPCA. This sunrise period will extend over a period of three months before the entry into force of the UPCA. The opt-out will become effective on the date of entry into force of the UPCA.
16 The budget of the UPC shall be financed by the court's own financial revenues, but it may be complemented at least in the transitional period as necessary, by contributions from the Contracting Member States (art. 36(1) UPCA).
17 International Intellectual Property Institute (IIPI) & United States Patent and Trademark Office (USPTO), Study of Specialized Intellectual Property Courts, 2012, available at http://iipi.org/wp-content/uploads/2012/05/Study-on-Specialized-IPR-Courts.pdf.
18 Rochelle C. Dreyfuss, 'The EU's Romance with Specialized Adjudication' (2016) 47 IIC, 887–890 and Federica Baldan & Esther van Zimmeren, 'The future role of the unified patent court in safeguarding coherence in the European patent system' 52 Common Market Law Rev., 1529–1577.

be replaced by a seat in Milan.[19] Moreover, some commentators have argued that the fact that the UPCA includes a reference to London is highly problematic and pragmatic solutions to establish the seat in another city may lead to fundamental legal challenges regarding its legality in the future.

Fourth, the UPCA stipulates that a Patent Mediation and Arbitration Centre is established (Art. 35 UPCA). The Centre shall provide facilities for mediation and arbitration of patent disputes falling within the scope of the UPCA. The Centre shall draw up a list of mediators and arbitrators to assist the parties in the settlement of their dispute. Even though mediation and arbitration in IP disputes is not uncommon and several national IP offices, WIPO and ICC offer such services as well, it is an important signal that the Centre is integrated in the institutional design of the UPC, which appears a less common phenomenon for international courts. This may imply that mediation and arbitration may be more strongly supported than in other international judicial settings. The judge-rapporteurs will explore with the parties the possibility for a settlement, including through mediation, and/or arbitration, by using the facilities of the Centre (Art. 52 UPCA) and their role will, hence, be crucial in advancing mediation and arbitration in the UPC context. As arbitration may be perceived as an internal "competitor" for the delicate position of the newly established UPC, in particular mediation may contribute to two other key objectives of the Unitary Patent Package, speeding up procedures and reducing the costs of litigation.

Fifth, another original feature of the UPC is the institutional design and operation of panels of the Court of First Instance and the Court of Appeal. The panels sit in a multinational composition, which is of course not uncommon for an international court. This multinational composition is combined with a multi-qualification composition; UPC judges consist of legally and technically qualified judges. Obviously, this is a characteristic which we also know from the EPO Boards of Appeal and some national jurisdictions. Yet, the combination of the multinational and multi-qualification composition is managed and realized in a fascinating way through the establishment of a "pool of judges" (Art. 18 UPCA).

The Pool of Judges is composed of all legally qualified judges and technically qualified judges from the Court of First Instance and includes at least one technically qualified judge per field of technology with the relevant qualifications and experience. The allocation of judges by the President of the Court shall be based on their legal or technical expertise, linguistic skills and relevant experience. The idea underlying this allocation of

---

19 In particular Italy had expressed an interest in establishing a seat in Milan, but also other Member States had made counter-proposals. In May 2023, the Italian government confirmed that Milan will host the third section of the central division. Laura King, 'Third seat of central division in Milan remains a priority for Italian government' (JUVE Patent Blog, 2 December 2022), https://www.juve-patent.com/news-and-stories/legal-commentary/third-seat-of-central-division-in-milan-remains-a-priority-for-italian-government/ (accessed 20 December 2022) and Amy Sandys, 'Italian government confirms Milan will host third UPC central division' (JUVE Patent Blog, 19 May 2023), https://www.juve-patent.com/people-and-business/italian-government-confirms-milan-will-host-third-upc-central-division/.

judges, is that in this manner the same high quality of work and the same high level of legal and technical expertise in all panels of the Court of First Instance will be guaranteed. How this allocation will actually happen in practice and whether indeed the expected high quality and high level of expertise will be available in all panels is still uncertain. Moreover, ensuring consistency in the case-law and practices developed in the various divisions will be an important task for the UPC; otherwise we may shift from a EPC system characterized by forum shopping to an UPC system which allows "division shopping".

Sixth, as indicated above, the first appointments of UPC judges concern especially part-time mandates, which will generally mean that those judges will still have another job. Most legally qualified judges will be judges in their national courts, but most technically qualified judges will be practicing patent attorneys in firms or in-house in industry. Clearly the UPCA and the Statute contain a lot of provisions to safeguard "the highest standards of competence and […] proven experience in the field of patent litigation" (Art. 15 UPCA), "judicial independence and impartiality" (Art. 16 UPCA)[20], a good command of at least one EPO official language (art. 2(2) Statute UPC). Whereas, comments on blogs and at conferences have shown that the general perception regarding the first aspect of competence and experience is covered, significant concerns persist regarding the second aspect with respect to the technically qualified judges. Art. 16(4) and (5) UPCA state that the "exercise of the office of technically qualified judges who are part-time judges of the Court shall not exclude the exercise of other functions provided there is no conflict of interests" and that "[in] case of a conflict of interest, the judge concerned shall not take part in proceedings".

The more specific rules governing conflicts of interest are set out in the Statute. According to Art. 7 Statute UPC judges sign a declaration that they shall respect the obligations arising from the position, in particular the duty to behave with integrity. Moreover, judges may not take part in the proceedings of a case in which they: (a) have taken part as adviser; (b) have been a party or have acted for one of the parties; (c) have been called upon to pronounce as a member of a court, tribunal, board of appeal, arbitration or mediation panel, a commission of inquiry or in any other capacity; (d) have a personal or financial interest in the case or in relation to one of the parties; or (e) are related to one of the parties or the representatives of the parties by family ties. Commentators have observed that technically qualified judges who work for big firms will likely often be in a position where one of these situations would arise or where there will be a perception of a conflict of interest. As parties to an action may object to a judge taking part in the proceedings on any of the grounds listed or where the judge is suspected of partiality, the

---

[20] "1. The Court, its judges and the Registrar shall enjoy judicial independence. In the performance of their duties, the judges shall not be bound by any instructions. 2. Legally qualified judges, as well as technically qualified judges who are full-time judges of the Court, may not engage in any other occupation, whether gainful or not, unless an exception is granted by the Administrative Committee. 3. Notwithstanding paragraph 2, the exercise of the office of judges shall not exclude the exercise of other judicial functions at national level."

fear is that this may be used strategically by some parties in the proceedings. Apparently, the Presidium is currently preparing a Code of Conduct, which also deals with this issue in more detail, which will be important for overcoming these concerns.

Seventh, in terms of the judicial independence of the judges, some authors have also criticized some other features of the appointment of the UPC judges.[21] They raise for instance the fact that they are appointed for a term of six years and can be reappointed, but are not appointed for life or until their retirement age (Art. 4 Statute UPC). These authors are also concerned that judges are appointed by the Administrative Committee, which is composed of one representative of each Contracting Member State (Art. 12 UPCA, Art. 3 Statute UPC), probably senior civil servants and not by a more independent body. Another issue mentioned relates to the procedure for the removal from office (Art. 10 Statute UPC), which would not provide the required human rights protection (access to a fair trial, access to justice) and safeguards for judicial independence. These (and other issues mentioned by these authors) are very fundamental limitations of the UPC's institutional design.

Eight, the procedure at the UPC is often described as a "frontloaded" procedure because the rules require parties to present both "an indication of the facts relied on" and "the evidence relied on, where available", in initial written pleadings. Therefore, we can expect to see evidence-heavy submissions from the outset in most UPC actions, similar to the procedures at the EPO and various national jurisdictions such as France, the Netherlands, and Germany. However, parties can seek permission to file evidence at later stages and one can expect parties to exploit these provisions. However, as the judges will have a lot of discretion to decide on such requests, we will need to see in practice whether judges are inclined to do so. In addition, in view of the frontloaded proceedings one may wonder whether the panels will prefer an expert-focused or a document-focused approach. Art. 53 UPCA lists "opinions of experts" as one of the types of evidence that can be used, and the procedural framework allows for expert evidence. However, again these provisions are at the discretion of the judge and it is hard to predict whether or not the judges will actually allow (or encourage) expert involvement in practice. In fact, UPC panels will always include a technically qualified judge if the proceedings involve patent validity, and such judges will be able to review and interpret scientific documents without expert assistance. The way the case will be managed in terms of these procedural issues by the judge may have an impact on the trustworthiness of the system.

Last but not least, the relationship between the UPC and the Court of Justice of the EU (CJEU) remains unique, complex and controversial.[22] The competences of the CJEU have been limited substantially during the negotiations on the Unitary Patent Package. As a court common to the Contracting Member States and as part of their judicial sys-

---

[21] See e.g. Leloup & Van Drooghenbroeck (2023), footnote 4.
[22] For more information, see Chapter 20.

tem, the UPC needs to collaborate with the CJEU to ensure the correct application and uniform interpretation of Union law, and request a preliminary ruling in accordance with Art. 267 TFEU if needed (Art. 21 UPCA). In fact, Contracting Member States are liable for damages caused by infringements of Union law by the UPC, including the failure to request preliminary rulings from the CJEU. Decisions of the CJEU shall be binding on the UPC. Nonetheless, in view of the not so positive reputation of the CJEU in the patent epistemic community in terms of developing patent and SPC case-law, it remains to be seen to what extent the UPC will live up to these obligations. This will be an important issue for assessing the performance of the UPC.

This list of nine unique features of the institutional design of the UPC shows many outstanding issues, a lot of uncertainty and scope for controversy. The way in which the UPC will address this uncertainty and develop its case-law and practices are vital for generating trust in the UPC.

15.3 Translating key concepts from the trust literature to the UPC setting

This section first focuses on the definition of trust and the trust relationship and different "levels" of trust, which is then linked to the importance of uncertainty in a trust relationship and the ABI-model as a tool for better understanding the assessment of trustworthiness of the UPC.

15.3.1 Defining trust, identifying the trust relationship and understanding the multilevel nature of trust within the context of the UPC

Trust as a social phenomenon has been examined from the angle of a panoply of sciences and social sciences, including psychology, economics, management, history, philosophy but also biochemistry, neuroscience and genetics.[23] As trust has been studied by many different disciplines, this has resulted in many definitions,[24] but a widely accepted definition is the one of Rousseau, et al.[25] Rousseau et al. state that "trust is a psy-

---

[23] Oliver Schilke et al., 'Trust in Social Relations' (2021) 47 *Annual Rev. Sociol.* 240; Denise M. Rousseau et al., 'Not So Different After All: A Cross-discipline View of Trust' (1998) 23(3) *The Academy of Management Review*, 393–404.
[24] Frederique Six & Koen Verhoest, 'Trust in regulatory regimes: scoping the field', in Six & Verhoest (eds.), *Trust in Regulatory Regimes*, Edward Elgar Publishing, 2017).
[25] Denise M. Rousseau et al., 'Not So Different After All: A Cross-discipline View of Trust' (1998) 23(3) *The Academy of Management Review*, 393–404.

chological state comprising the intention to accept vulnerability based upon the positive expectations of the intentions or behavior of another". Trust is, thus, a relational concept; an actor (trustor) trusts another actor (trustee) with respect to a certain future behavior (A trusts B to do X in the context of Y).[26]

In the context of the UPC, the trustor generally relates to the members of the patent epistemic community. Different from trust in criminal or civil courts, the general public ("public trust") does not seem very concerned by the UPC. The trustee could be the UPC, or more specifically a particular division, panel or UPC judge (see below, the concept of multilevel trust). Y will relate for instance to how discretion is managed by the UPC and the efficiency and fairness of the procedures and outcomes.

In the recent literature on trust, it is recognized that trust is a *multilevel concept*[27] which operates at the interpersonal (micro), (inter)organisational (meso) and system (macro) level. Interpersonal trust is the trust relationship existing between two individuals connected to different or the same organisation(s). Organisational trust concerns trust in organisations while system trust deals with trust in systems. In particular, at the macro-level, trust refers to the broader (sub-)system, its aims and values, and the adequacy with which these values are institutionalised and implemented.[28] The different levels of trust are nested into each other.[29]

In this context, the role of so-called "boundary spanners" is crucial. Boundary spanners are representatives of an organisation or entity. Highly competent boundary spanners are needed to represent the organization's aims and values and the associated roles and routines.[30] Individual UPC judges basically operate as boundary spanners for the UPC at the organizational level. UPC judges are not only representing aims and values, roles and routines of the UPC, but they are actually framing and developing them. Since the UPC begins in a way "from square one" with no vested or in-build trust based on history it will be up to the judges to represent the "face of the court"[31].

Perceived competence and abilities are essential signs of a boundary spanner's trustworthiness.[32] By contrast, an inadequate boundary spanner is likely to erode organizational trust. This explains why the announcement of the appointment of the UPC

---

26 Russel Hardin, *Trust and Trustworthiness* (Russel Sage Foundation 2002) and Bart Nooteboom, *Trust: forms, foundations, functions, failures and figures* (Edward Elgar 2002).
27 Ashley Fulmer & Kurt Dirks, 'Multilevel trust: A theoretical and practical imperative' (2018), 8(2) *Journal of Trust Research*, 137–141.
28 Frens Kroeger, 'Trusting Organizations: The Institutionalization of Trust in Interorganizational Relationships' (2012) 19 Organization 743, 746.
29 Susan P. Shapiro, 'The Social Control of Impersonal Trust' (1987) 93(3) American Journal of Sociology, 623–58.
30 Frens Kroeger, 'Trusting organizations± The institutionalization of trust in interorganizational relationships' (2012) 19 Organization, 743–763.
31 *Ibid.*
32 Jon M. Hawes et al., 'Trust Earning Perceptions of Sellers and Buyers' (1989) 9 *Journal of Personal Selling and Sales Management*, 1–8. See also below regarding the ABI model.

judges created such a buzz within the patent community. The perceived expertise and experience of the judges are important signals. In this respect, the allocation of judges from the pool of judges (Art. 18 UPCA) to the respective divisions of the Court of First Instance will be very important. The allocation of judges shall be based on their legal or technical expertise, linguistic skills and relevant experience. Ultimately, the UPC judges will only be able to fulfil their boundary spanner role appropriately if the allocation of judges guarantees the same high quality of work and the same high level of legal and technical expertise in all panels of the Court of First Instance.

The degree of trust in the representative of a certain trust level can feed back into other trust levels and may have spill-over effects in terms of the trustworthiness of the representative. For instance, if a new organization such as the UPC is created, trust in the organization's boundary spanner (i.e. micro-level) feeds back into the trustworthiness of the organization (i.e. meso-trust). After functioning several years, the UPC may have generated trust, which may subsequently spill-over to newly appointed UPC judges, who act as boundary spanners at the micro-level; even if they have less expertise and experience than the judges appointed in October 2022. Therefore, the interactions between the trustor and the boundary spanner affect the degree of trust in the organisation in a dynamic manner. Hence, adopting a multilevel perspective is important to understand trust dynamics, such as the relationship between interpersonal trust and inter-organisational trust. It emphasizes and explains the key role of individual UPC judges in building trust in the UPC at the organizational level.

15.3.2 Trust and uncertainty

Trust also implies uncertainty about the trustee's future behavior; it inevitably involves a kind of "a leap of faith" in which the "irreducible social vulnerability, and uncertainty [are suspended] as if they were favourably resolved".[33] This uncertainty is also prevalent with regard to the UPC. Although the legal framework is set through the UPCA, the Statute, the Rules of Procedure and other secondary rules published the last few months and available on the UPC website, quite some discretion is left to the court.[34] Some concrete and important examples relate to the importance of proportionality (Art. 42 UPCA), the role of the judge-rapporteur in the proceedings (e.g. Art. 52 UPCA), the appointment of courts experts (Art. 57 UPCA), the protection of confidential information (Art. 58 UPCA), injunctions (Art. 62–63 UPCA), the award of damages (Art. 68 UPCA) and the apportionment of legal costs (Art. 69 UPCA). The case-law of the UPC on these issues still needs to be developed. Of course, the UPC will not operate in a vacuum, as the judges

---

33 Guido Mollering, *Trust: reason, routine, reflexivity* (Elsevier, 2006).
34 Federica Baldan & Esther van Zimmeren, 'The future role of the unified patent court in safeguarding coherence in the European patent system' (2015)52 *Common Market Law Rev.*, 1529–1577.

will be inspired by prior case-law and practices in the Member States or at the EPO. Yet, as significant differences may exist between practices in Member States, uncertainty will remain a prime consideration for at least another decade. Even though the costs and uncertainty involved in parallel litigation in the current European system are significant, experienced patent attorneys and lawyers are used to navigating the existing legal landscape. Moreover, the potential consequences involved in a central attack before the UPC, in terms of the invalidity of the patent throughout the territory of the Contracting Member States are considerable. On the other hand, patent litigators are also excited about the new opportunities that the system is offering and eager to be at the forefront of the development of the new case-law. Therefore, decisions to opt-out or not involve a strategic cost-benefit analysis which is not straightforward and which require a careful case-by-case assessment.

15.3.3 Trust, trustworthiness and the ABI-model

Trust is strongly related to the assessment of the trustworthiness of the trustee, but the two concepts should not be confused. If there are clear signals that the trustee is not trustworthy, then reasonable arguments exist for not trusting the trustee – and to act upon that for instance by opting-out of the exclusive UPC jurisdiction and by relying on national courts.

Several factors explain why an actor is perceived as trustworthy or not and whether ultimately the trustor would be inclined to trust. Mayer et al. developed a model to assess the trustworthiness of the trustee focusing on the concepts of ability, benevolence, and integrity, the so-called "ABI model".[35] Each of the three factors varies on a spectrum. They may fluctuate independently from each other but can also be interrelated.

Mayer et al. define "ability" as that group of skills, competences, expertise and characteristics that enable a party to have influence within a specific domain. The UPC Advisory and Administrative Committee responsible for the appointment process have managed to select the "elite" of the European patent judiciary.[36] In addition, an extensive training program (e.g. linguistic skills, technical aspects of patent law, civil procedure) (Art. 19 UPCA and 11 Statute UPC) is foreseen to ensure a high level of expertise for all UPC judges, including those with limited experience. Some of these trainings have already started end of 2022.

---

35 Roger C. Mayer et al., 'An Integrative Model of Organizational Trust' (1995) 20 *The Academy of Management Review*, 709–734. This framework was originally developed to address interpersonal relationships within organizations, but it is nowadays commonly used to analyse and measure trust at the inter-organizational, meso level, and at the system, macro-level.
36 Amy Sandys, 'UPC divisions demonstrate clout with choice of experienced legal judges' (JUVE Patent Blog 20 October 2022), https://www.juve-patent.com/news-and-stories/people-and-business/upc-divisions-demonstrate-clout-with-choice-of-experienced-legal-judges/ (accessed 20 December 2022).

Many of the technically qualified UPC judges also have an impeccable reputation in terms of expertise and competences. However, for them the issue of the potential conflicts of interests is creating some challenges from the perspective of trustworthiness in view of their perceived integrity (see below).[37]

"Benevolence" is the extent to which a trustee is believed to seek the good for the trustor, aside from an egocentric profit motive. It focuses on the intentions of the trustor who is perceived to be positively oriented toward the trustee. In this respect, research regarding the US Court of Appeals for the Federal Circuit has highlighted the risk of a tunnel vision and pro-patent bias for judges who mainly deal with patent cases.[38] On the other hand, the Japanese experience with the IP High Court has shown that not all specialized courts have a pro-IP, pro-patent bias.[39] However, if through its case-law the UPC, or a specific division would give the impression of such a pro-patent bias, this will affect the level of benevolence perceived by the counterparties or companies with a limited IP portfolio. So, carefully considering who is in the position of the trustor is important in this respect.

"Integrity" involves the trustor's perception that the trustee adheres to a set of principles that the trustor finds acceptable, for example principles such as consistency, efficiency, impartiality and fairness. These principles are strongly enshrined in the UPCA, Statute and Rules of Procedure, but as the UPC judges have a lot of discretion in how the case is managed the actual implementation of these principles will be determinant for assessing integrity. Moreover, the mere perception of conflicts of interest may have a major impact on the trustworthiness of the UPC judges and ultimately the UPC. The Administrative Committee has pointed out its awareness of the issue and reassure observers that they are taking appropriate precautions. Moreover, some countries, such as the Netherlands, Denmark, Finland and Sweden have already had a positive experience with patent attorneys as part-time judges. Learning lessons from their experiences will be valuable for the UPC as well.

15.4 Concluding remarks

New organizational settings such as the UPC are an interesting context for studying the emergence of trust. Judges may play a central role in organizational and systems trust, when they act as boundary spanners for those levels. The importance attached by the

---

[37] Mathieu Klos, 'Patent attorney dominance among UPC technical judges leads to conflict debate' (JUVE Patent Blog 27 October 2022), https://www.juve-patent.com/news-and-stories/people-and-business/patent-attorney-dominance-among-upc-technical-judges-leads-to-conflict-debate/ (accessed 20 December 2022).
[38] Rochelle C. Dreyfuss, 'The EU's Romance with Specialized Adjudication' (2016) 47 *IIC*, 887–890.
[39] Federica Baldan, 'Judicial Coherence in Specialized Intellectual Property Courts: A Comparative Analysis of Japan and Europe' (IIP 2016), https://www.iip.or.jp/e/summary/pdf/detail2016/e28_05.pdf (accessed 20 August 2022).

European patent community to the appointment of the UPC judges clearly shows that individuals who share similar educational backgrounds, careers, expertise, beliefs, values and attitudes and are part of the same epistemic community, this may promote trust at the interpersonal and organizational level.[40]

As the role of the UPC judges as pro-active judge-rapporteurs and boundary spanners for the UPC will be determinant in building trust in the UPC, the ABI-model highlights the need to think about trustworthiness in terms of ability, benevolence and integrity. Even though, still quite some uncertainty exists regarding the actual allocation of judges, the profile of the pool of judges offers opportunities to compose balanced panels with high level expertise and extensive experience in patent litigation that allow for a careful development of court procedures and practices (ability). Nonetheless, in terms of benevolence and integrity the UPC judges should carefully balance party interests and the public interest and refrain from behavior which may be perceived as biased. Moreover, the UPC judges will need to be very meticulous in checking and avoiding potential conflicts of interest and – if necessary – recusing themselves. The adoption of a Code of Conduct in this regard will likely be helpful and may have a positive impact in terms of the judges perceived trustworthiness. However, also third parties can contribute to strengthening the trustworthiness of the UPC and its judges. Law firms and companies cannot use the fact that one of their attorneys has been appointed as a UPC part-time judge for marketing purposes; they should disperse any impression of bias or influence on the administration of justice.

It is clear that the global epistemic patent community will be watching the UPC closely, as an important experiment of a "one-of-its kind" institutional design. For many years to come, the support of the business and legal communities will be crucial in the UPC becoming a successful court. The UPC judges will need to eliminate any impression of dependence and partiality from day one. If any doubts about the independence and impartiality of individual judges would arise, the Court of First Instance and the Court of Appeal presidents will have to take consistent action. After all, it takes a long time to build trust, but trust can quickly erode. However, the patent community must also give the newly appointed judges "a chance to grow within their new positions" and to strengthen their trustworthiness.[41]

---

40 See also Majoral 2016 (examining the relationship between national courts and the CJEU within the context of the preliminary ruling procedure).
41 See also: Mathieu Klos, 'The UPC will succeed if its part-time judges have space to grow' (JUVE Patent Blog, 31 October 2022), https://www.juve-patent.com/news-and-stories/legal-commentary/the-upc-will-succeed-if-its-part-time-judges-have-space-to-grow/ (accessed 20 December 2022).

Stefan Luginbuehl, Matilda Titeca
16 The EPO within the Unitary Patent System

16.1 Introduction

The European patent system, under the European Patent Convention (EPC)[1] with the European Patent Office (EPO) as the executing body, has been extremely successful and has exceeded expectations.[2] When the EPC came into force it was expected that demand would plateau at around 30,000 filings a year, whereas in 2022 the EPO saw over 193,000 European patent applications.[3] The territorial scope is also continually expanding as 1 October 2022 saw Montenegro become the 39th State to accede to the EPC.[4]

The central body in the European patent system is the EPO which is an organ of the European Patent Organisation[5] dealing with the essential task of granting European patents[6]. It is the second largest intergovernmental institution in Europe after the European Commission. The central role of the EPO in the European Patent system was fixed by the Protocol on Centralisation, which was adopted with and is an integral part of the EPC.[7] The main task of the Protocol was to provide the EPO with a clear working structure to centralise the patent procedure.[8]

The attempts to create a system of common patent protection for the EU date back to 1959 but ever since the creation of the European Patent Organisation, and thus the EPO in 1977, the EPO has always been envisaged as having a central role in the system.

One of the first true attempts to create a common patent was the Community Patent, this was a single uniform patent for all member states of the European Community, and

---

1 Convention on the Grant of European Patents (European Patent Convention) (EPC).
2 Paul Braendli, 'The Future of the European Patent System' (1995) 26 IIC 813.
3 Ibid.
4 Montenegro accedes to the European Patent Convention [2022] Official Journal EPO A78.
5 Art. 4(2)(a) EPC.
6 Art. 4(3) EPC.
7 Protocol on the Centralisation of the European Patent System and on its Introduction (Protocol on Centralisation) (5 October 1973, as revised by the Act revising the EPC of 29 November 2000).
8 Alexandru Cristian Stenc, *European Patent Convention* (Kluwer, 2018) 714; Kurt Haertel, 'Das Protokoll über die Zentralisierung des europäischen Patentsystems und seine Einführung' (1973) 7 Mitteilungen der deutschen Patentanwälte 123.

Stefan Luginbuehl, PhD, Lawyer, Head of Department, European Patent Office.
Matilda Titeca, at time of writing, Trainee, European Legal Affairs, International Legal Affairs, European Patent Office.

https://doi.org/10.1515/9783110781687-016

which was implemented through the Community Patent Convention of 1975 (CPC).[9] The Community patent would have been granted on the basis of a separate application which was to be handled by the EPO. The CPC litigation system followed the organisation structure of the EPO and provided for the creation of a Revocation Division and Board within the EPO[10], thus envisaging powers for the EPO beyond the granting phase. The CPC was planned to enter into force at the same time as the EPC, however, never did despite several additional attempts, one of the reasons being the expensive and complicated translation regime it proposed.[11] Nevertheless, the establishment of a common patent for the territory of the EU has aways been considered essential for establishing an integrated market.[12]

In 2000, the European Commission tabled a proposal for a Community Patent Regulation[13] which envisaged the European Community acceding to the EPC and becoming a member of the European Patent Organisation.[14] Again the EPO had a central role as the granting body of the Community patent on the basis of a separate application and thus leading to a separation of application procedures. The EPO, however, rejected this approach of a separate treatment of patent applications depending on whether a Community Patent or classic European Patent was requested. It felt that it would diminish the common application and examination procedure provided for in the EPC and would lead to great difficulties in its practical implementation. The negotiations within the EU again proved to be very difficult, in particular no agreement on the proposed language regime, which focused more on the three language regime of the EPO, could be forged.

After multiple attempts, it became clear that a consensus between all the EU member states was not possible and so to break the deadlock, the Council decided on the basis of a request of 26 of the member states and a proposal by the European Commission[15] to authorise the creation of a unitary patent by way of 'enhanced cooperation'.[16]

---

9 Mauricio Troncoso, 'International Intellectual Property Scholars Series: European Union Patents: A Mission Impossible? An Assessment of the Historical and Current Approaches' (2013) 17 Marquette Intellectual Property Law Review 233.
10 Stefan Luginbuehl & Teodora Kandeva, The role of the European Court of Justice in the European Patent in Christophe Geiger/Craig Allen Nard/Xavier Seuba (eds.), Intellectual Property and the Judiciary, 2018, 207, at 208.
11 Justine Pila, 'The European Patent: An Old and Vexing Problem' (2013) 62 International & Comparative Law Quarterly 935.
12 Ibid 920.
13 Doc Com(2000) 412 of 1.8.2000.
14 Mauricio Troncoso, 'International Intellectual Property Scholars Series: European Union Patents: A Mission Impossible? An Assessment of the Historical and Current Approaches' (2013) 17 Marquette Intellectual Property Law Review 237.
15 Council Decision of 10 March 2011 authorising enhanced cooperation in the area of the creation of unitary patent protection [2011] OJ L76/53.
16 Justine Pila, fn 11.

The decision was taken to implement the unitary patent system on the basis of two separate regulations (see 16.2.1)[17] within the existing European patent legal framework under the EPC, i.e. Part IX of the EPC. This part of the EPC was introduced as an interface between the EPC and a prior embodiment of the unitary patent, the earlier mentioned CPC. It includes the legal, technical, and institutional framework for establishing a unitary patent within the existing EPC system.

16.2 Legal framework

16.2.1 The Unitary Patent Regulations

Under the framework of enhanced cooperation, the commission adopted the 'EU patent package', comprising two EU Regulations[18], which create a unitary patent for the 25 participating member states (participating states)[19] and the related translation requirements, as well as the Agreement on a Unified Patent Court (UPCA)[20]. The two Regulations were published on 31 December 2012 in the Official Journal of the European Union and entered into force 20 days thereafter. They became fully applicable on 1 June 2023 when the UPCA entered into force.[21]

Regulation 1257/2012 establishes a unitary patent system within the EU. It outlines that a European patent granted under the EPC, which has the same claims in all participating states, shall benefit from unitary effect in the participating states provided that its unitary effect has been registered in the Register for unitary patent protection.[22]

Regulation 1260/2012 complements the provisions of Regulation 1257/2012 and regulates the translation arrangements for European Patents with unitary effect. Regulation 1260/2012 particularly shows the integration of the new unitary patent system with the existing European patent system by reflecting largely the three language regime provided for under the EPC. This approach was taken due to the sensitivities that sur-

---

17 Regulation (EU) 1257/2012 of the European Parliament and of the Council of 17 December 2012 implementing enhanced cooperation in the area of the creation of unitary patent protection [2012] OJ L361/1, and Council Regulation (EU) No 1260/2012 of 17 December 2012 implementing enhanced cooperation in the area of the creation of unitary patent protection with regard to the applicable translation arrangements [2012] OJ L361/89.
18 Regulation (EU) 1257/2012 of the European Parliament and of the Council of 17 December 2012 implementing enhanced cooperation in the area of the creation of unitary patent protection [2012] OJ L361/1; Council Regulation (EU) 1260/2012 of 17 December 2012 implementing enhanced cooperation in the area of the creation of unitary patent protection with regard to the applicable translation arrangements [2012] OJ L361/89.
19 All EU member states with the exception of Croatia and Spain.
20 Agreement on a Unified Patent Court (UPCA) of 19 February 2013.
21 Art. 18(2) Regulation 1257/2012.
22 Art. 3 Regulation 1257/2012.

rounded the discussions on the translation regime and the costs involving multiple translations. Adopting a regime reflecting the EPC was consequently the most feasible.[23]

The Unitary Patent Regulations were drafted to fit into the existing EPC legal framework. This is important from a practical point of view, as if the Regulations were not within the confines of the EPC then the latter would have had to be amended. This would have involved a diplomatic conference and the involvement and adoption of the revised EPC by all the EPC contracting states. There were fears within the EU that this would have seriously delayed the process. However, it would have been hardly slower than what it proved to be as the EU member states have taken more than eleven years to complete the system.

16.2.2 Agreement on a Unified Patent Court (UPCA)

The UPCA, along with the two Regulations, is the third legal instrument in the Unitary Patent package. Unlike the Regulations, the UPCA is an international agreement which does not have direct effect in the EU member states. In order to be binding the states had to ratify the agreement according according to their own constitutional procedures. The UPCA was signed by 25 EU member states in February 2013 and entered into force on 1 June 2023. The Agreement is open only to EU member states. The United Kingdom, which was a UPCA signatory state, withdrew its ratification before the agreement entered into force.

The UPCA establishes the Unified Patent Court (UPC) which is a court common to all the UPCA states and thus part of their judicial system.[24] The UPC has exclusive competence for the UPCA states for actions concerning the infringement or threatened infringement of classic European patents, unitary patents, and supplementary protection certificates (SPCs); actions for declaration of non-infringement; and actions or counterclaims for revocations of such patents and SPCs.[25] Furthermore, the UPC has jurisdiction over decisions taken by the EPO in carrying out the tasks delegated to it concerning the unitary patent such as rejecting a request for unitary effect.[26] This is when the EPO comes into play again providing a limited interface between the two institutions.

16.2.3 Secondary legislation

On top of the three legal instruments just discussed, there are also secondary legal instruments that further implement the unitary patent system and which are of particular

---

23 Alfredo Ilardi, *The New European Patent* 1st edn, Hart (2015) 48.
24 Art. 1 UPCA.
25 Art. 32 UPCA.
26 Art. 9 Regulation 1257/2012; Art 32(1)(i) UPCA.

importance for the EPO: the Rules relating to Unitary Patent Protection (UPR)[27] and the Rules relating to Fees for Unitary Patent Protection (RFeesUPP).[28]

The UPR lay down the details on all the procedures related to administrative tasks given to and to be conducted by the EPO for the unitary patent system as established in the two Regulations. This includes the request for unitary effect, the compensation scheme for translation costs, the payment of the renewal fees, and the Register for unitary patent protection.

The RFeesUPP set the concrete amounts for all fees associated with the unitary patent to be paid to the EPO by the proprietor.[29] The RFeesUPP also outline the compensation for translation costs which some proprietors may be eligible for. It is pertinent to note in this regard that some provisions of the Rules relating to Fees under the EPC also apply to the unitary patent, for example how to pay fees to the EPO.

16.3 Role of the EPO from a governance perspective

16.3.1 Select Committee of the Administrative Council of the European Patent Organisation

Part IX of the EPC sets the framework for the implementation of the unitary patent in the existing European patent system. Article 145 EPC, together with Article 9(2) of Regulation 1257/2012, provides that the member states participating in the enhanced cooperation are to set up a Select Committee of the Administrative Council of the European Patent Organisation to ensure the governance and supervision of the additional tasks which are delegated to the EPO.[30] The Select Committee is a sub-body of the Administrative Council.

There were several proposals on how best to set up the Select Committee, in the end the Select Committee itself agreed in a decision at is inaugural meeting to set up the Select Committee of the Administrative Council, this decision was then recorded in the minutes.[31]

---

27 Rules relating to Unitary Patent Protection as adopted by decision of the Select Committee of the Administrative Council of the European Patent Organisation of 15 December 2015 and as last amended by decision of the Select Committee of the Administrative Council of 23 March 2022 (UPR) [2022] OJ EPO, A41.
28 Rules relating to Fees for Unitary Patent Protection (RFeesUPP) as adopted by decision of the Select Committee of the Administrative Council of the European Patent Organisation of 15 December 2015 (RFeesUPP) [2022] OJ EPO, A42,
29 Art. 2 RFeesUPP.
30 Art. 9 Regulation 1257/2012.
31 Stefan Luginbuehl, 'An Institutional Perspective I: The Role of the EPO in the Unitary (EU) Patent System' in Justine Pila and Christopher Wadlow (eds), *The Unitary EU Patent System* (Hart 2017) 51.

The Select Committee is not just a supervising body, but also establishes the level of renewal fees for the unitary patent, as well as the distribution scale of the renewal fees.[32] It works under its own rules of procedure.[33]

Currently, it is composed of representatives of the 24 participating states as well as observers such as the European Commission and the EPC contracting states which do not participate in the unitary patent system.[34]

16.3.2 Unified Patent Court (UPC)

To ensure an effective implementation and operation of the provisions of the UPCA the agreement itself establishes three committees namely, the Administrative Committee, the Budget Committee, and the Advisory Committee.

The Administrative Committee is in a powerful position as it has many decision making powers within the framework of the UPCA.[35] It is composed of one representative of each UPCA state with the EPO and the European Commission as observers.[36] The Administrative Committee, amongst other things, fixes the court fees, amends the Statute of the Court, adopts and amends the Rules of Procedure of the Court, and appoints the judges.[37]

The Budget Committee's main role, as the name would suggest, is to adopt the budget of the Court as proposed by the Presidium[38] and to approve the annual accounts and the annual report of the Court.[39] The Budget Committee is composed of one representative of each UPCA state and takes its decisions by a simple majority, unless it is adopting the budget, then a three-quarters majority is needed.[40]

Lastly, the Advisory Committee has the task of assisting the Administrative Committee with the appointment of the judges, the Administrative Committee appoints judges based on a list established by the Advisory Committee.[41] The Advisory Committee is com-

---

32 EPO, "Council bodies" <https://www.epo.org/about-us/governance/administrative-council/bodies.html> accessed 23 August 2022; Arts 12 and 13 Regulation 1257/2012.
33 Cf decision of the Select Committee of the Administrative Council of 25 June 2013, approving the Rules of Procedure of the Select Committee of the Administrative Council, SC/D 1/13, available at <https://www.epo.org/about-us/governance/documentation/documentation.html>.
34 Stefan Luginbuehl, 'An Institutional Perspective I: The Role of the EPO in the Unitary (EU) Patent System' in Justine Pila and Christopher Wadlow (eds), *The Unitary EU Patent System* (Hart 2017) 52.
35 Winfried Tilmann and Clemens Plassmann, *Unified Patent Protection in .Europe: A Commentary* (OUP, 2018) 334.
36 Art. 12(1) UPCA.
37 Arts. 36(3), 40(2), 41(2), 16(2), UPCA.
38 Art. 26(1) Statute of the Unified Patent Court.
39 Art. 32(3) Statute of the Unified Patent Court.
40 Art. 13(1) and (3) UPCA.
41 Ibid, art. 16.

posed of patent judges and practitioners in patent law and patent litigation who are proposed by the UPCA states.[42]

It is also pertinent to consider the role of the EPO within these Committees, which may not be apparent at a first glance. In the Administrative Committee the role of the EPO is two-fold, firstly, it has observer status. Although the EPO has no decision-making powers, this status keeps the EPO informed of the key decisions being made within the UPC, and shows that the EPO, along with the European Commission, is a key player in the unitary patent system. The second way in which the EPO plays a role is that the functions and composition of the Administrative Committee largely reflect those of the Administrative Committee that was proposed in the European Patent Litigation Agreement (EPLA). The EPLA was a proposal for a European Patent Court that preceded the UPCA, and which aimed at strengthening the enforcement of patent rights in Europe and was consequently open to accession to all EPC contracting states.[43] The Administrative Committee, as envisaged in the EPLA, is heavily inspired by the Administrative Council of the European Patent Organisation. The draft agreement even citing multiple Articles from Chapter IV of the EPC which outlines the Administrative Council, its functions, and its composition.[44] The Administrative Committee of the UPC therefore, can be seen to draw elements from the European Patent Organisation's Administrative Council, for example the composition, its powers, the voting rules, and the existence of observers.[45] Whilst this is not the EPO directly, it does show how the wider structure, the European Patent Organisation, of which the EPO is an organ, has influenced the UPC and its establishment.

16.4 Role of the EPO with regard to the Unitary Patent Procedure

16.4.1 Additional tasks for the European Patent Office

The EPC outlines in Article 143(1) that the group of contracting states who are, pursuant to Article 142(1) EPC, party to the special agreement may give additional tasks to the EPO. The EPO is obligated to carry out these tasks[46] but on the costs of the states that participate in the unitary patent scheme.[47] It further explains that to carry out these additional

---

42 Ibid, art. 14(2).
43 Draft Agreement on the establishment of the European patent litigation system, preamble.
44 See Draft Agreement on the establishment of the European patent litigation system, art 13.
45 Arts. 26(1), 33, 35, and 30 EPC.
46 Winfried Tilmann and Clemens Plassmann, *Unified Patent Protection in Europe: A Commentary* (OUP, 2018)187.
47 Art. 146 EPC.

tasks, special departments may be established within the EPO by the group of contracting states.[48]

Article 9(1) of Regulation 1257/2012 takes advantage of this provision and outlines the additional tasks to be carried out by the EPO 'in accordance with the internal rules of the EPO'. For this purpose, it was decided to establish a new department within the EPO, namely the Unitary Patent Protection Division which is entrusted to carry out the additional tasks delegated to the EPO.

The main tasks of the EPO include, receiving and examining requests for unitary effect, registering unitary effect or rejecting requests if the legal requirements are not met; setting up and administering a central unitary patent register; and collecting and administering the renewal fees for unitary patents.

16.4.2 Request for Unitary Effect

Proprietors of European patents may request their European patent to have unitary effect, to make such a request they must file a formal 'request for unitary effect' in writing with the EPO.[49] Upon the filing of the request, the EPO examines the request to see if it meets the substantive and formal requirements. If the requirements are met then the EPO will register unitary effect in the Register for unitary patent protection.[50] The Register for unitary patent protection is part of the European Patent Register, and the maintenance of which is another task delegated to the EPO via Article 9 of Regulation 1257/2012.[51] Such decision of the EPO can be appealed by the requester to the UPC via special procedures.[52]

16.4.3 Payment of fees

Article 9(1)(e) of Regulation 1257/2012 deems it the task of the EPO to collect and administer renewal fees and additional fees. With regards to renewal fees, the role of the EPO has two sides as the EPO both collects and redistributes the fees. The fees have to be paid to the EPO. It then retains 50 per-cent of the fees and distribute the remaining amount after deducting the costs related to the administration of the unitary patent by the EPO to the participating states according to a distribution key.[53] The decision of the level of

---

48 Art. 143(2) EPC.
49 Art. 9(1)(a) Regulation 1257/2012,
50 EPO, 'Unitary Patent Guide' (guide) (2022) 69.
51 Art. 9(1)(b) Regulation 1257/2012.
52 Rule 97 Rules of Procedure of the Unified Patent Court, available at <https://www.unified-patent-court.org/sites/default/files/rop_en_25_july_2022_final_consolidated_published_on_website_0.pdf>.
53 Art. 13(1) Regulation 1257/2012.

renewal fees for the unitary patent and of the distribution key is one specifically for the Select Committee.[54] Regulation 1257/2012 does outline the criteria for establishing the distribution key in a general sense but it does not establish the key concretely.[55] It thus comes as no surprise that it took several years and many financial simulations for the states participating in the unitary patent scheme to agree on the fee level and the distribution key.

16.5 Correlation of European Patent, Unitary Patent and national patent systems

16.5.1 From a true Community patent to an alternatively available patent for a group of EU member states

It was the basic idea in the 1970s when the EPC and the CPC were contemplated that the Community patent would again merge the bundle of patents provided by the European patent to a patent covering all of the EC members states. Against this background Article 142(1) EPC was formulated as follows:

Any group of Contracting States, which has provided by a special agreement that a European patent granted for those States has a unitary character throughout their territories, may provide that a European patent may only be granted jointly in respect of all those States.

This makes it clear that it was the basic intention of the legislator that the group of states would only create a European patent with unitary as soon as they decided to establish such patent for their territories, as it was created by Switzerland and Liechtenstein[56]. The possibility to choose a classic European patent for the states that make part of the group of states would not have been possible.

However, times have changed and also the approach for a European integration without a national fall back position. The discussions on the establishment of a unitary patent on the basis of an EU Regulation thus focused on the establishment of a European patent with unitary effect for the territories of the group of states next to the possibility to continue to request a classic European patent for the territory of the states participating in the unitary patent scheme.

Regulation 1257/2012 provides that a double protection by a European patent and a unitary patent is excluded for the territories of the states which are covered by the uni-

---

54 Ibid, art. 9(2).
55 Ibid, art. 13(2).
56 Treaty between the Swiss Confederation and the Principality of Liechtenstein on Patent Protection (Patent Treaty) of 22 December 1978, OJ EPO 1980, 407.

tary patent[57]. Interestingly enough several states which did not allow for simultaneous protection of European and national patents amended their national laws to allow simultaneous protection with the start of the unitary patent system. This includes France, Germany, and Estonia[58].

The initial approach of creating a true unitary territory among the EU member states and to replace the classic European patent for their territory was thus even more diminished by making it even possible to have a double protection by a unitary patent or classic European patent and a national patent.

This implies that the national legislators wanted to enable patent proprietors to maintain their national patent protection on their territory, even if the UPC revoked the corresponding Unitary or European patent. It is thus no surprise that the European Commission is rather critical about this approach. On the other hand, a new system can only be successful if the users believe and trust in it. Such trust must first be built and it seems easier if users maintain their well trusted systems and alternatives that they have successfully used so far. The basic idea of establishing a unitary patent full of political compromises that replaces the existing European patent was one of the reasons why the CPC never entered into force.

Nevertheless, the chosen approach should only provide for a first step, and a true and credible European integration requires that the classic European patents and the national patents in the long term be replaced by the unitary patent for the territory of the states that participate in the enhanced cooperation for unitary patent protection, and which are bound by the UPC Agreement. Anything else would only reveal that these states only acted as if they took half a step towards further European integration.

16.5.2 Co-existing EPO opposition and appeals proceedings before the EPO and the EPO Boards of Appeal, the Unified Patent Court and national courts

The unitary patent scheme leaves the EPC, and its existing framework untouched. As a consequence, the unitary patent is treated as any other European patent and is thus open to any opposition and appeal proceedings provided for in the EPC. An opposition against a granted European patent can be filed after grant by any person[59]. As a consequence, the European patent, irrespective of whether unitary effect was provided to that

---

57 Art. 4(2) and Nr 8 Preamble Regulation 1257/2012.
58 In France and Germany the national law even, contrary to the situation before, allows simultaneous protection by a national patent and a "classic" European patent, under the condition that the European patent was not opted-out from the jurisdiction of the UPC (Art. 83(3) UPC Agreement). In Estonia, the simultaneous protection is only allowed for Unitary Patents and national patents.
59 Art. 99ff EPC.

patent, will be maintained, revoked or limited with effect from the outset[60]. A decision of the opposition division may be appealed to the EPO Boards of Appeal[61] which again could possibly limit or revoke the European patent. However, the EPO route is only available during the first 9 months after the grant of the European patent. Several states, such as Germany, do not allow the filing of a revocation action as long as an opposition can be filed with the EPO. This is different from the UPC where a revocation action concerning a unitary patent or classic European patent can already be filed even if the 9 months opposition period has not yet expired or is still pending before the EPO. In case of parallel proceedings before the EPO opposition division or Boards of Appeal and the UPC, the UPC has in general no obligation to stay its proceedings. In order to a avoid possible diverging decision, the court may stay its proceedings if it can expect a rapid decision from the EPO[62]. For this purpose, the UPC can request an acceleration of opposition and appeals proceeding by the EPO or the Boards of Appeal[63].

The UPC competes with the EPO's opposition division and Boards of Appeal, since it has exclusive jurisdiction for revocation actions against unitary patents[64]. The UPC also shares its jurisdiction with the responsible national authorities of the UPCA states with regard to infringement and revocation actions concerning classic European patents for a transitional period of at least seven years[65]. During this period, the claimant has the possibility to apply alternatively to the previously competent courts in the UPCA states. Furthermore, the national courts and other authorities have exclusive jurisdiction for disputes concerning a patent application, a classical European patent or a Supplementary Protection Certificate (SPC), if a corresponding opt-out from the jurisdiction of the UPC has been declared according to Article 83(3) UPCA. From the perspective of the litigators using the European patent litigation system, the UPC thus also competes with the national courts of the states which are participating in the UPC. The race between the UPC and the national courts will be determined by the patent proprietors and claimants.

Finally, the court also competes with the national courts of those states, which are not participating in the UPCA. In cross-border infringement cases, there are concurring jurisdictions on European patents on the basis of the existing international instruments in Europe. Under these instruments, claimants are able to choose the competent court at the seat of the infringer or at the place where the infringement occurred.

Again, all these possibilities have to a big extent been introduced on the wish of the stakeholders who want to have a choice, and who first want to examine the new system

---

60 Art. 68 EPC.
61 Art. 106ff EPC.
62 Art 32(10) UPCA.
63 See also Notice of the EPO dated 17 March 2008, OJ EPO 2008, 221 with regard to acceleration of opposition proceedings in the case of pending infringement proceedings and Art 10(4) Rules of Procedure of the Boards of Appeal.
64 Art. 32(1)(d) UPCA.
65 Art. 83(1) UPCA.

before they give up their tried and tested procedures. It goes without saying that the UPC will only be successful if the stakeholders trust in it. However, the found solution comes at a high price; due to the parallel jurisdiction of the UPC and the national authorities and the possibility to opt-out patent applications, classic European patents, and SPCs from the jurisdiction of the UPC, national authorities continue to be responsible for disputes related to such rights for another 30 years. This is unique in the history of the creation of a court with "exclusive" jurisdiction and again questions the credibility of the states officially promoting European integration, where the national courts have parallel jurisdiction for an entire generation with the European court which aims at replacing them.

16.5.3 Role of the Court of Justice of the European Union (CJEU) and impact on the EPO and the European Patent System

16.5.3.1 The impact of rulings of the CJEU on the EPO

As a court common to the EU member states[66], the UPC has a duty provided for under the EU treaties to refer questions on the interpretation of EU law to the CJEU[67] and to request preliminary rulings.[68] These rulings are binding to the UPC.

As already raised in an earlier article[69], the fact that the EU was starting to act as legislator in an area that is regulated by the EPC provoked complicated institutional and sovereignty problems, given that the EPC is an international system outside the EU and includes 11 states that are not EU members, such as the Norway, Switzerland, and the United Kingdom. Neither the EPO nor the Boards of Appeal are directly part of the EU judicial framework, and thus they can neither submit questions to the CJEU on the interpretation of EU law, which was incorporated into the EPC, nor are they bound by any ruling of the CJEU.[70] However, for the time being, 27 of the EPC contracting states are bound by the CJEU's interpretation of EU law. This required a difficult balancing act at the European Patent Organisation when implementing the Brüstle v Greenpeace judgment by the CJEU[71] into the European patent system, suggesting via the examination guidelines that the EPO will take the judgment into account when interpreting the relevant provisions of the EPC Implementing Rules which reflect the EU Biotech Directive. These insti-

---

66 Art. 1(2) UPCA.
67 *See* Angelos Dimopoulos, *An Institutional Perspective II: The Role of the CJEU in the Unitary (EU) Patent System*, in Justine Pila and Christopher Wadlow (eds), *The Unitary EU Patent System* (Hart 2017) 57.
68 Art. 21 UPCA.
69 Stefan Luginbuehl, fn 31.
70 See decision of the Enlarged Board of Appeal of the EPO, G 2/06, OJ EPO 2009, 306, 317 et seq; Art. 23 (3) EPC.
71 Case C-34/10 Brüstle v Greepeace, (2011) ECR I-9849.

tutional tensions will further increase if more substantive patent law provided for in the EPC were to be interpreted by the CJEU.

16.5.3.2 The interpretation of substantive patent law provided for in the UPC Agreement by the CJEU

In connection with the definition of the exclusive rights under the unitary patent, it was already the aim of the CPC to unify further areas with effect for the then EC. This follows logically from the structure of the EPC.[72] These include, in particular, the exclusive rights to use the patent, for which the EPC refers to national law in accordance with the country of protection principle[73]. This objective of further promoting the EU internal market through the most uniform possible effects of a unitary patent has not changed with the EPO.

However, the definition of the scope of these rights and limitations (apart from its unitary nature) was removed again in the Regulation after severe criticism of the drafts. The same applies to the substantive rules on the unitary patent as an object of property. The United Kingdom in particular, but also highly qualified judges in the patent field[74] and lawyers[75], were concerned that the CJEU, and thus a court with no appropriate expertise, could have made binding pronouncements on substantive patent law. This would have jeopardised legal certainty[76]. The judges would even have seen the creation of a better patent litigation system in such a power of the CJEU as misguided[77]. As a result, these rules were moved[78] to the UPCA or deleted altogether[79], leaving them to the applicable national law.

While the CPC focused on the integration of substantive patent law into European Union law[80], this has been strongly diluted in the EPC Regulation by its deletion or shift-

---

72 Ingwer Koch & Dieter Stauder, Vereinbarung über Gemeinschaftspatente, 2. Auflage, Carl Heymanns, Köln 1997, 10.
73 Cf Art. 64(1) EPC.
74 Intellectual Property Judges Association (IPJA), Declaration of San Servolo, 2 November 2011.
75 EPLAW Resolution on the Draft Agreement 13751/11 of September 2, 2011.
76 See Ansgar Ohly, Auf dem Weg zum Einheitspatent und zum Einheitlichen Patentgericht, ZGE / IPJ 4 (2012) 419, at 439.
77 See Intellectual Property Judges Association (IPJA), Declaration of San Servolo, 2 November 2011.
78 See Christopher Wadlow, 'Hamlet without the prince': can the Unitary Patent Regulation strut its stuff without Articles 6 -8? und Hanns Ullrich, The Property aspects of the European Patent with Unitary Effect, 483; see also Ansgar Ohly, Auf dem Weg zum Einheitspatent und zum Einheitlichen Patentgericht, fn. 77, 426, and Erika Ellyne, European unitary patent: are we there yet?, Queen Mary Journal of Intellectual Property, vol 4 No. 1 (2014), 57, at 64ff; Avgi Kaisi, Finally a Single European Right for the EU? An Analysis of the substantive Provisions of the European Patent with Unitary Effect, EIPR 2014, 170, at 178.
79 See Mary-Rose McGuire, European Patent Package: das Zusammenspiel von EPVO, EPGÜ und nationalem Patentrecht, Mitt. 2015, 537, at 539.
80 Art. 25ff CPC.

ing to the EPC. This approach is also in contrast to the Community design[81] and the Union trademark[82]. As a consequence, the substantive patent law is also removed from the interpretation jurisdiction of the CJEU.

However, it is disputed whether the norms on the scope of protection of a unitary patent and their limitations, which have been shifted to the UPC, are not nevertheless subject to interpretation by the CJEU. It is argued that the right conferred by the unitary patent cannot be separated from the actual legal acts protecting this right, which define its scope, and therefore qualifies as Union law, even if these rights of use and the limitations now derive from national law and the UPC[83]. The following speaks against this: the CJEU has stated in its decision C-146/13 that the required uniformity of protection by the unitary patent, which the Regulation must ensure, results from the application of Article 5(3) and Article 7 Regulation 1257/2012. This ensures that certain national law is applicable in the territory of all participating states in which this patent has unitary effect. Even though the Regulation lacks an enumeration of the acts against which the unitary patent provides protection, this protection is unitary, since it applies to the unitary patent irrespective of the precise scope of the substantive protection provided by a unitary patent under the applicable national law according to Article 7 Regulation 1257/2012 in the territory of all Member States in which the patent has unitary effect[84]. Thus, the CJEU held that the right and the permissible acts flowing therefrom, which define the scope, can be separated from a Union law perspective and the latter can be left to national or international law. Thus, there is no competence of interpretation for the CJEU.[85]

However, should the CJEU nevertheless be of the opinion that this is Union law and that it can reach national or international law for interpretation via Article 5(3) Regulation 1257/2012, this would have consequences that would go far beyond the question of the scope of protection of the right. Furthermore, this could lead to the fact that the states participating in the enhanced cooperation will explicitly include other substantive law for their national patents in their national law in order to counteract possible disagreeable decisions of the CJEU. This is all the more to be feared as certain countries have deliberately not brought their substantive law, with effect for their national patents, in line with the UPCA in order to provide an alternative to the unitary patent or

---

81 See Art 19f Regulation (EC) 6/2002 of the Council of 12 December 2001 on Community designs.
82 See Art 9ff Regulation (EU) 2017/1001 of the European Parliament and the Council of 14 June 2017 on the European Union trademark.
83 Tilmann, The compromise on the uniform protection for EU patents, JIPLP 2013, 78, at 81.
84 EuGH C-146/13 Spanien vs Parlament und Rat vom 5. Mai 2015, Rn 47 ff. See also the criticla remarks by Josef Drexl, Einheitlicher Patentschutz durch Kollisionsrecht, in: Wolfgang Büscher/Willli Erdmann/Andreas Fuchs/Volker Michael Jänich/Michael Loschelder/Mary-Rose McGuire, Rechtsdurchsetzung, Festschrift für Hans-Jürgen Ahrens zum 70. Geburtstag, Carl Heymanns 2016, 165, 169ff.
85 See also Haedicke, Rechtsfindung, Rechtsfortbildung und Rechtskontrolle im Einheitlichen Patentsystem, GRUR 2013, 609, at 616.

European patent with effect on their territory. The consequence would be an even greater fragmentation of the law in Europe.

This should be an undesired development which would also have a negative impact on the EPO which is granting European patents and registering unitary patents.

16.6 Conclusion

With the UPC, a new judiciary in the form of an international organisation was created for, currently, 17 EU member states. This created a new player in the post-grant phase next to the EPO Boards of Appeal and all the national courts and other authorities of the 39 EPC contracting states. All these bodies apply and interpret substantive patent law established by the EPC. This includes in particular the extent of protection (Article 69 EPC), revocation grounds (Articles 138 and 139(2) EPC), and related patentability criteria (Articles 52–57 EPC).

The first instance of the UPC is organised in a decentralized way, i.e. there will be divisions for example in Copenhagen, Helsinki, Ljubljana, Lisbon, and of course Düsseldorf, Milan, Munich, The Hague and Paris. These chambers are staffed differently depending on the number of cases in their panels, i.e. either with one or two judges from the state hosting the Division. Depending on the Division, the local influence or interpretation tradition will therefore have a stronger or weaker influence.

Quite certainly there will be a really great atmosphere of departure in the UPC amongst judges and staff involved with a lot of momentum and above all interests to leave the national traditions behind and to look for new European solutions. Nevertheless, quite naturally or just because of this search for a new European solution, it will take some time until the different divisions will go more or less in the same direction in all questions of substantive uniform law. However, as already indicated the UPC does not have exclusive jurisdiction in the countries participating in the UPC Agreement. The courts that had jurisdiction still continue to have jurisdiction over the same patent disputes for the next 7 years. It will be particularly interesting to see whether these national courts will follow the jurisdiction of their big brother, or whether they will and perhaps want to explicitly distance themselves from it. The fact that many judges of the UPC only work part-time for the UPC and are therefore still active at the national level speaks in favour of a harmonization of jurisdiction. This is partly contradicted by legal policy requirements, since certain countries, such as for example France[86] have not explicitly adapted their substantive law to that of the UPCA, for example in the case of the Bolar ex-

---

86 Art. L613-5 d) of the French IP Code.

emption[87]. Therefore, in a relevant infringement case concerning a European patent, the national courts apply different substantive patent law than the UPC in the same infringement case, and this nota bene for a European patent which is valid for the same state. And then there are the national courts from the UK and Switzerland, two important patent nations in Europe. Will the courts of these states follow the UPC case law when it comes to interpreting the EPC? And last but not least, in Europe we already have a European patent court, at least as far as the question of the validity of a patent is concerned: the Boards of Appeal of the EPO. How will they behave towards the jurisdiction of the UPC? Certain EU politicians have already made their expectations clear in this respect and demanded that the Boards of Appeal should of course follow the UPC without hesitation. It is open whether they will really follow this request. It seems quite clear that these nations will increasingly turn away from the existing EPC system if they are not properly represented and heard, and a truly European discourse takes place among all the courts involved. It is thus crucial that the judges of the different courts in Europe take into account their judgments and jurisprudence, regularly meet and exchange views on controversial aspects of law. It is thus time to revive the European Patent Judges Symposium[88] which was halted in 2014.

---

[87] Art. 27(b) and (d) UPCA.
[88] Cf. <https://www.epo.org/law-practice/judiciary/documentation.html>.

Hanns Ullrich

17 The role of the Court of Justice of the European Union

17.1 The role of the CJEU in EU intellectual property in general

17.1.1 The provisions of the Treaties

Art. 19(1) TEU provides that the Court of Justice of the European Union "shall ensure that in the interpretation and the application of the Treaties the law is observed."
  Pursuant to Art. 19(3) TEU

> "The Court of Justice … shall, in accordance with the Treaties: a) rule on actions brought by…a natural or legal person; b) give preliminary rulings, at the request of courts or tribunals of the Member States, in the interpretation of Union law or the validity of acts adopted by the institution; …."[1]

Pursuant to Art. 263(1) TFEU the Court of Justice

> "shall review the legality of … acts of the Commission …. intended to produce legal effects vis-à-vis third parties. It shall also review the legality of acts of bodies, offices or agencies of the Union intended to produce legal effects vis-à-vis third parties."

Art. 263(2) TFEU states that for "this purpose" the Court shall have

> "jurisdiction in actions brought by a Member State, the European Parliament, the Council or the Commission on grounds of lack of competence, infringement of an essential procedural requirement, infringement of the treaties or of a rule of law relating to their application, or misuse of powers".

---

[1] Art. 19(3) lit. b) TEU is implemented by Art. 267 TFEU, which reads:
The Court of Justice of the European Union shall have jurisdiction to give preliminary rulings concerning:
a) the interpretation of the Treaties;
b) the validity and interpretation of acts of the institutions, bodies, offices or agencies of the Union.
Where such a question is raised before any court or tribunal of a Member State, that court or tribunal may, if it considers that a decision on the question is necessary to enable it to give judgment, request the Court to give a ruling thereon.
Where any such question is raised in a case pending before a court or tribunal of a Member States against whose decisions there is no judicial remedy under national law, that court or tribunal shall bring the matter before the Court.

Hanns Ullrich, Prof. (i.R.) Dr. iur., Dr. eh., MCJ (NY Univ.); Honorary professor, College of Europe, Bruges.

Pursuant to Art. 263(4) TFEU

> "Any natural or legal person may, under the conditions laid down in the first and second paragraphs, institute proceedings against an act addressed to that person or which is of direct and individual concern to them ...."

Art. 263(5) TFEU provides that

> "Acts setting up bodies, offices and agencies of the Union may lay down specific conditions and arrangements concerning actions brought by natural or legal persons against acts of these bodies, offices or agencies intended to produce legal effects in relation to them."

These rules of primary Union law describe and determine the central role the Court of Justice of the European Union has to fulfill as regards ensuring the autonomy of the legal order of the Union and the well-functioning of its system of complete and effective judicial protection in general, and, more particularly, as regards safeguarding the autonomy of the EU's system of intellectual property protection and the unity of its judicial implementation.

17.1.2 The role of the Court of Justice under Reg. 1257/2012 and under other EU intellectual property regulations compared

17.1.2.1 Review of the grant and of the validity of EU intellectual property rights

Little if anything of this role seems to be present in the system of European and European Union patent protection that Regulation 1257/2012 on the European patent with unitary effect (UP Reg.)[2] and the Agreement on a Unified Patent Court[3] establish and that, after half a century of continuously reduced ambitions of integrating it into the EU's legal and judicial order,[4] entered into application on 1 June 2023. While the deci-

---

[2] Regulation (EU) No. 1257/2012 of the European Parliament and of the Council of 11 December 2012 implementing enhanced cooperation in the area of the creation of unitary patent protection, OJEU 2012 L 361, 1.

[3] Agreement on a Unified Patent Court of 19 February 2013, OJEU 2013 L 175, 1.

[4] See *Rat der Europäischen Gemeinschaften*, „Erster Vorentwurf eines Übereinkommens über das Europäische Patent für den Gemeinsamen Markt" ausgearbeitet von der Sachverständigengruppe „Gemeinschaftspatent", Luxemburg 1970 (= GRUR 1970, 122), Art. 67 and 77, which provided for judicial review by the Court of Justice of the decisions of the Revocation Boards of the EPO regarding the Community patent and for a preliminary ruling procedure regarding the interpretation of the Agreement, respectively. These provisions became Art. 63 and 73 of the 1975 Convention for the European patent for the common market (Community Patent Convention), OJEC 1976 L 17, 1. For the subsequent developments see *Th. Jaeger*, The EU Patent: Cui bono et quo vadit? 47 CMLRev. 63, 79 et seq. (2010); *H. Ullrich*, EuGH und EPO im Europäischen Patentschutzsystem: Wer hat was zu sagen?, in: *A. Metzger* (ed.), Methodenfragen des Patentrechts, Tübingen (Mohr Siebeck) 2018, 229 (= Max-Planck-Institute for Innovation

sions of the European Union's Intellectual Property Office (EUIPO) and of the Community Plant Variety Office (CPVO) regarding the registration, revocation or invalidation of a Union trade mark, a Community design or a plant variety right are subject to judicial review by the General Court and, upon appeal in law, by the Court of Justice,[5] decisions regarding the grant or the revocation of a European patent by the European Patent Office (EPO) are subject to review only by the quasi-judicial Boards of Appeal of that Office[6], a non-EU international administrative body, even if the European patent at issue is, by virtue of the law, one of unitary EU-effect.[7] Due to the decentralized jurisdiction of national courts ruling as European Union trade mark or design courts on counterclaims for revocation or invalidation of an EU trade mark or a Community design in inter partes (infringement) proceedings, the Court of Justice will, upon request for a preliminary ruling (Art. 267 TFEU), decide upon the proper interpretation of the grounds for revocation or invalidation, which at this stage of the existence of EU industrial property titles are to be applied by the national courts.[8] By contrast, since, according to the majority opinion, Art. 138 EPC, which states the grounds of invalidity of European patents, is self-executory in the sense of being directly applicable, and since, at any rate,

---

and Competition, Discussion Paper No. 8, ssrn.com/abstract=2942199); *id.*, Le futur système de protection des inventions par brevets dans l'Union européenne – un exemple d'intégration (re-)poussée? Prop. Int. 2014 (53) 382 = ssrn.com/abstract=2464032, sub. II.B.2.a) with references.

5 Following an EUIPO internal, quasi-judicial review procedure, see Art. 66 et seq. 72 Reg. (EU) 2017/1001 of 14 June 2017 on the European Union trade mark (OJEU 2017 L 154, 1); Art. 55 et seq., 61 Reg. (EC) 6/2002 of 12 December 2001 on Community Designs (OJEC 2002 L 3, 1); Art. 67 et seq., 73 Reg. (EC) 2100/94 of 27 July 1994 on Community plant variety rights (OJEC 1994 L 227, 1); for a summary presentation see *Ullrich*, in *Metzger*, loc.cit. p. 232 et seq.

6 See *H. Ullrich*, The European Patent and Its Courts: An Uncertain Prospect and an Unfinished Agenda, 46 IIC 1, 4 et seq. (2015) with references. Although BVerfG (Federal Constitutional Court) of 8 November 2022, case 2 BvR 2480/10 et al., ECLI:DE:BVerfG:2022:rs20221108.2bvr248010, paras. 123 et passim, 165 et passim confirmed that the quasi-judicial review of the decisions of the EPO by its Technical Boards of Appeal complies with international minimum standards of judicial independence and fair trial, the facts remain, first, that these Boards form part of the EPO's organization and depend on the EPO as regards their financing, so also as regards their number, overall staffing and facilities, and, second, that as to their professional career the members of the Boards remain part of the EPO's administrative personnel.

7 See Art. 3(1) with Recital 7 Reg. 1257/2012; CJEU of 5 May 2015, case C-146/13, *Spain/European Parliament and Council*, ECLI:EU:C:2015:298; para. 29; for a critique see inter alia *Th. Mylly*, Hovering between intergovernalism and unionization: The shape of unitary patents, 54 CMLRev.1391, 1397 et passim (2017); *Th. Jaeger*, Nach l'Europe à la carte nun la loi européenne à la carte? Zur Erlaubnis der Umgehung der Unionsmethode nach dem Urteil in Rs.C-146/13 u.a., EuR 2015, 461, 471 et seq. For the problem resulting from the qualification of the unitary character of the UP as being merely accessory to the EPO granted patent see infra 17.2.1.2.(i).

8 By exception to the invalidation privilege of the CJEU regarding acts of the institutions and bodies of the Union (Art. 267(1) lit. b) TFEU), see *Th. Jaeger*, System einer Europäischen Gerichtsbarkeit für Immaterialgüterrechte, Berlin 2013, 89 et seq., 419 et seq.; *Ullrich* in *Metzger* (ed.), loc.cit., p. 234 et seq., both with references. By contrast, Art. 20, 21 Reg. 2100/94 reserve the invalidation or revocation of plant variety rights to the Community Plant Variety Office and to judicial review by the Court of Justice, see supra n. 5.

these grounds are not taken up by Reg. 1257/2012 but held to be those of the European "basis" patent,[9] their interpretation may a priori not be submitted to the Court of Justice under Art. 267 TFEU.

This means that, as a matter of principle, the Court of Justice as the supreme court of the European Union has hardly any role to play as regards the interpretation of the criteria of patent eligibility (concept of invention, exclusions from patentability, ordre public[10]) and the merit criteria of patentability (novelty, non-obviousness, sufficient disclosure/enablement) although they express a major part of a legislature's patent policy.[11]

---

9 See recital 7 Reg. 1257/2012 in fine, Art. 65(2) UPCA. For the misleading characterization of the relationship between the European patent and the unitary effect attributed to it by Art. 3(1) Reg. 1257/2012 see infra 17.2.1.2.(i).

10 However, as regards the unitary patent, it is by its very nature that the ordre public reservation (Art. 53, lit. a) EPC) must come within the CJEU's interpretation privilege under Art. 267 TFEU. In respect of the European patent with unitary effect (as distinguished from the European bundle patent), the refusal by the Enlarged Board of Appeal (of 25 November 2008, case G2/06, GRURInt 2010,230, 233 et seq., paras. 2 et passim) to submit to the CJEU a request for a preliminary ruling on the ground, inter alia, that the exclusions from patentability are a matter of international EPC law, is not convincing. The EU cannot accept a patent that is incompatible with its ordre public, the substance of which it must be able to itself determine, at the very least in respect of a patent that rests on Union law (comp. also infra n. 11). The next question then is whether the statutory exclusions that serve to specify the ordre public reservation, such as Rules 28 et seq. EPC Implementing Regulation, which mirror only Art. 5(1), Art. 6(2) Dir. 98/44 of 6 July 1998 on the legal protection of biotechnological inventions (OJEC 1998 L 213, 13), may really be exempted from the CJEU's jurisdiction under Art. 267 TFEU. The double split in pre grant/post grant control and public international/European Union law simply is inadequate.

Note that in order to grant patents centrally the EPO is almost obliged to apply an international standard whereas the reference in recital 39 of Dir. 98/44/EC to ethical or moral principles "recognized in a Member State" (in the German version "in the Member States"!) is explained by that the directive harmonizes national law. When transposed to the unitary patent, this reference must mean the group of Member States adhering to enhanced cooperation and to the UPCA. In any case, the conflict remains; for a detailed discussion see *Cl. Petersen, Th. Riis, J. Schovsbo*, The Unified Patent Court (UPC) in Action: How will the Design of the UPC Affect Patent Law? in *R. Ballardini, M. Noorgard, N. Bruun* (eds.), Transitions in European Patent Law – Influences of the Unitary Patent Package, Alphen adR (Kluwer) 2015, 37, 46 et seq.

11 It is only in the particular field of biotechnological inventions that the CJEU may at least indirectly exercise some limited control by interpreting, upon request by the UPC (or a national court), the criteria of patent eligibility and of patentability that Art. 1 to 5 Dir. 98/44/EC on biotechnological inventions (supra no. 10) harmonizes in respect of national patent law; comp. CJEU of 18 October 2011, case C-34/10, *Brüstle/Greenpeace*, Rep. 2011 I 9831 = ECLI:EU:C:2011:669; of 18 October 2014, case C-364/13, *International Stem Cell Corporation/Comptroller General of Patents*, ECLI:EU:C:2014:2451. This is so because post grant the grounds of invalidation the European patent and, consequently, also those of the unitary patent, come under national law (as harmonized by Dir. 98/44); see *Ullrich* in *Metzger* (ed.), loc.cit, 246 et seq. Member States may not escape harmonization by an international agreement among them and admit on their territories the co-existence of non-harmonized EPO-granted national patents. At any rate, it is surprising that the CJEU's power of control over the interpretation of harmonized national patent protection by Member States' courts seems to reach further than its power of judicial review over at least the interpretation of the Union's own system of patent protection. None of the Member States has given away that minimum of judicial review by their own courts that is the ex post control over the interpretation and ap-

17.1.2.2 Interpretation of the rules of substantive law of EU intellectual property protection

(i) Likewise, as regards the substance of a right of intellectual property, such as the definition of the infringing acts, the exceptions from protection and the determination of the scope of exclusive control over the protected subject matter, the system of unitary patent protection confers much less power of control on the Court of Justice than do the regulations on the EU trade mark, the Community design or the Community plant variety right. Under all of the latter, national courts, acting as EU trade mark or Community design courts or simply as ordinary courts of the Union, may, and, if courts of last instance, must request preliminary rulings by the Court of Justice on the interpretation of any of the terms of the almost full set of rules of substantive law of protection that Regulation No. 2017/1001, No. 6/2022 and No. 2100/94 establish (Art. 267 TFEU).[12] Since the breadth of this authority of the Court of Justice to interpret the substantive law of the Union's systems of industrial property protection is enlarged by the powers the Court has under Art. 267 TFEU to authoritatively interpret the harmonization directives regarding trade marks and designs,[13] in practice the Court of Justice holds a strong position of judicial control over the development of infringement law and related matters.[14]

(ii) By contrast, instead of setting forth the rules implementing both "the right to prevent any third party from committing acts against which that (unitary) patent provides protection throughout the territories" wherein the patent is of unitary effect (Art. 5(1) Reg. 1257/2012) and the "applicable limitations" to which it is subject (Art. 5(1) Reg. 1257/2012 in fine), Art. 5(3) in combination with Art. 7 Reg. 1257/2012 establish a referral mechanism to the national laws of the Member States participating in enhanced cooperation. This mechanism operates to the effect that, first, throughout the territory of actual

---

plication of the grounds of invalidity of national patents flowing from the grant of a European patent. How can the EU be assumed to have done so? After all, adopting EPO-granted patents as a basis for unitary patent protection means adopting the EPC as part of the EU's patent policy.

12 See Art. 9–16, 130 EU Trademark Reg.; Art. 19–22, 89 ComDesignReg.; Art. 13–16, 94 ComPlant Variety Rights Reg.

13 As to the infringing acts and exceptions see Art. 10–15 Directive (EU) 2015/2436 of 16 December 2015 to approximate the law of Member States relating to trade marks (OJEU 2015 L 336, 1), Art. 12–15 Directive 98/71/EC of 13 October 1998 on the legal protection of designs (OJEC 1998 L 289, 28).

14 The actual exercise of that power of control, however, is limited by national courts' willingness to submit requests for preliminary rulings. Pursuant to *CJEU*, Annual Report 2020, tab. IV, in 2020 out of a total of 555 requests only 11 related to intellectual property (copyright, designs and trademarks confounded); in 2021 it was 23 out of 566 (see *id.*, Annual Report 2021, tab. IV). These numbers are constant, see for former years *Ullrich* in *Metzger* (ed.), loc.cit. p. 236, n. 48. Note that the Court's experience with intellectual property matters is much broader since it has to take the appeals in law from the General Court's judgments on decisions of the EUIPO's Boards of Appeal (in 2020: 40 out of 282 judgements of the GenCt, in 2021: 61 out of 308 judgments of the GenCt).

enhanced cooperation each European patent with unitary effect is subject to a single national law of infringement and limitations, namely that of the residence or place of business of its owner. Second, due to the linkage between Reg. 1257/2012 and the Agreement on the United Patent Court,[15] it is ultimately the rules of substantive patent law of that Agreement that will apply to all unitary patents, so rules that originally had been taken over from the Community Patent Conventions to the defunct European and European Union Patent Court Agreement (EEUPC Agreement) and its predecessors as a matter of making these agreements work properly for the European bundle of national patents.[16] The result of this approach is that the rules of substantive law that govern the unitary patent, namely Art. 25 to 28 UPCA, rest on an agreement of public international law between the EU Member States participating in enhanced cooperation, and that, therefore, their interpretation seems to be outside the jurisdiction of the Court of Justice, it being limited by Art. 267 TFEU[17] to the interpretation of the Treaties and of the acts of the institutions and bodies of the Union.

Accordingly, the role that Reg. 1257/2012 retains for the Court of Justice to play seems to be limited by a dividing line that follows a formal distinction between Union law and public international law rather than a functional distinction between the tasks of the Court of Justice as a supreme court of general jurisdiction and those of the Unified Patent Court as a specialized court of combined legal and technical expertise.[18] Given the dual applicability of the UPCA to the European bundle patent and the unitary patent, the latter dividing line also appears to be more appropriate than a comparison between the rules that embrace the bundle of national patents forming the UPCA-type of a European patent on the one hand, and, on the other, the unitary patent protection that derives its legal authority from a Union regulation. Therefore, the following examination of the

---

15 See recital 9 and Art. 18(2) Reg. 1257/2012. Its confusingly worded subpara. 2 means only that the unitary effect will be triggered only if the UPCA was effective at the date of registration; it does not delink the unitary effect from the substantive law applicable to the unitary patent, see W. Tilmann in W. Tilmann, Cl. Plassmann (eds.), Unified Patent Protection in Europe, Oxford (OUP) 2018, Art. 18 Reg. 1257/2012, para. 3 (p. 275).
16 See Art. 29 et seq. Community Patent Convention 1975 (supra n. 4); Art. 25 et seq. Community Patent Convention 1985/89, OJEC 1989 L 401,9; Art. 14 a et seq. Draft Agreement on the European and Community Patents Court and Draft Statute – Revised presidency text (Council of the EU, Doc. 7928/09 of 23 March 2009). For the origin of the Draft EEUPC agreement in the semi-official, EPO-supported European Patent Litigation Agreement (EPLA), and the need to incorporate rules of substantive patent law into it see H. Ullrich, National, European and Community Patent Protection: Time for Reconsideration in A. Ohly, D. Klippel (eds.), Geistiges Eigentum und Gemeinfreiheit, Tübingen (Mohr Siebeck) 2007, 61, 79 et passim (= European University Institute, EUI-Working Paper, Law No. 2006/41); id., loc.cit., Prop.Int.2014(53), 382 sub II. B.2.a).
17 Irrespective of whether Art. 267 TFEU applies directly or by virtue of Art. 21 UPCA, the acts qualifying for interpretation by the CJEU are limited to acts of the Union, its bodies and agencies. For the proper qualification of Art. 25–28 UPCA see infra 17.2.1.2.
18 For the nature of the UPC as a specialized court see infra 17.2.2.2.(ii); E. van Zimmeren, UPC structure and procedure; this volume, chap. 18.

role of the Court of Justice will focus on how to draw the dividing line with due respect for the functions of the Court of Justice and of the Unified Patent Court as regards unitary patent protection.[19]

17.2 The role of the Court of Justice in the interpretation of the rules of substantive law of the unitary patent and the European bundle patent

17.2.1 The law covered by Art. 267 TFEU

17.2.1.1 Union law

(i) The rules of substantive law that come under the authority of interpretation of the Court of Justice are manifold. As regards the unitary patent they relate not only to the definition of unity and uniformity of protection (Art. 3 and 5 Reg. 1257/2012), including, possibly, the infringing and the exempted acts on which this contribution will focus,[20] but also to licenses of right (Art. 8 Reg. 1257/2012), to the acquisition of the unitary effect

---

[19] A new approach is the more justified as the rules of substantive law of the unitary patent always formed part of the proposed Community Patent Regulation until its last version (Art. 7–10 Proposal for a Council Regulation on the Community Patent – General Approach, *Council of the EU*, Doc. 16113/09 of 27 November 2009) and even of the compromise text of the fundamentally changed proposal made within the framework of enhanced cooperation (see Art. 6–9 Proposal for a Regulation implementing enhanced cooperation in the area of the creation of unitary patent protection – Analysis of the final compromise text, *Council of the EU*, Doc. 17578/11 of 1 December 2011) until they were transferred to the envisaged UPCA as a matter of satisfying the domestic policy interests of a Member State that disdained the Court and, before the entry into application of Reg. 1257/2012 and the entry into force of the UPCA, left the Union with no less disdain and no interest in further participation in the UPCA. For these developments, see *Ullrich*, loc.cit. Prop. Int. 2014(53) 382 sub II.B.b),(iv) with in n. 139 noting also the acclaim by certain circles of the patent law community.

[20] Infra sub. 17.2.1.2. Exhaustion of the right of exclusive distribution of the patent is expressly covered by Art. 6 Reg. 1257/2012 as it is in similar terms by Art. 15 Reg. 2017/1001 on the Union trade mark, Art. 21 Reg. 6/2001 on Community designs and Art. 16 Reg. 2100/94 on Community plant variety rights. Except for the latter, the differences do not result from the different nature of patents, trade marks or designs, but from legislative inconsistency. As primacy of Art. 34 et seq. TFEU will help overcoming them (comp. as regards Art. 7 Directive 89/104 on the approximation of the laws of trade marks CJEU of 11 July 1996, joint cases C-427/93, C-429/93 and C-430/93, *Bristol-Myers-Squibb/Paranova* et al, Rep. 1996 I 3457 =ECLI:EU:C:1996:282, paras. 24 et seq.), there is no need to discuss the matter in more detail here. For the same reason, Art. 28 UPCA on exhaustion of the UPC-type of European patents will not be specifically considered.

and its publication by registration (Art. 3(1), Art. 4 Reg. 1257/2012), and to the language regime provided for by Reg. 1257/2012.[21]

As regards, more particularly, the administration of requests for unitary effect, of licenses of right and of renewal fees, Art. 9(1) lit. a)–c) and lit. e) Reg. 1257/2012 oblige the Member States to give these tasks to the European Patent Office,[22] and Art. 9(3) Reg. 1257/2012 obliges them to ensure effective legal protection before a competent court against the decisions taken by the EPO in carrying out these tasks. Member States have done so by attributing jurisdiction to the UPC over actions covering these decisions by the EPO (Art. 32 (1) lit. (i) UPCA.[23] This means that decisions of the EPO on the acquisition of unitary effect of a European patent, so decisions on its very nature as a patent of Union-wide effect, on the maintenance of that effect and on Union-wide access to the protected invention are subject to review only by the UPC. Consequently, the Court of Justice's role is limited to interpret, upon request by the UPC for a preliminary ruling, the relevant terms and concepts of Reg. 1257/2012, such as the condition that, in order to qualify for unitary protection, the national patents forming the European bundle patent must contain the same set of claims.[24] While the answer to this issue appears to be self-evident and a matter of formality, other issues may be less easy to resolve, such as the limitation of unitary protection

---

21 Reg. (EU) 1260/2012 implementing enhanced cooperation in the area of unitary patent protection with regard to the applicable translation requirements, OJEU 2012 L 361, 89. Although the language regime is not merely a procedural matter (see H. Ullrich, Les régimes linguistiques limités des systèmes de la propriété industrielle de l'Union européenne: injustes mais inévitables, Rev.int.dr.écon (RIDE) 2020, 453), it cannot be considered here. However, the arguments submitted in the text regarding the application of Art. 267 TFEU to UPC-rulings relating to the EPO tasks listed in Art. 9(1) lit. a), c), e) Reg. 1257/2012 cover also the matters coming under Art. 9 lit. f) Reg. 1257/2012.

22 More precisely, it obliges Member States to exercise their powers under Art. 143 EPC accordingly, assuming that the group of Member States forming enhanced cooperation comes under Art. 142 EPC by virtue of Art. 1(2) Reg. 1257/2012, and does so despite the fact that only part of that group actually adheres to the UPCA and, thus, to the system of unitary patent protection; for the problem raised by Art. 1(2) Reg. 1257/2012 see Ullrich, loc.cit., Prop.Int. 2014 (53) 382 sub. II.B.1.c)(i), C.2.c) with references.

23 See UPC, Rules of Procedure, rules 85 et seq., rule 87 defining the grounds for annulling or altering a decision of the Office, namely infringement of Reg. 1257/2012 or Reg. 1260/2012, or of any rule relating to their application; infringement of any of the implementing rules of the EPO for carrying out the tasks referred to in Art. 9(1) Reg. 1257/2012; infringement of essential procedural requirements; misuse of power. The Rules of Procedure thus seem to solve the problem that Art. 9(1) and Art. 12 Reg. 1257/2012 only bind the Member States, not the European Patent Organization (see Mylly, loc.cit., 54 CMLRev. 1401 (2017)). However, the Rules of Procedure are only public international treaty law as delegated to the Administrative Committee of the UPC, see Art. 41 UPCA.

24 Given that it is the very purpose of the EPO to grant, through a centralized procedure, patents on the basis of a law common to the Contracting States, so at uniform conditions, the patents resulting from the European grant are bound to have the same set of claims, the main exception being due to Art. 139(2) EPC, see Rule 138 Implementing Rules. However, the consequences of this exception for the unitary effect are assessed differently; see Tilmann in Tilmann, Plassmann (eds.), loc.cit., Art. 3 Reg. 1257/2012, paras. 49, 53 et seq.; A. Hüttermann in A. Hüttermann (ed.), Einheitspatent und Einheitliches Patentgericht, Cologne (Carl Heymanns) 2012, paras. 147 et seq. Note that the wording of the German version of Art. 3 Reg. 1257/

upon amendment of the claims to the limits of amended claims (Art. 3(3) Reg. 1257/2012) or, more generally, to the substantive scope of the patent. Indeed, due precisely to Art. 3(1) and (3) Reg. 1257/2012, issues arising in these respects are likely to present a mixed character of Union law and EPC law (Art. 69 EPC), and, thus will arguably come also within the jurisdiction the CJEU has under the Art. 267 TFEU. Other issues may arise more indirectly, such as whether in view of the significance of the unitary effect for patent protection in the Internal Market the EPO's rules on the registration procedure and their application take due account of the requirements of administrative due process.[25] Similarly, the legality of the renewal fees that determine a patentee's willingness to acquire and maintain a unitary patent and, thus, the incentive effect of patents for innovation, rests on that these fees are fixed in full compliance with Art. 12 Reg. 1257/2012.[26] While, as such, the fee schedule and its amendments may not be subject to direct judicial review, their compatibility with Art. 12 Reg. 1257/2012 presents questions of interpretation of the criteria of Art. 12 Reg. 1257/2012 and of their enigmatic interplay that come under Art. 267 TFEU and its function of complementary judicial protection.[27]

(ii) In its opinion 1/09 on the (in)compatibility of the once envisaged Agreement on a European and European Union Patent Court (EEUPC)[28] the Court of Justice described the extent to which that court – and, consequently, now the UPC – would have to apply general Union law in addition to the Regulation on the Community patent, now the UP-Regulation 1257/2012, as covering "in particular regulations and directives in conjunction with which that regulation would, when necessary, have to be read, namely provisions relating to other bodies of rules on intellectual property, and rules of the FEU-Treaty concerning the internal market and competition law. Likewise, the PC (i.e. the EEUPC) may be called upon to determine a dispute pending before it in the light of the fundamental rights and general principles of European law ..."[29]

2012 ("gleiche Ansprüche") differs from the English ("same set of claim"), French ("même jeu de revendications") and Italian ("stessa serie di rivendicazioni") versions.
25 See Art. 41 EUChFR; for its origin in and development by the CJEU's case law see M. Ruffert, in Chr. Calliess, M. Ruffert (eds.), EUV- AEUV, 6th ed. Munich (C.H. Beck) 2022, Art. 41 GRCh, paras. 3, 10 et passim.
26 Even though – or because? – the criteria determining the level of renewal fees are in part dysfunctional, see Ullrich, loc.cit., Prop.int. 2014(53) 382 sub II.B.1.c), (ii).
27 See J. Schwarze, N. Wunderlich in U. Becker, A. Hatje, J. Schoo, J. Schwarze, (eds.), EU-Kommentar, 4th ed. Baden-Baden (Nomos) 2019, Art. 267 AEUV, para. 5; B. Wegener in Calliess, Ruffert (eds), loc.cit., EUV-AEUV, Art. 267 AEUV, para. 1. Given that Art. 12 Reg. 1257/2012 defines only the criteria that Member States have to respect in fulfilling their obligations under Art. 9(2) Reg. 1257/2012, it is only by using Art. 267 TFEU that a minimum of judicial protection against disproportionate levels of renewal fees can be ensured. The only direct remedy is an action for infringement of Union law to be brought by the Commission (see its reporting duties under Art. 16(2) Reg. 1257/2012) or by a Member State (Art. 263(2) TFEU) against the Member States actually adhering to the system of unitary patents.
28 See supra n. 16.
29 CJEU, op. 1/09 of 8 March 2011, Rep. 2011 I 1137=ECLI:EU:C:2011:123, para. 78; see also CJEU of 30 June 2011, case C-271/10, VEWA/Belgium, Rep. 2011 I 5815 = ECLI:EU:C:2011:442, para. 27.

Given the limited purpose and space of this contribution it is not possible to elaborate on how the interpretation these four categories of Union law may become relevant for the application of Reg. 1257/2012 by the UPC. A few merely summary remarks must suffice. As to reading the rules of unitary patent protection in the light of or by comparing them to other bodies of EU-rules on intellectual property, both the general principles of intellectual property and those rules of other areas of EU intellectual property come to mind that address the same issues as do Reg. 1257/2012 or the provisions of the UPCA implementing it (Art. 25–28 UPCA).[30] As regards the former, it is true that the absolute character of the exclusivity conferred by an intellectual property right varies with the type of that property, the "monopoly" character of, e.g., copyright or of plant variety rights being less pronounced than that of patents for inventions. For instance, independent creation or breeding by third parties are not encompassed by the exclusivity as are independent inventions by virtue of the principles of novelty and priority. Also, the infringing acts are defined differently for the various categories of intellectual property.[31] However, the common denominator of all intellectual property – and not a small one – is that, to the difference of tangible property in general, it serves a public policy goal that ought to inform its functional interpretation.[32] Another common feature is that the exceptions from the exclusivity of protection also need to be read with respect to their function rather than "narrowly",[33] in particular with a view to their in-

---

[30] For the relationship between Reg. 1257/2012 and the UPCA see infra 17.2.1.2..

[31] As to the latter comp., e.g., the catalogue of infringing acts of Art. 9 Reg. 2017/1001 on the EU trade mark, Art. 13 Reg. 2100/94 on community plant varieties, and, in particular Art. 2 to 4 of Directive 2001/29/EC of 22 May 2001 on the harmonization of certain aspects of copyright and related rights in the information society, OJEC 2001 L 167, 10 (no infringement by use of copyrighted work). Also, indirect infringement (Art. 26 UPCA) is not within the scope of copyright, the design right or the plant variety rights and regulated very specifically for trademarks (Art. 1 Reg. 2017/1001). For the category-specific limitations see following text.

[32] See H. Ullrich, Legal Protection of Innovative Technologies: Property or Policy?: In O. Granstrand (ed.), Economics, Law and Intellectual Property, Boston (Kluwer) 2003, 439, 466 et seq., 470 et seq.; id., Intellectual Property: Exclusive Rights for a Purpose – The Case of Technology Protection by Patents and Copyright, in Problemy Polskiego I Europejskiego Prawa Prywatnego (Festschrift M. Kepinski (K. Klaftkowska-Wasniowska, et al., eds.), Warsaw (Wolters Kluwer) 2012, 425, 433 et passim (= Max-Planck-Institute for Intellectual Property and Competition Law Research Paper No. 13-01=ssrn.com/abstract=2179511, sub. III.).

[33] For the established but ambivalent case law that tends to a narrow, yet teleological interpretation see as regards in particular copyright inter alia CJEU of 16 July 2009, case C-5/08, *Infopaq International/Danske Dagblades Forening*, Rep. 2009 I 6569 = ECLI:EU:C:2009:465, paras. 40 et 56 et seq.; of 4 October 2011, joint cases C-403/08 and C-429/08, *Football Association Premier League/QC Leisure* et al., Rep. 2011 I 9083 = ECLI:EU:C:2011:631, paras. 161 et seq.; of 1 December 2011, case C-145/10, *Painer/Standard VerlagsGmbH*, Rep. 2011 I 12533 = ECLI:EU:C:2011:798, paras. 109 et seq., 133; of 5 June 2014, case C-360/13, *Public Relations Consultants Association/Newspaper Licensing Agency*, ECLI:EU:C:2014:1195, paras. 23 et seq.; of 3 September 2014, case C-201/13, *Deckmyn/Vandersteen*, ECLI:EU:C:2014:2132, paras. 22 et seq.; of 29 November 2017, case C-265/16, *VCAST/RTI*, ECLI:EU:C:2017:913, para. 32.

terrelationship with exclusions from protection[34] or as expressions of countervailing rights.[35]

As to the specific rules of substantive law, systemic consistency of intellectual property protection by the EU requires that common concepts, such as those of the infringing acts (using, making, offering, putting on the market, importing, storing) be interpreted in the same way or different meanings explained by the particular nature of the intellectual property right at issue.[36] Likewise, exceptions from the exclusivity that rest on common concepts ask for consistent interpretation, in particular in case of conflicts between overlapping rights. Thus, Art. 27 lit. k) UPCA expressly transposes the decompilation rule of Art. 5, 6 Directive 2009/24/EC on the legal protection of software by copyright to both the unitary patent and the UPCA-type of European patents and, therefore, requires uniform interpretation. However, other examples are rare. One is private noncommercial use, another experimental use,[37] and still another the prior user right, the latter asking

---

34 See *L. Bentley*, Exclusions from Patentability and Exceptions to Patentees' Rights, Taking Exceptions Seriously, in Current Legal Problems 2011, 1, 5 et passim.
35 See inter alia *S. Dusollier*, Unlimiting limitations in intellectual property, in *G. Ghidini, V. Falce* (eds.), Reforming Intellectual Property, Cheltenham (E. Elgar) 2022, 64, 71 et seq.
36 See Art. 25 lit. a) UPCA, Art. 19 Reg. 6/2002 on the Community Design on the one hand, on the other, Art. 9 Reg. 2017/1001 on the EU trade mark and Art. 13 Reg. 2100/94 on Community plant variety rights. Despite the obvious differences, notions such as making, stocking/storing are the same; the notion of putting/placing on the market is determined by the CJEU's case law on exhaustion, see e.g. CJEU of 30 November 2004, case C-16/03, *Peak Holding/Axolin-Elinor*, Rep. 2004 I 11313 = ECLI:EU:C:2004:759, paras. 30 et seq.; of 3 June 2010, case C-127/09, *Coty Prestige Lancaster Group/Simex Trading*, Rep. 2010 I 4965 = ECLI:EU:C:2010:313, paras. 29 et seq.. Import is an infringing act under all regimes, and so is export under most regimes but, for good reason, not under Art. 25 UPCA.
Commonalities exist also as regards remedies for infringement that are harmonized by Directive 2004/48/EC of the Parliament and the Council of 29 April 2004 on the enforcement of intellectual property rights, OJEU 2004 L 157,45; see e.g. for the determination of claims to compensation *A. Hüttermann*, Die mögliche Bedeutung jüngster EuGH-Entscheidungen für das Einheitspatentsystem, Mitt.dt.PatAnw. 2021, 4 et seq.
37 For the former see Art. 27, lit. a) UPCA, Art. 20, lit. a) Reg. 6/2002 on the Community Design, Art. 1, lit. a) Reg. 2100/94 on Community plant variety rights; for the latter Art. 27, lit. b) UPCA, Art. 20, lit. b) Reg. 6/2002, Art. 15, lit.b) Reg. 2100/94. Despite their different wording the experimental use exceptions from the protection of a Community design or a Community plant variety right are generally read in the same narrow way as is the experimental use exception from patent protection; see for designs *D. Jestaedt* in *H. Eichmann* et al. (eds.), Designgesetz, Gemeinschaftsgeschmacksmusterverordnung, 6th ed. Munich (C. H. Beck) 2019, Art. 20 GGV, para. 7; *O. Ruhl* (ed.) Gemeinschaftsgeschmacksmuster, 3rd ed. Cologne (Carl Heymanns) 2019, Art. 20, paras. 8 et seq. (main purpose is to avoid conflicts of overlapping protection by patents and designs); for a broader reading *Chr. Spintig* in *G. Hasselblatt* (ed.), Community Design Regulation, 2rd ed. Munich (C.H. Beck) 2018, Art. 20 p. 10 et seq.; for plant variety rights *H. Leßmann, G. Würtenberger*, Deutsches und Europäisches Sortenschutzecht, 2nd ed. Baden-Baden (Nomos) 2009, p. 97 et seq.; *A. Metzger* in *A. Metzger, H. Zech* (ed.), Sortenschutzrecht, Munich (C.H. Beck) 2016, Art. 15 lit. c) Reg. 2100/94, Art. 14, 15 GSortV, paras. 13 et passim. However, there is still the question whether a broader reading of the experimental use exception in design law and patent law could have some merit, e.g. as regards experimental use in view of follow-on inventions, see e.g. *J. Straus*, Zur Zulässigkeit klinischer Un-

the more for uniform interpretation as its version in Art. 28 UPCA is in conflict with the principles of the Internal Market.[38]

The principles of the Internal Market may affect the exploitation of patent protection in various circumstances. Their impact on the exhaustion upon first sale of exclusive control over the distribution of patented products, in particular the extension of the principle of exhaustion to repackaged products, is too well-known to be presented here.[39] It is also well-known that exhaustion covers not only territorial restrictions of resale that run along Member States borders, but any territorial limitations, so not only those that a patentee or a licensee of the European bundle of national patents might wish to impose on its distributors as a matter of keeping the national territories separate. In addition, to the extent that national law applies, direct or indirect regulatory discrimination may present an issue under Internal Market principles.[40]

No less important are the rules on competition (Art. 101, 102 TFEU) that the UPC might have to apply in cases of patent infringement that come under its jurisdiction (Art. 32(1), lit.a) to c) UPCA).[41] This is so although the application of Art. 101 TFEU to restrictions in license agreements will come under its jurisdiction only if relevant for deciding on counterclaims concerning licenses (Art. 32(1) lit. a)–c) UPCA in fine),[42] litiga-

---

tersuchungen am Gegenstand abhängiger Verbesserungserfindungen, GRUR 1993, 308; see also infra n. 108.

38 See Art. 22 Reg. 6/2002 on the Community design (prior use within the Community), Art. 28 UPCA (prior use only in a Contracting Member State). As regards unitary patent protection it should not matter where in the EU the prior use takes place. The purpose of the prior use exception requires its extension to at least the entire Internal Market of enhanced cooperation; see Art. 12 Proposal for a Community Patent from its first to its last version, *Council*, Proposal for a Council Regulation on the Community Patent – General Approach of 27 November 2009 (Doc. 16113/09). As to the general conflict with the free movement/free establishment principles of the Internal Market see *H. Ullrich*, Gewerblicher Rechtsschutz und Urheberrecht im Binnenmarket in *U. Immenga, E.J. Mestmäcker* (eds.), Wettbewerbsrecht Bd. 1. EU/Teil 2, 5th ed. Munich 2012, p. 1662 (GRUR A, para 101).

39 For the recurring issues see only CJEU of 21 June 2018, case C-681/16, *Pfizer Ireland Pharmaceuticals/ Orifarm*, ECLI:EU:C:2018:484; of 12 February 2015, case C-539/13, *Merck Canada/Sigma Pharmaceuticals*, ECLI:EU:C:2015:351; for a summary of the case law *J. Rinken* in *R.Schultes* (Hrsg.); Patentgesetz mit EPÜ, 11th ed. Cologne (Carl Heymanns) 2022, § 9, paras. 28 et passim; *U. Scharen* in *B. Benkard* (ed.), Patentgesetz, 11th ed. Munich (C.H. Beck) 2015, § 9, paras. 19 et passim.

40 See *Ullrich* in *Immenga, Mestmäcker*, loc.cit. p. 1660 et passim (GRUR A, paras. 99 et passim).

41 In litigation concerning the revocation/invalidity of a unitary patent or an UPCA-type European patent (Art. 32(1), lit.d), e) UPCA) only the (in)validity of no challenge-clauses in license agreements, in cooperation agreements or in settlement agreements may become relevant; see Art. 5(1), lit.b) Commission Reg. 316/2014 of 21 March 2014 on the application of Art. 101 TFEU to categories of technology transfer agreements (OJEU 2014 L 93,17); *Commission*, Guidelines on the application of Art. 101 TFEU to technology transfer agreements (OJEU 2014 C 89,3), paras. 242 et seq.; as to pay-for-delay agreements see *M. Wolf* in *F. Säcker* et al. (eds.), Münchener Kommentar Wettbewerbsrecht, 3rd ed. Vol. 1, Munich (C.H. Beck) 2020, Grdl., paras. 1200 et seq.

42 A licensee's right to bring action before the UPC (Art. 47(2), (3) UPCA) may also depend on the compatibility of the license agreement with Art. 101 TFEU since Art. 101(2) TFEU operates ex lege and may be in-tion on licensing in general being outside the jurisdiction of the UPC as a highly specialized patent court, not a commercial court. By contrast, the exercise of the patent right by claiming infringement may come within its jurisdiction because Art. 101 TFEU applies whenever such exercise constitutes the object, means or result of a cartel, i.e. if it rests on or serves an agreement or a concerted practice in restraint of competition.[43] Given the broad variety of restrictions of competition that Art. 101 TFEU covers and the various potential infringers who, as victims of the restriction, might raise an "antitrust defense", Art. 101 TFEU may become relevant under various, albeit not too frequent circumstances.[44]

Likewise, Art. 102 TFEU, whose application depends on a patentee holding a dominant position on the relevant market, may come into play under various circumstances. The enforcement of illegally or even fraudulently acquired patents is a prominent, but rare example.[45] More frequently, the question may arise whether a patent, whose use is essential for practicing a widely practiced technical standard, is abusively exercised if enforced despite a general licensing commitment the patentee gave to the standard setting organization.[46] It is again only in exceptional circumstances that a market dominating patentee may be obliged to accommodate its enforcement practice with its duty to li-

---

voked by third parties whose interests are affected by restrictive agreements, see *K. Schmidt*, in *U. Immenga, E.J.-Mestmäcker* (*T. Körber* et al., eds.), Wettbewerbsrecht, Vol. 1, EU, 6th ed., Munich (C.H. Beck) 2019, Art. 101 Abs. 2 AEUV, para. 18.

43 See CJEU of 18 February 1971, case 40/76, *Sirena/Eda*, Rep. 1971, 69 = ECLI:EU:C:1971:3, paras. 9 et seq.; of 8 June 1971, case 78/70, *Deutsche Grammophon/Metro–SB-Großmärkte*, Rep. 1971, 487 = ECLI:EU:C:1971:59, para. 6; of 8 June 1982, case 258/78, *Nungesser/Commission*, Rep. 1982, 2015 = ECLI:EU:C:1982:211, para. 28; of 14 September 1982, case 148/81, *Keurkoop/Nancy Kean Gifts*, Rep. 1982, 2853 = ECLI:EU:C:1982:289, para. 27; *Wolf* in Säcker et. al. (eds.) Münchener Kommentar, loc.cit., Grdl. paras. 1206 et seq.

44 For instance, damages claimed for patent infringement may need to be examined as to whether the amount claimed rests on supra-competitive prices that, due to a pay-to-delay agreement and, thus, due to the absence of competition by generics, the patentee was able to ask for on the market, see only Adv.gen. *J. Kokott*, op. of 22 January 2020 in case C-307/18, *Generics (UK)/Competition and Market Authority*, ECLI: EU:C:2020:28, paras. 21 et seq.; *Commission*, Press release of 26 November 2020 (IP/20/2220) "Commission fines Teva € 60.5 million for delaying entry of cheaper generic medicines" (for details see case AT 39686, decision of 21 November 2020, C (2020) 8153 at para. 1245). Note that direct actions for damages resulting from a violation of Art. 101 TFEU do not come within the jurisdiction of the UPC, but within that of national courts.

45 See CJEU of 6 December 2012, case C-457/10 P, *Astra Zeneca/Commission*, ECLI:EU:C:2012:770.

46 See CJEU of 16 July 2015, case *Huawei Technologies/ZTE*, ECLI:EU:C:2015:477; for an analysis see *H. Ullrich*, FRAND Access to open standards and the patent exclusivity: Restating the principles, in Concurrences 2-2017, Art. No. 83890 = Max-Planck-Institute for Innovation and Competition Research Paper No. 17-04 (ssrn.com/abstract=2920660); see also BGH (German Federal Supreme Court) of 5 May 2020, case KZR 36/17, BGHZ 225, 260 = GRUR 2020, 961. Due to a settlement agreement the request for a preliminary ruling under Art. 267 TFEU by LG Düsseldorf (District Court Düsseldorf) of 26 November 2020, case 4c O 17/19, NZ KartR 2021, 61 was withdrawn. For a summary of national case law see *E. Bonadio, A. Tanwar*, Case law on standard essential patents in Europe, 22 ERA Forum 601(2021); for a general discussion *G. Ghidini*, Rethinking Intellectual Property, Cheltenham 2018, 345 et passim.

cense that may result from the indispensability of the use its patent for third parties wishing to bring an innovation of their own to a particular market.[47] An example may be presented by patents on follow-on inventions, whose exploitation is blocked due to that, as dependent patents, they infringe a prior patent.[48] More generally, issues of Art. 102 TFEU may arise in case a market dominating firms seeks to impose an abusively restrictive business practice on third parties by bringing patent infringement suits and/or by asking damages for patent infringement that mirror an abusive conduct rather than reasonable market conditions.

The common dominator of these and other issues of EU competition law is that they will arise only as defenses in litigation on the infringement of unitary patents and UPCA-type European patents, not as part of "antitrust actions", since these have to be brought before the "ordinary" courts of the Union, so typically before the commercial chambers or specialized competition law chambers of general civil courts.[49]

By contrast, fundamental rights as enshrined in the EU's Charter[50] may be relied upon in support of both the protection of intellectual property (Art. 17(2) TFEU) and the exceptions to it. Their main function in litigation between parties[51] is to inform the interpretation of relevant rules of existing law[52] and the weighing of conflicting inter-

---

[47] The principles, as first developed in respect of refusals to license the design rights for spare parts, then in respect of copyright, including copyright on data, were established by CJEU of 5 October 1988, case 53/87, *CICRA/Renault*, Rep. 1988, 6039 = ECLI:EU:C:1988:472; of 5 October 1988, case 238/87, *Volvo/Veng*, Rep. 1988, 6211= ECLI:EU:C:1988:477; of 6 April 1995, joint cases C-241/91 P and C-242/91 P, *RTE and ITV Publications/Commission*, Rep. 1995 I 743 = ECLI:EU:C:1995:98 ("Magill TV Guide"); of 29 April 2004, case C-418/01, *IMS Health/NDC Health*, Rep. 2004 I 5039 = ECLI:EU:C:2004:257. For an analysis see Th. Eilmannsberger, F. Bien in Säcker et al. (eds.), Münchner Kommentar, loc.cit. Art. 102 AEUV, paras. 474 et passim with references.

[48] See H. Ullrich, Patent Dependency under European and European Union Patent Law – A Regulatory Gap, in Max-Planck Institute for Innovation and Competition Research Paper Series No. 23-04 (=ssrn.com/abstract= 4339426) sub III.2.

[49] This jurisdictional split asks for mutual respect and avoidance of conflicts by a willingness to stay proceedings while the same issues are pending before the other jurisdiction and to request preliminary rulings by the CJEU that harmonize different judicial approaches to the same or similar issues of substantive law.

[50] Charter of Fundamental Rights of the European Union, OJEU 2016 C 202, 389.

[51] Including the indirect control of the compatibility of secondary EU law with the EU's legal order under Art. 267 lit. b) TFEU, see e.g. (early on before the adoption of the EUChFR) CJEU of 28 April 1998, case C-200/96, *Metronome Musik/Music Point HoKamp*, Rep. 1998 I 1953 = ECLI:EU:C:1998:172; of 12 September 2006, case C-479/04, *Laserdisken/Kulturministeriet*, Rep. 2006 I 8089 = ECLI:EU:C:2006:549, paras. 60 et seq. For a direct action for annulment of a copyright directive see recently CJEU of 26 April 2022, case C-401/19, *Poland/European Parliament and Council*, ECLI:EU:C:2022:297.

[52] For the limitation of patentability of biotechnological inventions by considerations of human dignity, see CJEU of 18 October 2011, case C-34/10, *Brüstle/Greenpeace*, Rep. 2011 I 9821= ECLI:EU:C:2011:669, paras. 33 et seq. referring to CJEU of 9 October 2001, case C-377/98, *Netherlands/Parliament and Council*, Rep. 2001 I 6229 = ECLI:EU:C:2001:525 paras. 69 et seq. concerning a direct action for the annulment of Directive 98/44 on the legal protection of biotechnological inventions (OJEU 1998 L 2013, 13).

ests.⁵³ Thus, while in the view of the Court of Justice Art. 17(2) EUChFR lends support to protecting patents at a high level, it does not require a narrow interpretation of the rules on competition as they apply to the exploitation of patents by market dominating patentees.⁵⁴ All in all, it seems that fundamental rights influence the interpretation and application of patent law only marginally,⁵⁵ and they hardly ever do so as countervailing rights supporting exceptions from patent protection.⁵⁶

As to the last point of reference to EU law the Court of Justice set in its opinion 1/09,⁵⁷ the general principles of EU law, it is by their very nature that most of them will be taken into consideration by the UPC as a matter of regular judicial practice. Therefore, principles such as the safeguard of legal certainty, the protection of legitimate expecta-

---

53 See as regards copyright protection inter alia CJEU of 9 March 2021, case C-392/19, *VG Bild-Kunst/Stiftung Preußischer Kulturbesitz*, ECLI:EU:C:2021:181, para. 54; of 29 July 2019, case C-476/17, *Pelham/Hütter*, ECLI:EU:C:2019:624, paras. 30 et passim; of 7 August 2018, case C-161/17, *Land Nordrhein-Westfalen/Renckhoff*, ECLI:EU:C:2018;634, paras. 41; of 15 September 2016, case C-484/14, *McFadden/Sony Music Entertainment*, ECLI:EU:C:2016:689, paras. 80 passim; of 3 September 2014, case C-201/13, *Deckmyn/Vandersteen*, ECLI:EU:C:2014; 2132; paras. 25 et passim; of 27 March 2014, case C-314/12, *UPC Telekabel Wien/Constantin Film Verleih*, ECLI:EU:C:2014:192, paras. 42 et passim; of 24 November 2011, case C-70/10, *Scarlet Extended/SABAM*, Rep. 2011 I 11959 = ECLI:EU:C:2011:771, paras. 41 et passim; see also CJEU of 29 January 2008, case C-275/06; *Promusicae/Teléfonica di España*, Rep. 2008 I 271= ECLI:EU:C:2008:54, paras. 61 per passim.
54 See CJEU of 16 July 2015, case C-170/13, *Huawei Technologies/ZTE*, ECLI:EU:C:2005:477, paras. 42, 57 et passim; of 30 January 2020, case C-307/18, *Generics/Competition and Markets Authority*, ECLI:EU:C:2020: 52, paras. 41, 137.
55 Fundamental rights may be more relevant in particular fields of patent protection than in patent law in general, for instance in the field of pharmaceuticals where the right to health (Art. 35 EUChFR) could inform the interpretation of the public interest when it comes to compulsory licensing or to determining whether injunctive relief from patent infringement is justified (see only *I. Haracoglou*, Competition Law and Patents, Cheltenham (E.Elgar) 2008, 701 et passim). However, since Reg. 1257/2012 refers compulsory licensing to national law (recital 10), and since Art. 32 UPCA does not confer jurisdiction over compulsory licensing on the UPC, the issue is outside the scope of this contribution. Yet, it is precisely because of the non-availability of compulsory licenses on the EU- and UPC-level that despite the reluctance of some national courts to withhold injunctive relief in view of an overriding public interest, such as patients' welfare, that the UPC will have to rethink the question of whether, in addition to the equities between the parties, fundamental rights of third parties affected should be taken into account when deciding on the appropriate remedies under Art. 62 to 65, 68 UPCA; for the controversy under national law see LG Düsseldorf of 7 July 2022, case 4c O 18/21, GRUR 2022, 1665; *Kl. Grabinski*, Injunctive Relief and Proportionality in Case of Public Interest in the Use of a Patent, GRUR 2021, 200; *M. Dani*, Proportionality in Patent Litigation on Medical Devices, 44 Eur.Int.Prop.Rev (EIPR) 567 (2022)).
56 Considering the various exceptions listed by Art. 27 UPCA it appears that almost half of them relate to system-inherent considerations of promoting innovation within the patent system (Art. 27 lit b)) or in related fields of technological property (Art. 27 lit. c)., lit. d), lit. i), lit. j), lit k)), the other concerning territorial exemptions (Art. 27 lit. f), lit. g), lit. h) or de minimis matters (Art. 27 lit. a), lit. e), see also infra sub 17.2.1.2.(iii).
57 Supra n. 29.

tions of parties[58] or the respect of the rule of proportionality, need not be presented here, even though the latter lends itself to debate, in particular as regards determining the appropriate remedy to acts infringing a patent.[59] Also, such fundamental principles of EU law as are its autonomy and primacy in relation to the law of Member States,[60] the autonomous interpretation of its rules[61] or the duty of Member States' authorities and courts to interpret national law in conformity with the relevant harmonization directives[62] need not be restated here. These principles form part of the reasons why the UPC had to be established as a court common to Member States rather than as an international court,[63] so determine the UPC's raison d'être and require full respect by it.[64] More particularly, they will generally inform the interpretation and application of the rules of substantive law of the UPC Agreement.

---

58 See e.g. CJEU of 16 July 2015, case C-170/13, *HuaweiTechnologies/ZTE*, ECLI:EU:C.2015:477, para. 64; of 29 June 1999, case C-60/98, *ButterflyMusic/Carosello*, Rep. 1999 I 339 =ECLI:EU:C:1999:333, para. 25.

59 For interim injunctive relief see recently CJEU of 28 April 2022, case C-44/21, *Phoenix-Contact/Harting Deutschland*, ECLI:EU:C:2022:309; for the broad discussion on the – legal or practical – indispensability of prohibitory injunctive relief see only *P. Blok*, A harmonized approach to prohibitory injunctions: reconsidering Art. 12 of the Enforcement Directive, 11 J.Int.Prop.L.&Pract. 56 (2016); *M. Leistner*, Unterlassungsverfügung im Einheitspatentsystem, GRUR 2022, 1633 with references; for the recent amendment of § 139 PatG (German Patent Act) see *A. Ohly*, Unverhältnismäßigkeit, Injunction Gap und Geheimnisschutz im Prozess, GRUR 2021, 1229, 1230 et seq. See also supra 55 and infra text sub 17.2.1.2.,(i) at n. 79.

60 For these principles see in addition to standard literature on EU law recently as regards the autonomy of the EU's legal order CJEU of 2 September 2021, case C-741/19, *Republic of Moldova/Komstroy*, ECLI:EU: C:2021:655, paras 43 et seq.; opinion 1/17 of 30 April 2019, ECLI:EU:C:2019:341, paras. 109 et seq. (Comprehensive Economic and Trade Agreement (CETA) Canada-EU); of 6 March 2018, case C-284/16, *Slowak Republic/Achmea*, ECLI:EU:C:2018:158, paras. 33 et seq., all with references. As regards primacy of EU law see CJEU of 6 October 2021, case C-487/19, *W.Z.*, ECLI:EU:C:2021:798, paras 142, 156 et seq.; of 22 June 2021 case C-439/19 *Latvijas Republikas/ Saeima*, ECLI:EU:C:2021:504, paras. 130 et seq.; of 18 May 2021, joint cases C-83/19, C-127/19, C-195/19, C-355/19 and C-397/19, *Asociatia "Forumul Judecatorilor din România"/Inspectia Judiciara*, ECLI:EU:C:2021:393, paras. 242 et seq., all with references; see also *M. Dougan*, The primacy of Union law over incompatible national measures: Beyond disapplication and towards a remedy of nullity? 59 CMLRev. 1301(2022); *V. Skouris*, Der Vorrang des Europäischen Unionrechts vor dem nationalen Recht, EuR 2021, 3.

61 This principle determines the uniform development and implementation of the EU's, "IP"-policy also in merely harmonized areas, such as copyright, see CJEU of 21 October 2010, case C-467/08, *Padawan/ SGAE*, Rep. 2010 I 10055 = ECLI:EU:C:2010:620, paras. 32 et seq. with references; of 13 February 2014, case C-466/12; *Svensson/ Retriever Sverige*, ECLI:EU:C:2014:76, paras. 34 et seq.; of 3 September 2014, case C-201/13, *Deckmyn/Vandersteen* ECLI:EU:C:2014:2132, para. 14; of 12 November 2015, case C-572/13, *Hewlett Packard Belgium/Reprobel*, ECLI:EU:C:2015, 750 para. 35; of 6 June 2016, case C-470/14, *EGEDA et al./Aministración del Estado*, ECLI:EU:C:2016:418, para. 38.

62 See recently CJEU of 28 April 2022, case C-44/21, *Phoenix Contact/Harting*, ECLI:EU:C:2022:309, paras. 50, 52 with references; for the methodology see inter alia *A. Wietfeld*, Die richtlinienkonforme Auslegung – Auslegungsmethode oder Zielvorgabe? JZ 2020, 485 with references.

63 See supra text at n. 28, 29.

64 As confirmed by the declaratory provisions of Art. 1(2), 20 UPCA.

17.2.1.2 The interdependence of Reg. 1257/2012 and Art. 25 to 27 UPCA

Although the spectrum of Union law that the UPC has to apply – if necessary by requesting the CJEU to give a preliminary ruling on its interpretation – appears to be rather broad, it covers only a presumably limited number of borderlines cases, albeit most likely important ones. The much larger number of typical infringement cases will involve the routine application of the criteria determining the infringing acts and the exceptions, so Art. 25 to 27 UPCA. The question whether their interpretation, if beyond routine,[65] comes within the scope of application of Art. 267 TFEU has raised a doctrinal controversy about the meaning of Art. 5(3) Reg. 1257/2012. According to one view, the wording "The acts against which the patent provides protection referred to in paragraph 1 and the applicable limitations shall be those defined by the law applied to European patents with unitary effect in the ... Member State whose national law is applicable ... in accordance with Article 7" constitutes a conflict of laws-rule ultimately referring to the UPCA as an international agreement whose interpretation is outside the CJEU's authority under Art. 267 TFEU.[66] Other authors see Art. 5(3) Reg. 1257/2012 as rule that, by referring to the law that in a Member State is applied to European patents with unitary effect, incorporates Art. 25–27 UPCA into Reg. 1257/2012, so into Union law, just as it does with any national law that according to Art. 7 Reg. 1257/2012 applies to the unitary patent, the result being that Art. 25–27 UPCA become a matter of Union law within the meaning of Art. 267 TFEU.[67]

This doctrinal controversy comes in the aftermath of the political controversy that resulted in shifting Art. 6 to 8 of the Draft Regulation on the European Patent with Unitary Effect to the UPC Agreement, the political purpose being to appease opposition against the CJEU taking jurisdiction over the unitary patent.[68] However, this political motivation of the re-arrangement of the legal rules applicable to the unitary patent is not sufficiently reflected by the legislative documents, let alone by the recitals of Reg.

---

[65] For the acte clair/acte éclairé doctrine of defining the need for preliminary rulings see infra 2.a),(ii).
[66] A. Haedicke, Rechtsfindung, Rechtsfortbildung und Rechtskontrolle im Einheitlichen Patentsystem, GRURInt 2013, 609, 616; hesitating V. Henke in Benkard, EPÜ, loc.cit., Vor B., paras 54 et seq.; in detail M. Yan, Das materielle Recht im Einheitlichen Europäischen Patentsystem und dessen Anwendung durch das Einheitliche Patentgericht, Baden-Baden (Nomos) 2017, 109 et seq., 139 et seq. Much of the criticism of CJEU of 5 May 2015, case C-146/13, *Spain/Parliament and Council*, ECLI:EU:C:2015:298 rests on the assumption that the entire UPCA, including its Art. 25 to 27, must be read as any convention of public international law, see inter al. *Jaeger*, loc.cit., EuR 2015, 463 et seq., 473 et seq.; *Mylly*, loc.cit.,54 CMLRev. 1385 et passim (2017); generally D. de Lange, EU patent harmonization policy: reconsidering the consequences of the UPCA, 16 J.Int.Prop.L.& Pract. 1078 (2021).
[67] See in particular Tilmann in Tilmann, Plassmann (eds.), loc.cit., EPUE Reg.,Art.5, paras 17 et seq; ibid, UPCA, Art. 21, para.24.
[68] See supra n 19.

1257/2012.[69] Therefore, the following presentation of the interrelationship of Union law and the UCPA' rules of substantive law (Art. 25 to 27) will focus on the objectives the legislature pursues by introducing unitary patents as part of its system of Union intellectual property and on the functions that the elements of protection of unitary patents are supposed to fulfill in this regard as compared to the UPCA-type of the European bundle patent.

(i) The point of departure is the nature of the European patent with unitary effect, which Art. 3(2), Reg. 1257/2012 characterizes in the same terms as do Art. 1(2) Reg. 2017/1001 with respect to Union trade marks and Art. 1(3) Reg. 6/2002 with respect to Community designs.[70] As such it comes into being by virtue of EU law (Art. 3(1), Art. 4 Reg. 1257/2012), it covers, by virtue of EU law (Art. 3(2) Reg. 1257/2012), the whole internal market to which enhanced cooperation extends rather than only some selected Member States as does a European bundle of national patents.[71] The attribution of unitary effect merges, by virtue of EU law (Art. 3(2) 2nd subpara. Reg. 1257/2012), the national patents within a European bundle patent into one single indivisible patent that is administered as such by the EPO, is subject to only one unitary EU renewal fee (Art. 11 Reg. 1257/2012), "may only be limited, transferred or revoked, or lapse", in respect of the entire area of enhanced co-operation(Art. 3(2), 2nd subpara. Reg. 1257/2012),[72] and confers, again by virtue of EU law (Art. 5(1) Reg. 1257/2012), upon its holder a right of exclusive use of unitary substance. Denying its "autonomous" character therefore, is as misleading as is the notion of the "accessory" nature of the unitary effect.[73] What matters is which law lends legal effect to it

---

[69] See *Haedicke*, loc.cit., GRURInt 2013,610, sub II. Recital 9 Reg.1257/2012 reads in relevant parts: "In matters not covered by this Regulation...the provisions of the EPC, the Agreement on a Unified Patent Court, including its provisions defining the scope of that right and its limitations, and national law, including rules of private international law, should apply".

[70] Pursuant to Art. 3(2) Reg. 1257/2012, the unitary patent shall, in addition to having equal effect, provide uniform protection. One wonders whether the distinction really matters. Art. 2 Reg. 2100/94 on plant variety rights does without any of these qualifications, probably because they are inherent in unitary protection.

[71] See infra sub (ii).

[72] Contra *Tilmann* in Tilmann, Plassmann (eds.), loc.cit., Art. 3 Reg. 1257/2012, paras. 57 et seq, who describes the unitary effect as a „block effect" as if the unitary patent were nothing else than a group of separate patents that are legally tied together by a string. That description may fit the UPCA-type of the European bundle patent (see text infra sub (ii)), not a unitary patent that, in addition to the attributes provided for by Art. 3(2) Reg. 1257/2012, as an object of property is governed by one law only (Art. 7 Reg. 1257/2012) as are all Union titles of intellectual property, see Art. 19 Reg. 2017/1001 on the Union trade mark, Art. 27 Reg. 6/2002 on the Community design; Art. 22 Reg. 2100/94 on Community plant variety rights.

[73] Art. 3(4) Reg. 1257/2012 with recital 7 in fine states what is elf-evident: the legal effects of a patent ceases with its revocation. The unitary effect is not an isolated attribute that is attached to a European patent, which, as such, continues to exist and from which it could be removed had the legislature not provided otherwise by Art. 3(4) Reg. 1257/2012. Upon grant, the European patent falls apart in as many territo-

and what kind of an effect this is, not which authority grants the patent.[74] This effect is "equal in all participating Member States", i.e., it is legally the same throughout the territory of enhanced cooperation.[75] Therefore, it is not only in respect of its legal basis that the unitary patent is an EU patent, but also in respect of the substantive scope of its protection, which is not only "uniform" as if equal in separate territories, but the same throughout the area of enhanced cooperation.[76] This holds true for both the subject matter scope of protection claimed (Schutzgegenstand), since Art. 3(1) Reg. 1257/2012 makes the identity of claims a conditio sine qua non of the European bundle patent becoming a unitary EU patent,[77] and for the substance of the right of exclusivity, i.e. its "contents" (Schutzinhalt) in terms of the uses of the protected subject matter that are the privilege of the patentee.

As regards the latter more particularly, Art. 5(1) Reg. 1257/2012 is of central importance in that it defines the core function of unitary patents as rights entitling the patentee to prevent third parties from committing acts that come under its right of exclusivity. Since this right is one unitary right, these acts must be the same throughout the area of enhanced cooperation. Hence, the definition of the infringing "acts against which that patent provides protection" must of necessity be legally identical wherever the protection applies. Put differently, this definition is a matter of Union law and Art. 5(3) Reg. 1257/2012, which for that definition refers to national law, must be understood accordingly. Therefore, *Tilmann* concludes that the infringing acts are prohibited by virtue of Union law and, thus, their definition by the national law to which Art. 5(3) in conjunction with Art. 7 Reg. 1257/2012 refers, has to be read into Art. 5(1) Reg. 1257/2012.[78] Indeed, the definition of the unitary patent as a preventive right means more than merely that the patentee is entitled to injunctive relief from infringing acts.[79] The preventive function of the exclusive right cannot be defined in the abstract or by reference

---

rially separate and independent patents as the patentee asked for in its application (Art. 79 EPC). It is only upon its subsequent registration as a unitary patent that by virtue of EU law (Art. 3(1) Reg. 1257/2012) these patents merge with retroactive effect into a single one (Art. 4(1), (2) Reg. 1257/2012).

74 Contra: *Haedicke*, loc.cit., GRURInt 2013,, 610, left column.
75 This is best expressed in the French version of Art. 3(2) Reg. 1257/2012 ("effets identiques"); see also Art. 1(2) Reg. 2017/1001 and Art. 1(3) Reg. 6/2002 ("les mêmes effets").
76 Comp. supra n. 70.
77 Thus, as for the classic European bundle patent, Art. 69 EPC is Janus-headed: It looks to both the (pre-grant) application and the (post-grant) infringement procedure. Therefore, due to Art. 3(4) Reg. 1257/2012, the determination of the subject matter scope of protection is as much a matter of Union law as is the unitary effect.
78 See *Tilmann* in *Tilmann, Plassmann* (eds.), loc.cit., Art. 5 Reg. 1257/2012, paras. 19, 20, 22 et seq.; ibid., Art. 21 UPCA, para. 24.
79 For the preventive nature of an intellectual property right that may entail the grant of injunctive relief from infringement see as regards copyright inter al. CJEU of 12 July 2011, case C-324/09, *L'Oréal/eBay International*, Rep. 2011 I 6011 = ECLI:EU:C:2011:474, paras. 131 et seq.; of 24 November 2011, case C-70/10, *Scarlet Extended/SABAM*, Rep. 2011 I 11959 = ECLI:EU:C:2011:771, para. 31; of 16 February 2012, case C-360/10, *SABAM/Netlog*, ECLI:EU:C:2012:85, para. 29.

only to the available remedies. It needs to be determined in relation to the nature and the breadth of the spectrum of the acts that form its economic substance and that, therefore, are to be prevented.[80] Conversely, the definition of these acts has to be interpreted and applied in the light of the preventive function of the rights flowing from the unitary patent. Therefore, even when assuming that there might be more than sheer political opportunism to the shift from incorporating the definition of the infringing acts and the exceptions into the text of the unitary patent regulation to a rule of reference to national law,[81] and that, consequently, *Tilmann's* conclusion is to be qualified as a way of circumventing the EU legislature's intentions, the point remains that there is a close link between the preventive function of unitary patent protection and the definition of the infringing acts that out to be respected rather than cut off. It is submitted that the rationale underlying the reference mechanism of Art. 5(3) Reg. 1257/2012 is to introduce a division of labour between the Court of Justice as the general and supreme court of the Union and the Unified Patent Court as a specialized, field of law-specific judiciary, and that, therefore, the referral to the national law that according to Art. 7 Reg. 1257/2012 is applicable to the European patent with unitary effect, should not be understood as a referral to rules of law that are outside the EU but as a referral to complementary rules of law that are meant to support unitary patent protection.[82] Art. 25 to 27 UPC must be read accordingly.

By providing that the acts infringing unitary patents and the exceptions to protection are to be defined by the national law that applies to the property aspects of the unitary patent (Art. 7 Reg. 1257/2012) Art. 5 (3) Reg. 1257/2012 ensures that, as regards infringement, the rules of only one national law will be applied so that "the scope of that right and its limitations (are) uniform in all Member States in which it has unitary effect" (Art. 5(2) Reg. 1257/2012). The purpose and function of the indirect referral to Art. 25 to 27 UPCA is to substitute to this patent per patent approach to safeguarding unity of protection, i.e. to a multitude of national laws, one single set of rules on the infringing acts and exceptions because this is the only way to ensure that all of the unitary patents are governed by identical rules. It is by reducing the number of applicable national laws and by superseding them as regards unitary patents, not by sort of international harmonization of national laws,[83] that the two step-referral mechanism of Art. 5(3) Reg. 1257/2012 achieves the simplification of unitary patent protection that is necessary for it to operate

---

[80] See only as regards copyright CJEU of 27 March 2014, case C-314/12, *UPC Telekabel Wien/Constantin Film Verleih*, ECLI:EU:C:2014:192, paras. 25 et seq., 34 et seq.
[81] See supra n. 19.
[82] It is only when read to this effect that CJEU of 5 May 2015, case C-146/13, *Spain/ Parliament and Council*, ECLI:EU:C:2015:298, paras. 48 et seq. (with para, 50 referring to recital 9 Reg. 1257/2012) makes at least some sense.
[83] Contra *Haedicke*, loc.cit., GRURInt 2013, 611, left column; *Yan*, loc.cit., p. 150.

efficiently as a system.[84] Art. 25 to 27 UPCA are, thus, a necessary supporting component of the system of unitary patent protection that implements Art. 5(1) Reg. 1257/2012 by defining the infringing acts and the exceptions.[85] This means that qualifying Art. 25 to 27 UCPA as parts of an international treaty, which the UPCA is, misses their function.[86] It is to serve as rules implementing Art. 5(1) Reg. 1257/2012, and they have to be read and interpreted accordingly.[87] This function as implementing rules of unitary patent protection will also help identifying the questions of interpretation that qualify for requests for preliminary rulings under Art. 267 TFEU. In cases that raise issues of enhancing or reducing the generally recognized level of protection or of broadening or limiting the scope of protection in view of new technological developments,[88] and, more generally, in cases of a principled change of case law or of an alleged need of jurisprudential

---

[84] It was precisely the impossibility for a common court of several States to handle the applicability of a multitude of national laws that once led the drafters of the European Patent Litigation Agreement and of the European and European Union Patent Court Agreement (see supra. n. 16) to provide for a full set of uniform international infringement rules regarding the European bundle patent. Think also of the problems that a multitude of applicable laws would create for firms owning a broad patent portfolio or wishing to trade patents.

[85] See for this supportive function also Art. 5(4) and Art. 16 Reg. 1257/2012. Clearly, should the Commission see a need for amending the definition of the infringing acts or for reforming the exceptions, whose proper operation the Commission has to monitor particularly (Art. 5(4) Reg. 1257/2012), making the necessary amendments most likely will demand broad efforts of finding consensus because the Contracting States of the UPCA might be tempted to form a reluctant majority in the EU's legislative process.

[86] CJEU of 12 November 1998, case C-162/98, *Hartmann*, Rep. 1998 I 7083 = ECLI:EU:C:1998:539, paras 8 et seq. concerned the interpretation of the provisions of an agreement on cooperation that some Member States concluded in order to facilitate the levying of a road toll provided for by a EU directive, but is not in point. The agreement was no necessary component for the implementation of the directive but the result of the Member States independent decision on how to best meet their obligations under the directive. As regards the UPC, Member States hardly have a way of establishing a common court other than by an international agreement of some kind. However, this does not mean that the rules of public international law apply equally to all parts of such an agreement. There is a difference between the institutional, the organizational and the financial rules on the one hand, and, on the other, the rules governing the relations between the organization and individuals, such as the rules on judicial procedure, and the rules of substantive law that apply to the conduct of the individuals in their relations on the market place, and that do so irrespective of possible controversies and judicial disputes. Since the latter rules implement unitary patent protection, they may not be modified or terminated like possibly other parts of the UPCA. Rather, the link needs to be respected that exists between the purpose and the functioning of unitary patent protection and these rules, be it only as a matter of Member States duty under Art. 4(3) TEU to assist the Union in carrying out its tasks, to facilitate the achievement of that tasks and to refrain from any measure which would jeopardize the attainment of the Union's objectives, see *E. Pistoia*, Outsourcing EU Law While Differentiating European Integration: The Unitary Patent's Identity in the Two "Spanish Rulings" of 5 May 2015, 41 Eur.L.Rev. 711, 719 (2016); contra: *Tilmann* in *Tilmann, Plassmann* (eds.), loc.cit., UPC Agreement, Introduction, paras. 1, 13 et seq.

[87] See *Yan*, loc.cit., p. 177 et seq.

[88] Comp. recitals 1 – 3, 8 Directive 98/44/EC on the legal protection of biotechnological inventions, OJEC 1998 L 213, 13. Artificial intelligence may raise such new issues not only as regards inventorship or stan-

"Rechtsfortbildung" the UPC may well wish to seek a preliminary ruling by the Court of Justice.[89]

(ii) This analysis is not altered by the fact that Art. 25 to 27 UPCA also apply to the infringement of the national patents that form the bundle of a European patent granted in respect of the Contracting States of the UPCA because here they play a different role. There function is not to specify the substance of a newly created type of patent as is the unitary patent, but to support the establishment of a centralized enforcement mechanism that, as a counterpart to the centralized grant of a set of national patents by the EPO, requires substituting the diversity of rules of substantive law of this set of national patents (Art. 2 (2), Art. 64(1), (3) EPC) by one coherent body of uniform international law. These national patents already have a – more or less similar[90] – substance of their own that as territorially independent and separate rights they draw essentially from the national laws to which they are subject. Consequently, it is to enable the UPC to adjudicate infringement on the basis of one law instead of a multitude of national laws that the Contracting States of the UPCA agreed to replace, in respect of the rules on infringement and on the exceptions, by rules of international convention law rather than merely to harmonize them. While this approach tightens the bundle around the national patents resulting from the centralized patent grant a bit closer together than harmonization of the then still applicable national laws would do, the configuration of these common rules of infringement law remains nevertheless within the collective control of the Contracting States exercising their sovereign powers independently from the Union.[91]

In addition, the applicability of the internationally uniform rules of Art. 25 to 27 UPCA to all the bundled patents that are covered by the centralized enforcement through the UPC (Art. 34 UPCA) obscures the fact that the UPC-type of European patents does not integrate them into one composite patent whose function would be similar to

---

dards of patentability (Art. 56, 83 EPC), but also as regards the definition of infringing acts and of the exceptions (Art. 25, 27 UPCA), see also infra n. 144.

89 The criteria relied upon by the U. S. Attorney general when recommending to the U. S. Supreme Court to grant or not to grant certiorari from judgments of the Court of Appeals for the Federal Circuit or by which the Supreme Court decides to actually grant or refuse certiorari might be helpful in determining the need for a preliminary ruling, see R. *Dreyfuss*, In Search of Institutional Identity: The Federal Circuit Comes of Age, 23 Berkeley Tech'y L.J. 787, 806 et seq. (2008); *id.*, An International Perspective I: A View from the United States, in *J. Pila, Chr. Wadlow* (eds.), The EU Unitary Patent system, Oxford 2015,145, 152 et seq.. Of course, this suggestion needs to be substantiated by a detailed comparative study, the obvious difference – and point of interest – being that since the CJEU has no power to refuse requests for preliminary rulings all depends on the UPC's willingness to submit such requests, see infra 17.2.2.2.,(ii).

90 Due to Art. 63, 64(2), 69 EPC and Art. 29 TRIPS it is mainly the rules on indirect infringement and on the exceptions (Art. 26, 27 UPCA) that may differ from Contracting Member State to Contracting Member State.

91 E.g. by a revision of the UPCA amending Art. 25 to 27 as they apply to the UPCA-type of a European patent.

the unitary patent.[92] To the contrary, a UPC-type European patent does not exist as such, but bundles the national patents only for more efficient enforcement. Each of them remains subject to national law as regards its administration, the determination of the renewal fees and their payment to the national treasury. They may lapse and be abandoned state-by-state and independently; they may be assigned separately territory by territory, and, as objects of property, they come under different national laws rather than under a single national law as does the unitary patent. As a consequence, the acquisition, maintenance, use and enforcement of a UPC-type European patent tend to follow an economic and legal logic that differs from that of the acquisition maintenance, use and enforcement of a unitary patent. The strategic perspective of patenting and licensing is not the Internal Market, but selected Member States with other Member States being left out or protected only indirectly,[93] i.e., it is one of territorially selective, targeted protection. Thus, as far as the UPCA-type of the European bundle of national patents is concerned, the uniformity of law that Art. 25 to 27 UPCA create serves mainly the individual interests of patentees in efficient enforcement of their national patents, not the unity of the Internal Market.

These interests are perfectly legitimate and the functional difference is but the consequence of the optionality of protection by either the unitary patent or the UPC-type of European bundle patent.[94] This optionality, however, means diversity. It does not allow qualifying Art. 25 to 27 UPCA as they apply to the unitary patent as rules of international law merely because they also apply to the patent that are bundled in a UPCA-type of European patent or because before its transformation the unitary patent is a European (bundle) patent. While in routine practice Art. 25 to 27 UPCA will generally be applied equally to either type of patent, their different nature and function needs to be respected. Accordingly, the Court of Justice might accept requests for preliminary rulings

---

[92] However, Art. 56 to 72 UPCA on remedies and the UPC's Rules of Procedure do not distinguish between the unitary patent and the European bundle patent, and the UPC's Table of Court Fees determines fixed and value-based fees indistinctively for litigation concerning either type of patent as if they were equal. While the value of the patent and that of its litigation may mirror the different territorial reach of the different types of patents, differences of the territories covered by UPCA-type European patents may become determinative, e.g., for granting injunctive relief, assessing damages and even for applying substantive law, e.g., for ascertaining whether there is indirect infringement across borders or for deciding whether an exception applies, such as exhaustion; comp. CJEU of 5 December 1996, joined cases C-267/95 and C-268/95, *Merck/Primecrown*, Rep. 1996 I 6285 = ECLI:EU:C:1996:468; of 21 June 2018, case C-681/16, *Pfizer Ireland/Orifarm*, ECLI:EU:C:2018:484.

[93] The criteria determining an applicant's choice between the unitary patent and the UPCA-type of the European bundle patent are complex and form part of the discussion on whether or not to opt out of the UPC system (Art. 83(3),(4) UPCA); see inter al. *Hüttermann* in *Hüttermann* (ed.), loc.cit, p 48 et seq. One of the many considerations is that protection needed for a regional market only may not justify the costs of a unitary patent, another that there is no need to cover the entire internal market by a unitary patent if unprotected territories do not have enough reward potential for competitors to invest in setting up the production facilities and distribution networks necessary for "imitating" products.

[94] See recital 26 Reg. 1257/2012.

even in cases involving the UPCA-type of European patents because it is "in the interest of the Union's legal order"[95] that the functionality of Art. 25 to 27 UPCA as rules implementing unitary patent protection be not distorted by the UPC's interpretation of these provisions of the UPCA as they apply to the UPCA-type of European patents. However indirect, ultimately an interpretative separation between the rules of substantive law of the UPCA as they apply to unitary patents and as they apply to the UPCA-type of patents would affect both the autonomous character of unitary patent protection that the Court of Justice sought to safeguard in its opinion 1/09[96] and its "raison d'être" as an expression of the Union's intention to determine its market integration and innovation policy by instruments of its own legal authority.[97]

(iii) As regards more particularly the exceptions from protection, they "limit" the patent's "effects"[98] by permitting ex lege certain uses of the protected subject matter that otherwise would constitute infringing acts. They thus form part of the definition of the substance of both the unitary patent and the UPCA-type of the European bundle patent.

---

95 Terminology borrowed from CJEU of 18 October 1990, joined cases C-297/88 and C-197/89, *Massam Dzodi/Belgian State*, Rep. 1990 I 3763 = ECLI:EU:C:1990:360, para. 37. The so-called *Dzodi* case-law of the CJEU stands for the Court's determination to safeguard the uniform interpretation of the rules of EU law irrespective of the circumstances in which they are to be applied, so also in cases that have no EU dimension, but are adjudicated on the basis of national rules that refer to EU rules, incorporate them or copy-paste them as a matter of ensuring equal treatment under EU harmonized and purely domestic regulation and/or of avoiding indirect discrimination, see inter alia CJEU of 8 November 1990, case C-231/89, *Gmurzynska-Bscher/Oberfinanzdirektion Köln*, Rep. 1990 I 4003 = ECLI:EU:C:1990:386, paras. 18 et seq; of 17 July 1997, case C-28/95, *Leur-Bloem/Inspecteur der Belastingdienst/Ondernemingen*, Rep. 1997 I 4161 = ECLI:EU:C:1997:369, paras. 25 et seq. with references; of 18 October 2012, case C-583/10, *USA/Nolan*, ECLI:EU:C:2012:638, paras. 45 et seq. with references; of 12 May 2016, case C-281/15, *Sahyouni/Mamisch*, ECLI:EU:C:2016:343, paras 25 et seq. with references. Clearly, the issues raised in the *Dzodi* line of cases differ from the issue at hand in that they concern legal references to EU law whereas there is no such reference in Art. 25, 26 UPCA. It is also true that the issue is not one of ensuring uniform interpretation as regards the rules applicable to unitary patent protection, which is why Haedicke, loc.cit., GRURInt 2013, 616 rejects the application of the *Dzodi* case-law. However, it is obvious enough that the interpretation by two major courts of the same rules that apply to two legally and economically different types of patents, which in different ways claim protection of EU dimension, is bound to result in frictions, particularly so as the interpretation given in view of the application of these rules to one type of patent will produce a preemptive effect on the interpretation of these rules in view of their application to the other type of patent. The prerogative of creating such effects may not lie with a (common) court of Member States but only with the Court of Justice of the EU.
96 See CJEU, op. 1/09 of 8 March 2011, supra n. 29, paras. 77 et passim (83).
97 See recital 4 Reg. 1257/2012, which needs to be read in conjunction with recitals 1 to 3, 8 Directive on the legal protection of biotechnological inventions, supra n. 88.
98 See the headline of Art. 27 UPCA. For the distinction between limitations of patentability and exceptions from the patent exclusivity see supra n. 34; *N. Lee*, Adding Fuel to Fire: A Complex Case of Unifying Patent Limitations and Exceptions through the EU Patent Package in *Ballardini, Norrgard, Bruun* (eds.), loc.cit., p. 207, 216 et seq.

Most of them are contained in the rather heterogeneous list set up by Art. 27 UPCA.[99] Leaving aside the usual exceptions provided for by international conventions (Art. 27, lit.f), g), h) UPCA),[100] the exceptions may be sub-divided in two groups that are of interest here. One group consists of those exceptions whose substance is determined by considerations of consistency of the Union's system of intellectual property, namely the need to ensure compatibility between patent protection and, first, the protection of plant variety rights by Reg. 2100/94 (Art. 27, lit.c) UPCA),[101] second, the protection of biotechnological inventions by national patent law as harmonized by Directive 98/44 (Art. 27, lit. i), j), l) UPCA),[102] and, third, copyright protection of computer programs as harmonized by Directive 2009/24 (Art. 27, lit. k) UPCA).[103] This group is of interest here[104] because it comes within the jurisdiction the Court of Justice has under Art. 267 TFEU irrespective of the qualification of the UPC Agreement as a treaty of public international law. The reason is either that, due to its direct effect, Union law applies anyway in the Member States of enhanced cooperation or that the national law that applies pursuant Art. 5(3) Reg. 1257/2012 or pursuant to Art. 2(2), Art. 64(1) EPC to the unitary patent or the UPCA-type of a European patent, respectively, needs to comply with the relevant directives and may be controlled as to its compliance by the Court of Justice.[105] Art. 27 UPCA may ensure a higher degree of uniformity of these exceptions than do the harmonized national laws, but it does not exempt it from the Court of Justice's jurisdiction under Art. 267 TFEU, let alone allow Member States to escape their duties under Union law.

The other group comprises three traditional exceptions from the patent exclusivity by which the legislature pursues rather different purposes. Art. 27, lit. a) UPCA concerns the very common de minimis exception of private non-commercial use; Art. 27, lit.e) relates to the profession-specific extemporaneous preparation of prescription medicines by pharmacies, and Art. 27, lit.b) UPCA covers "acts done for experimental purposes relating to the subject matter of the patented invention". The latter is not a general re-

---

[99] Although Art. 27 UPCA seems to represent a limited catalogue of exceptions, general rules of civil law, penal law or public law justifying specific uses, such as legitimate defense or emergency, may become relevant; see *Tilmann* in *Tilmann, Plassmann* (eds.), loc.cit., Art. 27 UPCA, paras. 31 et seq.
[100] For Art. 27, lit.f), lit.g) UPCA see Art. 5 ter Paris Convention for the Protection of Industrial Property. The EU is party to the WTO TRIPS Agreement Art. 2 of which incorporates Art. 1 to 12 Paris Convention.
[101] Since under Art. 15, lit.c) Reg. 2100/94 on Community plant variety rights breeding, discovering and developing other varieties do not constitute infringing acts, Art. 27,lit.c) UPCA ensures that in case of an overlap with patent protection of biotechnological material breeding is not considered as infringing the patent.
[102] Art. 27, lit.i), j) UPCA correspond to Art. 11(1), (2) Reg. 98/44 on the protection of biotechnological inventions.
[103] Art. 5, 6 Directive 2009/24/EC of 23 April 2009 on the legal protection of computer programs, OJEU 2009 L 111,16.
[104] Including Art. 27, lit.d) UPCA on the uses necessary in proceedings for the grant of a marketing authorization of medicinal products.
[105] See *Haedicke*, loc.cit., GRURInt 2013, 612 et passim (615).

search exception, not even a patent-specific one,[106] but an important component of the system of patent protection. It complements the disclosure requirement (Art. 83 EPC), which forms part of the public interest-quid pro quo of the patent privilege, by the right to try the invention for the purpose of finding out whether and how it really works. Its importance results from that it enables follow-on improvements and alternative inventions, and, thus, contributes to an overall well-functioning of patent protection as a system of incentivizing innovation.[107] Since its scope or at least its interpretation differs between Member States,[108] its uniform interpretation will matter for achieving the overall purpose of patent protection and of the unitary patent more particularly.

17.2.2 The relationship between the Court of Justice and the Unified Patent Court

17.2.2.1 On the application of Art. 267 TFEU by the UPC

(i) Certainly, there will be more questions of law that would justify requests for preliminary under Art. 267 TFEU than those presented above. They may relate to the interpretation of the EU regulations on the grant of supplementary certificates of protection[109] as they apply to national patents forming the UPCA-type of a European patent,

---

[106] See e.g. for Belgian law *G. Van Overwalle*, The Implementation of the Biotechnology Directive in Belgium and its After-Effects: The Introduction of a New Research Exemption and a Compulsory License for Public Health, 37 IIC 889, 905 et seq. (2006).

[107] See *H. Ullrich*, Patent dependency under European and European Union Patent Law – A Regulatory Gap, Max Planck Institute for Innovation and Competition Research Paper 23-04 2023 (ssrn.com/abstract=4339426); GRURInt 2023, forthcoming.

[108] See *V. Di Cataldo*, Towards a general research exemption, in *G. Ghidini, V. Falce* (eds.), Reforming Intellectual Property, Cheltenham (E.Elgar) 2022,18, 21 et seq.; *Th. Jaeger, J. Lukan*, A system fit for innovation? Part II: (Dis-) Advantages for follow-on inventors in the UP legal system, this Vol., Ch. 23.

[109] Reg. (EC) of the European Parliament and the Council of 6 May 2009 concerning the supplementary certificate for medicinal products (codified version), OJEU 2009 L 152,1; Reg. (EC) 1610/96 of the European Parliament and the Council of 23 July 1996 concerning the creation of a supplementary certificate for plant protection products, OJEC 1996 L 198,30. The application of Reg. 469/2009 and of the predecessor regulation resulted in a considerable number of preliminary rulings by the CJEU, frequently enough on rather specific issues; for details see *Max Planck Institute for Innovation and Competition*, Study on the Legal Aspects of Supplementary Protection Certificates (European Commission, ed.), Final Report Luxemburg (Office for Official Publications of the EU) 2018, sub 8.1.6., 8.4. and Part III, passim. Note that Art. 30 UPCA, while worded like Art. 5(1) Reg. 469/2009 and Art. 5(1) Reg. 1610/96, modifies the effect of these referrals to national patent law in that it creates a uniform bundle of certificates grafted on the national patents forming the UPCA-type of a European patent. That uniformity may be welcome by interested circles, but it entails a distortion of protection between the certificates that come under the UPCA and those separate certificates for patents that are outside the UPCA. Whether Member States may collectively create such a group effect of exclusive rights by agreement in an area that is covered by EU regulation is an open question.

but not (yet) to unitary patents since surprisingly the framers of Reg. 1257/2012 abstained from regulating the matter.[110] A broader range of issues of interpretation may result from the applicability of the WTO Agreement on Trade Related Aspects of Intellectual Property Rights (TRIPS) that comes within the exclusive competence the EU has under Art. 3(1), lit. e), Art. 207(1) TFEU and, as such, is to be observed by the EU and its Member States.[111] This concerns both the substantive law of patent protection and the procedural rules governing its enforcement.[112] However, as to the former, it is hard to see any TRIPS issues arising under the EU's current, rather strict system of patent protection;[113] as to the latter, they are codified by the Directive on the enforcement of intellectual property rights that precisely aims at implementing the provisions of the TRIPS Agreement within the EU's legal order.[114] The Directive establishes a set of rules on procedure and remedies that are common to all categories of intellectual property and, thus, invites requests for preliminary rulings with a view to ensuring systemic consistency of interpretation.[115] Yet another category of questions of interpretation that qualify under Art. 267 TFEU may result from the applicability of the EU's justice-related fundamental rights, in

---

110 In fact, the matter is not only highly complex in itself (see supra n. 109), but raises problems of centralization/decentralization since, being post grant the European patent, the grant of the certificates comes within the authority of national patent offices; see *R. Romandini*, Study on the options for a unified supplementary protection certificates (SPCs) system in Europe (European Commission, ed.), Luxemburg (Office of Official Publications of the EU) 2022, passim. See now Commission, proposal for a regulation on the supplementary certificate for medicinal products, COM (2023) 222 of 27 April 2023 and the related proposals COM (2023) 221, COM (2023) 223, COM (2023) 231, all of 27 April 2023.
111 See CJEU of 18 July 2013, case C-414/11, *Daiichi Sankyo/Sanofi-Aventis Deutschland*, ECLI:EU:C:2013:520, paras. 40 et passim; A. Dimopoulos, P. Vantsiouri; Of TRIPS and Traps: The interpretative jurisdiction of the Court of Justice of the European Union over Patent Law, 39 Eur.L.Rev. 210 (2014); A. Dimopoulos, An Institutional Perspective II: The Role of the CJEU in the Unitary (EU) Patent System, in *Pila, Wadlow* (eds.), loc.cit., p 57, 64 et passim; more reserved *Mylly*, loc.cit., 54 CMLRev.1410 et seq. (2017). Note that TRIPS, while binding on the EU legislature and authorities, does not have direct effect in the EU legal order; see CJEU of 15 March 2012, case C-135/10, *SCF/Del Corso*, ECLI:EU:C:2012:140, paras. 43 et seq. with references.
112 Art. 27 to 34 and Art. 41 to 50 TRIPS. For Art. 27 TRIPS see CJEU of 11 September 2007, case C-431/05, *Merck-Genericos/Merck*, Rep. 2007 I 7001 = ECLI:EU:C:2007:496; of 18 July 2013, case C-414/11, supra n. 111, paras. 63 et passim. For Art. 50 TRIPS see inter alia CJEU of 14 December 2000, joined cases C-300/98 and C-392/98, *Parfums Christian Dior/Tuk Consultancy*, Rep. 2000 I 11307 = ECLI:EU:C:2000:688; of 13 September 2001, case C-89/99, *Schieving-Nijstad* et al./*R. Groenveld*, Rep. 2002 I 5851 = ECLI:EU:C:2001:438.
113 New issues may arise should the EU reform its system of patent protection, e.g., by introducing rules on compulsory licensing of unitary patents and European patents; see *Commission*, Communication of 31 March 2022 (Ref.Ares (2020)2413270), Call for an impact assessment "Compulsory licensing in the EU" – Legislative proposal; see Commission Proposal for a Regulation on compulsory licensing for crisis management and amending Reg. (EC) 816/2006, COM (2023) 224 of 27 April 2023; see also supra n. 48.
114 See recital 4 et seq. Dir.2004/48/EC on the enforcement of intellectual property rights. Note that Dir 2004/48 applies "to any infringement of intellectual property rights as provided for by Community law or the national law of the Member State concerned", (Art. 2(1). Thus, since Member States may not by an agreement among them escape their obligations under EU law, Dir. 2004/48 covers also Art. 56 to 68 UPCA.
115 See supra 17.2.1.1.,(ii), text at n. 36.

particular Art. 47 EUChFR.[116] However, unless it wishes to fundamentally depart from the principles that the General Court observes when adjudicating EU intellectual property protection, the UPC is likely to consider the development of a procedural practice of its own to be its domaine réservé. The reason is not only that the UPCA expressly holds the UPC to principles of expediency, quality, fairness and proportionality,[117] but that the UPC is set up as a specialized court that by its specific expertise and practice caters to the particular complexity, urgency, costs and harsh business and economic consequences of patent litigation.

(ii) While the latter consideration hints already to the way in which the particular function and the identity or "Selbstverständnis" of the UPC will determine its willingness to use Art. 267 TFEU,[118] there are also distinct limits to the admissibility of requests for preliminary rulings that the Court of Justice has continuously developed through a by now well established case-law and that will support the UPC's likely inclination to abstain from such requests. Since this case-law is generally known, a short summary of the relevant principles may suffice.[119]

---

116 See *A. Haedicke*, Justizielle Grundrechte im Einheitlichen Patentsystem, GRUR 2014, 119. For the relationship between national (German) guarantees of fundamental rights and the EUChFR, in particular the judicial control of the application of the EUChFR by German authorities see BVerfG (Federal Constitutional Court) of 6 November 2019, case 1 BvR 276/17, BVerfGE 152, 216 = ECLI:DE:BVerfG:2019: rs20191106.1bvr027617 ("Right to be forgotten II").
117 See recitals 6, 12 UPCA; UPC, Rules of Procedure, Preamble; for details see *Fl. Paschold*, Verfahrensprinzipien des Einheitlichen Patentgerichts, Cologne (Carl Heymanns) 2018, 201 et passim, 373 et passim, 573 et passim.
118 See infra 17.2.2.2.,(ii). It is assumed here that the UPC constitutes a court common to the Contracting Member States as claimed in circular terms by Art. 1(2) UPCA, and that, as such, it qualifies under Art. 267 TFEU although it is not really integrated into the judicial systems of these Member States as required by CJEU, op. 1/09 of 8 March 2011, Rep. 2011 I 1137 = ECLI:EU:C:2011:123, para. 82 (European and European Union Patent Court Agreement); op. 2/13 of 18 December 2014, ECLI:EU:C:2014:2454, paras. 174 et seq., 198 (European Convention on Human Rights); judgment of 6 March 2018, case C-284/16, *Slowak Republic/Achmea*, ECLI:EU:C:2018:158, paras. 47 et seq. with references; comp. also CJEU, op. 1/17 of 30 April 2019, ECLI: EU:C:2019:341, paras. 120 et seq. (CETA). For the status of the UPC and the controversies accompanying its establishment see *De Visscher*, The constitutional foundations of the UPC, supra Ch. 14; *J. Alberti*, New developments in the EU system of judicial protection: The creation of the Unified Patent Court and its future relations with the CJEU, 24 Maastricht J. Eur.&Compar. L. 6, 12 et seq., 18 et seq. (2017); *Th. Jaeger*, Delayed Again? The Benelux Alternative to the UPC, GRURInt 2021, 1133; *W. Tilmann*, Das EPG aus der Sicht des EuGH, GRUR 2021,373; *Ullrich*, loc.cit., Prop.Int. 2014 (53) 382 subB.2.b), all with references. Whether or not the contradiction between the characterization of the UPC as a common court of Member States and its actual quality as an international court of Member States is only one of appearance or really one of substance, for the purpose of this contribution it is sufficient to note that Art. 21 UPCA makes Art. 267 TFEU fully applicable, be it by merely declaratory or by genuine referral. Note that Art. 22(1) UPCA limits liability to infringement of EU law by the Court of Appeal; see also infra n. 148.
119 See Art. 93 to 104 CJEU Rules of Procedure; *CJEU*, Recommendation to national courts and tribunals in relation to the initiation of preliminary ruling proceedings, OJEU 2012 C 338,1. In addition to standard lit-

First, the request must concern a "question préjudicielle" in the sense that the answer to the question submitted to the Court of Justice must relate to a legal issue the submitting court has to solve in order to render its decision. However, since it is for the submitting court to consider whether "a decision on the question is necessary to enable it to give judgment" (Art. 267(2) TFEU), and since that court is best placed to assess the relevance, i.e., determinative nature of the question, the Court of Justice will not control the "caractère préjudiciel" of the question unless it is obviously irrelevant, has become mute or does not arise from a genuine controversy.[120]

Second, the question must be formulated as an abstract one asking the Court of Justice how a rule of Union law is to be interpreted rather than as one asking it how that rule is to be applied to the facts of a case. However, as any legal rule reveals its meaning only when read against the backdrop of the circumstances to which it is supposed to apply, the Court of Justice requires the submitting court to set forth both the factual and the legal background within which the issue arises and why it arises.[121] Conversely, the Court of Justice tends to frame its preliminary ruling according to the factual and legal circumstances that condition its meaning and to expressly ask the submitting court to verify the existence of these circumstances and the criteria that determine the legal relevance and reach of its preliminary ruling.[122]

Third, in general, Member States' courts are under no duty to submit to the Court of Justice requests for a preliminary ruling on the interpretation of Union law. Rather, as "ordinary", i.e. general courts of the Union that are held to apply Union law they must also interpret it themselves (iura novit curia). They are only offered the option to request a preliminary ruling as a way out of the difficulties of interpreting rules that are authoritative in a multitude of languages, worded in the terminology of autonomous Union law, and in need of being read in the context of the Union's particular legal order and with a view to achieving its particular "finalité".[123] It is only courts "against whose

---

erature see *M. Broberg, N. Fenger*, Preliminary References to the European Court of Justice, 3rd ed. Oxford 2021. In the following, references are made to the German version "Das Vorabentscheidungsverfahren vor dem Gerichtshof der Europäischen Union", Baden-Baden 2014 (with additional reference to the relevant chapters in brackets).

120 See inter al. CJEU of 6 October 2021, case C-561)19, *Consorzio Italian Management/Rete Ferroviaria Italiana*, ECLI:EU:C:2021:799, paras. 34 et seq.; of 19 April 2018, case C-152/17, *Consorzio Italian Management/Rete Ferroviaria Italiana*, ECLI:EU:C:2018:264, paras. 37 et seq. with references; *Schwarze, Wunderlich* in *Schwarze* et al.(eds.), EU – Kommentar, loc.cit., Art. 267 AEUV, paras. 37 et seq. with references; *Broberg, Fenger*, loc.cit., p. 149 et seq. (Ch. 5, sub 2.), p. 151 et seq. (Ch. 5, sub 3.), 159 et seq. (Ch. 5, sub 4.), 186 et seq. (Ch. 5, sub 5.).

121 See Art. 94 CJEU Rules of Procedure; CJEU of 19 April 2018,, case C-152/17, supra n. 120, paras. 21 et seq.; of 6 October 2021, case C-561/19,, supra n. 120, paras. 68 et seq. with references; *Schwarze, Wunderlich* in *Schwarze* et al. (eds.), EU-Kommentar, loc.cit., Art. 267 AEUV, para. 31; *Broberg, Fenger*, loc.cit., p. 262 et passim (Ch.8, sub 3.).

122 For details see *Broberg, Fenger*, loc.cit., p. 371 et passim (Ch. 11, sub 3.).

123 CJEU of 6 October 2021, case C-561/2019, supra n. 120, paras. 28, 41 et seq.; CJEU op. 1/09 of 8 March 2011, ECLI:EU:C:2011:123, para. 83 (European and European Union Patent Court Agreement).

decisions there is no judicial remedy"[124] that for the sake of the autonomous and uniform interpretation of Union law are obliged to submit any question of interpretation to the Court of Justice.[125] However, even these courts may abstain from requesting a preliminary ruling if there is no real "question" in that the rule of Union law represents an "acte clair" or an "acte éclairé".[126] The former will lie "where the correct interpretation of EU law is so obvious as to leave no scope for any reasonable doubt".[127] The latter will lie where the Court already gave a ruling on the question of interpretation either at an earlier stage of the proceedings before the submitting court or in a similar case or where established case-law of the Court of Justice already resolves the point of law.[128]

Although this so-called CILFIT case-law primarily concerns the duties to which Art. 267 TFEU subjects Member States' courts of last instance, it also informs the application of Art. 267 TFEU in general. Thus, in acte clair/acte éclairé cases the Court of Justice may render its ruling by simple decision rather than by full judgment,[129] and lower courts may rely on the CILFIT case-law when dealing with parties' suggestions to submit an issue of interpretation of EU law to the Court of Justice. It is true that, due to the nature of preliminary ruling proceedings as inter-court dialogues, the parties are not in a procedural position to oblige a Member State court to request a preliminary ruling on a point of law they consider relevant.[130] However, they have a constitutionally secured right to be heard by the Member State court on all relevant points of law, which means that the court may not simply ignore a party's substantiated plea for submitting to the CJEU a true issue of interpretation of an obviously pertinent but ambiguous rule of EU law.[131] Also, the parties will

---

[124] Art. 267(3) TFEU. Accordingly, the Court of Appeal of UPC is under a general duty to request preliminary rulings.
[125] CJEU of 6 October 2021, case C-561/19, *Consorzio Italian Management/Rete Ferroviaria Italiana*, ECLI:EU:C:2021:799, paras. 27, 41, 49.
[126] For the well established CILFIT case-law see CJEU of 6October 1982, case 283/81, *C.I.L.F.I.T. et al./Ministero della Sanità*, Rep. 1982, 3415 = ECLI:EU:C:1982:335, paras. 6 et seq., 12 et seq.; recently confirmed and elaborated on by CJEU of 6 October 2021, case C-561/19, supra n. 125, paras. 27 et passim. For the CILFIT case-law see Adv.Gen. *M. Bobek*, opinion of 15 April 2021, case C-561/19, *Consorzio Italian Management/ Rete Ferroviaria Italiana*, ECLI:EU:C:2021:291, paras. 2 et seq., 18 et seq. proposing a modified approach that the Court did not adopt; for its development see *Broberg, Fenger*, loc.cit., p. 297 et passim (Ch. 6, sub 3.); *Th.Jaeger*, System einer europäischen Gerichtsbarkeit für Immaterialgüterrechte, Heidelberg 2013, 746 et seq., *id.*, CILFIT nach dem Urteil Consorzio: Rückenwind für den acte clair, EuZW 2022, 18.
[127] CJEU of 6 October 2021, case C-561/19, supra n. 125, para. 39, stressing at para. 40 "that the matter must be equally obvious to the other courts or tribunals of last instance of the Member States and to the Court of Justice".
[128] CJEU of 6 October 2021, case C-561/19, supra n. 125, para. 36, stressing at paras. 37 et seq. that a renewed or second request for a preliminary ruling on the same issue remains admissible.
[129] Art. 99 CJEU Rules of Procedure.
[130] CJEU of 6 October 1982, case 283/81, supra n. 126, paras. 7 et seq.; of 6 October 2021, case C-561/19, supra n. 125, paras. 27 et seq., 53 et seq.
[131] CJEU of 6 October 2012, case C-561/19, supra n. 125, para. 51 obliges only courts of last instance to formally justify their refusal to request a preliminary ruling by a reasoned decision. Lower courts may be

be heard by the Court of Justice in case the Member State court actually submits a request for a preliminary ruling.[132] After all, it is their litigation, they control its scope, procedure and termination by virtue of the principle of party autonomy, and it is their interests that in terms of legal certainty may be as much affected by a court's refusal to request a preliminary ruling as by the delivery of such ruling by the Court of Justice.

17.2.2.2 A division of labor

(i) Given that the Court of Justice considers the preliminary ruling proceeding of Art. 267 TFEU to be the cornerstone of the EU's judicial system,[133] given also the broad spectrum of rules that in the context of unitary and European patent litigation may raise issues of interpretation that come within the reach of Art. 267 TFEU, and given the detailed criteria that condition the application of the CILFIT case-law, the original fears seem to be justified that the adjudication of patent litigation by the Unified Patent Court might be unduly burdened by an additional layer of legal dispute. It may distract the Court from fulfilling its main function, and, due to the lack of patent law expertise of the Court of Justice, it might impair the predictability of the outcome of invalidity and infringement proceedings.[134] Leaving aside the profession-specific nervousness of some parts of the patent law community about the predictability of the outcomes of patent litigation that frequently enough results from seeking protection up to the legal borderlines of the patent system,[135] the facts are: First, the main function of the UPC as a specialized patent court will not be affected by it being subject to Art. 267 TFEU. The vast majority of cases

---

held by their procedural rules or practice to request a preliminary ruling from the CJEU if the parties so wish rather than refer them to the possibly even lengthier procedure of appeal up to a court of last instance, see *Broberg, Fenger*, loc.cit. p. 247 et seq. (Ch.7, sub 2.3). In fact, preliminary rulings originating from requests by lower courts constitute by far the majority of all preliminary rulings, see *CJEU*, Annual Report 2021, table XXIII.

132 Art. 97 CJEU Rules of Procedure.
133 See CJEU of 6 October 2021, case C-561/19, supra n. 125, para. 27; of 6 March 2018, case C-284/16, *Slowak Republic/Achmea*, ECLI:EU:C:2018:158, para. 37; op. 2/13 of 18 December 2014, ECLI:EU:C:2014:2454, para. 176 (Accession of the EU to the ECHR). Between 2/3 and 3/4 of the CJEU's caseload relate to Art. 267 TFEU proceedings, see *CJEU*, Annual Report 2020, Tab. II (75,64% out of 735 cases); *id*, Annual Report 2021, Tab. II (67,66% out of 838 cases). Due to the General Court's jurisdiction over actions brought by individuals against acts of the EU institutions and agencies, the second prong of the CJEU's jurisdiction, direct judicial protection, essentially comprises appeals in law from the General Court's decisions (17% of all cases in 2020, 26.61% in 2021 (*CJEU*, Annual Reports, ibid.).
134 See *Ullrich* in *Metzger* (ed.), loc.cit., p. 253 with references.
135 This nervousness is evidenced by the fact that parts of the patent law community do not even trust the UPC that they fought for; see the transitional and the opt-out rules of Art. 83 UPCA, including the prolongation of the transition period provided for by Art. 83(5) UPCA in case the patent law community is still not satisfied with the UPC, and see Art. 87 UPCA. This author knows of no court that has to adjudicate under a similar populist censorship.

will turn on technical and patent law-specific issues of validity and infringement with the correct determination of the subject matter scope of protection typically being at the center of the litigation. In addition, due to the centralized structure of the Unified Patent Court and due to the UPCA's rules on territorial jurisdiction,[136] a main objective underlying the creation of the UPC, which is to exclude the risk of conflicts between decisions of national courts relating to the same patent, will be met with.

Second, due precisely to its centralized structure, the use of Art. 267 TFEU by the Unified Patent Court will necessarily differ somewhat from that made and to be made by national courts since by its very function the UPC's Court of Appeal is to ensure the uniform application of the law that also constitutes the core function of the Court of Justice under Art. 267 TFEU.[137] However, it is not the uniform interpretation of the law as such that the Court of Justice seeks to ensure by virtue of Art. 267 TFEU but the systemic consistency, the full effect and the autonomy of the particular nature of Union law.[138] In accomplishing this comprehensive task the Court of Justice has come to assume a role of guidance of national courts that, by applying EU law, act as ordinary courts of the Union.[139] As a court common to Member States the UPC, however specialized and structured,[140] must also act as an ordinary court of the Union. More particularly, the profound embeddedness of the unitary patent and to a lesser extent also of the UPCA-type European patent into a broad range of EU law and principles[141] requires the UPC becoming included into the Art. 267 TFEU judicial dialogue with the CJEU. It is in this way that, by virtue of a comprehensive rather than a separate and isolated adjudicatory authority, the Union's patent policy as expressed by the purpose of protection, its substantive scope, its exceptions and enforcement rules will be transposed into judicial practice as an integrated part of the EU's legal order and of its overall system of intellectual property protection.

(ii) Accordingly, it would seem that there is a broad enough basis for a fruitful division of labor and for a dialogue between the Court of Justice and the Unified Patent Court.

---

136 Art. 33 UPCA. The remaining potential of conflicts with and between decisions of national courts regarding European patents may concern major markets, e.g. Poland, Spain.
137 For an earlier version of that evolving argument see *Ullrich*, The Court of Justice of the European Union: The Future European and EU Patents Court: Hierarchy, Complementarity, Rivalry, in *B. Hansen, D. Schüssler-Langeheine* (eds.), Patent Practice in Japan and Europe (Liber amicorum G. Rahn), Alphen adR 2011, 81, 86 et passim; *id.*, Die Entwicklung eines Systems des Gewerblichen Rechtsschutzes in der EU: Die Rolle des Gerichtshofs, in *P. Behrens* et al.(eds.), Ökonomische Analyse des Europarechts, Tübingen 2012, 147, 184 et passim; *id.*, in Metzger (ed.), loc.cit., p. 253 et passim (sub B.II.5.).
138 CJEU of 6 October 2021, case C-561/19, supra n. 125, paras. 27 et seq. with references.
139 CJEU, op. 1/09 of 8 March 2011, Rep. 2011 I 1137 = ECLI:EU:C:2011:123, para. 80 (European and European Union Patent Court Agreement). This characterization follows from that, due to the direct effect of Union law, Member States' courts have full jurisdiction over all matters that are not specifically attributed to the CJEU, see Art. 19(1), subpara. 2, Art. 19(3) TEU.
140 As are so many judiciaries of Member States, be it courts of labour law, social law or tax law etc.
141 See supra sub 17.2.1.

The latter will do its work as programmed by the UPCA and request preliminary rulings in the areas described here above[142] just as national courts would do, which, by the way, in the fields of intellectual property mostly are specialized courts. Being a technical expert court,[143] the UPC may even have a particular interest in seeking the interpretative advice of the Court of Justice in case new or highly controversial questions of Union law arise in litigation before it, in particular issues of hidden legislative policy or of new technologies or business practices[144] or issues cutting across other fields of intellectual property or related to the general legal order of the Union. After all, in the 70 years of its existence,[145] the Court of Justice built up an enormous case-law, became the lead authority for the interpretation and judicial development of Union law, shaped its characteristics and its effective operation, and has itself a broad and ever broadening experience in intellectual property and related fields. Certainly, the UPC's Court of Appeal is under a general duty to request preliminary rulings from the Court of Justice, in particular, albeit not only in case it wishes to depart from a ruling of the CJEU or from rulings of national courts of last instance.[146]

---

142 Sub 17.2.1.

143 For the structure and procedure of the UPC see *E. van Zimmeren*, supra. Ch. 15; for a broader role of the UPC see *F. Baldan, E. van Zimmeren*,The Future Role of the Unified Patent Court in the European Patent System, 52 CMLRev. 1529, 1560 et passim (2015), more critical *Petersen, Riis, Schovsbo* in *Ballardini, Norrgard, Bruun*, loc.cit., p. 42 et seq. The point of interest here is, first, that the panels of the local and the regional divisions must, upon request by one of the parties, include a technically qualified judge, and they will also be so composed whenever the panel asks for it (Art. 8(5) UPCA); second, that except in Art. 32(1), lit.i) UPCA cases the Central Division, which has broad jurisdiction (Art. 33(3), lit.b), lit.c); Art. 33(4) UPCA) is always sitting in a composition of two legally and one technically qualified judge (Art. 8(6) UPCA); third, that irrespective of the nature of the litigation even the Court of Appeal sits always in a composition of three legally and two technically qualified judges (Art. 9(1) UPCA), the only exception being Art. 32(1),lit. i) UPCA cases. Parties may be represented by patent attorneys instead of lawyers, and, if they assist lawyers, they have a right to speak (Art. 48(1), (2), (4) UPCA). Clearly, technical expertise is essential in many cases, particularly so in Art. 32(1), lit.b), lit.d), lit.e) UPCA cases, but such actions rarely come alone. Clearly also, the weight given to the vote of the technically qualified judge is considerable and even determinative in case the legally qualified judges are in disagreement.

144 See generally *D. Nicol*, The pendulum of patents, principles and products – from the industrial revolution to the genetic revolution, in *G. Ghidini, H. Ullrich, P Drahos* (eds.), Kritika – Essays on Intellectual Property, Vol. 5, Cheltenham (E.Elgar) 2021, 99; *R. Dreyfuss*, The challenges facing IP systems: researching for the future, in *P. Drahos, G. Ghidini, H. Ullrich*, Kritika – Essays on Intellctual Property, Vol. 4, Cheltenham (E.Elgar) 2020, 1, 3 et passim; for artificial intelligence more particularly see *J. Straus*, Artificial Intelligence and Patenting: Some Lessons from DABUS Patent Application, 44 Eur.Int Prop.Rev. 348(2022); *T. Dornis*, Künstliche Intelligenz als "Erfinder" – Perspektiven der Disruption im Patentrecht, Teil I, Mitt.PatAnw. 2020, 436, Teil II, Mitt.PatAnw. 2020, 477.

145 See only *I. Govaere*, Editorial: Une grande dame de 70 ans, forte et fragile, J.dr.eur. 2022 (no. 293) 413; *Schwarze* in *Schwarze* (ed.), EU-Kommentar, loc.cit., Art. 19 EUV, passim (paras. 15 et seq.); *B. Wegener* in *Calliess, Ruffert* (eds.), loc.cit., EUV – AEUV, Art. 19 EUV, passim (paras. 15 et seq.).

146 See CJEU of 6 October 2021, case C-561/19, *Consorzio Italian Management/Rete Ferroviaria Italiana*, ECLI:EU:C:2021:799, para. 49.

However, given both the broad discretion that courts enjoy as regards determining the "caractère préjudiciel" of a question of interpretation[147] and the practical non-enforceability of the obligation that Art. 267 TFEU and Art. 21 UPCA, respectively, create for the UPC, in particular for its Court of Appeal,[148] the well-functioning of the preliminary ruling mechanism will essentially depend on the UPC's willingness to take the initiative, so on what it comes to consider good judicial practice regarding the use of Art. 267 TFEU.[149] It is well known that the costs and delays caused by such requests will matter as will the position the parties take before the UPC.[150] But these factors alone do not explain the differences in the use of Art. 267 TFEU by national courts,[151] and they do not suffice for predicting the future practice of the UPC. Local divisions may tend to rely on the UPC's procedure of appeal and the authority of the Court of Appeal or they may, in particular cases, see the need to engage the CJEU's authority with much depending on how they define their position within the UPC's structure.[152] Likewise, when determin-

---

147 See supra 17.2.2.1., (ii).
148 Since there is no appeal, not even in law, from the decisions of the UPC's Court of Appeal, the only remedy is an action for liability under Art. 22 UPCA. Although the absence of a liability regime in the EEUPC Agreement was noted in a complementary consideration by CJEU in its op. 1/09 (of 8 March 2011, Rep. 2011 I 1137 = ECLI:EU:C:2011:123, paras. 86 et seq. with references), it is fraught with so many problems (causation, violation of a subjective right, evidence and scope of actual damage) as to make it a purely hypothetical sanction; see *Tilmann*, in *Tilmann, Plassmann*, eds., loc.cit., Art. 22 UPCA, paras 4 et seq.; generally K. *Havu*, Contemporary Member State Liability Case Law: on Causation and Harm, 47 Eur.L.Rev. 791 (2022). In addition, under Art. 22 UPCA liability is limited to the UPC's Court of Appeal infringing Union law although local or regional divisions may infringe Union law as well, e.g., by holding an act of an institution of the EU invalid; see Art. 267(1), lit.b) TFEU; CJEU of 22 October 1987, case 314/85, *Foto-Frost/Hauptzollamt Lübeck*, Rep. 1987, 4199 = ECLI:EU:C:1987:452, paras. 11 et seq. A little more promising may be an individual's right to bring a complaint to a Member State's constitutional court on grounds of violation of the fundamental right to be heard, see for Germany BVerfG (Federal Constitutional Court) of 30 August 2010, case 1 BvR 1631/08, GRUR 2010, 999 = ECLI:DE:BVerfG:2010:rk20100830.1bvr163108.
149 While Art. 38 Statute of the UPC refers to the procedure that Art. 93 et seq. CJEU Rules of Procedure establish, the Rules of Procedure of the UPC are silent as regards the procedure of the UPC in Art. 267 TFEU cases.
150 See supra n. 130; *Broberg, Fenger*, loc.cit., p. 225 et seq. (Ch.6, sub 3.4.4). On average, the preliminary ruling procedure takes 16 months, see *CJEU*, Annual Report 2021, table XIV. Art. 105 CJEU Rules of Procedure provides for an accelerated procedure, but most requests for it are dismissed, see *CJEU*, ibid. table XVII, XVIII.
151 For the (non-disclosed) motivation of courts to request or not to request preliminary rulings see *Broberg, Fenger*, loc.cit., p. 59 et passim (Ch.2, sub 3.3). It seems that subjective factors are of little influence; see M.*Broberg*, H. *Hansen*, N.*Fenger*, A Structural Model for Explaining Member State Variations in Preliminary References to the ECJ, 45 Eur.L.Rev. 599 (2020).
152 Note that the number of "voluntary" requests for preliminary rulings by lower instance courts by far surpasses that of "mandatory" requests by last instance courts (see CJEU, Annual Report 2021, Tag. XXIII), and that, possibly, lower courts may use Art. 267 TFEU as a way to bypass courts of last instance (see *Broberg, Fenger*, loc.cit., p. 65). For instance, a local or regional division may wish to overcome a precedent set by the Court of Appeal it considers to be obsolete or erroneous enough under patent law or procedural law or contrary to Union law, comp. LG Munich (District Court Munich) of 19 January 2021, case 21 O

ing its role in relation to the Court of Justice, the Court of Appeal needs to define its function as either that of a patent-specific enforcement court or that of a Union-specific common court of Member States in charge of adjudicating patent law in its EU context.[153] The Unified Patent Court will have to do so also with a view to the positions of courts of Member States that do not adhere to the UPCA, to the positions of national courts adjudicating national patent protection, and possibly to some degree also with a view to the positions of courts of non-EU States that are Contracting States of the EPC. Whether in these respects the UPC will accept support by the authority of the Court of Justice or rather avoid its shadow will not be seen before at least some years of developing a case-law of its own have passed.[154] Ultimately, the UPC, in its turn, will have to find its way to concepts, notions and an interpretation of the rules of a unified system of patent protection that are autonomous by reference to their origins in a multitude of co-existing and potentially rivalling national laws.

17.3 Outlook

The in part hybrid character of the unitary patent will not make it easier for the Unified Patent Court to accomplish this task. Presumably, as a common expert court of a considerable number of EU Member States, the UPC may acquire a strong position vis-à-vis the European Patent Office and its Boards of Appeal, which will contribute to further rectifying the balance between the administrative and the judicial branch of the European patent system.[155] However, adjudicating infringement litigation raises challenges of quite a different nature because these disputes arise when patent protection meets the reality of the market and of its general regulation. These realities cannot be simply left

---

16782/20, GRUR 2021, 466 requesting the preliminary ruling by CJEU of 28 April 2022, case C-44/21, *Phoenix Contact/Harting*, ECLI:EU:C:2022:309.

153 Which latter may also be a way of attaining the advantages of a specialized judiciary while avoiding its drawbacks; see generally *Jaeger*, System einer europäischen Gerichtsbarkeit, loc.cit., p. 449 et passim (506 et seq.); *S. Glazebrook*, A Specialist Patent or Intellectual Property Court for New Zealand? 12 J.World Int.Prop. 524 (2009); *I. Schneider*, Das Verhältnis zwischen allgemeinen Gerichten und Fachgerichten am Beispiel des Politikfelds Patentrecht und des europäischen Einheitlichen Patentgerichts in *B. Rehder, I. Schneider* (eds.), Gerichtsverbünde, Grundrechte und Politikfelder in Europa, Baden-Baden (Nomos) 2016, 125; *J. Schovsbo, T. Riis, C. Petersen*, The Unified Patent Court: Pros and Cons of Specialisation – Is there a Light at the End of the Tunnel?, 46 IIC 271 (2015); *Petersen, Riis, Schovsbo*, in *Ballardini, Norrgard, Bruun*, loc.cit., p 42 et seq.

154 The UPC will have to do so under conditions of a sort of test period (see supra n. 135) and of changed circumstances. The departure of the UK from the UPCA dims hopes for self-financing in the long term (see Art. 36 UPCA) and leaves London as a rivalling expert jurisdiction for high yield litigation and high quality judgments on European bundle patents; see *K. Cremers* et al, Patent Litigation in Europe, 44 Eur.J.Law Econ.1, 14 et seq. (2017) with references.

155 See supra n. 6 and accompanying text; *Petersen, Riis, Schovsbo*, in *Ballardini, Noorgard, Bruun*, loc. cit., p. 39 et seq.

out of consideration. In addition, the unitary patent adds a new dimension to patent protection in the EU in that, uno acto, it grants full protection throughout the entire area of enhanced cooperation and, thus, creates the same patent density everywhere rather than only in some lead States.[156] This rarely mentioned consequence entails the need for the Unified Patent Court to overcome by its jurisprudence the resistance of so many Member States against pronounced patent protection, a need that is the more compelling as the ultimate goal of unified patent protection is to also integrate both the still hesitating signatory States of the UPCA and the Member States that remain outside enhanced cooperation.[157] Just as the importance of the Court of Justice does not rest on the scope of the tasks alone that Art. 19 TEU confers upon it but on that, early on, it understood that the traditional concepts of public international law do not allow to adequately address the needs and realities of EU integration, the Unified Patent Court will have to develop its approach to getting the new layer of protection generally accepted that the unitary patent introduces into the existing patent system and, more generally, into the protection of industrial property in the European Union.

The Unified Patent Court will have to do so in a constructive way and as part of its mission within a judicial structure that is asymmetric and that it is supposed to complement. The General Court controls only the administrative branch of granting and revoking industrial property rights of the Union, namely trade marks, designs and plant variety rights, while infringement litigation, including validity challenges that typically arise within the context of such disputes, remains within the jurisdiction of Member State courts. Conversely, as regards unitary and UPCA-type European patents, the Unified Patent Court will exercise a centralized and exclusive jurisdiction over infringement and related matters while the administrative procedure of granting these patents is outside its control. Although the latter is also outside its jurisdiction the Court of Justice sees the granting procedure and its results of all the other Union rights of industrial property and, via Art. 267 TFEU, the entire fields of infringement of intellectual property, and it does so with a view to their context of general market regulation. There is no reason to narrow its perspective other than one of patent parochialism.

---

[156] Art. 89(1) UPCA both obscures this consequence and reveals its importance. As necessary as it may be to include the major patent Member States into the UPCA system, it is quite obvious that in the mid- to long-term the patent density of the Member State with highest patent coverage will automatically extend to all the other Member States. The fear of becoming dominated rather than integrated largely explains the reluctance of some Member States to adhere to the UPCA; see *A. Kupzok*, Law and Economics of Unitary Patent Protection in the European Union: The Rebel's Viewpoint, Eur.Int.Prop.Rev. 2014, 418, 424 et passim; *Z. Zawadzka*, The Unitary Patent Protection: A Voice in the Discussion from the Polish Perspective, 44 IIC 383 (2014).
[157] See Art. 20(2) TEU, Art. 328(2) TFEU.

Sam Granata
18 Rules of procedure of the UPC, a judge's perspective

18.1 Introduction

This chapter embodies a *"judge's"* perspective on the rules of procedure of the Unified Patent Court (hereafter referred to as "UPC")[1], and as such articulates a very personal view by *a* Belgian judge who considers himself *"legally qualified"*[2]. Therefore, as something as a standard (Belgian) judge does not exist, do not read into this contribution an opinion which is shared by all (Belgian) judges[3].

Further, this contribution will not entail a detailed overview of the structure and functioning of UPC or in depth analysis of its rules of procedure. For detailed studies reference can be made to other contributions in this book, specific books on the subject[4] and numerous on-line commentaries[5].

Finally, it is important to note that this contribution is based on some knowledge of the drafting process but most of all on the *"bare"* texts of the Unified Patent Court Agreement[6] (hereafter referred to a "UPCA"), the Statute and the Rules of Procedure[7] (when the notion *"Rule"* is used it will refer to these Rules). As such, besides non-binding interpretational views by the Preparatory Committee of the UPC regarding specific issues[8], no national court nor UPC-court has interpreted these rules and their interplay as yet. Therefore, it is reasonable that this *personal* perspective might be altered or adapted once the UPC is up and running and articles and rules have been the subject of such interpretation.

---

1 As explained later the *"rules of procedure of the UPC"* consist of an interplay between three levels of internal rules.
2 The panels of the Court of the UPC will be manpowered by legally and technically qualified judges.
3 If the term *"judge"* is used, it refers to any kind of gender, also would the term *"he"* or *"his"* be linked to this term.
4 See footnote 3 but also i.a. Tilmann, W. (editor), "Unified Patent Protection in Europe A Commentary", Oxford University Press, 2018, p. 2878, and the undoubtedly to be published books in the near future such as Augenstein, C., Wilson. A, Unified Patent Court Procedure: a Commentary, "Bloomsbury Publishing (to be published in November 2022).
5 Type as a search term *"rules of procedure UPC"* in any search engine and a multitude articles will be presented. Most of them being *"personal perspectives"*.
6 Agreement on a Unified Patent Court (2013/C 175/01) dated June 20, 2013.
7 More specifically the 18th Draft of the Rules (with its amendments up to 8 July 2022).
8 And expressed on their website www.unified-patent-court.org.

Sam Granata, Judge at the Court of Appeal Antwerp, Belgium and at the Benelux Court.

https://doi.org/10.1515/9783110781687-018

18.2 Levels of rules of procedure of the UPC

18.2.1 Hierarchy between the rules of procedure of the UPC

One of the inherent problems of the UPC, better of any international newly established court, was that it could not fall back on existing *"general"* rules of proceedings (of a Contracting Member State of the UPCA). Where most national centralized patent courts can rely *either* on *specific* national procedural law regarding patent proceedings *either* on *general* national procedural law, the UPC had to draft a new set of rules of procedure. In drafting these rules of procedure, the drafters seemed to have the ambition to identify specific procedural approaches in national (patent or general IP) law of the Contracting Member States which were regarded as contributing to the ideal patent procedure. This led to a mixture of rules of procedure finding their roots in common and civil law. After BREXIT, this in itself led to a strange situation that besides Ireland no other common law country is a signatory to the UPCA[9].

Before going into the rules themselves, one should keep in mind that the UPC will actually be governed by three internal levels of rules of procedure which refer to each other and are hierarchical. General rules are to be found in the UPCA itself. More detailed rules related to the functioning of the UPC are articulated in the Statute (annexed to the UPCA). The final and lowest level are the Rules which are focused on the proceedings itself and are the most detailed.

The term *"internal"* rules of procedure is used because the external primary rules are to be found in EU law. Where the UPCA prevails on the Statute and the Statute on the Rules, EU law prevails on the UPCA. When questioning a specific rule on its legality, a user of the UPC system will have to examine whether a Rule is in conformity with the Statute and the UPCA but at the end has to examine whether the UPCA (or Statute) is itself in conformity with EU law. To safeguard the conformity of the Rules with EU law, the European Commission played and will play an important (advisory) role in the drafting (and amending) process of the Rules. The original 18th draft of the Rules was examined in detail by the European Commission which gave its opinion, as it did and will for any later amendment[10].

A potential problem of this primacy of EU Law read together with the (internal) hierarchical structure of the rules of procedure of the UPC, could come into play if a Rule would be held not in conformity with EU Law but in conformity with the UPCA. Amend-

---

9 Malta is a Contracting Member State but its legal tradition seems a mixture of civil and common law. Therefore, it might be of importance for the interpretation of the Rules and the UPC as a whole that Ireland, after the Irish government announced on June 28th 2022 to hold a referendum (in 2023 or 2024) on the approval to ratify the UPCA, becomes part of the system.
10 Article 41 (2) UPCA.

ing such a Rule (to bring in line with EU law) could imply it to be in contradiction with the UPCA[11].

An example related to above could be the translation of the Enforcement Directive[12] in the UPCA and further elaborated in the Rules. The translation of the Enforcement Directive in the UPCA is not always literal. The UPCA foresees e.g. in an *"Order to Inspect Premises"* which in some ways differs from the actual *"Order to Preserve Evidence"*[13]. One of the differences is that under Article 60 (7) UPCA *"measures to preserve evidence"*[14] may be subject to the lodging of a security (or an equivalent assurance intended to ensure compensation) for any prejudice suffered by the defendant as provided under Article 60 (9) UPCA while this is not foreseen for the *"Order to Inspect Premises"*. However, the Rules with regard to the *"Order to Inspect Premises"*[15] state under Rule 199 (2) juncto Rule 196 (3) b the possibility to condition the enforceability to a security. As Article 7 (2) Enforcement Directive foresees *generally* for *any* measure to preserve evidence that it may be subject to the lodging by the applicant of adequate security or an equivalent assurance, the Rules seem in line with the Enforcement Directive but not with the UPCA. A UPC judge, bound by EU Law, could possibly allow such an security even if not foreseen in the UPCA.

18.2.2 The UPCA

The UPCA is the macro-level of the internal rules of procedure of the UPC. As mentioned the UPCA hierarchically embodies the highest internal rules. The UPCA sets the general principles to which the court (and its judges) should abide[16], which are further elaborated in the Statute and, essentially, in the Rules[17].

---

[11] Article 41 (2) second paragraph last sentence explicitly states that amendments may not contradict or alter the Agreement or the Statute. However, even in contradiction with the UPCA, a judge will always be obliged to apply EU Law and can set aside the contradicting UPCA (or Statute) articles.
[12] Directive 2004/48/EC of the European Parliament and of the Council of 29 April 2004 on the enforcement of intellectual property rights.
[13] The Order to Inspect Premises is mentioned in Articles 60 (3), 60 (4) and 60 (6) UPCA setting it apart from the Order to Preserve Evidence.
[14] As the title of this article (stating both measures as distinct) and Article 60 UPCA makes a difference between an "Order to Preserve Evidence" and an "Order to Inspect Premises" one could interpret "measure to preserve evidence" as being limited to an "Order to Preserve Evidence". This specifically could be derived from Article 60 (6) UPCA which makes a clear distinction between "a <u>measure</u> to preserve evidence" and a "<u>measure</u> to inspect premises".
[15] The Rules make procedurally no difference between the two mentioned orders (for obtaining such orders). See Rule 199 (2) (with regard to the *"Order to Inspect Premises"*) stating that the same Rules as stipulated under Rules 192 – 198 (with regard to the *"Order to Preserve Evidence"*) will apply ("*mutatis mutandis*").
[16] E.g. Article 17 UPCA (judicial independence and impartiality),
[17] Art. 41 UPCA states that details of the proceedings are lay down in the Rules.

The key-principles of the rules of procedure of the UPC are mentioned under Article 42 UPCA articulating the principles of *"proportionality"* and *"fairness"*. These principles are further shaped in the Rules (see infra).

The UPCA, as an (international) agreement, can only be modified by a new agreement to be signed by all Contracting Member States. As such, and as the signing of the UPCA was already a political roller coaster, it can be foreseen that, at least regarding procedural issues, no modification of the UPCA may be expected in the near future. Being of such a general nature regarding procedural issues, it will probably not be necessary to modify the UPCA as modifications can be made to the Rules based on decisions by the Administrative Committee (see infra).

18.2.3 The Statute

Under Article 2 UPCA the Statute is defined as the *"Statute of the Court"* as set out in Annex 1 of the UPCA. Further, this article stipulates that the Statute is an integral part of the UPCA. Throughout the UPCA several articles refer to the Statute regarding internal organizational issues[18]. Article 40 (3) UPCA states that the Statute should guarantee that the functioning of the Court is organized in the most efficient and cost-effective manner and should ensure equitable access to justice. Some articles of the Statute specifically clarify (in general terms) the functioning of UPC Judges[19].

Article 40 UPCA deals with the Statute itself and states under its second paragraph that the Statute may be amended by a decision of the Administrative Committee on the basis of a proposal by the Court or a proposal of a Contracting Member State after consultation with the Court[20]. Again, it states that such amendments should be in line with the UPCA itself.

The Statute states under its first article that it contains institutional and financial arrangements of the UPC. It goes beyond the object of this contribution to detail these insti-

---

[18] i.a. Article 4 (2) UPCA (regarding the procedure to elect the President of the Court of Appeal), Article 7 (3) and (5) UPCA (regarding the setting up of local and regional divisions), Article 10 (1) and (4) UPCA regarding the setting up of the Registry and the appointment of the Registrar), Article 11 UPCA regarding composition of, the duties of and adoption of decisions by of the Administrative Committee, Budget Committee and Advisory Committee), Article 16 UPCA (regarding the appointment procedure of the judges of the UPC), Article 18 UPCA (regarding the establishment of the Pool of Judges), Article 19 UPCA (regarding the training framework for judges of the UPC), Article 37 (regarding the Financing of the UPC), Article 57 UPCA (regarding the conflicts of interest of court experts), Article 82 (3) UPCA (regarding enforcement procedures).
[19] Article 17 UPCA (regarding the judicial independence and impartiality) and Article 78 UPCA (regarding decisions of the UPC and dissenting opinions).
[20] The term "*Court*" is defined in Article 2 UPCA as *"the Unified Patent Court created by this Agreement"*. I tend to understand under the term *"Court"* related to this Article 40 UPCA the *Presidium*.

tutional and financial arrangements, but the following articles (and principles) merit more insight as they are linked to the functioning of UPC judges.

Article 7 Statute deals with the impartiality of judges and does not seem to differ for written and/or unwritten principles that can be expected to apply in any Contracting Member State. Although this contribution has been written from the viewpoint of a *"legally qualified judge"*, the grounds listed under Article 7 (2) Statute seem of particular importance for *"technically qualified judges"*.

Somewhat novel for a Belgian judge is that in the event a judge considers that he should not take part in the judgement or examination of a particular case, he should inform his President (either First Instance or Court of Appeal). This president will then decide (and justify) whether the judge should not sit or make a submission in a particular case. Such a system implies that a judge needs to inform his President with the *reasons* (even these of a personal nature) why he should not take part in the judgement or examination of a particular case. This could imply, also because no appeal against such decision is foreseen, that even if a judge questions his impartiality that he can still be obliged to take part in the judgement or examination of a particular case.

To be complete, Article 7 (4) UPCA states that besides a personal consideration of a judge, also a party may object to a judge taking part in the proceedings on the grounds listed under Article 7 (2) Statute. The procedure to be followed is then detailed under Rule 346 (Application of Article 7 Statute) (as amended by the Administrative Committee on 8 July 2022[21]). In this procedure it will be in principle the president of the court to which the judge belongs who will decide whether an objection by a party is valid or not. In case of *"difficulty with the meaning of Art. 7 (5) Statute"* this president should refer to the Presidium. Where before this amendment there existed no safeguards for parties using such an objection to delay proceedings, the amended Rule 346.6. foresees that the panel may proceed with proceedings pending the decision by the respective President or Presidium.

As the Presidium was already mentioned a couple of times, notice should be given to Article 15 Statute dealing with this body. The Presidium will be composed of the President of the Court of Appeal (elected as the chairperson), the President of the Court of First Instance, two judges of the Court of Appeal and three judges from the Court of First Instance. The Registrar is also part of the Presidium (but as a non-voting member). The Presidium, among other functions, is responsible for proposals regarding amendments to the Rules[22].

An important chapter IV of the Statute is reserved for procedural issues. That deliberations are secret speaks per se[23]. The decision-taking process, and more specifically majority rules, are stipulated in Article 35 (1) Statute. That a process is set up, is impor-

---

21 Amendment 31 (to Rule 346) as adopted by the Administrative Committee of the UPC on 8 July 2022.
22 Article 15 (3)(a) Statute.
23 Article 34 Statute.

tant as it is possible that a panel of division sits in an even number of judges[24]. Should there be no majority the vote of the presiding judge shall prevail.

Article 21 (2) Statute states that in cases of *"exceptional importance"* (articulated as a decision which may affect the unity and consistency of the case law of the UPC)[25] a panel of the Court of Appeal of the UPC, on a proposal by the presiding judge, to which an action is assigned can refer it to the Full Court of Appeal. The presiding judge of the panel should request the President of the Court of Appeal and the two judges of the Court of Appeal member of the Presidium to appoint the judges of the full Court of Appeal[26]. The appointees should be the President of the Court of Appeal *"and not less than ten (legally and technically qualified) judges of the Court of Appeal"*[27]. If the UPC is up and running and more than two panels are formed, the full Court of Appeal should be increased by five (legally and technically qualified) judges for each additional panel. Where Article 35 (3) Statute states that a decision of this full Court of Appeal is only *"valid"* if it is taken by at least ¾ of the judges comprising the full court, Rule 238A (3) states that decisions of the Full Court of Appeal should be taken by no less than a ¾ majority of the judges, which seems to be a more coherent wording as such Full Court of Appeal may be expected to only take *"valid"* decisions. The question might arise what will happen with an action where such a majority cannot be reached and an opinion is expected from the Full Court of Appeal.

Finally, and novel for a number jurisdictions of Contracting Member States, it the possibility to provide in a dissenting opinion[28]. Such dissenting opinions should be provided in writing and signed by the judge expressing his decision. Article 78 (2) UPCA states that a dissenting opinion may only be expressed in *"exceptional circumstances"*. As there exists no clarification as to what is considered as *"exceptional"* it is the subjective decision of the dissenting judge which will prevail[29].

18.2.4 The Rules of Procedure

It is not the object of this contribution to detail the historical background of the Rules, but it should be noted that the Contracting Member States set up a *"Preliminary Committee"* in charge of preparing the practical arrangements for the *"early"* establishment and coming into operation of the UPC.

---

[24] This is the case if a technically qualified judge is added to a panel of three legally qualified judges of a local or regional division.
[25] A situation which is reiterated in Rule 238 A.
[26] Rule 238 A (2).
[27] They represent the initial two panels of the Court of Appeal.
[28] Article 36 Statute.
[29] It would seem beneficial that dissenting opinions should be scarce to non-existent, as it would not be opportune that the lack of dissenting opinion is perceived as if the decision is taken by consensus.

The Preparatory Committee focused on five streams, one of which was the legal framework[30]. This legal framework stream was divided in several sub-streams, with the most important for this contribution the Rules of Procedure (Group). Although initially it was the idea that this group was staffed with experts and the Preliminary Committee would take more political approaches, national interests were prominently present during the discussions in the sub-streams. This presence of national interests was more or less minimized by the fact that sub-stream worked on proposals which were drafted by a select Drafting Committee of expert judges and lawyers[31].

As already mentioned the rules of procedure of the UPC are indeed a mixture of civil and common law best practices in patent law proceedings. The influence of common law can be derived (e.g.) from the non-hierarchical ranking of the means of evidence and means of obtaining evidence[32]. Contrary to civil law traditions written evidence is placed on the same level as *"hearing and questioning of witnesses"* and *"hearing and questioning of experts"*. This finds its way in the actual proceedings before the UPC where it seems that cross-examination may be part of the proceedings. The possibility of such cross-examination constitutes as such an alternative means of evidence, compared with e.g. Belgium, where expert and witness opinions are simply submitted in writing and only exceptionally allowed during the oral hearing. The possible importance of hearing witnesses and experts became somewhat more prominent upon amending Rule 112 (conduct of the oral hearing) approved on 8 July 2022[33]. Where the old Rule 112.2.(b) indicated that witnesses and experts could only be heard *"if ordered during the interim procedure"* by the Judge-Rapporteur, the amended Rule 112.2.(b) seems to indicate that hearing of witnesses and experts is a *standard* for the oral hearing. The explanatory notes to the amendment do not indicate whether the hearing of the witnesses and experts is dependent of the order by the Judge-Rapporteur[34].

18.3 The driving principles of *"proportionality"* and *"fairness"* as a matter of trust in the UPC judge

Where civil law orientated countries seem to explicitly articulate specific conditions for a judge to examine and motivate in his decision, the rules of procedure of the UPC are

---

30 The others were financial aspects, IT, facilities and HR and training.
31 Members of the Drafting Committee were Mr. Kevin Mooney (UK), Mr. C. Floyd (UK), Mr. K. Grabinski (DE), Mr. W. Tilmann (DE), Mrs. Pérard (FR), Mr. Véron (FR) and Mr. W. Hyong (NL).
32 Rule 170 (2).
33 Amendment 15 (to Rule 112) as adopted by the Administrative Committee of the UPC on 8 July 2022.
34 Such order might still be a condition as would the hearing be held as a norm, no order to hear expert and witnesses would seem necessary. Indeed Rule (Rule 104) was not amended on 8 July 2022.

structured in such a way that they leave a high(er) level of discretion to its judges. The UPC judges should be led in their decision taking by standards of *"fairness"* and *"proportionality"*.

The principle of *"proportionality"* is introduced in the 6th paragraph of the preambule of the UPCA where it is stipulated that the decisions of the UPC should strike *"a fair balance between the interests of right holders and other parties and considering the need for proportionality and flexibility"*;

A specific article in the UPCA is later reserved to these principles where Article 42 (1) UPCA states that *"the Court shall deal with litigation in ways which are proportionate to the importance and complexity thereof"*. In its second paragraph it states that *"The Court shall ensure that the rules, procedures and remedies provided for in this Agreement and in the Statute are used in a fair and equitable manner and do not distort competition"*. As such the court should take into consideration not only the interest of the parties but also on a macro-level the principles of *"competition"*.

These principles of proportionality and fairness are further articulated in the Preamble of the Rules under paragraph 2 with a direct reference to article 42 UPCA and re-iterating the principles of proportionality, flexibility, fairness and equity. In the third paragraph of this preamble it is further elaborated that proportionality should be ensured *"by giving due consideration to the nature and complexity of each action and its importance"*.

To clarify the trust awarded to a UPC judge, one could refer to the Order to Preserve Evidence by comparing national Belgian legislation to the rules of procedure of the UPC taking a different approach as to the decision taking process.

A Belgian judge having to decide on a Belgian *"Order to Preserve Evidence"* (translated into Belgian law as an Order for Descriptive Measures and a separate Order for Seizure Measures) is guided by stringent rules laid down in the article 1369bis (Belgian) Judicial Code. This article states under its third paragraph that the judge when deciding on an Order to Preserve Evidence *"should investigate"* (i) whether *prima facie* the intellectual property right (and as such the patent) is valid and (ii) whether there exist indications of an actual or future infringement of this intellectual property right. When deciding on a seizure order (as a subsequent order to preserve evidence and separate to the order for obtaining descriptive measures) the judge *"should investigate"* (i) whether *prima facie* the intellectual property right (and as such the patent) is valid (ii) whether the infringement cannot reasonably be disputed and (iii) whether, after having weighed the interest of the parties (including the common interest), the facts and the evidence introduced by the applicant are of such a nature that the actual seizure reasonably can be justified. In other words, the test which a Belgian judge has to apply is explicit. Belgian procedural law does not, and specifically regarding the decision on an application for an order to obtain descriptive measures (and if the conditions are met) allow a judge based on proportionality grounds to refuse an order.

The UPCA and Rules take a different approach. Neither the UPCA nor the Rules, demand the UPC judge to investigate or motivate specific conditions when deciding on an application for obtaining an order to preserve evidence. Article 60 UPCA[35] states that *"(a)t the request of the applicant which has presented reasonably available evidence to support the claim that the patent has been infringed or is about to be infringed the Court may, even before the commencement of proceedings on the merits of the case, order prompt and effective provisional measures to preserve relevant evidence in respect of the alleged infringement, subject to the protection of confidential information"*. Rules 192 through 199 detail the procedure which should be followed when deciding on an application to obtain an *Order to Preserve Evidence*. Where Rule 194 specifically state as its title the *"examination of the application for preserving evidence"*, such examination is limited to the discretion of the court to (i) inform the defendant about the application and invite him to lodge an objection to the application (ii) summon the parties to an oral hearing, (iii) summon the applicant to an oral hearing without the presence of the defendant or (iv) decide on the application without having heard the defendant. In exercising *"this discretion"* the court should consider (i) the urgency of the action, (ii) whether the reasons for not hearing the defendant appear well-founded and (iii) the probabilities that evidence may be destroyed or cease to be available[36]. The Rules as such do not provide guidance to the UPC judge, but neither to the applicant, which *"conditions"* should be met to allow or refuse an application for an Order to Preserve Evidence as such. The UPC judge will be guided by the general principles of article 60 UPCA and has to decide whether *"reasonably available evidence"* was introduced to *"support the claim that the patent has been infringed or is about to be infringed"*. In making this decision he will have to deal with the application *"in ways which are proportionate to the importance and complexity"* of the litigation[37]. That proportionality will be essential in the decision of the UPC judge is even further stressed in the wording of article 60 UPCA which states that the judge *"may"* order the measure to preserve relevant evidence even if reasonably available evidence was introduced. This seems to mean that based on proportionality considerations (and not in the least the interest of other parties) a UPC judge can still refuse such an order.

The above seems to mean, comparing the UPC and Belgian approach, that regarding an Order for Descriptive Measures and in case the two mentioned conditions are met, the Belgian judge is obliged to allow such an order while the same judge acting as UPC judge can deny such order if he would find the application not-proportionate.

In other words the UPCA read together with the Rules seem to leave a high degree of discretion to the UPC judge. The rules of procedure of the UPC seem to put more trust in its judges than the same judge can expect in his national (Belgian) procedural law.

---

[35] A transposition of article 7 Enforcement Directive.
[36] Important to note but not object of this contribution is that whether or not a protective letter was introduced is not an element to be taken into consideration and this opposite to the elements to be taken into consideration in an order for preliminary measures (see Rule 209– Examination of the application for provisional measures).
[37] Article 42 (1) UPCA.

Although such trust in a judge should be applauded, on the other hand, especially in the first years, this undoubtedly implies uncertainty and unpredictability regarding the proportionality standards to be applied by the UPC judge.

In line with the above, the word *"may"* has led to extensive interpretative discussions related to permanent injunctions upon an infringement decision by the UPC judge. Article 63 (1) UPCA states that the *"Court may grant injunction against the infringer"*. Here again proportionality seems to be introduced regarding the decision for an injunction even after the infringement was found to be proven. The wording of article 63 (1) UPCA seems to be in contradiction with article 25 UPCA stating that *"a patent shall confer on its proprietor the right to prevent any third party not having the proprietor's consent"* followed by deeds or actions which are normally the object of an injunction. It should be noted that the national approaches seem to differ regarding an automatic injunction (without taking into consideration proportionality). In Germany and Italy a proportionality test seems to be introduced in their national procedural law, but is only in exceptional cases applied. In the Netherlands proportionality is considered, while in Belgium it is only considered in decisions regarding permanent injunctions against intermediaries. An argument which could be used in arguing that proportionality should not play a role in decisions regarding permanent injunctions (if the infringement was decided upon), is an *a contrario* reasoning regarding the decision taking applicable to applications for provisional measures in the Rules. Rule 211 clearly states that the Court *"shall in the exercise of its discretion weigh up the interests of the parties and, in particular, take into account the potential harm for either of the parties resulting from the granting or the refusal of the injunction"*. This is indeed a proportionality test which cannot be identified in the Rules regarding permanent injunctions. On the other hand reference should be made to the hierarchy between the rules of procedure where the UPCA prevails (and where the word *"may"* is clearly stated and where the principle of proportionality under article 42 is dependent of the nature of the decision).

18.4 Pragmatic versus legalistic approach

Another principle which clearly dictates the functioning of the UPC (and as such the decision-making process of the UPC judges) is its pragmatic approach. Such an approach can be identified in the drafting process of the Rules finding its origin in Article 41 (2) UPCA stating that the Rules shall be adapted by the Administrative Committee on the basis of *"broad consultation with the stakeholders"*. Proof of this broad consultation of the stakeholders is that two drafts (the 15th dated May 31, 2013 and the 17th dated October 31, 2014) were subject to public consultations. Based on the received comments the 18th draft emerged on July 1, 2015, was presented on July 10, 2015 and was published on October 19, 2015. This version was altered after a meeting with the Drafting Committee in March 2017 and the final version was published on the website of the UPC on April 10, 2017. After this publication several amendments were adopted by the Administrative

Committee of the UPC on 8 July 2022.[38] These last amendments were not the subject of *"broad"* consultations, but were discussed rather within a limited framework of stakeholders (and in particular patent lawyers and judges) of whom the identity is not made public.

This pragmatic approach can also be read into the *"flexibility"* principle articulated in the already mentioned 6th paragraph of the Preambule of the UPCA and the 2nd (regarding the applications and the interpretation Rules) and especially 4th paragraph of the Preambule of the Rules. In this 4th paragraph it is stipulated that flexibility should be ensured by applying the procedural rules in a flexible and balanced manner *"with the required level of discretion for the judges to organize the proceedings in the most efficient and effective manner"*.

Such a pragmatic approach is, at least for civil law judges, not very common. Where in first instance (at least in Belgium in the Enterprise Court) a more pragmatic approach (sometimes) could influence the decision-making process, the question will be whether such a flexible and pragmatic approach is what can be expected from the Court of Appeal of the UPC (and especially as EU Law prevails on the (internal) rules of procedure). A legalistic view can be found to be very unpragmatic and not very flexible, but has the advantage that it provides legal certainty. A system driven by flexibility, may at the end lead to legal uncertainty for the clients of the UPC, the parties. Finding a balance between a flexible system and legal certainty for its users will therefore be one of the important issues for the UPC (and especially its Court of Appeal).

18.5 The Judge-Rapporteur

The Judge-Rapporteur[39] is a key-player in the UPC system. The Judge-Rapporteur is the case manager of the proceedings and fulfils an important function throughout the UPC proceedings up to the oral hearing. It would lead to far to list all the decisions and orders he can take[40], but the importance of his function as a case manager is explicit during the *"interim procedure"*[41]. During this phase of the procedure the Judge-Rapporteur should make all necessary preparations for the oral procedure (during which the presiding judge will take over the case management[42]). These preparations may include an interim conference with the parties. He may order to provide further clarifications on specific points, to answer specific questions, produce evidence and lodge

---

38 Resulting to a number of amendments to the 18th version of the Rules.
39 Only the legally qualified judge can be appointed as judge rapporteur.
40 As a personal note, and especially during the start-up years, it would seem opportune that either the Judge-Rapporteur on his own motion (Rule 102 (1)) either on request of the parties (Rule 102 (2)) that a decision is referred to the panel.
41 Rule 101–110.
42 Rule 111.

specific documents[43]. If a party fails to comply with an order, he can even give a decision by default.

Where also on a national (at least Belgian) level there seems to be shifts from a relatieve passive judge (leaving case management more or less to the parties and their lawyers) to an active judge, this shift is only prominent for a national (Belgian) judge during the oral phase, the UPC has introduced such case management as being the responsibility of the Judge-Rapporteur ánd has introduced that such case management should be organized before the oral hearing.

Such approach is beneficial not only for the time limits the UPC has imposed itself as ideal regarding decisions on infringement and validity[44] but also for the parties.

The phase of proceedings during which the actual case management is expected from the Judge-Rapporteur might further play an important role in view of the Judge-Rapporteur as a settlement seeker[45]. In national (Belgian) proceedings a judge will normally only play this role during oral hearings, which is the ultimate phase of litigation and in most cases too late. By explicitly stating that the Judge-Rapporteur's task is also to seek settlements and by moving this task to a phase before the oral phase, could increase chances to reach a settlement.

18.6 The UPC as one-stop-shop for patent disputes

By extension to the above the second part of the cited sentence of Rule 104 (d) should be highlighted. Not only should the Judge-Rapporteur explore the possibilities of a settlement but he could also explore the possibilities to make use of the facilities of the *Patent Mediation and Arbitration Center*. Although this center is often critically perceived and important issues might need to be clarified regarding its competence, I wish to highlight that having a "*court*" (decision-taking above the parties) and an "*ADR-center*" (decision-taking above and between the parties) under one roof could be beneficial in dispute resolution, which again should be applauded.

As this center will (as may expected at least during the start-up years of the UPC) be activated if a proceeding has already been initiated before the Court, arbitration might not play a major role compared to mediation. Specifically regarding damages and costs (i.e. after a decision has been taken regarding the infringement and/or the validity) the

---

43 Rule 103.
44 See Consideration 7 of the Preambule UPCA where it is stated that decisions (in first instance) should be taken within a year.
45 Rule 104 (d) states that the interim procedure should enable the Judge-Rapporteur to "*explore with the parties the possibilities to settle the dispute (...)*".
The settlement-seeker-function should be part of any job description of a judge and he should encourage and guide parties to a settlement. A judge taking a decision should be indeed the last resort to resolve a dispute.

PMAC might be able to lead parties to a mediated-settlement. The director of this center and specifically the interplay between the Court and the Center will play an important role in its possible success.

18.7 Conclusion

National procedural interpretative issues are often the gist of national proceedings, even if such rules exist since decades or more. Factual circumstances seem to give rise to different opinions and approaches which demand an interpretative decision on procedural rules which were considered set.

It seems unrealistic that the rules of proceedings of the UPC are of such a nature that no interpretative issues would exist when the first cases (and facts) are introduced before UPC. What is more, interpretative issues may especially arise for the UPC as its rules of procedure can be identified as a mixture of common and civil law, cherry-picking and introducing the best national patent litigation practices into an international patent court.

Interpretative issues may further arise given the driving principles of *"proportionality"*, expressing the trust given to UPC judges, and *"flexibility"*, giving air to a pragmatic and less legalistic approach.

It will be up to the Court of Appeal of the UPC to find a balance between these principles leading to more legal certainty for its users. This should not considered an issue but rather an opportunity to further construct the most ideal patent litigation proceedings which in its turn might find its way into national patent proceedings.

This contribution further proves that the drafters of the UPCA, Statute and Rules have introduced a modern body of rules of procedure taking into consideration the needs of the parties and procedural economy. These procedural rules express a shift which already can be identified in national procedural law, whereby the functioning of the judge is aligned to what may be expected from a judge as decision taker ánd active settlement seeker. Especially the case-management-approach (helped by a performant CMS-system and the phase of the proceedings where such case management is exercised) will most probably lead to an up-to-date court system. As such the UPC judge, and specifically the Judge-Rapporteur, might evolve from a case manager to a true litigation manager.

Guillaume Dubos, Stéphanie Rollin de Chambonas, Thomas Leconte

19 The user in the UPC

In addition to the more general considerations outlined elsewhere in this Handbook, it is worthwhile to consider the UPC from the viewpoint of its users. These include, of course, the parties to future litigation, e.g., patent holders (hereafter patentees) on one hand, and alleged infringers and claimants for, e.g., revocation of the patent on the other hand, but also professionals such as attorneys and patent attorneys who will represent the parties.

In a broader sense, third parties who wish to access the UPC's decisions and orders as well as the written pleadings will also be "users" of the UPC.

In the following, we provide some practical considerations from the viewpoint of each of these users in turn, based on our experience. (References to the Rules of Procedure are to those which were adopted by decision of the Administrative Committee on 8 July 2022, and which entered into force on 1 September 2022.)

19.1 Opting out and in: beware of the torpedoes

With the UPC being expected to finally start operations in the first semester of 2023, there has been ample time to discuss the legal provision for opt-out, Article 83(3) UPCA (as well as Article 83(4) UPCA, which provides for "opt-in" after an opt-out).

As a reminder, the framework is as follows:
- by default, all EPs will be subject to the jurisdiction of the UPC;
- however, during the transitional period of 7 years starting from the entry into force of the UPCA, national courts will retain concurrent jurisdiction over revocation and infringement actions.[1] Furthermore, patentees will be able to opt out from the exclusive jurisdiction of the UPC;[2]
- once a patent has been opted out, patentees will have the option to withdraw their opt-out and fall back within the exclusive jurisdiction of the UPC at any time, including after the transitional period ("opt-in").[3]

---

[1] UPCA, art 83(1).
[2] UPCA, art 83(3), 2nd sentence.
[3] UPCA, art 83(4).

Guillaume Dubos, Partner, Abello IP Firm, Paris.
Stéphanie Rollin de Chambonas, Lawyer, Abello IP Firm, Paris.
Thomas Leconte, European Patent Attorney, Abello IP Firm, Paris.

https://doi.org/10.1515/9783110781687-019

Said otherwise, during a 7-year period starting in 2023, the UPC and national courts will have concurrent jurisdiction, but patentees will be able to escape the jurisdiction of the UPC by opting out, and then get back in by opting in. Afterwards, the UPC will have exclusive jurisdiction (except for patents which have been opted out at the latest one month before the expiry of the transitional period).[4]

It should be noted that new Rule 5A of the Rules of Procedure provides a mechanism for eliminating fraudulent or otherwise unauthorised opt-outs in a short amount of time.[5]

Thus, an existing EP portfolio can be managed according to two broad approaches: do nothing, in which case the UPC will have jurisdiction over the EPs;[6] or opt-out some or all EPs to remove them from the jurisdiction of the UPC.

The latter approach will require more active management, not only to request all the opt-outs, but also to select which EPs to opt-out. For large patent portfolios, this can constitute a significant amount of work within the short time frame before the end of the so-called "sunrise period".[7]

The main catch is that an opt-out is only possible if no action has yet been brought before the UPC regarding the relevant patent.[8] Thus, a patentee who contemplates opting out for any number of patents should do so as quickly as possible, and ideally even before the entry into force of the UPCA. Otherwise, a cunning competitor may bring a quick action before the UPC (such as revocation, or even declaration of non-infringement) which would irreversibly prevent any opt-out.

Patentees may think that the safest way to approach the issue would be to simply opt-out their entire portfolio considering the possibility to opt back in later, for example just before launching an infringement action before the UPC. However, there is another catch here: opt-in is only possible if no action has been brought before any national court regarding the relevant patent while it was opted out.[9] This opens up another strategy for competitors, who could prevent opt-in and thus the jurisdiction of the UPC, by simply launching a minor action involving the patent before a national court of any UPCA Contracting Member State.

Finally, a last catch regarding opt-out is that, while a legal person can opt-out *its* EPs, it cannot opt-out *itself* from the jurisdiction of the UPC: another patentee can still sue it

---

4 UPCA, art 83(3), penultimate sentence.
5 Rule 5A.2 provides that *"The Registrar shall decide on the Application for removal* **as soon as practicable**"; and Rule 5A.3 provides for a one-month time limit for applying for review of the decision on the Application for removal.
6 UPCA, art 32(1) and art 83(3).
7 This sunrise period is foreseen e.g. in Rule 5.12 of the Rules of Procedure, according to which applications to opt-out *"accepted by the Registry before the entry into force of the Agreement shall be treated as entered on the register on the date of entry into force of the Agreement"*.
8 UPCA, art 83(3), 1st sentence.
9 UPCA, art 83(4).

for infringement before the UPC. Therefore, there is no way to escape entirely from any sort of proceedings before the UPC. In view of the potentially powerful effects of a decision by the UPC (see below), this should be taken into account when deciding whether to opt-out or not, since opting out one's full portfolio could lead to an inability to mount counter-offensive actions before the UPC on equal terms.

Therefore, there is no easy answer as to whether to opt out or not from the UPC. Without careful consideration and anticipation, patentees risk having the choice made for them by their competitors.

19.2 Procedural aspects: the devil is in the details

A very important, yet often overlooked aspect of the UPC lies in the constraints provided for by its Rules of Procedure. These mainly entail three topics: the speed of the proceedings, their costs, and the language in which they will be conducted. These do not only impact claimants and defendants, but also their lawyers and the Court itself.

The first topic is the speed of the proceedings, and it is perhaps the one which will have the most significant effect on patent litigation in Europe over the long term. The preamble of the Rules of Procedure provides that a case shall be conducted in such a way that the final oral hearing will normally take place within one year, starting from the date of receipt of the summons, i.e. after the statement of claim has been recorded and checked by the Registry.[10] This time frame is vastly different from virtually all current judicial systems in Europe, except for some fast-track proceedings (with the provision that existing fast-track proceedings can usually fall back into the normal track proceedings in case of delay). In general, most patent cases currently last at least 6 months longer and in several cases even longer, sometimes significantly so.

The obvious consequence is that the parties, and their counsels, will have a much shorter timeframe to build their case, while the UPC will have to be dimensioned to handle cases quickly. While this should have limited effect regarding claimants, who by definition can prepare well in advance, the situation will be quite different for defendants.

Without reviewing the various deadlines in detail, we shall take an example: starting from the service of the statement by the Registry under Rule 271, defendants to an infringement action will have 3 months to lodge their Statement of defence,[11] which may include a counterclaim for revocation.[12] If the infringement action was not anticipated, this means that the alleged infringer will have to conduct prior art searches, find revocation grounds, and build their case on infringement, all within the 3-month period. In parallel, defendants will also have to raise any preliminary objection (such as lack of jur-

---

10 Rules of Procedure, Rule 17.4.
11 Rules of Procedure, Rule 23.
12 Rules of Procedure, Rule 25.1.

isdiction of the division) within one month of the summons,[13] or else they will be considered as having submitted to the jurisdiction and competence of the Court.[14]

This is also compounded by the principle of concentration set forth in point 7 of the preamble, and by the fact that subsequent pleadings after the Statement of defence (i.e., the rejoinder) are limited to matters raised in the reply of the claimant,[15] meaning the defendant will have to be as complete as possible in their first Statement of defence.

The situation is likewise, but reversed, for a revocation action, with the patentee having to file a counterclaim for infringement within 2 months[16] (of course, the patentee could also decide to launch a separate action later on).

It should be noted that the Rules of Procedure do contain some provisions allowing for flexibility on the deadlines. The preamble specifies that more complex actions may require more time, and various rules give leeway for extension of the deadlines,[17] additional pleadings[18] and further discussions.[19] Nevertheless, the same rules also allow for shortening the proceedings.

Although it is of course not possible to predict how the practice will develop and some higher flexibility may be expected during the first few years, there is little doubt that eventually patent litigation before the UPC will have to be conducted within much shorter time frames than is the norm nowadays in most jurisdictions.

In practice, this means that both legal departments and law firms will have to be organized to be able to tackle these constraints, starting with making sure that there is available manpower at short notice.

The second topic is the cost of the proceedings, meaning here the court fees, not the attorney fees. These are set out in the rules on court fees and recoverable costs. Without reviewing them in detail, it is worth noting that the costs are not insignificant: for example, any revocation claim will entail a fixed fee (of 20,000 € for a revocation action, and 11,000 € for a revocation counterclaim), while infringement actions will incur a variable fee of up to 325,000 €, depending on the value of the action.

While this is not unusual for some European jurisdictions, such as Germany, the situation is quite different for countries with virtually no court fees, such as France. The costs will be recoverable by the successful party, albeit in the context of a separate proceedings.[20]

---

[13] Rules of Procedure, Rule 19.1.
[14] Rules of Procedure, Rule 19.7.
[15] Rules of Procedure, Rule 29(c).
[16] Rules of Procedure, Rule 49.
[17] Rules of Procedure, Rule 9.3, for example.
[18] Rules of Procedure, Rule 36.
[19] For example, after the closure of the written procedure at the behest of the judge-rapporteur: Rules of Procedure, Rule 103.1.
[20] Rules of Procedure, Part 1, Chapter 5.

The rules do provide for a fee reduction for small companies, but only of 40 %, meaning that any action would still require paying the fees upfront, on top of the attorney fees, under penalty of default.

Although this will likely not significantly impact large companies, this may give pause to smaller ones, especially those coming from countries not currently having court fees.

Lastly, the language of the proceedings will also have practical consequences. As per the UPCA, the rules are as follows:
- for revocation actions (thus before the central division), the language of the proceedings will be the language of the patent as granted (i.e., English, German, or French, in view of the EPC);[21]
- for other actions before local or regional divisions, this will be the official language (or one of them) of the relevant Member State hosting the division, or the language designated by the States in case of a regional division;[22]
- in case of mutual agreement, parties will be able to elect the language in which the patent was granted, subject to approval by the relevant division.[23]

There are some other minor rules which we will not detail here.

The important aspect is that parties will more likely need to handle European-wide cases in a language they are not familiar with. Of course, the Rules of Procedure do provide for translation in various cases and for interpretation of oral proceedings. Nevertheless, outside of some exceptions, the costs of these will have to be borne by the parties and the translations will have to be done in the short timeframe of the proceedings. Furthermore, considering this timeframe, if the usual law firm of a company is not able to handle the language of the proceedings, such company will have to quickly designate an alternate representative, if only to raise a preliminary objection.

Overall, UPC patent litigation will be quicker, more expensive, and potentially in many more languages than today, while at the same time carrying higher stakes. The name of the game is likely to be anticipation: of legal and technical defence as soon as possible (i.e., cease-and-desist letters), of the dimension of legal teams, and of a panel of available legal representatives.

19.3 The UPC as a "one-stop shop" for users

From the point of view of the patentees, the UPC is highly attractive in the context of cross-border patent disputes, because a single, unified enforcement action allows them

---

21 UPCA, art 49(6).
22 UPCA, art 49(1); see also UPCA, art 49(2).
23 UPCA, art 49(3); see also UPCA, art 49(4).

to obtain relief for infringing activities happening in all Contracting Member States at the same time.

In practice, the ability of patentees to assert their patents on a large scale will be greatly enhanced, compared the previous setup where an action before each national court of those States where the patent is in force was necessary.

Patentees will also enjoy enhanced legal certainty within the EU, as the scenario where different courts in different countries reach conflicting decisions regarding the same patent is eliminated.

Another appealing feature for patentees using the UPC is the possibility to obtain pan-European injunctions prohibiting any further infringement when the Court has found a patent is infringed.[24] Therefore, a single injunction with pan-European effect may be obtained from the UPC, which will greatly simplify enforcement for patentees. However, it should be noted that granting such injunctions is left to the discretion of the UPC; injunctions will not be automatically granted. For comparison it is interesting to note that, in some Contracting Member States like France, as a rule, judges automatically grant an injunction in case infringement is found. It will be interesting to observe if and to what extent the local divisions of the UPC, in France and Contracting Member States with similar practices, will continue with their national particularism and grant automatic injunctions, and whether their practice will influence local divisions seated in other Contracting Member States.

From the above, it is plain that the UPC will be attractive for patentees from the viewpoint of enforcement. However, to give a complete picture, it also is worth mentioning that the aforementioned advantages of the UPC will have a flipside: patentees are exposed to central revocation of their UP and non-opted out EP, across all Contracting Member States and in States where the EP is validated.

In practice, that means that a patentee who wishes to not expose a specific, valuable EP to a revocation action before the UPC, must actively remove the patent from the UPC jurisdiction by opting out (see above). Some patentees will wish to review their patent portfolio well before the start of operations of the UPC, in order to be ready to opt out at the start of the so-called "sunrise period" and thereby avoid a central invalidity action by a challenger as soon as the UPC opens.

19.4 National patents: not (yet?) out of the picture

In view of the risk of central revocation, some patent applicants might want to secure double patent protection for their valuable and strategic patents. By "double patent protection" we mean obtaining a UP and a national patent for one or more Contracting Member States, for the same invention and the same applicants.

---

24 UPCA, art 63(1).

A few Contracting Member States have implemented legislation which will allow double patent protection. For instance, in France, when the UPCA will enter into force, it will be possible to obtain double patent protection via (i) a French national patent and (ii) a UP or a non-opted-out EP.[25] This contrasts with the present situation, where patent protection via a EP validated in France and a French national patent is not possible, because the latter ceases to have effect insofar as it covers the same invention as the former.[26] Germany has also implemented similar provisions.

While we have not searched for comparable legislation in other Contracting Member States, we expect that, since both France and Germany have allowed double patent protection, risk-adverse (and well-funded) patent applicants can at least consider filing French and/or German national patent applications in addition to an EP application leading to a UP (or non-opted-out EP) for the same subject-matter after the UPCA has entered into force. This can allow them, e.g., to assert the national patent in case infringement is limited to France and/or Germany, before the relevant national jurisdictions, while refraining from asserting the UP before the UPC (bearing in mind that the defendant might still start a revocation action before the UPC, however, but the associated costs and constraints are higher than before national courts, see above).

19.5 Forum shopping with the UPC and its impact on its users' actions

Although one of the main aims of the UPC is to limit forum shopping,[27] the UPCA in fact allows patentees to engage in forum shopping when suing an alleged infringer. Indeed, Article 33(1) allows the patentee to choose between the following divisions: before the local or regional division of the Contracting Member State where the infringement (actual or threatened) has or may occur *or* before the local or regional division of the Contracting Member State where the alleged infringer has its residence or principal place of business *or* before the central division (when the defendant has no place of business in

---

25 *Ordonnance* no. 2018-341 of 9 May 2018 related to the Unitary patent and the Unified Patent Court amends art L.614-13 of the French Intellectual Property Code to provide that the EP without opt-out can coexist with the French patent and creates art L.614-16-3, which will provide that a French patent covering the same invention as a UP can coexist with the UP. Said *ordonnance* will enter into force on the day the UPCA enters into force.
26 French Intellectual Property Code, art L.614-13, as of September 30, 2022.
27 UPCA, Recital 2 (*"the significant variations between national court systems are detrimental for innovation"*), Recital 5 (*"to enhance legal certainty by setting up a Unified Patent Court for litigation relating to the infringement and validity of patents"*).

a Contracting Member State, or if the Contracting Member State has no local division and does not participate in a regional division).[28]

In contrast, potential infringers are in a less favourable position than patentees, for two main reasons. Firstly, they are exposed to being sued, at the choice of the patentees, before any one of several regional or local or central divisions. If a patentee decides to file an infringement action before a division located in another Contracting Member State than the one where the defendant has its residence or principal place of business, the defendant will be forced to defend himself in a country and in a language which he may not know and understand, and within a short time frame, which can make it harder to mount an effective defence in time. Secondly, unlike the patentee, a potential infringer has a more limited forum choice, as the revocation action or action for declaration of non-infringement must be introduced before the central division[29] (except for counterclaims for revocation, which may be raised before the relevant local or regional division). For revocation claimants located in a country other than the three[30] Contracting Member States where the sections of the central division will be set up, this jurisdictional rule may constitute an impediment to their actions.

These forum shopping opportunities offered by the UPC might result in an over-concentration of patent cases in just a few forums and a competition between courts to attract litigants. When choosing a local division, some patentees will likely look for divisions they are familiar with and/or where judges will already have extensive experience in patent law. This should be the case at least before the German, French, Italian and Dutch local divisions – where, due to a high volume of patent cases (more than fifty per calendar year) before the jurisdictions of those Contracting Member States, there will be two legally qualified judges who are nationals of the Contracting Member States hosting the division.

Only practice and experience will tell how users of the UPC will use the flexibility offered by the UPC in the choice of the forum.

In a worst-case scenario, patentees' overwhelming preference for certain forums may result in situation similar to the one in the United States, where certain district courts have established an image as the *"go-to jurisdiction for patent litigation"*– such as the Eastern District of Texas,[31] or more recently the Waco Division of the Western District of Texas.[32]

---

[28] UPCA, art 33(1).
[29] UPCA, art 33(4).
[30] At the time of writing of this chapter, it seems that Milan may be a serious candidate for housing the life sciences section of the UPC's central division, which was to be seated in London before Brexit.
[31] Brian J. Love & James Yoon, "Predictably Expensive: A Critical Look at Patent Litigation in the Eastern District of Texas", 20 Stanford Technology Law Review (STLR) 1 (2017).
[32] J. Jonas Anderson & Paul R. Gugliuzza, "Federal Judge Seeks Patent Cases", Duke Law Journal, Vol. 71, p. 419, 2021.

However, we believe such a scenario will not materialize in the UPC system, for the following reasons.

Firstly, the UPCA creates a more unified substantive patent law, since it provides that the UPC shall base its decisions on Union Law, the UPCA, the EPC, international agreements binding on all the Contracting Member States, and national law.[33] Moreover, the fact the UPC system has one Court of Appeal in Luxembourg should produce consistent case law, and rein in divisions inclined to issue rulings with too much "national flavour", so to speak. In the same vein, the existence of unified procedural rules will likely reduce the motivation to engage in forum shopping or judge shopping, in contrast e.g. to United States district courts, which may and sometimes do establish local rules for patent cases.

Secondly, the judges in all local and regional divisions will be *"legally qualified"* judges for patent cases,[34] and upon request by one of the parties, the UPC will appoint an additional *"technicaly qualified"* judge with qualifications and experience in the field of the technology concerned.[35] Therefore, all UPC divisions should have judges with expertise in patent law, which arguably should reduce the motivation to engage in forum shopping. Moreover, local and regional divisions will be multi-national,[36] which should further contribute to have consistent case law and expertise shared among all local divisions.

19.6 Means of evidence: a large and complete toolbox for users

Users of the UPC will certainly be pleasantly surprised by the large toolbox offered to the parties by the UPCA to prove their allegations.[37] Article 53 UPCA contains a long (and non-exhaustive) list of means of evidence, including hearing the parties, requests for information, production of documents, hearing witness, opinions by experts, inspection, experiments and sworn statements in writing (i.e., affidavits).

Some of these means of evidence will be new for many practitioners, in particular the hearing of witnesses and/or experts. Such hearings may be obtained in the following situations: on request from a party,[38] if the Court orders it of its own motion, or where a

---

[33] UPCA, art 24(1).
[34] UCPA, art 8(2), (3), (4).
[35] UPCA, art 8(5).
[36] UPCA, art 8(2), (3), (4).
[37] Article 54 UPCA provides for the familiar rule according to which the burden of the proof of facts shall be on the party relying on those facts.
[38] Rules of Procedure, Rule 176 and Rule 181.

written statement proffered by one party is challenged by the other party.[39] The Court may put questions to the witness/expert, and, under the control of the Court, the parties may put questions to the witness/expert which are limited to adducing admissible evidence.

Such hearings, which are not common practice in many continental jurisdictions such as France, has attracted our attention as patent litigators, as they may provide an opportunity to reinforce the probative interest and value of written witness/expert statements proffered in patent cases. Indeed, in France, it is quite common for parties to proffer written experts' reports to support some specific validity and/or infringement allegations, and/or to rebut the other party's allegations, which can lead to a multiplication of reports which add complexity to the case. Before the UPC, being able to question the experts in person will enable the judges and the parties alike to shed light on specific points of the written reports, sometimes unclear or challenged, which should provide useful information to the Court.

Counsel will need to spend time and resources preparing the expert/witness for such hearings, since experts may be directly questioned by the presiding judge, the judges of the panel,[40] and the parties (and accordingly by the adverse parties).[41] Under such circumstances, although the UPC system offers many means of evidence which should be useful for the parties to prove their allegations in patent disputes, it can be debated whether parties will have sufficient time to fully use them during proceedings, considering the very short time frames foreseen in the Rules of Procedure.

In view of the short deadlines mentioned above, some parties might have difficulty using the different tools available for providing evidence. Indeed, in infringement cases, the defendant seeking to offer oral witness and/or expert evidence will need to apply for a hearing very quickly after receiving the complaint, since it has only three months to study the case, contest the infringement allegations, possibly prepare a counterclaim for revocation of the patent and search for prior art in support of the counterclaim. In addition, the hearing should be held within a reasonable time before the end of the three months, for the defendant to take into account the statements of the expert and/or the witness for its defence. Similarly, the claimant will also be obliged to promptly react within the two-month time limit if he wishes an expert and/or witness to be heard to rebut statements made by the defendant's to and/or experts.

It is possible that the Court will grant additional time to parties wishing to gather more evidence in the course of the proceedings, in the context of the flexibility allowed by the Rules of Procedure. It will be interesting to see how the local and regional divisions will use their discretion to enable UPC practitioners to gather all the evidence they need during the proceedings.

---

39 Rules of Procedure, Rule 177 and Rule 181.
40 Rules of Procedure, Rule 178.4.
41 Rules of Procedure, Rule 178.5.

However, it is not certain that such flexibility will encourage the parties to seek all possible evidence during the written and interim procedure. This is because the Rules of Procedure explicitly require the parties to *"set out their full case as early as possible in the proceedings"*.[42] This limitation of facts and legal grounds very soon in the proceedings will effectively compel the parties to present all their evidence from the outset of the first instance proceedings. Even though Rule 13 leaves a little freedom to the parties as to when evidence can be provided to the Court,[43] considering the short time limits foreseen for the actual proceedings, it is likely that UPC practitioners will prefer to collect all possible evidence before starting infringement proceedings on the merits.

19.7 UPC-style *saisie*: less powerful than the French *saisie-contrefaçon*?

According to Article 60 UPCA, the Court may order (even before the commencement of proceedings) measures to preserve evidence and to inspect premises. Such measures may include *"detailed description"*, with or without the taking of samples, or the *"physical seizure"* of the infringing products, and in appropriate cases, the materials and implements used in the production and/or distribution of those products and the documents relating thereto. The Court may also order an inspection of premises. To obtain such measures, the claimant must present reasonably available evidence to support the claim that the patent has been infringed or is about to be infringed. The measures ordered by the Court may be conducted before the commencement of the proceedings, or during the proceedings, to preserve relevant evidence in respect of the alleged infringement. Importantly, these measures can be requested, before proceedings, by the claimant on an *ex parte* basis so as to benefit from the "surprise effect", e.g. in cases where any delay is likely to cause harm to the patentee or when there is a risk of evidence being destroyed.

Practitioners in some EU jurisdictions will already be familiar with these measures, as they stem from Article 7 of the IP Enforcement Directive 2004/48/EC of 29 April 2004. They are highly similar to the French *saisie-contrefaçon*, which is widely used in France before infringement proceedings on the merits, since it enables a bailiff to enter premises and to seize evidence, without warning to the defendant, so that evidence of infringement can be obtained very efficiently and at a moderate cost.

However, we point out that the UPC seizure procedure is not strictly identical to the French *saisie-contrefaçon*. Notably, the former is arguably more burdensome, from the

---

42 Rules of Procedure, Preamble, paragraph 7.
43 Rule 13 of the Rules of Procedure requires the statement to contain the evidence relied on where available, and an indication of any further evidence which will be offered in support.

viewpoint of the patentee, than the French *saisie-contrefaçon* in at least the following respects:
- The seizure is not available of right like in France;[44] it must be motivated (Article 60 UPCA provides that the *"Court **may** [...] order prompt and effective provisional measures"*);
- the urgency must be justified;
- the claimant must specify the reasons for which the proposed measures are needed to preserve relevant evidence;
- if the order is requested on an *ex parte* basis, the reasons why the defendant should not be heard must be indicated;
- the claimant must present reasonably available evidence to support his claim;
- the evidence collected must be limited to use in the proceedings on the merits on the case otherwise ordered by the Court whereas, with the French *saisie-contrefaçon*, they can be used for another case (even a foreign case).

There is also a major difference between the UPC system and the French one: in France, there is no "protective letter system" – which, to a certain extent, guarantees the effectiveness of the *saisie-contrefaçon*. Indeed, the system of the protective letter – incorporated in Rule 207 of the Rules of Procedure – might lessen the chances to obtain a seizure on an *ex parte* basis, as it gives potential defendants the opportunity to file a letter with the Court which requests that it be given notice of any application for provisional measures. Even in case of an *ex parte* application for a seizure, the Court thus shall have the discretion to inform the potential infringer about the application or summon the parties to an oral hearing.[45]

Time will tell how the local divisions will rule on applications for seizure, and whether they will make the *inter partes* procedure the rule and the *ex parte* one the exception.

Overall, patent owners will certainly regret that the *saisie-contrefaçon* was not taken as a model in the Rules of Procedure, while alleged infringers will be relieved by the limitations of the UPC seizure.

---

44 Article L.615-5 of the French Code of Intellectual Property provides that *"Infringement may be proven by any means. To this end, any person entitled to bring an infringement action* **shall be entitled** *to have carried out, at any place and by any bailiffs, if necessary assisted by experts appointed by the plaintiff, by virtue of an order made on request by the competent civil court, either a detailed description, with or without taking samples, or the actual seizure of the allegedly infringing products or processes and any document relating thereto. The order may authorise the actual seizure of any document relating to the allegedly infringing goods or processes in the absence of the latter"*.
45 Rules of Procedure, Rule 209.

19.8 Access to decisions, orders, and written pleadings: some lingering question marks

While more than a few concerns regarding public access to the docket of the UPC have been appeased by the final version of the Rules of Procedure, in our opinion, some others may only be appeased by the actual practice of the Registry.

After it had been briefly suggested that not all orders and decisions should be published,[46] the final version of Rule 262 provides that decisions and orders will be published by default, only following redaction of personal data within the meaning of the GDPR and of confidential information.[47] In our opinion, this was absolutely necessary to ensure the development of a consistent case law, which is especially important for a jurisdiction having such a high number of effectively delocalized Courts.

On the other hand, there will be a possibility for third-parties to access pleadings and evidence *"upon reasoned request to the Registry"*, by decision of the judge-rapporteur after consulting the parties,[48] and then only 14 days after the request, during which the parties may request that certain information be kept confidential.[49] This provision is complemented by a fresh Rule 262A, which allows to request that some information is kept confidential or restricted to "confidentiality clubs".

In our opinion, too liberal a standard on the access to pleadings by third parties would not only raise confidentiality concerns, despite the aforementioned provision; it may also discourage parties to seek amicable settlement in the course of the proceedings. Considering the principle of concentration and the required content of the statement of claims, this would effectively mean that any third-party gaining access to such written pleadings would gain valuable information. This is especially true for revocation actions/counterclaims, meaning patent owners would be discouraged to agree to settle a case considering the risk of having another action quickly launched by another party.

19.9 Conclusion

Regardless of whether one decides to opt-out or not their EPs, there is no way to totally escape patent litigation before the UPC: accordingly, all users would be well advised to start preparing right away, especially in consideration of the many specific provisions in the Rules of Procedure. We expect that many future parties to litigation will want to re-

---

46 Simmons & Simmons LLP, "Final UPC Rules of Procedure approved – with some important changes" (*JUVE Patent*, 18 July 2022) <https://www.juve-patent.com/sponsored/final-upc-rules-of-procedure-approved-with-some-important-changes/> accessed 30 September 2022.
47 Rules of Procedure, Rule 262.1(a).
48 Rules of Procedure, Rule 262.1(b).
49 Rules of Procedure, Rule 262.2.

tain the possibility of participating in the UPC, at least to be able to mount counter-offensive actions.

As we have seen above, some open questions will only be definitively settled by the practice adopted by the UPC's divisions and by its Registry. The first few years of operation of the UPC will be decisive in setting the course for its (eventual) exclusive jurisdiction over European patent litigation within the UPCA Contracting Member States – and are therefore well worth watching closely.

Klara Polackova Van der Ploeg
20 Unified Patent Court and international law

20.1 Introduction

While by no means a new theme,[1] the Covid-19 pandemic has made the tension between intellectual property protection and public health ever more concrete. As the world watched the speed with which effective Covid-19 vaccines were developed with awe, issues of both absolute and relative vaccine access—that is, both their availability for distribution and at what cost to public budgets—became the subject of much attention among both lawyers and the wider public. The perception that patent law, as it normally applies, might be standing in the way of public health or people's right to health, was only amplified by the proposal and subsequent negotiations and adoption of the TRIPS Covid waiver,[2] which WTO member states adopted ostensibly to speed up manufacturing and ease access to the Covid-19 vaccines.

Regardless of whether it was necessary or whether it has delivered on its stated purpose,[3] the TRIPS Covid waiver illustrates the intertwinement of international patent law

---

[1] See, e.g., Laurence Helfer, 'Human Rights and Intellectual Property: Conflict or Coexistence?' (2003) 5 *Minnesota Intellectual Property Review* 16; Estelle Derclaye, 'Intellectual Property Rights and Human Rights: Coinciding and Cooperating.' in Paul Torremans (ed), *Intellectual property rights and human rights: enhanced edition of Copyright and human rights* (2008); Jakob Cornides, 'Human Rights and Intellectual Property: Conflict or Convergence' (2004) 7 Journal of World Intellectual Property 135; Hans Morten Haugen, 'Patent Rights and Human Rights: Exploring Their Relationships' (2007) 10 The Journal of World Intellectual Property 97; Holger Hestermeyer, *Human Rights and the WTO* (Oxford University Press 2008) ch IV; Laurence Helfer and Graeme Austin, *Human Rights and Intellectual Property: Mapping the Global Interface* (Cambridge University Press 2011); P Xiong, 'Patents in TRIPS-plus Provisions and the Approaches to Interpretation of Free Trade Agreements and TRIPS: Do They Affect Public Health?' (2012) 46 Journal of World Trade 155; Jennifer Sellin, *Access to Medicines: The Interface between Patents and Human Rights. Does One Size Fit All?* (Intersentia 2014).
[2] Waiver from Certain Provisions of the Trips Agreement for the Prevention, Containment and Treatment of COVID-19: Communication from India and South Africa, WTO doc IP/C/W/669 (2 October 2020) <https://docs.wto.org/dol2fe/Pages/SS/directdoc.aspx?filename=q:/IP/C/W669.pdf&Open=True> accessed 7 December 2022 Ministerial Decision on the TRIPS Agreement, WTO doc WT/MIN(22)/30; WL/L/1141 (22 June 2022) <https://docs.wto.org/dol2fe/Pages/SS/directdoc.aspx?filename=q:/WT/MIN22/30.pdf&Open=True> accessed 29 May 2023.
[3] See, e.g., Andrew Green, 'WTO Finally Agrees on a TRIPS Deal. But Not Everyone Is Happy' (*Devex*, 17 June 2022) <https://www.devex.com/news/sponsored/wto-finally-agrees-on-a-trips-deal-but-not-everyone-is-happy-103476> accessed 24 October 2022.

Klara Polackova Van der Ploeg, Assistant Professor, University of Nottingham.
I am grateful to Daniel Stewart and Narine Ghazaryan for comments on earlier drafts. Thanks also to Daniela De Zubiria Velasquez, Laura-Jayne Parle and Hwee Teo for their assistance in relation to this chapter.

https://doi.org/10.1515/9783110781687-020

with norms, values, and interests that may traditionally have been viewed as extraneous to the legal regime, as well as the salience of the normative interplay between different branches of international law. Both regime interplay and the tension between protection of private property interests and sovereign regulation in public interest are topics familiar to international law: they regularly arise in practice and have been extensively explored in the literature.[4]

While in the past, specialized branches of international law, such as international trade law, international criminal law, international investment law or international patent law may have been viewed—at least by some—as autonomous and essentially isolated (so-called 'self-contained') legal regimes, the current dominant approach in international law is integrationist. International lawyers chiefly conceptualize international law as a coherent legal system, which involves a body of common (or general) rules and contains different specialized branches, to which the common rules apply and which interact within the international legal system. While most writing on so-called 'fragmentation' and unity of international law was primarily motivated by efforts to maintain the coherence of international law as a legal order,[5] this thinking proves useful at times of increased public awareness and attention to the implications of technical legal rules for common good,[6] which make it increasingly difficult—if it were ever right as a matter of policy—to present specialized legal regimes as self-contained and disjointed.

These considerations have significant bearing on international courts and tribunals operating within the framework of international law and the cases before them. As the UPC starts developing its own jurisprudence, and the UPC's judges, staff, litigating parties, their representatives and others involved with the UPC are presented with the opportunity to define in practical terms its role, reputation and success, this Handbook provides an apposite opportunity to consider the significance and implications of international law for the UPC's decision-making. This chapter therefore offers some reflections from the perspective of international law as both a legal order and a discipline that will hopefully prove useful to those bringing and deciding UPC cases. Following a brief consideration of the UPC's nature as an international court, this chapter draws on insights from the practice of other international courts and tribunals and international legal literature to consider the relationship between the UPC and international law through the lens of four key topics: (i) international law as the law governing the UPC's jurisdiction and a part of the law applicable to the disputes before it; (ii) the interplay between patent law and other branches of international law from the perspective of the

---

[4] See sections 'Patent Law and Other International Law: From Regime-Conflict to Regime-Cooperation' and 'Functions and Authority of International Courts: Strengthening the UPC's Decision-Making' below.
[5] See section 'Patent Law and Other International Law: From Regime-Conflict to Regime-Cooperation' below.
[6] See, e.g., Waheed Hussain, 'The Common Good' in Edward Zalta (ed), *The Stanford Encyclopedia of Philosophy* (Spring 2018, Metaphysics Research Lab, Stanford University 2018) <http://plato.stanford.edu/archives/spr2018/entries/common-good/> accessed 14 November 2022.

current state of the debate on international regime interaction; (iii) considerations of the UPC's roles as an international court; and (iv) human rights-related obligations of business under international law.[7] As a way of conclusion, the chapter reflects on the experience of international investment law and investor-state arbitration to highlight possible parallels with international patent law and the UPC and to offer possible lessons from that field of international law.

20.2 UPC as an international court

The UPC has several comparatively unusual institutional features among international courts and tribunals.[8] While a body separate from the EU or any single EU member state, it has strong institutional, procedural and substantive links to EU law and the CJEU, as well as the courts and law of the EU member states who are parties to the UPCA—the UPC's founding treaty[9] (the 'Contracting Member States',[10] CMSs), including a position within the CMSs' domestic judicial systems.[11] Although the specialized court is endowed with exclusive jurisdiction over most actions relating to EPs and UPs,[12] patentees may opt out from this jurisdiction during the seven-year transitional period.[13] While the court may hear cases to which CMSs will be a party,[14] the vast majority of disputes before the UPCs will not involve state litigants.

Despite its unusual features, many of which reflect the fragmented nature of European patent law and the politics of European patent integration,[15] the UPC is an international court. It is established and primarily governed by a treaty—that is an international agreement concluded between states in written form and governed by international law.[16] It is through this treaty, the UPCA, that the CMSs have conferred on the UPC the jurisdiction to settle disputes relating to EPs and UPs; and in formal terms, the UPC's authority is based on the CMSs consent with the UPCA. It is consequently the UPCA that primarily governs the UPCs' jurisdiction, powers, as well as its relationship with the EU

---

[7] Every international court and tribunal of course operates within limits of its constitutive instruments and in that sense the context of its decision-making is unique. However, there are commonalities across institutions.
[8] Cesare Romano, Karen Alter and Yuval Shany (eds), *The Oxford Handbook of International Adjudication* (OUP 2014), esp part II.
[9] Agreement on the Unified Patent Court [2013] (UPCA).
[10] UPCA art 2(c).
[11] UPCA arts 1, 20 and 21.
[12] UPCA arts 1 and 32.
[13] UPCA art 83(3)-(4).
[14] UPCA arts 46 and 47.
[15] Christopher Wadlow, 'An Historical Perspective II: The Unified Patent Court' in Justina Pila and Christopher Wadlow (eds), *The Unitary EU Patent System* (Bloomsbury 2017).
[16] Vienna Convention on the Law of Treaties [1969] ('VCLT') art 2(1).

and national laws and institutions.[17] By virtue of being a treaty, the UPCA is governed by international law and must therefore be interpreted in accordance with the international law on treaty interpretation memorialized primarily in the Vienna Convention on the Law of the Treaties (VCLT).[18] The VCLT reflects customary international law (and therefore applies universally, regardless of whether a state is a party to it or not),[19] and international courts and tribunals rely on VCLT Articles 31–33 as the rules of interpretation as a matter of course[20] (even if international legal scholarship has questioned the extent to which the VCLT provisions really capture the actual processes of treaty interpretation).[21]

20.3 International law as the UPC's governing law

The UPC's international legal foundations anchor the relevance of international law for its decision-making. In particular, international law is essential as (i) the law governing

---

[17] Tilmann and Plassman therefore go too far if they assert that the UPC must apply EU law before the UPCA. Such approach would effectively involve putting the cart before the horse. See Winfried Tilmann and Clemens Plassmann (eds), *Unified Patent Protection in Europe: A Commentary* (Oxford University Press 2018), 470–71 (commentary on art 24).

[18] VCLT arts 31–33. According to the basic rule, a treaty is to be interpreted in good faith in accordance with the ordinary meaning to be given to the terms of the treaty in their context and in the light of its object and purpose (Article 31(1)). The relevant context should include the preamble of the UPCA and the UPC's Statute. Additionally, the VCLT directs that subsequent agreement or practice by the parties in relation to the treaty and 'any relevant rules of international law applicable in the relations between the parties' should be taken into account, together with the context (Article 31(3)). When the meaning is ambiguous or obscure, or the general rule on interpretation leads to an absurd or unreasonable result, the VCLT points to preparatory works (drafting history) of the UPCA and the circumstances of the UPCA's conclusion, as supplementary means of interpretation (Article 32). As the UPCA has been authenticated in English, French and German, if a difference in meaning between the authentic texts should be identified and cannot be resolved using Articles 31 and 32, the meaning which best reconciles the texts needs to be adopted (Article 33(4)).

[19] See, e.g., Anthony Aust, *Modern Treaty Law and Practice* (Cambridge University Press 2007) 232 and the cases cited therein.

[20] Vast literature explores VCLT arts 31–33. See, e.g. Joseph Klingler, Yuri Parkhomenko, and Constantinos Salonidis (eds), *Between the Lines of the Vienna Convention?: Canons and Other Principles of Interpretation in Public International Law* (Wolters Kluwer 2018) 359–385; Oliver Dörr and Kirsten Schmalenbach (eds), *Vienna Convention on the Law of Treaties: A Commentary* (2nd edn Springer 2018) 559–651; Mark Villiger, *Commentary on the 1969 Vienna Convention on the Law of Treaties* (Nijhoff 2009) 415–464.

[21] Andrea Bianchi, Daniel Peat and Matthew Windsor, *Interpretation in International Law* (Oxford University Press 2015); Anne van Aaken, 'The Cognitive Psychology of Rules of Interpretation in International Law' (2021) 115 American Journal of International Law 258; Sotirios-Ioannis Lekkas and Panos Merkouris, 'Interpretation of International Law: Rules, Content, and Evolution' (2022) 69 Netherlands International Law Review 183.

the UPC's jurisdiction; (ii) a part of the law applicable to the disputes before it (i.e., the substantive law governing the resolution of the disputes before it—the regularly referred to as 'applicable law');[22] and (iii) the source of the UPC's procedural law.[23] It is the first two aspects that warrant particular attention in the context of the UPC and will therefore be explored here.[24]

While jurisdictional clauses determine the scope of international courts and tribunals' jurisdiction, and thus the matters they may hear,[25] applicable law clauses generally specify the choice of the law to determine the merits of a dispute.[26] Although jurisdictional and applicable law clauses in a treaty operate in tandem (and in the case of the UPC are particularly intertwined), they are distinct,[27] and the law governing jurisdictional issues is independent of the law applicable to the merits of a case.[28]

---

22 UPCA art 24 ('Sources of law').
23 UPCA part III, Annex I (Statute of the UPC) and Rules of Procedure of the Court (UPCA art 42).
24 The concepts of jurisdiction of international courts and applicable law, including their interplay, raise complex legal issues; only a few basic points are made here. Key writings include Lorand Bartels, 'Jurisdiction and Applicable Law Clauses: Where Does a Tribunal Find the Principal Norms Applicable to the Case before It' in Tomer Broude and Yuval Shany (eds), *Multi-Sourced Equivalent Norms in International Law* (Bloomsbury 2011); Yuval Shany, *Questions of Jurisdiction and Admissibility before International Courts* (Cambridge University Press 2015); Christoph Schreuer, 'Jurisdiction and Applicable Law in Investment Treaty Arbitration' (2014) 1 McGill Journal of Dispute Resolution 1; Matina Papadaki, 'Compromissory Clauses as the Gatekeepers of the Law to Be "Used" in the ICJ and the PCIJ' (2014) 5 Journal of International Dispute Settlement 560; Sienho Yee, 'Article 38 of the ICJ Statute and Applicable Law: Selected Issues in Recent Cases' (2016) 7 Journal of International Dispute Settlement 472; Dafina Atanasova, 'Applicable Law Provisions in Investment Treaties: Forever Midnight Clauses?' (2019) 10 Journal of International Dispute Settlement 396. The discussion in this chapter focuses only on the points most relevant for the UPC.
25 See, e.g., John Collier and Vaughan Lowe, *The Settlement of Disputes in International Law: Institutions and Procedures* (Oxford University Press 2000) 239; Dafina Atanasova, 'Applicable Law Provisions in Investment Treaties: Forever Midnight Clauses?' (2019) 10 Journal of International Dispute Settlement 399.
26 Yas Banifatemi, 'The Law Applicable in Investment Treaty Arbitration' in Katia Yannaca-Small (ed), *Arbitration Under International Investment Agreements: A Guide to the Key Issues* (Oxford University Press 2010), 191.
27 See, e.g., *Mox Plant case (Ireland v United Kingdom)*, Annex VII Arbitral Tribunal, Order No 3, 24 June 2003, para 19 (there is a 'cardinal distinction' between jurisdiction and applicable law); *Eurotunnel*, Partial Award, Permanent Court of Arbitration, 30 January 2007, para 152. For commentary, see, e.g., Schreuer (n 24) 6; Bartels (n 24) 123–125; Papadaki (n 24) 565–559; Jarrod Hepburn, 'Applicable Law in TPP Investment Disputes' (2016) 17 Melbourne Journal of International Law 1, 5–6.
28 See, e.g., Schreuer (n 24) 2, 24.

20.3.1 Jurisdiction

Jurisdictional issues are primarily determined by reference to the legal instrument(s) establishing jurisdiction[29]—in the case of the UPC, the UPCA—and common (general) international law operationalizing the treaty (in particular the law of treaties, which provides rules governing the existence, applicability, interpretation, suspension and termination of treaty norms, and the law of international responsibility).[30] UPCA Article 32(1), in conjunction with Article 1, specify the UPC's subject-matter jurisdiction (jurisdiction *ratione materiae*).[31] However, Article 32(1) provides for the legal bases for claims within the court's jurisdiction only in relation to the actions for compensation for licences of right.[32] In relation to all the other matters within the UPC's exclusive jurisdiction, claims can consequently be based on any of the sources listed in the UPCA's applicable law clause—Article 24 entitled Sources of law.

An applicable law clause is irrelevant for jurisdictional purposes when the jurisdictional clause expressly defines the legal bases for claims within the court's jurisdiction (such as, for example, by stating that the court may hear 'disputes relating to the interpretation and application of the treaty', thus specifying that in order for claims to fall within the court's or tribunal's jurisdiction, they must be based on the provisions of the treaty containing the jurisdictional clause).[33] However, when the jurisdictional clause does not specify the legal bases for a claim, while the instrument establishing jurisdiction contains an applicable law clause, claims based on any of the norms included in the applicable law clause generally fall within the court's jurisdiction.[34]

UPCA Article 24 refers to international law (the UPCA, the EPC, and the 'other international agreements applicable to patents and binding on all the Contracting Member States'), EU law and national laws of the CMSs, and this broad scope is clearly a consequence of the complex and fragmented nature of the substantive patent law in Europe.[35]

---

29 See, e.g., Schreuer (n 24) 6; *Daimler Financial Services AG v. Argentine Republic*, ICSID case no ARB/05/1, Award of 22 August 2012, para 50.
30 Schreuer (n 26) 25.
31 UPCA art 32(1) sets out the matters over which the UPC has exclusive subject-matter jurisdiction, subject to the arrangements for the transitional period and the opt-out system (UPCA art 83).
32 UPCA art 32(h); Bartels (n 24).
33 See, e.g., Atanasova (n 24) 399–400; Bartels (n 24) 120, 124. An example of such treaty is the United Nations Convention on the Law of the Sea (UNCLOS), whose jurisdictional clause in art 288(1) specifies UNCLOS as the sole basis for claims within the UNCLOS tribunals' jurisdiction. UNCLOS' applicable law clause in art 293(1) does not expand this scope of jurisdiction. See, e.g., *Arctic Sunrise (Netherlands v. Russia)*, UNCLOS Annex VII, PCA case no 2014-02, Award of 14 August 2015, paras 188 and 192; Peter Tzeng, 'Jurisdiction and Applicable Law Under UNCLOS' (2016) 126 Yale Law Journal 242.
34 Atanasova (n 24); Bartels (n 24). Still, this does not merge the law governing the jurisdiction and the law applicable to the merits of a dispute: cf (n 30) and the discussion below.
35 Federica Baldan and Esther Van Zimmeren, 'The Future Role of the Unified Patent Court in Safeguarding Coherence in the European Patent System' (2015) 52 Common Market Law Review 1531.

However, the UPCA's reliance on the applicable law clause for the determination of the scope of the UPC's subject-matter jurisdiction, combined with the comparatively comprehensive list, ultimately leaves ambiguous the identity of the specific rules that may provide the legal basis for claims before the UPC, and thus the precise scope of the UPC's subject-matter jurisdiction.[36]

International rules of treaty interpretation can potentially sustain a range of interpretations as to what the law included in UPCA Article 24 is, and, consequently, what precise claims are within the UPC's jurisdiction and may be raised in infringement, declarations of non-infringement, revocation and other actions relating to the EPs or UPs.[37] First, it is open to interpretation which international agreements binding on all the CMSs are 'applicable to patents'. On a narrow reading, such agreements would presumably include the Paris Convention,[38] the PCT, and TRIPS. However, on a broader reading, the term could include many other treaties to which all the CMSs are a party and which have some bearing on the scope and enjoyment of patent rights, including human rights treaties (such as the ECHR, the European Social Charter,[39] the International Covenant on Civil and Political Rights[40] and the International Covenant on Economic, Social and Cultural Rights[41]), environmental treaties (such as the Paris Agreement,[42] the Minamata Convention on Mercury[43] and Stockholm Convention on Persistent Organic Pollutants[44]), as well other treaties (such as the Plant Genetic Resources Treaty).[45]

Additionally, the practice of international courts and tribunals has shown that the scope of subject-matter jurisdiction may go beyond the bases explicitly stipulated in the jurisdictional instrument. As a matter of principle, an international court or tribunal can only rule on claims within its jurisdiction, i.e., those which are specified by the law governing its jurisdiction.[46] However, international courts and tribunals have regularly

---

36 See, e.g., G Fitzmaurice, The Law and Procedure of the International Court of Justice (vol 2, Grotius Publications Limited 1986) 524; Massimo Benedettelli, 'Determining the Applicable Law in Commercial and Investment Arbitration: Two Intertwined Road Maps for Conflicts-Solving' (2022) 37 ICSID Review – Foreign Investment Law Journal 687, 712, 719.
37 UPCA art 32 in conjunction with art 1.
38 Paris Convention for the Protection of Industrial Property [1883].
39 European Social Charter [1961].
40 International Covenant on Civil and Political Rights [1966].
41 International Covenant on Economic, Social and Cultural Rights [1966].
42 Paris Agreement [2015].
43 Minamata Convention on Mercury [2013].
44 Stockholm Convention on Persistent Organic Pollutants [2001].
45 International Treaty on Plant Genetic Resources for Food and Agriculture [2001].
46 For example, in the *Application of the Convention on the Prevention and Punishment of the Crime of Genocide (Bosnia and Herzegovina v Serbia and Montenegro)* (Merits) [2007] ICJ Reports 43, where the jurisdiction of the International Court of Justice was based on the 1951 Genocide Convention, the court stated that: 'The jurisdiction of the Court in this case is based solely on Art IX of the Convention. [...] It follows that the Court may only rule on the disputes between the Parties to which that provision refers [..] It has

faced (i) claims (by the claimant or the defendant) based on rules extraneous to the jurisdictional title; and (ii) claims that would be outside of the court's or tribunal's jurisdiction if brought independently. While the former is typically framed as a problem of interpretation of the scope of the jurisdictional title, the latter involves an issue of so-called incidental jurisdiction.

The *Pulp Mills (Argentina v Uruguay)* case[47] provides an example of the interpretation of the jurisdictional title scenario. In this case, Argentina argued, *inter alia*, that certain provisions of the relevant jurisdictional instrument—the 1975 Statute of the River Uruguay—should be read as referral (*renvoi*) clauses incorporating into the Statute obligations under multilateral environmental treaties, including the 1973 Convention on International Trade in Endangered Species of Wild Fauna and Flora, and the 2001 Stockholm Convention on Persistent Organic Pollutants). Argentina argued that these referral clauses endowed the International Court of Justice (ICJ) with jurisdiction to determine whether Uruguay had complied with its obligations under these treaties[48]—an argument which the ICJ rejected in that case.[49]

The *Enrica Lexie (Italy v India)* case[50] illustrates the issue of incidental jurisdiction. In this arbitration, Italy challenged India's exercise of jurisdiction over an incident involving the killing of two Indian fishermen by Italian marines and instituted an arbitration under the United Nations Convention on the Law of the Sea ('UNCLOS'). Italy argued, inter alia, that India could not exercise criminal jurisdiction over the marines, because they were entitled to functional immunity under general international law. Although under UNCLOS Article 288(1), the tribunal's jurisdiction extended to 'dispute[s] concerning the interpretation or application of this Convention' and, in the tribunal's view, UNCLOS did not address personal immunities,[51] the tribunal accepted jurisdiction over the immunity claim as an 'incidental issue' necessary for the determination of

---

no power to rule on alleged breaches of other obligations under international law, not amounting to genocide, particularly those protecting human rights in armed conflict' (para 147).
47 *Case Concerning Pulp Mills on the River Uruguay Case (Argentina v Uruguay)* (Judgment) [2010] ICJ Reports 14.
48 Ibid, paras 53 and 56.
49 The ICJ stated that: 'the rules ... contained in multilateral conventions to which the two States are parties, ... ha[d] no bearing on the scope of the jurisdiction conferred on the Court under Article 60 of the 1975 Statute, which remains confined to disputes concerning the interpretation or application of the Statute.' Ibid, para 66. For another example of an international court or tribunal refusing to expand its subject-matter jurisdiction through interpretation, see *Arctic Sunrise* (n 33) paras 188, 192 and 198 (relating to the claim for a declaration that Russia had violated the International Covenant for Civil and Political Rights by arresting and detaining the Greenpeace activists aboard the ship).
50 *The 'Enrica Lexie' Incident (Italy v India)*, UNCLOS Annex VII, PCA case no 2015-28, Award of 21 May 2020.
51 Ibid, paras 795–802.

which state was entitled to exercise jurisdiction over the incident—the principal issue of interpretation and application of UNCLOS.[52]

While the expansion of an international court's jurisdiction through incorporation of other, extraneous rules within the jurisdictional instrument through interpretation (that is, in the absence of a proper referral clause) would typically be viewed as an excess of authority, incidental jurisdiction has been considered a component of international courts and tribunals' inherent (implied) powers.[53] Due to their generally limited subject-matter jurisdiction, incidental jurisdiction allows international courts and tribunals to adjudicate claims that would ordinarily be outside of their subject-matter jurisdiction, but which are essential to the settlement of the issues over which they do have jurisdiction[54]—a common occurrence in particular in relation to defenses.[55] The characterization of an issue as incidental to a dispute necessarily involves evaluative determinations and in that sense may be problematic. However, incidental jurisdiction generally enables international courts and tribunals to protect both the coherence of their proceedings[56] (by ensuring a proper application of international law) and the unity of international law as a legal order (a theme explored below).

20.3.2 Applicable law

Similar—though not identical—issues arise also in relation to the law governing the resolution of disputes, i.e., the applicable law.[57] On merits, the core issue for the UPC to determine is the scope of the rights and obligations involved, such as those of EP/UP patentees and third parties. The role of UPCA Article 24 as the applicable law clause is to specify the rules that delimit the scope of such rights and obligations (although the multiplicity of the sources of law under this provision will no doubt raise complex problems

---

52 Ibid, para 809. See also *Certain German Interests in Polish Upper Silesia (Germany v Poland)*, PCIJ Series A no 6, Judgment of 25 August 1925 (Preliminary Objections), 18; *Certain German Interests in Polish Upper Silesia (Germany v Poland)*, PCIJ Series A no 7, Judgment of 25 May 1926 (Merits), 25. Cf *Chagos Marine Protected Area Arbitration (Mauritius v. United Kingdom)*, UNCLOS Annex VII, PCA case no 2011-03, Award of 18 March 2015.
53 See, e.g., the recent AJIL Unbound Symposium on 'Incidental Jurisdiction', which also discusses disagreements about certain aspects of the doctrine. 116 AJIL Unbound 160–190.
54 James Gerard Devaney, 'Introduction to the Symposium on Incidental Jurisdiction' (2022) 116 American Journal of International Law 160; Peter Tzeng, 'Incidental Jurisdiction', *Max Planck Encyclopedia of International Procedural Law [MPEiPro]* (2022), para 1.
55 For example, when applying a treaty provision permitting measures that are 'necessary' to protect a state's national security interests, the court may, for this purpose, need to interpret and apply international rules on the use of force. Bartels 118–119.
56 Matina Papadaki, 'Incidental Question's as a Gatekeeping Doctrine' (2022) 116 AJIL Unbound 170.
57 James Gerard Devaney, 'Introduction to the Symposium on Incidental Jurisdiction' (2022) 116 American Journal of International Law 160.

of which source(s) govern(s) a specific legal question and what the interplay between concurrently applicable sources is).

International law applicable to the merits of the disputes before the UPC again includes not only the UPCA, EPC and 'other international agreements applicable to patents' (interpreted narrowly or broadly). International law also enters the UPC's applicable law indirectly as a part of EU law[58] and a part of the CMSs' national.[59] When an aspect of a dispute is governed by EU or national law, international law will be a part of that law to the extent of its incorporation or may impact the construction of that law. Additionally, as 'a treaty can never be applied in isolation from the broader legal system in which it was created',[60] international law operationalizing the treaty (in particular treaty law and law of international responsibility) is also again a part of the applicable law.[61] Even though UPCA Article 24 is relevant for both jurisdictional and merits issues in the UPC, the principled distinction between the law governing the jurisdiction and the law governing the resolution of the dispute manifests in the potentially distinct content of these laws.[62] While international courts and tribunals, such as the ICJ, the International Criminal Court and UNCLOS tribunals, generally take a strict view of their jurisdiction,[63] they tend to adopt a broader approach to applicable law and regularly use external rules to interpret and determine the content of their 'own' law.[64]

VCLT Article 31(3)(c) has been the most important normative vehicle for bringing external norms within treaties, as it identifies any (additional) norms that an interpreter needs to consider when determining treaty issues such as the scope of a right, including any limitation on it, possible exceptions, existence of obligations etc.[65] Reflecting

---

58 See, e.g., Katja Ziegler, 'The Relationship Between EU Law and International Law' in Dennis Patterson and Anna Södersten (eds), *A Companion to European Union Law and International Law* (John Wiley & Sons, Incorporated 2016). EU law includes the treaties entered into by the EU, such as TRIPS. Accordingly, TRIPS rules enter the UPC's decision-making in three ways: under the UPCA, under EU law and as part of domestic law by virtue of CMSs being TRIPS parties.
59 See, e.g., Dinah Shelton, *International Law and Domestic Legal Systems: Incorporation, Transformation, and Persuasion* (Oxford University Press 2011).
60 See, e.g., *Appeal Relating to the Jurisdiction of the ICAO Council (India v Pakistan)* (Merits) [1972] ICJ Rep 46, para 32; *United States Diplomatic and Consular Staff in Tehran (United States of America v Iran)* (Merits) [1980] ICJ Rep 3, paras 53–54.
61 Atanasova (n 24) 401, 417; Banifatemi (n 26) 207–208; Papadaki (n 24) 580–582.
62 The determination of the content of the applicable law is distinct from the choice of law process of what law will apply to the resolution of the dispute. Banifatemi (n 26) 191.
63 See, e.g., James Crawford, 'Jurisdiction and Applicable Law' (2012) 25 Leiden Journal of International Law 471, 479; Gudrun Hochmayr, 'Applicable Law in Practice and Theory: Interpreting Article 21 of the ICC Statute' (2014) 12 Journal of International Criminal Justice 655, 662; Lan Ngoc Nguyen, 'Jurisdiction and Applicable Law in the Settlement of Marine Environmental Disputes under UNCLOS' (2021) 9 The Korean Journal of International and Comparative Law 337, 352.
64 See, e.g., Nguyen ibid.
65 Papadaki (n 24) 537. A vast body of literature explores the operation of VCLT art 31(3)(3). For introduction, see, e.g., Panos Merkouris, 'Principle of Systemic Integration', *Max Planck Encyclopedia of Interna-*

customary international law,⁶⁶ and expressing the so-called principle of systemic integration, the rule compels a treaty interpreter to take into account 'any relevant rules of international law applicable in the relations between the parties'.⁶⁷ It demands treaties to be interpreted 'by reference to their normative environment'⁶⁸ (which involves not just treaty rules but also customary international law and perhaps even soft law instruments⁶⁹, and external rules consequently play a key interpretative role in the proper construction of the regime-specific rules.⁷⁰

For example, while the ICJ in the *Pulp Mills* case refused to expand its subject-matter jurisdiction by incorporating certain treaty and customary rules within the 1975 Statute, it did interpret the Statute in light of the customary law requirement to conduct environmental impact assessment, and consequently considered the obligations imposed by the Statute to include that requirement.⁷¹ Other international adjudicators such as the WTO Appellate Body⁷² and the vast majority of investment arbitration tribunals,⁷³ have taken a more reserved approach, choosing narrow interpretations of their applic-

---

tional Law [MPEPIL] (2020); Campbell McLachlan, 'The Principle of Systemic Integration and Article 31(3)(c) of the Vienna Convention' (2005) 54 International & Comparative Law Quarterly 279; Duncan French, 'Treaty Interpretation and The Incorporation of Extraneous Legal Rules' (2006) 55 International & Comparative Law Quarterly 281.
66 See, e.g., Arbitral Award of 31 July 1989 (Guinea-Bissau v Senegal) (Merits) [1991] ICJ Rep 53; Maritime Delimitation and Territorial Questions between Qatar and Bahrain (Qatar v Bahrain) (Merits) [1995] ICJ Rep 18, para 33; Territorial Dispute (Libyan Arab Jamahiriya v Chad) (Merits) [1994] ICJ Rep 6, para 41; Japan–Taxes on Alcoholic Beverages, Appellate Body Report of 1 November 1996, WTO doc WT/DS8,10,11/AB/R.
67 VCLT art 31(3)(c).
68 Study Group of the International Law Commission, Report on the Fragmentation of International Law: Difficulties Arising from the Diversification and Expansion of International Law, finalized by Martti Koskenniemi, UN doc A/CN.4/L.682 (13 April 2006), para 413.
69 Anne Peters, 'The Refinement of International Law: From Fragmentation to Regime Interaction and Politicization' (2017) 15 International Journal of Constitutional Law 671, 693; Jan Klabbers, 'Reluctant Grundnormen: Articles 31(3)(C) and 42 of the Vienna Convention on the Law of Treaties and the Fragmentation of International Law' in Matthew Cravens, Malgosia Fitzmaurice and Maria Vogiatzi (eds), Time, History and International Law 58 (Martinus Nijhoff 2007) 141, 159.
70 Peters (n 69) 693.
71 *Pulp Mills* (n 47) para 204.
72 *Mexico – Tax Measures on Soft Drinks and Other Beverages* (Appellate Body Report) (2006) WTO doc WT/DS308/AB/R, para 78; Joost Pauwelyn, 'Interplay between the WTO Treaty and Other International Legal Instruments and Tribunals: Evolution after 20 Years of WTO Jurisprudence' (10 February 2016) <https://papers.ssrn.com/abstract=2731144>, 11. The Appellate Body used general international law mainly to fill procedural gaps on issues such as the burden of proof, evidence, good faith, due process. Pauwelyn ibid, 26.
73 See, e.g., *CMS Gas Transmission Company v The Republic of Argentina*, ICSID case no ARB/01/8, Award of 12 May 2005; *Sempra Energy International v The Argentine Republic*, ICSID case no ARB/02/16, Award of 28 December 2007. Cf *Urbaser S.A. and Consorcio de Aguas Bilbao Bizkaia, Bilbao Biskaia Ur Partzuergoa v. The Argentine Republic*, ICSID case no ARB/07/26, Award of 8 December 2016.

able law. Nevertheless, VCLT Article 31(3)(c) has been a focal point of treaty interpretation in international adjudication and necessarily also impacts the interpretation of the UPCA, the EPC, Paris Convention, TRIPS and other treaties.

20.4 UPC's interpretative autonomy

As the preceding paragraphs explain, international law frames and enters the UPC's decision-making through multiple entry points. There are open questions regarding the scope of the UPC's subject-matter jurisdiction and the construction of its applicable law, which sophisticated parties before the UPC may strategically exploit, and which the UPC will need to settle in its jurisprudence.[74] The UPC will thus need to make significant interpretative choices, which will not only determine case outcomes,[75] but also shape its institutional standing and its relationships with the CJEU and other bodies involved in European patent protection, including the EPO and national courts.

By virtue of the competence-competence principle, which endows international courts and tribunals with the power to determine the scope of their jurisdiction and the manner in which they exercise this jurisdiction,[76] the UPC enjoys significant interpretative autonomy.[77] This autonomy includes the determination of issues such as which treaties 'relate to patents';[78] which specific rules may provide the basis for claims in the UPCA Article 32 proceedings; as well as what common (general) and specialized international law, such as human rights, environmental or health law, bears on an issue before

---

[74] Pauwelyn has argued that every international court or tribunal must make five key 'interpretation choices' regarding its (i) dominant hermeneutic (text, party intent or underlying objective); (ii) timing (original or evolutionary interpretation); (iii) activism (work-to-rule or gap-filling approach); (iv) case-by-case analysis or rule of precedent; (v) its positioning in relation to the outside world, in particular, linkage to other treaties and tribunals (self-contained or systemic interpretation). Joost Pauwelyn and Manfred Elsig, 'The Politics of Treaty Interpretation: Variation and Explanations Across International Tribunals' in Jeffrey Dunofff and Mark Pollack (eds), *International Law and International Relations: Taking Stock* (Cambridge University Press, 2013) 445.
[75] Atanasova, (n 24) 397; Banifatemi (n 26).
[76] See, e.g., Yoshifumi Tanaka, *The Peaceful Settlement of International Disputes* (Cambridge University Press 2018) 142.
[77] See, e.g., in relation to applicable law: '[I]f the text of the treaty provides for several applicable laws, without providing a hierarchy or a rule as to which law should apply to a particular issue, and there is a dispute between the parties as to the law that should apply to decide a particular issue in dispute, it is for the arbitral tribunal to conclude what the applicable law is ... [T]here may be many different approaches or conclusions that tribunals have adopted or made in the past, and ... there are differing views on how the law should be ascertained.' *Total SA v Argentine Republic*, ICSID case no ARB/04/1, Decision on Annulment of 1 February 2016 paras 196–97.
[78] See UPCA art 24(1)(d) and the discussion in section 'International Law as Governing Law' above.

the UPC and should therefore be introduced within the applicable law and with which relative dispositive weight.[79]

In many respects, a key choice for the UPC will relate to EU law and the UPC's relationship with the CJEU. While the UPC must apply EU law, respect its primacy,[80] and refer questions of EU law to the CJEU through the preliminary question procedure[81] (with the CJEU decisions being binding on the UPC),[82] it is for the UPC to position itself vis-à-vis EU law and the CJEU—for example, by clarifying in which aspects of its decision-making it implements EU law, and consequently must respect the CJEU's purview. There are significant portions of substantive patent law, such as that relating to the creation and existence of an EP, which are clearly not subject to EU law, as well as large grey areas as to which parts of EU law apply and how.[83] Afterall, the desire to limit the CJEU's role in patent litigation was a major reason for the establishment of the UPC, the creation of, the multi-layered system of patent protection in Europe (including the incorporation of most substantive UP rules in the UPCA rather than secondary EU legislation), and the design of the UPC as an institution compliant with the EU treaties yet distinct from the EU.[84]

The UPC will also need to give specific content to its relationship with international law, including how to apply international law in its decision-making. Significantly, the UPC is not required to follow the CJEU's approach to international law. Considering the UPC's distinct institutional context and its role of a specialized international court, the

---

[79] Cf Kabir Duggal and Nicholas Diamond, 'Human Rights and Investor–State Dispute Settlement Reform: Fitting a Square Peg into a Round Hole?' (2021) 12 Journal of International Dispute Settlement 291, 302 (on discretion of investment arbitration tribunals).
[80] UPCA arts 20 and 24(1)(a).
[81] UPCA art 1.
[82] UPCA art 21.
[83] This applies both to substantive patent law issues and questions such as whether the EU Charter of Fundamental Rights applies to the UPC. See, e.g., Winfried Tilmann and Plassmann Clemens, 'The Primacy of Union Law, Liability and Responsibility of the Contracting Member States' in Winfried Tilmann and Clemens Plassmann (eds), *Unified Patent Protection in Europe: A Commentary* (Oxford University Press 2018) 445–446; Clement Salung Petersen and Jens Schovsbo, 'Decision-Making in the Unified Patent Court: Ensuring a Balanced Approach', *Intellectual Property and the Judiciary* (Edward Elgar 2018) 238; Angelos Dimopoulos, 'An Institutional Perspective II: The Role of the CJEU in the Unitary (EU) Patent System' in Justine Pila and Christopher Wadlow (eds), *The Unitary EU Patent System* (Bloomsbury 2017), 61–62, 75–76; Tuomas Mylly, 'A Constitutional Perspective' in Justine Pila and Christopher Wadlow (eds), *The Unitary EU Patent System* (Bloomsbury 2017), 83.
[84] See, e.g., Tuomas Mylly, 'A Constitutional Perspective' in Justine Pila and Christopher Wadlow (eds), *The Unitary EU Patent System* (Bloomsbury 2017); Angelos Dimopoulos, 'An Institutional Perspective II: The Role of the CJEU in the Unitary (EU) Patent System' in Justine Pila and Christopher Wadlow (eds), The Unitary EU Patent System (Bloomsbury 2017), 62–63; Thomas Jaeger, 'Shielding the Unitary Patent from the ECJ: A Rash and Futile Exercise' (2013) 44 International Review of Intellectual Property and Competition Law 389.

strong constitutionalist, inward-looking[85] (and also criticized)[86] approach of the CJEU to international law may neither be appropriate nor viable. Given the UPC's independent treaty foundations, its approach to international law will determine its relationship with EU law rather than vice versa.

With the UPC facing such a range of interpretative choices, the following sections situate the available alternatives against the background of some of the leading debates within international law.

20.5 Patent law and other international law: from regime-conflict to regime-cooperation

The proposition that the UPC may be required under international law to consider or even apply international legal rules beyond those that may have traditionally been viewed as 'patent law' engages a topic widely explored in international legal scholarship—that of regime interplay.

In international law, the interest in regime interplay has been connected to a doctrinal debate on 'fragmentation of international law'.[87] Both an analysis and an articulation of disciplinary anxieties, the fragmentation debate centered around the proposition that because of the dynamic growth of new and specialized international legal regimes after 1989, the rise of new actors beside states, including new international courts and tribunals, and the prominence of new types of international norms beyond the recognized sources[88] (all in the context of a decentralized structure of international law defined by the absence of a central legislator), international law had been disintegrating and therefore losing coherence and its quality and legitimacy as a legal order (system).[89] Three aspects were perceived as particularly problematic: the existence of a plurality of

---

85 Ziegler (n 58) 43.
86 See, e.g., Grainne de Burca, The EU, the European Court of Justice and the International Legal Order after Kadi (2009) 51(2) Harvard International Law Journal.
87 The leading document in the topic was the 'fragmentation report' of the International Law Commission, an authoritative body of international law experts appointed by the UN General Assembly. ILC (April 2006) (n 68); Draft conclusion of the work of the Study Group, UN doc A/CN.4/L.682/Add.1 (2 May 2006); Study Group of the International Law Commission, Report on the Fragmentation of International Law: Difficulties Arising from the Diversification and Expansion of International Law, UN doc A/CN.4/L.702 (18 July 2006).
88 Peters (n 69) 673.
89 For an excellent overview of the debate and the different facets of fragmentation, see Peters (n 71). See also Bruno Simma and Dirk Pulkowski, Of Planets and the Universe: Self-Contained Regimes in International Law, (2006) 17 European Journal of International Law 483; Mario Prost, *The Concept of Unity in International Law* (Bloomsbury 2012); Luca Pasquet, 'De-Fragmentation Techniques', *Max Planck Encyclopedia of International Procedural Law [MPEiPro]* (2018), para 1.

potentially overlapping international jurisdictions and the related risk of divergent judicial decisions; the possible normative conflicts between norms belonging to different legal regimes with different goals; and the purportedly self-referential attitude of interpreters operating within a regime.[90]

While the debate initially focused on understanding, conceptualizing, and evaluating the fragmentation, it later concentrated more on developing principles and procedures for solving conflicts[91]—both in terms of defining of what constitutes a normative conflict and the available techniques for the resolution of such conflict—and coordination of different regimes. The view of specialized regimes as self-contained, delinked from other international legal regimes as well as common (general) international law has been discredited,[92] in particular as international courts and other actors [have] developed a range of techniques to coordinate the various subfields of international law.[93] Some commentators have also argued for understanding fragmentation not only as an existential threat to international law but also as a potential for productive uses of the multiplicity of international regimes to generate a denser, more finetuned and more adequate international law.[94]

Peters has observed that 'either/or' techniques for dealing with normative conflict (such as lex specialis or hierarchy concepts), which aim for the application of one norm over a potentially conflicting other norm stemming from a different source or regime, have often been replaced with techniques aimed at seeking compatibility 'not only in a "negative" sense, but also in a supportive ("positive") sense' by facilitating the cumulative application of norms arising from different regimes, and thus the achievement of the objectives of (also) other treaties.[95] Presumption of compatibility and harmonious interpretation have become some of the leading interpretative maxims that international courts and tribunals use when dealing with international rules rooted in different regimes.[96] Normative conflicts before international courts and tribunals are actually rare due to the widespread use of such 'rapporchement' or 'de-fragmentation' techni-

---

90 Pasquet ibid, para 3.
91 Peters (n 69) 674.
92 Simma and Pulkowski (n 89); ILC (April 2006) (n 68) para 492; Peters (n 69) 675.
93 For a detailed discussion of the techniques, see Peters (n 69) 682–694; Pasquet (n 89) paras 31–51; Ralf Michaels and Joost Pauwelyn, 'Conflict of Norms or Conflict of Laws?: Different Techniques in the Fragmentation of Public International Law' (2012) 22 Duke Journal of Comparative & International Law 349.
94 Bruno Simma, Fragmentation in a Positive Light, 25 Michigan Journal of International Law 845 (2004); Karen Alter & Sophie Meunier, The Politics of International Regime Complexity, 7 Perspectives on Politics 13 (2009); Colin Murray & Aoife O'Donoghue, A Path Already Travelled in Domestic Orders? From Fragmentation to Constitutionalisation in the Global Legal Order, 13 International Journal of Law in Context 1 (2017); Peters (n 69) 672, 680–682.
95 Peters (n 69) 682–694.
96 See, e.g., *Al-Jedda v UK*, 2011 ECtHR para 102 (app no 27021/08); *United States—Standards for Reformulated and Conventional Gasoline*, Appellate Body Report, WTO doc WT/DS2/9 (20 May 1996), 17; Peters (n 71) 690–694; Pasquet (n 89) paras 46–51. There is a general presumption against conflict in international law. Hepburn (n 27) 7; Joost Pauwelyn, *Conflict of Norms in Public International Law: How WTO Law Relates to Other Rules of International Law* (Cambridge University Press 2003) 240.

ques[97] (although there are certainly limits to how far the presumption of compatibility can go for a reasoning to remain convincing).[98]

The presumption of compatibility of international legal obligations unless there is a clear indication to the contrary (such as a priority or conflict clause in a treaty[99] or other 'clear or explicit wording'[100]) reflects some basic principles of international law. Because states are bound by their international legal obligations (pacta sunt servanda) and are presumed to comply with their obligations in good faith, any law-making (be it directly by states, such as through the conclusion of a new treaty or indirectly through acts of their international organizations) must be interpreted as producing 'effects in accordance with existing law and not in violation of it'.[101] This implies that 'when multiple norms bear on a particular issue, they should, to the extent possible, be interpreted in a way to produce a single set of compatible obligations'.[102] As a consequence, the presumption gives effect to norms from other subfields.

The debate on fragmentation has arguably led to a shift in the understanding of regime interplay in international law from one of regime-conflict to one of regime-cooperation. From the perspective of international law, European patent law is a regional international legal regime, which—just as international intellectual property law—is a part of a broader international legal system.[103] The conceptualization of international law as a unified legal order, characterized by regime-cooperation between its various subfields, compels the UPC to take account of this broader normative environment when determining the principal issues before it, such as the scope of patent rights, limitations, exceptions, patentability, grounds for revocation or what constitutes adequate remuneration. The systemic perspective means that the treaties within the UPC's 'own' law are presumed to be compatible with other treaties to which all the CMSs are party to and must be interpreted as such. The content of the UPC's 'own' law, including the scope of any rights and obligations involved, is thus delimited not only by that law, but by all the international legal norms bearing on the issue at hand.

As explained, the development of the integrative approach to international law and its interpretation was largely motivated by international lawyers' concerns about the unity and legitimacy of international law as a legal order. However, 'de-fragmentation'

---

97 Peters (n 69) 698; Pasquet (n 89); Tamar Megiddo, 'Beyond Fragmentation: On International Law Integrationist Forces' (2019) 44 *Yale Journal of International Law* 115.
98 See, e.g., Pasquet (n 89) paras 50–51.
99 A priority or conflict clause specifically regulates the relationship between treaties. Nele Matz-Lück, 'Treaties, Conflict Clauses', *Max Planck Encyclopedia of International Law [MPEPIL]* (2006). EPC art 150 on the 'Application of Patent Cooperation Treaty' is such a clause.
100 See, e.g., *Al-Dulimi v Switzerland*, 2016 ECtHR para 140 (app no 5809/08).
101 *Right of Passage over Indian Territory (Portugal v. India)*, Preliminary Objections, 1957 ICJ Rep. 125, 142.
102 ILC (April 2006) (n 68) 25, para 42.
103 In relation to international intellectual property law, Henning Grosse Ruse-Khan, The Protection of Intellectual Property in International Law (Oxford University Press 2016).

techniques are also suited to mediate competing interests and values embedded in different specialized regimes, and thus counter outcome-related legitimacy attacks on such regimes—an issue explored in the next section.

20.6 Functions and authority of international courts: strengthening the UPC's decision-making

Specialized institutions, including international courts, naturally tend to approach matters before them from the vantage point of their own specialism and the rules and normative preferences of the relevant regime.[104] For example, investment courts and tribunals have traditionally understood investment cases as economic disputes about governmental interference with internationally protected foreign investments. Human rights courts typically view matters before them from a humanist perspective as narratives of affront on innate human dignity. WTO panels regularly identify themselves as the guardians of free trade with particular sensitivity to the values underpinning the global trading system.

This partial approach arises for both organizational and sociological reasons. Founding instruments articulate specific institutional mandates, and in the case of specialized international courts and tribunals, define a limited subject-matter jurisdiction.[105] The specialized jurisdiction restricts both the kinds of cases that can come before the court or tribunal and shapes the way in which parties plead these cases. Officials tend to be chosen specifically for their expertise in the respective area of law and are likely to have internalized the relevant regime's value system, which results in expertise and mission bias in determining the relevance (both absolute and relative) of legal norms, values and interests to be protected, and typically translates into maximalist protective positions.[106] The inclination to disregard norms external to the specialized regime may arise from the lack of familiarity with other areas of international law; be a strategy to avoid potential normative conflicts; or result from conflation of subject-matter jurisdiction with questions of applicable law. However, influential players, both state

---

104 Cf ILC (April 2006) (n 68), 245. See also Ziegler (n 58) 82.
105 The ICJ is the only international court of general subject-matter jurisdiction.
106 Ernst-Ulrich Petersmann, 'Human Rights in International Investment Law and Adjudication: Legal Methodology Question' in Julien Chaisse, Leïla Choukroune and Sufian Jusoh (eds), *Handbook of International Investment Law and Policy* (Springer 2021); Yuval Shany, *Questions of Jurisdiction and Admissibility before International Courts* (Cambridge University Press 2015) 110. See also Peters (n 71) 674; Koskenniemi and Leino have noted how '[e]ach institution speaks its own professional language and seeks to translate that into a global Esperanto, to have its special interests appear as the natural interests of everybody.' Martti Koskenniemi and Päivi Leino, 'Fragmentation of International Law? Postmodern Anxieties' (2002) 15(3) Leiden Journal of International Law 553, 578.

and non-state, often also utilize specialized legal regimes to advance their particular interests in ways which would not be possible in more general fora.[107] Such actors will consequently favor judicial decision-making, which interprets the confines of 'its' regime narrowly, as such decision-making will support their effort to identify the special interest with general interest and gain dominance within the international arena.[108] Regardless of which dynamic proves dominant in the context of a specific institution, the result is a degree of structural normative bias.[109]

The risk of such narrow specialist approach has also been noted in relation to the UPC.[110] Because of its features, such as the specialized, limited jurisdiction, the inclusion of technical judges on judicial panels as well as the involvement of European patent attorneys as representatives (that is technical specialists who will typically lack broader legal education), the UPC has been structurally designed to focus on technical aspects of patent disputes and favor technology-based values, to the exclusion of broader policy considerations.[111]

While international courts and tribunals are dispute settlement bodies,[112] (and the UPCA specifically spells out the UPC's dispute settlement function in its very first article),[113] their role goes beyond the settlement of a specific dispute between the disputing parties (even if some adjudicators maintain otherwise).[114] International legal scholarship has challenged a one-dimensional understanding of international courts and tribunals and espoused their other important functions, including the stabilization of normative expectations through restatement and enforcement of existing law; law-making through clarification of law; as well as control and legitimation of authority exercised by others.[115] The proper exercise of these other functions requires international courts and

---

107 Koskenniemi and Leino ibid 578.
108 Grosse Ruse-Khan (n 103) 6.
109 See Martti Koskenniemi, 'The Politics of International Law—20 Years Later' (2009) 20(1) European Journal of International Law 7, 9.
110 See, e.g., Clement Salung Petersen and Jens Schovsbo, 'Decision-Making in the Unified Patent Court: Ensuring a Balanced Approach' in Christophe Geiger, Craig Nard and Xavier Seuba (eds) *Intellectual Property and the Judiciary* (Edward Elgar 2018), 233 and other publications by the authors, including Clement Salung Petersen, T Riis and Jens Schovsbo, 'The Unified Patent Court: Pros and Cons of Specialization – Is There a Light at the End of the Tunnel (Vision)?' (2015) International Review of Intellectual Property and Competition Law, 271–274.
111 Ibid.
112 Cf, e.g., international criminal courts. See Romano, Alter and Shany (n 8).
113 UPCA art 1.
114 See, e.g., *Romak SA (Switzerland) v. The Republic of Uzbekistan*, PCA case no AA 280, UNCITRAL Award of 26 November 2009, para 171.
115 Armin Von Bogdandy and Ingo Venzke, 'On the Functions of International Courts: An Appraisal in Light of Their Burgeoning Public Authority' (2013) 26 Leiden Journal of International Law 49. For alternative taxonomies, see, e.g., Dinah Shelton, 'Form, Function, and the Powers of International Courts' (2009) 9 Chicago Journal of International Law; Stephan Schill, 'System-Building in Investment Treaty Arbitration and Lawmaking' (2011) 12 German Law Journal 1083.

tribunals to consider the wider implications of their adjudication beyond the confines of a particular dispute, and points them in the direction of decisions and reasoning that do not contradict other international law.

Virtually all international courts and tribunals face some legitimacy challenges,[116] be it because of their origins, processes or outputs.[117] However, for some international courts and tribunals, it has arguably been precisely their inability to convincingly engage with the law, values and interests beyond their 'own' that has detrimentally impacted both persuasiveness of their reasoning[118] and public perceptions of their authority and legitimacy and led to profound challenges of the legal regime. Investor-state dispute settlement (ISDS) is a case in point.[119]

ISDS provides a particularly strong enforcement mechanism of international investment law, the full potency of which has materialized with the boom of investor-state arbitrations in the late 1990's and 2000's.[120] However, ISDS has become the subject of major criticisms and legitimacy challenges by both lawyers[121] and the public,[122] as investment arbitration tribunals have found states around the world have violated their obligations

---

[116] Cesare Romano, Karen Alter and Yuval Shany, 'Mapping International Adjudicative Bodies, the Issues, and Players' in Cesare Romano, Karen Alter and Yuval Shany (eds), *Oxford Handbook of International Adjudication* (2013), 16.
[117] Andreas Follesdal, 'Survey Article: The Legitimacy of International Courts*' (2020) 28 Journal of Political Philosophy 476, 476–477.
[118] Ragnar Nordeide, 'The ECHR and Its Normative Environment: Difficulties Arising from a Regional Human Rights Court's Approach to Systemic Integration' in Ole Kristian Fauchald and André Nollkaemper (eds), *The Practice of International and National Courts and the (De-)Fragmentation of International Law* (Bloomsbury 2014), 117.
[119] Investor-state arbitration typically involves the resolution of a dispute by an arbitral tribunal established under a bilateral treaty on the promotion and protection of foreign investments (BIT), an investment chapter in a bilateral or multilateral trade agreement or an investment contract. In a treaty-based investor-state arbitration, an 'investor', a national of one of the treaty parties, brings a claim against the host state of its investment—another treaty party, for a violation of standards of protection defined in the relevant treaty, including protection against unlawful expropriation, 'fair and equitable treatment', 'full protection and security', non-discrimination, etc. The discussion of ISDS draws on Klara Polackova Van der Ploeg, 'Investor Obligations: The Transformative and Regressive Impacts of the Business and Human Rights Framework' (2023, forthcoming).
[120] Jonathan Bonnitcha, Lauge Poulsen and Michael Waibel, *The Political Economy of the Investment Treaty Regime* (Oxford University Press 2017) 1. According to the UN Conference on Trade and Development (UNCTAD), there have been 1190 known investment arbitration to date (as of 7 December 2022). See <https://investmentpolicy.unctad.org/investment-dispute-settlement> accessed 7 December 2022.
[121] See, e.g., Michael Waibel et al (eds), *The Backlash Against Investment Arbitration: Perceptions and Reality* (Kluwer, 2010); Suzanne Spears, 'The Quest for Policy Space in a New Generation of International Investment Agreements' (2010) 13 Journal of International Economic Law 1037; Jean Kalicki and Anna Joubin-Bret (eds), *Reshaping the Investor-State Dispute Settlement System: Journeys for the 21st Century* (Brill Nijhoff, 2015); OECD, 'Investment Treaties: The Quest for Balance—Summary' (14 March 2016); David Schneiderman, 'International Investment Law's Unending Legitimation Project' (2017) 49 *Loyola University Chicago Law Journal* 229; Jane Kelsey, 'The Crisis of Legitimacy in International Investment Agreements and Investor-State Dispute Settlement' in Richard Ekins and Graham Gee (eds.), *Judicial Power and*

under investment treaties and ordered to pay investors vast sums of compensation,[123] often for taking non-discriminatory good faith regulatory measures in public interest, such as for protection of health, environment, human and workers' rights, or in situations of economic crises.[124]

Although by no means the only factor, a significant reason behind the controversy and backlash against ISDS and international investment law has been the narrow, self-referential approach to the interpretation of investment treaties that most investment tribunals have adopted. As the bulk of investment treaties do not explicitly refer to non-investment considerations, most tribunals have refused to take into account investment treaties' broader normative context, including competing international legal obligations of states and other public interests and instead opted for an expansive interpretation of the scope of investor protections.[125] This approach has produced arbitral decisions, which have been broadly viewed as overreaching on protection of private property while denying host states' 'right to regulate' in public interest.[126] The practice has fueled the ISDS' existing legitimacy crisis and led to the significant demand for a reform of both substantive and procedural aspects of the international investment legal regime and even calls for termination of investment treaties and abolition of ISDS.[127]

---

the Left (London: Policy Exchange, 2017); Malcolm Langford and Daniel Behn, "Managing Backlash: The Evolving Investment Treaty Arbitrator?," 29(2) *European Journal of International Law* (2018), 551–580.

122 See, e.g., Claire Provost & Matt Kennard, The Obscure Legal System That Lets Corporations Sue Countries, *The Guardian* (Jun. 10, 2015), <https://www.theguardian.com/business/2015/jun/10/obscure-legal-system-lets-corportationssue-states-ttip-icsid> accessed 28 June 2022.

123 Jonathan Bonnitcha et al, 'Damages and ISDS Reform: Between Procedure and Substance' (2021) *Journal of International Dispute Settlement* 1; Rachel Wellhausen, 'Recent Trends in Investor–State Dispute Settlement' (2016) 7(1) *Journal of International Dispute Settlement* 117; Vera Weghmann and David Hall, 'The Unsustainable Political Economy of Investor–State Dispute Settlement Mechanisms' 87 (2021) *International Review of Administrative Sciences* 1. See also Bettina Müller and Cecilia Olivet, 'ISDS in Numbers. Impacts of Investment Arbitration against African States' (Transnational Institute 2019) 6–7.

124 See examples in Barnali Choudhury, 'Investor Obligations for Human Rights' (2020) 35 *ICSID Review – Foreign Investment Law Journal* 82, 86. For a particularly poignant critique, see Daria Davitti et al, COVID-19 and the Precarity of International Investment Law. *Medium* (6 May 2020) <https://medium.com/iel-collective/covid19-and-the-precarity-of-international-investment-law-c9fc254b3878> accessed 28 June 2022.

125 See (n 73).

126 See, e.g., Yulia Levashova, *The Right of States to Regulate in International Investment Law: The Search for Balance Between Public Interest and Fair and Equitable Treatment* (Kluwer, 2019).

127 See, e.g., UNCTAD, 'Investment Policy Framework for Sustainable Development' (New York: UNCTAD, 2015); UNCTAD, 'UNCTAD's Reform Package for the International Investment Regime' (New York: UNCTAD, 2018) and UNCTAD, 'International investment agreements: Reform Accelerator' (New York: UNCTAD, 2020); United Nations Commission on International Trade Law (UNCITRAL), 'Report of Working Group III (Investor-State Dispute Settlement Reform) on the work of its thirty-fourth session (Vienna, 27 November–1 December 2017)', UN doc no A/CN.9/930/Rev.1 (19 December 2017); Mohammad Hamdy, 'Redesign as Reform: A Critique of the Design of Bilateral Investment Treaties' (2019) 51 Georgetown Journal of International Law 255, 267–270. Similar trends aimed at incorporation of 'other' interests may be

There are important institutional and other differences between the UPC and ISDS. Nevertheless, the ISDS experience seems instructive for the UPC because both dispute settlement mechanisms involve highly specialized economic areas of law, strong protective regimes of private rights, an initially isolationist conception of the judicial function,[128] and a deep and consequential interplay between public and private interests. Similarly to ISDS, 'the impact and importance of UPC decision-making will extend beyond the direct interests of the parties in individual cases. Firstly, enforcement of patent law involves delineating the scope of patent rights and may involve deciding the validity of patents, both of which also involve a general societal interest. Secondly, the UPC will through its case-law also be shaping patent policy'[129]—and indirectly other public policies. The opening anecdote of the Covid-19 vaccines illustrates such wider impact of patent law and the reality of its relevant audiences going beyond those of patent specialists. To its benefit, the UPC is procedurally better positioned to engage with broader interests and parties beyond the litigants than ISDS, not least through the third-party intervention procedure.[130]

20.7 Obligations of commercial patentees and other businesses

International law initially developed as an interstate legal order that regulated state conduct. However, the circle of international law's addressees has gradually been expanding to include international (governmental) organization, individuals, and collective non-state entities, such as business corporations. Nowadays, international law directly regulates such entities' conduct, including through its formal sources, such as treaties. Contemporary international law not only confers rights on business corporations and other non-state entities (such as through UPCA Articles 25 and 26) but also imposes obligations on them: business corporations owe international legal obligations un-

---

observed elsewhere, for example in the Court of Arbitration for Sport, which has been criticized as insufficiently engaging with human rights. A Duval, 'Lost in Translation? The European Convention on Human Rights at the Court of Arbitration for Sport' (2022) 22 International Sports Law Journal 132; S Chanda and K Saha, 'An Analytical Study of the Human Rights Concerns before the CAS with Reference to Caster Semenya' [2022] International Sports Law Journal.
128 Yanwen Zhang, 'The Judicial Function of Investment Tribunals: Taking Foundational Assumptions Seriously' (2022) 25 Journal of International Economic Law 129.
129 Petersen and Schovsbo (n 110) 232.
130 An intervention under UPC Rules of Procedure rules 313–317 provides third parties, including states, with an opportunity to provide information and arguments, which the court may take into consideration in its decision-making (as long as the intervener establishes a legal interest in the result of the case). Cf Nicole Bürli, *Third-Party Interventions before the European Court of Human Rights: Amicus Curiae, Member-State and Third-Party Interventions* (Intersentia 2017).

der international humanitarian law, law of the sea, international aviation law, civil liability treaties etc.[131] Many recent investment treaties in fact include provisions on investor conduct in an effort to (i) rectify to some extent the original normative asymmetry of investment treaties, which traditionally conferred rights on investors and imposed obligations only on host states; and (ii) force investment arbitration tribunals to consider investors' conduct when deciding their claims against host states, which they were previously reluctant to do.[132]

Arguably the most impactful development in international law in relation to the regulation of business entities has been the introduction of the business and human rights (BHR) framework, epitomized in the 2011 United Nations (UN) Guiding Principles on Business and Human Rights (UNGPs).[133] The BHR framework involves a categorical demand for accountability of business corporations (in the language of the UNGPs the 'business enterprises') for business-related human rights abuses, and articulates the 'responsibility to respect human rights' as a 'global standard of expected conduct'.[134] While the UNGPs are a soft-law instrument, and the concept of 'responsibility' to respect does not involve a strict legal obligation (standing in contrast to the legal 'duty' of states to protect human rights), the normative demands vis-à-vis businesses go beyond mere suggestions for voluntary undertakings.[135] The international BHR framework has also instigated domestic legislation around the world, including in the UK, France, Australia, the Netherlands, Germany, Switzerland, Norway,[136] and at the EU level.[137] International or-

---

[131] See, e.g., Klara Polackova Van der Ploeg, 'The Functional Threshold: Direct International Legal Regulation of Collective Nonstate Entities and the Law of International Peace and Security' (2020) 53 New York University Journal of International Law and Politics 71, 73–75.

[132] Van der Ploeg (n 119). See, e.g., Economic Community of West African States (ECOWAS) Supplementary Act on Investments [2008] ch III; Morocco-Nigeria BIT [2016] arts 14, 17(2) and (3), 18, 19(1)(a) and (b), 20, 21(1); Turkey-Ghana BIT [2016] art 13(1); Ethiopia-Qatar BIT [2017] art 14; Democratic Republic of the Congo-Rwanda BIT [2021] ch III; Indonesia-Switzerland BIT [2022] art 14.

[133] Human Rights Council, 'Guiding Principles on Business and Human Rights: Implementing the United Nations "Protect, Respect and Remedy" Framework', UN doc A/HRC/17/31 (21 March 2011) ('UNGPs'). This discussion draws on Van der Ploeg (n 119).

[134] UNGPs, note 139, commentary to principle 11.

[135] Florian Wettstein, *Business and Human Rights* (Cambridge University Press 2022) 188–189.

[136] Modern Slavery Act 2015 (UK); Code de commerce 2017, arts L225-102-4 and 5 (Duty of Vigilance Act) (France); Modern Slavery Act 2018 (Australia); Wet Zorgplicht Kinderarbeid 2019 (Child Labour Due Diligence Law) (The Netherlands); Lieferkettensorgfaltspflichtengesetz 2019 (Act on Corporate Due Diligence Obligations in Supply Chains) (Germany); Code des obligations 2021, art 964 (amendment on conflict minerals and child labour due diligence law) (Switzerland); Åpenhetsloven 2021 (Transparency Act) (Norway).

[137] Directive 2014/95/EU of the European Parliament and of the Council of 22 October 2014 as regards disclosure of non-financial and diversity information by certain large undertakings and groups, *Official Journal of the European Union*, L 330/1, 15.11.2014, and its forthcoming amendment, Council of the European Union, 'New rules on corporate sustainability reporting: provisional political agreement between the Council and the European Parliament', <https://www.consilium.europa.eu/en/press/press-releases/2022/06/21/new-rules-on-sustainability-disclosure-provisional-agreement-between-council-and-european-parliament> accessed 28 June 2022; Regulation (EU) 2017/821 of the European Parliament and of

ganisations, including the OECD[138] and the International Finance Corporation (IFC),[139] have incorporated UNGPs into their policies and guidelines, as have major business corporations and industry organizations.[140] In the recent *Milieudefensie v Shell* case,[141] in which the Hague District Court ordered Shell to reduce its CO_2 emissions, the court used the UNGPs as one of the sources to interpret domestic law and determine the content of the unwritten duty of care provided for in the Dutch Civil Code[142]—opining that the UNGPs expressed a 'widespread international consensus that human rights that human rights offer protection against the impacts of dangerous climate change and that companies must respect human rights'.[143]

For the UPC's decision-making, the significance of the BHR framework and the broader changes within international law to regulate not only states but also non-state entities lie primarily in the attention that these developments draw to the potentially detrimental or outright illegal conduct of the regime's core rights-holders—the patentees—who are dominantly private (non-state) persons. Strong protective regimes, such as international investment law or patent law, may be disposed or even initially designed to focus exclusively on the protection of the core rights involved (such as those of patentees) and disregard the rights-holders' own legal obligations or responsibilities. However, the experience of ISDS again illustrates the risks involved in such a singular focus: another significant factor in ISDS' current legitimacy crisis has been the practice of the majority of tribunals to interpret investment treaties as providing widespread rights for investors, even in circumstances in which an investment has significant detrimental impacts on local communities or the environment, or when the investor engages

---

the Council of 17 May 2017 laying down supply chain due diligence obligations for Union importers of tin, tantalum and tungsten, their ores, and gold originating from conflict-affected and high-risk areas, *Official Journal of the European Union*, L 130/1, 19.5.2017; Regulation (EU) 2020/852 of the European Parliament and of the Council of 18 June 2020 on the establishment of a framework to facilitate sustainable investment and amending Regulation, *Official Journal of the European Union*, L198/13, 22.6.2020; and the forthcoming Human Rights Due Diligence Directive—see European Commission, 'Proposal for a Directive on Corporate Sustainability Due Diligence and Annex' (23 February 2022), <https://ec.europa.eu/info/publications/proposal-directive-corporate-sustainable-due-diligence-and-annex_en> accessed 22 March 2022.

138 2011 OECD Guidelines for Multinational Enterprises, ch 4.

139 International Finance Corporation, 'Environmental and Social Performance Standards: 2012 Guidance Notes', <https://www.ifc.org/wps/wcm/connect/9fc3aaef-14c3-4489-acf1-a1c43d7f86ec/GN_English_2012_Full-Document_updated_June-14-2021.pdf?MOD=AJPERES&CVID=nXqnsJp> accessed 28 June 2022.

140 See examples in René Wolfsteller and Yingru Li, 'Business and Human Rights Regulation After the UN Guiding Principles: Accountability, Governance, Effectiveness' (2022) 23 *Human Rights Review* 1, fn 12; Alvise Favotto and Kelly Kollman, 'When Rights Enter the CSR Field: British Firms' Engagement with Human Rights and the UN Guiding Principles' (2022) 23 *Human Rights Review* 21.

141 *Milieudefensie v Royal Dutch Shell Plc*, Hague District Court, C/09/571932 (Judgment of 26 May 2021). English translation available at <https://uitspraken.rechtspraak.nl/#!/details?id=ECLI:NL:RBDHA:2021:5339> accessed 9 December 2022.

142 Ibid, paras 4.4.11-4.4.21.

143 Ibid, para 4.1.3.

in conduct criminal under the host states' domestic law—that is in circumstances in which such rights may be difficult to justify to the public.

20.8 Conclusion: building a new international court

When reflecting on his experience as an inaugural member of the WTO Appellate Body, Claus-Dieter Ehlermann observed that 'from the very beginning' all the seven adjudicators were 'aware that [they] had to build up the reputation, acceptability, and the ensuing legitimacy of the Appellate Body from scratch' and that they were determined 'to contribute to the strength and authority of this new institution.'[144] The UPC judges and officials no doubt share these resolutions.

The UPC is anchored in international law: international law defines its judicial powers and is essential in the resolution of the disputes before it. However, as it establishes itself as a new international court, the UPC will need to make a number of salient interpretative choices on the UPCA and wider international law that will define the parameters of its operation and decision-making. It is these choices that will determine not only case outcomes, but also the public perceptions of the UPC's authority and legitimacy. If recent international legal scholarship and practice suggest anything, the UPC will be best served by an integrative approach to (its) international law—especially given patent law's significant distributive effects.

---

144 Claus-Dieter Ehlermann, 'Reflections on the Appellate Body of the WTO' (2003) 6 Journal of International Economic Law 695, 695.

Miłosz Malaga
21 The patent with unitary effect and competition law

21.1 Introduction

The discussion regarding relation between exercise of IPRs and competition law constitutes one of most interesting subjects in the law of EU internal market. There seems to be an inherent collision between rules introducing and maintaining internal market, including competition law, and national laws establishing protection of intellectual property. The former introduce free movement of *inter alia* goods and services as well as aim to abolish any obstacles to that movement. On the other hand, under IPRs proprietors enjoy the rights to prevent the use of protected inventions, including prevention of imports. Thus, further questions arise whether specific types of conduct of IPRs proprietors are compatible with internal market and competition law.

Both EU legislation and the Court's case law provide certain solutions to these issues, so that both IPRs and competition law would be adequately balanced in order to serve the same purposes, namely proper functioning of the internal market and competitive EU economy.

In this context, introduction of the unitary patent raises questions whether it could affect the current balance between IPRs and competition law.[1] Further, it can be debated if the existing mechanisms will be suitable to ensure full effectiveness of the internal market and competition law when confronted with exercises of the new patent.

Thus, this chapter aims to discuss if the unitary patent may anyhow impact the existing interplay between EU competition law and intellectual property rights; and if so, which characteristics of the unitary patent system may occur particularly challenging in that context.

21.2 Intellectual property rights in the internal market

Before discussing the interplay between EU competition law and the European unitary patent, it is worth to outline the broader internal market context. The establishment of the

---

[1] S. Anderman, *A Competition Law Perspective II: The Relationship between Patents and Competition Rules*, The Unitary EU Patent System, J. Pila, Ch. Wadlow (eds), 2015, p. 129.

Miłosz Malaga, PhD, Assistant Professor, Chair of European Law, Faculty of Law and Administration, Adam Mickiewicz University in Poznań, Poland; m.malaga@amu.edu.pl, ORCID: 0000-0001-9969-9066.

internal market has always been among the EU's key objectives and is now introduced in Article 3 (3) TEU. Further, as it follows from Article 26 TFEU, "the Union shall adopt measures with the aim of establishing or ensuring the functioning of the internal market, in accordance with the relevant provisions of the Treaties" and the internal market itself "shall comprise an area without internal frontiers in which the free movement of goods, persons, services and capital is ensured in accordance with the provisions of the Treaties".

Thus, the said removal of internal frontiers is firstly achieved by introduction of the "four freedoms" that are predominantly addressed to Member States. These provisions are further supplemented by *inter alia* competition rules that are mostly addressed to undertakings, but serve the same purpose of establishment and maintenance of the internal market. Therefore, understanding of key principles regarding the intersection between IPRs and internal market rules will be very similar for the four freedoms and competition law.

In the context of IPRs, the most relevant prohibitions include free movement of goods, and to lesser extent, freedom to provide services.[2] Among provisions on free movement of goods, Article 34 TFEU has had the key meaning for the development of the internal market, largely through the Court's case law. The said provision prohibits Member States from introducing any measures having equivalent effect quantitative restrictions in imports. This is one of the key concepts in internal market and, following the Court's case-law, it may also include exercise of IPRs.

Against that background, the Court developed the so-called theory of existence-exercise dichotomy, according to which EU Treaty freedoms and competition law may constrain the exercise of an IPR, but that does not affect the *existence* (or grant) of this right.[3] This approach was introduced in *Consten Grundig*,[4] a competition law case, and then settled in subsequent judgments that distinguished 'regular' and 'abusive' ways of exercising IPRs.[5]

The discussed prohibition is balanced with exceptions included in Article 36 TFEU, which include protection of IPRs. In this context the Court implemented into EU law the doctrine of exhaustion of IPRs, according to which the subject matter of IPRs includes the right of first marketing. However, when the first marketing occurs, the proprietor can no longer prevent any re-sales of goods of lawfully marketed goods.[6] The principle

---

2 S. Enchelmaier, *A Competition Law Perspective I: Competition Law Aspects of European Patents with Unitary Effect*, The Unitary EU Patent System, J. Pila, Ch. Wadlow (eds), 2015, p. 112.
3 Anderman (n 1), p. 131–132; M. Malaga, *The European Patent with Unitary Effect: Incentive to Dominate? A Look From the EU Competition Law Viewpoint*, IIC – International Review of Intellectual Property and Competition Law, 2014, 45:6, p. 632.
4 Judgment of the Court of 13 July 1966, C-56/64 Consten Grundig, EU:C:1966:41.
5 See e.g. judgments of the Court: of 29 February 1968, C-24/67 Parke Davis, EU:C:1968:11; of 5 October 1988, C-238/87 Volvo Veng, EU:C:1988:477.
6 See to that effect the judgment of the Court of 17 October 1990, C-10/89 CNL-SUCAL, EU:C:1990:359, paragraph 12; Enchelmaier (n 2), p. 115; G. Westkamp, *Intellectual property, competition rules, and the emer-*

of exhaustion is well recognised and included across various IPR legislation, including Article 6 UPR.

The interplay between free movement provisions and IPRs can be summarised as follows.[7] Firstly, in absence of harmonisation of IPRs on EU level, conditions and scope of intellectual property protection is determined on national level. Secondly, the Treaties do not affect *existence* of IP protection in national laws, however they might limit *exercise* of proprietors' rights. Thus, thirdly, free movement provisions recognise specific subject-matter of IPRs and level of protection stemming from these rights. However, fourthly, free movement provisions impose limitations on exercise of IPRs since, if abusive or otherwise excessive, it will be contrary to the discussed legislation. Fifthly, following the principle of exhaustion, if the IPR proprietor places or consents to place their goods or services on the market, they no longer can prevent use or onward sales of these goods or services.

21.3 EU Competition legal framework

As it follows from Article 3 (3) TEU and Protocol 27 to the Treaty, internal market "includes a system ensuring that competition is not distorted". Thus, competition law serves the same purposes as the discussed four freedoms and constitutes the other integrating factor as well as an instrument to establish and maintain the internal market.[8] Therefore, generally the approach and rules regarding the interplay between exercise of IPRs and internal market remain the same in relation to the intersection between intellectual property and competition law.

Competition law mostly applies to actions taken by certain type of individuals, i.e. undertakings, and not Member States. Since IPR proprietors are usually private parties (or, undertakings), execution of these rights will be more often covered by competition law and not the Treaty freedoms.

EU competition rules include most of all prohibition of anti-competitive agreements (Article 101 TFEU) and abuse of dominant position (Article 102 TFEU). Further, they contain regulations on control of concentrations (or, mergers and acquisitions) as well as Article 106 TFEU regarding state aid (under which Member States shall not grant selective advantages to undertakings). Control of concentrations and state aid have less in

---

ging internal market: some thoughts on the European exhaustion doctrine, Marquette Intell Prop Law Rev 11(2), p. 207–212.
[7] D.T. Keeling, *Intellectual Property Rights in EU Law. Volume I. Free Movement and Competition Law*, 2003, p. 28.
[8] Enchelmaier (n 2), p. 115; W. Frenz, *Handbook of EU Competition Law*, 2016, p. 3; J. Faul, A. Nikpay (eds.), *The EU Law of Competition*, 2014, p. 183–184.

common with exercise of IPRs[9] and thus will not be discussed further in the present chapter.

Article 101 (1) TFEU prohibits "all agreements between undertakings, decisions by associations of undertakings and concerted practices which may affect trade between Member States and which have as their object or effect the prevention, restriction or distortion of competition within the internal market". It further specifies that such agreements include *inter alia* agreements that fix purchase or selling prices, limit or control production, markets technical development or investment, share markets etc. It follows from Article 101 (2) TFEU that such agreements shall be automatically void.

Thus, Article 101 TFEU deals with contractual or consensual relations between undertakings. Such arrangements or decisions on what to do together may be of interest of competition authorities especially if such undertakings are actual or potential competitors. Traditionally, anti-competitive agreements are divided into two categories: horizontal (agreements concluded between competitors) and vertical (between suppliers and customers, or undertakings active on different levels of the value chain) ones.[10]

However, Article 101 (3) TFEU contains an exception to the discussed prohibition. If agreements caught by Article 101 (1) TFEU satisfy conditions stipulated in Article 101 (3) TFEU, they are valid, enforceable and do not require any prior decision to that effect.[11] The discussed provision requires that such agreements:
1) contribute to improving the production or distribution of goods or to promoting technical or economic progress;
2) allow consumers a fair share of the resulting benefit;
3) include restrictions that are indispensable to the attainment of these objectives;
4) do not afford the parties the possibility of eliminating competition in respect of a substantial part of the products in question.

Article 101 (3) TFEU may be applied either individually to specific agreements or generally, by way of "block exemption regulations". In individual matters, the discussed provision provides a defence against allegations on Article 101 TFEU infringements. The parties to the restrictive agreements may also benefit from block exemptions detailed in specific regulations on that regard.[12]

Article 102 TFEU serves the fundamental goals of the Treaties to ensure that the internal market is not distorted. It does so by prohibiting dominant undertakings from abusing their position on given markets. Importantly, the said provision does not pre-

---

9 See however the Commission's decisions in Google / Motorola Mobility and Microsoft / Nokia for developments regarding interplay between competition law and standard essential patents.
10 Faul, Nikpay (n 8), p. 189.
11 Ibid., p. 307.
12 See for instance the Commission Regulation (EU) 2022/720 of 10 May 2022 on the application of Article 101(3) of the Treaty on the Functioning of the European Union to categories of vertical agreements and concerted practices, OJ L 134, 11.5.2022, p. 4–13.

vent possession or creation of dominant position and only prohibits abuses of such position.

The dominant position is defined in the Court's case-law as a "position of economic strength enjoyed by an undertaking that enables it to prevent effective competition being maintained on the relevant market by giving it the power to behave to an appreciable extent independently of its competitors, customers, and ultimately consumers".[13] Such dominant position occurs on a given, relevant market which needs to be distinguished on a product and geographic basis. According to the Commission's Market Definition Notice[14], a "relevant product market comprises all those products and/or services which are regarded as interchangeable or substitutable by the consumer, by reason of the products' characteristics, their prices and their intended use" whereas "the relevant geographic market comprises the area in which the undertakings concerned are involved in the supply and demand of products or services, in which the conditions of competition are sufficiently homogeneous and which can be distinguished from neighbouring areas because the conditions of competition are appreciably different in those area"[15]. Naturally, the narrower the relevant market definition, the greater the undertaking's market power and consequently the likelihood of holding a dominant position.

Since holding dominant position is not illegal under competition law, even if it results from holding certain IPRs, the discussed rules cannot be used to bring such dominant position to an end, for instance by compulsory licensing.[16]

Only abuse of dominant position is prohibited by Article 102 TFEU. The provision also includes an open list of such abusive conducts. These consist of *inter alia* directly or indirectly imposing unfair purchase or selling prices or other unfair trading conditions; limiting production, markets or technical development to the prejudice of consumers or applying dissimilar conditions to equivalent transactions with other trading parties, thereby placing them at a competitive disadvantage. Indeed, undertakings holding dominant positions may be regarded as having special responsibility and limited freedom regarding their market conduct.

---

[13] Judgment of the Court of 14 February 1978, C-27/76 United Brands, EU:C:1978:22, paragraph 65.
[14] Commission on the definition of relevant market for the purposes of Community competition law, OJ C 372, 9.12.1997, p. 5–13; currently under review (see the Commission's Staff Working Document – Evaluation of the Commission Notice on the definition of relevant market for the purposes of Community competition law of 9 December 1997, SWD(2021) 199 final, 12.7.2021).
[15] The Market Definition Notice, paragraphs 7–8.
[16] J.T. Lang, European competition law and intellectual property rights – a new analysis, ERA Forum (2010) 11, p. 422.

21.4 EU Competition law and intellectual property rights

21.4.1 Principles

As discussed above, general rules governing the interplay between competition law and IPRs are similar to those developed in the field of Treaty freedoms. Historically, exclusive IPRs were regarded as inherently conflicting with competition. However, currently these two areas are more described as serving similar purposes (such as ensuring undistorted competition in factors like innovation or quality) and thus there is rather a need to balance these forms of competition than any structural conflict.[17] Therefore, significant scope of IPRs is regarded as justified also from competition law perspective. As in the case of the Treaty freedoms, generally exercise that is inherent to IPRs (or, the specific subject matter) is not infringing competition law.[18]

In any event, intellectual property is without prejudice to the application of competition law[19] and certain ways of exercise of IPRs may trigger application of Articles 101–102 TFEU. They need to be however accompanied with "additional abusive conduct"[20] that would extend beyond given IPR's specific subject matter. Indeed, in addition to already outlined *Volvo Veng* and *Parke Davis*, in *Magill*, a purely competition case, the Court provided for a concept of exceptional circumstances, in which the "exercise of an exclusive right (...) may involve abusive conduct".[21] This approach was confirmed in other landmark judgments regarding the IPRs and competition law interplay.[22] Such circumstances need to be however defined individually in each case as their precise scope might depend on the type of anti-competitive conduct. For instance, in matters regarding refusal to licence, these exceptional circumstances include the facts that such refusal: (1) relates to a product or service indispensable to the exercise of a particular activity on a neighbouring market; (2) is of such a kind as to exclude any effective competi-

---

[17] J. Turner, *Intellectual Property and EU Competition Law*, 2010, p. 3; G. Ghidini, *Innovation, Competition, and Consumer Welfare in Intellectual Property Law*, 2010, p. 11–16.
[18] O. Kolstad, Competition law and intellectual property rights – outline of an economics-based approach, J. Drexl (ed.), *Research Handbook on Intellectual Property and Competition Law*, 2008, p. 11.
[19] That rule is also confirmed in Article 15 UPR.
[20] J.T. Lang, European competition law and intellectual property rights – a new analysis, ERA Forum (2010) 11, p. 422.
[21] Judgment of the Court of 6 April 1995, C-241/91 P RTE, EU:C:1995:98, paragraph 50.
[22] Judgment of the Court of 29 April 2004, C-418/01 IMS Health, EU:C:2004:257, paragraphs 35–36; judgment of the Court of First Instance of 17 September 2007, T-201/04 Microsoft, EU:T:2007:289, paragraphs 321–331 and to certain extent judgment of the Court of 16 July 2015, C-170/13 Huawei, EU:C:2015:477, paragraphs 46–47.

tion on that neighbouring market and (3) prevents the appearance of a new product for which there is potential consumer demand.[23]

21.4.2 IPRs and anti-competitive agreements

The most typical, potentially anti-competitive agreements regarding IPRs include contracts on exclusive licensing or transferring intellectual property rights as long as they may partition the internal market or separate the EU from other markets by limiting parallel imports. An undertaking may own parallel IPRs in different states and grant exclusive licenses in one or some of these states. Even if such conduct does not contain any restrictions outside the scope of IPR and merely transfers some of the rights, it still may have the effect of preventing competition at the expense parallel importers that would otherwise be active in the market.[24] Further, assignments or exclusive licences may prevent, restrict or distort competition by significantly strengthening one's market power. This would be the case for instance if a number of undertakings assign their multiple IPRs to a single licensee.[25]

Other commonly discussed infringements of Article 101 TFEU with respect to IPRs include restrictions on resale or use of products placed on the market, restrictions on other activities outside scope of valid IPRs as well as within scope of these rights. Further, contracts may include no-challenge clauses, i.e. provisions in which the parties commit not to challenge their IPRs.[26]

Patent settlements may also infringe Article 101 TFEU.[27] For instance, in pharmaceutical markets, they may delay entry of generic drugs in return for a value transfer or result in extending the patent's exclusionary zone, going beyond its geographic scope.[28] To that end, these are especially the reverse-payment patent settlements (or, "pay-for-delay" settlements) which may provide for such a delay. In other words, the patent proprietor pays their potential competitors so as to prevent them from entering the market in a particular period[29] and thus restricts competition. Most discussed Commission's

---

[23] Judgment of the Court of First Instance of 17 September 2007, T-201/04 Microsoft, EU:T:2007:289, paragraph 332.
[24] Turner (n 17), p. 52–53.
[25] Ibid., p. 52–53.
[26] Ibid., p. 55–56.
[27] *3rd Report on the Monitoring of Patent Settlements* (period: January-December 2011), published on 25.07.2012; http://ec.europa.eu/competition/sectors/pharmaceuticals/inquiry/patent_settlements_report3_en.pdf.
[28] Ibid., p. 2.
[29] D. W. Hull, The Application of EU Competition Law in the Pharmaceutical Sector [in:] *Journal of European Competition Law & Practice* Volume 5 Issue 5 (October 2012), p. 479.

decisions on reverse-payment settlements include Cephalon,[30] Lundbeck[31] and Servier.[32]

Lundbeck and Servier decisions were challenged to the Court under actions for annulment (Article 263 TFEU). In *Lundbeck*, the Court provided the criteria under which dispute settlement agreement between a patent proprietor and a generic medicinal products manufacturer may be regarded as contrary to EU competition law.[33] These are further discussed by Advocate General Kokott in her two opinions in *Servier*.[34]

However, many of discussed agreements, if concluded by parties within vertical relations, may benefit, among others, from block exemptions, as detailed in the Commission Regulation 2022/720 on the application of Article 101 (3) of the Treaty to categories of vertical agreements and concerted practices. As follows from Article 2 (3) and (1) of the said Regulation, in essence the exemption applies to vertical restraints relating to the assignment to the buyer or use by the buyer of IPRs, provided that those provisions do not constitute the primary object of such agreements and are directly related to the use, sale or resale of goods or services by the buyer or its customers.

21.4.3 IPRs and abuse of dominant position

Abuse of dominant position seems to be the key and most often discussed prohibition in the context of interplay between competition law and exercise of IPRs. Firstly, one can distinguish more "typical" and relevant for IPRs forms of abuse, such as refusals to supply and licence, tying or excessive pricing.[35] Secondly, as the list of types of abuses is not exhaustive and exercise of IPRs may occur in very specific circumstances, one may identify more modern and "IPR-specific" conducts. These include *inter alia* regulatory or litigation abuses, patent hold-up or actions regarding the specific status of standard essential patents. They may occur along every sector, however two industries in which potential anti-competitive harm through exercise of IPRs has arisen are pharmaceuticals as well as information and communication technology (ICT).[36]

---

30 Case COMP/39.686 Cephalon.
31 Case COMP/39.226 Lundbeck.
32 Case COMP/39.612 Perindopril (Servier) – case brought under both Articles 101 and 102 TFEU.
33 Judgment of the Court of 25 March 2021, Lundbeck v Commission, C-591/16 P, EU:C:2021:243, paragraphs 113 et seq.
34 Opinions of Advocate General Kokott of 14 July 2022, Commission v. Servier, C-176/19 P, EU:C:2022:576; Servier v. Commission, C-201/19 P, EU:C:2022:577.
35 S. Anderman, H. Schmidt, *EU Competition Law and Intellectual Property Rights. The Regulation of Innovation*, 2011, p. 91.
36 Faul, Nikpay (n 8), p. 492.

21.4.3.1 Refusal to supply and licence

With respect to refusal to supply, it was established also out of the context of IPRs that once an undertaking is found in dominant position and is possessing deep essential facilities, it may not anymore refuse the access to the crucial infrastructure for performance of the others. As long as such access is really necessary (and not just facilitating the competitors' market performance), it shall be offered on the so-called FRAND conditions (i.e. fair, reasonable and non-discriminatory).[37] Those observations remain relevant in cases when such essential facilities are protected by IPRs.[38] In these terms, refusal to supply may take the particular form of refusal to licence or refusal to continue to licence. Abusive conduct may be combined with a refusal to manufacture (or to allow for it) products which customers actually need or to buying a patent for desirable invention, which is afterwards neither used nor subject to license, yet only suppressed with an aim of preventing competition.[39]

The question of determining FRAND royalties is particularly significant in the field of standard essential patents (SEPs). These cover technical standards, access to which is indispensable to enter certain markets. SEP holders may not only impose licence conditions that are not FRAND, but also engage in other anti-competitive conducts, such as patent ambush or abusive litigation.[40]

21.4.3.2 Tying

Tying constitutes "selling or leasing a product on the condition that the buyer or lessee would also purchase or lease another product from the seller"[41] and is explicitly forbidden in Article 102 (d) TFEU. Indeed, in the Court's case-law this form of abuse is to certain extent specific for exercise of IPRs and may hinder one's engagement in technological integration.[42] As the Court ruled in *Tetra Pak II*,[43] "any independent producer is free (…) to manufacture consumables intended for use in equipment managed by others, unless in so doing it infringes a competitor's intellectual property rights". In other words, if sales of a product protected by an IPR were tied to sales to an unprotected one, there

---

37 Judgment of the Court of 26 November 1998, C-7/97 Bronner, EU:C:1998:569, paragraphs 38–41.
38 J. T. Lang, *The principle of essential facilities in European Community competition law – the position since Bronner*, Journal of Network Industries I, 2000, p. 376.
39 Ibid., p. 388.
40 See further: judgment of the Court of 16 July 2015, C-170/13 Huawei, EU:C:2015:477; D. Geradin, *European Competition Law, Intellectual Property Law and Standardization*, J. Contreras (ed.), The Cambridge Handbook of Technical Standardization Law. Competition, Antitrust and Patents, 2008, p. 78–93.
41 Anderman, Schmidt (n 35), p. 127.
42 Ibid., p. 142.
43 Judgment of the Court of First Instance of 6 October 1994, T-83/91 Tetra Pak, EU:T:1994:246, paragraph 83.

would be an abuse of dominant position due to the extension of that IPR to a product, which itself is not protected.[44]

21.4.3.3 Excessive pricing

Excessive pricing is expressly prohibited by Article 102 (a) TFEU and constitutes an exploitative abuse, directly harming the consumers. However, with respect to patents, competition law recognises that the right to ask a higher price lies within the very essence of incentives deriving from an IPR.[45] Therefore, the proprietor maintains the right to "recoup their losses" and enjoy a "fair return" from their inventive efforts.[46] Thus, identifying the balance between that perspective and excessive pricing with respect to IPRs becomes particularly difficult and needs to be conducted on a case-by-case basis.[47]

21.4.3.4 Regulatory and litigation abuses

These types of IPRs abuses can be best explained on the example of pharmaceutical sector. Firstly, one may distinguish strategies regarding misuse of process or of patent system, e.g. as they took place in *AstraZeneca*[48] case. The abusive conduct consisted in changing the pharmaceutical shape in which the product was marketed and consequently withdrawing the market authorisation granted for that very version, on which the generics (products offered by competitors) would rely as well. More generally, in pharmaceutical sector, the originators may apply patent filing strategies with a foreclosure effect.[49] They may either seek to maximise the exclusivity period or extend the exclusivity well beyond the expiry of the patent.[50] Thus, dominant undertakings would either file a multitude of patent applications for the same original compounds, generating therefore several layers of defence (so-called patent cluster) or divide a single patent into several narrower "divisional patents".

Another example of such potential abuse is recent Teva case, in which the Commission issued a statement of objections, claiming that the company might have intended to delay competition on one of pharmaceutical markets by artificially extending patent

---

44 Anderman, Schmidt (n 35), p. 142.
45 Ibid., p. 144.
46 Judgment of the Court of 5 October 1988, C-53/87 CICRA v Renault, EU:C:1988:472, paragraph 17.
47 Anderman, Schmidt (n 35), p. 159.
48 Judgment of the General Court of 1 July 2010, T-321/05 AstraZeneca, EU:T:2010:266.
49 M. Siragusa, *The EU Pharmaceutical Sector Inquiry. New Forms of Abuse and Article 102 TFEU*, G. Caggiano et al., Competition Law and Intellectual Property, A European Perspective, 2012, p. 179.
50 Ibid., p. 180.

protection and systematically spreading misleading information about a competing product that was going to enter the market.[51]

Overall, regulatory abuses may include supply of misleading information to extend patent validity, withdrawal of marketing authorisation to restrict entry of generics, certain patent filing strategies.

On the other hand, IPRs proprietors may engage into vexatious and artificial litigation in order to increase the competitors' costs or prevent their market entry, especially if proceedings are lengthy and costly. This is particularly related to the question of injunctions in IPRs cases, which can effectively prevent production and sales of products before infringement of IPR is confirmed in a final judgment. Such injunction strategies may also occur abusive from competition law perspective.[52]

21.4.3.5 Patent hold-ups and patent trolling

Although these notions might have slightly different meaning, they can be generally described as "deceptive conduct (...) by not disclosing the existence of the patents and patent applications which is later claimed were relevant to the adopted standard".[53] Thus, the proprietor would use their IPR with the intention to demand licence fees or initiate burdensome infringement proceedings rather than to protect an invention.[54] Such conduct can be abusive within meaning of Article 102 TFEU and the Commission already in 2006 noted that patent trolls had the potential to "threaten the entire industry with a court order no matter how minor the feature that has been patented is".[55]

21.5 The Unitary Patent and EU competition law

As discussed in detail in the present handbook, introduction of the European patent with unitary effect involves significant and structural changes for functioning of the patent system in the EU. These may as well impact the current view on the intersection between competition law and patents, which is based *inter alia* on the premise that patent

---

51 See the Commission's press release: https://ec.europa.eu/commission/presscorner/detail/en/IP_22_6062.
52 See e.g. the Commission's decision in Motorola Mobility case, as described in a press release: https://ec.europa.eu/commission/presscorner/detail/en/IP_14_489.
53 Case COMP/38.636 *Rambus*; paragraph 27.
54 T. Pohlmann, M. Opitz, *Typology of the patent troll business*, R&D Management, Volume 43, Issue 2, 2013, p. 104.
55 *Future patent policy in Europe*. Public hearing – 12.7.2006, Consultation paper by the European Commission (http://ec.europa.eu/internal_market/indprop/docs/patent/hearing/preliminary_findings_en.pdf); p. 11.

laws are national. Thus, the mere transition onto European level may have certain implications in terms of striking proper balance between the two perspectives. At the same time, the UP package involves more substantial and detailed changes, such as introduction of regime for translations or dedicated court and procedure. The present section discusses firstly general issues regarding the envisaged entry into force of the system and secondly, more specific matters that might be particularly interesting for application of competition law.

Article 15 UPR confirms the already discussed general rule that the "Regulation shall be without prejudice to the application of competition law and the law relating to unfair competition". Consequently, competition law may still limit certain ways of exercise of the patent. However, it is worth to remind that following the Court's unfavourable opinion,[56] provisions regarding the proprietor's essential rights to prevent the use of invention were transformed from the UPR to Articles 25–26 UPCA. Indeed, the UPCA expressly recognises primacy of Union law (Article 20) and does refer to internal market and competition in the preamble. However, technically exercise of the proprietor's rights relies on the Agreement concluded by Member States and not EU law as such. Consequently, introduction of the system does not seem to bring any structural changes as regards the source of exercised rights, compared to situation before entry into force of the UP.

Compatibility of the envisaged system with EU law was to certain extent subject to judicial discussion under Treaty provisions on enhanced cooperation. It follows from Article 326 TFEU that enhanced cooperation, among others, shall not distort competition between Member States. This can be interpreted as a prohibition to introduce through enhanced cooperation measures that create new challenges in application of EU competition law. Infringement of that provision constituted one of the pleas brought by Italy and Spain in their actions for annulment of the decision authorising enhanced cooperation for Unitary patent Regulations.[57] Although it was voiced that employing enhanced cooperation in the field of unitary patent protection would "almost necessarily entail a distortion of competition",[58] neither the Advocate General in his opinion, nor the Court found infringement of Article 326 TFEU. The Court confirmed however, that its review concerned only legality of the decision authorising enhanced cooperation, and not the underlying substantive Regulations.[59] However, due to the Treaty's wording and structure, distortion of competition could not constitute a standalone plea in actions for an-

---

[56] Opinion 1/09 of the Court of 8 march 2011, EU:C:2011:123.
[57] See judgment of the Court of 16 April 2013, C-274/11 and C-295/11 Spain and Italy v Council, EU:C:2013:240.
[58] H. Ullrich, *Enhanced cooperation in the area of unitary patent protection and European integration*, ERA Forum 2013, 13(4).
[59] Further on that matter see: M. Malaga, *The European Patent with Unitary Effect: Incentive to Dominate? A Look From the EU Competition Law Viewpoint*, IIC – International Review of Intellectual Property and Competition Law, 2014, 45:6, p. 625.

nulment of these Regulations.[60] Thus, it remains an open question whether entry into force of the system in its current shape would not distort competition and the internal market.

There are valid arguments that introduction of the UP will not require much adaptation of the existing principles regarding the interplay between IPRs and competition law. Any potential anti-competitive conduct, such as territorial limitations for licensing, are already known from the existing system, thus there are mechanisms that can prevent any distortions in the internal market.[61] Competition rules will remain to provide an external regulation to the internal regulations regarding the unitary patent. It is also unlikely that the new patent system could rely on competition law to create new problems in terms of misuse of patents. It is noted that the competition cases will be by necessity few and restricted to rare and exceptional circumstances.[62]

However, one may raise a few points of concern regarding the impact of the new system on application of competition law and effectiveness of its specific tools.

Firstly, introduction of the system may have implications for identification of dominant position of given undertakings and consequently for effectiveness of Article 102 TFEU. As discussed, dominant position occurs on a given relevant, product and geographic, market. Defining a relevant market is thus a tool to determine market power,[63] which naturally becomes lower vis-à-vis any wider market definition. The Commission's Notice on the definition of relevant market does not refer to IPRs as a factor which may have an impact on the market definition. However, the territorial scope of IPR is often equal to the scope of geographic market,[64] which due to the principle of IPRs territoriality implies national geographic markets.

In this context, since UP will enjoy the same (unitary) effect in all participating Member States, the scope of patent protection will be unified and thus the geographic market may be redefined more broadly, to the territories of those countries. This results from the fact that obtaining a patent with the same set of claims in those Member States could result in providing for sufficiently distinguished conditions of competition.[65]

As a result, geographic market perspective might change from several national markets to one market covering the participating Member States. Therefore, market power of a given patent proprietor might be assumed as accordingly lower. This could lead to a situation in which, under the new regime, certain patent proprietors would be no

---

60 See in that regard the judgment of the Court of 5 May 2015, C-146/13 Spain v Parliament and Council, EU:C:2015:298.
61 Enchelmaier (n 2), p. 128;
62 Anderman (n 1), p. 143.
63 Anderman, Schmidt (n 35), p. 42.
64 Ibid., p. 43; Turner (n 17), p. 83.
65 M. Malaga, *The European Patent with Unitary Effect: Incentive to Dominate? A Look From the EU Competition Law Viewpoint*, IIC – International Review of Intellectual Property and Competition Law, 2014, 45:6, p. 640–641.

more regarded as dominant and thus their anti-competitive conduct would not be any more caught by Article 102 TFEU. Should that be the case, competition authorities need to be particularly careful when estimating the proprietors' market power to ensure effectiveness of the discussed prohibition.

Secondly, the patent's unitary effect will leverage the scope of intellectual property protection, but also may accordingly enhance the scope for proprietor's anti-competitive conduct. Since the scope of protection is going to cover participating Member States and not each state separately, decisions on infringement will be delivered with respect to that wider area and thus improve the proprietor's ability to impact the market. Therefore, certain abuses – especially those related to infringement claims, such as patent trolling – may be easier to carry out and have greater commercial significance. That certainly would require the authorities' attention when applying competition law with respect to the UP.

Thirdly, the translations regime might be of particular concern with respect to possible regulatory abuses. As discussed in this handbook, the main rule for translations is that if the patent is granted in either English, German or French, no further translations are required. Therefore, there will be potential infringers who do not know that language and thus the exact patent's scope. Translation of the patent would be submitted by the proprietor only in the event of a dispute, i.e. in most cases after infringement occurs.

Such structure of the translations regime may in the first step imply that a patent is less "visible" to potential infringers and in the second step – incentivise proprietors to abuse the system, for instance by providing "imperfect" translations in the event of a dispute. It remains open, whether such conduct could be regarded as abuse of dominant position, compared to other regulatory abuses outlined in this chapter.

21.6 Conclusions

As discussed in this chapter, the established legal framework for accommodating the relation between IPRs and competition law works efficiently to balance these two areas. Also types of anti-competitive use of IPRs are well identified and tools to combat such abuses seem to be effective. In that context, introduction of the unitary patent does not seem to bring significant structural changes, which could not be remedied by the currently working system.

However, one may identify certain points that competition authorities may need to pay more attention to when applying competition law to exercise of the unitary patent. As discussed above, particular challenges may arise from potential redefinition of geographic market. Since the patent protection will cover all participating Member States, also the relevant market's geographic scope might be wider than national and thus estimation of the proprietor's market power artificially lowered. At the same time, unitary patent proprietors obtain, due to the unitary effect itself, a powerful tool that might leverage their ability to distort competition, for instance by filing abusive infringement claims also with respect to territories that so far were less affected by such conducts. Finally, the translations arrangements seem to create enough room for regulatory abuses. That results from the fact that unitary patents will be translated to languages other than English, German or French in the event of the dispute. Therefore, the system may be less transparent for potential infringers speaking other languages. If dispute occurs, such additional translations are not binding and therefore the proprietor might be tempted to include there certain inaccuracies in their favour.

Thomas Jaeger, Johannes Lukan

22 A system fit for innovation?
Part I: (Dis-)incentives for potential patentees in the UP legal framework

22.1 Introduction

When is a patent system fit for innovation? Bearing in mind that the key objective of patent regulation is to encourage investments in innovation in an optimal and functional manner,[1] the argument will be made in the following that a balance must be struck between two main interests in order to attain this goal: On the one hand, easy, fast, legally secure and inexpensive access to patent protection[2] with a solid substantive, territorial and temporal scope will provide incentives for investment in R&D.[3] The first part of this bipartite contribution will therefore be dedicated to an analysis of the incentives and obstacles the UP legal framework provides in this respect.

On the other hand, access to patentable knowledge for follow-on research also needs to be ensured within a patent system. However, these issues are reserved for the second part of this paper, which will conclude with an overall assessment of whether the UP and its surrounding legal framework succeed in striking a fair balance between these two interests, ie a balance between protecting patented 'senior' innovation on the one hand and facilitating 'junior' innovation on the other.[4]

---

[1] Cf eg Miłosz Malaga, 'The European Patent with Unitary Effect: Incentive to Dominate?' (2014) 45 IIC 621, 631; Pedro Henrique D. Batista and Adrian Gautschi, 'Stoffschutz' in Reto M. Hilty and Thomas Jaeger (eds), *Europäisches Immaterialgüterrecht* (Springer 2018) 407, 411.
[2] Already in the follow-up document to its 1997 Green Paper, the Commission quoted the European Parliament as noting that a reformed patent system must be 'simple, rapid, legally certain, accessible and not involve excessive expenditure' in order to promote innovation, Commission, 'Promoting Innovation through Patents: The Follow-Up to the Green Paper on the Community Patent and the Patent System in Europe' COM(1999) 42 final, 8. Cf also recital 4 UP Reg (Regulation [EU] 1257/2012 of the European Parliament and of the Council of 17 December 2012 implementing enhanced cooperation in the area of the creation of unitary patent protection [2012] OJ L361/1).
[3] Geertrui Van Overwalle and Esther van Zimmeren, 'Functions and Limits of Patent Law' in Erik Claes, Wouter Devroe and Bert Keirsbilck (eds), *Facing the Limits of the Law* (Springer 2009) 415, 421; Herbert Zech, 'Brauchen wir ein Patentrecht?' (2021) 8 ifo Schnelldienst 3, 3.
[4] This terminology is inspired by Zhiqian Wan and Samuel Meng, 'A Case for a Limited Breeding Exemption from Patent Protection' (2018) 49 IIC 636, 645f.

Thomas Jaeger, Professor of European Law, University of Vienna.
Johannes Lukan, University Assistant (prae doc) at the Department of European, International and Comparative Law, University of Vienna.

https://doi.org/10.1515/9783110781687-022

22.2 Easy, fast and legally secure access to UPs?

In contrast, this first part of the paper serves to prepare some of the ground for that endeavour. As was already indicated at the beginning, it will be discussed here how (i) easy or difficult, (ii) (in)expensive and (iii) fast or slow it is to obtain (and maintain) patent protection under the UP system as compared to cross-border protection of an invention in Europe through an ordinary bundle patent under the EPC. After all, these factors were identified as potential (dis-)incentives for investment in innovation at the outset. A fourth subsection is specifically dedicated to uncertainties as regards the law applicable to the UP as an object of property. Some other issues of legal (in)security will be addressed along the way. Moreover, the costs of UP protection will be assessed together with its territorial scope from a cost-benefit perspective and the duration of the application process will be appraised considering the related issue of the term of protection. Whereas the second part of the paper is more specifically dedicated to the central question of whether or not the UP legal framework establishes a functional balance for innovative activities, where appropriate, related matters will already be discussed in this first part.

22.2.1 Easy access: the EPO as a central granting authority and the language regime

The major advantages of the UP in terms of simplicity of access are certainly its favourable language regime for potential patentees and the fact that patentees need not approach any national patent offices.

22.2.1.1 The request for unitary effect as a replacement of national validation

For UPs, national validation still required after the grant of a classic EP is replaced by a single procedure for obtaining unitary effect, which can be applied for within one month after the grant of an EP with an identical set of claims in respect of all the EU Member States participating in the enhanced cooperation.[5] Due to the dependence of a UP on a classic EP, the former is said to have an accessory nature.[6]

---

[5] Cf art 3 UP Reg (n 2) and rule 6 UPR (Rules relating to Unitary Patent Protection as adopted by decision of the Select Committee of the Administrative Council of the European Patent Organisation of 15 December 2014 and as last amended by decision of the Select Committee of the Administrative Council of 23 March 2022, OJ EPO 2022, A41); cf also EPO, *Unitary Patent Guide* (2nd edn 2022) para 44.

[6] Recital 7 UP Reg (n 2); Aisling McMahon, 'An Institutional Examination of the Implications of the Unitary Patent Package for the Morality Provisions: a Fragmented Future too Far?' (2017) 48 IIC 42, 52.

In contrast, after a European bundle patent has been granted, applicants have to 'nationally validate' it in some or each of the designated states, generally by filing translations of the patent claims and description in the official languages of the designated countries with the respective national patent offices. While states that are parties to the London Agreement[7] provide for some relief in this respect, by waiving the translation of either only the patent description or also the claims,[8] a UP's description only has to be translated into one additional language in any case[9] (while the claims have to be submitted in all three official languages of the EPO pre-grant already).[10] If the application is in French or German, an English translation of the UP's description is required.[11] If it is in English, the patent claims and the description can be translated into any other official language of the EU.[12] When a UP is thus combined with a European bundle patent in the sense that designations for EU Member States are included, where unitary effect is not (yet) possible, a translation into the language of such a country can be (re-)used for this purpose.[13] Additional translations only need to be furnished in the case of legal disputes.[14]

22.2.1.2 Downsides to the language regime?

The downside of this arrangement, according to some authors,[15] is that market participants might inadvertently infringe patents published in languages other than those they speak. Due to this concern (among others), ratification of the UPCA is not to be expected

---

7 Agreement on the application of Article 65 of the Convention on the Grant of European Patents, OJ EPO 2001, 550.
8 For more details cf eg Annette Kur, Thomas Dreier and Stefan Luginbuehl, *European Intellectual Property Law* (2nd edn, Edward Elgar 2019) 123; Andreas Wiebe, *Wettbewerbs- und Immaterialgüterrecht* (4 edn, facultas 2018) 67f.
9 Cf Art 6(1) Language Reg (Council Regulation [EU] 1260/2012 of 17 December 2012 implementing enhanced cooperation in the area of the creation of unitary patent protection with regard to the applicable translation arrangements [2012] OJ L361/89).
10 Cf Art 14(6) EPC.
11 Art 6(1)(a) Language Reg (n 9).
12 Since Art 6(1)(b) Language Reg (n 9) refers to 'any other official language of the Union', this is arguably not restricted to the languages of the Member States participating in the enhanced cooperation.
13 EPO, *UP Guide* (n 5) para 58.
14 Cf Art 4 Language Reg (n 9).
15 Eg Malaga (n 1) 639. Concerning the same issue in the context of the London Agreement, Grabenwarter, 'Verfassungsrechtliche Fragen eines Beitritts Österreichs zum Londoner Übereinkommen' (2010) 59 ÖBl 209, 210ff.

in Czech Republic[16] and Hungary[17] any time soon, whilst Poland has not even signed the UPCA to date.

For patentees, however, the language regime of the UP appears favourable. What is more, since UPs are in any case published in English, the main language of research in engineering as well as natural sciences,[18] the aforementioned concerns might be overstated. Even if a patent infringement occurs due to the infringer's lack of proficiency in English, at least any criminal consequences of a patent infringement provided for in national law will regularly fail due to the criminal law requirement of intent.[19] Admittedly, this does not exclude civil liability.

From a different angle, however, it is even regrettable that English has not been adopted as the *only* language of the UP: According to reports on the preparations of the UP package, Spain might have joined the project under the mutual concession that Germany and France had also renounced the use of their official languages.[20]

22.2.1.3 Centralised collection of renewal fees

Returning to the EPO acting as a central administrative authority for the holders of UPs, another advantage in the administration of UPs post-grant is that only a single renewal fee is payable to the EPO directly[21] as opposed to classic EPs, where each year several annual fees are due to the national patent offices corresponding to the designations of the patent.

22.2.2 Value for money: costs and territorial scope of protection

The level of these fees is another significant factor in whether stakeholders, and SMEs in particular,[22] will use the UP system or whether they will prefer to stay with traditional

---

[16] Anonymous, 'Legal and financial concerns: Czech Republic will not ratify UPCA any time soon' (13 September 2019) <patentblog.kluweriplaw.com/2019/09/13/legal-and-financial-concerns-czech-republic-will-not-ratify-upca-any-time-soon> accessed 13 September 2022.
[17] Anonymous, 'Constitutional Court of Hungary rules Unified Patent Court Agreement cannot be ratified' (29 June 2018) <patentblog.kluweriplaw.com/2018/06/29/constutional-court-hungary-rules-upca-cannot-ratified/?doing_wp_cron=1568397191.8276090621948242187500> accessed 13 September 2022.
[18] Pieter Callens and Sam Granata, *Introduction to the Unitary Patent and the Unified Patent Court* (Kluwer 2013) 12.
[19] Grabenwarter (n 15) 211.
[20] Callens and Granata (n 18) 12f; Matthias Lamping, 'Patentrecht' in Hilty and Jaeger (n 1) 464, 470, 494.
[21] Art 9(1)(e) and art 11 UP Reg (n 2).
[22] Cf Luke McDonagh, *Exploring Perspectives of the Unified Patent Court and Unitary Patent Within the Business and Legal Communities* (Report commissioned by the UK's IPO 2014) 32.

EPs or even resort to national patents.[23] Given the accessory nature of UPs, any fees payable to the EPO pre-grant are exactly the same as those for their classic counterparts.[24] Since the procedure for obtaining unitary effect is free of charge,[25] a comparison with the costs for an ordinary EP boils down to the level of renewal fees. Besides, of course, as pointed out above,[26] translation costs can be saved with a UP, which are also considered to be a significant spending factor relating to EPs.[27]

According to the UP Reg,[28] the level of renewal fees shall be set by the Select Committee of the Administrative Council at the EPO, which consists of representatives of the EU Member States participating in the enhanced cooperation (regardless of whether they have signed the UPCA).[29] Their discretion in setting the renewal fees is restricted, inter alia, by the conditions that these fees shall be progressive, take into account the situation of SMEs and reflect the level of the national renewal fees to be paid for the average geographical coverage of current EPs taking effect in the participating Member States.[30] The idea was thus to get the additional territorial protection that a UP offers compared to an 'average EP' as a bonus, free of charge.

22.2.2.1 What is an 'average' EP?

However, the average geographical coverage of an EP appears to vary according to the stage of patent life: Since 2009, the designation fee payable to the EPO pre-grant is a lump sum, irrespective of the number of designations.[31] Therefore, it is likely that at the beginning of patent life, when renewal fees are generally low, EPs will be validated in all the contracting states to the EPC where there are no additional translation requirements,[32] even if protection should not really be needed there. Towards the end of patent

---

[23] After the seven-year transitional period provided for in art 83 UPCA has expired, it will no longer be possible to opt-out classical EPs from the jurisdiction of the UPC. For this reason, it is unlikely, but conceivable, that national patents will make a revival in the late 2020s, cf Alan Johnson, 'Looking Forward: A User Perspective' in Justine Pila and Christopher Wadlow (eds), The Unitary EU Patent System (Hart 2015) 179, 188.
[24] Johnson (n 23) 187.
[25] EPO, *UP Guide* (n 5) para 34.
[26] At n 9.
[27] Cf eg Bruno van Pottelsberghe and Didier Francois, *The Cost Factor in Patent Systems* (CEPR Discussion Paper No 5944/2006) 14; Commission, 'Enhancing the patent system in Europe' (Communication) COM(2007) 165 final 17f.
[28] Art 9(1)(e) and (2) UP Reg (n 2) read in conjunction with Art 12 thereof.
[29] Art 9(2) UP Reg (n 2).
[30] Art 12(1)(a) and (3)(a) UP Reg (n 2).
[31] Notice from the European Patent Office dated 26 January 2009 concerning the 2009 fee structure, OJ EPO 2009, 118, para 3.3.
[32] Due to the London Agreement or due to the fact that the EP is already available in the official language of the respective country.

life, however, when renewal fees are generally high, it is common practice to 'prune' designations and only validate in jurisdictions which are either important to the patentee, eg because there is a sufficient market for the invention to be sold or used, or a competitor is also established there, or if the country in question simply provides for low renewal fees.[33]

Due to it thus being unclear what an 'average' EP is, there was the fear that the renewal fees for UPs would be set at the equivalent of six or more designations.[34] However, these fears have not materialised. The abovementioned[35] Select Committee has set the fees at a relatively moderate level in 2015.[36] According to the EPO's *UP Guide*, this supposedly corresponds to the four participating EU Member States where classic EPs were most often validated in 2015.[37] It remains unclear which specific states are referred to here. This depends on whether the four Member States where the most EPs were validated in 2015 in absolute terms (patents still in force) or those where most patents were validated in relative terms (eg EPs that were granted in 2015 and also validated in a certain Member State that same year) were (allegedly) taken as the basis for the adoption of the level of renewal fees for a UP.[38]

22.2.2.2 Dependence of territorial coverage on the status of ratifications

What seems odd about the renewal fees for UPs is that they do not depend on the countries included in the respective UP's territorial scope. This is so, because for any 'generation' of UPs uniform protection will only be awarded for the countries having ratified the UPCA at the time of registration of unitary effect and remain restricted to these states, irrespective of any subsequent ratifications. This conditionality in relation to the status of ratifications provided for in art 18(2) UP Reg[39] has been explicitly approved by the CJEU.[40] As Germany[41] has the only state, apart from those that had already ratified

---

33 Kur, Dreier and Luginbuehl (n 8) 89; Johnson (n 23) 188; McDonagh (n 22) 23f.
34 Johnson (n 23) 189.
35 At n 28.
36 Cf art 2 RFeesUPP (Rules relating to Fees for Unitary Patent Protection as adopted by decision of the Select Committee of the Administrative Council SC/D 2/15 of 15.12.2015, OJ EPO 2016, A40).
37 EPO, *UP Guide* (n 5) para 37.
38 For specific relative (patents validated for the first time) and absolute (patents still in force) numbers cf EPO, *Statistics 2020* (Doc no CA/F 5/21) 18ff.
39 N 2.
40 Case C-146/13 *Spain v Parliament and Council* [2015] ECLI:EU:C:2015:298, para 107.
41 German ratification has been a prerequisite for the entry into force of the UPCA, which took place on the first day of the fourth month after the deposit of the German instrument of ratification, ie on 1st June 2023 (art 89 UPCA), cf UPC, 'The Provisional Application Phase and the UPC's expected timeline' (6 April 2022) <www.unified-patent-court.org/news/provisional-application-phase-and-upcs-expected-timeline> accessed 13 September 2022. In order to allow applications pending before that date to also benefit from

the agreement earlier, that has still ratified the UPCA before its entry into force, the territorial scope of protection of the first generation of UPs will comprise 17 out of 25 Member States participating in the enhanced cooperation, respectively 17 out of the 24 Member States[42] having signed the UPCA, namely Austria, Belgium, Bulgaria, Denmark, Estonia, Finland, France, Germany, Italy, Latvia, Lithuania, Luxembourg, Malta, the Netherlands, Portugal, Slovenia and Sweden.[43] Even though unitary effect can only be granted for EPs with the same set of claims in respect of *all* the Member States participating in the enhanced cooperation, regardless of the status of ratifications,[44] the obligation to designate all of these countries in the initial EP application does not entail additional costs. This is so, because the EPO prescribes a flat designation fee regardless of the number of designations[45] and subsequent national validation in states where unitary effect is not (yet) possible is optional. Any subsequent ratifications of the UPCA – and therefore a widening of the territorial scope of the following generations of UPs – will possibly only be reflected in the level of renewal fees five years from the entry into force of the UPCA, when the first adjustment of the UP fee structure is scheduled.[46]

Anyhow, it appears fair that for protection in – at the beginning – 17 states, patent holders would pay the equivalent of the renewal fees for the four participating Member States where classic EPs are most often validated (whatever that truly means). By contrast, it seems unjustified that a proprietor of a 'first generation UP' should pay the national renewal fees for protection in eg Ireland or Romania on top if it also wishes to also validate the patent there (in that case as a classic EP) whereas for later applicants these countries might also be included in the price already.

22.2.2.3 Who will use the system?

While in most of the other industrial sectors it is currently common to seek patent protection in no more than three or four European states, pharmaceutical companies are referred to as virtually the only companies that regularly seek pan-European patent protection.[47] Yet it is these very pharma firms, which could save a substantial amount of

---

the new system, 'Requests for delay in issuing the decisions to grant a European patent' and/or 'Early requests for unitary effect' could already be filed during the 'sunrise period', ie between the deposit of the German instrument of ratification and the entry into force of the UPCA, cf EPO, 'Supporting users in an early uptake of the Unitary Patent' <www.epo.org/applying/european/unitary/unitary-patent/transitional-arrangements-for-early-uptake.html> accessed 13 September 2022.
42 Poland participates in the enhanced cooperation but has not signed the UPCA to date.
43 Cf <www.consilium.europa.eu/de/documents-publications/treaties-agreements/agreement/?id=2013001> accessed 13 September 2022.
44 Cf art 3 UP Reg (n 2), rule 6 UPR (n 5) and EPO, *UP Guide* (n 5) para 44.
45 Cf at n 31.
46 Cf art 7 RFeesUPP (n 36).
47 Johnson (n 23) 189; McDonagh (n 22) 23.

money for translations and renewal fees by making use of UP protection, that will most likely not take up the new system. For big players in the pharmaceutical industry, the additional costs for a classic EP are not seen as a significant issue. In this perception, the difference in costs is outweighed by the legal security that is offered by the existing system, as opposed to the uncertainties associated with placing valuable patents under the jurisdiction of the newly founded UPC, notably with the risk of central revocation. It is therefore expected that the pharma sector will continue to rely on classic EPs and opt them out of UPC-jurisdiction, at least until a settled body of case law of the new court system – comprising various local and regional divisions as well as a central division and a Court of Appeal – has emerged.[48]

It will therefore most likely be smaller market players, who cannot afford the luxury of placing legal certainty over costs, that will be the first ones to apply for UP protection and test the new system. For these actors, the 'free lunch'[49] which represents the protection in a significant number of further states, as compared to the three or four European states for which protection is currently commonly sought, will arguably outweigh the fact that the abovementioned[50] practice of pruning an EP towards the end of patent life in order to reduce costs is not available for UPs.

22.2.2.4 The compensation scheme

An additional incentive for SMEs – whose situation is after all to be taken into account under art 12(2) UP Reg[51] when determining the level of the fees – was created in art 8ff UPR,[52] read in conjunction with art 4 RFeesUPP[53] according to which a lump sum of 500 euros is granted to, inter alia, natural persons or SMEs based in the EU if they filed their initial EP application in a language other than the three official languages of the EPO and thus had to produce a full translation[54] into English, French or German at the outset of the procedure.

22.2.2.5 Licenses of right

Moreover, renewal fees are reduced by 15 percent if a patentee files a statement on a license of right to be registered in the Register for UP protection with the EPO, ie that it is

---

48 Johnson (n 23) 189; McDonagh (n 22) 23.
49 Cf Johnson (n 23) 189.
50 At n 33.
51 N 2.
52 N 5.
53 N 36.
54 Cf at n 9.

prepared to non-exclusively license the invention to anyone in return for appropriate consideration.[55] This is intended to provide an incentive for patentees not to 'block' others from using their inventions and thus to facilitate follow-on innovation. However, compared to the 50 percent reduction from German national renewal fees granted for a license of right entered into the German patent register,[56] it seems that a more ambitious discount could have been adopted here.

In sum, regarding the UP's value for money, it seems that the Commission's initial goal to substantially decrease the astronomical costs of patent protection covering all – or at least the main part – of the EU's territory in order to incentivise investment in innovation and improve competitiveness with the cheaper US- and Japanese frameworks respectively,[57] has been more or less achieved. The most significant issue that remains in this regard (next to the truncated territorial scope of protection) is the optionality[58] of the new regime, so that those who can afford it may forego the lower costs in exchange for more legal certainty until a body of established case law by the UPC has been developed.

22.2.3 Duration of the granting procedure and temporal scope of protection

Another objective pursued with the initiative for a Community patent and later with that for an EU patent had been an acceleration of the granting process,[59] arguably in order to further incentivise investment in R&D. Since with the UP package a 'transformation approach' was adopted instead of a 'delegation approach' – to the effect that the EPO does not directly grant a UP on behalf of the EU but rather an EP is 'transformed' into a UP post-grant[60] – the average duration of the pre-grant phase for obtaining a UP will be the same as for classic EPs.[61] Given the need of an additional post-grant procedure in order to convert a European bundle patent (if applicable, partially) into a UP, the proceedings for grant even take slightly longer as compared to EPs, albeit a UP would be granted with retroactive effect to the date of publication of the mention of the grant of the EP on which it is based in the European Patent Bulletin.[62]

---

55 Art 12 UPR (n 5); art 3 RFeesUPP (n 36).
56 Cf § 23 PatG.
57 Commission, 'Enhancing the patent system in Europe' (Communication) COM(2007) 165 final 2f.
58 For other issues connected with this optionality, cf Hanns Ullrich, *National, European and Community Patent Protection: Time for Reconsideration* (EUI Working Paper LAW No 2006/41) 40.
59 Commission, 'Enhancing the patent system in Europe' (Communication) COM(2007) 165 final 12.
60 Lamping, 'Patentrecht' (n 20) 472.
61 EPO, *UP Guide* (n 5) para 19.
62 Recital 8 and art 4 UP Reg (n 2).

22.2.3.1 The EPO's improved timeliness

Due to recent endeavours by the EPO, however, such as the fast-track 'PACE'-program (participation in this program is free, but must be requested using EPO form 1005)[63] and subsequently the 'Early Certainty from Search'-initiative (which relates to all patent applications examined by the EPO[64] and the introduction of which therefore in turn led to a strong reduction in 'PACE'-requests),[65] the pre-grant phase has been significantly sped up in general. In cases where the claims of an EP application have already been deemed patentable by a so-called Office of Earlier Examination participating in a Patent Prosecution Highway (PPH) programme together with the EPO (eg in cases of international applications under the PCT entering the European phase), an additional acceleration of processing can be requested with EPO form 1009.[66]

22.2.3.2 The importance of patent quality

In spite of the improved timeliness,[67] the quality of patents granted by the EPO has seemingly not decreased. On the contrary, the EPO was elected number one among the world's five largest patent offices (referred to as the 'IP5', ie CNIPA, EPO, JPO, KIPO and USPTO) for the quality of its patents in 2021 for the twelfth time in a row in a survey conducted by Intellectual Asset Management Magazine (IAM).[68] Particularly the opposition system under the EPC is seen as an important feature to ensure the quality of patents in international comparison.[69]

Upholding a high quality of patents is important, because even if 'trivial', low quality patents can be challenged in opposition or revocation proceedings (which requires resources), once granted and unchallenged, they can be used like scarecrows to deter

---

[63] Notice from the European Patent Office dated 30 November 2015 concerning the programme for accelerated prosecution of European patent applications ('PACE'), OJ EPO 2015, A93; EPO, 'Changes to PACE programme from 1 January 2016' (1 January 2016) <www.epo.org/news-events/news/2016/20160101.html> accessed 13 September 2022.
[64] EPO, 'Improving timeliness' <www.epo.org/about-us/annual-reports-statistics/annual-report/2016/highlights/improving-timeliness.html> accessed 13 September 2022.
[65] Kur, Dreier and Luginbuehl (n 8) 119.
[66] EPO, 'Patent Prosecution Highway (PPH)' <www.epo.org/applying/international/patent-prosecution-highway.html> accessed 13 September 2022; WIPO, 'PCT-Patent Prosecution Highway Program (PCT-PPH and Global PPH)' (26 July 2022) <www.wipo.int/pct/en/filing/pct_pph.html> accessed 13 September 2022.
[67] For specific numbers cf EPO, *Annual Review 2021* (2022) 53.
[68] Cf EPO, *Annual Review 2021* (2022) 42.
[69] OECD, *Patents and Innovation: Trends and Policy Challenges* (2004) 28.

competitors and thereby impede follow-on innovation.[70] Similar considerations apply to low quality patent *information* published in the respective registry.[71]

Even if by and large, patents granted by the EPO are perceived to be of a rather high quality by international standards,[72] it seems important to maintain an effective possibility for 'private enforcement' of patent quality as a safety net for erroneous decisions of the office. It is thus to be hoped that the possibility of revocation of UPs in opposition proceedings, which – as compared to an action for revocation at the UPC[73] – is relatively cheap for interested third parties,[74] is not 'stricken down' by the CJEU once the system starts to operate. This could happen due to concerns that the EPO, as an authority located outside the complete system of judicial remedies in EU law ensured inter alia by arts 267 and 344 TFEU, may annul an EU law-based right in the time window where unitary effect has already been granted and the nine-month opposition period has not yet expired. It remains to be seen in this context whether the CJEU will accept the legal fiction contained in art 3(3) UP Reg,[75] according to which unitary effect 'shall be deemed not to have arisen to the extent that the European patent has been revoked or limited', and thus overlook this seemingly blatant violation of the autonomy of EU law.[76] If, however, the current design of opposition procedures were to be declared incompatible with the EU treaties by the CJEU, it would be important to provide for an equivalent alternative, as the possibility of bringing much more expensive revocation actions before the UPC alone cannot fulfil the function of private enforcement of patent quality.

---

[70] Reto M. Hilty and Christophe Geiger, 'Patenting Software? A Judicial and Socio-Economic Analysis' (2005) 36 IIC 615, 637, 640; Van Overwalle and van Zimmeren (n 3) 417.
[71] Cf Julian Pénin and Daniel Neicu, 'Patents and Open Innovation: Bad Fences Do Not Make Good Neighbours' (2018) 25 I-JIEM, 57, 64ff; Matthias Lamping et al, 'Declaration on Patent Protection – Regulatory Sovereignty under TRIPS' (2014) 45 IIC 679, 690; Hilty and Geiger (n 70) 634f; Ullrich, *National, European and Community Patent Protection* (n 58) 31f.
[72] Van Overwalle and van Zimmeren (n 3) 417.
[73] The fee for a revocation action at the UPC's Court of First Instance is 20.000 euros, cf R.47 Rules on Court fees and recoverable costs adopted by the Preparatory Committee for the UPC on 25 February 2016 (albeit in case of success, fees are recoverable by virtue of art 69 UPCA).
[74] The opposition fee at the EPO is currently 840 euros, cf art 2(1) No 10 Rules relating to Fees of 20 October 1977 as adopted by decision of the Administrative Council of the European Patent Organisation of 7 December 2006 and as last amended by decision of the Administrative Council of 15 December 2021, OJ EPO 2022, A2.
[75] N 2.
[76] Thomas Jaeger, 'Alternatives to the UP and the UPC' in Luc Desaunettes-Barbero, Fernand de Visscher, Alain Strowel and Vincent Cassiers (eds), *The Unitary Patent Package & Unified Patent Court: Problems, Possible Improvements and Alternatives* (Ledizioni 2023) 591, 598f); McMahon (n 6) 52.

22.2.3.3 The unheard call for a differentiated approach

Returning to the EPO's improved timeliness – besides, speed has also been increased with regard to opposition proceedings[77] – there is arguably no need to introduce patent term adjustments for the UP, as they have recently been inserted into Chinese, Japanese or Korean patent law for certain cases of non-culpable delays in the granting procedure.[78] On the contrary, depending on the industry-sector, an investment in innovation that has led to the grant of a patent might well be amortised long before the expiry of the maximum protection period of 20 years from the date of the filing of the application,[79] provided by art 63(1) EPC.[80]

Such 'temporal overprotection', which occurs when the investments made in the patent have already long been recouped, may diminish the competitive pressure necessary as an incentive for renewed investment in innovation and/or block cumulative innovation by third parties.[81] Even if a patent protects outdated technology, as might frequently be the case in sectors such as IT, where innovation cycles are short, it can still play a role in newer technologies and thus be instrumentalised as a blocking patent.[82] However, the UP package fails to address these economic realities.

Even if a reduction of the term of patent protection *per se* would currently run counter to art 33 TRIPS[83] (which generally provides for a term of patent protection of at least twenty years), this would arguably not have barred the legislator from laying down an attenuated (reduced) substantive scope of protection after a certain period of time has lapsed.[84] Contrary to what is envisaged in the UP package, the timespan after which a patent holder could, for instance, lose its right to injunctive relief[85] and be reduced to a claim for appropriate remuneration, should arguably differ according to the field of technology and be determined according to statistical surveys on the respective amortisation period of investment in R&D across the various industry sectors.

A limitation of this kind would not constitute a discrimination between different fields of technology, since under art 27(1) TRIPS,[86] differentiation based on objective cri-

---

77 For specific numbers cf EPO, *Annual Review 2021* (2022) 53.
78 EPO, 'Speeding up the patent granting process – Patent term adjustments on their way through Asia' (25 October 2021) <www.epo.org/searching-for-patents/helpful-resources/patent-knowledge-news/2021/20211025b.html> accessed 13 September 2022.
79 Reto M. Hilty and Thomas Jaeger, 'Gesamtanalyse und Erkenntnisse' in Hilty and Jaeger (n 1) 665, 673f.
80 Art 63(1) also applies to the UP, as the latter *is* an EP to which unitary effect is awarded post-grant, cf Art 2(c) UP Reg (n 2); Case C-146/13 *Spain v Parliament and Council* [2015] ECLI:EU:C:2015:298, para 29.
81 Hilty and Jaeger (n 79) 673f.
82 Hilty and Jaeger (n 79) 674.
83 Agreement on Trade-Related Aspects of Intellectual Property Rights [1994] OJ L 336/214.
84 Hilty and Jaeger (n 79) 675; OECD (n 71) 6.
85 Cf Matthias Lamping, 'Ergänzender Leistungs- und Investitionsschutz' in Hilty and Jaeger (n 1) 174, 174.
86 N 83.

teria is permitted.[87] Furthermore, the suggested arrangement could be designed to pass the three-step-test provided for by Art 30 TRIPS,[88] which subjects limitations of patent protection to a proportionality requirement: Arguably, a rule of this kind would be 'limited' for the purpose of the first step of the test, ie it would not go beyond what is necessary to achieve its aim of facilitating cumulative innovation. Also, the patent holder would retain its marketing opportunities by and large, since the scope of protection would only be reduced once investments are regularly already amortised in the respective sector. Thus, the second step of the test seems to be met, according to which an exception may not 'unreasonably conflict with a normal exploitation of the patent', ie it must not render illusory the chances of recouping the patent holder's investment. As its chances of amortisation would be maintained, the patent proprietor's interests would also not be outweighed by the benefits of potential users under the third step of the test, which requires that an exception does not 'unreasonably prejudice the legitimate interests of the patent owner, taking into account of the legitimate interests of third parties'.[89]

22.2.3.4 The UP and SPCs

While, as was just shown, an undifferentiated term of patent protection could be dysfunctional in terms of promoting innovation in certain sectors (like IT) requiring only low investments or having typically short amortisation periods,[90] other sectors show the opposite picture: Particularly in the pharmaceutical sector, investments in R&D can regularly be comparatively high and product testing and market authorisation can take a considerable amount of time.[91] Against this background, it is possible to extend the term of patent protection of medicinal products and pesticides subject to a market authorisation procedure with SPCs for a period of up to five additional years.[92]

However, while it is theoretically already possible to use a UP as a basic patent for national SPCs with the respective limited territorial scope of protection, there are no provisions for a 'unitary SPC' yet. Still, meanwhile the Commission has tabled four proposals for regulations for both unitary SPCs and a single, unified procedure for obtaining a bundle of national SPCs for pharmaceutical and plant protection products respec-

---

87 Hilty and Jaeger (n 79) 675.
88 N 83.
89 Lamping et al, 'Declaration on Patent Protection' (n 71) 687f; Lamping, 'Ergänzender Leistungs- und Investitionsschutz' (n 85) 179.
90 At n 81.
91 Hilty and Jaeger (n 79) 674.
92 Cf art 2 and art 13 Regulation (EC) No 469/2009 of the European Parliament and of the Council of 6 May 2009 concerning the supplementary protection certificate for medicinal products (Codified version) [2009] OJ L152/1.

tively, according to which, curiously enough, the EUIPO (which has so far only dealt with trade marks and designs) will act as the central granting authority.[93] The option of receiving a bundle of national SPCs in a single procedure before the EUIPO, which has been proposed by the Commission, is unfortunate, as if the future possibility of obtaining SPCs after a centralised procedure would have been restricted to UPs as basic patents, this would have provided an additional incentive for pharmaceutical and herbicide companies to utilise the UP system, since, as stated above,[94] it is currently expected that big pharma players will stay with classic EPs and opt them out of the UPC's jurisdiction, at least until uncertainties about the new court chambers' attitudes and viewpoints are clarified by the emergence of settled case law.[95]

22.2.4 Uncertainties regarding the law applicable to the UPC as an object of property

While insecurities of the kind just mentioned are inherent in the establishment of a new court system and might be resolved over time, other ambiguities vested in the system will likely not disappear by themselves. An important example is the question of the applicable law to a UP as an object of property, which harbours uncertainties that could have been avoided in the drafting of the currently ambiguous art 7 UP Reg.[96] For these issues, including inter alia the conditions for the transfer of a UP, its use as a security or its fate in enforcement proceedings,[97] art 7(1)(a) UP Reg[98] declares applicable the national law of the Member State having ratified the UPCA[99] where 'the applicant had its residence or principal place of business on the date of filing of the application for the European patent', *'according to the European Patent Register'* (emphasis added). It is neither clear from the wording whether a registered office or a possibly unregistered, administrative seat is referred to here, nor can the applicable national law be unequivocally determined in cases where the entry in the register differs from the true state of affairs.[100] The same holds true for art 7(1)(b) UP Reg[101] which applies subsidiarily to

---

93 <ec.europa.eu/commission/presscorner/detail/en/qanda_23_2455> accessed 23 May 2023.
94 At n 47.
95 Johnson (n 23) 189; McDonagh (n 22) 23.
96 N 2.
97 Tilman Müller-Stoy and Florian Paschold, 'European patent with unitary effect as a property right' (2014) 9 JIPLP 848, 856f; Hanns Ullrich, *The Property Aspects of the European Patent with Unitary Effect: A National Perspective for a European Prospect?* (Max Planck Institute for Intellectual Property and Competition Law Research Paper No 13–17) 6; Jaeger, 'Alternatives to the UP and the UPC' (n 76) 595.
98 N 2.
99 The exact wording is '[it] shall be treated in its entirety and in all the participating Member States as a national patent of the participating Member State *in which that patent has unitary effect*' (emphasis added), cf Müller-Stoy and Paschold (n 97) 851.
100 Müller-Stoy and Paschold (n 97) 855.

art 7(1)(a) and refers to the national law of the Member State having ratified the UPCA[102] where the applicant had '*a* place of business' (emphasis added) at the relevant time, thus *any* place of business, in turn, 'according to the European Patent Register'. In cases of joint applicants, the situation of the applicant indicated first on the application is decisive.[103] Subsidiarily to all these situations, German law applies.[104] Given that each year, more than 80 percent of EP applications are filed by applicants seated either outside of the 'UP territory' or in Germany, it is expected that German law will apply to most UPs as objects of property.[105]

It has been convincingly argued in literature that in all other cases, most likely only the place of business appearing in the European Patent Register is relevant in the interest of legal certainty.[106] For the situation referred to in art 7(2)(b) UP Reg[107] an option to indicate *a* seat of business in a Member State having ratified the UPCA to be published in the Register for UP protection (which is part of the European Patent Register)[108] was especially introduced in rule 16(1)(w) UPR,[109] as there has previously been no need for the publication of such information. However, the interpretation according to which solely the entry in the register is relevant is but one of the approaches the UPC might take in this respect. This is also acknowledged by the EPO, which indicates in its *UP Guide* that the patentee 'must take care to provide the correct information […]. This is not only relevant for the proprietor but also for third parties, for whom incorrect information may have adverse legal consequences.'[110]

22.2.4.1 Disadvantages of the available interpretative options

Arguably, the interpretation referred to above[111] is prone to abuse and comes down to a free choice of the applicable law if the EPO does not increase the requirements for proof that the information indicated on the application is correct.[112] However, also the other possible interpretation, according to which the true state of affairs is decisive, has a significant downside, namely that when it comes to litigation, patent proprietors could proceed

---

101 N 2.
102 Cf n 99.
103 Art 7(2) UP Reg (n 2).
104 Art 7 (3) UP Reg (n 2).
105 Müller-Stoy and Paschold (n 97) 851; Thomas Jaeger, 'Das BGB als gesamteuropäisches Innovationsgesetz?' (2012) 68 JZ 1070, 1071; EPO, *Patent Index 2021 – Statistics at a glance* (2022) 3.
106 Müller-Stoy and Paschold (n 97) 855.
107 N 2.
108 Cf art 2(e) UP Reg (n 2).
109 N 5.
110 EPO, *UP Guide* (n 5) para 55.
111 At n 106.
112 Müller-Stoy and Paschold (n 97) 855.

tactically as regards the revelation of the 'truly' applicable law.[113] Whichever interpretation the UPC will follow, in both cases the choice of the preferred law could also effectively be achieved by mandating a trusted third party established in the respective state to file the patent application and subsequently transfer it to the economic owner, should one of the available jurisdictions turn out to be particularly attractive for UP proprietors.[114]

22.2.4.2 Impact on patent value

Trading partners to whom a UP is transferred or licensed need to know what the law is, eg concerning the questions whether a license is furnished with an *erga omnes* effect, which formal requirements apply to transfer of ownership etc.[115] Even if the applicable law is clear because the registered and administrative seats of the patentee were identical at the time of the application and were also correctly indicated to the EPO, the answers to these questions are often enough hidden in the general civil code of the respective country or even in case law.[116] Accordingly, depending on how simply and/or favourably these issues are regulated in the available legal regimes, the law applicable to a UP as an object of property might have a positive or negative effect on its value.[117] Also, since patents are typically licensed or transferred in packages covering a technology, when such a package is compiled by acquiring patents from different owners, the possible diversity of the applicable legal regimes may cause problems.[118] In this context, the expected predominance of German law as the applicable statute[119] could lead to 'German UPs' being regarded as the 'gold standard', adversely affecting the value of all other UPs. These uncertainties may disincentivise the utilisation of the new system and therefore – albeit admittedly very indirectly – constitute an obstacle to investment in R&D.

22.2.4.3 Which alternatives would have been available?

The disadvantages referred to above could have been easily avoided if a similar approach as in the EU Trademark Reg,[120] the Community Design Reg[121] or the Community

---

113 Müller-Stoy and Paschold (n 97) 854.
114 Müller-Stoy and Paschold (n 97) 855.
115 Ullrich, *Property Aspects* (n 97) 8f.
116 Ullrich, *Property Aspects* (n 97) 8f.
117 Ullrich, *Property Aspects* (n 97) 10f.
118 Ullrich, *Property Aspects* (n 97) 11.
119 Cf at n 104.
120 Regulation (EU) 2017/1001 of the European Parliament and of the Council of 14 June 2017 on the European Union trade mark (codification) [2017] OJ L154/1.
121 Council Regulation (EC) 6/2002 of 12 December 2001 on Community designs [2002] OJ L3/1.

Plant Variety Rights Reg[122] had been adopted. As in these regulations, some of the most important questions in this context could have been directly addressed in the UP Reg[123] or the UPCA, leaving only their implementation in detail to national law,[124] such as guarantees that the UP *is* subject to insolvency or levy in execution[125] or rules on the position of licensees with regard to standing in infringement proceedings.[126] Furthermore, as laid out above,[127] the approach taken in the UP Reg[128] of leaving the legal system relevant for questions concerning the UP as an object of property unchanged throughout the entire lifespan of the patent arguably causes more problems than it contributes to legal certainty. Instead, one could have opted for the position that the EU Trade Mark Reg, the Community Design Reg and the Community Plant Variety Rights Reg take in this regard, namely that with a change of seat or ownership, the applicable national law changes according to the seat of the current owner.[129] This would have at least solved the issue of patent packages whose components are subject to different legal regimes and prevent the emergence of different values for UPs depending on the national law applicable to them. The necessary legal certainty could have been achieved by introducing an obligation of patentees to file an information on transfers of UPs as well as transfers of seat with the EPO to be published in the register, as such events are currently only entered in the register at the request of an interested party.[130] As an accompanying measure, effects vis-à-vis third parties could have been made conditional on such entries, unless the person concerned knew of the transfer.[131]

22.3 Interim conclusion

The first part of this contribution analysed and assessed whether or not the UP legal framework provides for easy, inexpensive, fast and legally secure access to patentability in

---

122 Council Regulation (EC) 2100/94 of 27 July 1994 on Community plant variety rights [1994] OJ L227/1.
123 N 2.
124 Ullrich, *Property Aspects* (n 97) 6f.
125 Cf arts 23 and 24 EU Trade Mark Reg (n 120), arts 30 and 31 Community Design Reg (n 121) and arts 24 and 25 Community Plant Variety Rights Reg (n 122).
126 Cf art 25(3) EU Trade Mark Reg (n 120) and art 32(2) Community Design Reg (n 121).
127 At n 118.
128 N 2.
129 Cf art 19(1) EU Trade Mark Reg (n 120), art 27(1) Community Design Reg (n 121) and art 22(1) Community Plant Variety Rights Reg (n 122).
130 Cf EPO, *UP Guide* (n 5) para 114; rule 22 Implementing Regulations to the Convention on the Grant of European Patents of 5 October 1973 as adopted by decision of the Administrative Council of the European Patent Organisation of 7 December 2006 and as last amended by decision of the Administrative Council of the European Patent Organisation of 15 December 2020, OJ EPO 2020, A132.
131 Cf art 27 EU Trade Mark Reg (n 120), art 33 Community Design Reg (n 121) and 23(4) Community Plant Variety Rights Reg (n 122).

order to promote investment in R&D. The picture that unfolded based on this analysis is by and large positive. In terms of easy access, the replacement of the national validation procedures for EPs with the centralised proceedings for obtaining unitary effect as well as the rationalisation of the payment of renewal fees can be mentioned in favour of the UP system. Concerning timeliness, the status quo, which is by no means bad, remains unchanged.

However, there are also some aspects that still call for improvement. For instance, we have identified shortcomings in the areas of value for money and legal certainty. From a cost-benefit perspective, it is an issue that the territorial coverage of a UP is dependent on the status of ratifications of the UPCA at the time the request for unitary effect is granted and then remains frozen for the entire patent life. Even if additional Member States become available for UP protection during the term of the patent, patentees will thus still have to pay the respective national renewal fees on top. As regards legal security, besides the uncertainties associated with the establishment of a new court system, ambiguities regarding the national law applicable to the UP as an object of property remain that are a cause for concern for both patent holders and third parties.

Yet, the question raised in the title as to whether the UP legal framework truly constitutes a 'system fit for innovation' can only be answered after a more comprehensive analysis, including an assessment of the exceptions and limitations to the substantive scope of UP protection that promote cumulative innovation. A definite answer to that question is thus reserved for the second part of this contribution, which deals specifically with the latter issue.

Thomas Jaeger, Johannes Lukan
23 A system fit for innovation? Part II: (Dis-)advantages for follow-on inventors in the UP legal framework

23.1 Introduction

The first part of this contribution has been concerned with the question of whether the UP legal framework provides for easy, fast, legally secure and inexpensive access to patents with a solid breadth of protection. However, as was already indicated therein at the outset, these qualities alone do not suffice for a patent system to truly deserve the label 'fit for innovation', regardless of how well it performs in these fields. Much rather, it must also ensure access to patentable knowledge for follow-on research, including so-called dependent or cumulative innovation[1] (eg enhancements of earlier generations of technologies). This second part of the paper is dedicated to some of the various tools that are available in that respect. These instruments range from the disclosure requirement as a procedural obligation to excluding certain subject matter from patentability or limiting the scope of patent protection, thus allowing either free or remunerated (compulsory licensing) use of already patented inventions in the respective field or for the respective purpose (eg for research activities).[2]

It is evident that in this matter one person's joy is another one's sorrow: While it is important to keep patentability or the scope of patent protection limited and balanced to encourage follow-on innovation, care must be taken not to unduly diminish the incentives for potential patentees to invest in R&D in the first place.[3]

---

[1] Cf eg Matthias Leistner, 'Towards an Access Paradigm in Innovation Law?' (2021) 70 GRUR Int 925, 926; Alberto Galasso and Mark Schankerman, 'Patents and Cumulative Innovation: Causal Evidence from The Courts' (2015) 130 QJE 317, 317ff; Steven Anderman, 'A Competition Law Perspective II: The Relationship between Patents and Competition Rules' in Justine Pila and Christopher Wadlow (eds), *The Unitary EU Patent System* (Hart 2015) 129, 137.
[2] Cf Geertrui Van Overwalle and Esther Van Zimmeren, 'Functions and Limits of Patent Law' in Erik Claes, Wouter Devroe and Bert Keirsbilck (eds), Facing the Limits of the Law (Springer 2009) 415, 417f.
[3] Zhiqian Wan and Samuel Meng, 'A Case for a Limited Breeding Exemption from Patent Protection' (2018) 49 IIC 636, 645; Anderman (n 1) 138; OECD, *Patents and Innovation: Trends and Policy Challenges* (2004) 10.

Thomas Jaeger, Professor of European Law, University of Vienna.
Johannes Lukan, University Assistant (prae doc) at the Department of European, International and Comparative Law, University of Vienna.

Ultimately, this second part of the contribution will therefore seek to examine whether the UP and its surrounding legal framework succeed in striking a fair balance between these two interests. Can the new[4] rules claim the label 'fit for innovation', because they reconcile protecting patented 'senior' innovation and facilitating 'junior innovation' better than the existing legal framework that applies to 'classic' EPs?[5] The starting hypothesis is that they cannot. In the following, we will thus scrutinise the initial assumption that the UP framework provides for an imbalance between an excessively broad scope of patent protection as opposed to overly limited exceptions, corresponding to a general trend in IP law towards overprotection that could be observed over the last four decades.[6] If specific deficiencies are detected, suggestions for improvement will be made.

23.2 Substantive scope of protection and applicable limitations – a functional balance?

Just as regarding the treatment of a UP as an object of property, which constituted one of the main topics of the first part of this paper, the UP Reg[7] refers to national law also concerning the substantive scope of UP protection[8] and its limitations. According to art 5(3) UP Reg,[9] the rights conferred on a UP proprietor 'shall be those defined by the law [...] in the participating Member State whose national law is applicable to the European patent with unitary effect as an object of property'.[10] In fact, however, the only important issue that is truly left to that statute apart from the questions pertaining to the UP as an object

---

4 Although the UP Reg (Regulation [EU] 1257/2012 of the European Parliament and of the Council of 17 December 2012 implementing enhanced cooperation in the area of the creation of unitary patent protection [2012] OJ L361/1) and the Language Reg (Council Regulation [EU] 1260/2012 of 17 December 2012 implementing enhanced cooperation in the area of the creation of unitary patent protection with regard to the applicable translation arrangements [2012] OJ L361/89) already formally came into force in early 2013, their applicability was only triggered by the entry into force of the UPCA on 1st June 2023, which took place on the first day of the fourth month after the deposit of the German instrument of ratification to the UPCA, cf UPC, 'The Provisional Application Phase and the UPC's expected timeline' (6 April 2022) <www.unified-patent-court.org/news/provisional-application-phase-and-upcs-expected-timeline> accessed 13 September 2022.
5 This terminology is inspired by Wan and Meng (n 3) 645f.
6 OECD (n 3) 17f; Matthias Lamping et al, 'Declaration on Patent Protection – Regulatory Sovereignty under TRIPS' (2014) 45 IIC 679 (681).
7 N 4.
8 In this contribution, this and similar terms are used exclusively to refer to the 'rights conferred' by a UP. For the technical distinction between the 'protection which is conferred' and the 'rights which are conferred' by a patent cf *Mobil Oil* [1989] EPO Enlarged Board of Appeal G 2/88, OJ EPO 1990, 93, para 3.2.
9 N 4.
10 Art 5(3) UP Reg (n 4).

of property is probably the applicable law on damages and compensation in cases of infringement. This is so because the material coverage of protection is indirectly governed by arts 25ff UPCA, which have to be implemented by all the contracting states having ratified the agreement.

The latter provisions form the main topic of the second part of this contribution, as the answer to the question of whether or not the UP legal framework provides for an overprotection of patentees' interests to the detriment of follow-on innovation heavily depends on the material breadth of UP protection. Some other questions pertaining to this balance have already been dealt with in the first part of this contribution, eg where a discount on renewal fees available to patentees offering a license of right was noted[11] or where a differentiated approach was advocated, according to which the substantive scope of patent protection would be reduced over time, depending on the amortisation of investments in a given industry sector.[12] This second part of the paper will now address questions of substantive patent law concerning the aforementioned balance – and ultimately the UP system's fitness for innovation. In this context, issues of patentability, which belong here for the sake of completeness, will be kept brief, while the main focus will lie on limitations to patent protection that relate to the promotion of follow-on innovation.

23.2.1 No changes with regard to patentability?

Like other issues pertaining to the shape of the right, the question of patentability too has a bearing on the functionality of the patent regime and the balance between protecting existing patents and facilitating cumulative innovation. When inventions in a given field of technology are considered patentable in principle, the prospect of obtaining patents might on the one hand arguably incentivise investments in R&D. On the other hand, the mere risk of patent infringements and the associated costs might at the same time have a deterrent effect to research.[13]

The UP package does not address patentability due to the UP's accessory nature[14] and thus leaves this issue to the EPC. A chance has been missed here to induce more clarity and thereby to consolidate currently divergent application of arts 52ff EPC. At present, numerous substantial divergences in the interpretation of the requirements of

---

11 At n 55 thereof.
12 At n 84 thereof.
13 Reto M. Hilty and Christophe Geiger, 'Patenting Software? A Judicial and Socio-Economic Analysis' (2005) 36 IIC 615, 633; Richard Gold and Yann Joly, 'The Patent System and Research Freedom: A Comparative Study' (WIPO, Doc. SCP/15/3, 2010, Annex VI) 6.
14 Cf Recital 7 UP Reg (n 4). The EPO does not directly grant a UP, but rather an EP is converted into a UP post-grant.

protection (eg the criteria of novelty and inventive step)[15] or the reach of exceptions from patentability (eg whether the exclusion of 'essentially biological processes for the production of plants or animals'[16] from patent eligibility also extends to products obtained therewith)[17] exist between the EPO's boards of appeal, national courts and legislators as well as the EU institutions. The current system does nothing to improve this situation and to establish a truly homogeneous body of patent law across the 'UP territory'.

23.2.2 A case for a purpose-bound compound protection

Between patentability on the one hand and the substantive scope of patent protection (ie limitations) on the other lies the question of whether UP-applicants should be able to obtain absolute protection for previously unknown or previously unmanufacturable isolated biological material or chemical substances, or conversely, whether purpose-bound protection for the respective use of the compound would be more appropriate. As laid out above,[18] the UP package leaves the determination of the possible subject matter of a patent to the EPC, which, in turn, does not take a clear stance on this issue.[19] The law is certain only with regard to DNA-sequences, the patentability of which is subject to an indication of the functions they perform under the CJEU's interpretation of the EU Biotechnology Dir,[20] which was (as a consequence of the obligation of the EU Member States to bring EPC practice in line with EU law) also taken over by the EPO.[21] Consequently, the protection conferred by such a patent is likewise limited to DNA sequences that, in the material in which they are incorporated, perform the functions indicated in the patent specifications.[22]

---

15 For the different approaches of the EPO and the German courts concerning the so-called 'doctrine of inherency', cf Markus Ackermann, 'Die „inhärente" Trennlinie zwischen BGH und EPA' (2022) 124 GRUR 683ff; cf also *Mobil Oil* [1989] EPO Enlarged Board of Appeal G 2/88, OJ EPO 1990, 93, para 10.1.
16 Art 4(1) Directive 98/44/EC of the European Parliament and of the Council of 6 July 1998 on the legal protection of biotechnological inventions [1998] OJ L 213/13.
17 Cf Christopher Then, *Technical briefing: How should the exclusions in Article 53(b) be interpreted to make them effective* (Discussion paper for 'No Patents on Seeds!', February 2017) 1ff; Rudolf Kraßer, 'Die Rote Taube wird 50 – zur Entwicklung des Patentschutzes von Verfahren zur Züchtung von Pflanzen und Tieren' (2018) 67 GRUR Int 1138, 1144ff. Meanwhile, the EPO's Enlarged Board of Appeal has reversed its controversial position on the patentability of plants derived from conventional breeding, albeit notably without retroactive effect on pending EP applications, cf *Pepper* [2020] EPO Enlarged Board of Appeal G 3/19, OJ EPO 2020, A119, paras XVIIIff, XXIX.
18 At n 14.
19 Pedro Henrique D. Batista and Adrian Gautschi, 'Stoffschutz' in Reto M. Hilty and Thomas Jaeger (eds) *Europäisches Immaterialgüterrecht* (Springer 2018) 407, 421.
20 N 16.
21 Cf Matthias Lamping, 'Weiterentwicklungen' in Hilty and Jaeger (n 19) 464, 487f.
22 Case C-428/08 *Monsanto v Cefetra* [2010] ECLI:EU:C:2010:402, para 43ff.

As regards patents on chemical substances, however, different interpretations of the EPC remain possible.[23] In this field, the EPO and its boards of appeal[24] as well as, prominently, the German BGH[25] have so far decided in favour of an 'absolute compound protection'.

This approach has been criticised in literature, as where an invention can have multiple functions or uses, some of them unknown at the time when a patent is granted, affording absolute protection to the 'first comer'[26] may disincentivise third parties to perform further research in order to detect unknown characteristics of the substance in question and put them to new uses.[27] Provided that chemical compound protection was indeed absolute, 'second comers' could only apply for dependent patents for any further innovative applications of the substance developed by them.[28] If the patent proprietor then proves unwilling to grant a license, they might not be able to commercialise their invention at all, as the conditions for 'compulsory dependency licenses'[29] under art 31 TRIPS[30] include, among others, the high threshold that the second invention 'shall involve an important technical advance of considerable economic significance'. In contrast, there appears to be very limited causal contribution by the patentee when a patented substance is used by third parties for new, previously unexpected purposes. By being able to claim royalties for such uses that it could never have expected, the patent proprietor is overcompensated with an additional reward that arguably goes beyond what is necessary to promote the original investment in R&D.[31]

In the absence of any guidance from both the UP Reg[32] and the UPCA, the interpretation of the relevant provisions of the EPC continues to be controversial. It remains open

---

23 Pedro Henrique D. Batista, 'Grundrechtliche Dimension des Stoffschutzes' in Hilty and Jaeger (n 19) 421, 432.
24 *Mobil Oil* [1989] EPO Enlarged Board of Appeal G 2/88, OJ EPO 1990, 93, para 5.
25 BGH GRUR 1972, 541, 544 – Imidazoline.
26 This terminology is inspired by Esther van Zimmeren and Geertrui Van Overwalle, 'A Paper Tiger? Compulsory License Regimes for Public Health in Europe' (2011) 42 IIC 4, 21.
27 Batista and Gautschi (n 19) 409; Batista (n 23) 431; Matthias Lamping, 'Ergänzender Leistungs- und Investitionsschutz' in Hilty and Jaeger (n 19) 174, 176f identifying this as an issue also with cross-sectional technologies like nanotechnology; Lamping et al, 'Declaration on Patent Protection' (n 9) 685f; Götting, 'Kritische Bemerkungen zum absoluten Stoffschutz' (2009) 111 GRUR 256ff; Geertrui Van Overwalle, 'The Implementation of the Biotechnology Directive in Belgium and its After-Effects. The Introduction of a New Research Exemption and a Compulsory Licence for Public Health' (2006) 37 IIC 889, 903; as regards specifically the first medical indication of a substance, Frederik Fortmann, *Der Patentschutz von neuen Wirkungen bei bereits bekannter Verwendung* (Springer 2021) 100ff.
28 Batista (n 23) 426.
29 This formulation is inspired by Matthias Leistner, 'The Requirements for Compulsory Dependency Licenses: Learning from the Transformative Use Doctrine in Copyright Law' in Reto M Hilty and Kung-Chung Liu (eds), *Compulsory Licensing: Practical Experiences and Ways Forward* (Springer 2013) 221.
30 Agreement on Trade-Related Aspects of Intellectual Property Rights [1994] OJ L 336/214.
31 Lamping, 'Ergänzender Leistungs- und Investitionsschutz' (n 27).
32 N 4.

what the UPC will do in this regard, ie whether it will follow the EPO's stance of an absolute compound protection in infringement actions or whether it will open yet another line of divergent jurisprudence to the advantage of follow-on innovation.

Suggestions have been made to improve this unsatisfactory status quo: The most far-reaching option for the UP system would have been to explicitly restrict compound protection to the function(s) indicated in the patent application.[33] An option that would have also accommodated patent holders would have been to grant the patentee a grace period during which it enjoys absolute protection and can extend the claims to further functions of the compound detected during that period. After the expiry of such a period, the patent proprietor would be left with purpose-bound protection until the end of the patent term.[34]

23.2.2.1 How could such adaptions be made?

In terms of practical feasibility, however, any of these proposals would require an amendment, respectively a clarification of the patentability criteria under the EPC or its Implementing Regulations[35] (provided that the UP's accessory nature[36] was to remain untouched). This would require at least a three-quarters majority of the delegates of the 38 EPC member states in the EPO's Administrative Council, if one opts for the minimal variant of merely amending the Implementing Regulations,[37] as was done when the Biotechnology Dir[38] was incorporated into the EPC – a politically questionable approach.[39]

Alternatively, a limitation of the substantive scope of patent protection could have been (and could yet be) introduced in the UP Reg,[40] the UPCA or via a separate an EU directive, to be implemented only in the UP territory or in the EU as a whole respectively. Since the EPC delegates the determination of the rights conferred on a patentee and the exceptions therefrom on its state parties,[41] the EU is thus competent to legislate instead of its Member States based on the internal market clause of art 114 TFEU.[42] As regards

---

33 Batista (n 23) 431f.
34 Similarly, Batista (n 23) 432.
35 Implementing Regulations to the Convention on the Grant of European Patents of 5 October 1973 as adopted by decision of the Administrative Council of the European Patent Organisation of 7 December 2006 and as last amended by decision of the Administrative Council of the European Patent Organisation of 15 December 2020, OJ EPO 2020, A132.
36 Cf n 14.
37 N 35.
38 N 16.
39 Lamping, 'Weiterentwicklungen' (n 21) 487.
40 N 4.
41 Cf art 64 EPC.
42 Both the Biotechnology Dir (n 16) and Directive 2004/27/EC of the European Parliament and of the Council of 31 March 2004 amending Directive 2001/83/EC on the Community code relating to medicinal

the content of such a limitation, it could, for example, provide that 'the rights conferred on a patent proprietor do not extend to the use of a patented substance for purposes which were not part of the state of the art at the time the patent was granted'. The UPC would be bound to apply such a limitation, either as part of the national law governing the rights a UP confers on its proprietor according to art 5(3) UP Reg[43] (in case of a directive, once it is implemented), or simply as 'Union law', which is, curiously, even mentioned before the agreement itself among the sources that the UPC 'shall base its decisions on' according to art 24 UPCA. Unfortunately, the hierarchy between these two legal sources (the UP Reg[44] and the UPCA) in their application by the UPC remains unclear.[45]

23.2.3 The applicable limitations – more of the same

As regards the exceptions to patent protection that are actually contained in art 27 UPCA, a well-known picture unfolds. Instead of modernising patent law to render it fit for innovation in the 21st century, the UPCA perpetuates a conservative, backward-looking approach known from older national patent acts.

23.2.3.1 Limitations stemming from the CPCs

Most of the UPCA's limitations, in particular the 'private use exception' under art 27(a) UPCA and the 'general research exception' under art 27(b) UPCA, had already been included in the failed drafts for the 1st and 2nd Community Patent Convention (CPCs) of 1975[46] and 1989.[47] Consequently, at least the 'older' EU Member States had already voluntarily incorporated them into national legislation in order to prepare for accession to these conventions.[48] This does not mean, however, that these provisions were imple-

---

products for human use [2004] OJ L136/34, which introduced the 'Bolar exception' into EU law, were based on what is art 114 TFEU today.
43 N 4.
44 N 4.
45 Thomas Jaeger, 'Alternatives to the UP and the UPC' in Luc Desaunettes-Barbero, Fernand de Visscher, Alain Strowel and Vincent Cassiers (eds), The Unitary Patent Package & Unified Patent Court: Problems, Possible Improvements and Alternatives (Ledizioni 2023) 591, 594f.
46 Cf art 31 Convention for the European Patent for the Common Market (Community Patent Convention) [1976] OJ L 17/1.
47 Cf art 27 Agreement relating to Community patents [1989] OJ L 401/1.
48 Wan and Meng (n 3) 642; Christopher Wadlow, 'Hamlet without the prince: Can the Unitary Patent Regulation strut its stuff without Articles 6–8?' (2013) 8 JIPLP 207, 208–211; Lionel Bently, 'Introduction' (WIPO, Doc. SCP/15/3, 2010, Annex I) 34; Lamping, 'Ergänzender Leistungs- und Investitionsschutz' (n 27) 182; Thomas Jaeger and Matthias Lamping 'Fehlstellungen im europäischen Recht' in Hilty and Jaeger

mented in the same terms across those Member States. Linguistic deviations from the CPCs' 'model limitations' existed from the outset.[49] In some cases, model exceptions were also subsequently amended after national regulatory autonomy had been restored with the failure of the CPCs.[50] Accordingly, the respective provisions are interpreted differently in the judicial practice of the different Member States.[51]

23.2.3.2 Limitations stemming from EU directives

Other limitations included in art 27 UPCA stem from EU directives, such as the 'Bolar exception' under art 27(d) UPCA,[52] the 'farmer's privilege' concerning plants and animals under art 27(i) and (j) UPCA[53] as well as the exhaustion of rights with regard to patented self-replicating biological material where its multiplication or propagation necessarily results from the application for which the biological material was marketed, according to art 27(l) UPCA.[54] Nevertheless, this does not mean that *these* exceptions have previously been fully harmonised in the Member States either. Particularly with regard to the Bolar exception, gold plating has apparently occurred in some Member States,[55] which will be discussed in more detail below.[56]

Finally, the only exceptions contained in art 27 UPCA that have not yet been included as limitations to the rights of patentees *per se* in the CPCs[57] or EU directives so far are the 'decompilation exception' for software under art 27(k) UPCA and the 'breeder's privilege' concerning plants under art 27(c) UPCA. However, these limitations are not truly new to EU (related) regulation either, as the decompilation exception had already

---

(n 19) 191, 192; Holzapfel, 'Die patentrechtliche Zulässigkeit der Benutzung von Forschungswerkzeugen (2006) 108 GRUR 10, 11.
49 Wadlow (n 48) 209–211;
50 Gold and Joly (n 13) 30; Van Overwalle (n 27) 905ff.
51 Wadlow (n 48) 209–211.
52 Cf art 10(6) Directive 2001/83/EC of the European Parliament and of the Council of 6 November 2001 on the Community code relating to medicinal products for human use [2001] OJ L 311/67 as amended by Directive 2004/27/EC (n 42).
53 Cf art 11 Biotechnology Dir (n 16); Denis Borges Barbosa and Karin Grau-Kuntz, 'Exclusions from Patentable Subject Matter and Exceptions and Limitations to the Rights' (WIPO, Doc. SCP/15/3, 2010, Annex III) 64f; Van Overwalle (n 27) 904; Jaeger and Lamping (n 48) 202f.
54 Cf art 10 Biotechnology Dir (n 16); Barbosa and Grau-Kuntz (n 53) 53f, 64; Richard Gold and Alain Gallochat, 'The European Biotech Directive: Past as Prologue' (2001) 7 ELJ 331, 346.
55 Cf Hans-Rainer Jaenichen and Johann Pitz, *Research Exemption/Experimental Use in the European Union: Patents Do Not Block the Progress of Science* (Cold Spring Harb Perspect Med 2015) 6ff; Esther Pfaff, '"Bolar" Exemptions – A Threat to the Research Tool Industry in the U. S. and the EU?' (2007) 38 IIC 258, 271ff.
56 At n 72.
57 N 46–47.

existed as a limitation to the copyright of software producers in the Software Dir.[58] The breeder's privilege had already similarly[59] been laid down as an exception from the rights of proprietors of plant variety rights in the Community Plant Variety Rights Reg[60] as well as in the national law of individual Member States, such as Germany, which already explicitly provide for a breeder's exception as a limitation of the rights of patent holders in their national patent acts.[61] In this context, the UPCA thus merely ensures that what is permitted under plant variety rights and copyright law cannot be prohibited under the cloak of patent law.

The first conclusion that must be drawn with regard to the limitations contained in art 27 UPCA is therefore that old wine in new skins[62] might not be enough in order to establish a truly fair balance between protecting patented senior innovation on the one hand and facilitating junior innovation on the other. The following sub-sections will focus specifically on the limitations pertaining to this balance, namely the applicable exceptions from protection that facilitate research. It is submitted that these limitations are the breeder's privilege, the Bolar exception and the general research exception.

23.2.3.3 The breeder's privilege – why not also exempt new animal breeds?

First, with regard to the breeder's exception, the extension of this 'privilege' from plant variety rights to patent law is to be welcomed both in terms of coherence and functionality of the IP system. Breeders may utilise plants containing patented gene sequences[63] free of royalties in order to try and develop new plant varieties. If they succeed, the patent proprietor may – unlike under the parallel limitation in the Community Plant Variety Rights Reg[64] – however still prohibit the commercialisation of the new

---

58 Cf arts 5 and 6 Directive 2009/24/EC of the European Parliament and of the Council of 23 April 2009 on the legal protection of computer programs (Codified version) [2009] OJ L 111/16; Jaeger and Lamping (n 48) 202f.
59 For subtle differences as to the scope of these limitations in patent law and plant variety protection law respectively cf Axel Metzger, 'Der Schutzumfang von Patenten auf Pflanzen nach den EPA-Entscheidungen „Brokkoli II"/„Tomate II"' (2016) 118 GRUR 549, 554f.
60 Cf art 15(c) Council Regulation (EC) 2100/94 of 27 July 1994 on Community plant variety rights [1994] OJ L227/1.
61 Cf § 11(2a) PatG; BT-Drs 15/1709, 9, 15; Claudia Schreider, Patentierung in der Tierzucht – im Spannungsfeld zwischen geistigem Eigentum und Agrobiodiversität (kassel university press 2019) 150.
62 The non-official drafts for the limitations contained in the CPCs (n 46–47) which were copied and pasted into the UPCA date back to the early sixties, cf. Hanns Ullrich, *National, European and Community Patent Protection: Time for Reconsideration* (EUI Working Paper LAW No 2006/41) 31.
63 Whether plants and animals as such are patentable under art 4(1)(a) Biotechnology Dir (n 16) has been subject to debate in the past. Meanwhile, the EPO's Enlarged Board of Appeal has given in to the prevailing view that they are not, albeit without retroactive effect, cf *Pepper* [2020] EPO Enlarged Board of Appeal G 3/19, OJ EPO 2020, A119, paras XV.2ff, XXIX.
64 N 60. Cf Metzger (n 59) 554f.

variety[65] (which seems problematic in terms of incentivising research) or claim royalties for such commercialisation[66] (which seems adequate, provided that the patented gene sequence still performs its original function).[67]

Still, the question arises, why a similar arrangement for animals was not equally included in the UPCA. Admittedly, such an extension would be likely to encounter difficulties because the breeder's privilege in the plant sector refers to 'plant varieties', whereas the term 'animal breed' cannot be reliably defined to the same extent.[68] In German literature, it is therefore argued that a possible breeder's privilege in the animal sector could not be designed completely in parallel to the respective arrangement in the plant sector.[69] Nonetheless, as the farmer's privilege concerning animals under art 27(j) UPCA does not apply to breeding activity *per se* (due to the condition of an 'agricultural purpose'),[70] there is a call for the introduction of a breeder's privilege, the continued absence of which could have an inhibiting effect on follow-on innovation in the animal breeding sector.[71] Nevertheless, even though this issue has not been addressed in the UPCA, the transfer of the breeder's privilege for plants from plant variety protection to patent law was a step – albeit a small one – in the right direction.

23.2.3.4 The Bolar- and the general research exceptions: a race to the bottom?

In contrast, as far as the Bolar privilege and the general research exception are concerned, the UPCA may indeed result in limiting the rights to free use of patented inventions by UPs, EPs as well as national patents compared to the status quo. This is so, because in Member States forming part of the UP territory where the implementation of the Bolar exception contained in the Dir on the Community Code Relating to Medicinal Products for Human Use[72] has been 'gold plated', it is unlikely that a broader design of this restriction can be maintained in respect of the aspirations of the UP Reg[73] to provide

---

65 Compulsory dependency licenses can only be granted under the same demanding condition as foreseen by art 31(l)(i) TRIPS (n 30), namely that the new plant variety or invention constitutes significant technical progress of considerable economic interest, cf art 12(3)(b) Biotechnology Dir (n 16).
66 Schreider (n 61) 150.
67 Cf our argument for a purpose-bound compound protection at n 26.
68 Peter Henning Feindt, Claudia Fricke et al, *Patentrecht und landwirtschaftliche Tierzucht. Grundlagen, Problembereiche, Handlungsempfehlungen* (Stellungnahme des Forschungsprojekts "Biopatente in der Tierzucht" und des Friedrich-Löffler-Instituts für Nutztiergenetik 2014) 20.
69 Schreider (n 61) 151; Henning, Feindt et al (n 68) 13.
70 Cf art 11(2) Biotechnology Dir (n 16).
71 Henning, Feindt et al (n 68) 13.
72 Cf art 10(6) Dir on the Community Code Relating to Medicinal Products for Human Use (n 52) as amended by Dir 2004/27/EC (n 42).
73 N 4.

UP holders with 'uniform' rights and limitations.[74] The same holds true for the general research exception, which has so far only been voluntarily aligned to a certain extent as it was part of the CPCs from 1975 and 1989 respectively (from where it has now been copied verbatim into the UPCA).[75]

Even if broader national exceptions were to be left in place, it remains unclear whether the UPC will apply national transpositions at all in accordance with art 5(3) UP Reg[76] or rather rely on art 24(1)(b) UPCA and base its decisions directly on the agreement[77] – in monist countries, of course, this effectively does not make any difference. Even if the UPC adopted the first approach and were to base its decisions on the applicable national transposition of the UPCA – notably for the whole UP territory[78] – it would most likely bring any deviations into harmony with the original text of the UPCA through consistent interpretation.

Furthermore, the UPCA does not only align the material scope of patent protection in the UP territory as regards UPs, but it also harmonises the rights and limitations conferred by classic EPs in the territory of its state parties.[79] Finally, with regard to 'purely' national patents, Belgium, for instance, has already scheduled an alignment of its national patent law with the UP upon its entry into force in order to comply with its domestic constitutional requirement of equal treatment.[80]

23.2.3.4.1 The general research exception – bulldozing the Belgian approach

Turning to the general research exception contained in art 27(b) UPCA in particular, this provision reads: 'The rights conferred by a patent shall not extend to [...] acts done for experimental purposes *relating to the subject matter* of the patented invention' (emphasis added). As this provision allows license-free experimentation on patented inventions with the possible aims of further enhancing them or developing alternative technology, it is probably the most important limitation to the rights of patent proprietors in terms of promoting follow-on innovation.[81]

---

74 Art 5(2) UP Reg (n 4).
75 Cf at n 46.
76 N 4.
77 Cf at n 43. Assuming the latter option eg Olivier Mignolet, François Jonquères, Estelle Thiebaut and Hannelore Daems, 'Research and Bolar Exemptions from UPC, Belgian and French Perspectives', in Desaunettes-Barbero, de Visscher, Strowel and Cassiers (n 45) 493, 496.
78 Cf art 5(3) UP Reg (n 4).
79 Cf art 2(e) read in conjunction with art 26f UPCA.
80 Nicolas Carbonelle and Domien Op de Beeck, 'Europe: seeking competitive research exemptions in view of the UPC Agreement – the Belgian example' (7 May 2018) <www.twobirds.com/en/insights/2018/belgium/europe-seeking-competitive-research-exemptions-in-view-of-the-upc-agreement-the-belgian-example> accessed 13 September 2022; Mignolet, Jonquères, Thiebaut and Daems (n 77) 499
81 Other research activities covered by the core area of the research exception include eg testing the functionality of the invention or determining its field of application, cf Wan and Meng (n 3) 642f.

Given its CPC-background,[82] many European countries already provide for a general research exception, with the notable exception of Austria.[83] The opposite approach, in terms of a very broad research exception is (still) represented by Belgium. Since 2005, in this country, the royalty-free experimental use of patented inventions is not limited to experiments *on* the patented invention, thus *relating to its subject matter*, but also extends to experiments (other than those with a purely commercial purpose)[84] *with* a patented invention, thus to its use as a *research tool*.[85] This latter term does not only comprise mechanical apparatuses, such as microscopes, but also biotechnological and chemical tools such as cell lines, monoclonal antibodies or reagents.[86] In between the Belgian and Austrian extremes lie differently nuanced national variations of the provision, which, however, generally seem to be confined to performing research *on* a patented invention, thus excluding its use as a research tool whereas they are applicable irrespective of the commercial or non-commercial purpose of the research.[87]

With the UPCA, on the one hand, an express general research exception will be introduced for the first time into Austrian law, which is to be welcomed in the interest of promoting cumulative innovation but is of course long overdue. On the other hand, however, in Belgium, a legislative act narrowing down its exceptionally broad research exception to the version contained in the UPCA has already been adopted, which will enter into force together with the UPCA.[88] It has been said that this was necessary in order to comply with Belgian constitutional requirements as regards equality and non-discrimination between the holders of UPs and those of national patents.[89]

It is debatable whether the possibility of experimenting *with* patented research tools should be royalty-free, as it has been the case in Belgium. On the one hand, free production and use of these items improves access of researchers to the instruments they need, especially when alternatives to the patented invention are not available. On the other hand, however, the possibility of experimenting with research tools without having to purchase them might deprive the owners of the respective patents of their main marketing opportunity, thereby lowering the incentives to even develop new tools.[90] Therefore, an argument for the extension of the former Belgian approach to the whole UP territory is not necessarily what we want to get across here. The point of cri-

---

82 Cf at n 46 and at n 75.
83 Cf Wan and Meng (n 3) 643.
84 Van Overwalle (n 27) 907; Carbonelle and Op de Beeck (n 80).
85 Carbonelle and Op de Beeck (n 80); Van Overwalle (n 27) 905ff; Gold and Joly (n 13) 30; Mignolet, Jonquères, Thiebaut and Daems (n 77) 504.
86 Wan and Meng (n 3) 642.
87 Wan and Meng (n 3) 642f; Jaenichen and Pitz (n 55) 3ff; Gold and Joly (n 13) 29ff, 39ff.
88 Carbonelle and Op de Beeck (n 80).
89 Carbonelle and Op de Beeck (n 80); Mignolet, Jonquères, Thiebaut and Daems (n 77) 499.
90 Gold and Joly (n 13) 42; Frank-Erich Hufnagl, 'Ausweitung des Forschungsprivilegs in Europa und den USA – Verschiebung der Grenzen zwischen Patentschutz und Versuchsfreiheit bei Arzneimitteln' (2006) 28 PharmR 209, 214.

tique is rather that instead of striving for an adequately balanced solution on the use of research tools and drafting a research exception fit for the 21st century, the legislator merely copied and pasted a narrow limitation that is nearly 50 years old into the UPCA, thereby bulldozing broader national research exceptions.

In the sense of a middle way, the Swiss approach could have been (and could yet be) adopted, for example. In this country, a statutory basis for a claim to a compulsory licence for patented biotechnological research tools exists since 2008.[91] Given that the UP package only regulates general exceptions,[92] however, and leaves compulsory licensing to the 'participating Member States as regards their respective territories',[93] this solution does not seem feasible for the UP package, albeit it would of course be desirable that the approach concerning compulsory licenses would be changed entirely.[94]

Another possible reform that would not have to overcome the current approach to compulsory licensing would be to introduce a statutory exception to use patented research tools subject to appropriate remuneration.[95] As for the determination of the appropriate fee, such a statutory authorisation could be combined with a disclosure requirement for licenses concerning research tools so that the related compensation for certain categories of such tools would be made transparent.[96] Alternatively, it might also be worth looking into the approach taken by the farmer's exception contained in art 27(i) UPCA under which farmers other than small farmers are required to pay an equitable 're-seeding fee' to the holder of the patent for the propagation of the protected material on their own holding. The determination of the amount of this remuneration is governed by a Commission implementing reg, which declares, inter alia, agreements between farmers' and IP-holders' organisations notified to the Commission to be decisive.[97]

In contrast to these proposals, the current design of the general research exception in art 27(b) UPCA is an archetypical example of the backward-looking approach of the UP system and the manifold missed chances to modernise it and enhance its functionality.

---

91 Marcin Rodek, 'Lebenswissenschaften' in Hilty and Jaeger (n 19) 433, 440f; Claudia Seitz, 'Art. 40b' in Markus Schweizer and Herbert Zech (eds), *Patentgesetz (PatG)* (1st edn, Stämpfli 2019).
92 Cf art 27 UPCA.
93 Cf recital 10 UP Reg (n 4).
94 Cf at n 129.
95 Cf Rodek (n 91) 441.
96 Rodek (n 91) 441.
97 Cf art 5(4) Commission Regulation (EC) No 1768/95 of 24 July 1995 implementing rules on the agricultural exemption provided for in Article 14 (3) of Council Regulation (EC) No 2100/94 on Community plant variety rights [1995] OJ L173/14 as amended by Commission Regulation (EC) No 2605/98 of 3 December 1998 [1998] OJ L328/6.

23.2.3.4.2 Bringing broader Bolar exceptions into line

Even more severe concerns than with regard to the general research provision exist in the context of the so-called 'Bolar'[98] exception, which was introduced in the EU in 2004, with the insertion of art 10(6) into the Dir on the Community Code Relating to Medicinal Products for Human Use.[99] This provision reads: 'conducting the necessary studies and trials [...] and the consequential practical requirements [with a view to obtaining market authorisation for generic, hybrid generic or biosimilar medicinal products][100] shall not be regarded as contrary to patent rights'. By virtue of the reference in art 27(d) UPCA, this exception and the parallel provision concerning veterinary medicinal products have been incorporated into the UP legal framework.

A look at different EU Member States' legislation shows us that in some of these countries, the Bolar exception was implemented more broadly than the Directive would have required. For instance, the German,[101] Italian[102] and probably also the French[103] Bolar provisions are – like in the US[104] – not limited to the development of generic products (including hybrid generics and biosimilars) but also allow trials and experiments on patented compounds with the view to obtaining a market authorisation for *any* innovative drug without a license. Furthermore, the territorial scope of, for example of the German,[105] Italian[106] and possibly also the French[107] Bolar exceptions are currently not limited to aspired market authorisation in the EU or its Member States but also extend to trials and experiments for obtaining a market authorisation *outside* the EU.

Upon the entry into force of the UPCA, eg the German, Italian or French Bolar exceptions will indirectly be set back to the narrower version contained in the Dir on the Community Code Relating to Medicinal Products for Human Use.[108] This will arguably occur

---

98 For the background of the Bolar exception, which originated in the US and owes its name to the party of a legal dispute, cf Pfaff (n 55) 260; Dietmar Buchberger, 'Bolar Provision' (2006) 28 PharmR 106, 108.
99 Dir on the Community Code Relating to Medicinal Products for Human Use (n 52) as amended by Directive 2004/27/EC (n 42).
100 On the difference between the three, cf EMA, 'Generic and hybrid applications' <www.ema.europa.eu/en/human-regulatory/marketing-authorisation/generic-medicines/generic-hybrid-applications> accessed 13 September 2022; EMA, 'Biosimilar medicines: marketing authorisation' <www.ema.europa.eu/en/human-regulatory/marketing-authorisation/biosimilar-medicines-marketing-authorisation> accessed 13 September 2022.
101 § 11(2b) PatG; Jaenichen and Pitz (n 55) 6; Pfaff (n 55) 273; Alfred Keukenschrijver, '§ 11' in Alfred Keukenschrijver (ed), *Patentgesetz* (9th edn, de Gruyter, 2020) para 20.
102 Jaenichen and Pitz (n 55) 9.
103 Jaenichen and Pitz (n 55) 8; Carbonelle and Op de Beeck (n 80); Mignolet, Jonquères, Thiebaut and Daems (n 77) 508f.
104 Pfaff (n 55) 268.
105 Jaenichen and Pitz (n 55) 6.
106 Jaenichen and Pitz (n 55) 9.
107 Jaenichen and Pitz (n 55) 9; Mignolet, Jonquères, Thiebaut and Daems (n 77) 509.
108 Cf art 10(6) Dir on the Community Code Relating to Medicinal Products for Human Use (n 52) as amended by Directive 2004/27/EC (n 42).

to the detriment of future follow-on innovation and specifically holds true for the narrowing-down of broader national Bolar provisions from *any* innovative drugs to generics (including hybrid generics and biosimilars). The Commission's recent initiative to amend the Bolar exception, which is contained and explained in art 85 as well as recitals 63 and 64 of the proposal for a codification of the Union Code Relating to Medicinal Products for Human Use (COM 2023[192] final) does not provide for any conceptual change in this latter respect, although it does envisage a welcome extension of the purposes of the studies and trials covered by the Bolar exemption beyond the sole objective of market authorisation. As the UPC is bound to base its decisions on 'Union law' according to art 24 UPCA, respectively the limitations provided by the relevant national (implementing) legislation by virtue of art 5(3) UP Reg, the reference in art 27 (d) UPCA would arguably not even have to be unanimously updated to the new Bolar provision in order for the UPC to be able to apply it (cf at n 43). Yet, given its insufficiencies, a need exists for the UPC to fill the blanks left by the legislator by interpreting the wording of the updated 'unitary Bolar exception' (once it is adopted, respectively implemented by the MS) broadly in order to reach similar outcomes to the ones that had previously already been achieved. However, until a consistent jurisprudence has emerged, it might not least depend on the provenance of the judges[109] forming the different panels within the local and regional divisions of the UPCA whether they take a strict or more lenient approach to the scope of the Bolar exception, namely depending on the approach to the provision taken by the country in which the respective judges have received their judicial training.[110]

Instead of factually narrowing down the Bolar exception (at least in some respects), an argument has been made in literature that it should rather have been extended to other products subject to a market authorisation procedure, eg pesticides, as a 'Bolar-plus clause'. According to this view, a differentiation between medicinal products and other technologies subject to market approval lacks coherence and might even contravene the prohibition of discrimination contained in art 27(1) TRIPS[111].[112] In this respect, the Canadian Patent Act, which already contains a general 'regulatory review exception'[113] and whose conformity with TRIPS[114] has been affirmed in 2000 by a WTO dispute settlement panel,[115] could serve as a model.

---

109 For the nationality requirements regarding the composition of the panels of the UPC's local and regional divisions, cf art 8 UPCA.
110 For other issues where the early court practice of different local and regional divisions of the UPCA might differ from one another depending on the origin of the judges cf Alan Johnson, 'Looking Forward: A User Perspective', in Pila and Wadlow (n 1) 179, 184 ff.
111 N 30.
112 Rodek, (n 91) 441f.
113 Cf s 55.2(1) Patent Act.
114 N 30.
115 Cf WT/DS114/R (17 March 2000) *Canada – Patent Protection of Pharmaceutical Products*, Report of the Panel, para 7.2ff.

23.2.4 Compulsory licenses and limitations to injunctive relief under the UP legal framework

TRIPS[116] is also an important determinant for the availability of compulsory licenses and possible limitations of patent holders' rights to injunctive relief. These will be the two final examples of ill balancing between protecting patented senior innovation and facilitating junior innovation in the UP package discussed here.

23.2.4.1 The relation between individual and general limitations to patent holders' rights

Whereas exceptions and limitations to patent protection are generally applicable and their permissibility under international law is subject to the three-step-test[117] laid down in art 30 TRIPS,[118] compulsory licenses are individual concrete acts subject to art 31 TRIPS[119] and art 5A Paris Convention[120].[121] Similarly, the denial of an injunction is assessed on on an individual basis and needs to comply with arts 44(2) and 31(h) TRIPS, ie the patentee must receive adequate remuneration. It is debated whether compulsory licenses are additionally subject to the three-step-test under art 30 TRIPS,[122] as according to some, arts 30 and 31 TRIPS[123] should form a coherent system.[124]

23.2.4.2 The link between compulsory licenses and limitations to injunctive relief

In terms of their factual consequences, compulsory licenses on the one hand and the refusal by a court to grant an injunction in patent infringement proceedings (due to considerations of proportionality)[125] on the other, both tools are similar. Indeed, each of them has the effect that the patent proprietor may (temporarily) not prevent a third party to use its invention and is limited to remuneration – in the case of compulsory licensing in the form of a license fee, in the case of the refusal of an injunction in the form

---

116 N 30.
117 Cf the first part of this contribution at n 88.
118 N 30.
119 N 30.
120 Paris Convention for the Protection of Industrial Property of 20 March 1883, as last amended on 28 September 1979.
121 Lamping, 'Ergänzender Leistungs- und Investitionsschutz' (n 27) 182.
122 N 30.
123 N 30.
124 Lamping, 'Ergänzender Leistungs- und Investitionsschutz' (n 27) 181.
125 Julia Schönbohm and Natalie Ackermann-Blome, 'Products, Patents, Proportionality – How German Law Responds to 21st Century Challenges' (2020) 69 GRUR Int 578, 580ff.

of damages or compensation. The link between these two instruments is also illustrated by the example that German courts have – until a recent legislative change[126] – traditionally almost automatically granted injunctions in cases of patent infringements. According to them, limiting patent proprietors to damages would have circumvented the procedure for obtaining a compulsory license.[127]

One difference between the two tools, of course, is that the utilisation of the patented invention regularly remains unlawful if merely the injunction is refused or limited in patent infringement proceedings.[128] What is more, obviously, the hope in the denial of injunctive relief cannot fully replace the legal certainty that a (compulsory) license offers.

The ill-designed exclusion of compulsory licenses from the UP package will be assessed in more detail in the following. Subsequently, it will be examined which possibilities the UPCA provides for limiting or excluding injunctive relief in cases of patent infringements and whether this can mitigate to some extent the absence of compulsory licenses in the system.

23.2.4.3 Compulsory licenses left untouched

According to recital 10 UP Reg,[129] compulsory licenses for UPs 'should be governed by the laws of the participating Member States as regards their respective territories'. This is unfortunate, as the possibility for obtaining a compulsory license in respect of the whole UP territory in a centralised procedure would have been a suitable option to promote follow-on innovation in the face of the right of UP holders to, in principle,[130] prevent the use of their inventions transnationally by way of a single injunction from the UPC.[131] In contrast, should a patent proprietor be unwilling to license its invention on appropriate terms, a license seeker would have to initiate parallel proceedings to obtain compulsory licenses in all the Member States having ratified the UPCA in order to gain access to the UP territory.[132] The recently published initiative for a 'Union Compulsory Licence' that is envisaged to be granted by the Commission for the whole territory of the EU, on the other hand, will be narrowly limited to patents relating to 'crisis-relevant products' according to the proposal (cf COM[2023] 224 final).

---

126 Cf § 139(1) PatG as amended by the '2. PatMoG', BGBl 2021 I S 3490.
127 Schönbohm and Ackermann-Blome (n 125) 580ff.
128 Sven Vetter, 'Der patentrechtliche Unterlassungsanspruch nach dem 2. PatMoG' (2022) 14 ZGE 87, 92.
129 N 4.
130 Cf at n 188.
131 Cf Art 25f UPCA.
132 Reto M. Hilty and Thomas Jaeger, 'Gesamtanalyse und Erkenntnisse' in Hilty and Jaeger (n 19) 665, 695; Jaeger and Lamping (n 48) 195.

23.2.4.4 A missed opportunity

What is more, due to high thresholds and lengthy procedures, national compulsory licensing options[133] are currently almost never put to effect.[134] Yet, the international framework would have left so many possibilities for the drafters of the UP package to provide for an effective, central compulsory licensing regime for the entire UP territory. Neither art 31 TRIPS[135] nor 5A Paris Convention[136] contain any restrictions concerning the reasons for which compulsory licenses may be foreseen. Therefore, in principle, any private or public interest worthy of protection could be taken into consideration.[137] As regards the design of compulsory licenses, there are some specifications under art 31 TRIPS[138] and art 5A Paris Convention[139] that must be adhered to, such as that the license seeker must have previously made efforts to obtain a voluntary license under art 31(b) TRIPS,[140] that the license shall be authorised predominantly for the supply of the domestic market under art 31(f) TRIPS[141] or that, if the compulsory license is granted on the ground of failure to put the patented invention to (sufficient) use (in the absence of any other public interest),[142] a period of three years must have elapsed after the grant of the patent under art 5A(4) Paris Convention.[143]

Only with regard to compulsory dependency licenses, ie if the use is authorised to permit the exploitation of a second, dependent patent, art 31(l)(i) TRIPS[144] provides for the demanding requirement that 'the invention claimed in the second patent shall involve an important technical advance of considerable economic significance in relation to the invention claimed in the first patent.' However, this last provision presupposes the existence of two patents.[145] In order to allow for the commercialisation of non-patented follow-on inventions, compulsory licensing arrangements could thus have been foreseen in the UP package without having to comply with this high threshold. Indeed, it seems to be a problem in some Member States that there only exists a specific provision

---

133 For an overview of the most common grounds for compulsory licenses laid down in the Member States, cf Lamping, 'Ergänzender Leistungs- und Investitionsschutz' (n 27) 186.
134 Christian Heinze 'Patent Law and Climate Change – Do We Need an EU Patent Law Directive on Clean Technology?' (2021) 70 GRUR Int 554, 560; Schönbohm and Ackermann-Blome (n 125) 579; Hilty and Geiger (n 13) 642; Jaeger and Lamping (n 48) 200; Rodek (n 91) 439ff; Hilty and Jaeger (n 132) 695.
135 N 30.
136 N 120.
137 Lamping, 'Ergänzender Leistungs- und Investitionsschutz' (n 27) 180.
138 N 30.
139 N 120.
140 N 30.
141 N 30.
142 Lamping, 'Ergänzender Leistungs- und Innovationsschutz' (n 27) 186.
143 N 120.
144 N 30.
145 Christian Osterrieth, 'Technischer Fortschritt – eine Herausforderung für das Patentrecht? Zum Gebot der Verhältnismäßigkeit beim patentrechtlichen Unterlassungsanspruch' (2018) 120 GRUR 985, 988.

on compulsory dependency licenses that is conditional upon the second invention being patented itself,[146] with the effect that if that were not the case, the license seeker would have to rely on more general grounds such as 'the public interest' in order to obtain a compulsory license.[147] Furthermore, compulsory dependency licenses should arguably also have been made available under the UP legal framework where follow-on inventions are yet to be made[148] and the general research exception does not apply, thus in particular where enabling cumulative innovation is dependent on the utilisation of patented research tools.[149]

Most importantly however, in the light of the current length of national proceedings for the grant of compulsory licenses, if they were still to be added to the UP system, the central granting authority, be it the Commission, the EUIPO or the UPC, should be furnished with the power to rapidly grant provisional compulsory licenses in return for the deposit of a financial guarantee.[150]

23.2.4.5 A proportionality requirement for injunctions

Unlike what is the case with compulsory licenses, however, the UPCA contains a presumably sufficient set of provisions for the possible limitation of injunctive relief. The inclusion of a proportionality requirement for the granting of injunctions in the UPCA corresponds to international standards, as is shown, for instance, by the new German arrangement in § 139(1) PatG[151] or the judicial practice in the US and the UK.[152] Art 62(2) UPCA explicitly refers to proportionality in the case of provisional injunctions. With regard to permanent injunctions, art 63(1) UPCA reads that the UPC 'may' (and not 'shall') grant an injunction when a patent infringement is found. This provision is supplemented by a general requirement of proportionality and fairness under art 42 UPCA. Furthermore, by virtue of art 24(1)(a) UPCA, the UPC has to consider art 3(2) IP Enforcement Dir,[153] which also provides for a proportionality requirement and a prohibition of abuse of law in this context as well as art 12 IP Enforcement Dir,[154] according to which the infringer of an IP right can be ordered merely to pay pecuniary compensation if it

---

146 Rodek (n 91) 439.
147 Cf eg § 24(1) and (2) PatG in Germany.
148 Rodek (n 91) 439.
149 Cf the Swiss approach, reported at n 91.
150 Rodek (n 91) 441.
151 Cf n 126.
152 Cf Schönbohm and Ackermann-Blome (n 125) 582f.
153 Directive 2004/48/EC of the European Parliament and of the Council of 29 April 2004 on the enforcement of intellectual property rights [2004] OJ L 195/16.
154 N 153.

acted unintentionally and without negligence, the enforcement of an injunction would cause it disproportionate harm and this appears satisfactory for the injured party.[155]

23.2.4.5.1 Why are proportionate injunctions essential for a functional patent system?

The importance of not automatically granting injunctions in cases of patent infringements cannot be overstated. In the telecommunications sector, for instance, patent density is very high. It is estimated that around 250 000 patents are implemented in a single smartphone.[156] In such circumstances, it seems impossible or at least disproportionate to assess the scope of patent protection fully and beyond doubt at the stage of the development of a new product.[157] If in such a situation an injunction is granted without a use-by period, even if the patent infringement only relates to a small component of the smartphone, this provides the patent proprietor with significant leverage.[158] On the side of the patent infringer, it may constitute disproportionate hardship, especially if it is difficult to develop a workaround, when other parts need to be adapted as a result of the removal of the patented component or if due to an adaption a new market authorisation is necessary.[159] Most importantly, R&D activities could be discontinued if it cannot be ruled out that at a later date, the marketing of the developed product would have to be stopped due to an unexpected patent infringement.[160]

It is thus essential that under the UPCA, the UPC will be equipped with the aforementioned competences[161] to deal adequately with the respective cases, albeit it would have been desirable to also furnish it with a demonstrative catalogue of considerations to be taken account at the exercise of its discretion.[162] Without an explicit provision to this effect in the UPCA, there is also[163] a risk here of diverging judicial practice of the different panels within the local and regional divisions of the UPC in their early days, possibly depending on where the respective judges have received their judicial training.[164]

---

155 Osterrieth (n 145) 988f; Lamping, 'Ergänzender Leistungs- und Investitionsschutz' (n 27) 189; Jaeger and Lamping (n 48) 198f.
156 Schönbohm and Ackermann-Blome (n 125) 579.
157 Osterrieth (n 145) 985; Jaeger and Lamping (n 48) 198.
158 Schönbohm and Ackermann-Blome (n 125) 579.
159 Osterrieth (n 145) 986.
160 Osterrieth (n 145) 985.
161 At n 152.
162 Jaeger and Lamping (n 48) 199.
163 For the initial risk of diverging interpretations of the scope of the Bolar exception by different local and regional chambers cf at n 109.
164 Cf eg the former practice of the German courts to almost automatically grant injunctions mentioned at n 127. For the nationality requirements regarding the composition of the panels of the UPC's local and regional divisions, cf art 8 UPCA. For other issues where the early court practice of different local and re-

23.2.4.5.2 Which factors are to be taken into consideration?

It is advocated that, apart from the factors laid down in art 12 IP Enforcement Directive mentioned above,[165] the UPC should take the following considerations into account when deciding whether or not to grant an injunction or to limit an injunction with a use by period: First and foremost, it ought to be decisive whether the parties are in a (potential) competitive relationship with each other and whether the infringement thus leads to an erosion of the market shares of the patentee to the benefit of the infringer. If that is not the case, there is regularly no genuine interest in injunctive relief, but pecuniary compensation in the amount of the lost license fees is adequate.[166] Further considerations to be taken into account are, inter alia, whether the patentee has waited strikingly long before filing an action,[167] whether the proportion of the protected technology in the overall product is high or low,[168] the possibility of a workaround,[169] the complexity of the market situation with regard to patent rights,[170] potential adverse effects for third parties connected with an injunction[171] (eg where medical products would be put off the market),[172] whether the infringer has sought a license after learning of the infringement[173] and, if applicable, the fact that the patent proprietor does not (seriously) use or license its invention itself.[174] Finally, and most importantly for our purposes, the UPC should include in its considerations whether the infringer contributes to a further development of the state of the art with its product.[175]

Ultimately, while it seems beneficial that the granting of injunctive relief is made subject to a proportionality requirement in the UPCA, this cannot replace the unavailability of unitary compulsory licenses. Even if similar effects might be achieved when the balancing exercise results in favour of the infringer, this should never go as far as incentivising third parties to disregard the rights of patent proprietors.[176]

---

gional divisions of the UPCA might differ from one another depending on the origin of the judges cf Johnson (n 110) 184 ff.

165 At n 154.
166 Jaeger and Lamping (n 48) 196.
167 Schönbohm and Ackermann-Blome (n 125) 583; Jaeger and Lamping (n 48) 196.
168 Commission, 'Setting out the EU approach to Standard Essential Patents' (Communication) COM (2017) 712 final 10; Osterrieth (n 145) 992; Jaeger and Lamping (n 48) 198.
169 Osterrieth (n 145) 992.
170 Jaeger and Lamping (n 48) 198.
171 Commission, 'Setting out the EU approach to Standard Essential Patents' (Communication) COM(2017) 712 final 10.
172 Schönbohm and Ackermann-Blome (n 125) 579, 583.
173 Osterrieth (n 145) 991.
174 Osterrieth (n 145) 992; Jaeger and Lamping (n 48) 197.
175 Schönbohm and Ackermann-Blome (n 125) 583.
176 Jaeger and Lamping (n 48) 199; Alina Wernick, 'Substantive Aspects of Compulsory Licences', in Desaunettes-Barbero, de Visscher, Strowel and Cassiers (n 45) 515, 523ff..

23.2.4.6 Presumed incompatibility with EU law of individual restraints of patent protection

While the preceding sections have sidestepped this matter and described the operation of compulsory licenses and possible restrictions of injunctive relief as intended by the drafters of the UP package, there is still a final concern of central importance that affects both and overshadows all other issues in this context: By virtue of EU law, neither national authorities nor the UPC might actually be entitled to hollow out the rights conferred by a UP on an individual basis.

Whereas the general limitations contained in Art 27 UPCA provide for a narrower substantive scope of patent protection by statute from the outset already (cf Art 5(1) UP Reg),[177] compulsory licenses and possible restrictions of injunctive relief are necessarily subject to a further individual decision by a national authority or the UPCA, respectively. Yet, under art 19 TEU and the settled case law of the CJEU, Member State courts and other national authorities may generally not (and are not competent to) annul an act of EU law or diminish its scope and effects under any circumstances. This task is, in principle, reserved exclusively to the CJEU. It follows that whenever national courts or the UPC (which operates based on the fiction that it is also a court of the Member States)[178] harbour doubts as to the validity of an EU legal act or wish to restrict its scope, they are obliged to make a reference for a preliminary ruling to the CJEU (*Foto-Frost*-Doctrine).[179]

A UP, albeit not granted by an EU authority (due to the 'transformation fiction'[180]) is nonetheless an individual right of the patent holder, based on, granted by and guaranteed under EU law (the UP Reg)[181] by virtue of art 3(1) and (2) UP Reg,[182] in short: an EU-law based right.

Consequently, from an EU law perspective, neither national courts and authorities, nor the UPC have jurisdiction to detract from the scope of the UP by granting a compulsory license or limiting injunctive relief.[183] A punctual, procedurally limited exception to the *Foto-Frost*-Doctrine only applies where EU legislation delegates the competence to invalidate or restrict EU-law based rights to Member State courts.[184] Such delegations have, notably, been included in the EU Trade Mark Reg[185] and the Community Design

---

177 N 4.
178 Cf art 21 UPCA.
179 Case 314/85 *Foto-Frost v Hauptzollamt Lübeck-Ost* [1987] ECLI:EU:C:1987:452, para 15f, 17.
180 Cf the accessory nature of the UP described in n 14.
181 N 4.
182 N 4.
183 Thomas Jaeger, 'Reset and Go: The Unitary Patent System Post-Brexit' (2017) 48 IIC 254, 279.
184 Thomas Jaeger, *System einer Europäischen Gerichtsbarkeit für Immaterialgüterrechte* (Springer 2013) 90f.
185 Art 124(d) EU Regulation (EU) 2017/1001 of the European Parliament and of the Council of 14 June 2017 on the European Union trade mark (codification) [2017] OJ L154/1.

Reg.[186] Importantly, these exceptions to the duty to submit questions on the validity of EU law acts to the CJEU do not also relieve courts of last instance of their obligation to refer questions of interpretation of EU law to the Luxembourg court within the limits of the *CILFIT*[187]-Doctrine.[188]

The UP Reg,[189] however, does not contain any express authorisation to this effect. Therefore, any limitations of UPs by way of individual court decisions are most likely unlawful without a prior referral to the CJEU. For the sake of completeness, it should be noted here that this problem of lack of jurisdiction to autonomously limit UPs on an individual basis also applies to revocation actions before the UPC. It is emphasised that the UPC would therefore always have to refer questions on the validity of UPs to the CJEU for a preliminary ruling too. This is probably not the swift and efficient invalidity procedure that the drafters of the UP package had in mind and, like so many other issues, calls for a correction in the UP Reg.[190]

23.3 Overall conclusion: a system fit for innovation?

This contribution comprehensively analysed and assessed, in its first part, the incentives and disincentives the UP legal framework offers for potential patentees and, in this second part, whether the scope of the rights conferred by a UP is sufficiently balanced in order to also promote follow-on innovation. Based on these analyses, in sum, a mixed picture emerges.

While the evaluation of the rules forming the topic of the first part of this contribution was by and large positive, the results for this second part are more nuanced and less favourable. With respect to the hypothesis that the substantive scope of UP protection would provide for an imbalance in favour of patent holders over patent users that pursue follow-on innovation, it has emerged from the analysis that the situation is dissatisfactory in many ways indeed, rendering the system partially dysfunctional. For instance, the only new exception contained in the UPCA with respect to facilitating follow-on innovation is the breeder's exception and also this provision has merely been extended from plant variety protection to patent law. What is more, the bulldozing of the Belgian general research exception can hardly be offset by the little ray of light that such a provision will be introduced in express terms in Austria for the first time. As far as the Bolar exception is concerned, we are witnessing a de facto full harmonisation at an underdeveloped level. What is more, on the one hand, it remains a major downside

---

186 Art 81 (c) and (d) Council Regulation (EC) 6/2002 of 12 December 2001 on Community designs [2002] OJ L3/1.
187 Case C-283/81 *CILFIT v Ministero della Sanità* ECLI:EU:C:1982:335, para 21.
188 Jaeger, *System Gerichtsbarkeit* (n 184) 91.
189 N 4.
190 N 4.

of the system that the participating Member States have shied away from providing for unitary compulsory licenses in the UP Reg.[191] On the other hand, the proportionality assessment prescribed for the UPC before granting injunctions may partially fill that void and facilitate third party access to protected knowledge. However, in the absence of an explicit derogation from the *Foto-Frost*-Doctrine in the UP Reg,[192] allowing the UPC to restrict the rights conferred by a UP on an individual basis, it is doubtful under EU law whether this possibility in its current design may even be used in practice.

In sum, the hypothesis that the UP legal system provides for overprotection of patentees to the detriment of follow-on innovation could not be falsified here: On the contrary, the analysis confirmed the initial assumption that the UP system is not fully in balance and contains many elements which are detrimental to innovation and therefore dysfunctional from a patent-intrinsic perspective. In order for the UP system to earn the label 'fit for innovation', substantial improvements are thus still called for. Selected initial suggestions in this regard have been made throughout this contribution, but the list and the work are far from complete.

---

[191] N 4.
[192] N 4.

Maximilian Haedicke
24 Patent mediation

24.1 Introduction

Although there is a high level of IP expertise in many courts, IP mediation is playing an increasingly important role. The great flexibility and the adaptability of the mediation process to the individual needs of the parties makes mediation attractive for various types of IP disputes. While judgments rendered by the courts are usually limited to granting or denying injunctive relief and/or damages, the outcomes of mediation can be as varied as the interests of the parties. The mediation process can be constantly redefined and adapted to the needs of the parties. Apart from some basic principles, there are no strict procedural rules. In contrast to court and arbitration proceedings, the parties do not give the conflict resolution out of their hands at any point – an outcome is only reached if all parties agree.

24.1.1 Definition and legal basis

'Mediation' means a structured process, however named or referred to, whereby two or more parties to a dispute attempt, on a voluntary basis, to reach an agreement on the settlement by themselves of their dispute with the assistance of a mediator (Art. 3 (a) of the European Mediation Directive)[1]. 'Mediator' means any third person who is asked to conduct a mediation in an effective, impartial and competent way, regardless of the denomination or profession of that third person and of the way in which the third person has been appointed or requested to conduct the mediation. (Art. 3 (b) of the European Mediation Directive). The mediation process is characterized by the voluntary nature and autonomy of the parties and the impartiality of the mediator, i.e. his or her interest in the goals and needs of each party.

Mediation can be used to resolve a wide range of conflicts in a variety of areas, including family and estate disputes, but also intellectual property disputes.[2] Legal provi-

---

[1] Directive (EU) 2008/52/EC on certain aspects of mediation in civil and commercial matters [2008] OJ L136/3.
[2] Felix Steffek, 'Internationales Recht' in Reinhard Greger, Hannes Unberath and Felix Steffekt (eds), *Recht der alternativen Konfliktlösung* (2nd edn, C H Beck 2016) 444.

Maximilian Haedicke, Professor of Intellectual Property Law, University of Freiburg and Judge at the Unified Patent Court, Central Division, Paris.

sions regulating mediation, whether at national, European or international level, must therefore be broad and flexible.

Relevant provisions are the Mediation Directive[3] (applicable to cross-border mediation proceedings within the EU), a European Code of Conduct for Mediators published by the European Commission[4] and mediation rules of various ADR institutions, e.g. the DIS,[5] ICC,[6] WIPO[7] and the European Institute for Conflict Management (EUCON).[8] There are also mediation rules of the Unified Patent Court.[9] Rules on mediation at the international level have been created by the Singapore Convention on Mediation as a multilateral treaty.[10]

24.1.2 Guiding principles

Mediation proceedings are based on five fundamental principles: Confidentiality, voluntariness, openness, impartiality and legal information.

---

3 Directive (EU) 2008/52/EC on certain aspects of mediation in civil and commercial matters [2008] OJ L136/3.
4 Euromed Justice, 'European Code of Conduct for Mediators' <https://www.euromed-justice.eu/en/system/files/20090128130552_adr_ec_code_conduct_en.pdf> accessed 08 October 2021.
5 Deutsche Institution für Schiedsgerichtsbarkeit e V 'DIS Mediation Rules' <https://www.disarb.org/fileadmin//user_upload/Werkzeuge_und_Tools/DIS_Mediation_Rules_V.pdf> accessed 08 October 2021.
6 International Chamber of Commerce, 'Mediation Rules' <https://iccwbo.org/dispute-resolution-services/mediation/mediation-rules/> accessed 08 October 2021.
7 World Intellectual Property Organization, 'Regeln für das Mediationsverfahren der WIPO' <http://www.wipo.int/amc/de/mediation/rules/index.html> accessed 08 October 2021.
8 Europäisches Institut für Conflict Management eV, 'Mediationsordnung' <http://www.eucon-institut.de/mediation/mediationsordnung/>.
9 The UPC Mediation Rules are available at Unified Patent Court, 'Mediation Rules' <https://www.unified-patent-court.org/sites/default/files/upc_mediation_rules.pdf> accessed 08 October 2021.
10 Formally 'United Nations Convention on International Settlement Agreements Resulting from Mediation'. For more details on the Singapore Convention on Mediation see <https://www.singaporeconvention.org/> accessed 14 October 2021. The EU and Germany have not signed the treaty, for further information see Haedicke/Kükenhöhner 'Mediation of IPR Disputes' in Edward Elgar, *Research Handbook on Intellectual Property Rights and Arbitration* (to be published in 2023). Additionally, a Model Law was developed to serve the different countries in adopting a uniform standard for international mediation, Formally 'UNCITRAL Model Law on Commercial Mediation and International Settlement Agreements Resulting from Mediation', amending the UNCITRAL Model Law on International Commercial Conciliation (2002). Singapore Convention on Mediation, 'Background to the Model Law' <https://www.singaporeconvention.org/model-law/about> accessed 14 October 2021; Singapore Convention on Mediation, 'Text of the Model Law' <https://www.singaporeconvention.org/model-law/text> accessed 14 October 2021. If interested, any state can enact the Model Law on Mediation or use it as a basis, Norel Rosner, 'The new UNCITRAL instruments on international commercial settlement agreements resulting from mediation – an insider's view' (2018) TMD – Nederlands-Vlaams tijdschrift voor mediation en conflictmanagement 30, 36.

24.1.2.1 Confidentiality

A most important pillar of mediation is **confidentiality**. It must be maintained at all times in accordance with Art. 7 of the Mediation Directive. Unless the parties agree otherwise, neither mediators nor those involved in the administration of the mediation process shall be compelled to give evidence in civil and commercial judicial proceedings or arbitration regarding information arising out of or in connection with a mediation process. While the mediator is subject to a legal duty of confidentiality, the parties themselves can decide whether and to what extent they want to keep the proceedings confidential. As a rule, a possible agreement on how to handle the confidentiality of the parties is discussed and recorded in writing at the beginning of the proceedings.

24.1.2.2 Voluntariness

Mediation may only result in a solution (mediation agreement/settlement agreement) that all parties agree to. The parties must consent to all procedural steps and all issues addressed in mediation. Furthermore, the parties can terminate the mediation at any time.

24.1.2.3 Openness

The parties must be willing to share the necessary information – if necessary, the confidentiality agreement can be adapted during the mediation process. Only fully informed parties can take informed decisions.

24.1.2.4 All-Partiality / neutrality

The mediator is subject to the principle of **all-partiality**, often also referred to as neutrality or impartiality. The mediator must understand all parties to the conflict. In some cases, this requires intensive engagement with the parties, if necessary also in individual discussions. It is also said that the mediator is on both/all sides. In this context, the term "all-partiality" is preferable to "neutrality".

24.1.2.5 Legal information

The parties need all the necessary information to be able to make an informed and responsible decision. This presupposes that the parties know exactly what their options are in court proceedings and from a legal point of view. There is thus a need for **legal information**. The parties need to understand the legal implications of their decisions. Before signing a final agreement, it is therefore essential that the parties seek legal advice. In IP mediation, the parties will in most cases be professionals who are already aware of their legal situation. In any case, it is essential that all parties consult their lawyers.

24.1.3 The course of IP mediation proceedings

The mediation process can be structured entirely according to the needs of the parties. Nevertheless, a certain framework that provides the necessary structure is helpful. There are certain steps that have proven to be purposeful and which mediators will generally follow.

24.1.3.1 First contact

First, one or sometimes all parties make initial contact with the mediator, typically by phone or email. The parties usually explain roughly what the conflict is about without going into too much detail. Depending on the complexity of the case, it may be necessary for the mediator to familiarize himself with the content of the conflict and the patent before the mediation begins. Usually, the parties are asked to provide the mediator with summaries of the case and their positions. It is important that information gathering is not done unilaterally with one party, but with all parties (whether during the mediation process or in advance), in order to preserve the mediator's impartiality and not to lose the trust of one party in advance.

24.1.3.2 Preparation

In complex cases, it may be useful for the mediator to look into the matter before the first meeting. In patent disputes in particular, the mediator may need time to consider the patent in depth. Due to the flexibility of the process, there is no clear distinction between the issues which need to be addressed in the preparatory phase and what is to be addressed in the opening phase of the mediation. The mediator provides the guidelines and can thus respond individually to the parties and their specific requirements.

Organizational details such as location, date, time, language and participants need to be clarified and agreed upon before the first meeting. It is important that all participants have decision-making power.[11] The parties can decide whether they bring their lawyers, which is usually recommended in IP disputes.

---

[11] Stefan Kessen and Markus Troja '§ 14 Ablauf und Phasen einer Mediation' in Fritjof Haft and Katharina von Schlieffen (eds), *Handbuch Mediation* (3rd edn, C H Beck 2016), 335.

The mediator may ask each party for a summary of the case, which he will make available to the other party in the interest of transparency.[12] In addition to the technical details of the patent, the mediator can thus familiarize himself in advance with the facts of the case and the positions of the parties.[13] It also gives the other party the opportunity to gain a new insight into the other party's point of view.[14]

Transparency of the preparatory process is the first basis for trust in the mediator and the mediation process itself. To this end, the mediator may also provide the parties with an agenda in advance.[15]

Pending court proceedings between the parties should be suspended until the end of the mediation.[16]

24.1.3.3 Opening – Phase I

In the opening phase the parties meet the mediator and the actual mediation begins. As already mentioned, the mediation process is flexible. Therefore, the mediator usually starts by explaining his mediation process and the basic principles of the process to the parties and their lawyers.

Then the mediator assesses whether mediation is the right process for the parties to resolve their conflict. To this end he will ask the parties about their expectations of the process. At this stage of the mediation process the mediator tries to get the parties thinking about and imagining the future rather than holding on to the past.[17]

Finally, a mediation agreement may be drawn up in which all details and stipulations (e.g. special rules on confidentiality), payment obligations, termination options and liability issues are recorded.[18]

---

[12] Cf. Haedicke/Kükenhöhner 'Mediation of IPR Disputes' in Edward Elgar, *Research Handbook on Intellectual Property Rights and Arbitration* (to be published in 2023).
[13] Ha Haedicke/Kükenhöhner 'Mediation of IPR Disputes' in Edward Elgar, *Research Handbook on Intellectual Property Rights and Arbitration* (to be published in 2023).
[14] Cf. Haedicke/Kükenhöhner 'Mediation of IPR Disputes' in Edward Elgar, *Research Handbook on Intellectual Property Rights and Arbitration* (to be published in 2023).
[15] Haedicke/Kükenhöhner 'Mediation of IPR Disputes' in Edward Elgar, *Research Handbook on Intellectual Property Rights and Arbitration* (to be published in 2023).
[16] Cf. on this Oberlandesgericht Oldenburg, decision of 21 February 2008, court number 8 U 186/07, ECLI: DE:OLGOL:2008:0221.8U186.07.0A, BeckRS 2008, 8299 (Oldenburg Higher Regional Court).
[17] Haedicke/Kükenhöhner 'Mediation of IPR Disputes' in Edward Elgar, *Research Handbook on Intellectual Property Rights and Arbitration* (to be published in 2023).
[18] Cf. for exact legal classification Maximilian Haedicke, 'Mediation im Patentrecht' in Maximilian Haedicke and Henrik Timmann (eds), *Handbuch des Patentrechts* (2nd edn, C H Beck 2020) 1559; Cf. Haedicke/Kükenhöhner 'Mediation of IPR Disputes' in Edward Elgar, *Research Handbook on Intellectual Property Rights and Arbitration* (to be published in 2023).

24.1.3.4 Exploration of facts and identification of issues – Phase II

Even if the parties have exchanged statements prior to the actual mediation process, it is necessary to discuss the facts and exchange information so that the parties can ensure that the mediator has considered the facts as they appear to the parties.[19] The mediator has the opportunity to ask specific questions and must make sure that he has understood the facts. The mediator simultaneously promotes the understanding of one party for the point of view of the other party.[20] By making an effort to understand both parties and giving both parties an equal opportunity to comment on the facts, the mediator maintains his or her "impartiality".[21] This strengthens the parties' trust in both the mediator and the process. Behind this background, the core of mediation can be built on the basis of a common set of facts.

Frequently, the parties will be asked to make opening statement. This gives each party the opportunity to explain the issues and problems relevant to them.

In the following, the parties are requested to identify the topics which they wish to discuss and for which they hope to reach an agreement. The topics to be discussed can be narrowed down to one subject matter of the conflict, e.g. patent infringement or a dispute about a license agreement. The topics can also be broad. For example, the entire future cooperation with all relevant topics may be dealt with in mediation.

24.1.3.5 Working through the areas of conflict – Phase III

Now each individual topic is considered. For this purpose, all relevant information is identified in detail before a topic is dealt with.[22] The discussion of the facts on a particular issue lays the foundation for a consensual resolution of the dispute.[23] It is the mediator's task to disclose the needs and interests of the parties and thus to free them from their entrenched positions.[24] The underlying needs and interests may become comprehensible to the other party and, when disclosed, lead to a mutual recognition of the re-

---

[19] Cf. Jan Malte von Bargen '§ 10 Mediation in Verwaltungssachen' in Michael Quaas, Rüdiger Zuck and Michael Funke-Kaiser (eds), *Prozesse in Verwaltungssachen* (3rd edn, Nomos 2018) 1049, 1061.
[20] Haedicke/Kükenhöhner 'Mediation of IPR Disputes' in Edward Elgar, *Research Handbook on Intellectual Property Rights and Arbitration* (to be published in 2023).
[21] Haedicke/Kükenhöhner 'Mediation of IPR Disputes' in Edward Elgar, *Research Handbook on Intellectual Property Rights and Arbitration* (to be published in 2023).
[22] Cf. Stefan Kessen and Markus Troja '§ 14 Ablauf und Phasen einer Mediation' in Fritjof Haft and Katharina von Schlieffen (eds), *Handbuch Mediation* (3rd edn, C H Beck 2016) 338.
[23] Cf. Jan Malte von Bargen '§ 10 Mediation in Verwaltungssachen' in Michael Quaas, Rüdiger Zuck and Michael Funke-Kaiser (eds), *Prozesse in Verwaltungssachen* (3rd edn, Nomos 2018) 1049, 1061.
[24] Cf. Stefan Kessen and Markus Troja '§ 14 Ablauf und Phasen einer Mediation' in Fritjof Haft and Katharina von Schlieffen (eds), *Handbuch Mediation* (3rd edn, C H Beck 2016) 339.

spective needs.[25] The mediator ensures that both parties can understand each other. Understanding, however, merely means understanding the needs and interests of the other party, not agreeing with them. If possible, common interests should be identified.[26] In order to find a long term solution that all parties can agree to, it is crucial that there is some mutual understanding.[27]

24.1.3.6 Negotiation and problem solving – Phase IV

Once the parties have gained some understanding of their respective needs, it is time to look carefully at the options for possible solutions. Brainstorming is used to find as many different and creative solutions as possible, so that solutions can be identified that might not have been considered by the parties before. The goal, of course, is to find options that are beneficial to both parties, creating a win-win situation.[28] Subsequently, the individual options are evaluated by each party and can be freely discussed and negotiated. Options will be assessed for practicality, involving or consulting with others as appropriate.[29] The proposed solutions must take into account the interests of both/all parties.[30]

At this stage, the shuttle method can be useful. This method is described in more detail later in the section "Role of the mediator". By using this method, the parties can consider different options in confidential discussions with the mediator without having to inform the other party directly. The mediator can act as a coach for the individual parties.

The aim is to end up with a collection of options that together form the solution and to which all parties can say "yes". This process is repeated for each issue so that in the end there are solutions for all the issues that the parties wanted to discuss.

---

25 Cf. Doris Morawe, *Mediation und Gesundheit* (1st edn, Springer 2017) 30; fundamentally Roger Fisher, William Ury and Bruce Patton, *Getting to yes* (3rd edn, Random House Business Books 2012) 42ff.
26 Jan Malte von Bargen '§ 10 Mediation in Verwaltungssachen' in Michael Quaas, Rüdiger Zuck and Michael Funke-Kaiser (eds), *Prozesse in Verwaltungssachen* (3rd edn, Nomos 2018) 1049, 1061.
27 See Roger Fisher, William Ury and Bruce Patton, *Getting to yes* (3rd edn, Random House Business Books 2012) 24 ff, 42ff.
28 Stefan Kessen and Markus Troja '§ 14 Ablauf und Phasen einer Mediation' in Fritjof Haft and Katharina von Schlieffen (eds), *Handbuch Mediation* (3rd edn, C H Beck 2016) 351.
29 For further information see Michael Groß, *IP-/IT-Mediation* (3rd edn, R&W 2018) 76.
30 Stefan Kessen and Markus Troja '§ 14 Ablauf und Phasen einer Mediation' in Fritjof Haft and Katharina von Schlieffen (eds), *Handbuch Mediation* (3rd edn, C H Beck 2016) 350.

24.1.3.7 Drafting a final agreement – Phase V

The solutions found in mediation are recorded in a legally binding settlement agreement. Before the agreement is signed, both parties discuss the agreement with their lawyers.

24.1.3.8 Enforcement of mediation settlements

The enforceability of a mediation result is not handled uniformly in different jurisdictions. The Mediation Directive leaves room for determining the enforceability of mediation agreements:

Art. 6 (1) of the Mediation Directive states that Member States shall ensure that [...] the parties [...] may request that the content of a written agreement reached in mediation be made enforceable, Art. 6 (2) provides that [t]he content of the agreement may be made enforceable by a court or other competent authority in a judgment or decision or in an authentic instrument in accordance with the law of the Member State in which the request is made.[31]

In the **unitary patent system,** enforceability is regulated as follows:

The agreements reached in mediation are enforceable (Art. 35 (2), Art. 82 UPCA). According to Rule 365.1 of the Rules of Procedure of the UPCA[32], *the court shall confirm the settlement by a decision of the court [...] if the parties so request, and the decision may be enforced as a final decision of the court.* Rule 365.2[33] states that *the court may, at the request of the parties, order that the details of the settlement are confidential.*

In 2020, the **Singapore Convention on Mediation** (SCM)[34] entered into force. It creates a harmonised legal framework agreement on the recognition and enforcement of mediation settlements.[35] The aim of the agreement is to ensure enforcement also in countries where the agreement has not been concluded. However, the EU and Germany have not signed the agreement.[36]

---

[31] Accordingly enforceability varies from country to country; Since mediation agreements are enforceable like a contract in Germany, a court title in the form of a final judgment is necessary for enforceability.
[32] Rule 365.1 of the UPC Rules of Procedure 18th draft of 19 october 2015.
[33] Rule 365.2 of the UPC Rules of Procedure 18th draft of 19 october 2015.
[34] 'The United Nations Convention on International Settlement Agreements Resulting from Mediation' (New York, 20 December 2018).
[35] United Nations Commission On International Trade Law 'United Nations Convention on International Settlement Agreements Resulting from Mediation (New York, 2018) (the "Singapore Convention on Mediation")' <https://uncitral.un.org/en/texts/mediation/conventions/international_settlement_agreements> accessed 06 October 2021.
[36] For more details on this see Haedicke/Kükenhöhner 'Mediation of IPR Disputes' in Edward Elgar, *Research Handbook on Intellectual Property Rights and Arbitration* (to be published in 2023).

24.1.4 The role of the mediator

24.1.4.1 General

The essential task of the mediator is to disentangle the parties from their deadlocked positions and, without decision-making power, to help the parties find a solution that satisfies all their needs and to which all parties can agree. The lack of decision-making power distinguishes the mediator from the judge or arbitrator. By finding out the real needs, the underlying causes, the obvious interests and the consequences of the conflict, the mediator helps the parties to move away from their entrenched positions, and to talk about possible solutions. The exact role of the mediator may vary depending on the conflict and the personality of the parties and the personality of the mediator.[37] If necessary, the mediator can act only as a moderator (facilitative mediation) or actively intervene (evaluative mediation).[38]

In the process of finding a solution, in the phase of collecting options and finding possible solutions, the mediator can also participate actively – depending on the wishes of the parties. However, the parties retain control over the process itself and the outcome at all times.[39]

In the end, there should be a solution tailored to the interests of the parties according to their own ideas, which the parties have worked out under the guidance and with the help of the mediator, without the mediator deciding on the outcome of the mediation. In summary, one could say that *the mediator is responsible for the mediation process, but not for the outcome.*[40]

24.1.4.2 The mediator's techniques for conflict resolution

Depending on the individual case, the mediator uses different methods to determine the interests behind the positions.[41]

---

[37] Cf. Matthias Wendland, *Mediation und Zivilprozess* (1st edn, Mohr Siebeck 2018) S. 392 ff.; see also Margellos/Bonne/Humphreay/Stürmann § 1.02 [B]; For a detailed discussion of the mediator's role and, in particular, the techniques of various mediators see also Leonard L. Riskin, Understanding Mediators' Orientations, Strategies, and Techniques: A Grid for the Perplexed, Harvard Negotiation Law Review 1 (1996), S. 7, 23 ff.

[38] Leonard L. Riskin, Understanding Mediators' Orientations, Strategies, and Techniques: A Grid for the Perplexed, Harvard Negotiation Law Review 1 (1996), S. 7, S. 26 ff.

[39] Matthias Wendland, *Mediation und Zivilprozess* (1st edn, Mohr Siebeck 2018) 177 f.

[40] Volpert, *Mediation – eine Alternative zum streitigen Verfahren auch im Gewerblichen Rechtsschutz?*, Mitt. 2008, 170, 171.

[41] A detailed discussion can be found in Leonard L. Riskin, Understanding Mediators' Orientations, Strategies, and Techniques: A Grid for the Perplexed, Harvard Harvard Negotiation Law Review 1 (1996), S. 7 ff., 25 ff.

Especially in patent law (but also in other areas of law), where confidentiality is frequently of essence for the parties, the parties need confidential discussions alone with the mediator to make their real interests and needs known. In such situations, the so-called *shuttle mediation* (*caucusing*) is often used. In shuttle mediation, the parties are in separate rooms, and the mediator works alternately with one party and the other. He "shuttles" from one party to the other, thus enabling the parties to talk openly with the mediator about their situation.[42] The content of the conversations is confidential unless one party allows the mediator to pass on what has been said to the other party. At the end of each individual conversation, the mediator asks what information may be disclosed to the other party.

The shuttle procedure can be used at different points in the mediation process. It is particularly useful when the mediation process stalls or even threatens to reach an impasse.

For example, shuttling during option collection can be used to confidentially discuss individual options in all their facets without jeopardizing the final outcome. In this way, individual options are not discarded from the outset for fear of torpedoing the outcome.

24.1.4.3 Special requirements for mediators in patent disputes

Patent law is a highly specialized area of law. It is therefore essential that the mediator has expertise in this field of law. Patent law knowledge not only ensures faster familiarization and is helpful in finding flexible solutions, but also creates trust in the person of the mediator and in his ability to understand the legal and economic interests and thus help the parties to identify the relevant issues and find appropriate solutions.[43]

24.1.5 Opportunities and challenges of mediation in general

The speed and the comparatively low costs offer an advantage over court or arbitration proceedings. In principle, mediation is also possible in highly escalated conflicts, as the parties do not even have to be in the same room, especially if shuttle mediation is applied. Since the parties make all the decisions and actively seek the solution, they are taken out of their passive victim role and they take active control of the resolution of the

---

42 A more detailed explanation can be found in Karl Heinz Blasweiler '§ 21 Shuttle-Mediation' in Fritjof Haft and Katharina von Schlieffen (eds), *Handbuch Mediation* (3rd edn, C H Beck 2016) 487ff.
43 Cf. Peter Chrocziel and Friedrich von Samson-Himmelstjerna '§ 39 Mediation im Gewerblichen Rechtsschutz' in Fritjof Haft and Katharina von Schlieffen (eds), *Handbuch Mediation* (3rd edn, C H Beck 2016) 907.

conflict. Moreover, in mediation, the resolution of the conflict is based on the underlying needs and interests and not only on legal provisions.[44]

Mediation is particularly suitable when future cooperation is necessary or desired. As far as the escalation level is concerned, mediation can be helpful up to the highest escalation levels. *The mediator is the fence on the cliff, while the court would act as the emergency doctor.*[45]

A solution is only reached in a mediation process if all parties agree with the outcome and with the necessary procedural steps. Therefore, despite all the mediator's efforts, it may not be possible to reach a decision.

There is a possibility that mediation may be abused to obtain information. To counteract this from the outset, a confidentiality agreement is essential. The possibility of the process being exploited to gain time and information can never be completely ruled out, as is the case with other forms of negotiation.

24.2 Patent conflicts suitable for mediation

24.2.1 Licence agreements

Patent- and know-how licence agreements:

Disputes may arise in particular over the amount of the licence fee, the scope of the activity owed or the quality of the goods and services provided. Patent and know-how licence agreements are often characterised by a long duration of the contractual relationship and the need of trust for future cooperation. Therefore, these contracts benefit from a positive relationship between the parties which can be accomplished by mediation.

SEP/FRAND disputes

SEP/FRAND issues[46] are particularly suitable for mediation. The confidentiality of the proceedings and of the outcome may be advantageous. WIPO also refers to mediation as an option for cost- and time-efficient FRAND determination.[47]

---

44 See also Matthias Wendland, *Mediation und Zivilprozess* (1st edn, Mohr Siebeck 2018) 34 ff.
45 Haedicke/Kükenhöhner 'Mediation of IPR Disputes' in Edward Elgar, *Research Handbook on Intellectual Property Rights and Arbitration* (to be published in 2023).
46 *Picht* presents in his essay *Schiedsverfahren in SEP/FRAND-Streitigkeiten (GRUR 2019, 11)* the situation of the various parties involved within a SEP/FRAND conflict.
47 WIPO, https://www.wipo.int/amc/en/center/specific-sectors/ict/frand/, last accessed 17.03.2022.

Research and development agreements

Unresolved conflicts, for example over technical, personal or financial issues, can cause damage and make future cooperation more difficult.[48] Especially in such cases it is important to avoid conflicts from the outset.

24.2.2 International and complex disputes

While the international nature and complexity of the legal issues undoubtedly present challenges for a mediator,[49] mediation allows the parties to choose a mediator whom they consider to be competent. Thus, mediation offers an advantage when the case would otherwise be handled by an inexperienced court. Parallel proceedings in different countries are also eliminated. If necessary, technical experts can be involved in the mediation process; thus, it is not only possible to find a quick solution in a short time, but also to deal with the facts of the case in depth.[50] Moreover, the parties themselves are most familiar with the complex conflict, so that a procedure in which the parties themselves decide on the outcome may seem appropriate.

24.2.3 Disputes requiring confidentiality

Shuttle mediation in particular offers the possibility of finding a solution without having to disclose confidential information to the other party.[51] Mediation is therefore particularly suitable for proceedings where there is a risk of confidential information being disclosed in civil proceedings.[52]

---

48 Cf. Michael Groß, *IP-/IT-Mediation* (3rd edn, R&W 2018) Rn. 94.
49 Cf. Peter Chrocziel and Friedrich von Samson-Himmelstjerna '§ 39 Mediation im Gewerblichen Rechtsschutz' in Fritjof Haft and Katharina von Schlieffen (eds), *Handbuch Mediation* (3rd edn, C H Beck 2016) . 28f.
50 Peter Chrocziel and Friedrich von Samson-Himmelstjerna '§ 39 Mediation im Gewerblichen Rechtsschutz' in Fritjof Haft and Katharina von Schlieffen (eds), *Handbuch Mediation* (3rd edn, C H Beck 2016) Rn. 18.
51 Despite the applicability of §§ 16–20 GeschgehG through § 145a PatG (German law), shuttle mediation, for instance, can offer even greater confidentiality.
52 Peter Müller, 'Advantages of Mediation in the IP Area' in Théophile Margellos, Sophia Bonne, Gordon Humphreys and Sven Stürmann (eds) *Mediation: Creating Value in International Intellectual Property Disputes* (Wolters Kluwer 2018) 60.

24.2.4 Further advantages of mediation

Often the driving force for the dispute lies in interests and motives outside the actual subject matter of the dispute. Mediation takes into account the individual concerns, needs and requirements of the parties.[53] A mediator tries to understand both sides – also through individual meetings and discussions – and therefore explores the interests, motivations and needs of both parties. The mediator gains a more comprehensive insight into the economic, and if necessary, personal situation of each party. The mediator helps to find a solution that also includes issues that are outside the subject matter of the dispute.[54] Thus, with the mediator's help, solutions can sometimes be found that neither party had thought of before.

A court case ends with a winner and a loser. Not only do court proceedings themselves carry the risk of escalation, but the win-lose situation created by a trial and judgment also fuels the conflict. So if the parties want or need a future or even long-term cooperation, it is helpful to base this relationship on a win-win solution. Mediation aims at finding satisfactory solutions for the future. Mediation is useful in long-term business relationships.[55]

Mediation offers the possibility to include a variety of options in solutions. The options are not limited by subject matter. Out-of-the-box thinking can lead to more complex, but thereby also individually suitable solutions, whereas a court judgment is limited by the parties' motions.

Especially when the parties are under time pressure, mediation can offer a quick path to a solution. In mediation, the parties are in control of the duration of the proceedings. Since the parties choose the mediator themselves, they can inquire whether the mediator is available for speedy proceedings.

Particularly suitable for mediation are conflicts whose basis are on the personal level and/or emotionally charged. Problems on the personal level often spill over. Thus, it is also not surprising that patent–related conflicts – despite their technical nature – also touch upon the personal level or may have rooted in personal relationships. Examples are long-term license agreements that fail due to personal misunderstandings. Patent disputes between competitors that can be burdened and inflamed by decades of personal dislike. Especially in the case of employee inventions, emotions can lead to patent disputes. Lack of appreciation, diverging corporate cultures, the wrong tone or private problems can be the reason for the conflict.

---

53 Cf. Peter Chrocziel and Friedrich von Samson-Himmelstjerna '§ 39 Mediation im Gewerblichen Rechtsschutz' in Fritjof Haft and Katharina von Schlieffen (eds), *Handbuch Mediation* (3rd edn, C H Beck 2016) Rn. 82.
54 Cf. Peter Chrocziel and Friedrich von Samson-Himmelstjerna '§ 39 Mediation im Gewerblichen Rechtsschutz' in Fritjof Haft and Katharina von Schlieffen (eds), *Handbuch Mediation* (3rd edn, C H Beck 2016) Rn. 4.
55 Matthias Wendland, *Mediation und Zivilprozess* (1st edn, Mohr Siebeck 2018) 32 ff.

24.3 Conclusion

In some jurisdictions a patent law dispute can be settled relatively quickly and inexpensively in court. The real added value of mediation lies in the confidentiality, the inclusion of all interests (including economic and personal ones), the fact that an agreement is only reached with the consent of all parties and thus in the predictability of the outcome and in the flexibility with regard to the terms of reference, the implementation and the results. In addition, mediation can be even more cost- and time-efficient. If mediation fails and no solution is found, the path to court proceedings (or arbitration) is still open. Due to the increasing complexity of patent cases, their multinational causes and effects, and the rising costs of litigation, the importance of mediation will increase in the future.

Alan Johnson
25 Litigation strategies and bifurcation

25.1 Introduction

The importance of strategic thinking in patent litigation was drummed into your author at the very beginning of his career as an Articled Clerk at Bristows by his Principal, David Brown. David was renowned for mixing his sporting metaphors (in this case, chess, cards and horse racing), and explained that "litigation is like a game of chess, you keep your cards close to your chest, and it's a question of first past the post". Breaking down this amusing but insightful analogy:

Chess: International patent litigation, like a game of chess, whilst governed by rules, involves potentially complex strategies;

Cards: Keeping your opponent guessing as to the strength of your hand and your tactics can result in an advantage as the opponent is caught by surprise; and

Racing: The first decision is usually the most important and can be commercially decisive. As a client once confided: "if you've lost at first instance, it's all very well telling your commercial people that it'll be different on appeal, or we will win elsewhere …"

So with the advent of the UPC, the chess board becomes even more complex, with more potential tactics and opportunities for keeping an opponent guessing and caught off guard. However, the importance of the first decision remains a key consideration. The UPC provides a new option with, for the first time, the potential for a pan-European (or at least to some extent multi-national) decision on infringement and validity and a potential injunction.

The existing system is considered in more detail elsewhere in this book, but for present purposes it is worth emphasising that both in the present system and in the UPC, there are very different types of cases where commensurately different considerations apply. Types of cases cannot be classified simply, and can be "sliced and diced" in a number of different ways, but looking at the potential impact of the UPC, the factors which influence tactics in the present system include:

1. The geographic scope of the patent portfolios of all parties involved;
2. Is the market essentially European in nature such that an injunction in one country would block the product on a continental basis;
3. Is one particular country the seat of manufacture or a particularly important market, and hence has a particular significance;
4. How valuable is the market overall, and hence what level of investment in litigation can be contemplated? In this regard, the relative importance of the European market can vary enormously from case to case, but very generally speaking will always

Alan Johnson, Consultant, Hogan Lovells International, London.

be secondary to the US market, and indeed increasingly secondary to other, particularly far-eastern markets, a factor which is also reflected in a reduction in recent decades of the geographic scope of patent protection sought and/or maintained by patentees in Europe;
5. Where might one party or the other perceive (for whatever reason, rightly or wrongly) that it has the best chance of success?

To take examples of different types of patent cases, the pharmaceutical model is generally to have protection in all (or nearly all) states via the EPC route, but the markets may be regarded as basically national in character. Nonetheless, save in the case of blockbuster drugs, litigation may presently often be limited to Germany and the UK, plus perhaps one or two other countries for particular local reasons. On the other hand in technology cases, where the market is often regional in nature, protection may exist in only two or three countries (usually including Germany and the UK) because that is all that is required, and may be via EPs or national patents (or both types may be involved when considering the portfolios of all parties involved).

Taking these examples, one may in both cases see disputes starting with infringement actions brought in Germany, with retaliatory nullity / revocation actions in Germany and the UK, the latter in turn spawning a counterclaim for infringement in the UK. There may additionally also possibly be actions elsewhere for particular local reasons, depending upon the geographical extent of protection, the value of the individual local markets, and of course, where one party or another believes it may score a victory which will influence the overall outcome, that is the terms of an eventual settlement.

By contrast to these international cases, there may be purely national cases, as is the case in many national German and French cases, and cases in the UK Intellectual Property Enterprise Court or in the Patents Court but subject to the Shorter Trial Scheme (where costs-capping is likely to be introduced in 2023 with a cap on recoverable costs of £500,000).

Currently, whether in the big international disputes or in purely national cases, the question of whether the patents were granted nationally or by the EPO will make not a great deal of difference subject to the influence of any pending EPO oppositions and occasional attempts to obtain pan-European relief in the case of EPs (but strictly limited to interim injunctive relief or requests for a declaration of non-infringement (DNI)). In the new system, however, whether patents are national or European will very obviously be of critical importance so far as concerns the choices available, as will whether EPs are unitary or not, and if not, whether opted out or not. These additional factors, plus the complex structure of the UPC itself with its mix of central, local and regional divisions, the possibility of bifurcation, and the uncertainties inevitable with any brand new system, make for a hugely more complex system with many more possibilities. For better or for worse, the new system provides so many more tactical options that it is inevitable that there will be "gaming" of the system, especially in the early years; and to revert to the chess analogy, it is not so much that more pieces have been introduced on the board, but that the game will become three dimensional. Even the simplest national cases will have the potential to become more complicated by the existence of the UPC if the patent involved is an EP which has not been opted out. In that regard, it is likely that many patentees will simply not have the time or inclination to opt out, and in the case of smaller entities, even know that it is an option. To take a typical smaller national German case, a company in Germany threatened with an infringement suit may, if the patent has not been opted out, seek to seise the UPC jurisdiction by seeking revocation in the UPC central division so as to avoid the possibility of an infringement action in Germany and the possibility of an "injunction gap" between the quick regional infringement decision and the slower federal nullity decision.

Whilst bearing strongly in mind that, in any one case, the facts will be different and limiting of options to some extent, and also that each of the facets of the UPC system which give rise to new options will have to be looked at in conjunction with all the other facets (old and new), the individual new facets of the UPC are now considered.

25.2 Forum shopping within the UPC

It may seem counterintuitive to suggest that in a single court, litigants will consider themselves better off fighting in one division than another. In theory this should not be the case, but this is not a "roving court" as propounded by Sir Robin Jacob where the panel would be drawn from a central pool and sit at a local court if necessary. Instead, there are local and regional divisions with (usually) a majority of local judges. One only has to look at a comparable system, that of the United States, to see that some divisions may be preferred over others. The dominating reason will usually be that litigants will consider their chances better in one division than another, but another factor in the UPC may be language, that is the relative ease for that party (and/or difficulty for the opponent) of conducting proceedings in a particular language.

A preliminary warning, which is outside the scope of this chapter to consider in detail, is that in considering the options, one must of course, first establish what options as to choices of local, regional or central division are actually available. In brief, these questions of jurisdiction and competence include consideration of first Article 31 UPCA and the recast Brussels Regulation (international jurisdiction); second Article 32 UPCA (types of proceedings); and third Article 33 UPCA (competence as between UPC divisions).

Due to the different possibilities which arise for litigants in different positions as patentees and non-patentees, and both before and after commencement of proceedings, it is convenient to consider the perspective of the parties in three different situations:

The claimant (whether patentee or non-patentee)
The non-patentee defendant; and
The patentee defendant

25.2.1 The claimant perspective

As stated above, there are likely, in the UPC, to be two main factors influencing the choice of division (when a choice is available), namely language and the ultimate outcome.

As to language, in some situations there will be no choice, notably in central division revocation and DNI cases, where the case must be brought in the language of the patent(s). These cases aside, and when considering infringement actions, it is highly probable, despite the regrettable absence of the UK from the system, and hence the lack of native English speakers among judges and practitioners, that the use of English as the language of the court will be usual, especially given Rule 14(2)(c) known colloquially as the "English limited" rule applicable to infringement actions. That this is so is clear from the use of the English language at the Venice meetings of European patents judges over the past two decades. However, claimants can, subject to being overruled by the Judge-Rapporteur, choose from among the languages available, and importantly, the choice of local or regional division may itself open up choices not available in other divisions, or reduce the chances of the Judge-Rapporteur overturning the claimant's choice. For example, a German company may prefer to bring its case in a German division so as to choose the German language to the detriment of a non-German defendant; or a French company to choose the French local division so as to choose the French language to the detriment of a non-French defendant.

More often, however, it will not be language which will be the main factor in the claimant's choice of one division over another, but rather a view on which division is most likely to hand down a favourable decision, either final or interim / procedural. Why such a view on potential diversity of results may be held by a claimant may arise from a variety of different factors, usually associated with the weighting in most divisions of local judges with traditional local views – something that has been termed the "couleur locale" which is inevitable in the early years especially, despite the inclusion on all panels of at least one non-local judge, and harmonisation through appeals and case law. Three distinct categories may be mentioned: interpretation of substantive law, attitude to injunctive relief (both interim and final), and procedural issues.

Despite the fact that substantive law should be the same under Articles 25–29 UPCA, differences at least initially are likely. For example, what constitutes an actionable act of infringement? Is the grant of a marketing authorisation for a pharmaceutical enough to constitute a threat of infringement either alone or if combined with certain other factors? What of internet offers for sale in a particular language?

The attitude to the grant of preliminary injunctions may be very important in some cases. This may include attitudes to delay; whether it is possible to limit the relief requested on an interim basis to only some Contracting States (Article 76(1) UPCA); and what cross-undertakings are appropriate? In parenthesis this issue may give rise to differing tactics for would-be infringers who may seek to launch in smaller Contracting State markets so as to be able to argue that there has been delay in invoking UPC relief.

Then there is the attitude to grant of final injunctions, and the extent to which alternative relief may instead be granted, for example in the case of life-saving medicines, and in second medical use cases where an injunction should obviously not prevent a first use under an expired patent.

The attitude to procedural aspects may also be important in certain cases, for example in the case of process patent cases where some aspects of infringement case may be within the sole knowledge of the defendant. Will a *saisie* be granted? If not, will an early inspection or disclosure likely be ordered? What will be the attitude to amendment of the pleaded case if new information becomes available at a relatively late stage due to disclosure being given after close of pleadings? Such procedural aspects will be the responsibility of the Judge-Rapporteur, whose identity will not be known before the case is begun, but nonetheless, in a division with two local judges, there may be an obvious possibility of a local judge being appointed to this role and the consequent "couleur locale". At the oral hearing itself, to what extent will cross-examination be permitted, and will it be by the court or by the parties' advocates? (Such matters are especially looked upon as important by US corporations used to the US system.) Under this heading, a further factor may be the attitude to bifurcation, a topic which is worthy of a more detailed examination.

To bifurcate or not to bifurcate?

As will be well known to all reading this book, bifurcation in Germany and other countries arises from the local constitutional position. In Germany, validity is a federal matter, whilst infringement is a regional matter. This system has long given German regional courts a competitive advantage in the patent litigation market. It is true that the UK system permits of bifurcation, but it is immensely rare in practice – just one case this century to the best of your author's knowledge. Hence a patentee with a strong infringement case but a patent of questionable validity will be attracted to Germany, and even a patentee with a strong patent may prefer to have the possibility of a relatively quick infringement decision without the bother of dealing with validity (at least not fully due to the lengthier procedures in the Federal courts) before an injunction is potentially available. Ironically from a German perspective, the participation by Germany in the UPC gives up most if not all of this marketing advantage because the UPC system has what may be described as optional bifurcation, rather than it being mandatory. Its existence is as a result of a political compromise, and is in many ways a very unsatisfactory one.

The possibility for bifurcation arises by virtue of Art 33(3) UPCA which reads as follows:

> (3) A counterclaim for revocation as referred to in Article 32(1)(e) may be brought in the case of an action for infringement as referred to in Article 32(1)(a). The local or regional division concerned shall, after having heard the parties, have the discretion either to:

(a) proceed with both the action for infringement and with the counterclaim for revocation and request the President of the Court of First Instance to allocate from the Pool of Judges in accordance with Article 18(3) a technically qualified judge with qualifications and experience in the field of technology concerned.
(b) refer the counterclaim for revocation for decision to the central division and suspend or proceed with the action for infringement; or
(c) with the agreement of the parties, refer the case for decision to the central division.

Hence, the procedure is that if an infringement action is met with a counterclaim for revocation, the division seised of the infringement action must decide whether to bifurcate the case by sending the counterclaim to the central division, and if so what to do with the infringement action in the interim. The mechanism for doing this is set out in the Rules of Procedure, Rule 37, which prescribe that the decision is only made after the case has been pleaded, and usually after the close of the written procedure. Hence, the parties will not know for certain how the court will deal with the matter until at least several months into the case, and likely not until after about eight months or more after commencement of proceedings. Rule 37 prescribes that the parties must be given an opportunity to be heard, and it is to be expected that a practice will develop that parties will, at least briefly, express their views on bifurcation in the written pleadings. Whilst this may give the parties more certainty if they are in agreement (though even then, the Court may take a different view), it is plain that the delay in knowing how the action will proceed is unsatisfactory, and that there is the possibility of the infringement action being delayed, and even stayed, if there is bifurcation.

Against this background, one may question whether in practice any division is likely to order bifurcation? Whilst the answer cannot be certain, it seems improbable that bifurcation in the UPC will be anything other than a rarity, restricted to cases where the infringement issue is simple, and/or the validity issue is very complex, and/or other factors are in play such as if the EPO is expected imminently to issue a final decision on validity. Whilst this cannot be anything more than indicative, expressions of views by the potential UPC judiciary at Venice meetings have suggested that even those judges from bifurcation jurisdictions are unlikely to yield their jurisdiction to the central division. Why would they want to do so, competent as they are to hear all aspects of a patent case? If so, then the norm will be that actions where counterclaims for revocation are made will be heard in full by the local or regional divisions (or in the central division in cases where no local or regional division has jurisdiction) rather than there being any routine bifurcation.

From the tactical perspective, the crucial point is that a claimant cannot do anything to guarantee bifurcation: it is not a matter of it simply opting for a bifurcated procedure, since the other party or parties must be heard too, and it is ultimately the court which will decide. At the very least, a claimant seeking bifurcation must realise that its chances are probably low of being granted its request; and worse still that if granted, the consequence could include the stay of the infringement part of the proceedings pending the decision of the central division, in other words a case of being "careful what you wish for". Having regard to that possibility, it seems unlikely that claimants will even ask for bifurcation, and the political compromise will turn out to have been made pointlessly.

One other matter must, however, be mentioned under the heading of bifurcation, due to the very curious combined effects of Articles 47(4) & (5) UPCA. In its totality, Article 47 (entitled "Parties") regulates the issue of who can bring patent proceedings. Article 47(4) is *permissive* of patentees joining in actions brought by licensees, rather than requiring the patentee to be joined either as a co-claimant or as a co-defendant (as is the case in the UK). Hence, (and this could, of course, be contrived between cooperating patentees and licensees) if the licensee sues and the patent owner declines to join the action, Article 47(4) requires a defendant to sue the patentee in the central division for revocation. As will be appreciated, this will give rise to a *de facto* bifurcated case. Quite what the two divisions seised of these plainly related actions will then do will be a matter of case management. The difficulty arises that there are no rules on transfers dealing with this specific situation. One would hope that the divisions would talk to each other and agree, preferably that only one division should deal with the case, but that cannot be guaranteed, and it is possible that in some situations patentees might try this tactic so as to see whether an advantage might be gained.

25.2.2 The non-patentee defendant perspective

A defendant sued in one particular local division has very few options available to it within the UPC. All it may do is potentially contest jurisdiction, or in some very limited circumstances request a transfer to the Central Division. This fact may of course, cause potential defendants involved in pre-litigation correspondence or discussions to take their own pre-emptive action, whether in the UPC or in national courts as discussed further below.

25.2.3 The patentee defendant perspective

One of the possible pre-emptive steps a potential defendant may take is to "clear the way" with a Central Division UPC revocation and/or DNI action. Whilst users should be aware that there are different rules affecting these two types of actions, basically the system nullifies the potential benefits to the non-patentee claimant since the patentee defendant retains its options. It may simply counterclaim for infringement in the Central Division, but equally it may still issue separate infringement proceedings in any local or regional division as if the Central Division action had never been started, with the revocation action being stayed automatically, and the DNI action stayed automatically if the infringement action is brought within three months of the DNI and the same parties are involved.

25.2.4 Conclusions on the "balance of power"

From this analysis it will clearly be seen that in the UPC system, it is the patentee which has the choices and the options, even when it is defendant. Whilst there are no extra options for a non-patentee defendant in a UP case, the cases in the early years will be predominantly non-opted out EPs. This leads us to consider what else a potential defendant might do when threatened with proceedings in the UPC's initial years, which in turn brings us to the complex topic of the transitional period (which also provides patentees with yet further options).

25.3 Forum shopping between national and UPC jurisdictions in the transitional period

The concept of the transitional period arose because it was obviously necessary to decide if the new system should apply only to patents applied for at the EPO after the UPCA came into force; or only to newly granted patents; or to all existing patents. Naturally it was realised that if only newly applied for (or even granted) patents were within the system, it would be many years before the UPC had enough cases to justify the major investment in its being set up. Equally, it was considered unfair to impose upon patentees a new system of litigation which they could not be said to have "signed up to" simply by reason of having prosecuted their patents in the EPO rather than in national patent offices. Many patentees considered that the UPC should not apply to their existing EPs (including any SPCs) at all, or they should be able to opt them in rather than having to opt them out, or at least that they should be able to opt them out for the whole of the life of the patent. In the end a political compromise was reached, and the system permits of an opt out for the life of the patent which can be made during a period of seven years after commencement of the system, with a review after five years and the possibility of an extension of the opt out period for up to a further seven years. Also, it was later decided that there should be no fee for opting out. Hence, for better or for worse, it gives rise to the potential for jurisdictional fights as between the UPC and national courts of Contracting States, and indeed non-participating EPC state courts for the reasons which are explained below

To begin it is worth mentioning one ambiguity in the relevant article of the UPCA, that is Article 83. The article permits certain types of actions to be brought in national courts despite the coming into force of the UPC. The list, for some reason, does not include DNIs. It is therefore possible that there could be a dispute as to whether a DNI brought in a national court in respect of a non-opted out EP is permissible under the UPCA. This has been the subject of much discussion, and the general consensus is that this is an oversight, such that DNIs can indeed be brought nationally during the transitional period. Note, however, that such a dispute would be decided by the national court, not the UPC and hence it remains conceivable that this could be the cause of some difficulties.

One major problem with the opt out procedure is that it requires affirmative action by patentees, and this affirmative action is not necessarily straightforward. Beyond mentioning this, however, the procedure is beyond the scope of this chapter, save to note a potential trap for the unwary that the final iteration of the rules (some, including your author, would say surprisingly) requires an opt out in resect of all designations of an EP, including those designations outside the Contracting States, including states who are arguably not eligible to join the UPC system such as Switzerland. We will return to this shortly.

In any event, one is left with a body of non-opted out patents where a potential defendant receiving a threat of patent proceedings may be able to seise either the UPC jurisdiction or a national jurisdiction. Also, potential defendants will be aware that an opt out can be withdrawn (once). Therefore a patentee may decide to opt out a patent to avoid a pre-emptive central division revocation action, but then surprise a defendant by withdrawing its opt out and commence UPC proceedings seeking a pan-European injunction and damages. This effectively means that in *any* case arising in the transitional period (even if the patent is opted out) a potential defendant should have in mind that it may find itself in the UPC. What might a potential defendant then do? It may consider that UPC proceedings are not in its best interests, including taking into account that as explained above, it is the patentee which has the advantage of choice within the UPC. For that reason, a defendant may decide that in response to a threat of proceedings, it will initiate them itself in its preferred national court, seeking to revoke and/or seek a DNI. Further, knowing this, patentees, may decide that they would rather not forewarn a potential defendant of its plans to litigate and "shoot first". In other words, the existence of the UPC transitional provisions may actually cause a rush to the courts, a most unfortunate, but seemingly inevitable consequence.

Other problems arising from transitional regime

Another question should also be considered here. Does the existence of a national action in the transitional period exclude the possibility of UPC actions in respect of other designations of the EP in suit? The answer may seem that it obviously should. It would seem faintly ridiculous that the system should permit of anything other than a "clean" system whereby all litigation in Contracting States was either within or without the UPC. Were this not the case, a potential defendant could for example seek to revoke the Dutch designation of an EP, but that then later the patentee could sue for infringement in the UPC and cause the defendant to counterclaim for revocation in the UPC also. However, Article 83 is not drafted so as to require a "clean" system, and there is nothing which prevents such a scenario. Therefore it is necessary to consider this issue more deeply.

At the heart of this question is whether or not EPs have a unitary character. Your author's view the answer is that once granted they clearly do not. As it is often described, what results from the grant of an EP is a "bundle" of patents of national character. Circumstances have arisen in the past when claims were granted by the EPO in different forms in different countries, and although central amendment is now routine, national amendment proceedings also remain routine and will usually result in the subject national designations being limited in scope. Then of course there are national revocation proceedings which may result in that designation being revoked in its entirety. Hence, for EPs (other than new UPs) there is nothing irrational in the concept that parallel national and UPC proceedings should exist.

One then needs to consider other provisions of the UPCA. Two are particularly relevant. First is Article 34 which states that "Decisions of the Court shall cover, in the case of a European patent, the territory of those Contracting Member States for which the European patent has effect". The other is Article 76(1) which states that: "The Court shall decide in accordance with the requests submitted by the parties and shall not award more than is requested."

Hence, although Article 34 may point the other way, it would seem likely that at the very least in response to the above exemplified revocation action in the Netherlands, a patentee could seek an injunction and damages in respect of other EP designations by bringing UPC proceedings specifically excluding the Netherlands and possibly even including the Netherlands because the Dutch Court in our example is seised only of the claim for revocation.

In such a scenario what would a defendant do? Would it counterclaim in the UPC for revocation of all designations, or just for the non-Dutch designations? Or would it argue that because of Article 34, and notwithstanding any limitations of the relief sought by the patentee (and hence restrictive of the UPC's powers to order remedies under Article 76(1)), Article 34 meant that it could not limit its case to exclude the Netherlands and hence the whole UPC action was unlawful?

Further, could the patentee seek a stay of the Dutch proceedings, despite that Court being first seised, particularly if the Defendant chose to seek revocation over the whole of the EP including the Dutch designation?

There are no easy answers to these questions, and inevitably therefore, until the points are decided, there will be uncertainty and satellite litigation of a jurisdictional type, possibly involving both the UPC and national courts which might conceivably give rise to conflicting decisions.

25.4 Anti-suit injunctions

The above-explained problems of the transitional period lead on to another topic which potentially arises both in respect of the specific type of issue raised above, and the wider problem of the exact relationship between the UPC and national courts of non-Contracting States. Let us begin with Contracting States and the above-mentioned transitional period regime.

As explained, it is unclear what might occur if a potential defendant reacted to a threat of litigation in the UPC by bringing (for example) revocation proceedings in the Dutch courts. One solution to the consequent problems outlined above would be for the potential defendant also to ask Dutch Court to grant an anti-suit injunction preventing the patentee from then bringing UPC proceedings in respect of either just the Dutch designation, or that and all other designations. Naturally, it would be for the Dutch Court to make that decision, and given the uncertainty and complications which could arise from parallel Dutch and UPC proceedings, one can well see the Dutch Court agreeing to such a request.

This possibility, of course, gives rise to the question of what a patentee foreseeing such a possibility might do? One obvious response would be to "shoot first" and bring UPC proceedings. Alternatively, it might bring an anti-anti-suit proceeding in the UPC to head off any pre-emptive national anti-suit proceedings. Either way, one is driven to the same conclusion as mentioned above, that the existence of the transitional arrangements may cause a rush to court and interim jurisdictional disputes.

A similar problem also exists with non-Contracting State designations where, as prefaced above, the opt out regime (as included in the Rules of Procedure as finalised prior to adoption on 8 July 2022) requires that designations of non-Contracting States also be opted out. The note explaining this late-in-the-day amendment to R.5 adding this requirement states that the old wording was inconsistent with the "indivisible nature" of the opt-out. That reasoning is, however, circular as the desire to prevent patents in Contracting States having different opt out status does not require the same of patents in non-Contracting States. However, more significantly, the note also states that the previous wording implied that "the UPC solely has jurisdiction over UPCA Contracting Member States which is not the case". This can easily be read as clearly signalling an expectation that the UPC will exercise jurisdiction in respect of EPs of non-Contracting States. That it can do so in similar fashion to the way in which national courts already exercise jurisdiction in some cases (when validity is not in issue (DNIs) and in provisional measures cases) is not surprising. However, this must raise alarm bells that rather more is in mind, including matters such as the so-called "long-arm" jurisdiction postulated by Maître Pierre Veron.

All of this raises the likelihood of pre-emptive measures including possibly anti-suit injunctions in respect of a wider class of national court, including perhaps most significantly in respect of the UK. Thus, a potential defendant threatened with European patent proceedings in respect of a non-opted out patent (or even an opted out one given the potential to withdraw the opt out) may also wish to consider pre-emptive measures in non-Contracting States. For example, a Swiss-based company threatened with UPC proceedings may consider applying for an anti-suit injunction from the Swiss courts to prevent any UPC action claiming relief in respect of the Swiss designation. Indeed, it may go further and seek an anti-suit injunction in respect of all designations, perhaps particularly in circumstances where it has already begun revocation or DNI proceedings in the national court of a Contracting State.

25.5 Conclusions – a more uncertain world for European patent litigation

From this analysis one can see that there are numerous new tactical permutations which will arise when the UPC goes live. Unless and until each of the new tactics has been tried out (and doubtless many more not covered in this short chapter will be dreamt up) it is impossible to say with any certainty how matters will unfold. What *is* certain is that attempts will always be made to gain an advantage of one sort or another through innovative tactics. These attempts will not all succeed, but neither will they all fail. At the very least there will be a period, perhaps of several years, where it will not be possible to say with any certainty how a matter will evolve. A particular problem is that it is not just the UPC which needs to make rulings, but also national courts, whose views may differ from the UPC and/or indeed from other national courts. Decisions may even vary within nations, such as Germany with its particular system of regional courts, or even the UK with its separate jurisdictions in Scotland and Northern Ireland in addition to the much larger England & Wales jurisdiction.

One obvious consequence of all of this is also that initial cases which involve jurisdictional disputes of one kind or another will very likely be subject to significant delays in the hearing of the substantive dispute. The result may be a hesitance among patentees to litigate in the UPC initially until others have tested the system, at least with their "crown jewels". That said a counter-view expressed by many patentees is that they wish to try out the system themselves early on so as to shape its jurisprudence. Also, some patentees with large portfolios which can be "sliced and diced" among national courts and different divisions within the UPC may already be gearing up to use the system to their advantage. Owners of large Standard Essential Patent portfolios are an obvious example. Hence, the only safe prediction to make about how the system may evolve, and the extent to which it will be used in the early months and years, is that both matters are entirely unpredictable.

Matthias Lamping, Christoph Rademacher

26 Patent litigation strategies in Germany: maneuvering the evolving landscape of bifurcation

Abstract: Germany is the most relevant venue for patent litigation in Europe. By some metrics, German courts decide more patent infringement cases than courts in any other country in the world, and, depending on the year, patent infringement filings at German courts account for more than 70% of all infringement filings across Europe. This chapter will highlight the role of bifurcating infringement and validity determination as the chief reason behind such popularity of German courts. The chapter will therefore introduce the contours of bifurcation under German law as well as at the Unified Patent Court (UPC); as a backdrop, it will also introduce the experience of the Japanese system, which used to operate a German-style bifurcation and abolished such bifurcation approximately 20 years ago. The chapter will conclude by discussing the different strategic options that parties to patent disputes encounter both in Germany and at the UPC.

26.1 Bifurcation of proceedings

26.1.1 Germany

26.1.1.1 Basic structure, legal basis and effect

Section 143 of the German Patent Act provides for subject-matter jurisdiction of regional courts to hear first-instance infringement disputes.[1] Pursuant to the authorization also stemming from such provision, the German state governments have delegated in-

---

[1] Section 143 of the German Patent Act: (1) The civil divisions of the regional courts shall have exclusive jurisdiction, irrespective of the value in dispute, over all actions in which a claim from one of the legal relationships regulated under this Act is asserted (patent litigation cases). (2) The Land (federal state) governments shall be authorised to assign, by statutory instrument, patent litigation cases for the districts of more than one regional court to one such regional court. The Land governments may delegate this authorisation to the Land departments of justice. In addition, the Länder may, by agreement delegate duties incumbent upon the courts of one Land to the competent court of another Land, in whole or in part.

Matthias Lamping, is Senior Research Fellow at the Max Planck Institute for Innovation and Competition, Munich.
Christoph Rademacher, is Professor of Law at Waseda University, Tokyo.

fringement cases to 12 regional courts.² The regional courts of Düsseldorf, Mannheim, and Munich have become the most prominent courts that hear the bulk of patent infringement cases in Germany. Decisions are made by panels of three judges who have studied law, but who usually do not have any formal technical training. Infringement decisions can be appealed to the higher regional courts that have jurisdiction for the respective originating regional court district. In principle, higher regional courts review the regional courts' case *de novo*, i.e., they have discretion to consider additional facts and do not need to rely on the facts as they have been determined by the regional courts.

Infringement courts are not competent to make decisions with respect to the validity of a patent. Such lack of competence is derived from Section 65 of the German Patent Act, which stipulates the jurisdiction of the Federal Patent Court (*Bundespatentgericht, BPatG*) to hear disputes in which the lack of validity of German patents is asserted.³ When the Federal Patent Court was established in 1961, it replaced the trial and appeals board of the German Patent and Trademark Office (*Deutsches Patent- und Markenamt, DPMA*) that had reviewed patent rejections as well as patent grant decisions of the patent office since 1936. The impetus for the establishment of the Patent Court came from a 1959 decision of the Federal Administrative Court, which held that the then-existing review structure in which an administrative institution was tasked with reviewing its own decisions without immediate recourse to an independent judicial review would constitute a violation of the constitutional principle of the separation of powers pursuant to Article 20(2) of the Ger-

---

2 The following regional courts have been delegated, pursuant to the following assignment authority: Regional Court of Berlin for the states of Berlin (Act of 20.11.1995, GVBl. BLN 96, 105) and Brandenburg (Act of 15.12.1995, GVBl. BR 95, 689; Act of 20.11.1995, GVBl. BLN 96, 105; GVBl. BR 95, 288); Regional Court of Braunschweig for the state of Niedersachsen (Act of 22.1.1998, GVBl. 98, 66); Regional Court of Düsseldorf for the state of Nordrhein-Westfalen (Act of 13.1.1998, GV. NW 98, 106); Regional Court of Erfurt for the state of Thüringen (Act of 1.12.1995, GVBl.TH 95, 404); Regional Court of Frankfurt (Main) for the states of Hessen (Act of 26.8.1960, GVBl. 60, 175 (for patents), Act of 27.8.1987, GVBl. 87 I,163 (for utility models)) and Rheinland-Pfalz (Act of 4.8.1950, GVBl.HE 50, 251, GVBl.R-P 50, 316 (patents)); Regional Court of Hamburg for the states of Bremen, Hamburg and Schleswig-Holstein (Act of 18.5.93, GBl.BR 93, 154; Act of 2.2.1993, GVBl.HH 93, 33; Act of 27.9.1993, GBl. SH 93, 497; Act of 6.11.1993, GVOBl.M-V 93, 919; Act of 17.11.1992 between BR, HH, SH and M-V, GVBl.HH. 93, 33; BlPMZ 95, 236)); Regional Court of Leipzig for the state of Sachsen (Act of 14.7.1994, GVBl. 94, 1313); Regional Court of Magdeburg for the state of Sachsen-Anhalt (Act of 5.12.1995, GVBl.LSA 95, 360); Regional Court of Mannheim for the state of Baden-Württemberg (Act of 20.11.1998, GBl. BW 98, 680); Regional Court of München I for Munich; Regional Court of Nürnberg-Fürth for Nürnberg and Bamberg (Act of 2.2.1988, § 18 Bayer. GVBl. 88. 6, 9), and Regional Court of Saarbrücken for the state of Saarland (no delegation, as there is only one regional court in Saarland).
3 The German Federal Supreme Court (Bundesgerichtshof, BGH) has confirmed that infringement courts should not make decisions with respect to the validity of asserted patents (cf. BGH, Decision of April 6, 2004 – Case No. X ZR 272/02 – Druckmaschinen-Temperierungssystem, published in GRUR 2004, 710). See e.g. Philip Moritz Cepl, in: Philip Moritz Cepl & Ulrike Voß (eds.), *Prozesskommentar Gewerblicher Rechtsschutz und Urheberrecht*, 3rd ed. 2022, ZPO § 148, para. 101; Thomas Kühnen, *Handbuch der Patentverletzung*, 15th ed. 2023, Ch. E, para. 901.

man Constitution.[4] As a response, the German legislator established the Federal Patent Court, which decides assertions of invalidity through revocation actions in panels that consist of two legally-trained judges and three judges with a technical background.[5]

The validity of an issued patent can also be challenged through commencing opposition proceedings at the DPMA or the European Patent Office (EPO), though such proceedings can only be initiated within nine months after issuance of the patent.[6] As long as an opposition action can be filed or is pending, no revocation action can be filed at the Federal Patent Court.[7]

26.1.1.2 Requirements for a stay of the infringement procedure

While infringement courts cannot hold an asserted patent invalid, they can, upon request of a party, decide to stay the infringement proceedings until the Patent Court – or, in case of opposition proceedings, the patent office conducting those proceedings – determines the validity of the asserted patent.[8] For the infringement court to consider whether or not such a stay is appropriate, the party requesting the stay – i.e. typically the alleged infringer – has to have commenced revocation proceedings at the Patent Court or opposition proceedings at the patent office. Furthermore, the infringement court usually has to believe the patent to be infringed in order to consider a stay.[9] The burden of proof rests on the defendant.[10]

---

4 German Federal Administrative Court (Bundesverwaltungsgericht, BVerwG), Decision of June 13, 1959 – Case No. IC 66. 57, published in NJW 1959, 1507.
5 Section 67 of the German Patent Act.
6 Section 59 of the German Patent Act for patents issued by the DPMA; Section 99 of the European Patent Convention (EPC) for patents issued by the EPO.
7 Section 81(2) of the German Patent Act.
8 Section 148 of the German Code of Civil Procedure.
9 Section 148 of the German Code of Civil Procedure requires that the infringement court's decision depends on the determination of the validity (*Vorgreiflichkeit*). If the infringement court finds the patent not to be infringed, it can decide the infringement contention without having to wait for the determination of validity. See e.g. Higher Regional Court of Munich, Decision of March 20, 2014 – Case No. 6 U 187/13, published in BeckRS 2014, 20370. Only in exceptional cases where the determination of infringement despite certain doubts on the validity would clearly violate the principle of economic efficiently use of court and party resources, e.g. if certain factual determination necessary to finally resolve the infringement assertion are particularly resource-consuming (see Regional Court of Mannheim, Decision of March 30, 2012 – Case No. 7 O 41/08, published in BeckRS 2013, 14993), or if the determination of the appropriate scope of the asserted patent's claim relies on the outcome of the validity procedure (cf. German Federal Supreme Court (BGH), Decision of June 5, 2018 – Case No. X ZR 58/16, published in BeckRS 2018, 12357), the infringement court can stay the infringement cases without having found infringement. The requirement to appoint an independent expert by the court for an infringement determination, which usually requires the use of a considerable amount of resources, would not constitute a reason to stay the infringement pro-

Traditionally, infringement courts have taken a rather conservative stance towards staying infringement procedure due to validity concerns argued in another venue.[11] Accordingly, courts stayed infringement proceedings usually only if they were presented with technology that strongly indicated a lack of novelty and that was not presented and reviewed during the prosecution of the patent.[12] Allegations of a lack of an inventive step would usually not convince a court to stay the infringement proceedings, especially if the patentee could make a reasonable argument to defend the existence of an inventive step.[13] In addition to the factors related to the 'quality' of the patent at issue, the infringement court also needs to take into consideration the judgments of foreign courts.[14] While decisions of the EPO or other courts of EPC member states on the same patent – to be more precise: on another 'part' of the 'same' European patent – are not binding on German courts, they need to consider such decisions in the interest of legal certainty and harmonization within EPC territory.[15] Arguably, the same applies to decisions of the EPO's Boards of Appeal.[16]

Not surprisingly, infringement courts almost always stay infringement proceedings if the asserted patent has been declared invalid in a parallel revocation proceed-

---

ceeding even if the court has considerable doubts regarding the validity of the patent, see Kühnen, *supra* note 3, para. 918.

10 See Ulrike Voß, in: Uwe Fitzner, Sebastian Kubis & Theo Bodewig (eds.), *BeckOK Patentrecht*, 27th ed. 2023, Vor §§ 139–142b (Verletzungsprozess), para. 191; Philip Moritz Cepl, *supra* note 3, ZPO § 148, para. 118.

11 For a detailed discussion of the case law from the early post-war period until the 1980s see Falk Freiherr von Maltzahn, *Die Aussetzung im Patentverletzungsprozeß nach § 148 ZPO bei erhobener Patentnichtigkeitsklage*, GRUR 1985, 163.

12 German Federal Supreme Court (BGH), Decision of November 11, 1986 – Case No. X ZR 56/85 – Transportfahrzeug, published in GRUR 1987, 284; Regional Court of Hamburg, Decision of May 2, 2013 – Case No. 327 O 370/12, published in BeckRS 2013, 14999.

13 Higher Regional Court of Düsseldorf, Decision of December 21, 2007 – Case No. 2 U 58/05 – Thermocycler, published in GRUR-RR 2007, 259; Regional Court of Düsseldorf, Decision of December 18, 2012 – Case No. 4 b O 16/11 U, published in BeckRS 2013, 14797; Regional Court of Mannheim, Decision of March 8, 2013 – Case No. 7 O 139/12 – Seitenaufprall-Schutzeinrichtung, published in GRUR-RR 2013, 449; Regional Court of Mannheim, Decision of February 18, 2011 – Case No. 7 O 100/10, published in BeckRS 2011, 4156.

14 See Philip Moritz Cepl, *supra* note 3, ZPO § 148, para. 138.

15 See German Federal Supreme Court (BGH), Decision of April 15, 2010 – Case Xa ZB 10/09 (BPatG) – Walzenformgebungsmaschine, published in GRUR 2010, 950. This requires, however, that the substantive law on the basis of which the foreign patent was revoked or amended is comparable to the legal basis on which the patent is being challenged in Germany (cf. Regional Court of Düsseldorf, Decision of January 22, 2015 – Case No. 4 a O 136/13, published in BeckRS 2015, 15910).

16 As a side note: The fact that the patent holder does not commercialize the patented invention by manufacturing and/or selling products (i.e that the patent holder is a non-practicing entity) is not considered to be a factor that should affect the court's decision to stay or not to stay (cf. Regional Court of Düsseldorf, Decision of October 30, 2014 – Case No. 4 a O 92/13, published in BeckRS 2014, 20491).

ing,[17] and are on the other hand very unlikely to stay if the basis for a revocation action or an opposition procedure has been assessed and dismissed either by the Patent Court or in opposition proceedings.[18]

In general, revocation and opposition proceedings are treated equally when it comes to the question of whether infringement proceedings should be stayed. However, some courts are more willing to stay in case of pending opposition cases than revocation cases. The reason is the difference regarding the burden of rendering evidence and proof.[19] In opposition proceedings it rests on the patent applicant, in revocation proceedings on the claimant.[20]

26.1.1.3 Communication between Patent Court and infringement courts

One of the fundamental institutional fairness concerns raised with respect to the interplay of infringement and validity decision-making in Germany is that especially first-instance infringement courts will almost always arrive at an infringement decision long before the Patent Court decides validity. More than 50 % of first-instance infringement decisions conclude with a finding of infringement, and a finding of infringement usually corresponds with the court issuing an enforceable injunction. This dynamic, also illustrated in Figure 1 below, has the potential to put excessive pressure on the infringer, who might have good reasons to challenge the validity of the asserted patent, but who might effectively be forced to withdraw such validity challenge and settle the dispute at conditions that would be very patentee-favourable given an imminent injunction that would often come with significant economic costs for the infringer.

---

[17] Higher Regional Court of Düsseldorf, Decision September 20, 2007 – Case No. 2 U 42/06, published in BeckRS 2008, 7892; Regional Court of Munich, Decision of February 12, 2015 – Case No. 7 O 9443/12, published in BeckRS 2015, 7460.
[18] Regional Court of Düsseldorf, Decision of December 16, 2010 – Case No. 2 U 89/09, published in BeckRS 2011, 8599.
[19] See Regional Court of München I, Decision of September 21, 2017 – Case No. 7 O 15820/16, para. 91, published in GRUR-RS 2017, 125777.
[20] German Federal Supreme Court (BGH), Decision of January 23, 1990 – Case No. X ZR 75/87 (BPatG) – Feuerschutzabschluss, published in GRUR 1991, 522.

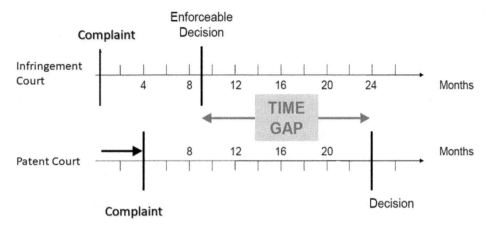

Figure 1: German Injunction Gap

The dynamics of having such 'injunction gaps' might be acceptable if the validity of patents issued by the DPMA or the EPO would usually withstand revocation actions at the Federal Patent Court. Studies on the outcome of revocation actions in Germany show, however, that the majority (more than three quarters) of patents that are challenged at the Federal Patent Court are found to be either fully or at least partially invalid.[21]

Years surveyed	# proceedings	Fully invalid	Partially invalid	Validity confirmed
2010–2013	392	171 (43.62 %)	139 (35.46 %)	82 (20.92 %)
2018–2020	221	83 (37.56 %)	94 (42.53 %)	44 (19.91 %)

Figure 2: Revocation Statistics

These studies also show that the rates of invalidity determination were even higher for patents issued for inventions in the telecom and software area, an area that tends to attract a large portion of the patent litigation in Germany.[22] Given the tendency of many patentees in such industries to enforce their patent portfolios with the primary goal of accomplishing an economically favorable settlement rather than excluding competitors from the market through permanent injunctions, the injunction gap of the German bi-

---

21 Peter Hess, Tilman Müller-Stoy & Martin Wintermeier, *Sind Patente nur Papiertiger?*, Mitteilungen der deutschen Patentanwälte 2014, 439; Tilman Müller-Stoy, Anna Giedke & Julian Große-Ophoff, *Aktuelle Vernichtungsquoten im deutschen Patentnichtigkeitsverfahren*, GRUR 2022, 142.
22 For 2010–2013, the rates reported in the telecom and software industry were as follows: fully invalid: 58 %; partially invalid: 30 %; validity confirmed: 12 %. For 2018–2020, the rates improved somewhat, with the following rates reported: fully invalid: 30 %; partially invalid: 52 %; validity confirmed: 18 %.

furcation system became particularly valuable for such patentees and particularly unfair for alleged infringers.

A number of commentators, both from legal practice and academia, noted the lack of fairness that the combination of a bifurcated system, a restrictive practice of allowing stays, and a high invalidation rate of challenged patents provided.[23] Attempting to address this concern, the German government presented a rather pragmatic approach by forcing parties and the Patent Court to expedite parts of the revocation procedure:[24] pursuant to Section 83(1) of the Patent Act, the Patent Court has to indicate "aspects which will presumably be of particular significance" for the validity decision to the parties "as early as possible". The requirement to provide such indication, usually referred to as a qualified indication (qualifizierter Hinweis), was added to the Patent Act in 2009. The indication of such aspects that the Patent Court considers to be of particular significance is based on the Patent Court's preliminary assessment of the challenged patent's validity, taking into consideration the courts views on all validity challenges raised.[25]

Before 2022, the Patent Court usually issued its qualified indication about 15 months after the filing of the revocation action,[26] albeit almost one year before the final validity decision, but usually still significantly later than the first-instance decision on infringement.[27] In its 2021 Patent Act amendment, the legislator followed the government draft and amended Section 83 of the Patent Act by adding a provision pursuant to which the qualified indication has to be issued within six months after serving the revocation action to the parties.[28] To enable the Patent Court to expedite its initial validity assessment, the revised law provides for more rigid timelines for the parties: the plaintiff is now re-

---

[23] Kühnen, *supra* note 3, para. 928; Léon E. Dijkman, *Does the Injunction Gap Violate Implementers' Fair Trial Rights Under the ECHR?*, GRUR Int. 2021, 215; id., *Does the Injunction Gap Violate Implementer's Fair Trial Rights Under the Charter?*, GRUR 2022, 857; Christof Keussen, *Das Trennungsprinzip im Patentrecht – ein Auslaufmodell?*, GRUR 2021, 257; Peter Meier-Beck, *Bifurkation und Trennung: Überlegungen zum Übereinkommen über ein Einheitliches Patentgericht und zur Zukunft des Trennungsprinzips in Deutschland*, GRUR 2015, 929; Reto Hilty & Matthias Lamping, Trennungsprinzip, Quo Vadis?, in: Achim Bender, Klaus Schülke & Volker Winterfeldt (eds.), *50 Jahre Bundespatentgericht – Festschrift zum 50-jährigen Bestehen des Bundespatentgerichts am 1. Juli 2011*, 2011, 255; Christoph Rademacher, *Expertise, Efficiency, Equity – Searching for an Appropriate Degree of Bifurcation of Patent Infringement and Validity*, Plenary talk at the 36th Annual Congress of ATRIP, October 25, 2017; Tobias Wuttke & Peter Guntz, *Wie weit reicht die Privilegierung des Klägers durch das Trennungsprinzip?*, Mitt. 2012, 477.
[24] Similarly, Rademacher, *id.*, at 9.
[25] An example of a 'qualified indication' (*qualifizierter Hinweis*) is provided in Alfred Keukenschrijver, *Patentnichtigkeitsverfahren*, 7th ed. 2021, Ch. 5, para. 211.
[26] Arwed Burrichter, Der qualifizierte Hinweis nach § 83 Abs. 1 PatG (Teil 1), in Thomas Kühnen (ed.), *Festschrift 80 Jahre Patentgerichtsbarkeit in Düsseldorf*, 2016, at 82.
[27] If the qualified indication was issued prior to the infringement court issuing its infringement decision, infringement courts tend to defer to substantiated qualified indications.
[28] Zweites Gesetz zur Vereinfachung und Modernisierung des Patentrechts, BGBl. 2021 I 3490. The revision discussed here has been in force since May 2022.

quired to immediately serve the complaint after filing it to the Patent Court,[29] and the patent owner has to substantiate its response to the invalidity complaint within two months after receiving the complaint.[30] These revised timelines put significant pressure on the parties and on the court. That said, especially the patentee can prepare for invalidity assertions in advance by conducting a thorough analysis of the patent before filing an infringement action, which is often the trigger event for a parallel revocation action.

The first qualified indications that have been issued by the Patent Court starting from December 2022 under the new six-month time limit seem to provide for reasoning that is of comparable depth to that of qualified indications issued before the implementation of the time limit. At the same time, it remains questionable whether the Patent Court will be able to continue to provide reliable thoughts on patent validity within the significantly shorter time period.[31] Also, the revision of the procedure at the Patent Court will not have any direct impact on the procedure and the timeline of opposition proceedings at the DPMA or the EPO, and revocation actions that trigger the court having to issue the qualified indication can still not be initiated before the lapse of the nine-month opposition period or after the resolution of opposition procedures.[32]

Despite the concerns mentioned above, the expedition of the qualified indication is an important first step to introduce an objective assessment of patent validity into the infringement proceedings and thus to ensure more fairness for alleged infringers. Whether this first step will really close the German 'injunction gap' will largely depend on the clarity and the substance of the reasoning of the qualified indication. Even prior to the 2021 reform, German infringement courts have refused staying infringement proceedings if the qualified indication has not clearly indicated a position on the validity of the challenged patent[33] or if its reasoning has been deemed somewhat insufficient.[34] At the same time infringement courts and commentators have acknowledged the importance of a well-reasoned qualified indication that conveys a clear position of the Patent Court on the prospects of the validity challenge.[35] If the Patent Court can continue to is-

---

29 Section 82 (1) of the German Patent Act.
30 Section 82 (3) of the German Patent Act.
31 Rather sceptical: Ansgar Ohly & Martin Stierle, *Unverhältnismäßigkeit, Injunction Gap und Geheimnisschutz im Prozess: Das Zweite Patentrechtsmodernisierungsgesetz im Überblick*, GRUR 2021, 1229, 1238–39; Keussen, *supra* note 23, at 259; Thomas Voit, in: Schulte (ed.), *Kommentar zum Patentgesetz*, 11th ed. 2022, § 83 PatG, para. 6.
32 Section 81 (2) of the German Patent Act. The hesitancy of the legislator to amend this section and to enable an alleged infringer to immediately file a nullification action at the Patent Court was one aspect of the law that was strongly criticized by commentators (see e.g. Keussen, *supra* note 23, at 260).
33 See e.g. Higher Regional Court of Düsseldorf, Decision of July 21, 2018 – Case No. I-2 U 19/17.
34 Regional Court of Munich, Decision of September 29, 2021 – Case No. 21 I 9793/21, published in GRUR-RS 2021, 37988.
35 See e.g. Higher Regional Court of Karlsruhe, Decision of February 22, 2010 – Case No. 6 U 71/08; Higher Regional Court of Düsseldorf, Decision of December 2, 2019 – Case No. I-2 U 48/19; Higher Regional Court of Düsseldorf, Decision of March 3, 2021 – Case No. I-2 U 25/20, published in GRUR-RS 2021, 1830; see also Küh-

sue qualified indications that live up to such standard, infringement courts will have no choice but to stay an increasing number of patent infringement proceedings going forward, resulting in a German patent enforcement system that will be significantly less tilted in favor of patentees.

26.1.2 Unified Patent Court

26.1.2.1 Institutional structure of the UPC

Charged to adjudicate disputes with respect to the validity and infringement of unitary patents, the UPC has been established under the auspices of the EU[36] as a "court common to the Contracting Member States" of the EU.[37] It is thus part of the Member States' "judicial system, with exclusive competence in respect of European patents with unitary effect [unitary patents] and European patents granted under the provisions of the EPC".[38]

The UPC's institutional structure is that of a two-level judiciary, with a Court of First Instance (CFI) and a Court of Appeal (CoA). The CFI comprises a central division as well as local and regional divisions.[39] The central division has its seat in Paris with a section in Munich (and possibly another one in Milan);[40] the local and regional divisions are established according to the country's or region's case-load.[41] At all levels, the panels are multinational.[42] They sit in a composition of three judges and are chaired by a legally qualified judge, though the parties may agree to have their case heard by a single legally qualified judge.[43] Panels of the central division sit in a composition of two legally quali-

---

nen, *supra* note 3, para. 947; Martin Chakraborty, Der qualifizierte Hinweis nach § 83 Abs. 1 PatG (Teil 2), in: Thomas Kühnen (ed.), *Festschrift 80 Jahre Patentgerichtsbarkeit in Düsseldorf*, 2016, at 111.
36 As part of the legislative package implementing enhanced cooperation: Regulation (EU) No. 1257/2012 of the European Parliament and the Council of 17 September 2012 implementing enhanced cooperation in the area of the creation of unitary patent protection, OJ 2012 L 361/1; Council Regulation (EU) No 1260/2012 of 17 December 2012 implementing enhanced cooperation in the area of the creation of unitary patent protection with regard to the applicable translation arrangements, OJ 2012 L 361/89.
37 Rec. 7 and Article 1 of the Agreement on a Unified Patent Court of 19 February 2013 (UPCA), OJ 2013 C 175/1.
38 Ibid.
39 Article 7(1) UPCA.
40 Article 7(2) UPCA. The Paris seat hosts the President's Office and deals with cases on performing operations, transporting, textiles, paper, fixed constructions, physics, and electricity. The Munich section hears cases related to mechanical engineering, lighting, heating, weapons, and blasting. Before Brexit, the London section was supposed to hear cases on human necessities, chemistry, and metallurgy. Whether these fields will be allocated to a new section (Milan has been discussed, for example) or distributed among Paris and Munich has not been decided yet (cf. Annex II to the UPCA).
41 Article 7(3) to (5) UPCA.
42 Articles 8 and 9 UPCA.
43 See also Rules 38(a), 17(2), and 345(6) UPC RoP.

fied judges and one technically qualified judge,[44] while panels of the local/regional divisions sit in a composition of three legally qualified judges. Upon request by one of the parties or where the panel deems it appropriate, an additional technically qualified judge with qualifications and experience in the field of technology concerned can be allocated to the panel. Panels of the CoA sit in a multinational composition of five judges, three legally qualified and two technically qualified.[45] All panels are chaired by a legally qualified judge.

The presiding judge of the panel to which an action has been assigned designates one legally qualified judge as judge-rapporteur (which may also be himself).[46]

26.1.2.2 Jurisdiction of the UPC

The UPC has exclusive jurisdiction over all revocation[47] and infringement[48] litigation regarding European and unitary patents.[49] Consequently, all European and unitary patents will be governed by the substantive rules laid down in the UPC Agreement[50] once the transitional period has expired and the opt-out possibilities have been exhausted.[51] If an action for revocation or a counterclaim for revocation is successful, the UPC may revoke the patent, either entirely or partly, on the grounds referred to in Articles 138(1) and 139(2) of the EPC.[52]

26.1.2.2.1 Opposition, revocation, and limitation proceedings at the Patent Office

As mentioned above, up to nine months after the publication of the European or unitary patent grant, anyone may give the EPO notice of opposition to the patent, except for the proprietor.[53] The patent proprietor may request the revocation or limitation of the patent after grant, for example if new prior art is discovered by the patentee or brought up by an alleged infringer.[54]

---

44 Except for actions within the meaning of Article 32(1)(i) UPCA. Here, the panel consists of three legally qualified judges (Article 8(6) UPCA).
45 Except for actions within the meaning of Article 32(1)(i) UPCA (Article 9(2) UPCA).
46 Rule 18 UPC RoP.
47 Article 32(d) to (e) UPCA.
48 Article 32(a) to (c) and (f) UPCA.
49 Articles 32 and 2(g) UPCA.
50 See, in particular, Articles 25 to 29 UPCA.
51 Article 83 UPCA.
52 Article 65(1) and (2) UPCA.
53 Article 99 of the EPC.
54 Article 105a of the EPC.

Since the EPO is entrusted with the task of granting both European and unitary patents,[55] all these proceedings (opposition, revocation, and limitation) are governed by the EPC.[56] This will be the case even after the transitional period has expired. To facilitate coordination between the EPO and the UPC, the parties are required to inform the UPC of any pending revocation, limitation, or opposition proceedings before the EPO, and of any request for accelerated processing. The UPC may stay its proceedings when a rapid decision may be expected from the EPO.[57]

26.1.2.2.2 Actions for infringement and counterclaim for revocation

Actions for infringement, injunction, and damages are brought before the CFI's local/regional division competent for the territory in which the actual or threatened infringement has occurred or may occur,[58] or where the defendant[59] has its residence or (principal) place of business.[60]

In case of a counterclaim for revocation, the local/regional division concerned has, after having heard the parties,[61] the discretion either to:[62]

- (1) proceed with both the action for infringement and the counterclaim for revocation and request the President of the CFI to allocate to the panel a technically qualified judge with qualifications and experience in the field of technology concerned;[63]
- (2) refer the counterclaim for revocation to the central division and suspend or proceed with the action for infringement;[64] or
- (3) with the agreement of the parties, refer the entire case to the central division.[65]

Only the second option bifurcates the case. However, in contrast to the German situation (*supra* at I.A.1) where infringement and invalidation proceedings are handled by two institutionally independent courts (at least at instances lower than the Supreme Court), the case remains within the sphere of UPC system.

---

55 Rec. 5 and Article 9 of Regulation (EU) No. 1257/2012.
56 Article 99 et seq. EPC; Rules 75 et seq. of the EPC's Implementing Regulations.
57 Article 33(10) UPCA; Rule 295(a) UPC RoP.
58 Article 33(1)(a) UPCA.
59 In the case of multiple defendants, one of the defendants.
60 Article 33(1)(b) UPCA. If the defendant has no residence or place of business within the territory of the Contracting Member States, the action may be brought before the central division (ibid.).
61 See also Rules 37(1) and 264 of the Rules of Procedure of the Unified Patent Court (UPC RoP).
62 As soon as practicable after the closure of the written procedure the panel shall decide by way of order, setting out brief reasons for its decision, how to proceed (Rule 37(1) and (2) UPC RoP).
63 Article 33(3)(a) UPCA.
64 Article 33(3)(b) UPCA.
65 Article 33(3)(c) UPCA.

Where the panel decides to effectively bifurcate infringement and validity proceedings by referring the counterclaim to the central division, the local/regional division panel
- *may* stay the infringement proceedings pending a final revocation decision; and
- *shall* stay the infringement proceedings where there is a high likelihood that the relevant claims of the patent will be held to be invalid on any ground.[66]

At the central division, the counterclaim for revocation is assigned to a panel by the Registrar.[67] As soon as practicable after service of the statement of defence, the judge-rapporteur shall, after consulting the parties, set a date and time for an interim conference (where necessary) and set a date for the oral hearing; he or she may set one alternative date.[68]

Where the panel of the local/regional division hearing the infringement action decides not to stay the proceedings, the judge-rapporteur is responsible for communicating to the central division the dates set for the interim conference and for the oral hearing.[69] The judge-rapporteur of the panel of the central division, on the other hand, needs to accelerate proceedings before the central division. He or she shall endeavour to set a date for the oral hearing on the revocation action prior to the date of the oral hearing of the infringement action.[70]

Any party may lodge an application for allocating a technically qualified judge to the panel hearing the counterclaim for revocation.[71] The judge-rapporteur may request the President of the CFI to allocate a technically qualified judge after consulting the presiding judge and the parties.[72]

---

[66] Rule 37(4) UPC RoP (own emphasis); see also Rule 118(2)(b) UPC RoP, which applies also in relation to opposition proceedings at EPO.
[67] Rules 38(a), 17(2), and 345(3) UPC RoP. Where an action involves a single patent having a single classification, or where it involves more than one patent and a majority of the patents have a single classification, it is allocated to the seat or the section of the central division appropriate to that classification (Rules 38(a), 17(3)(a) and (b) UPC RoP). Where that is not the case, the action is assigned to the panel at the seat or the section appropriate to the first classification of either the single patent or, where the action involves more than one patent, the patent first listed in the statement of claim (unless the presiding judge considers another panel more appropriate) (Rules 38(a) and 17(3)(c) UPC RoP).
[68] Rules 38(d), 28, and 101(1) UPC RoP.
[69] Rule 37(5) UPC RoP.
[70] Rule 40(b) UPC RoP.
[71] Rule 33(1) UPC RoP. The application shall be lodged as early as possible in the written procedure (Rule 33(2) and (3) UPC RoP).
[72] Rule 34 UPC RoP.

26.1.2.2.3 Actions for declarations of non-infringement and revocation

Questions of bifurcation can also arise out of a declaratory judgement action (DJA), i.e. an action seeking a declaration of non-infringement[73] and/or patent revocation, which are brought before the central division.[74] Even after the commencement of such DJA, the patentee (or licensee entitled to commence proceedings)[75] can bring an action for infringement of the same patent, either before the central division or before any competent[76] local/regional division.[77]

In the latter case, the local/regional division handling the infringement action has, after having heard the parties, the discretion either to:[78]

- (1) suspend or proceed with the action for infringement;[79] or
- (2) with the agreement of the parties, refer the case to the central division.[80]

Also, the alleged infringer may lodge a counterclaim for revocation at the local/regional division. This is possible under the UPC even if a standalone revocation action is already pending before the central division.[81] It is now up to the local/regional division to decide whether to:[82]

- (1) proceed with both the action for infringement and the counterclaim for revocation;[83]
- (2) refer the counterclaim for revocation to the central division (i.e. supposedly to the panel which is already handling the standalone action for revocation) and suspend or proceed with the action for infringement;[84] or
- (3) with the agreement of the parties, refer the entire case to the central division.[85]

Unless otherwise agreed by the parties, the panel appointed in the central division to hear the revocation action has to stay all further proceedings pending a decision of the local/regional division on how to proceed.[86] When making such decision, the local/regional division has to take into consideration how far the revocation action in the central

---

73 See also Article 33(6) UPCA.
74 Article 33(4) UPCA.
75 See Article 47(2) to (5) UPCA.
76 Article 33(1) UPCA.
77 Article 33(5) UPCA.
78 Article 33(5) and 33(3) UPCA and Rule 75 UPC RoP.
79 Article 33(3)(b) UPCA.
80 Article 33(3)(c) UPCA.
81 See Rule 75(3) UPC RoP.
82 Rule 75(3) UPC RoP and Article 33(3) UPCA.
83 Article 33(3)(a) UPCA.
84 Article 33(3)(b) UPCA.
85 Article 33(3)(c) UPCA.
86 Rules 75(3) and 37 UPC RoP.

division has advanced prior to the stay.[87] This is likely to give rise to systemic competition between the central division and local/regional divisions as they may develop case law with different views on certain validity issues.

Where the panel of the local/regional division decides to reunite proceedings (i.e. to proceed with both the action for infringement and the counterclaim for revocation), the parties and the judge-rapporteur may request the allocation of a technically qualified judge to the panel.[88] Under these circumstances, the fate of the standalone revocation action pending at the central division action is unclear; the situation is not regulated by the UPC's rules of procedure.

Where the panel of the local/regional division decides to refer the counterclaim to the central division,[89] or, with the agreement of the parties, refer the entire case to the central division,[90] the provisions on staying infringement proceedings,[91] language of proceedings,[92] accelerating proceedings before the central division,[93] and the written procedure[94] apply *mutatis mutandis*.[95]

For the sake of completeness, it should be mentioned that the defendant in an action for revocation pending before the central division may also file a counterclaim for infringement.[96] It is unclear whether the counterclaim needs to be brought at the central division or can also be brought at a competent local/regional division, which would bifurcate the case.

26.1.3 Japan

As a side note, we would like to introduce Japan's experience with determining infringement and validity as Japan has evolved from a jurisdiction with German-type bifurcation to a jurisdiction that allowed invalidity defences about twenty years ago.

If Germany is considered a paradise for patentees, Japan has acquired the reputation of being the opposite. During the 1990s, patent enforcement in Japan was known to be unpredictable and erratic.[97] Concerns included the difficulty in obtaining evidence, lack of guidance by the court during the course of litigation, difficulties to find qualified

---

87 Rule 75(4) UPC RoP.
88 Rule 75(5) UPC RoP.
89 See Article 33(3)(b) UPCA.
90 See Article 33(3)(c) UPCA.
91 Rule 37(4) UPC RoP.
92 Rule 39 UPC RoP.
93 Rule 40 UPC RoP.
94 Rule 41 UPC RoP.
95 Rule 75(5) UPC RoP.
96 Rules 43(2)(b) and 49(2)(b) UPC RoP.
97 This was at least a prominent view amongst foreign commentators, see e.g. Christopher Heath, *Erlangung und Durchsetzung von Patentrechten in Japan*, GRUR Int. 1998, 555.

counsel with sufficient expertise in patent litigation as well as insufficient explanation of the reasoning for court decisions.[98] The establishment of the IP High Court in 2005 was a central cornerstone of the government's effort to strengthen intellectual property protection in Japan. The government was hoping to establish Japan as an IP-based nation and to promote the IP High Court as an Asian hub for patent dispute resolution. Despite significant efforts, none of these lofty objectives were ever accomplished. If anything, the reputation for Japan as a venue for patent litigation has become even worse. The number of patent infringement cases that are filed in Japanese courts remain at around 150 cases per year, placing Japan in between India and Taiwan in terms of patentee popularity.[99] The reluctance to commence litigation in Japanese courts is mainly due to the harsh prospects that patentees faced when initiating patent litigation in the more recent past.[100] A survey that reviewed patent litigation features of 29 leading jurisdictions around the world showed that Japan had the third-lowest patentee win rate for litigation concluded between 2006 and 2016, with a win rate reported to be as low as 24%.[101] Just like in Germany – but of course with diametrically opposed results – the interplay of infringement and validity determination is arguably one of the main contributors to the attractivity of Japan as a patent litigation venue.

First-instance infringement proceedings in Japan are heard by the Tokyo District Court and the Osaka District Court.[102] Both courts have established court divisions that specialize on intellectual property disputes, including but not limited to patent infringement proceedings. Cases are typically heard by panels of three legally-trained judges who usually do not have any formal technical training. District court decisions can be appealed at the IP High Court, which has been established as a special court within the premises of the Tokyo High Court.[103]

Assertions of invalidity of issued patents have traditionally fallen under the jurisdiction of the Trial and Appeal Department (TAD) of the JPO. Patents that have been issued by the JPO can be challenged at any time in an invalidation trial pursuant to Article 123 of the Patent Act. Invalidation trials are heard by panels of three or five adminis-

---

98 Id., at 561–563.
99 Michael C. Elmer & C. Gregory Gramenopoulos, *Global Patent Litigation: How and Where to Win*, 3rd ed. 2019, at 2–4.
100 While the traditional and maybe socially-inherent hesitation of Japanese companies and individuals to resolve disputes in court litigation that "classic" academics such as the late Professor Takeyoshi Kawashima argued for (see e.g. Takeyoshi Kawashima, *Nihonjin no Hō Ishiki* (The Legal Consciousness of Japanese people), 1967, at 139) might still be somewhat of a factor here, the active role that Japanese companies play in litigating patents outside Japan tend to show that such factor would be a rather minor one.
101 Elmer & Gramenopoulos, *supra* note 99, at 2–7 through 2–12. The only two jurisdictions that showed lower win rates than Japan were Taiwan and Chile.
102 Article 6(1) of the Japanese Code of Civil Procedure.
103 Article 6(3) of the Japanese Code of Civil Procedure, Article 2(1) of the Law for Establishing the IP High Court.

trative judges, which are in essence senior patent examiners.[104] Article 123 (1) of the Patent Act lists a number of possible reasons that can be the basis for the validity challenge. An invalidation trial can only be brought by an interested party, which would include a person against whom such patent has been or is likely to be asserted. While invalidation trials can only be brought by interested parties, another avenue to challenge the validity of a Japanese patent that is open to anybody is to commence a post-grant opposition procedure. Post-grant oppositions can only be filed within six months after the grant of the patent.[105] Unlike invalidation trials which are conducted through oral proceedings,[106] post-grant opposition procedures are primarily conducted through an exchange of documents.[107] While the specific characteristics and the procedure of invalidation actions at the JPO have changed significantly over the last decades, the JPO has, since its establishment during the Meiji era, been the only institution that had the authority to invalidate a Japanese patent, making the Japanese system very similar to the German system of bifurcated infringement and validity determination.

Like under the German system, Japanese infringement courts have the option to stay infringement proceedings pending the determination of the validity of the asserted patent by the JPO.[108] Unlike German infringement courts, however, Japanese judges were not content with such rather limited scope of decision-making.[109] In 1991, the Osaka District Court held in dicta that a court tasked with determining infringement should review the validity of a patent in case of serious and apparent grounds of invalidity. It went on to review the validity of the asserted patent, and concluded that the patent was valid and infringed.[110] Six years later, the Tokyo High Court initiated a seismic change when it held that the enforcement of a patent which is highly likely to be invalid would constitute an abuse of right.[111] The Supreme Court confirmed the reasoning of the Tokyo High Court in 2000,[112] which opened the route for alleged infringers to challenge the va-

---

104 Invalidity trials are conducted between two adversary parties, but the characteristics of the procedure are more similar to an administrative litigation than to civil procedure. Most notably, the TAD plays are more active role than a court in a civil lawsuit as it can carry out proceedings ex officio (pursuant to Article 152 of the Japanese Patent Act), can ignore facts admitted by a party (Article 151 of the Japanese Patent Act) and can consider grounds that have not been pleaded by a party (pursuant to Article 153 (1) of the Japanese Patent Act). See Nobuhiro Nakayama, *Tokkyo-hō* (Patent Law), 4th ed. 2019, at 267.
105 Article 113 of the Japanese Patent Act.
106 Article 145 of the Japanese Patent Act.
107 Article 118 (1) of the Japanese Patent Act.
108 Article 168 of the Japanese Patent Act.
109 Not only judges, but also academics started to question the traditional role of infringement courts, and argued that courts should also consider validity arguments during infringement litigation. See Naohiko Tatsumi, *Tokkyo Shingai Soshō Ni Okeru Tokkyo Hatsumei No Gijutsuteki Han'i To Saibansho No Kengen* (Technical Scope of the Patented Invention and the Authority of the Court in Patent Infringement Litigation), Nihon Kōgyō Shoyūken Hō Gakkai Nenpō, No. 17 (1993), at 41.
110 Osaka District Court, October 30, 1991, published in Hanrei Jihō Vol. 1407, at 34.
111 Tokyo High Court Judgment, September 10, 1997, Chiteki Saishū Vol. 29, No. 3, at 819.
112 Supreme Court Judgment, April 11, 2000, Minshu Vol. 54, No. 4, at. 1368.

lidity of asserted patents not only in validity proceedings at the JPO, but also in infringement proceedings at the district court. The possibility to challenge the validity of patents in district court proceedings was codified through Article 104-3 of the Patent Act in 2004.

The effect of a court finding a patent to be invalid is different from the effect of such decision at the JPO: while the court decision binds only the parties and therefore has a somewhat relative effect, the JPO's decision to invalidate renders the patent invalid with retroactive and *erga omnes* effect.[113] Patent owners, who were hoping to benefit from the reform of the Japanese patent litigation system initiated with a pro-patent policy in mind, found themselves trying to defend the validity of any asserted patent in two different venues that employed different standards of review and that, at least in the early days of these so-called double-track proceedings, often enough arrived at conflicting decisions.[114] In the last decade, the JPO enhanced the resources of the TAD, ensuring that the JPO would conclude a parallel validity challenge before the district court completes its own validity review. District court judges are therefore usually able to review the validity determination of the TAD before releasing their own decision on validity, which has improved the consistency between the two decision-making institutions.

26.2 Implications for litigation

26.2.1 General remarks

The most important factor that drives a patentee's choice of litigation forum is usually the size of the covered market and the exposure of the alleged infringer. Thus, the fact that a successful infringement action at the UPC will typically provide a patentee with an injunction for the entire UPC territory, i.e. much of the EU, is a strong argument for considering the UPC as a preferable patent enforcement venue. On the other hand, many patentees are concerned that their key patents may become subject to a central validity challenge leading to a loss of patent protection for the entire territory. Given that such central validity challenge is not possible for traditional European patents once the opposition procedure has lapsed, a considerable percentage of patent owners especially in the pharmaceutical industry are expected to opt-out their key patents. A growing amount of case law will establish more certainty on patentability standards and the likelihood of unitary patent validity challenges to prevail, which will refine the choices that a patent holder searching for a patentee-friendly venues will be able to make.

Before approaching a potential infringer, a patentee should not only analyse the likelihood of prevailing with infringement assertions, but also carefully screen its pa-

---

113 Article 125 of the Japanese Patent Act.
114 See e.g. Junko Kobayashi, *Daburu-torakku Mondai ni taisuru Kangaekata Kaisei Teian ni mukete* (Towards a Proposal to Revise the Way of Thinking about the Double-Track Problem), Patento Vo. 63–8 (2010), 92.

tent portfolio by attempting to anticipate possible validity challenges. On the other hand, a party that is preparing to develop a product or a service that may infringe third-party patents should conduct a thorough freedom-to-operate (FTO) analysis before committing substantial resources for such development process. If such FTO analysis detects problematic patents, the party should consider the success chances of filing an invalidation action, either through opposition at the patent office, or – depending on whether the patent is a unitary patent or a European patent that the patentee has opted-out – by proactively filing a revocation action at the German Federal Patent Court or at the UPC.

26.2.2 Litigating in Germany

26.2.2.1 Timing of revocation and infringement

In German patent litigation, the alleged infringer has a number of defenses at its disposal[115] – the invalidity of the asserted patent is not one of them. Parties are therefore well advised to file a revocation action or a counterclaim for revocation of the patent-in-suit as soon as possible, ideally even before infringement proceedings are initiated.[116] However, since it is not mandatory under German law to issue a warning letter before bringing an infringement action, this may not always be possible. Unless the alleged infringer is aware of the potential infringement, it is difficult to take precautionary measures. The same applies to the possibility of filing a 'torpedo' action in another EU member state and thereby force the German infringement court to stay proceedings.[117]

The timing is also relevant for the stay of infringement proceedings in relation to pending opposition or revocation proceedings. The longer the alleged infringer waits to bring an action for revocation or file a counterclaim for revocation, the less inclined the

---

[115] Such as: that the infringing act does not fall within the scope of protection; a right to use the patented invention (e.g. on the basis of a licence or prior use; usurpation (widerrechtliche Entnahme) of the invention by the patentee (see German Federal Supreme Court (BGH), Decision of February 1, 2005 – Case No. X ZR 214/02 – Schweißbrennerreinigung, published in GRUR 2005, 567); a competition law claim to use the patented invention (see Court of Justice of the European Union (CJEU), Case C-170/13 – Huawei Technologies, ECLI:EU:C:2015:477); that the patent is exhausted; or that the claim to injunctive relief is forfeited (see Regional Court of Düsseldorf, Decision of March 26, 2009 – Case No. 2 U 108/03, published in BeckRS 2010, 21550).
[116] See Thomas Kühnen, *supra* note 3, para. 810; Philip Moritz Cepl, *supra* note 3, ZPO § 148, para. 144.
[117] See Article 29(1) of Regulation (EU) No 1215/2012 of the European Parliament and of the Council of 12 December 2012 on jurisdiction and the recognition and enforcement of judgments in civil and commercial matters (recast), OJ 2012 L 351/1, which states that "where proceedings involving the same cause of action and between the same parties are brought in the courts of different Member States, any court other than the court first seised shall of its own motion stay its proceedings until such time as the jurisdiction of the court first seised is established".

infringement courts will be to stay proceedings.[118] On the other hand, the more time goes by before the patent holder brings an action for infringement (although he/she knew or should have known about the potential infringement), the more inclined the courts will be to stay proceedings.[119]

26.2.2.2 Stay of infringement proceedings

With regard to the stay of infringement proceedings (supra at 26.1.1.2), there is only so much the parties can do. On the side of the patent holder, one possibility is to defend the patent only in part in parallel opposition or revocation proceedings, thereby increasing the chances that the amended claims will be upheld (i.e. that the patent will only be partially invalidated). For the question of whether to stay or not, the infringement court will have to consider the claims in their amended (limited) form even if the opposition or revocation verdict is not yet final,[120] provided that the claims are enforced unconditionally and not just by 'pleading in the alternative'.[121] According to some courts, the enforcement of limited claims reduces the probability that infringement proceedings will be stayed.[122] According to others, it is the opposite: the fact that there is no final decision on the scope of the patent in its amended (limited) form rather speaks in favour of a stay of proceedings.[123] The alleged infringer (i.e. the claimant in the revocation proceedings), on the other hand, may lodge a request for accelerated proceedings to facilitate the alignment between infringement and revocation proceedings and increase the chances of a stay of proceedings.[124]

Going forward, German infringement courts will likely stay infringement actions if the alleged infringer files a revocation action at the Patent Court early enough and on the basis of significant validity concerns. In light of an increasing number of stays, one

---

118 See Philip Moritz Cepl, *supra* note 3, ZPO § 148, para. 144.
119 See Mes, *Patentgesetz Gebrauchsmustergesetz*, 5th ed. 2020, § 139, para. 365.
120 German Federal Supreme Court (BGH), Decision of May 6, 2010 – Case No. Xa ZR 70/08 (OLG Düsseldorf) – Maschinensatz, published in GRUR 2010, 904.
121 See Thomas Kühnen, *supra* note 3, para. 844 et seq.; Philip Moritz Cepl, supra note 3, ZPO § 148, para. 153.
122 See Philip Moritz Cepl, *supra* note 3, ZPO § 148, para. 153; Klaus-J. Melullis, Zur Notwendigkeit einer Aussetzung des Verletzungsprozesses bei Anpassungen der Schutzansprüche an Bedenken gegen deren Schutzfähigkeit, in: Wolfgang Büscher et al. (eds.), *Festschrift für Joachim Bornkamm zum 65. Geburtstag*, 2014, p. 713 et seq.
123 See, for example, Higher Regional Court of Munich, Decision of December 8, 1989 – Case No. 6 W 3050/89 – Regal-Ordnungssysteme, published in GRUR 1990, 352; Regional Court of München I, Decision of September 21, 2017 – Case No. 7 O 15820/16, para. 90, published in GRUR-RS 2017, 125777; Regional Court of Mannheim, Decision of 23 May, 2006 – Case No. 2 O 150/05 (not published), confirmed by Higher Regional Court of Karlsruhe, Decision of July 13, 2006 – Case No. 6 W 52/06.
124 See Thomas Kühnen, *supra* note 3, para. 810.

may also see an even higher number of determinations of invalidity by the German Patent Court, given that the injunction gap would largely disappear and that infringers with good validity challenges will no longer be forced to settle and withdraw their pending revocation actions. At the same time, as there is still no institutionalized expedited framework for communication between infringement courts and the DPMA or the EPO during opposition procedures, a party who is likely to infringe a patent should consider relying on a third-party straw man to commence opposition proceedings so that infringer himself can commence a revocation action at the Patent Court and benefit of the expedited qualified indication after the opposition period lapses.

26.2.2.3 Compensation for injury caused by enforcement

If a judgment declared provisionally enforceable is reversed or modified (see also *infra* at 26.2.3.3), the plaintiff – i.e. the patent holder – shall be obligated to compensate the defendant – i.e. the 'infringer' of the amended or revoked patent – for the damages he/she has suffered by the judgment being enforced, or by the payments he/she had to make, or any other actions he/she had to take in order to avert enforcement.[125] After the final judgment, the infringer can bring an action for "restitution" (i.e. an action for retrial of the case)[126] to set aside the infringement judgment as far as it has lost its legal basis with the amendment or revocation of the patent.[127]

For the defendant in an infringement case, these provisions provide for certain protection against the negative consequences of an injunction gap. The patent holder assumes the risk of enforcing an infringement judgement before the conclusion of validity proceedings.[128]

26.2.3 Litigating before the UPC

During the public consultation on the rules of procedure of the UPC, stakeholders expressed concern about the CFI's local and regional divisions' discretion to bifurcate pro-

---

[125] Section 717(2) of the German Code of Civil Procedure. To ensure that the defendant receives compensation, provisionally enforceable judgments require the deposition of a security (Section 709).
[126] Section 580(6) of the German Code of Civil Procedure.
[127] See Higher Regional Court of Düsseldorf, Decision of December 19, 2019 – Case No. 2 U 41/19 – Messsensoren II, published in GRUR-RR 2020, 414; German Federal Supreme Court (BGH), Decision of January 10, 2017 – Case No. X ZR 17/13 (OLG Düsseldorf), published in GRUR 2017, 428.
[128] See e.g. German Federal Supreme Court (BGH), Decision of May 25, 1970 – Case No. VI ZR 199/68 (München), published in NJW 1970, 1459, 1461; see also Anja Lunze, in: Cepl & Voß (eds.), *supra* note 3, ZPO § 717, para. 4; Tobias J. Hessel & Maximilian Schellhorn, *Die Rückabwicklung des vorläufig vollstreckten Unterlassungstitels im Patentrecht*, GRUR 2017, 672, 673.

ceedings. The general sentiment of the German judges that will be sitting on the local divisions' panels is that bifurcation will probably be the exception rather than the rule. Judge Zigann, for example, believes that German judges will seize the power given to them "to decide the case and dismiss a nullity action or invalidate a patent themselves [...] more often than not".[129] Firstly, the nature of the proceedings is different. Patent validity cases before the Federal Patent Court are subject to the 'Offizialmaxime', which means that the court is obliged to investigate validity (to some extent) on its own motion. The UPC has no such obligation; it will not investigate any prior art beyond what the defendant has presented.[130] The amount of resources that the UPC needs to consider to render a decision on the validity of the patent is therefore more limited. Secondly, the UPC is subject to stricter timelines than German courts. The final oral hearing on the issues of infringement and validity at first instance is supposed to take place within one year[131] and the procedural time limits for filing motions and responding to them are generally rather short.

26.2.3.1 Infringement actions brought by licensees

One way to maintain bifurcated proceedings is for the patentee to have a licensee sue for infringement. Where an infringement action is brought by a licensee and the patent holder does not take part in the proceedings,[132] a counterclaim for revocation is excluded. To contest the validity of the enforced patent, the defendant (i.e. the alleged infringer) needs to bring a standalone action for revocation against the proprietor before the central division.[133] The proceedings remain bifurcated unless the local/regional division that handles the infringement action decides, with the agreement of *both* parties, to refer the entire case to the central division.[134]

As a consequence, if the patent holder wants to ensure – for whatever reason – a bifurcation of proceedings, he/she should have a licensee bring the infringement action. The potential infringer may anticipate that and bring an action for declaration of non-infringement before the central division,[135] but that will not help. Once the patent holder or an exclusive licensee brings an infringement action before a local or regional division, the action for declaration of non-infringement pending before the central division will need to be stayed.[136]

---

129 Matthias Zigann, *Unified Patent Courts Will Hardly Bifurcate Proceedings*, Kluwer Patent Blog of February 16, 2015.
130 Ibid.
131 Recital 7 of the Preamble to the UPC RoP.
132 Article 47(5) UPCA.
133 Articles 47(5) and 33(4) UPCA.
134 Article 33(3)(c) UPCA.
135 Article 33(4) UPCA.
136 Article 33(6) UPCA.

26.2.3.2 Parallel revocation and counterclaim

If an action for revocation is pending before the central division, the UPC leaves it up to the defendant (i.e. patent holder) to decide whether to bifurcate or not. An action for infringement by the patentee (or a licensee entitled to commence proceedings)[137] relating to the patent which is subject to the revocation action may be brought either before the central division (no bifurcation) or any competent[138] local/regional division (bifurcation).[139] If proceedings are initiated at a local/regional division, the only way to reunite them is if both parties agree to refer the case to the central division; which seems unlikely if one assumes that the claimant's decision to bring the action before a local/regional division – instead of the central division where the revocation action is pending – was deliberate. Up to here, the patent holder holds the whip hand.

The alleged infringer may, however, react by lodging a counterclaim for revocation at the local/regional division. In this case, the local/regional division is back in the game and may actually 'hijack' the entire case. It may refer the counterclaim for revocation to the central division and suspend or proceed with the action for infringement, or it may proceed with both the action for infringement and the counterclaim for revocation.[140] It will still not be the infringer who is in charge of deciding whether proceedings are bifurcated or not, but it will also not be the patent holder. The decision will rest on the panel of the local/regional division.[141]

26.2.3.3 Compensation for injury caused by enforcement

Where during an infringement action an enforceable decision or order of the UPC (such as a preliminary injunction) is subsequently varied or revoked, the UPC may order the party which has enforced such decision or order, upon the request of the party against whom it has been enforced, to provide appropriate compensation for any injury caused by the enforcement.[142] However, there is a difference between the UPC Agreement and German procedural law (*supra* at 26.2.2.3) in that regard. The situation under the UPC is more favourable to patent holders, because an obligation to compensate the infringer

---

[137] See Article 47(2) to (5) UPCA.
[138] Article 33(1) UPCA.
[139] Article 33(5) UPCA.
[140] Articles 33(3)(a) and (b) UPCA. Referring the entire case to the central division would require the agreement of both parties (Article 33(3)(c) UPCA).
[141] Limited only by the constraints of Rule 75(4) UPC RoP.
[142] Rule 354(2), 1st sentence, UPC RoP. The enforcement of a decision of the UPC may be subject to the provision of security or an equivalent assurance to ensure compensation for any damage incurred or likely to be incurred if the decision is enforced and subsequently revoked, in particular in the case of injunctions (Article 82(2) UPCA and Rule 352(1) UPC RoP).

only exists "during" the infringement action. If the patent is amended or revoked *after* the *conclusion* of the infringement action, the UPC may order, upon the request of the infringer, that a decision or order made pursuant to the finding of infringement ceases to be enforceable.[143] Under the UPCA there is no possibility to bring a restitution action.

This can be problematic if a patent is subject to multiple infringement actions and the patent is amended or revoked as a result of a later action. For prior actions that have already been concluded by a final verdict, the invalidity judgment only has *ex nunc* effect. The infringer of the amended or revoked patent has no right to be compensated. The same problem arises if the infringed patent is subject to revocation, limitation or opposition proceedings before the EPO, and the UPC does not make use of the possibility to stay proceedings.[144]

The magnitude of the problem depends on the degree of alignment between infringement and revocation proceedings. If there is no injunction gap, there is no problem.

26.3 Concluding remarks

It will be interesting to see is how much and what kind of litigation the different divisions of the CFI will be able to attract. Since the central division will only handle infringement issues in cases of declaratory judgement actions or if the parties agree to refer the case to it, the bulk of infringement proceedings will be heard by local and regional divisions, with the expectation being that the German local divisions may attract most of such infringement proceedings in light of the patentee-friendly reputation that its judges enjoy. Arguably, the central division's most important 'clients' are thus the infringers (i.e. revocation claimants). Given the expected tendency of the UPC to not bifurcate infringement and revocation proceedings and given the introduce of the expedited qualified indication by the German Patent Court, the significance of bifurcation as a strategic litigation consideration factor will probably diminish in Europe.

---

[143] Rule 354(2), 3rd sentence, UPC RoP (own emphasis).
[144] Article 33(10) UPCA; Rule 295(a) UPC RoP.

Part 3: **Co-existence and alternatives**

Marc Mimler

27 The co-existence between EPC and patents with unitary effect

27.1 Introduction

After decades of futile attempts to establish a comprehensive European patent framework, we will soon see the granting of European Patents with unitary effect (UPs) by the European Patent Office (EPO). For some this represents a giant and long-awaited leap forward for the European patent system: After over 70 years of trials and tribulations, UPs will provide another option for patent protection in Europe which are litigated before a common court, the Unified Patent Court (UPC). For many others, the system will be a disappointment as it showcases what might have been achievable. Many concerns have been raised outlining the short fallings of the UP system which would rather constitute a "step back" rather than forward. Among the various points which have been brought forward are the rules on co-existence of UPs and other European, aka classical European bundle patents. Co-existence of IP rights, in particular within the European framework, is not something uncommon. Such co-existence of IP rights on EU and on national level can be seen in relation to the law of trade marks and that of design rights.

With regards to the rules of co-existence presented within this chapter, the devil, as so often, lies in the details. Rather than ending the decade long fragmentation of patent law in Europe, the new system may add to its complexity by providing additional layers of fragmentation. The setup of the system born out of a compromise will lead to complex rules of applicability with regard to co-existence between the various layers of co-existence of UPs and other European patents as well as to their adjudication: Their co-existence basically hinges on the question whether the new UPC will have competence to adjudicate these or not. Finally, national patents are also part of the mix as they will remain available under the new system. This chapter will first trace the historical reasons that have led to the rules of co-existence. It will then outline the occurrence and features of the co-existence of UPs and European patents as well as their rules on adjudication and will then conclude by raising some critical points for the current and future debate.

Marc Mimler, is Senior Lecturer in Law, City Law School; City, University of London, email: marc.mimler@city.ac.uk.

27.2 Main Body

27.2.1 Historical background

At this stage, a few words regarding the historical developments that have led to a system of co-existence between a classical European patent and the UP are required. They revolve very much around the different objectives of the two main institutional drivers for European patent policy in the last decades. On the one hand, the young European Economic Community (EEC) saw patents as an important field of activity and set up a Working Group Patents in 1959.[1] This work cumulated in the Community Patent Convention (CPC) of 1975 which was based on safeguarding the free movement of goods protected by patents, and hereby eliminating trade distortions within the Community[2] by providing community-wide unitary patent rights. This first version of a Community Patent Convention, however, never came into force due to the failure of some countries to ratify it.[3] Later attempts to revive the project, such as the CPC 1989,[4] also failed.

On the other hand, the efforts initiated within the institutional framework of the Council of Europe culminated in the arguably most relevant moment in European patent policy: The completion of the Munich Conference of 1973 delivered the EPC[5] which established the European Patent Organisation, along with the EPO as its core organ for granting patents. The Convention's primary aim was to provide for a pragmatic solution for industry and commerce by reducing the cost of securing patent protection across national boundaries within Europe and would include countries outside the EEC. Once

---

[1] Kurt Haertel, 'Die geschichtliche Entwicklung des europäischen Patentrechtes' in Friedrich-Karl Beier, Kurt Haertel and Gerhard Schricker (eds) *Europäisches Patentübereinkommen, Münchner Gemeinschaftskommentar* (Carl Heymanns Verlag 1984) [38].

[2] Convention for the European patent for the Common Market, Preamble. – Records of the Luxembourg Conference on the Community patent 1975 (Office for Official Publications of the European Communities 1982) 295.

[3] Those were Ireland and Denmark – see Albrecht Krieger, 'The Luxembourg Convention on the Community Patent – A Challenge and a Duty' [1988] IIC 143, 145–146; Pieter Callens and Sam Granata, *Introduction to the Unitary Patent and the Unified Patent Court* (Wolters Kluwer 2013) 8. However, the substantive provisions of the CPC with regards to the post-grant phase of patents, such as the rules on infringement, were adopted in many national patent laws of EU member states.

[4] This was an amended version of the CPC 1975 and was envisaged as an international agreement and was signed in Luxembourg again on 15th of December 1989 – 1989 89/695/EEC, OJ EEC L 401, 30.12.1989, 1–27. Similarly, to the CPC 1975, this Agreement failed to enter into force. See: Pieter Callens and Sam Granata, *Introduction to the Unitary Patent and the Unified Patent Court* (Wolters Kluwer 2013) 8–9.

[5] The European Convention relating to the Formalities required for Patent Applications and the Convention on the Unification of Certain Points of Substantive Law on Patents for Invention formed the bases for the EPC – Richard Arnold, 'An Overview of European Harmonization Measures in Intellectual Property Law' in Ansgar Ohly A and Justine Pila (eds), *The Europeanization of Intellectual Property Law* (Oxford University Press 2013) 26.

granted, the patent holder would enjoy protection in the contracting member states of the EPC designated in the application[6], while enforcement of such patents would be subject to the applicable national law.[7] It was initially foreseen that the Community Patent system would be operating alongside the wider EPC system with the EPO as the granting office of Community patents.[8] As the attempts to create such unitary patent rights have been in vain, the EPC system would, albeit, become a success story.

This schism in European patent policy has not only had ramifications for the users of the system.[9] It also provided two institutional gravity centres which would not be easy to reconcile.[10] This "original sin" of the European patent system would stick out as a sore thumb of the ever-integrating European economies.[11] The EU's attempts to provide for unitary patent rights were given new momentum when the deadlock caused largely due to disagreements over the applicable language regime was resolved, or some might say, were "bulldozed over", by the Council of the EU's authorisation of enhanced cooperation with respect to the creation of unitary patent protection.[12] The legislative instruments which form the Unitary Patent Package would task, inter alia, the EPO with granting UPs[13] and set up a unified form of adjudication for UPs and some European patents with the UPC.[14] However, the system is widely regarded as falling short with the ambitious

---

6 See Articles 64(1), 79 EPC.
7 Subsection (3) of Article 65 states *expressis verbis* that "[a]ny infringement of a European patent shall be dealt with by national law." However, an opposition proceeding may be launched after the grant of the patent. The grounds for an opposition (Article 100 EPC) relate to pre-grant matters and do not relate to post-grant patent law. Therefore, the provisions within the EPC regarding opposition proceedings are of procedural nature.
8 Article 1(2) CPC 1975.
9 Here, the need of parallel litigation of the so-called "bundle patents", increases costs for patent holders. Defendants conversely had to face litigation in various jurisdictions which, according to the European Commission would be risky and cumbersome particularly for small and medium enterprises (SMEs) – (Enhancing the patent system in Europe' (COM (2007) 165 final)). Other issues surround forum shopping and decreased incentives to settle cases (Thomas Jaeger, Reto Hilty, Josef Drexl and Hanns Ullrich, 'Comments of the Max Planck Institute for Intellectual Property, Competition and Tax Law on the 2009 Commission Proposal for the Establishment of a Unified European Patent Judiciary' [2009] IIC 817, 823.) Finally, the situation is exacerbated where national courts diverged on their findings of infringement of identical patents granted by the EPO as in the schoolbook example of the so-called "Epilady" cases -see: Matt Fisher, *Fundamentals of Patent Law – Interpretation and Scope of Protection* (Hart Publishing 2007) pp. 246.
10 See, for instance, Plomer's discussion on this matter – Aurora Plomer, 'A Unitary Patent for a (Dis)United Europe: The Long Shadow of History' [2015] IIC 508–533.
11 Mihály Ficsor, 'Coexistence of national patents, European patents and patents with unitary effect' [2013] ERA Forum 95, 98.
12 Council Decision 2011/167/EU of 10 March 2011 authorising enhanced cooperation in the area of the creation of unitary patent protection (OJ 2011 L 76, p. 53).
13 Regulation (EU) No 1257/2012, Recital 5.
14 Agreement on a Unified Patent Court [2013] OJ C 175/1. Herewith "UPCA".

proposals of the past and has been subject to criticism.[15] First, the UP does not provide for an EU right as such, since it currently does not cover the entire territory of the Union, and as such its Internal Market. It only involves the territories of such EU Member taking part in the enhanced collaboration and among these only those who have ratified the UPCA, as explained below. Thus, it inevitably will not resolve the territorial fragmentation of patent law within the EU and would require the additional protection through national patents.[16] Secondly, the adjudication of European patents designated in non-EU members which was foreseen in a previous proposal has become impossible by Opinion 01/09 of the Court of Justice.[17] Thus, the "original sin" will not be atoned by this system and the rules on co-existence discussed below in this chapter stand witness for this.

27.2.2 Occurrence

The reiteration of the historical development culminating with the launch of the Unified Patent court in April 2023 showcases the many hurdles which the UP had to take. It will add another layer of patent protection aside national and European patents and thus raises questions as to the relationship between these layers. The title of this chapter may lead to the assumption that a mere co-existence between traditional European and UPs will occur in future. A closer look at the specific structure of the unitary patent package, however, reveals a co-existence of 4 types of patents: a.) European Patents with unitary effect (i.e. UPs), b.) Ordinary European Patents, c.) European Patents which have been withdrawn from the jurisdiction of the Unified Patent Court, and finally d.) national patents.[18] Each of these will be discussed below.

---

15 Vincenzo di Cataldo, 'Competition (or confusion?) of models and coexistence of rules from different sources in the European patent with unitary effect: Is there a reasonable alternative?' [2014] Queen Mary Journal of Intellectual Property 195, 195.
16 Reto M. Hilty, Thomas Jaeger, Matthias Lamping and Hanns Ullrich, 'Max Planck Institute for Intellectual Property and Competition Law, 'The Unitary Patent Package: Twelve Reasons for Concern' [2012] 1. <https://www.ip.mpg.de/fileadmin/ipmpg/content/stellungnahmen/mpi-ip_twelve-reasons_2012-10-17_01.pdf> accessed 28 November 2022.
17 Case C-1/09, Opinion of the Court (Full Court, 8 March 2011) para. 82.
18 Di Cataldo and Hilty et al., provide a similar separation in their respective papers – Vincenzo di Cataldo, Competition (or confusion?) of models and coexistence of rules from different sources in the European patent with unitary effect: Is there a reasonable alternative? [2014] Queen Mary Journal of Intellectual Property 195, 198–199; Reto M. Hilty, Thomas Jaeger, Matthias Lamping and Hanns Ullrich, 'Max Planck Institute for Intellectual Property and Competition Law, 'The Unitary Patent Package: Twelve Reasons for Concern' [2012] 1. <https://www.ip.mpg.de/fileadmin/ipmpg/content/stellungnahmen/mpi-ip_twelve-reasons_2012-10-17_01.pdf> accessed 28 November 2022.

27.2.2.1 European Patents with unitary effect (i.e. UPs)

The life of a UP commences once the applicant chooses to file a request for unitary effect within a month after the mention of the grant in the European Patent Bulletin.[19] This option then eliminates the selection of national patents in the participating jurisdictions pursuant to Article 4(2) Regulation 1257/2012.[20] Before this very moment the application remains an international or European application and will pursue the same granting process as other European patents. A UP will have unitary effect only within those jurisdictions which are participating in the enhanced collaboration pursuant to Article 3 (1) and Article 2 of the Regulation 1257/2012 and that additionally have ratified the UPCA. Its unitary effect is stipulated by what Jaeger calls "a transformation fiction"[21] by which uniform protection and equal effect within the territory of all participating Member States shall be provided.[22] In addition to this, Regulation 1257/2012 reinforces the unitary effect by prescribing that it "may only be limited, transferred or revoked, or lapse, in respect of all the participating Member States" though it may be licensed for only parts of these territories.[23] Since the new system wishes to leave the currently available options untouched[24], the UP constitutes an additional option available to the applicant aside the traditional European or national patents, as mentioned above.

Striking is also the particular terminology used for this new form of patent protection: Rather than being labelled as EU patent, the name "European patent with unitary effect" can be explained with its turbulent inception. The 2 Regulations of the so-called patent package[25] were conceived by enhanced cooperation[26] which created a group of EU Member States participating while others do not. Thus, the title "EU patent" would not adequately reflect that nature of UPs as they do not cover the entire territory of the EU. Additionally, rather than creating a sui generis right as envisaged within the proposal in the 2000 Regulation, it will consist of a right that derives "from a bundle of national patents of identical (territorial and substantive) scope".[27] The current system thus

---

19 Rules relating to Unitary Patent Protection, Rule 6 (1).
20 "that European patent is deemed not to have taken effect as a national patent in their territory on the date of publication of the mention of the grant in the European Patent Bulletin."- Regulation (EU) No 1257/2012, Article 4(2).
21 Thomas Jaeger, 'All Back To Square One? – An Assessment of the latest proposals for a patent and court for the internal market and possible alternatives' [2012] IIC 286, 294.
22 Regulation (EU) No 1257/2012, Article 3(1).
23 Regulation (EU) No 1257/2012, Article 3(2).
24 Regulation (EU) No 1257/2012, Recital 26.
25 Regulation (EU) No 1257/2012 and Council Regulation (EU) No 1260/2012 of 17 December 2012 implementing enhanced cooperation in the area of the creation of unitary patent protection with regard to the applicable translation arrangements [2012] OJ L 361/89.
26 Article 20 TEU.
27 Thomas Jaeger, 'All Back to Square One? – An Assessment of the latest proposal for a patent and court for the internal market and possible alternatives' [2012] IIC 286, 291.

presents itself as a "bastard system" claiming "EU-origin but disclaim[ing] EU character."[28]

27.2.2.2 Classical European Patents falling within the jurisdiction of the UPC

The UPCA foresees that a classical European patent granted by the EPO but which does "not benefit from unitary effect by virtue of Regulation (EU) No 1257/2012"[29] will fall within the jurisdiction of the UPC. This applies both to granted European Patents still valid when the UPCA enters into force or such granted after that date[30], as well as European patent applications which are pending at the entry of force of the UPCA or such filed after that date.[31]

27.2.2.3 European Patents which do not fall within the jurisdiction of the UPC

Several types of classical European patents will not fall within the jurisdiction of the new Court. The reasons, however, differ and the status of such patents falling outside the Court's jurisdiction may change over time. The first type of European Patents which will not fall within the UPC's jurisdiction are of course those of non-EU Member States, such as Switzerland, Turkey, Norway, as well as the United Kingdom after its departure from the EU in 2020. In the past, several initiatives were launched which sought to provide for an all-encompassing European patent litigation framework with the aim of addressing the original sin of leaving litigation of European Patents granted by the EPO to national courts. For instance, the European Patent Litigation Agreement (EPLA) initiative sought to provide for such system of adjudication which would include European Patents of both EU and Non-EU states. EPLA was initially not favoured by the European Commission[32] but received wide support by relevant stake holders.[33] The Commission's later attempt to adopt features of EPLA along with a Community jurisdiction[34] was dis-

---

28 Hanns Ullrich, 'Harmonizing Patent Law: The Untameable Union Patent' [2012] MPI research paper No. 12-03, 5. Similarly, Eck, who finds that the EP with unitary effect is somewhat national as well as EU patent. – Matthias Eck, 'Europäisches Einheitspatent und Einheitspatentgericht – Grund zum Feiern?' [2014] GRUR Int, 114, 115.
29 UPCA, Article 2 (e).
30 UPCA, Article 3 (c).
31 UPCA, Article 3(d).
32 Erika Ellyne, 'European unitary patent: are we there yet?' [2014] Queen Mary Journal of Intellectual Property 57, 60–61.
33 Jochen Pagenberg, 'Industry, Legal Profession and Patent Judges Press for Adoption of the European Patent Litigation Agreement (EPLA)' [2006] IIC 46, 46.
34 Communication from the Commission to the European Parliament and the Council – Enhancing the patent system in Europe, COM/2007/0165 final, C.

missed by Opinion 01/09 of the Court of Justice which stipulated that the UPC needed to be a court common to the EU Member States, such as the Benelux court.[35] This excluded the UPCs jurisdiction beyond EU Member States and shut the door to a combined adjudication of European Patents validated in non-EU Member States within a one box stop adjudication system.

The second type of European Patents falling within this category are such validated in EU Member states which currently do not participate in the enhanced collaboration authorised by the European Council in 2011.[36] Currently, this is the Kingdom of Spain which has been very vocal against the current system as underlined by the cases brought before the CJEU,[37] and Croatia which only joined the EU on the 01st of July 2013, i.e., after enhanced collaboration was authorised on 10th of March 2011.[38] As to the UK: While having participated in the enhanced collaboration, the country's departure from the EU made its continuing participation impossible under the current legal framework which would entail application of EU law and the involvement of the CJEU and consequently also withdrew its ratification of the UPCA in 2020.[39] However, the mechanism of enhanced collaboration does not perpetually exclude not participating EU Member States from joining at a later stage. Article 2(a) of Regulation (EU) No 1257/2012 provides that the status of a "Participating Member State" can be achieved not only by having participated in the original Council decision 2011/167/EC. It may also be achieved by virtue of a decision pursuant to Article 331(1) TFEU which provides the possibility to Member States to participate in an enhanced collaboration in progress. Italy, who did not participate in the enhanced collaboration initially, has joined in 2015.[40] Croatia and Spain which currently do not take part may therefore participate later. This would consequently mean that European Patents validated in their countries may be subject to the jurisdiction of the UPC at a later stage.

The third type of such European Patents relates to those validated in participating EU Member States that have yet to ratify the UPCA. While Article 2 of Regulation (EU) No 1257/2012 prescribes that the unitary effect extends to those EU Member States that have taken part in the enhanced collaboration, a UP's territorial scope also depends on the ratification of the UPCA. This is because of the derogation of Articles 3(1), 3(2) and

---

[35] Case C-1/09, Opinion of the Court (Full Court, 8 March 2011) para. 82.
[36] Council Decision 2011/167/EU of 10 March 2011 authorising enhanced cooperation in the area of the creation of unitary patent protection (OJ 2011 L 76/53).
[37] Joined Cases C-274/11 and C-295/11 *Spain and Italy v Council*, Judgement of the Court (Grand Chamber) EU:C:2013:240; C-146/13 *Kingdom of Spain v European Parliament*, Council of the European Union, Judgement of the Court (Grand Chamber) EU:C:2015:298; C-147/13, *Kingdom of Spain v European Parliament*, Council of the European Union, Judgement of the Court (Grand Chamber) EU:C:2015:299.
[38] Council Decision 2011/167/EU of 10 March 2011 authorising enhanced cooperation in the area of the creation of unitary patent protection (OJ 2011 L 76/53), Article 2.
[39] HC Deb 20 July 2020 vol 678 HCWS395.
[40] Commission Decision (EU) 2015/1753 of 30 September 2015 on confirming the participation of Italy in enhanced cooperation in the area of the creation of unitary patent protection" [2015] OJ L 256/19.

4(1) as laid out within Article 18 (2) of Regulation (EU) No 1257/2012 . The provision determines that the unitary effect of an UP does not extend to such participating Member States that have not given exclusive jurisdiction to such European patents to the UPC.[41] This is done through ratification of the UPCA by the participating Member State.

Currently, of the 24 signatories of the UPCA 16 have deposited their ratification.[42] This means that the initial scope of the UP will be limited to those participating member States which have already ratified the UPCA.[43] Once the outstanding participating Member States have ratified the UPCA after its entry into force, European patents validated within their jurisdiction would be considered to be falling within the ambit of the UPC "on the first day of the fourth month after the deposit of the instrument of ratification or accession."[44] Increasing ratifications will, however, not have retroactive effect on the territorial scope of the UP which makes it variable: It will initially extend to those participating Member States which have ratified the UPCA when the Agreement comes into force while its territorial scope will increase with a rising number of ratifications.[45] Finally, Poland, as a Participating Member State of the enhanced collaboration, has not signed the UPCA which means that UPs will currently not extend to its territory.[46]

Finally, a fourth type of classical European patents will be able to escape the jurisdiction of the UPC for a limited period. This relates to such European Patents which, while being validated within one or more participating Member States, have been withdrawn from the jurisdiction of the UPC pursuant to Article 83(3) UPCA.[47] This so-called "Opt-Out" provides for a transition arrangement which grants the adjudication of certain issues[48] before national courts or other competent authorities. Thus, opted-out European patents will remain subject to the jurisdiction of the contracting Member States of the EPC where they are validated. Importantly, this transitional arrangement will be in place for 7 years after the UPCA has been in force. This date will be set once Germany fi-

---

41 UPCA, Article 32.
42 As of the 28th November 2022 – <https://www.consilium.europa.eu/en/documents-publications/treaties-agreements/agreement/?id=2013001> accessed 28 November 2022.
43 Luke McDonagh, European Patent Litigation in the Shadow of the Unified Patent Court (Edward Elgar 2016) 113.
44 UPCA, Article 89 (2).
45 Mihály Ficsor, 'Coexistence of national patents, European patents and patents with unitary effect' [2013] ERA Forum 95, 108.
46 The Opinion of Advocate General Bot delivered on 18 November 2014 held that a refusal to ratify the Agreement may violate the principle of sincere cooperation laid down in Article 4(3) TEU – Case C-146/13 *Kingdom of Spain v European Parliament, Council of the European Union*, EU:C:2014:2380, Opinion of the AG Bot. The AG suggests that "the participating Member States must take all appropriate measures to implement enhanced cooperation, including ratification of the UPC Agreement, as such ratification is necessary for its implementation." – ibid. [179].
47 This equally applies also to patent applications and supplementary protection certificates (SPCs).
48 I.e., this relates to actions "for infringement or for revocation of a European patent or an action for infringement or for declaration of invalidity of a supplementary protection certificate issued for a product protected by a European patent" – UPCA, Article 83(1).

nally deposits its instrument of ratification or accession.[49] However, this transitional arrangement may be extended for another 7 years subject to the outcome of a consultation of the users of the system and a survey on how many cases are still brought before national courts conducted after 5 years of the entry into force of the UPCA and will be subject to the decision of the Administrative Council of the Court.[50] However, after this potential extension period has lapsed, the UPC will have exclusive jurisdiction over all European patents which are validated within participating Member States and where the UPCA has been ratified. Finally, European Patents with unitary effect, of course, are not eligible for an opt-out.

Opting out of the exclusive jurisdiction of the Unified Patent Court will be possible for such European patents which have been granted or applied for before the end of the transitional period. The Court's Registry needs to be notified of this at least one month before the lapse of this period.[51] The notification can be done via the Court's Case Management System, and all opt out requests and opted out patents, applications and SPCs will be publicly available via the UPC's website. Article 89 (1) of the UPCA provides that, once all criteria for it to come into existence are met, the Agreement will come into force after a four-month period and the UPC can start operating.[52] Thus, a "sunrise period" of 3 months for notifying the Court's Registry about opting out European patents, as well as European Patent applications and SPCs, is planned.[53] This is necessary to allow patent owners or applicants to validly opt-out their rights from the UPCs exclusive jurisdiction. Otherwise, an opt-out may be barred by an infringer filing an action for revocation or a negative declaratory action before the UPC which would manifest the UPCs jurisdiction pursuant to Article 83(3) UPCA.[54] This provides breathing space for owners or applicants in order to avoid rushed decisions. An opt-out can be withdrawn unless an action has been brought before a national court as Article 83(4) UPCA suggests. Once the opt-out is withdrawn, another opt-out will not be possible.

The availability of the opt-out can be explained by the reservation of certain stakeholders against a new and untried court system. It provides proprietors of European Pa-

---

49 While the required 13 instruments have been deposited already, Article 89 (1) UPCA also mandates that this ought to include "the three Member States in which the highest number of European patents had effect in the year preceding the year in which the signature of the Agreement takes place." As the Agreement was signed on the relevant year was 2012. Initially, this would have been France, Germany and the United Kingdom but due to Brexit Italy is the country of reference in lieu of the United Kingdom. Once Germany submits its instrument, the UPCA will come into force on the first day of the fourth month after the notification was deposited.
50 UPCA, Article 85 (3).
51 UPCA, Article 83 (3).
52 UPCA, Article 89(1).
53 European Patent Office, 'FAQ on the Unified Patent Court (UPC)' <https://www.epo.org/applying/european/unitary/upc/upc-faq.html> accessed 28 November 2022.
54 Lea Tochtermann, 'Law to be applied to a European Patent after an opt out according to Art. 83 (3) UPCA' [2018] GRUR 337, 338.

tents and of applicants thereof with the option not to place "all eggs into one basket", by risking a central attack with the UPC invalidating their European Patents within participating Member States, either in a stand-alone invalidation or after such counterclaim is raised in infringement proceedings.[55] Some proprietors therefore may reserve their "crown jewel patents" for an opt out.[56] However, the impact of such central attack may not be as severe as feared due to the currently limited territorial effect of UPs. In addition, EPs validated within the UK as one of the largest and important jurisdictions of EPC countries will not fall within the UPCs jurisdiction. Pagenberg, however, predicted in a paper from 2012 that 90 % of users would choose an opt out.[57]

27.2.2.4 National patents

Last but not least, the UP system does not affect the possibility for applicants to obtain national patent rights via the national application route or EPO route. This form of patent protection will be particularly relevant within EU Member States which are not taking part in the enhanced collaboration or such where the ratification or accession to the UPCA is still outstanding, as discussed above. Another interesting question arises in relation to "double patenting", i.e., the situation where patents in relation to the same invention are granted or are validated for the same applicant/owner within the same country.[58] With regards to the permissibility and ambit of double patenting of national and classical European patents, Article 139 (3) EPC leaves this decision to national laws of contracting member states. The preamble of Regulation (EU) No 1257/2012, however, states that double protection in Contracting participating Member States by classical European patents and UPs ought to be avoided.[59] Consequently, this then does not rule out the possibility of double patenting of classical national patents and UPs[60] which again requires to be resolved by national law.[61]

---

[55] Lea Tochtermann, 'Law to be applied to a European Patent after an opt out according to Art. 83 (3) UPCA' [2018] GRUR 337, 342.
[56] Luke McDonagh, European Patent Litigation in the Shadow of the Unified Patent Court, (Edward Elgar 2016) 148.
[57] Jochen Pagenberg, 'Die EU-Patentrechtsreform – zurück auf Los?' [2012] GRUR 882, 586.
[58] *Double Patenting T 0318/14*, Boards of Appeal of the EPO – 7.2.2019, EP:BA:2021:G000419.20210622, para 17.
[59] "Where unitary patent protection takes effect, the participating Member States should ensure that the European patent is deemed not to have taken effect on their territory as a national patent, so as to avoid any duplication of patent protection." – Regulation (EU) No 1257/2012, Recital 8.
[60] Regulation (EU) No 1257/2012, Recital 8.
[61] Regulation (EU) No 1257/2012, Recital 26.

27.2.3 Adjudication and substantive law

The co-existence between European patents and UPs as discussed above hinges on the UPCs exclusive jurisdiction. But what does this mean for the adjudication of these different layers of patent protection in practice? The UPCA provides the Court with exclusive "competence" to adjudicate in respect to UPs but also in relation to European Patents validated in one or more of the 24 participating Member States, subject to their ratification of/accession to the UPCA.[62] But many European patents still remain outside the ambit of the Court which is why the current set up does not resolve old issues and has the potential to create new ones: It maintains the current scenario where parallel national litigations become necessary and brings in the UPC, as a brand-new and therefore untested forum, into the mix.

27.2.3.1 The UPC's exclusive competence

As mentioned, the Court will have exclusive competence in relation to UPs[63] and European patents which falling within the category as discussed in 2.2.b.). Article 32 UPCA refines this by stating that the Court will have exclusive competence in relation to actions for actual or threatened infringements and related defences, actions for declaration of non-infringement, actions for provisional and protective measures and injunctions, actions for revocation and counterclaims for revocation. The Court will apply a plethora of sources of law, ranging from EU law, the UPCA, the EPC and national laws. Importantly, the substantive provisions on patent infringement and exceptions thereof are not found within the Regulation (EU) No 1257/2012. They initially were in the proposal of the Regulation within articles 6–8 but have subsequently been placed within the UPCA.[64] This odd occurrence is most probably based on the scepticism of some EU member states[65] and practitioners towards the role of the CJEU[66] on the highly technical subject matter of patent law.[67] It gives the impression that the creators of the system sought

---

62 UPCA, Article 32.
63 In addition, SPCs will also fall within the jurisdiction of the UPC, unless opted out or originated from a European patent which has been opted out – Articles 32(1) a). b.) d.) and e.) with Article 83(3) UPCA.
64 Erika Ellyne, 'European unitary patent: are we there yet?' [2014] Queen Mary Journal of Intellectual Property 57, 64–65.
65 In particular, the United Kingdom – Vincenzo di Cataldo, 'Competition (or confusion?) of models and coexistence of rules from different sources in the European patent with unitary effect: Is there a reasonable alternative?' [2014] Queen Mary Journal of Intellectual Property 195, 202.
66 Jochen Pagenberg, 'Die EU-Patentrechtsreform – zurück auf Los?' [2012] GRUR 582, 587.
67 Matthias Eck, 'Europäisches Einheitspatent und Einheitspatentgericht – Grund zum Feiern?' [2014] GRUR Int. 114, 116.

to limit the role of the CJEU with regards to substantive patent law[68] and might be based on its decision practice in other fields of IP.[69]

The new system will not touch on the possibility to file for opposition procedures before the EPO's boards pursuant to Articles 99-105b EPC. Within the UPC's organisational structure, infringement claims can be brought before local or regional divisions of the courts depending on where the alleged infringement occurred. The Central division will be competent for revocation actions unless this is brought as a counterclaim in which case it can adjudicated along with the infringement action or may be transferred to the central division.[70] Additionally, the Central division has exclusive jurisdiction over declarations of non-infringement.

The UPC will be the "new kid on the block" in a world of established and widely trusted European and national patent institutions. It, therefore, has to earn the trust of its future users. This somehow explains the initially limited competence of the Court which inevitably will grow over time. How the UPC will operate and how its users will respond to its practice remains to be seen. The availability of the "opt-out" can be regarded to address the reservations by stake holders against an untested body of patent adjudication. It provides time to "wait and see" how the new court will operate and therefore serves to earn trust of the users over the years.[71] Other trust building initiatives have been devised, from establishing an advisory committee[72] to the extensive training of prospective UPC judges. But even with growing exclusive competence over time, the UPC cannot fulfil the bold ambitions to overcome the "schism" between the EPC and EU patent frameworks.

27.2.3.2 Competence of national courts and applicable law

National courts will still play an important role even after the UPC opens its doors. As discussed, the classical European Patents discussed in point 2.2.c.) will remain to be adjudicated before national courts. But as the number of participating member states rises, and as more participating Member States submit their instruments of ratification or accession, the territorial scope of the UPC's competence will increase. Additionally, the possibility to opt out classical European patents from the UPC's exclusive competence will seize once the transitional period, and a possible extension thereof, lapses. Finally,

---

68 Michael Nieder, 'Materielles Verletzungsrecht für europäische Bündelpatente in nationalen Verfahren nach Art. 83 EPGÜ' [2014] GRUR 627, 627.
69 Luke McDonagh, *European Patent Litigation in the Shadow of the Unified Patent Court* (Edward Elgar 2016) 90.
70 UPCA, Article 33(3).
71 Winfried Tilmann, 'Das europäische Patentpaket vor dem Start' [2022] GRUR 1099.
72 Unified Patent Court, 'Administrative Committee' <https://www.unified-patent-court.org/en/organisation/administrative-committee> accessed 28 November 2022.

national patents granted by national patent offices will remain to exists. National substantive and procedural law will apply to these patents pursuant to Article 64 (3) EPC.

The question arises, however, which substantive law will apply to European Patents which have been opted out of the UPCs exclusive competence pursuant to Article 83 (3) UPCA. Article 3 c.) UPCA provides that the UPCA's provisions are applicable with regards to a "European patent which has not yet lapsed at the date of entry into force of this Agreement or was granted after that date." This, of course refers to such European patents falling within the competence of the UPC as discussed above.[73] Importantly, Article 3 c.) UPCA adds that this rule is "without prejudice to Article 83". This means that even where an opt-out was declared, the substantive rules of the UPCA, i.e. Articles 25 – 30 UPCA, may apply before national courts instead of current national legislation.[74] Tochtermann, however, argues that national law would still be applicable in such case and that the CJEU may be called to decide on this matter.[75] As to the practical consequence of this question, Nieber does not anticipate that this will change much of legal practice in Germany.[76]

27.3 Conclusion

What the previous lines have demonstrated is that the rules on co-existence are a prime example of the heightened complexity that this new European patent system will bring. This has already been foreseen by the Max Planck Institute in its paper published in 2012.[77] The culmination of the Unitary Patent Package with the official arrival of the UPC will add a layer of complexity to the current European patent framework at large which is expressed through the various forms of fragmentation. This fragmentation occurs within the applicable legal rules, but also will be seen along territorial and institutional lines and moreover within that of markets in Europe.

From a legal perspective, the UPC will lead to procedural fragmentation since the competences between national and UPC competences to adjudicate European patents are shared. The arrival of the UPC provides yet another avenue where patents may be li-

---

[73] Mihály Ficsor, 'Coexistence of national patents, European patents and patents with unitary effect' [2013] ERA Forum 95, 107.
[74] Michael Nieder, 'Materielles Verletzungsrecht für europäische Bündelpatente in nationalen Verfahren nach Art. 83 EPGÜ' [2014] GRUR 627, 628.
[75] Lea Tochtermann, 'Law to be applied to a European Patent after an opt out according to Art. 83 (3) UPCA' [2018] GRUR 337, 339–342.
[76] Michael Nieder, 'Materielles Verletzungsrecht für europäische Bündelpatente in nationalen Verfahren nach Art. 83 EPGÜ' [2014] GRUR 627, 633.
[77] Reto M. Hilty, Thomas Jaeger, Matthias Lamping and Hanns Ullrich, 'Max Planck Institute for Intellectual Property and Competition Law, 'The Unitary Patent Package: Twelve Reasons for Concern' [2012] 1. <https://www.ip.mpg.de/fileadmin/ipmpg/content/stellungnahmen/mpi-ip_twelve-reasons_2012-10-17_01.pdf> accessed 28 November 2022.

tigated though the amount of case load initially managed by the Court may be limited. This, of course, will grow over time, and the dynamic nature of the increasing exclusive jurisdiction of the UPC as to the territories of participating Member States it covers, means that patent holders need to bear this in mind in their decision-making process. The arrival of the UPC will also provide for more fragmentation as to substantive law. UPs will be subject to the EPC, the 3 instruments of the unitary patent package and the UPCA.[78] But national law will also remain relevant, in particular as to the UP as an object of property[79] but also with regards to the rules of voluntary and compulsory licensing.[80] It remains to be seen how the UPC will address this conundrum of applicable norms. Moreover, the Court will never fully champion the role of harmoniser of European patent law due to those European patents which remain outside its competence though its role may yet become more and more persuasive over the years. But there are doubts that even after the lapse of the transitional period, the UPC will assist in providing a "higher level of uniformity than some of the existing national courts do at present."[81]

These last points also indicate an increasing institutional fragmentation since the UPC adds another player to the European patent framework, in addition to the EU along with the CJEU, the EPO with its granting office and its Boards as forum of patent adjudication and finally national courts. Particularly interesting will be the evolving relationship with the EPO Boards where there is overlapping competence, such as in relation to the patentability requirements and it remains to be seen whether the UPC can provide for a meaningful voice here in relation to the sometimes-diverging approaches taken by national courts and the Boards of the EPO. Ultimately, the institutional and legal fragmentation creates a fragmentation in the European market. This may not be "fully compatible with the original ideas of the European Treaties" when the opposite situation is in the process of being created.[82] This applies particularly to non-participating Member States and would result in a more severe situation than under the current system.[83] But Tillmann rightly points at the potential for improvement[84] which the system provides.[85] But, sins cannot be undone, only forgiven.

---

78 UPCA, Art. 24(1).
79 Regulation 1257/2012, Art. 7.
80 Regulation 1257/2012, Recital 10.
81 Jan Smits and William Bull, 'The Europeanization of Patent Law: Towards a Competitive Model' in Ansgar Ohly A and Justine Pila (eds), *The Europeanization of Intellectual Property Law* (Oxford University Press 2013) 50.
82 Vincenzo di Cataldo, 'Competition (or confusion?) of models and coexistence of rules from different sources in the European patent with unitary effect: Is there a reasonable alternative?' [2014] Queen Mary Journal of Intellectual Property 195–212, 200.
83 Thomas Jaeger, 'All Back To Square One? – An Assessment of the latest proposals for a patent and court for the internal market and possible alternatives' [2012] IIC 286, 290.
84 Regulation 1257/2012, Arts. 5(4), 16(1).
85 Winfried Tilmann, 'Das europäische Patentpaket vor dem Start' [2022] GRUR 1099.

Karen Walsh
28 Institutional coexistence: the necessity of judicial dialogue and cooperation in the UPC

28.1 Introduction

The harmonisation of patent law in Europe through the introduction of a unitary patent system has been an enduring goal for policy makers in the area for decades.[1] It appears that in 2023, a unitary patent system will finally enter into force.

The establishment of the European Union (EU) unitary patent system will have a significant impact on the European patent system. It introduces a unitary patent and unified patent court for a number of EU Member States.[2] The unitary patent will provide patentees with a single patent covering participating EU Member States. The Unified Patent Court (UPC) will make cross-border decisions on matters of validity and infringement relating to unitary patents and European patents for applicable Member States.[3] Following a lengthy transitional period, it will have exclusive jurisdiction over such patents. As is its main purpose, the EU unitary patent system will likely have a substantial influence on the harmonisation of patent law across Europe. However, and despite its potential benefits regarding harmonisation, there are some remaining concerns, especially when considering the European patent system as broadly defined to include countries both inside and outside the EU.

Focusing mainly on post-grant matters, and particularly on the functioning of the UPC, this chapter will argue that the post-grant harmonisation of patent law in Europe, to the extent that this is possible and desirable,[4] cannot rely solely on the EU unitary pa-

---

[1] For a history of attempts towards a unitary patent system, see: J Pila, 'An Historical Perspective I: The Unitary Patent Package' and C Wadlow 'An Historical Perspective II: The Unified Patent Court' in J Pila and C Wadlow (eds), *The Unitary EU Patent System* (Hart Publishing 2014).
[2] Not all EU Member States have signed up to the EU unitary patent system. This will be detailed further below.
[3] European patents denote patents applied for through the European Patent Office.
[4] Ensuring a responsible patent system that considers the legal, social and ethical implications of its decisions requires an adaptable system that can change direction if necessary.

Karen Walsh, is Assistant Professor in Law, Maynooth University. The author would like to thank the editors, Duncan Matthews and Paul Torremans, and Aisling McMahon and Naomi Hawkins for their comments on previous drafts of this work. This chapter has been informed by research undertaken with the support of the British Academy and Department for Business, Energy and Industrial Strategy (Reference number: SRG1819 \190316). All links last accessed on 10.12.22.

https://doi.org/10.1515/9783110781687-028

tent system. To assist with the development of a consistent system overall, communication between divisions within the UPC, and between the UPC and external institutions will be key.[5] Judicial dialogue and cooperation, that is, the process of judges considering or discussing relevant decisions and interpretations of other courts, and taking a coordinated approach where possible, will be essential in achieving this goal.[6]

Following an examination of the UPC, its structure and composition, and where it is situated in the context of the broader European patent law landscape, this chapter will discuss the potential limitations regarding harmonisation through the UPC and suggest a way forward to address associated concerns. The main suggestion in this regard is the promotion and encouragement of judicial dialogue and cooperation as a means of reducing possibilities for divergence in decision-making both inside and outside the UPC. The intentional addition of such a practice into UPC procedure would have several key advantages. This chapter will go on to discuss this mechanism and how it could fit within the UPC context. It will conclude by advocating for judicial dialogue and cooperation as a necessary additional tool to assist in the promotion of a coordinated and further harmonised European patent system.

28.2 The UPC

The EU unitary patent system is legislatively unique. It consists of two EU Regulations on unitary patent protection and an international agreement on a Unified Patent Court (UPCA).[7] Following numerous failed attempts and years of negotiations, in 2012, twenty-five out of the twenty-seven EU Member States at the time adopted the EU Regulations.[8] In 2012/2013, a different combination of twenty-five out of twenty-seven EU Member States signed the UPCA.[9] At the time of writing, the unitary patent system is expected to

---

5 These external institutions include national patent offices, national courts dealing with patent law matters, the European Patent Office and its Examining/Opposition Divisions and Boards of Appeal, and the Court of Justice of the European Union.

6 See: K Walsh, 'Promoting harmonisation across the European patent system through judicial dialogue and cooperation' (2019) 50(4) *International Review of Intellectual Property and Competition Law* 408.

7 Council Regulation (EU) 1257/2012 of the European Parliament and of the Council of 17 December 2012 implementing enhanced cooperation in the area of the creation of unitary patent protection [2012] OJ L 361/1; Council Regulation (EU) 1260/2012 of the European Parliament and of the Council of 17 December 2012 implementing enhanced cooperation in the area of the creation of unitary patent protection with regard to the applicable translation arrangements [2012] OJ L 361/89; and Agreement 2013/C on a Unified Patent Court [2013] OJ L 175/01 (UPCA).

8 At this point, the United Kingdom was an EU Member State and Croatia was not. All EU Member States apart from Spain and Italy agreed to the Regulations. Italy agreed at a later point. Croatia has not yet approved the Regulations.

9 At this point, the United Kingdom was still an EU Member State and Croatia was not. All EU Member States apart from Spain and Poland signed the UPCA. With a change of government in Italy, there was also a change in decision relating to the unitary patent system. Poland decided not to sign the UCPA based on a

enter into force from June 2023.[10] So far, twenty-five EU Member States are party to the Regulations and sixteen EU Member States have ratified the UPCA. The ratification of the UPCA by Germany (expected in December 2022/January 2023) is the final condition to be fulfilled before the system can enter into force.[11]

The two EU Regulations introduce the unitary patent and the applicable translation regime. The unitary patent will provide patentees with a single patent that covers a significant portion of the EU. It will guarantee uniform protection across all participating Member States.[12] Compared to alternative routes to patent protection in Europe, the new language regime will reduce the number of translations required on application/validation.[13] The UPCA establishes the UPC, which aims to provide users with expert opinions on patentability, patent infringement and more, in a timely, efficient and cost-effective manner. It is a purpose-built, specialised, patent court. As this chapter will predominantly focus on the potential impact of the UPC on the harmonisation of the European patent system, some further detail is required.

The UPC is made up of a Court of First Instance, a Court of Appeal and a Registry. The Court of First Instance is divided into local and regional divisions, as well as a central division. Contracting Member States can establish up to four local divisions (depending on its caseload) or choose to participate in a regional division.[14] The central division will be based in Paris and has a section in Munich.[15] It will hear all actions related to re-

---

study reporting that the unitary patent system would be detrimental to Polish businesses, particularly small and medium sized enterprises (Deloitte, 'Analysis of prospective economic effects related to the implementation of the system of unitary patent protection in Poland' (1 October 2012)). Croatia has not yet signed the UPCA.

10 Originally planned for April 2023, the start date was postponed following pleas from industry representatives to delay the sunrise period until the Case Management System is more functional. See: A Merelle Ward, 'Calls to push back the UPC sunrise period as 89 % have not been able to obtain/authenticate security devices needed to access Case Management System' (*IPKat*, 29 November 2022) available at https://ipkitten.blogspot.com/2022/11/update-calls-to-push-back-upc-sunrise.html; and A Merelle Ward, 'UPC and Sunrise start dates pushed back by 2 months to 1 March 2023' (*IPKat*, 05 December 2022) available at https://ipkitten.blogspot.com/2022/12/breaking-upc-and-sunrise-start-dates.html. The sunrise period is incredibly important as it provides users with only three months to opt out any relevant European patents from the EU unitary patent system.
11 Article 89 UPCA.
12 Article 5 Regulation 1257.
13 Regulation 1260.
14 Germany is the only Contracting Member State thus far to indicate the establishment of more than one local division. These are expected in Düsseldorf, Hamburg, Mannheim and Munich. Estonia, Latvia, Lithuania, Norway and Sweden are expected to establish a regional division.
15 It is expected that another section will be established elsewhere in due course. Prior to the United Kingdom's departure from the EU and subsequently, the unitary patent system, the intention was that this section be located in London. Since then, Milan have come forward to bid for this section: A Sandys, 'Italian Government officially fields Milan for UPC central division' (*Juve Patent*, 11 September 2020) available at www.juve-patent.com/news-and-stories/people-and-business/italian-government-officially-fields-milan-for-upc-central-division/.

vocation and declarations of non-infringement unless these have already been raised at a local division. Each seat of the central division will deal with different areas of technology. The Court of Appeal is based in Luxembourg and will hear appeals from all divisions of the Court of First Instance. The Registry will deal with the day-to-day operations of the UPC, including all administrative and procedural tasks. There will also be a Mediation and Arbitration centre in Ljubljana and Lisbon.

Each division of the UPC will include a multinational panel of judges from Contracting Member States. At local divisions, the panel will comprise of three legally qualified judges. Depending on the number of cases heard by the division, panels will include either one or two local judges with one or two judges from different Contracting Member States.[16] At regional divisions, the panel will include three legally qualified judges, with two from Contracting Member States within the region and one from another Contracting Member State.[17] There will also be an option to appoint an additional technically qualified judge at both local and regional divisions.[18] At the central division, the panel will consist of two legally qualified judges from different Contracting Member States and one technically qualified judge. At the Court of Appeal, the panel will be made up of five multinational judges. There will be three legally qualified judges and two technically qualified judges.

Most of the judges have now been appointed.[19] Many are familiar names in the patent field and have extensive expertise in patent law decision-making. There is also a Training Centre for judges located in Budapest to ensure a high level of quality from UPC judgments.

The UPC will have jurisdiction over unitary patents and European patents validated in Contracting Member States.[20] It will have extensive competence for most relevant actions.[21] During the transitional period of seven years (which is extendible to fourteen years), national courts will also retain jurisdiction over European patents validated therein.[22] There is the potential for patentees to opt out European patents from the unitary patent system during this time.[23] The UPC will base its decisions on, in order, Union

---

16 Article 8(2–3) UPCA.
17 Article 8(4) UPCA.
18 Article 8(5) UPCA.
19 See: 'Unified Patent Court judicial appointments and Presidium elections' (*UPC Website*, 19 October 2022) available at https://www.unified-patent-court.org/en/news/unified-patent-court-judicial-appointments-and-presidium-elections.
20 Jurisdiction can be established in accordance with the Brussels I Regulation (Regulation (EU) 1215/2012 of 12 December 2012 on jurisdiction and the recognition and enforcement of judgments in civil and commercial matters [2012] OJ L 351/1) or the Lugano Convention (Convention on jurisdiction and the recognition and enforcement of judgments in civil and commercial matters [2007] OJ L 339/3).
21 Article 32 UPCA.
22 Article 83 UPCA.
23 Article 83 UPCA.

law, the UPCA, the European Patent Convention,[24] other applicable international agreements, and national law.[25]

Overall, the main aims of the unitary patent system are to provide a simple, cost-effective patent system providing uniform protection and enforcement across participating EU Member States, and as a result, reduce costs and improve legal certainty for users. These aims reflect the perceived problems associated with the pre-existing European patent law landscape.

Prior to the introduction of the unitary patent system, no matter which route to patent protection a patent applicant takes in Europe, be it through national or regional systems, the result will essentially be equivalent to a national patent, providing protection in validated countries only, and enforced at national level, with very limited options for cross-border enforcement. For example, there is the possibility for central revocation of a European patent at the European Patent Office during the opposition period, but this must occur within nine months of grant.[26] It is also possible for national courts to make a cross-border decision on patent infringement, but this is only in the rare circumstances where the validity of the patent is not in question. If invalidity is raised, either as an action or as a counterclaim to infringement, each national court must decide on this matter.[27]

In practice, this can result and has resulted in multiple patents being granted for the same invention in different territories, not necessarily with identical claims,[28] divergent interpretations of substantive patent law among the institutions involved, as well as divergence in parallel proceedings.[29] Applying for and maintaining a large

---

[24] Convention on the Grant of European Patents of 5 October 1973 (European Patent Convention) (EPC), amended in 2000.
[25] Article 24 UPCA.
[26] Article 99 European Patent Convention.
[27] For more on cross-border enforcement, see: J Brinkhof and A Ohly, 'Towards a Unified Patent Court in Europe' in J Pila and A Ohly (eds), *The Europeanization of Intellectual Property Law: Towards a Legal Methodology* (Oxford University Press 2013); and E-J Min and JC Wichard, 'Cross-border Intellectual Property Enforcement' in RC Dreyfuss and J Pila (eds), *The Oxford Handbook of Intellectual Property Law* (Oxford University Press 2017).
[28] Given differences in, for example, the way in which inventive step is decided in various countries and at the European Patent Office, patent applications can be redrafted to be more tailored towards the offices they are being sent to. Limitations or amendments may also be requested in some jurisdictions and not others.
[29] Parallel proceedings occur where two or more national courts are deciding on the same issues in relation to the same patent. The most famous example of such parallel proceedings is *Improver v Remington* where different decisions on infringement were made across Europe. For these decisions in England & Wales, Germany and the Netherlands, which were among others, see: *Improver Corp v Remington Consumer Product Ltd* [1990] FSR 181; Decision of the Oberlandesgericht Düsseldorf, 21 November 1991 – 2 U 27/89 '*Improver*', translated in 'Improver Corp & Sicommerce AG v Remington Products Inc' (1993) 24 IIC 838; Decision of the Gerechtshof, translated in (1993) 24 IIC 832. For more on the presence of divergent decisions across Europe, see: K Cremers, M Ernicke, F Gaessler, D Harhoff, C Helmers, L McDonagh, P Schliessler and N Van Zeebroeck, 'Patent Litigation in Europe' [2016] *European Journal of Law and Economics*

portfolio of patents across Europe is also time-consuming and expensive for patentees.[30]

By contrast, the unitary patent will provide cross-border uniform protection for participating EU Member States and the UPC will make cross-border decisions on validity and enforcement. This will undoubtedly have a major impact on the European patent system, though for which users this system will be most beneficial is contentious. Although the unitary patent system includes specific provisions for small and medium sized enterprises and individual inventors, a number of external studies have shown that this system may not be as beneficial to these groups as claimed.[31]

In relation to the questions raised by this chapter, the UPC has been framed by proponents as a future harmonising power in the European patent system with the potential to resolve the perceived problem of institutional fragmentation in the European patent system.[32] However, the unitary patent system will not replace previously existing systems or institutions. It will add to them.

This raises a concern regarding the UPC and harmonisation in a broader context. The impact of this will be especially significant post-grant partly due to the internal construction of the UPC, but mainly due to its unknown future relationship with existing institutions.

28.3 Harmonisation and the UPC

While the unitary patent system will have a harmonising impact on patent law in Europe, there have also been numerous criticisms raised against it, and it has faced hurdle

---

available at http://link.springer.com/article/10.1007/s10657-016-9529-0; SJH Graham and N Van Zeebroeck, 'Comparing Patent Litigation Across Europe: A First Look' (2014) *17 Stanford Technical Law Review* 655; P-O Bjuggren, B Domeij and A Horn, 'Swedish Patent Litigation in Comparison to European' (2015) *5 Nordisk Immateriellt Rättsskydd* 504; S Luginbuehl, *European Patent Law: Towards a Uniform Interpretation* (Edward Elgar 2011) 10; and F Baldan, *Judicial Coherence in the European Patent System* (Edward Elgar 2022) Chapter 3.

30 See European Commission Memo, 'Patent reform Package – frequently asked questions' available at http://europa.eu/rapid/press-release_MEMO-12-970_en.htm?locale=en.

31 This was the main reason Poland decided not to participate in the Unified Patent Court thus far. See: Deloitte, 'Analysis of prospective economic effects related to the implementation of the system of unitary patent protection in Poland' (1 October 2012); and D Xenos, 'The Impact of the European Patent System on SMEs and National States and the Advent of Unitary Patent' (2020) 36(1) *Prometheus – Critical Studies in Innovation* 51.

32 For example, according to the European Patent Office, 'Unified Patent Court; Benefits' available at https://www.epo.org/applying/european/unitary/upc.html: 'The UPC will provide a better framework for all parties involved in patent litigation in Europe. In particular, costs will be reduced as parties will not need to engage in parallel patent litigation in different member states. Diverging decisions from different national courts on infringement and validity of the same patent *will cease* as the UPC develops a truly European case law, thus enhancing legal certainty for all users.' (emphasis added).

after hurdle along the path towards entry into force.[33] Many of these concerns are valid and need to be addressed, but we have reached the point where this will need to be achieved in the functioning of the new system.

In the context of this chapter, the main issues that require further discussion relate to the UPC as a harmonising body, its approach towards decision-making, and its possible future interactions with pre-existing institutions. This is because, as mentioned, it is undeniable that the UPC will have a significant impact on the harmonisation of European patent law, and it is likely that it will provide expert and well considered perspectives on patent law interpretation. However, we must bear in mind that it will be one of multiple institutions functioning in this area. While UPC decisions will likely be highly influential outside the UPC, it does also have the potential to cause divergence in many ways, which will be considered in more detail immediately below. As a result, institutional coexistence, both inside and outside the UPC, will be incredibly important.

First, there is a potential for divergence within the UPC. Its internal construction, described above, is complex. Given the presence of so many divisions of the UPC Court of First Instance (multiple local divisions, at least one regional division, as well as the central division which has multiple sections), there is some risk of divergence here, particularly on the commencement of the system. Adding to this complexity is the possibility for bifurcation in the UPC. Bifurcation occurs where one court, or in the UPC instance, division, decides on the validity of a patent and another court/division decides on infringement. According to the UPCA, if a counterclaim for revocation is actioned at a local or regional division, the option is available to bifurcate and refer the counterclaim to the central division.[34] Although it has been suggested that such bifurcated proceedings will be rare,[35] this has the potential to cause further issues in the functioning of the system.

It is quite likely that as the UPC begins to hear cases using newly formed judicial panels of multinational composition, there will be a period where conflicts may arise – both within panels and between divisions. Any divergence among judges on the same panel will have to be resolved immediately for the case to progress. This itself will be interesting from a dialogue perspective. It is quite possible that judges from Contracting

---

[33] For a roundup of initial criticisms, see: R Hilty, T Jaeger, M Lamping and H Ullrich, 'The Unitary Patent Package: Twelve Reasons for Concern' [2012] *Max Planck Institute for Intellectual Property & Competition Law Research Paper* No 12-12 available at http://papers.ssrn.com/sol3/papers.cfm?abstract_id=2169254. Hurdles have included but are not limited to the United Kingdom's decision, by referendum, to leave the EU, which had knock on implications for the EU unitary patent system, and two constitutional complaints that were filed with the German Constitutional Court.

[34] Article 33(3) UPCA. The division has three options – it can hear the case as a whole, refer the counterclaim to the central division, or refer the entire case to the central division.

[35] This has been elaborated upon by the newly appointed President of the Court of Appeal of the UPC, Klaus Grabinski, at a European Patent Office Conference on 17 November 2022, 'The Unitary Patent system – a game-changer for innovation in Europe', available at https://www.youtube.com/watch?v=cLbl-Ay8Wv0, from 06:15:07–06:17:52.

Member States whose approach differs on, for example, exceptions to patentability, will be on the same UPC panel. If, or when, this happens, the panel will have to come to a mutually acceptable decision. How they do so will be of great interest and could serve as an example of how to negotiate a common approach towards diverging areas. Divergence between panels may also occur, which may take longer to resolve. For example, a local division in the Netherlands could approach patentability or inventive step differently when compared to a local division in Austria. This type of divergence is not highly concerning because is expected that the Court of Appeal will deal with any issues of uncertainty or divergence of this kind in a clear and consistent manner; however, how long it will take for a case to come before the Court of Appeal is unclear. The longer this takes the more uncertainty will be created as other UPC divisions will be able to align with either of the directions taken. Prompt decisions from the UPC Court of Appeal will be required to prevent any ambiguity.

The second and greater concern is the potential for divergence between the UPC and pre-existing institutions. In this context, the geographic scope of the UPC is relevant. Although the unitary patent system was designed to cover the EU in its entirety, not all EU Member States are taking part and not all who had decided to take part in the past have ratified the UPCA.[36] There are also countries outside the EU, and therefore outside the EU unitary patent system, that are still part of the European patent system.[37] As a result, numerous patents will still exist for the same invention in different territories and therefore, different institutions will still come to different conclusions on the interpretation of the law, or on whether a similar/identical patent has been infringed in more than one jurisdiction. While the UPC may provide one answer, this does not ensure that, for example, national courts tasked with the same question or interpreting the same provision will provide the same answer. Prior to the introduction of the UPC, divergence in decisions on the interpretation of patent law provisions and divergence in parallel proceedings were observed among different levels of national courts, between national courts in different countries, and between national courts, the Boards of Appeal of the European Patent Office, and the Court of Justice of the European Union.[38] Divergence is nothing new. However, with the addition of the UPC, which combines a number of European countries but not all, a new supranational system and institution is added to this list. More and more decisions will be made by all institutions involved – some will align, and some will not.

Additionally, the possibility of divergence is intensified by the UPC given the likelihood of an expansive transitional period. For up to fourteen years the UPC and national

---

[36] For the current list of ratifications, see: https://www.consilium.europa.eu/en/documents-publications/treaties-agreements/agreement/?id=2013001.
[37] For example, countries that are party to the European Patent Conventions but not the EU (Albania, Iceland, Liechtenstein, Macedonia, Monaco, Norway, San Marino, Serbia, Switzerland, Turkey and the United Kingdom).
[38] See: fn (29).

courts will have jurisdiction over European patents, and European patents can be opted in and out of the system mainly at will.[39] Therefore, a situation could emerge where a division of the UPC and a national court is deciding on essentially the same issues.[40] For example, a revocation action could be taken before a national court and a case of infringement and invalidly on the same patent could be brought before the UPC. As *lis pendens* would not necessarily operate in such a situation given the differences between the actions, one can hope but not presume that either the national court or the relevant division of the UPC would stay proceedings until a decision has been reached by the court first seized. Otherwise, there will be another new situation where divergent decisions can arise.

This overall potential for divergence is heightened again because it is not clear how the UPC will approach decision-making. It could be guided by the enormous amount of European patent law precedent already decided in the European patent system by national courts and by the Boards of Appeal of the European Patent Office, it could start from scratch, or it could use a combination.

Although the unitary patent system may eventually have its desired effect internally through UPC Court of Appeal decisions, and will have an influence more broadly, it cannot control how institutions outside this system will make decisions. Given this potential for divergence in the European patent system, less formal mechanisms that promote convergence where possible, such as judicial dialogue and cooperation, should be introduced and encouraged within the UPC and beyond.

28.4 The necessity of judicial dialogue and cooperation in the UPC

Judicial dialogue and cooperation is the process of judges considering or discussing relevant decisions and interpretations of other courts, and taking a coordinated approach where possible, as a means to promote harmonisation.[41]

---

[39] Opting in and out of the system will be possible unless an action has been taken against the patentee. If opted out and a case is taken to a national court, the patentee cannot then decide to opt in. The same applies vice versa – if opted in and a case is taken to the UPC, the patentee cannot then decide to opt out.

[40] For a detailed analysis on this issue, see: PLC Torremans, 'An International Perspective II: A View from Private International Law' in J Pila and C Wadlow (eds), *The Unitary EU Patent System* (Hart Publishing 2015).

[41] For more detail on this concept see: K Walsh, 'Promoting harmonisation across the European patent system through judicial dialogue and cooperation' (2019) 50(4) *International Review of Intellectual Property and Competition Law 408*; and K Walsh, *Fragmentation and the European Patent System* (Hart Publishing 2022).

As explored elsewhere, judicial dialogue and cooperation has been used to good effect in multiple situations, both inside and outside the patent system.[42] The European patent system is the ideal scenario for the successful implementation of such a mechanism because patent laws in Europe are all based on the European Patent Convention. Although the European Patent Convention has three official versions (English, French and German), and has been implemented into national laws in a number of different languages, which has sometimes caused issues in interpretation,[43] the general outlook is that because the laws are the same, the interpretation of the law should also be aligned.

In practice, we have already seen multiple courts across Europe supporting the consideration of court decisions from other jurisdictions.[44] We have seen the Boards of Appeal of the European Patent Office refer to national court decisions and vice versa.[45] We have seen Supreme Courts require explanations in the reasoning of decisions that deviate from an approach taken in previous decisions.[46] We have even seen Supreme Courts change decades of practice in favour of a harmonised European approach towards patent infringement.[47] Of course, there are certain limitations to judicial dialogue and cooperation. As a process it is ad hoc, informal and irregular, and we must also be aware of the potential for courts stepping in where matters should be decided by the legislature. However, on balance, in a system with so many layers and so much room for divergence, it becomes a necessity. To ensure that future harmonisation attempts in the European patent system are considerate of the variety of approaches that exist towards matters such as patentability, exclusions, exceptions, infringement and more, it is essential that judicial dialogue and cooperation is also incorporated in the functioning of the UPC.

As mentioned, how the UPC will approach decision-making is so far unclear. It could use European patent law precedent from national courts and the Boards of Appeal of the European Patent Office, although this does raise the question as to which precedent.[48] It

---

42 For a view on fragmentation and judicial dialogue and cooperation from an international law perspective, see: K Walsh, *Fragmentation and the European Patent System* (Hart Publishing 2022) Chapter 4.
43 T19/90 *Oncomouse* of 03.10.1990, 4.2.
44 For a few examples, see: *Merrell Dow Pharmaceutical Inc v Norton & Co Ltd* [1996] RPC 76; *Grimme Maschinenfabrik v Derek Scott (t/a Scotts Potato Machinery)* [2010] EWCA Civ 1110; *Warner-Lambert Company LLC v Generics (UK) Ltd t/a Mylan and another* [2018] UKSC 56; Decision of the Bundesgerichtshof, 5 May 1998 – X ZR 57/96 'Zahnkranzfräser (Gear rim mill)'; Decision of the Bundesgerichtshof, 15 April 2010 – Xa ZB 10/09 'Walzenformgebungsmaschine (Roller-forming-machine)'.
45 See, for example: G5/83 *Second medical indication* of 05.12.1984.
46 See: Decision of the Bundesgerichtshof, 15 April 2010 – Xa ZB 10/09 'Walzenformgebungsmaschine (Roller-forming-machine)'.
47 See: *Actavis v Eli Lilly* [2017] UKSC 48.
48 There are numerous approaches towards the interpretation of the criteria for patentability found across Europe. For example, approaches towards determining whether there has been an inventive step can differ, and until recently, approaches towards determining infringement had also diverged more drastically. For more, see: K Walsh, 'Promoting harmonisation across the European patent system

could decide to do something completely different and begin UPC case law from scratch. However, more likely is that the judges of the UPC will decide upon something in the middle – to use what they consider to be the 'best of' approaches towards the interpretation of European patent law.

Implementing a 'best of' approach would be an excellent opportunity for judicial dialogue and cooperation. To decide on how the UPC will approach, for example, inventive step, the judges involved, who will be from a variety of Contracting Member States and have expertise and training in patent law decision-making, could consider past decisions and judgments on inventive step in the European patent system and the various approaches that are and have been taken across Europe in national courts and by the Boards of Appeal of the European Patent Office. While doing this, they could also speak to judges in other UPC divisions and with judges from outside the UPC to enhance their knowledge and understanding of the approaches that exist and the reasoning behind them. Finally, with that information in hand, they can decide on which is the best approach for the UPC.

It is expected that judicial dialogue and cooperation will already be happening to some degree within the UPC. For its internal functioning, it is crucial that all divisions of the UPC are sending a clear and coordinated message. Indeed, multiple mock trials have already occurred to demonstrate the potential functioning of the UPC.[49] There are plans in place for judicial meetings of the UPC to take place in order to manage responses and discuss developments in the system.[50] Federica Baldan and Esther van Zimmeran have also previously identified numerous additional tools that are being used by the UPC to promote convergence, including the training of judges and the incorporation of multinational panels.[51] They also suggest that dissenting opinions and amicus curiae briefs should be included as features in the UPC to make further progress on a coherent approach.[52] A combination of all such tools will go a long way towards a more consistent system.

It is likely that the judges of the UPC will also engage with external judicial meetings, such as those organised by the Patent Academy of the European Patent Office.[53] En-

---

through judicial dialogue and cooperation' (2019) 50(4) *International Review of Intellectual Property and Competition Law* 408.
49 See for example, the most recent mock trial held in Paris on 21 November 2022 organised by UJUB (Union pour la Juridiction Unifiée du Brevet/Union for the Unified Patent Court), available at https://www.opinews.com/ujub2022/. Previous mock trials are available at https://www.veron.com/ujub-mock-trials/?lang=en.
50 Article 19(3) UPCA.
51 F Baldan and E van Zimmeren, 'The Future Role of the Unified Patent Court in Safeguarding Coherence in the European Patent System' (2015) 52 *Common Market Law Review* 1529, 1571–1575.
52 Baldan and van Zimmeren, 1571–1575.
53 The informal meeting of judges is discussed further in: K Walsh, *Fragmentation and the European Patent System* (Hart Publishing 2022). For information on the most recent forum, see: 'European Judges' Forum 2022' (*EPO Website*, 26 October 2022) available at https://www.epo.org/news-events/news/2022/20221026.html.

gaging in such meetings is already a vital part of informal harmonisation in the European patent system and will be even more important on the entry into force of the EU unitary patent system.

Intentionally including judicial dialogue and cooperation in the UPC as an additional mechanism could result in several key advantages such as the development of a common approach toward patentability; the development of a common approach towards patent infringement; and the development of a common approach towards other post-grant matters. Importantly though, progress through judicial dialogue and cooperation also leaves open the possibility for gaining additional clarity on areas of divergence.

The European patent system will always have elements of difference. By engaging with judicial dialogue and cooperation, judges do not have to agree – often, they will not. However, if the process is engaged with and reasons are given for diverging from a previously decided case on the same patent or issue, this will highlight where discussions and analysis can be focussed on in the future.[54] Including greater scope for judicial dialogue and cooperation within the UPC is still possible and doing so would mitigate many risks associated with the potential for divergence that exists and will continue to exist within the European patent system.

28.5 Conclusion

The introduction of the EU unitary patent system will be the biggest change to the European patent system in decades. Interested parties all around the world will be watching as the first unitary patent is granted by the European Patent Office, as the UPC decides on its first case, and at how the system develops therefrom.

Although unitary by name, the system stops short of being unitary by nature. As a standalone system, its geographic scope is limited, and it has a complicated internal court structure that may lead to internal divergence in the short term. When considered from the perspective of the European patent system more broadly, it will add to the complex nature of this system. It will exist alongside multiple national patent systems, the European Patent Office and its Boards of Appeal, and the Court of Justice of the European Union. As the EU unitary patent system will now be a part of the European patent system, it is likely that divergent approaches towards patent law interpretation and divergent decisions in parallel proceedings that have previously been observed will continue to occur to some extent. Therefore, the advancement of post-grant harmonisation in the European patent system cannot depend on the EU unitary patent system alone.

In order to reduce the risks associated with divergence in the European patent system, to the extent that is possible and desirable, this chapter has suggested that it is ne-

---

[54] For more on this point, see: K Walsh, *Fragmentation and the European Patent System* (Hart Publishing 2022).

cessary to include the additional mechanism of judicial dialogue and cooperation, the process of judges considering or discussing relevant decisions and interpretations of other courts, and taking a coordinated approach where possible, within the UPC process and beyond. Doing so would have several key advantages. It would continue the development of consistent approaches towards patentability, towards enforcement and towards other post-grant matters where possible, considering the variety of approaches that already exist before coming to a conclusion on the way forward.

Even if it were possible or desirable, the European patent system will never be fully unified. Instead, what we can and should strive for is an adaptable system that can consider the legal, social, and ethical implications of patent law, as well as accommodating technological developments in the area. We should be striving for a system that is responsible, current and considered. To achieve this will require a consistent and up to date dialogue among the parties involved in the European patent system and beyond. For the European patent system, judicial dialogue and cooperation can play a key role in achieving this by allowing discussions to continue and adapt where necessary, and by raising diverging points that need to be considered in more depth. With the introduction of the UPC, this will be even more important.

Tamar Khuchua

29 The role of the CJEU in European patent law from a procedural perspective

Introductions

The Court of Justice of the European Union (CJEU or the Court)[1] has been created as a supranational court to guarantee the harmonised application of EU law in all EU Member States.[2] Its role is tremendous in all areas of law where the EU has established its exclusive or shared competence including in the field of intellectual property law which, according to the Court, falls into the category of shared competence when it comes to the establishment of IP rights within the Union.[3] Hence, based on the EU's legislative acts which either create EU level IP rights[4] or harmonise the national laws[5] in the field of in-

---

[1] For the purposes of this chapter, the term CJEU or the Court is adopted to refer to the Court of Justice and not to the entire institution that also includes the General Court.
[2] Vincent Cassiers and Alain Strowel, 'Intellectual Property Law Made by the Court of Justice of the European Union' in Christophe Geiger, Craig Allen Nard and Xavier Seuba (eds), *Intellectual Property and the Judiciary* (Edward Elgar 2018) 176; Joseph Kenneth Yarsky, 'Hastening Harmonization in European Union Patent Law Through a Preliminary Reference Power' (2017) 167, INT'l & Comp. L. Rev. 167, 187.
[3] See, Joined Cases C-274/11 and C-295/11, *Spain and Italy v Council*, EU:C:2013:240, paras 24–25. The Court stated that the issues falling within the sphere of Article 118, TFEU are shared competences for the purposes of Article 4(2), TFEU and of Article 20(1), TEU, as it does not fall within the TFEU's Chapter, "Rules on Competition" which in turn, is the EU's exclusive competence based on the Article 3(1)(b), TFEU. However, as for the EU's external competence, the Court has held in Case C-414/11, *Daiichi Sankyo and Sanofi-Aventis Deutschland*, EU:C:2013:520, that all TRIPS provisions fall within the common commercial policy category and thus EU's exclusive competence based on the Article 3, TFEU. See in this regard, Anna Wilińska-Zelek, Milosz Malaga, 'EU Competence and Intellectual Property Rights. Internally Shared, Externally Exclusive?!' (2017) 1 Środkowoeuropejskie Studia Polityczne 27.
[4] For example, trade mark and community design rights created by the Regulation (EU) 2017/1001 of the European Parliament and of the Council of 14 June 2017 on the European Union trade mark, OJ L 154, 16.6.2017, p. 1–99 (EUTM Regulation) and Council Regulation (EC) No 6/2002 of 12 December 2001 on Community designs.
[5] For example, in the copyright field, the EU has adopted several directives, e.g. Directive (EU) 2019/790 of the European Parliament and of the Council of 17 April 2019 on Copyright and Related Rights in the Digital Single Market and Amending Directives 96/9/EC and 2001/29/EC (Text with EEA Relevance) OJ L 130, 17.5.2019, p. 92–125. In the trade mark field, there is Council Directive 89/104/EEC of 21 December 1988 to approximate the laws of the Member States relating to trade marks OJ L 40, 11.2.1989, p. 1–7 (EU Trade mark Directive).

Tamar Khuchua, PhD in Law (University of Strasbourg and Queen Mary University of London under the Marie Sklodowska Curie Action ITN-EJD, EIPIN-Innovation Society). Currently a post-doctoral research fellow at Sciences Po Paris within the French-German research project UNIFIED in collaboration with the University of Heidelberg.

tellectual property, the questions may fall within the CJEU's jurisdiction. Apart from the substantive legal instruments, the acts related to exercising such IP rights, such as the EU Enforcement Directive 2004/48/EC,[6] also bring issues related to IP rights under the scrutiny of the CJEU, particularly from a procedural point of view. As a supranational court, the Court's competence does not entail direct involvement in private legal disputes of any kind, it is reserved for cases where the correct interpretation or application of EU law needs to be guaranteed in an EU's supranational legal order, as it co-exists with national legal orders. Given these characteristics of the Court, first, it is worth outlining the available EU legal instruments in the field of patent law in the EU that trigger the CJEU's competence in this area as well as the legal avenues considered by the EU Treaty leading to the CJEU's binding case law. In this regard, the chapter presents the types of cases that have resulted from these avenues with a particular focus on the interpretation of the Enforcement Directive by the Court. Hence, after this introductory section, the chapter identifies the EU's stance in patent law and the available case law of the CJEU, then, the main objectives and the nature of the Enforcement Directive are highlighted followed by the detailed analysis of four judgments of the Court of Justice handed down concerning the procedural guarantees as foreseen by that Directive in relation to the enforcement of patent rights. In particular, two cases concern the provisional measures (Article 9(1) and 9(7)), one case concerns the reimbursement of legal costs (Article 14) and the last case is on the provisional measure (Article 9) in the context of the interpretation of competition law (Article 102, TFEU). Finally, the chapter provides reflections on how the new Unified Patent Court (UPC) can function in the light of the EU's procedural safeguards and the respective case law of the Court of Justice. Concluding remarks are provided in the conclusion of the chapter.

29.1 EU Legislation in patent law and the CJEU's current role in the patent field

In contrast to the other IP rights EU's legislation on patent law is relatively limited.[7] Despite the Article 118 of the Treaty on the Functioning of the European Union (TFEU) that lays the ground for the creation of intellectual property rights in the EU, including patent rights, up to now an EU patent right has not been adopted. Alongside the national

---

6 Directive 2004/48/EC of the European Parliament and of the Council of 29 April 2004 on the enforcement of intellectual property rights, OJ L 157, 30.4.2004, p. 45 (Enforcement Directive, Directive 2004/48/EC or the Directive).
7 See in this regard, Elisabeta Zirnstein, 'Harmonization and Unification of Intellectual Property in the EU' (2005) Published Scientific Conference Contribution, University of Primorska, 293, 298–298; Tamar Khuchua, 'Different Rules of the Game – Impact of National Court Systems on Patent Litigation in the EU and the Need for New Perspectives' (2019) 10(2) JIPITEC, 257, 267.

patents, the only regional patent right that operates based on the intergovernmental agreement – the European Patent Convention (EPC)[8] – is the so called "classical" European patent which may also be attributed a unitary effect in the EU upon the patent application at the European Patent Office (EPO), based on the EU Regulation 1257/2012[9] after its entry into force. Therefore, a directly applicable EU legal instrument which would give rise to the CJEU's rulings on EU patent rights is not yet in place.

However, since the scope of protection of biotechnological inventions varies in different national legal systems, the EU Directive on biotechnological inventions was adopted[10] in 1998 to harmonise the national laws in this regard. Despite its harmonising nature, the Directive has led to ambiguities for national courts on numerous occasions, particularly concerning the patentability of human embryonic stem cells that led to the CJEU's interference on this issue in the cases *Brüstle*[11] and *International Stem Cell*[12] where the CJEU has provided a balanced approach, taking into account differences in legal and cultural frameworks between the EU Member States and thus providing a broad definition of a human embryo.[13] Other legislative instruments adopted on the EU level that have also led to the CJEU's judgments are the Regulations on Supplementary Protection Certificates for pharmaceutical and for plant products.[14] These Regulations have also been brought to the attention of the Court that has decided on the substantive issues, such as when an active ingredient can be considered as protected by a basic patent in force and therefore, the protection extended by a supplementary protection certificate.[15] As for the procedural aspects of patent law, the most relevant EU legislation in this regard is the EU Enforcement Directive 2004. This Directive has incorporated most of the TRIPS Agreement provisions from its 3rd Chapter[16] and has set minimum stan-

---

8 European Patent Convention of 5 October 1973 as revised by the Act revising Article 63 EPC of 17 December 1991 and the Act revising the EPC of 29 November 2000 (European Patent Convention).
9 Regulation (EU) No 1257/2012 of the European Parliament and the Council of 17 December 2012 implementing enhanced cooperation in the area of the creation of unitary patent protection, OJ L 361, 31.12.2012, p. 1–8. (1257/2012).
10 Directive 98/44/EC of the European Parliament and of the Council of 6 July 1998 on the legal protection of biotechnological inventions 1998, OJ L 213, 30.7.1998, p. 13– 21 (Biotechnology Directive).
11 Case C-34/10, *Oliver Brüstle v Greenpeace* e.V. EU:C:2011:669.
12 Case C-364/13, *International Stem Cell Corporation v Comptroller General of Patents, Designs and Trademarks*, EU:C:2014:2451.
13 Regarding *Brüstle* case see Karen Walsh, 'The Unitary Patent Package, the Court of Justice of the European Union, and Brexit: (Ir)reconcilable?' (2019) Intellectual Property Quarterly, 1, 13.
14 Council Regulation (EEC) No 1768/92 of 18 June 1992 concerning the creation of a supplementary protection certificate for medicinal products, OJ L 182, 2.7.1992, p. 1–5; Regulation (EC) No 1610/96 of the European Parliament and of the Council of 23 July 1996 concerning the creation of a supplementary protection certificate for plant protection products, OJ L 198, 8.8.1996, p. 30–35.
15 See for example, Case C-322/10 *Medeva v Comptroller General of Patents, Designs and Trade Marks* ECLI:EU:C:2011:773.
16 See in this regard, Rafał Sikorski, 'Towards a More Orderly Application of Proportionality of Patent Injunctions in the European Union' (2022) 53 IIC, 31, 32.

dards for IP protection through enforcement, mainly focusing on the fight against counterfeiting in the trade mark and copyright fields.[17] Nevertheless, since its adoption, the CJEU has issued a few but noteworthy rulings in the patent field, particularly concerning the application of provisional measures by national courts in the light of the mentioned Directive coupled with the EU competition law provisions. It is precisely the procedural aspects seen through the prism of the CJEU that are central to this chapter, as these interpretations provide a solid foundation for the approximation of laws to ensure harmonised and competition law compliant patent enforcement in the EU.

29.2 Avenues leading to CJEU judgments on patent enforcement and available case law

Of the four most important avenues leading to CJEU jurisdiction within the EU, in particular 1. an action directed at an EU institution seeking the annulment of its act[18] or an action for its failure to act[19]; 2. an action directed against a Member State due its breach of EU law[20]; 3. an appeal action against the decisions of the General Court brought to the Court of Justice[21]; and 4. preliminary references submitted to the CJEU by national courts[22], it is the fourth procedure that mostly trigger cases on the interpretation of substantive patent protection as well as the procedural aspects of patent enforcement at the CJEU. Preliminary rulings have long been deemed the most powerful tools for the CJEU to exert its harmonising impact in the EU.[23]

Statistically, when searching for any kind of document issued by the Court of Justice in relation to the Directive 2004/48/EC without accounting for any specific time period, i.e. since the entry into force of the Directive until today (September 2022), and without any limitation of subject matter, out of all 197 search results[24] – judgments, judgment summaries, judgment information, abstracts, operative parts of the judgments, Advocate General opinions, applications as well as working documents labeled as "request for a preliminary ruling" found in the CJEU's official Curia case law database, 42 judgements can be found (available in full or only with their operative parts, summaries, abstracts or

---

[17] See, Florence Hartmann-Vereilles, 'Achievements in Civil Intellectual Property Enforcement and Recent Initiatives Within the Digital Single Market Strategy on the Regulatory Environment for Platforms and Online Intermediaries' (2017) 18 Era Forum, 1.
[18] Article 263, TFEU.
[19] Article 265, TFEU.
[20] Article 263, TFEU.
[21] Article 256, TFEU.
[22] Article 267, TFEU.
[23] See in this regard, Morten Broberg, Henrik Hanse and Niels Fenger, 'A Structural Model for Explaining Member State Variations in Preliminary References to the ECJ' (2020) 45(5) E. L. Rev. 599.
[24] InfoCuria Case-law, <https://curia.europa.eu/jcms/jcms/j_6/en/> accessed 28 September 2022.

as an information).[25] Out of these 42 judgments 36 cases have derived from the preliminary requests of national courts, followed by three actions against Member States to fulfill their obligations, two appeals brought to the Court of Justice to set aside the judgments of the General Court and only one action for annulment of a decision of the EU institution (in this case the Council). Concerning the subject matter, majority of the cases were raised in relation to the approximation of laws (20) followed by freedom of establishment (6). As for the related IP issue in these proceedings, they vary, yet copyright is the most frequently invoked IP right related to the implementation of the Enforcement Directive, followed by trade marks. (See the Table 1 below).

Table 1: Share of subject matters and IP rights amongst judgments of the Court of Justice mentioning the Directive 2004/48/EC

#	Subject Matter	Total number of judgments	IP rights concerned
1	Approximation of laws	20	Copyright and related rights (8) Trade mark (5) Patent (3) Utility model (1) Other (3)[26]
2	Freedom of establishment	6	Copyright and related rights (4) Trade mark (1) Other (1)[27]
3	Freedom to provide services	1	Copyright (1)
4	Agriculture and fisheries	1	Community Plant Variety Rights (1)
5	Competition	2	Patents (2)
6	Intellectual, industrial and commercial property – trade mark	5	Trade mark (5)[28]
7	Intellectual, industrial and commercial property	1	Trade mark (1)
8	Free movement of goods	1	Copyright and related rights (1)

---

25 For one case one corresponding judgement is counted (either available fully or only with its operative part as well as abstract, summary or information). In case all types of documents are available for one case, the judgment count is also only one).
26 The rest of the three cases concerned the European Commission's action against Member States regarding the failure to transpose the Directive 2004/48/EC into national laws within the prescribed time-limit.
27 One remaining case concerned the reimbursement of legal costs, however, as the entire judgment is not available on Curia case law database, it is not possible to identify the specific IP right concerned.
28 In four cases, the issue of trade mark was raised in the context of the EUTM Regulation while the EU Trade mark Directive was discussed only in one case.

Table 1: (continued).

#	Subject Matter	Total number of judgments	IP rights concerned
9	Area of freedom, security and justice – judicial cooperation in civil matters	3	Community design (1) Trade mark (1) Patent (1)
10	Principles, objectives and tasks of the Treaties	1	Neighboring rights (1)
11	Provisions governing the institutions	1	Copyright and related rights (1)

Out of these 42 judgments concerning specific IP rights, six are related to patents. In particular, one concerns jurisdiction and recognition of judgments in the area of freedom, security and justice and judicial cooperation in civil matters; in three cases the proceedings are on the approximation of laws, out of which, one case deals with the costs and two cases with interim and provisional measures. Finally, in the two remaining cases the patent issue is related to competition, one involving the relationship between seeking an injunction and the dominant position, and another involving agreements, decisions and concerned practices between patent holders and manufacturers of generic products. All six cases have emerged within the preliminary reference mechanism.

Despite the small number of patent related CJEU cases involving procedural aspects, these rulings are worth studying as they provide guidance not only for the national courts but also for the potential litigants. These cases are directly linked to the attainment of the Treaty objectives regarding effective IP protection, the protection of fundamental rights, including in court proceedings, and fair competition practices. As the procedural aspects deriving from the Directive 2004 are the focus of this chapter, the four patent cases directly related to the provisions of this Directive will be analysed in detail, thus leaving aside one case on the Brussels I Regulation 44/2001[29] in the context of cross-border IP litigation[30] and the other case on the 'by object' or 'by effect' restriction of competition through patent settlements between an originator and a generic manufacturer.[31]

---

[29] Council Regulation (EC) No 44/2001 of 22 December 2000 on jurisdiction and the recognition and enforcement of judgments in civil and commercial matters (Brussles I Regulation).
[30] The Case C-406/09 *Realchemie Nederland*, ECLI:EU:C:2011:668 concerned the recognition of an order imposing a fine within the meaning of the Brussels I Regulation. The small portion of the case touched upon the question whether the costs related to an exequatur procedure fell within the Article 14 of the Directive 2004/48/EC to which the answer of the Court was affirmative.
[31] Case C-307/18 *Generics (UK) and Others*, ECLI:EU:C:2020:52. See in this regard, Sophie Lawrence, Edwin Bond, Francion Brooks, Matthew Hunt, Helena Connors and Isobel Thomas, 'Patent Settlement Reach the CJEU; Pay-TV Licensing Commitments Annulled; Commission Analysed Patent Licensing Programmes: A Survey of Developments at the Intersection between Competition Law and IP Law in the Past Year' (2021) 12(4) Journal of Competition Law and Practice 338.

29.3 Guaranteeing an EU-law compliant patent enforcement procedure within national courts based on the Enforcement Directive

The Enforcement Directive is the central instrument for harmonising private enforcement of IP rights, including the patent enforcement procedure in the EU. EU legislative interference in the sphere of private enforcement is rather exceptional, which is why this Directive has been considered to be an ambitious initiative that touches upon procedural issues.[32] In particular, due to the disparities in the procedural guarantees available for the IP enforcement, such as the application of provisional measures to preserve evidence, damages to be granted, or remedies available to the rightsholder,[33] that in turn may lead to the lack of confidence on the part of IP rights holders, lack of investment in innovation and thus a weakening of substantive IP rights,[34] the Directive was adopted on the basis of Article 114 TFEU with the aim to provide "effective means of enforcing intellectual property rights" in the internal market.[35] These means are understood as different "measures, procedures and remedies".[36] At the same time, the technology driven increase in rich patent portfolios in pharmaceutical, electronic or communication sectors as well as the accumulation of patents amongst patent assertion entities have triggered abuse and aggressive litigation strategies.[37] Therefore, the Directive operates in a challenging global context where IP enforcement mechanisms can be used to abuse the system under the pretext of IP protection. For this reason, Article 3(2) of the Directive underlines that "those measures, procedures and remedies shall also be effective, proportionate and dissuasive and shall be applied in such a manner as to avoid the creation of barriers to legitimate trade and to provide for safeguards against their abuse." This Article echoes Article 41 of the TRIPS Agreement and is also rooted in Articles 34 and 36 TFEU that seek to strike a fair balance between the free movement of goods and services on the one hand, and IP rights protection, on the other.[38] Observing fundamental rights as recognised by the Charter of Fundamental Rights of the European Union (the Charter) is also highlighted by the Directive.[39] Hence, in addition to the effec-

---

[32] Folket G. Wilman, 'A Decade of Private Enforcement of Intellectual Property Rights under IPR Enforcement Directive 2004/48: Where do We Stand (and Where might We Go)? (2017) 42(4) E. L. Rev. 509, 512.
[33] Recital 7, Enforcement Directive.
[34] ibid Recital 9.
[35] ibid Recital 3.
[36] ibid Article 1.
[37] See in this regard, Sikorski (n 16) 33; Concerning abuse of patent rights see, Amandine Léonard, 'Abuse of Rights' in Belgian and French Patent Law – A Case Law Analysis' (2016) 7 JIPITEC, 30; Regarding the Patent Assertion Entities' strategies see, Shawn P. Miller, 'Who is Suing Us? Decoding Patent Plaintiffs since 2000 with the Stanford NPE Litigation Dataset' (2018) 21 Stan. Tech.L. Rev. 235.
[38] Regarding Article 34 and 36 TFEU, see, Cassiers and Strowel (n 2) 178–179.
[39] Recital 32, Enforcement Directive.

tive IP enforcement, the second main message of the Directive is to balance the interests of parties by adopting the proportionality principle, which also leads to the consideration of public interest.[40] For attaining these objectives, the Directive contains provisions on evidence,[41] right of information,[42] provisional and pecuniary measures,[43] corrective measures,[44] injunctions,[45] alternative measures,[46] damages[47] and legal costs.[48] However, the interpretation of these norms largely depends on the courts of the Member States, resulting in either pursuing a strong enforcement policy or rather a weaker one in favor of alleged infringers.[49] For instance, judicial authorities may order "the information on the origin and distribution networks of the goods and services" if the claimant's order is "justified and proportionate"[50] – the vagueness of these notions is undoubtful.[51] The calculation of damages can also vary from court to court, depending on what kind of enforcement is pursued,[52] to name just a few examples. Due to existing disparities and uncertainties, the European Commission, after its report on the Directive issued in 2010,[53] has also published the guidance in the form of the Communication Paper.[54]

Hence, striking a fair balance is not an easy task for the national courts in IP enforcement proceedings. This may explain the overall number of preliminary references submitted to the CJEU for the interpretation of different elements of the Directive, which is quite high considering the fact that the Directive is a relatively recent piece of legislation in the EU.[55]

---

40 Wilman (n 32) 515.
41 Articles 6 and 7, Enforcement Directive.
42 ibid Article 8.
43 ibid Article 9.
44 ibid Article 10.
45 ibid Article 11.
46 ibid Article 12.
47 ibid Article 13.
48 ibid Article 14.
49 See in this regard, Marcus Norrgård, 'The Role Conferred on the National Judge by Directive 2004/48/EC on the Enforcement of Intellectual Property' (2005) 6 Era Forum 503, 506–507.
50 Article 8, Enforcemenet Directive, see in this regard, ibid, 509.
51 See, Norrgård (n 49) 509.
52 ibid.
53 See, Christophe Geiger, Jacques Raynard and Caroline Roda, 'What Developments for the European Framework on Enforcement of Intellectual Property Rights? A Comment on the Evaluation Report Dated December 22, 2010' (2011) 33(9) EIPLR 543.
54 Communication from the Commission to the European Parliament, the Council and the European Economic and Social Committee, Guidance on Certain Aspects of Directive 2004/48/EC of the European Parliament and of the Council on the Enforcement of Intellectual Property Rights, Brussels, 29.11.2017, COM (2017) 708 final.
55 Even though the Enforcement Directive was adopted in 2004, and the deadline for national transposition was set for 2006, most of the Member States were late with the implementation, the last Member State being Luxembourg, transposing the Directive in 2009. See in this regard, Commission Staff Working

In the trade mark and copyright context, the CJEU clarified most of the provisions of the Directive, which have been discussed in detail elsewhere.[56] However, procedural guarantees for the patent enforcement have remained in shadow in the scholarly literature, with some exceptions,[57] calling for the analysis of these few identified cases – two pertaining to interim and provisional measures, one to legal costs and one to competition (abuse of a dominant position). The analysis is particularly relevant in the context of the upcoming UPC which will also be required to observe the CJEU's case law whenever relevant.[58]

29.3.1 CJEU rulings on interim and provisional measures in patent enforcement

In order to prevent any "imminent infringement", Article 9(1) of the Directive provides the possibility of requesting an interlocutory injunction against an alleged infringer. It is in this context that the Court of Justice, in case *Phoenix Contact*, has been asked for a preliminary ruling by the regional court in Munich in the dispute between the two technology companies concerning the European patent held by Phoenix Contact.[59] Particularly, the referring court was interested in whether the practice of the higher regional courts in Germany, which refused to grant interim reliefs when the patent in question had not yet survived the opposition procedure before the EPO or the invalidity proceedings before the Federal Patent Court of Germany (*Bundespatentgericht*), was compatible with Article 9(1) of the EU Directive.[60]

The Court stressed that the objectives of the Directive should be recalled and that each case should be treated individually by national courts when they decide upon the provisional measures.[61] The purpose of the provisional measure stipulated in Article 9

Document Analysis of the Application of Directive 2004/48/EC of the European Parliament and the Council of 29 April 2004 on the Enforcement of Intellectual Property Rights in the Member States, Brussels, 22.12.2010, SEC (2007) 1589 final, Annex 1.

56 In the context of trade mark disputes, see for example cases, C-427/15, *New Wave SZ*, EU:C:2017:18, C-580/13, *Coty Germany*, EU:C:2015:485; In the context of copyright see for example cases, C-275/06, *Promusicae*, ECLI:EU:C:2008:54; C-314/12, *UPC Telekabel Wien*, ECLI:EU:C:2014:192. See, Wilman (n 32) 509.

57 Pedro Henrique D. Batista and Gustavo Cesar Mazutti, 'Comment on "Huawei Technologies" (C-170/13): Standard Essential Patents and Competition Law – Howe Far does the CJEU Decision Go?' (2016) 47 IIC 244.

58 According to the Article 21, UPC Agreement, the UPC, "[a]s a court common to the Contracting Member States and as part of their judicial system […] shall cooperate with the Court of Justice of the European Union to ensure the correct application and uniform interpretation of Union law, as any national court, in accordance with Article 267 TFEU in particular. Decisions of the Court of Justice of the European Union shall be binding on the Court".

59 Case C-44/21, *Phoenix Contact*, ECLI:EU:C:2022:309.

60 ibid para 27.

61 ibid para 31.

(1) of the Directive is, according to the Court, precisely to stop the infringement immediately before the final decision on infringement is taken, in order to avoid any irreparable harm caused to the IP rights holder.[62] This goes to the heart of the Directive that set as its objective an effective IP enforcement.[63] The Court argued that as the patent in question was confirmed to be valid, the case law of national courts predominantly rendered the procedural guarantees to protect IP right ineffective.[64] To mitigate the risk that the defendant might suffer from an interim relief, the Court, by referring to Article 3(2) of the Directive, emphasised the necessity to balance the interests of parties in order to avoid an abusive conduct by a patent holder.[65] Thus, the Court recalled all possibilities provided by the Directive (Articles 9(5) (6) and (7)) that ensure that the rights of the defendant are preserved and that the abuse of provisional measures is avoided, for instance by granting a compensation to the defendant.[66] Interestingly, German national law did not contain any rule whereby the issuance of an interim injunction is subject to the condition that the patent in question must have been held valid by a court decision,[67] but it was only the national courts that followed this line of reasoning. Therefore, the Court of Justice called for precluding such case law which was clearly contrary to the objectives of Article 9(1) of the Directive.[68]

With this decision, the Court of Justice averts the burden imposed on patent holders in German proceedings. In many parts of the judgment it can be noted that the Court frequently highlights that IP rights must be protected effectively, for instance when the Court states that the Directive is only a minimum standard and that the national legislation, and ultimately the courts, can only provide a higher level of protection[69] and not a lower one. The pro-IP protection character of the judgment is also noticeable when the Court mentions the presumption of validity of patents granted at the EPO.[70] With this judgment, the German courts are now obliged to disregard the additional criterion for applying provisional measures that will perhaps make the German courts even more attractive for patent holders.[71] As this case is very recent, dating to 28 April 2022, it remains to be seen how the case law in Germany will further develop, and if the Court of Justice will receive similar questions in the future.

---

62 ibid para 32.
63 ibid.
64 ibid para 40.
65 ibid para 42.
66 ibid paras 45–47.
67 ibid para 51.
68 ibid para 52–54.
69 ibid para 38.
70 ibid para 41.
71 Sandra Mueller, 'Through the Fire? Not Anymore – European Court of Justice strengthens Rights of Patent Owners in Germany', 17 May 2022, <https://www.iptechblog.com/2022/05/through-the-fire-not-any more-european-court-of-justice-strengthens-rights-of-patent-owners-in-germany/> accessed 2 September 2022.

Another case in relation to preliminary measures provided in Article 9 of the Directive which is also relatively new – dating to 12 September 2019 – is *Bayer Pharma*.[72] This time the issue in question was Article 7(9) of the Directive which is a counterbalancing provision and provides that in case no infringement or threat of infringement has been found, the courts can, upon the request of the defendant, order the applicant to pay appropriate compensation for the injury caused by the provisional measures.

The case concerned a pharmaceutical product of Bayer for which the patent application was still pending at the Hungarian patent office when the two competitors started marketing their generic products in Hungary.[73] Once the patent was granted, the patent owner requested a preliminary injunction to stop the marketing of the alleged infringers' products and in addition, to provide the guarantees.[74] The provisional measures had been granted, but were then revoked due to some procedural defects.[75] Moreover, the patent was later found to be invalid[76] and thus, the infringement proceedings were also stopped.[77] The two defendants subsequently asked for a compensation for their losses caused by the provisional measures.[78] In these circumstances, the Hungarian national court, the Budapest Hight Court, discontinued the proceedings and asked the Court of Justice how the "appropriate compensation" provided in Article 9(7) of the Directive should be interpreted and whether national legislation under which a party shall not be compensated for the loss if he has not taken any action to avoid the said loss, shall not apply.[79] In other words, the question was whether the defendant's action or inaction in experiencing the loss, in this case the marketing of the products despite the pending patent application, played a role in deciding the issue of compensation.[80]

According to the Court, as the Article 9(7) of the Directive does not make any reference to national law, it must be given an autonomous and uniform interpretation,[81] since otherwise the objective of the Directive to ensure an equivalent, homogenous and high level of protection would be compromised.[82] In this regard, the national authorities

---

72 Case C-688/17, *Bayer Pharma*, ECLI:EU:C:2019:722.
73 ibid para 16.
74 ibid para 21.
75 ibid para 23.
76 ibid para 26.
77 ibid para 28.
78 ibid para 31.
79 ibid para 34.
80 Eszter Szakás, 'Launch at Risk' – Article 9(7) of the Enforcement Directive interpreted by the CJEU in C-688/17 (Bayer), concluding that when a patent is subsequently revoked it does not automatically follow that the preliminary injunction was unfounded', Kluwer Patent Blog, 23 September 20019, <http://patentblog.kluweriplaw.com/2019/09/23/launch-at-risk-article-9-7-of-the-enforcement-directive-interpreted-by-the-cjeu-in-c-688-17-bayer-concluding-that-when-a-patent-is-subsequently-revoked-it-does-not-aut/> accessed 2 September 2022.
81 Case C-688/17, *Bayer Pharma*, ECLI:EU:C:2019:722, para 41.
82 ibid para 44.

must provide their national courts with the power to grant such "appropriate compensation"[83]; it is therefore up to the national courts to find out what the "appropriate" compensation would be in the specific circumstances of the case.[84] The Court submitted that the mere fulfilment of the criteria of Article 9(7), particularly the lifting of provisional measures or the cessation of infringement or threat of infringement, does not automatically oblige the national courts to grant a compensation.[85] In the given context, as the defendants were marketing their products while the patent application was pending, the applications for the provisional measures could not be considered as "unjustified," even if they were later set aside.[86] Otherwise it would be discouraging for the IP rightsholders to apply for such provisional measures available under Article 9 of the Directive.[87] Most importantly, the national courts should determine whether the possibility of receiving a compensation foreseen by Article 9(7) is not abused.[88] Therefore, the Court of Justice found that the national law prohibiting the grant of compensation for the party that had not acted to avoid the loss, was not incompliant with Article 9(7) and with the concept of "appropriate compensation", as long as it allowed the national courts to observe all the objective circumstances to determine whether the tool of compensation had been abused or not.[89]

Hence, automatic compensations imposed on patent holders are not welcomed by the CJEU and a cautious approach is instructed before concluding whether the defendant has suffered from preliminary injunctions. Based on these two cases, it can be argued that the possibilities to put a heavy burden on the patent holders when it comes to the application of preliminary measures are minimised by the Court. In one case, national case law that hinders the way to preliminary measures employed by patent holder is overturned, and in another, automatic compensation to be provided by the patent holder is restrained. The latter case is particularly relevant for the system where an "injunction gap" may occur due to the bifurcated judicial system to which Hungary and Germany belong. The Unified Patent Court has also adopted this system, therefore, the CJEU's balanced approach exhibited in *Bayer Pharma* will be most probably followed by the UPC as it will be under the obligation to observe EU law, in this case the Enforcement Directive, when dealing with cross-cutting substantive patent issues.

---

83 ibid para 50.
84 ibid para 51.
85 ibid para 52.
86 ibid paras 63–64.
87 ibid para 65.
88 ibid para 70.
89 ibid para 71.

29.3.2 The issue of reimbursement of legal costs in patent proceedings clarified by the CJEU

Article 14 of the Enforcement Directive states that "Member States shall ensure that reasonable and proportionate legal costs and other expenses incurred by the successful party shall, as a general rule, be borne by the unsuccessful party, unless equity does not allow this." However, it is not always clear what shall be included in the costs to be reimbursed by a losing party. This question gave rise to the case *United Video Properties*, which originated from the dispute in Belgium between United Video Properties and Telnet concerning the former's patent.[90] In particular, United Video Properties brought a patent infringement action against Telnet and requested an injunction to cease the infringement and pay the costs.[91] The Commercial Court in Antwerp dismissed the infringement action, declared the patent invalid and ordered the claimant to pay procedural costs amounting to EUR 11 000.[92] The United Video Properties subsequently appealed the judgment at the Court of Appeal, however, it later discontinued its appeal.[93] Telnet, in addition to the granted damages, requested reimbursement of lawyer's and patent specialist's fees,[94] but Belgian legislation sets EUR 11 000 as a ceiling for the proceedings at each instance and, moreover, according to the case law of the Court of Cassation, any additional reimbursement can only be made if there is a fault on the applicant's side when bringing an action resulting in these additional costs.[95] Telnet submitted that such legislation and case law were contrary to Article 14 of the Directive, which is why the Court of Appeal of Antwerp stopped its proceedings and asked the Court of Justice whether 1. a national legislation giving courts the flexibility to take into account the specificities of a case at hand and setting a ceiling on the costs associated with lawyer's assistance and 2. national case law making the reimbursement of additional expert costs conditional on fault, were in compliance with Article 14 of the Directive.[96]

Regarding the first question, the Court has traditionally employed a teleological reasoning, specifying that the question of costs must be read in the light of the objectives of the Directive and that the substantial part of the costs must be reimbursed in order to ensure the enforcement of intellectual property rights.[97] At the same time, the Court highlighted that the unsuccessful party can only bear "reasonable" and "proportionate" costs,[98] which is up to the national courts to determine. Therefore, the Court's answer to

---

90 Case C-57/15, *United Video Properties*, ECLI:EU:C:2016:611.
91 ibid para 14.
92 ibid para 15.
93 ibid para 16.
94 ibid.
95 ibid para 17.
96 ibid para 19.
97 ibid para 22.
98 ibid paras 26, 29.

the first question is that a national legislation allowing the courts to take into account the specific features of each individual case and a law setting the limit for reimbursement, can be justified as long as the set rates take into account the costs incurred for the given proceedings in the Member State concerned,[99] whereas a legislation setting "significantly below the average rate" would not be acceptable.[100]

As for the second question, here the court adopted a literal approach and held that the "other costs" mentioned in Article 14 of the Directive are not specified anywhere, and therefore the technical expert's fees are not excluded in principle.[101] At the same time, the Court noted that a broad interpretation of Article 14 would blur the line between the costs associated with the court proceedings under Article 14 and the damages considered under Article 13 which articulates upon the infringer's faultand reads as follows: "knowingly, or with reasonable grounds to know engaged in an infringing activity." Consequently, the Court's response to the second question is that the national rules subjecting the reimbursement of "other costs" to the fault of the unsuccessful party, is not acceptable as long as those other costs of a technical advisor are "directly and closely" linked to a judicial action.[102] Although these terms are open to interpretation, the Court has at least defined which costs are not directly and closely linked to the court action, such as the general observation of the market,[103] or the "costs of identification and research."[104]

The question of costs of representation in patent proceedings has become especially relevant in the context of the Unified Patent Court where litigation will require particular preparation due to the new legal instruments and court proceedings. The short deadlines imposed on defendants are also considered to be particularly challenging and require the involvement of multiple lawyers in the preparation of the defence at the UPC.[105] Hence, the rule on incurring costs by an unsuccessful party, also considered by the UPC Agreement[106], will be alarming for the parties prior to deciding upon bringing an action to the new court. Nevertheless, with the aforementioned CJEU judgment, the risk of reimbursing of expensive representation costs is somewhat mitigated, as not every prior effort put in the preparation by a party will be counted as a cost "directly and closely" related to the litigation at the UPC.

---

99 ibid para 25.
100 ibid para 26.
101 ibid para 34.
102 ibid para 40.
103 ibid para 39.
104 ibid para 35.
105 For instance, according to the Rule 23 of the Rules of Procedure of the UPC, the defendant will have only three months for the preparation of a Statement of defence.
106 Article 69, Unified Patent Court Agreement 2013 (UPC Agreement).

29.3.3 CJEU providing guidance on procedural guarantees in patent enforcement in the light of EU competition law

The thin line between the protection of IP and the concerns of competition is a well-known issue that is appropriately covered in academic literature.[107] The case in point – *Huawei Technologies* – is a representation of how patent enforcement can potentially conflict with the principles of fair competition and the CJEU's guidance in this regard. The case originated from proceedings between Huawei Technologies and the German corporation ZTE concerning the alleged infringement of a standard essential patent granted by the EPO in the field of telecommunication as established by European Telecommunications Standards Institute (ETSI).[108] Given that the dominant position of Huawei Technologies was undisputed, the regional court of Düsseldorf asked the Court of Justice 1. whether it constituted an abuse of that dominant position if the applicant, that had committed to grant licences on FRAND terms, brought an action for an injunction against the alleged infringer, in cases where the infringer had shown its willingness to negotiate a licencing agreement or, would there be an abuse only if in addition to the willingness, an offer to conclude the licencing agreement had been submitted by the infringer and 2. how each of the scenarios should have been concretely exhibited in order to conclude whether there was an abuse or not.[109] The question was particularly relevant in the context of the pre-existing contrasting practices – on the one hand, of the German Federal Supreme Court in the *Orange Book* case, where the standard user's defences were limited by requiring him to submit an unconditional offer as well as the payment of a licencing fee, and, on the other hand, the Commission's approach, according to which the standard user's mere willingness to become a licencee would be sufficient to prohibit the SEP holder from seeking an injunction, without establishing the objective criteria for "willingness".[110] In view of these two extreme references, in one case the intricate conditions required from the defendant (SEP user) and in another case with some leeway given to them, the German court sought clarification from the CJEU.

The CJEU's balanced response to the question of whether seeking an injunction, the rendering of accounts, the recall of products and damages constitutes an abuse of a dominant position within the meaning of Article 102 was a middle ground between the *Orange Book* case law and the Commission's approach. At the outset, the Court underlined that balance should be found between on the one hand, free competition and on the other

---

[107] See, for example, Joseph Strauss 'Patent Application: Obstacle for Innovation and Abuse of Dominant Position under Article 102' (2010) 1(3) Journal of European Competition Law & Practice 189; Hanns Ullrich, 'Mandatory Licensing under Patent Law and Competition Law: Different Concerns, Complementary Roles' in Reto Hilty and KC Liu (eds) *Compulsory Licensing MPI Studies on Intellectual Property and Competition Law*, vol 22 (Springer 2015).
[108] Case C-170/13, *Huawei Technologies*, ECLI:EU:C:2015:477, para 2.
[109] ibid para 39.
[110] ibid paras 30–34.

hand, the protection of intellectual property rights and effective judicial protection.[111] Even though the right to bring an action for infringement cannot in itself be considered an abuse of a dominant position, in exceptional circumstances, it may however be qualified as abusive.[112] In particular, the CJEU observed that in this specific case, the question concerned not any patent but a standard-essential patent that is granted only on condition that the patent holder licences on FRAND terms,[113] thus creating legitimate expectations for third parties that such licences will be granted.[114] Refusal to do so can indeed be considered as an abusive conduct, yet the specific circumstances of the case must be observed in the light of the objectives of the Directive 2004/48 and the Article 17(2) concerning the IP protection as well as Article 47 of the Charter on the access to a tribunal.[115]

Consequently, the Court provided the objective elements that may contribute to defining a possible abuse. According to the CJEU, the SEP holder does not infringe Article 102 by bringing the prohibitory injunction if he has submitted a prior notice or has engaged in the consultation with the alleged infringer.[116] Moreover, it is up to the SEP holder to specify the nature of the infringement as it is not always easy to be aware of the specific essential patent, since standards consist of many such patents.[117] The SEP holder should then submit a written offer for a licencing agreement on FRAND terms, specifying the royalty fees[118] to which the alleged infringer has not diligently responded.[119] At the same time, the CJEU also set out the obligations that the alleged infringer must fulfill in order to be able to rely on the abuse of a dominant position by an SEP holder as a ground in its defence. These are: no delaying tactics in responding to the offer,[120] submission of a counteroffer also with FRAND terms in case of a disagreement with the initial offer,[121] and providing the security for the past uses of the SEP from the moment the counteroffer is refused.[122] The CJEU also held that legal proceedings seeking a render of accounts or an award of damages do not amount to an abuse of a dominant position as these requests relate to past actions and do not impact the competitors' ability to enter the market.[123] Moreover, although the issue was not raised when speaking of procedural guarantees, the Court held that the defendant's parallel action against the

---

111 ibid para 42.
112 ibid paras 46–47.
113 ibid paras 50–51.
114 ibid para 53.
115 ibid para 57.
116 ibid para 60.
117 ibid paras 61–62.
118 ibid para 63.
119 ibid para 71.
120 ibid para 65.
121 ibid para 66.
122 ibid para 67.
123 ibid paras 74–76.

validity or essentiality of a patent shall not be "criticised" as these are not checked by the standardisation body.[124]

This judgment is an outstanding example among the Courts' many rulings, where a clear and objective guidance is set out for the national courts and the SEP holders willing to enforce their patent rights without infringing the competition rules. As a result, the heavy burden of identifying the infringement and preparing the licencing agreement offer is lifted from the SEP users, who are in an inferior position compared to the SEP holder in terms of the knowledge about the value of a patent, while at the same time the Court maintained the possibility to fight against the infringement even by a dominant SEP holder, as long as the latter cautiously follows the steps explained in the judgment. Such a decision minimises the risks associated with the over and under enforcement of patents, also known as "hold-up" (instrumentalising the licence agreements for hindering access to market by competitors, e.g. by setting high royalty fees) and "hold-out" (setting low or no royalty fees by the SEP users, thereby jeopardizing IP rights enforcement).[125] These types of judgments serve as a reminder that even though patents are very technical in nature, they can "become a matter of general interest."[126] The *Huawei* case is of particular importance when it comes to reconciling competition and patent law requirements, which will also be one of the main preoccupations of the UPC.

29.4 The future role of the CJEU in procedural aspects of patent enforcement at the UPC

The new and (still upcoming) Unified Patent Court will have exclusive jurisdiction over disputes concerning European patents with unitary character and, ultimately European patents.[127] Even though this court is based on an international agreement and not EU law, it will co-exist with the existing judicial order of the EU and, particularly, the established case law of the Court of Justice. The UPC Agreement explicitly refers to EU law as its source of applicable law in the Article 24(1). In addition, the very same preliminary reference mechanism is also considered for the UPC in Article 21 of the UPC Agreement. In particular, the UPC, as a court common to the Contracting Member States "shall cooperate with the Court of Justice of the European Union to ensure the correct application and uniform interpretation of Union law, as any national court, in accordance with Article 267 TFEU," rendering the CJEU's decisions binding on the

---

124 ibid para 69.
125 See on this case, Batista and Mazutti (n 57) 348–349.
126 Hanns Ullrich, 'Patent Protection in Europe: Integrating Europe into the Community or the Community into Europe? (2002) 5 EUI Working Paper Law 1, 5.
127 According to the Article 83, UPC Agreement, during the transitional period of seven years, the European patents can still be challenged before national courts.

UPC.[128] In terms of co-existence of two courts, the beforementioned article is the central provision. When it comes to the Regulation 1257/2012, it is assumed in the literature that the preliminary references will be submitted regarding its Article 5 that is on the unitary effect and the rights derived from it. Other substantive norms regarding which the preliminary references are likely to be raised relate to the Biotechnology Directive, one of the rare pieces of EU substantive patent legislation. However, the UPC, like any national court, will also apply the rules of procedure and thus, it may well be that the procedural aspects in the context of patent enforcement will be the subject of dialogue between the UPC and the Court of Justice.

Legally, the UPC contains those procedural guarantees provided in the EU Enforcement Directive. It is even argued that the entire UPC Agreement is "a collective transposition of the rules" of this Directive.[129] Indeed, in principle all provisions of the Directive are provided in Chapters 3 and 4 of the UPC Agreement, and some of the provisions are in parts even repeated literally, for example the issue of preserving evidence,[130] the provisional and protective measures,[131] damages[132] or legal costs.[133]

As for the Rules of Procedure of the UPC, the *travaux préparatoires* illustrate that after the discussion on these rules between the Member States' delegations, such as, legal aid, court fees, recoverable costs, etc., the European Commission was asked to examine their compatibility with the *acquis communautaire*.[134] In principle, the rules are detailed explanations of the provisions set out in the UPC Agreement, spread through the five main parts: on the Procedures before the Court of First Instance, on Evidence, on Provisional Measures, on Procedures before the Court of Appeal and General Provisions.[135]

While formally speaking the UPC is ready to co-exist with the CJEU, the types of references and therefore, the interference of the CJEU in patent enforcement, as it has done in the illustrated national cases, will only be seen once the UPC enters into force. As of now, it can be argued that the judicial law-making of the CJEU is always characterised by a "balanced" approach and observation of the proportionality principle in the light of EU legal principles, including fundamental rights. If the UPC's powers in relation to ordering the production of evidence, or inspection of premises will be called for the CJEU's scrutiny through the preliminary reference mechanism, the CJEU will continue its line

---

128 Article 21, UPC Agreement.
129 Wilman (n 32) 518.
130 Article 60, UPC Agreement and Article 7, Enforcement Directive.
131 Article 62, UPC Agreement and Article 9, Enforcement Directive.
132 Article 68, UPC Agreement and Article 13, Enforcement Directive.
133 Article 69, UPC Agreement and Article 14, Enforcement Directive.
134 EPO, '17th European Patent Judges' Symposium, Tallin, 9–12 September 2014' (2015) 5, Supplementary Publication – Official Journal of EPO, p. 27, <https://www.epo.org/law-practice/legal-texts/official-journal/2015/etc/se5/2015-se5.pdf> accessed 19 August 2020.
135 Rules of Procedure of the Unified Patent Court, 2017.

of case law and ensure to guide the UPC in terms of application of procedural rules in the same way as the Court guides the national courts. The CJEU's balanced approach will be particularly essential as patent enforcement directly affects the protection of fundamental rights and has far-reaching societal implications in some fields, such as the medical sector.[136] However, as there is no appeal mechanism of the UPC's decisions at the Court of Justice, it will be up to the UPC itself or individuals – the parties in disputes before the UPC – to initiate the preliminary references to the CJEU.[137] To mitigate the concerns, it is important to note that the judges of the UPC will come from national courts that are used to dealing with the EU legislation and CJEU case law, the examples of which were discussed above. This experience will be a valuable attribute for serving as a judge at the UPC.

29.5 Conclusion

The importance attached to the effective enforcement of intellectual property rights in the EU is undeniable as evidenced by the adoption of the Directive 2004/48/EC. As it is an instrument setting minimum standards, its implementation varies amongst national legislations and courts. This may explain the overall number of preliminary references submitted to the CJEU seeking clarification of the provisions of the Directive. As far as the procedural guarantees and enforcement of patents are concerned, there are only a few CJEU rulings, but their analysis allows some conclusions to be drawn. Firstly, the Court is aware of the importance of the patent enforcement, which is often underlined by referring to the objectives of the Directive and the context in which it was adopted. Secondly, despite the need to ensure the protection of the rights of patent owners (as was seen in cases *Phoenix Contact and Bayer Pharma)*, the Court reinforces the balanced approach towards patent holders' interests on the one hand, and their competitors and the general public, on the other. The procedural norms explained by the Court concerning the use of preliminary measures, the reimbursement of legal costs and the final injunctions demonstrate how cautious the Court is about a reasonable and proportionate approach, reminding us that these are not straightforward issues and that each case shall be treated individually within its legal and economic context (for example that the reimbursable costs must be calculated based on the national context as stated in *United Video Properties case*). Finally, these cases, particularly the *Huawei* case, demonstrate that the Court of Justice is in full capacity to provide a very detailed examination of patent issues, especially when they are discussed in the context of EU competition law. The Court's guidance is clear and applicable by national courts. Such ruling is particularly

---

136 See in this regard, Aurora Plomer, 'The Unified Patent Court and the Transformation of the European Patent System' (2020) 51 IIC 791, 794.
137 ibid.

essential in times when the specialised European Unified Patent Court is about to enter into force, as the authority of the Court of Justice must be maintained when it comes to the interpretation and the application of procedural guarantees deriving form EU law, including fundamental rights in patent enforcement. Only if the role of the Court of Justice as a guardian of EU law is ensured, the harmonious co-existence of the two courts and thus, balanced patent enforcement can be achieved.

Naomi Hawkins
30 Gene patents in the EPC and the European patent with unitary effect

30.1 Introduction

Modern human genomics research has captured the public imagination, with its potential to improve understandings of human physiology and enhance health. At the same time, despite the hopes of new diagnostic and therapeutic products, concerns have focused on the ways in which the patent system has permitted the appropriation of the human genome to private ownership through patents. In the early days of identifying and sequencing elements of the human genome, many patents were granted,[1] and fears quickly crystalised around the potential for an anti-commons effect that would inhibit or constrain research.[2] There were also widespread worries about the potential for these patents to negatively impact patient care, although the actual extent of this problem remains contested.[3]

However, the patents to which these early concerns apply are no longer in force. The human genome project was completed, publishing a model human genome sequence, moving the state of the art beyond the point at which the patenting of a human genome sequence *per se* would be possible.[4] While isolation of genes may now be routine and non-patentable, genetics and genomics research and genetic medicine in clinical practice nonetheless continues to advance. There are thus new forms of genetic and genomic inventions, with associated new questions for patent law to address. It is the

---

[1] K Jensen and F Murray, 'Intellectual Property Landscape of the Human Genome' (2005) 310 Science 239; MM Hopkins and others, *The Patenting of Human DNA: Global Trends in Public and Private Sector Activity (The PATGEN Project)* (SPRU, Science and Technology Policy Research, University of Sussex, Brighton 2006).
[2] MA Heller and RS Eisenberg, 'Can Patents Deter Innovation? The Anticommons in Biomedical Research' (1998) 280 Science 698.
[3] Secretary's Advisory Committee on Genetics Health and Society (SACGHS), *Gene Patents and Licensing Practices and Their Impact on Patient Access to Genetic Tests* (2010); Naomi Hawkins, 'The Impact of Human Gene Patents on Genetic Testing in the United Kingdom' (2011) 13 Genetics in Medicine 320; J Kaye, N Hawkins and J Taylor, 'Patents and Translational Research in Genomics' (2007) 25 Nature Biotechnology 739; A Schissel, JF Merz and MK Cho, 'Survey Confirms Fears about Licensing of Genetic Tests' (1999) 402 Nature 118; MR Henry and others, 'DNA Patenting and Licensing' (2002) 297 Science 1279; AL Caplan and J Merz, 'Patenting Gene Sequences' (1996) 312 British Medical Journal 926; JF Merz and MK Cho, 'What Are Gene Patents and Why Are People Worried about Them?' (2005) 8 Community Genetics 203.
[4] Rochelle C Dreyfuss, Jane Nielsen and Dianne Nicol, 'Patenting Nature—a Comparative Perspective' (2018) 5 Journal of Law and the Biosciences 550.

Naomi Hawkins, Professor in Intellectual Property Law, University of Sheffield.

ways in which these questions are arising, and will arise, in the EPC and UPC systems that is the focus of this chapter. It argues that there are three areas where the intersection of the existing and future European Patent Law system with new genetics and genomics research will give rise to important challenges: *ordre public* and morality; concerns related to access to medicine; and questions of divergence of patent law and policy approaches to gene patents.[5]

30.1.1 Definition of gene patents

A gene patent is a term which may include various different types of inventions. It has been used in the academic literature primarily to refer to a patent which includes a claim over nucleic acids, either DNA or RNA.[6] Thus, any patent which claims DNA or RNA sequences as products, or the processes to make or identify them, would fall within the scope of what is considered to be a gene patent.[7] Both coding and non-coding DNA is included in this definition, as are diagnostic method patents. Patents claiming isolated DNA sequences have been most controversial in popular and academic circles,[8] but it has been argued that claims to methods of diagnosis are also problematic, and in practice difficult to invent around.[9]

This broadly inclusive definition continues to be appropriate and is adopted for this chapter. The types of technology which it covers have increased with the development of the science of genomics. As already highlighted, new patents on isolated genes are now rare, and almost all that were granted have now long expired.[10] Many simple methods of diagnosis patents have also expired, and such patents will now be unlikely to meet the patentability criteria, because they form part of the state of the art, or are unlikely to be sufficiently inventive. But other forms of genetic and genomic inventions continue to be

---

5 Much of the innovation in genetics and genomics continues to be focused on human health, although the scope for genetics and genomics in animal health and wider ecology is also clear. However, this chapter is primarily focused on gene patents in human health.
6 Aisling McMahon, 'Gene Patents and the Marginalisation of Ethical Issues.' (2019) 41 European Intellectual Property Review 608; Nuffield Council on Bioethics, *The Ethics of Patenting DNA: A Discussion Paper* (Nuffield Council on Bioethics 2002); Naomi Hawkins, 'Human Gene Patents and Genetic Testing in Europe: A Reappraisal' (2010) 7 ScriptEd 453; R Cook-Deegan and C Heaney, 'Patents in Genomics and Human Genetics' (2010) 11 Annu Rev Genomics Hum Genet 383.
7 This is essentially the same as the definition used by Paradise, Andrews and Holbrook in J Paradise, L Andrews and T Holbrook, "Patents on Human Genes: An Analysis of Scope and Claims" (2005) 307 *Science* 1566.
8 Secretary's Advisory Committee on Genetics, Health and Society (SACGHS), *Public Consultation Draft Report on Gene Patents and Licensing Practices and Their Impact on Patient Access to Genetic Tests* (2009), 22–23.
9 I Huys and others, "Legal Uncertainty in the Area of Genetic Diagnostic Testing" (2009) 27 Nature Biotechnology 903.
10 Dreyfuss, Nielsen and Nicol (n 4).

formed and to, at least *prima facie*, satisfy patentability criteria. Current and recent case law reflects developments in genomics – thus more recent cases have moved from a consideration of whether isolated genes are patentable,[11] to more complex diagnostic methods such as non-invasive prenatal diagnosis,[12] and genome editing technologies.[13] As might be expected, given the significant lag between patent filing and litigation, patents are being filed on ever newer forms of genetic and genomic inventions in fields as diverse as pharmacogenetics, prenatal diagnostics and human gene editing, and seem likely to form the subject matter of patent challenges in the future.

Gene patents continue to generate important legal questions. The case law around the patenting of isolated gene sequences generated international divergence in approaches. The narrow focus of these decisions means that questions around eligibility have not been definitively settled and continue to be a potential source of challenge for new genetic inventions. Objections to patents on the grounds of morality and ethics continue, and these new genetic inventions give rise to ever more difficult ethical conundrums especially around questions of balancing fair access and incentives for innovation. Additionally, the divergent approaches taken by different jurisdictions to the resolution of these questions pose difficulties for a field that is global in nature.

30.1.2 Current technical landscape

The first gene patents were for fragments of DNA such as expressed sequence tags. As the human genome project progressed, many human genes, partial gene sequences, and mutations associated with disease were patented, both as products *per se*, and also in forms that claimed methods of diagnosis. In the past, the gene patents relevant to diagnosis have been categorised as falling within four broad areas: product claims to iso-

---

11 Such as for example in *Association for Molecular Pathology v Myriad Genetics Inc* 569 US 576 (2013); *Alice Corp v CLS Bank International* 573 US 208 (2014); *D'Arcy v Myriad Genetics Inc* [2015] HCA 35; *Howard Florey/Relaxin* [1995] EPOR 541 (EPO (Opposition Division)).
12 See for example *Ariosa Diagnostics Inc v Sequenom Inc*, 788 F.3d 1371 (Fed Cir, 2015) *Illumina, Inc v. Ariosa Diagnostics, Inc*, 952 F.3d 1367 (Fed Cir, 2020), modified and reissued following a petition for rehearing filed by Defendants-Appellees, 967 F.3d 1319 (Fed Cir, 2020), *Illumina, Inc v Premaitha Health Plc* [2017] EWHC 2930, *Sequenom, Inc. v Ariosa Diagnostics, Inc.* [2019] FCA 1011 and discussion in Dianne Nicol and Jane Nielsen, 'Non-Invasive Prenatal Testing and the Resilience of the Patent System' in Naomi Hawkins (ed), *Patenting Biotechnical Innovation: Eligibility, Ethics and Public Interest* (Edward Elgar 2022); Naomi Hawkins and others, 'The Continuing Saga of Patents and Non-Invasive Prenatal Testing' (2019) 39 Prenatal Diagnosis 441.
13 See for example *Broad Institute, Inc v Regents of the University of California*, No 106,048, (P.T.A.B., February 15, 2017), *Regents of the University of California v Broad Institute Inc.*, No 2017–1907 (Fe. Cir. September 10, 2018), T 0844/18 (CRISPR-Cas/BROAD INSTITUTE) of 16.1.2020 and discussion in Duncan Matthews and others, 'The Role of Patents and Licensing in the Governance of Human Genome Editing : A White Paper' (2021) [2.2.2].

lated DNA or RNA molecules; product claims for diagnostic kit tests; process claims for methods of diagnosis through genetic testing; and product claims to gene chips and microarrays.[14]

The state of scientific research and clinical practice has moved on from these relatively simple gene patents. The possibilities of genetics in research and in useful application have moved well beyond the mere isolation of a string of nucleotides. Sequencing technologies have become more precise, faster and cheaper. Instead of testing a single change in a person's DNA by carrying out a complex series of chemical reactions one by one, now exomes (the coding region of the genome) or the whole genome can be sequenced, generating vast quantities of information. Beyond the structure of the genome itself, there is also increased understanding of epigenetics, the non-permanent changes which affect gene expression,[15] and its relationship to disease. This also is leading to useful clinical applications, and associated patents.[16]

Diagnostic use continues to be one of the main clinical application of genetics, and more advanced diagnostics across the medical sphere rely heavily on genetic technologies. More targeted, specific and useful cancer diagnostics draw on epigenetic understandings,[17] and the identification of fragments of genetic material in the blood of patients (cell free DNA or circulating tumour DNA) can identify cancer growth and spread in a focused, targeted and non-invasive manner.[18] Better understandings of the interaction of genes, and the combination of small contributions to disease risk across the whole genome are resulting in more advanced diagnostics through predictive and multigene tests. These may be useful for diseases known to have clear genetic causes, such as particular cardiac conditions caused by a variety of genes,[19] for prognostic value in some cancers,[20] or in the future it is hoped that they may serve predictive value in

---

[14] Naomi Hawkins, 'Human Gene Patents and Genetic Testing in Europe: A Reappraisal' (2010) 7 SCRIPTed 454; Secretary's Advisory Committee on Genetics Health and Society (SACGHS), *Gene Patents and Licensing Practices and Their Impact on Patient Access to Genetic Tests* (2010) 13–14; E Kane, 'Patent-mediated Standards in Genetic Testing' [2008] Utah L Rev 836-874, 845.

[15] United States Centers for Disease Control, 'What is epigenetics?', <https://www.cdc.gov/genomics/disease/epigenetics.htm#:~:text=Epigenetics%20is%20the%20study%20of,body%20reads%20a%20DNA%20sequence> accessed 27 October 2022.

[16] Joanna Wisniowska, 'Epigenetic Inventions : Lessons for the European Patent System' (2020) 42 European Intellectual Property Review 707.

[17] See for example James E Barrett and others, 'The WID-CIN Test Identifies Women with, and at Risk of, Cervical Intraepithelial Neoplasia Grade 3 and Invasive Cervical Cancer' (2022) 14 Genome Medicine 1.

[18] See for example M Cisneros-Villanueva and others, 'Cell-Free DNA Analysis in Current Cancer Clinical Trials: A Review' (2022) 126 British Journal of Cancer 391.

[19] For a recent statement about the use of genetic testing in cardiac disease see Arthur AM Wilde and others, 'European Heart Rhythm Association (EHRA)/Heart Rhythm Society (HRS)/Asia Pacific Heart Rhythm Society (APHRS)/Latin American Heart Rhythm Society (LAHRS) Expert Consensus Statement on the State of Genetic Testing for Cardiac Diseases' (2022) 19 Heart Rhythm e1.

[20] For example, genetic tests are used to guide treatment in light of prognostic information. For a review of the field, see Jennifer K Litton, Harold J Burstein and Nicholas C Turner, 'Molecular Testing in Breast

some common complex diseases. Pharmacogenetics guides the better targeting of prescription drugs, and the avoidance of serious side effects in those who have genetic predispositions.

Gene editing technology is also a growth area. Since 2009, CRISPR gene editing has permitted specific and much more precise editing of genomic sequences than was previously possible.[21] This important platform technology has also been the subject of patent applications and associated litigation.[22] The use of gene editing techniques permits the possibility of effective gene therapy, the modification or manipulation of the expression of a gene or the alteration of the biological properties of living cells for therapeutic use. The possibility of clinical use of gene therapy presents hugely exciting opportunities for the expansion of genetic medicine.[23] Such developments which seemed doomed to failure due to the lack of precision and the associated risks in the past[24] are now on the horizon. Research is advancing and clinical trials are ongoing,[25] and the widespread use of gene therapy for rare disease looks to be a real possibility in the future.

Like any new field of technology, the innovative products and processes associated with genetics can be and are the subject of patents. Each of the types of new field discussed here has had some level of patent activity. Diagnostics continue to be a fertile field of patent activity, and the technologies underpinning cell-free diagnosis have been patented, and those patents vigorously litigated.[26] Similarly, CRISPR patents have been

---

Cancer' (2019) 39 American Society of Clinical Oncology educational book. American Society of Clinical Oncology. Annual Meeting e1.

21 For an explanation of gene editing and CRISPR see National Human Genome Research Institute, 'What is Genome Editing?' <https://www.genome.gov/about-genomics/policy-issues/what-is-Genome-Editing> accessed 27 October 2022.

22 Oliver Feeney and others, 'Patenting Foundational Technologies: Lessons From CRISPR and Other Core Biotechnologies' (2018) 18 The American Journal of Bioethics 36; Aisling McMahon, 'Biotechnology, Health and Patents as Private Governance Tools the Good, the Bad and the Potential for Ugly' [2020] Intellectual Property Quarterly 161; Duncan Matthews, 'Access to CRISPR Genome Editing Technologies: Patents, Human Rights and the Public Interest', *Access to Medicines and Vaccines* (Springer 2022); D Matthews, T Minssen and A Nordberg, 'Balancing Innovation, 'Ordre Public' and Morality in Human Germline Editing: A Call for More Nuanced Approaches in Patent Law' (February 16, 2022). Queen Mary Law Research Paper No. 379/2022, Available at SSRN: https://ssrn.com/abstract=4036406; Duncan Matthews and others (n 13).

23 Xavier M Anguela and Katherine A High, 'Entering the Modern Era of Gene Therapy' (2019) 70 Annual Review of Medicine 273; Karen Bulaklak and Charles A Gersbach, 'The Once and Future Gene Therapy' (2020) 11 Nature Communications 1.

24 For a summary of the problems of gene therapy in the past see Anguela and High (n 23).

25 For a registry of ongoing clinical trials in advanced therapeutics maintained by the Cell and Gene Therapy Catapult in the UK see: Cell and Gene Therapy Catapult, 'Clinical trials database', <https://ct.catapult.org.uk/resources/clinical-trials-database> accessed 27 October 2022.

26 For an exploration of patents in non-invasive prenatal testing see: Hawkins and others (n 12); Nicol and Nielsen (n 12).

the subject of ongoing debate and litigation.[27] The patenting in this field, as well as the controversies and the litigation, seems set to continue and grow.

30.2 Patents on genes – the historical concerns

This author has previously argued that gene patents test the traditional assumptions and boundaries of the patent system.[28] Cases and academic commentary have focused around questions of patent eligibility, including the questions of patentable subject matter, novelty, non-obviousness and industrial application, as well as the exceptions to and exclusions from patentability. Challenges to gene patents on these grounds in Europe have largely been unsuccessful – genetic material has been treated as no different to any other naturally occurring chemical, and while some patents have been narrowed, on the whole, gene product and methods of diagnosis patents have been upheld in Europe.[29]

Patents for and associated with human genetic material touch on deeper questions about the role of the patent system, the morality and ethics of patenting information and the nature of DNA as being fundamental to the human self. Beyond the consideration of technical questions of patent eligibility, broader moral and ethical concerns have been consistently raised around the potential for patents to impact on access to fruits of innovation.

The cases and commentary in this field disclose two broad concerns of this nature: first, an ethical objection to the ownership or commodification of the human genome per se, and secondly, concerns about the potential for gene patents to negatively impact access to medicine.[30] The first concern is arguably primarily theoretical, and whilst it interests some bioethicists,[31] and it evident in some early cases,[32] it has become less prevalent with time. The second concern generated much discussion and empirical work examining impact on access to diagnostic testing in the late 1990s and early 2000s and continues to persist.

As early as 1997, Merz, Cho and colleagues were publishing papers arguing against disease gene patenting on the basis that it was detrimental for patient access to diagnos-

---

27 For a summary of CRISPR patenting issues see Jacob S Sherkow, 'Patent Protection for CRISPR: An ELSI Review' (2017) 4 Journal of Law and the Biosciences 565.
28 Hawkins, 'Human Gene Patents and Genetic Testing in Europe: A Reappraisal' (n 14).
29 See discussion in Naomi Hawkins, 'A Red Herring – Invalidity of Human Gene Sequence Patents' (2016) 38 European Intellectual Property Review 83; Hawkins, 'Human Gene Patents and Genetic Testing in Europe: A Reappraisal' (n 14).
30 Discussed in Hawkins, 'A Red Herring – Invalidity of Human Gene Sequence Patents' (n 29).
31 See for example David B Resnik, *Owning the Genome: A Moral Analysis of DNA Patenting* (State University of New York Press 2004).
32 Such as for example in *Howard Florey/Relaxin* [1995] EPOR 541 (EPO (Opposition Division)).

tic testing,[33] and a number of empirical studies were published which found that patents were having a significant negative effect on the provision of genetic testing by US clinical genetics laboratories.[34] In contrast, a later study conducted for the Secretary's Advisory Committee on Genetics, Health and Society concluded that that gene patents did not cause wide or lasting barriers to patient or clinical access to genetic tests in the USA and that while patents may have resulted in limitation of testing to certain laboratories licensed to offer the test, this need not result in reduced patient access.[35] In Australia, Nicol and Neilsen reported that diagnostic facilities conducting clinical genetic testing in Australia had not experienced the same degree of patent enforcement activity reported by Merz and colleagues in the USA, but that many laboratories expressed concerns about the impact of gene patents on genetic testing services. Respondents on the whole did not pay royalties and had not been approached by many patent holders. They were largely prepared to pay reasonable royalties for test kits but were concerned about licence fees in the case of home-brew tests.[36]

In Europe, empirical work indicated that gene patents generally did not have a deleterious impact on access. Empirical studies in the mid 2000s reported that laboratories had little experience of dealing with patents, and that the public sector was ill-prepared to license patented technology for use in clinical testing. Studies showed low levels of awareness of patent law and gene patents generally, and few licences either being granted or negotiated, but very little evidence, beyond some specific limited examples, of patents causing access problems for genetic diagnostics in public sector laboratories.[37]

Although the expressed concerns around patient access have not abated, more recent literature continues to show that gene patents do not have a major impact on simple diagnostic tests.[38] However, the reasons for this lack of impact are mostly related to widespread lack of engagement with the law, and the lack of enforcement, related to the

---

[33] JF Merz and others, 'Disease Gene Patenting is a Bad Innovation' (1997) 2 Molecular Diagnostics 299.
[34] JF Merz and others, 'Diagnostic Testing Fails the Test' (2002) 415 Nature 577; MK Cho and others, 'Effects of Patents and Licenses on the Provision of Clinical Genetic Testing Services' (2003) 5 J of Molecular Diagnostics 3.
[35] Secretary's Advisory Committee on Genetics Health and Society (SACGHS), Gene Patents and Licensing Practices and Their Impact on Patient Access to Genetic Tests (2010) 38–46.
[36] D Nicol and J Nielsen, Patents and Medical Biotechnology: An Empirical Analysis of Issues Facing the Australian Industry – Occasional Paper No 6 (Centre for Law and Genetics, Faculty of Law, University of Tasmania, Hobart 2003) 198–207.
[37] S Gaisser and others, 'The Phantom Menace of Gene Patents' (2009) 458 Nature 407; Hawkins, 'The Impact of Human Gene Patents on Genetic Testing in the United Kingdom.' (n 3).
[38] Johnathon Liddicoat, Tess Whitton and Dianne Nicol, 'Are the Gene-Patent Storm Clouds Dissipating? A Global Snapshot.' (2015) 33 Nature Biotechnology 347; Johnathon Liddicoat and others, 'Continental Drift? Do European Clinical Genetic Testing Laboratories Have a Patent Problem?' (2019) 27 European Journal of Human Genetics 997.

small size of the market for single gene diagnostics, rather than appropriate patent grant, licensing and enforcement.[39]

The reality of the wider market for genomic medicine, in the form of multigene panel tests, companion diagnostics, NIPT and genomic medicine with wider population relevance, as outlined above, means that the impact of patent law will likely grow. Accordingly, it is important to consider the ways in which the law in this area is developing.

30.3 Gene patents in European patent law – current pressing questions

Although some key legal questions have been clarified, and scientific developments mean that some previously pressing questions are no longer relevant, the application of the law in this area to new fields continues to raise important and interesting questions.

Against this background, this chapter argues that there are three areas where the intersection of the existing and future European Patent Law system with new genetics and genomics research will give rise to important challenges. The remainder of this chapter explores these three areas: *ordre public* and morality; concerns related to access to medicine; and questions of divergence of patent law and policy approaches to gene patents. It also suggests the ways in which the law in this area might develop in light of current and future changes.

30.3.1 Ethics and morality – the application of the morality exclusion

Since the first genetic inventions, there has been debate about the moral and ethical aspects of gene patents. Despite various failed attempts to challenge patents on these grounds, the ethical concerns about gene patents continue, and there remains considerable scope for these objections to be raised in relation to future genetic inventions. Inventions which in the future use genetic methods to develop routine clinical applications, including most product patents or for new methods of diagnosis, seem, following the approach in past cases, to not be sufficiently ethically contentious to enliven the prohibitions. However, gene editing, especially where there is potential to modify the germline genome, raises novel questions which have not previously been considered in the case law, and where there is potential for the morality and ethics provisions in patent law to be significant.

---

[39] Naomi Hawkins, 'Patents and Non-Invasive Prenatal Testing: Is There Cause for Concern?' (2020) 47 Science and Public Policy 655.

There are both general and specific morality provisions in European Patent Law, giving rise to important case law under the EPC system, and which will likely arise under in the unitary patent system also. The first, general prohibition is found in Article 53(a) EPC, which provides that:

European patents shall not be granted in respect of:

(a) inventions the commercial exploitation of which would be contrary to "ordre public" or morality; such exploitation shall not be deemed to be so contrary merely because it is prohibited by law or regulation in some or all of the Contracting States

The more specific provisions are found in Rule 28(1)(a)-(d) of the Implementing Regulations of the EPC 2000, which were incorporated into the EPC following the introduction of the EU Biotech Directive.[40] Rule 28(1) provides:

Under Article 53(a), European patents shall not be granted in respect of biotechnological inventions which, in particular, concern the following:
(a) processes for cloning human beings;
(b) processes for modifying the germ line genetic identity of human beings;
(c) uses of human embryos for industrial or commercial purposes;
(d) processes for modifying the genetic identity of animals which are likely to cause them suffering without any substantial medical benefit to man or animal, and also animals resulting from such processes.

In terms of Art 53(a), in gene patent cases, as in other cases on the provision, the prohibition has been interpreted narrowly.[41] In the *Howard Florey/Relaxin* case the Opposition Division suggested that "patents would not be granted for inventions which would universally be regarded as outrageous", and there, a patent for a gene encoding a pregnancy hormone was not prohibited by Art 53(a).[42] Instead, the arguments of the opponent were rejected by the Opposition Division, which held that the patent did not in fact involve the patenting of human life, abuse of pregnant women or slavery,[43] but that DNA, a chemical substance, should be treated in the same manner as other chemical substances. Similarly, in *Breast and Ovarian Cancer/University of Utah*, the Art 53(a) prohibition was not engaged.[44] There, an opponent argued that there was a contravention of the morality provisions occasioned by failure to obtain specific consent to commercial exploitation of research results from the donor of cells used to derive the invention, and the absence of any benefit sharing agreement. Another opponent argued that the socio-economic conse-

---

[40] The provisions of Directive 98/44 on the Legal Protection of Biotechnological Inventions (Biotechnology Directive) were implemented by the European Patent Organisation into the Implementing Regulations of the EPC, to ensure a consistent approach to biotechnology patents.
[41] Karen Walsh and Naomi Hawkins, 'Expanding the Role of Morality and Public Policy in European Patent Law' in Paul Torremans (ed), *Intellectual Property and Human Rights* (Wolters Kluwer 2020).
[42] *Howard Florey/Relaxin* [1995] EPOR 541 (EPO (Opposition Division)).
[43] *Howard Florey/Relaxin* [1995] EPOR 541 (EPO (Opposition Division)), 6.3.
[44] T1213/05 *Breast and Ovarian Cancer/University of Utah* of 27.9.2007.

quences of the patent should be taken into account in relation to Art 53(a), suggesting that the patent would be detrimental to human dignity because it would result in increased costs for patients and would also influence the way in which diagnosis and research would be organised in Europe in a manner disadvantageous to both patients and health care professionals. These arguments were rejected by the Board.

This narrow interpretation of the Art 53(a) prohibition has limited its application in relation to gene patents. The EPO and national courts have been reticent to view genetic inventions as anything other than chemical in nature, and have accordingly refused to acknowledge any ethical dimension to the patenting of DNA due to its informational nature. There is potential that this very narrow approach may be broadening, in light of more recent case law where the Board of Appeal interpreted Article 53(a) with an explicit focus on human dignity. They found that *ordre public* had to be seen "as defined by norms that safeguard fundamental values and rights such as the inviolability of human dignity and the right of life and physical integrity."[45] However, it remains to be seen whether this case signals a broader movement in the case law. Under current approaches, it seems likely that the majority of patents for simple genetic inventions, or for diagnostic or therapeutic products based on DNA but which do not involve embryos or gene editing, will continue to fall outside the scope of the morality provisions.

Of the specific provisions in r28, it is r28(1)(c), uses of human embryos for industrial or commercial purposes, which has received the most interpretation in case law.[46] In the line of cases from the Boards of Appeal, it is possible to discern a general reluctance to examine morality in any substantive sense, and a narrow focus on the specific aspects of how the invention was made, rather than an engagement with broader questions of whether the use of an embryo should be permitted and in what circumstances.[47] The interpretation of the provisions by the CJEU on the other hand has linked morality in patent law to the concept of human dignity, noting that the context and aims of the Biotech Directive were to "exclude any possibility of patentability where respect for human dignity could thereby be affected."[48] The possibility of widening the scope of morality in this way, and drawing on the wider body of EU law and its interpretation of human dignity does open the door to a broader and more fully developed conception of morality in European Patent Law. With the enhanced role of the CJEU in the UPC system,[49] the scope

---

[45] T149/11 *Method and device for processing a slaughtered animal or part thereof in a slaughterhouse* of 24.01.2013, Reasons 2.5; Walsh and Hawkins (n 41).
[46] Walsh and Hawkins (n 41).
[47] Walsh and Hawkins (n 41).
[48] Case C-34/10 *Oliver Brüstle v Greenpeace* ECLI:EU:C:2011:669, para 34. These questions are explored further in: Justine Pila, 'A Constitutionalized Doctrine of Precedent and the *Marleasing* Principle as Bases for a European Methodology' in Ansgar Ohly and Justine Pila (eds) *The Europeanization of Intellectual Property Law: Towards a European Legal Methodology* (OUP 2013) 233–240; Walsh and Hawkins (n 41).
[49] H Ullrich, 'The role of the CJEU' in D Matthews and P Torremans (eds), Research Handbook on European Patent Law: The European Patent Convention, the European Patent with Unitary Effect and Unified Patent Court (De Gruyter, 2023). The role of the CJEU is discussed further below.

for the development of the law in this manner seems clear. Accordingly, the potential for morality to be expanded, with a deeper connection to human dignity principles, should not be ignored. This possible widening may have important implications for the patentability of new genetic inventions. While morality arguments in relation to gene patents in the past, notably gene sequence patents, were given short shrift, there is more scope for argument in relation to patents for gene editing in clinical practice.

To date, much of the patent litigation in relation to gene editing has taken place in the USA, where there is no equivalent provision, and morality is not an explicit ground for revocation of patents. Current litigation over CRISPR patents in Europe has focused on formalities associated with priority, but has not to date explored potential Art 53(a) objections,[50] and patents for gene editing technologies have not been invalidated on this basis. But it is reasonable to suppose that questions of human dignity are enlivened where the patented technology might alter the human genome, and therefore, morality objections may have some traction in future cases.

There are obvious potential ways in which the other rule 28(1) provisions, may be relevant for future gene patents. However, because these rules are drafted in specific terms, it is entirely feasible that the majority of gene patents will be able to be drafted in ways that fall outside their scope. To the extent that future gene editing patents may seek to modify the germ line genetic identity of human beings, then r28(1)(b), which prohibits processes for modifying the germ line genetic identity of human beings will be relevant. Many existing patents limit their claims to avoid falling within the scope of this provision.[51] Modification of the germ line remains ethically contentious, and most countries prohibit human genetic germline modification.[52] However, more recent technological innovations which have shown that safe and precise gene editing is possible have meant that the debate is being reframed and questions about the ethical position are being re-examined.[53] Recently, the European Society of Human Genetics has explored these questions, and made recommendations that both basic and pre-clinical research regarding germline gene editing can be justified with conditions, that clinical germline gene editing might become a responsible intervention in the future after adequate pre-clinical research and that the prohibition of human germline modification needs re-

---

50 BROAD INSTITUTE/CRISPR-Cas (T844/18) [2021] E.P.O.R. 9; [2020] 1 WLUK 623 (EPO (Technical Bd App)).
51 Matthews (n22).
52 Françoise Baylis and others, 'Human Germ Line and Heritable Genome Editing: The Global Policy Landscape' (2020) 3 CRISPR Journal 365.
53 See for example Guido De Wert and others, 'Human Germline Gene Editing: Recommendations of ESHG and ESHRE' (2018) 26 European Journal of Human Genetics 445; Guido De Wert and others, 'Responsible Innovation in Human Germline Gene Editing: Background Document to the Recommendations of ESHG and ESHRE' (2018) 26 European Journal of Human Genetics 450; Kelly E Ormond and others, 'Human Germline Genome Editing' (2017) 101 American Journal of Human Genetics 167; Margaret Waltz and others, 'The View from the Benches: Scientists' Perspectives on the Uses and Governance of Human Gene-Editing Research.' (2021) 4 The CRISPR Journal; Floor M Goekoop and others, 'Systematic Scoping Review of the Concept of "Genetic Identity" and Its Relevance for Germline Modification' (2020) 15 PLoS ONE.

newed discussion among relevant stakeholders, including the general public and legislators.[54] While the advance towards a more nuanced approach to this question outside of the patent law context may be possible, it remains difficult to see how the explicit prohibition in r28(1)(b) could be read down or otherwise limited, especially in light of the approach of the Boards of Appeal and the CJEU to the r28(1)(c) prohibition on the uses of human embryos for industrial or commercial purposes. However, it is potentially arguable that gene editing for therapeutic purposes would fall outside the prohibition, even if it amounted to germline gene editing, following the approach of the CJEU in *Brüstle*[55] and *ISCC*[56], that the exclusion does not affect inventions for therapeutic or diagnostic purposes which are applied to the human embryo and are useful to it.[57] In the absence of this interpretation however, should there be a widespread consensus that germline gene editing is desirable, and patents associated with it similarly desirable to enhance innovation in this field, then legislative modification of r28(1)(b) may be required to enable those patents.

30.3.2 Addressing access concerns

Beyond the morality provisions in patent law, concerns continue to be expressed about the potential for patents to limit access to medicine. Such access concerns are beyond the narrow confines of the morality provisions, but nonetheless raise important ethical questions. Gene patent cases have long acted as a lighting rod for concern. For example, the *Myriad* case is said to be 'emblematic of the fear that patents on human genetic material would have an adverse impact on access to useful technologies, both for research and for clinical use'.[58]

These access concerns seem unlikely to abate as genomic medicine becomes more widespread. Non-invasive prenatal testing (NIPT), examining cell-free foetal DNA, a form of diagnostic testing which is offered to pregnant woman to identify foetal abnormality, has generated significant concerns about patent-mediated access problems.[59] Similar testing technology to cell free foetal DNA testing is increasingly relevant in can-

---

54 De Wert and others, 'Human Germline Gene Editing: Recommendations of ESHG and ESHRE' (n 52).
55 Case C-34/10 *Oliver Brüstle v Greenpeace* ECLI:EU:C:2011:669.
56 Case C-364/13 *International Stem Cell Corporation v Comptroller General of Patents, Designs and Trade Marks* ECLI:EU:C:2014:2451.
57 Drawing on recital 42 of the Biotech Directive. Duncan Matthews and others (n 13) [2.3.2.2]; Matthews (n 22).
58 Timothy Caulfield et al., 'Evidence and Anecdotes: An Analysis of Human Gene Patenting Controversies' (2006) 24 Nature Biotechnology 1091.
59 Hawkins and others (n 12); Megan Allyse and others, 'Non-Invasive Prenatal Testing: A Review of International Implementation and Challenges' (2015) 7 International Journal of Women's Health 113; Ashwin Agarwal and others, 'Commercial Landscape of Noninvasive Prenatal Testing in the United States.' (2013) 33 Prenatal Diagnosis 521.

cer diagnostic testing, which suggests that these access concerns will continue to arise in new fields of clinical application of technology.

However, whilst patient access to patented inventions may still be a concern, the nature of the current and future access concerns seems likely to be different to the historical access problems. The more complex nature of current and future genomic medicine means that there is much less of a linear relationship between the patent and the innovation. Early forms of genetic tests were relatively straightforward and could be conducted in hospital laboratories, using routine, well-accepted and non-inventive procedures.[60] The patented inventions in such cases were often very simple, such as an isolated DNA sequence for the disease-causing gene or a method of diagnosis. Such inventions could be easily recreated in a hospital laboratory from the primary literature, without reference to the patent, and there was little industry involvement. Such an environment led to widespread patent non-compliance, with few consequences.[61]

In contrast, the translational process for more recent genetic inventions, including diagnostics and therapeutics, is far more complicated.[62] Because the inventions are more complex, they require more sustained development and often clinical trials. There is thus much greater investment required, and much greater risk. As a result, the later stages of the development of an innovation into clinical use is increasingly undertaken by industry.[63] Because of the more complex nature of the invention, there is therefore less debate about the rights and wrongs of the existence of the patents, and more acceptance of the difficulties of innovation, with the associated need for patent protection, or at least, more recognition of the closer nature of genomic patents to other more traditional patent mediated biomedical innovation.

However, for inventions which are of a broad nature, or where there are patents for platform technologies, such as CRISPR, there remain concerns about the potential implications of gene patents to have a problematic impact on access to fundamental medical technologies across a wide range of clinical applications. The potential for the cost of access to, for example, gene editing technologies, to accentuate existing inequalities, such as by limiting access to curative technologies is high.[64]

Solutions to these access problems arguably arise primarily from areas beyond patent law. As McMahon argues, these access concerns have been marginalised within pa-

---

[60] For an explanation see for example T Strachan, AP Read and DJ Matthes, *Human Molecular Genetics 2* (2nd ed BIOS Scientific, Oxford 1999) 407.
[61] Hawkins, 'The Impact of Human Gene Patents on Genetic Testing in the United Kingdom.' (n 3); S Gaisser and others (n37).
[62] Eleftheria Zeggini and others, 'Translational Genomics and Precision Medicine: Moving from the Lab to the Clinic' (2019) 365 Science 1409; For a review of some of the challenges of translational research in cancer genomics see Oriol Pich and others, 'The Translational Challenges of Precision Oncology' (2022) 40 Cancer Cell 458.
[63] Nicol and Nielsen (n 12); Dianne Nicol and others, 'International Divergence in Gene Patenting' (2019) 20 Annual Review of Genomics and Human Genetics 519.
[64] Matthews (n 22).

tent law itself,[65] and the most effective solutions to the problems have arisen from areas adjacent to patent law, such as contract law. Recent proposals to ensure access have suggested recourse to licensing models for example.[66] In this sense, they mirror the contract and competition law-based solutions proposed in the mid-2000s around patent pools and clearing houses to avoid the perceived risks of patent thickets and royalty stacking in field of genetic diagnostics.[67] Most of these solutions were not implemented in any systematic or widespread way in practice because the anticipated problems failed to materialise. For single gene testing, with a very small number of affected patients, primarily in the public sector, with small returns and little commercial involvement, few patent problems arose in Europe.[68] Instead, widespread wilful blindness, coupled with little enforcement, meant that access problems were largely averted.[69] As genomic medicine moves away from single gene tests, to more complex forms of diagnostics, including non-invasive prenatal testing (NIPT), complex cancer genomic testing and whole genome methods, the situation will change. This has already been evident in relation to NIPT, where much greater engagement and compliance with patents is evident, with patents an important factor driving the costs and therefore access to this technology.[70] In an environment where patents are widespread and routinely engaged with, rather than ignored, as is the case where there is greater commercial involvement, licensing will be increasingly important. As a result, licensing models will be an important means to ensure fair access.[71]

These access difficulties are not specific to gene patents however, and they are arising in other fields of biotechnology, as well as other areas of technology with pressing public interest concerns, such as climate change technology.[72] The balance between pa-

---

65 McMahon, 'Gene Patents and the Marginalisation of Ethical Issues.' (n 6).
66 Aisling McMahon, 'Accounting for Ethical Considerations in the Licensing of Patented Biotechnologies and Health-Related Technologies: A Justification' in Naomi Hawkins (ed), *Patenting Biotechnical Innovation: Eligibility, Ethics and Public Interest* (Edward Elgar Publishing 2022).
67 Geertrui van Overwalle, *Gene Patents and Collaborative Licensing Models: Patent Pools, Clearinghouses, Open Source Models, and Liability Regimes* (Cambridge University Press 2009); E van Zimmeren and others, 'A Clearing House for Diagnostic Testing: The Solution to Ensure Access to and Use of Patented Genetic Inventions?' (2006) 84 Bulletin of the World Health Organisation 352; B Verbeure and others, 'Patent Pools and Diagnostic Testing' (2006) 24 Trends in Biotechnology 115; G van Overwalle and others, 'Models for Facilitating Access to Patents on Genetic Inventions' (2006) 7 Nature Reviews Genetics 143.
68 Hawkins, 'The Impact of Human Gene Patents on Genetic Testing in the United Kingdom' (n 37); Gaisser and others (n37); Liddicoat, Whitton and Nicol (n 38).
69 Hawkins, 'The Impact of Human Gene Patents on Genetic Testing in the United Kingdom' (n 37); Hawkins, 'Patents and Non-Invasive Prenatal Testing: Is There Cause for Concern?' (n 39).
70 Hawkins, 'Patents and Non-Invasive Prenatal Testing: Is There Cause for Concern?' (n 39).
71 McMahon, 'Gene Patents and the Marginalisation of Ethical Issues.' (n 6); McMahon, 'Accounting for Ethical Considerations in the Licensing of Patented Biotechnologies and Health-Related Technologies: A Justification' (n 65); van Overwalle (n 66).
72 Abbe EL Brown, *Intellectual Property, Climate Change and Technology: Managing National Legal Intersections, Relationships and Conflicts* (Edward Elgar 2019).

tentability and access remains important, and the ways in which those acting to safeguard the public interest, such as governments, research institutes and research funders, are able to leverage their bargaining power in negotiations around licensing is vital to ensuring that all avenues to protect the public interest are explored.[73]

30.3.3 Divergence of approaches – does the UPC offer possibilities for increased harmonisation?

A key feature that has shaped the landscape of gene patents more recently is the divergent approaches to ostensibly similar legal rules which govern the granting of patents as well as their scope, internationally.[74] Although the broad rules of patent law are internationally harmonised, through international conventions including the Paris Convention and the TRIPS agreement, there remains considerable divergence in the approach taken on key questions which are of great relevance to gene patents.[75] The divergence between the USA and Europe is of particular note here, and is the main focus of this section of the chapter.[76]

The primary area of divergence internationally which has attracted recent commentary is around the question of patentable subject matter.[77] Both *Myriad*[78] and *Mayo*[79] have imposed important limitations on patentable subject matter in the USA, and reversed the previously expansive approach which resulted in widespread gene patenting in the USA. In contrast, isolated gene sequences remain patentable in Europe under the EPC, and the narrow interpretation in the exclusion of diagnostic methods has meant that process patents are also widely available.[80]

There remain other important distinctions between European and US patent law. Notably, Europe has both morality[81] and diagnostic and medical methods exceptions[82]

---

[73] For an exploration of the public interest in this area see Naomi Hawkins (ed), *Patenting Biotechnical Innovation: Eligibility, Ethics and Public Interest* (Edward Elgar 2022).
[74] Nicol and Nielsen (n 12).
[75] Dreyfuss, Nielsen and Nicol (n 4); Nicol and Nielsen (n 12).
[76] Europe and the USA are two very significant patent jurisdictions and divergence between approaches has important implications for business. It is acknowledged that there is also a significant market outside of these two regions, and patent law divergence in those jurisdictions is also relevant to global markets, but analysis of this divergence is beyond the scope of this work.
[77] See for example Mateo Aboy and others, 'How Does Emerging Patent Case Law in the US and Europe Affect Precision Medicine?' (2019) 37 Nature Biotechnology 1118; Nicol and others (n 62); Nicol and Nielsen (n 12).
[78] *Association for Molecular Pathology v Myriad Genetics Inc* 569 US 576 (2013).
[79] *Mayo Collaborative Services v Prometheus Laboratories* Inc 566 US 66 (2012).
[80] Hawkins, 'Human Gene Patents and Genetic Testing in Europe: A Reappraisal' (n 14).
[81] Art 53(a) EPC and Rule 28(1)(a)-(d) of the Implementing Regulations of the EPC 2000, discussed above.
[82] EPC art 53(c).

which are not found in the USA in the same form. Similarly, the experimental use exception exists in more expansive forms in Europe than in the USA.[83] Such differences often result from historical differences in the evolution of patent legislation in these jurisdictions, and are underpinned by differing legislative provisions. These flexibilities are permitted by the TRIPS agreement. The extent to which harmonisation is possible is therefore variable depending on the legislative differences in question.

In contrast to the position as between Europe and the USA, there is relatively little divergence in the rules which are applied to gene patents between contracting states of the EPC. In this respect, there is a degree of consistency necessitated both by the harmonised legislative framework of the EPC, as well as the streamlined grant procedure, including the opposition procedures. Much of the divergence that does exist is either of narrow impact, resolved by a different route to the same ultimate outcome or resolved through changes to ensure consistency in approach, such as the approach to industrial application in relation to genetic inventions, where the UK adopted an approach to harmonise with the EPO position.[84] A notable exception however, is the approach to morality, which remains a point at which EU member states, and EPC contracting states continue to take different approaches, especially as relates to the moral status of the embryo.[85] It may be anticipated that divergent approaches to morality questions around new genetic inventions in areas such as gene editing, for example, might similarly arise. Whether any such differences are significant for patents in practice remains to be seen.

An important question is whether the changes to the European patent law and policy landscape which are imminent with the UPC have the potential to address any divergence. As outlined above, the differences in approach between major patent offices has been highlighted as problematic by industry. It seems clear that there is no direct route by which such harmonisation between, for example, the approach of US courts and the Unitary Patent Court, is possible. However, it is argued below that a degree of convergence, if not harmonisation, of standards and approaches in the gene patent space might be possible through the operation of the UPC, through first, the unified post-grant forum for decision making, second, the potential role of the CJEU in relation to morality, and finally, the persuasive force of the decisions of the tribunals in this area.

---

83 T Cook, *A European Perspective as to the Extent to which Experimental Use, and Certain Other Defences to Patent Infringement, Apply to Differing Types of Research: A Report for the Intellectual Property Institute* (Intellectual Property Institute, London 2006) 28; *Clinical Trials II* [1998] RPC 423.
84 *Human Genome Sciences v Eli Lilly* [2011] UKSC 51.
85 For a discussion of the approach to these questions see Aurora Plomer and Paul Torremans, *Embryonic Stem Cell Patents : European Law and Ethics* (Oxford University Press 2009); Aurora Plomer, 'The European Group on Ethics: Law, Politics and the Limits of Moral Integration in Europe' (2008) 14 European Law Journal 839.

30.3.3.1 A single forum

It is a central goal of the UPC that the single forum will lead to consistency in approach to post-grant questions.[86] While some level of divergence, such as to accommodate matters where there are national differences in approach may be expected to continue, some harmonisation seems likely. Some of the key questions around morality and ethics may continue to prove contentious, and be refractory to harmonisation, but some of the more technical questions may be less controversial.

There will be procedural reasons why a single forum may bring business advantages to patent holders and litigants.[87] These are similar for all types of patents and areas of technology, although there may be particular reasons why gene patent holders or litigants in relation to gene patents may find the UPC system advantageous.

Indeed, in relation to gene patents, the opposition procedure at the EPO was used extensively to oppose and in a number of cases, narrow the scope of gene patents.[88] It was used to facilitate a number of public interest challenges, in ways that would not have been possible had it been necessary to litigate on each patent in each jurisdiction across EPO member states.[89] It is therefore plausible that the UPC system will be used similarly to enable more, or more effective, challenges to patents for public interest reasons by non-typical patent litigants, including public sector organisations, patient groups, or special interest groups. Such factors may at the same time encourage patent holders to opt out of the UPC system where possible, which would limit these opportunities for challenge. However, ultimately, as the single forum becomes more widely used, it may be anticipated that it will lead to enhanced consistency overall.

30.3.3.2 The role of the CJEU

The CJEU has had a significant impact in relation to the interpretation of the provisions of the Biotech Directive, with key relevance for gene patents.[90] The Biotechnology Direc-

---

86 Walsh, K. 'Promoting Harmonisation Across the European Patent System Through Judicial Dialogue and Cooperation' (2019) 50 IIC 408; Leon Dijkman and Cato Van Paddenburgh, 'The Unified Patent Court as Part of a New European Patent Landscape: Wholesale Harmonization or Experiment in Legal Pluralism?' (2018) 26 European Review of Private Law 97.
87 EPO, 'Unitary Patent Guide' <https://www.epo.org/applying/european/guide-up/html/e/uppg_a_v.html> accessed 16 December 2022. There are also potentially a number of procedural reasons why patent applicants may find the UPC to be of advantage. As these are reasons that are business decisions and less likely to be specific to the nature of genetic inventions, they are not considered within this article.
88 Perhaps most notably in relation to breast cancer gene patents, as discussed in Louise Hatherall, 'Procedural issues in public interest patent challenges' (2022) 44 E.I.P.R. 198.
89 Louise Hatherall 'Procedural issues in public interest patent challenges' (n88).
90 Important cases include for example *Monsanto v Cefetra* (Case C-428/08) [2012] 3 CMLR 7 and Case C-34/10 Oliver Brüstle v Greenpeace e.V. ECLI:EU:C:2011:669.

tive has been important for gene patent law and policy. In particular, the provisions in Art 5, specifying the limits of patentability of human genetic material and the specific morality provisions in Art 6 have provided specific standards to be applied by the EPO and national patent offices, as well as national courts and the CJEU. The CJEU has interpreted the morality provisions of the Biotechnology Directive as being founded on the principle of human dignity, which provides a vital interpretative principle.

In this respect, the Biotech Directive will operate as a thread of continuity, and the role of the CJEU will be expanded in the new UPC system. There is potential scope for the jurisprudence of the CJEU to have important implications for aspects of the gene patent debate, particularly insofar as ethics is involved. The current approach, with human dignity as the underpinning principle, shows potential for providing a coherent basis for the development of a body of jurisprudence around the morality questions discussed above.[91] With the CJEU as the ultimate arbiter within the UPC system of questions of EU law, CJEU precedent will have added force over its current role in the European patent system. Of course, should the involvement of the CJEU develop an expanded approach to morality drawing on human dignity, it is likely that such an approach would take European patent law further away from the USA, which recognises no such role for morality.

30.3.3.3 Persuasive standards

The pre-grant case law of the Boards of Appeal of the EPO has provided a body of jurisprudence which has been drawn upon by member states and has provided a central source of law which has enabled some level of harmonisation, at least in relation to questions of eligibility. Similarly, the UPC case law will provide authority for national courts, and it can be anticipated that, even for states that are outside the system, such as the UK, the decisions will have persuasive force. It can therefore be anticipated that the UPC may drive a degree of harmonisation in this manner, although it is also the case that such harmonisation is not guaranteed.[92]

Beyond the European patent system, there may also be scope for the implementation of the UPC to bring about a degree of international harmonisation. If there is a single harmonised approach within Europe, supported by a body of persuasive authority, then it has added force in other jurisdictions, which might be more inclined to take a similar approach.

The extent to which such harmonisation might be expected as between Europe and the USA may be limited however, due to divergent statutory approaches. In this respect,

---

[91] Walsh and Hawkins (n 41); Justine Pila, 'Adapting the Ordre Public and Morality Exclusion of European Patent Law to Accommodate Emerging Technologies' (2020) 38 Nature Biotechnology 555.
[92] Karen Walsh, *Fragmentation and the European Patent System* (Hart 2022).

the Biotechnology Directive is key. The divergence in approach to isolated substances as set out in Article 5 of the Biotechnology Directive, and as interpreted by case law, and the products of nature doctrine in the USA will remain, and this will limit the harmonisation on patent scope. Similarly, the different approaches to morality will limit the adoption of the European approach in the USA, as set out earlier. However, the widespread lack of satisfaction with the US approach to these questions[93] may result in changes in the law, either through legislative efforts or judicially.[94] Should the change arise through case law, then strong and consistent as well as legally and logically defensible precedents from the UPC might prove to be persuasive to a US court.

The potential for the introduction of the UPC to result in harmonisation of standards and approaches towards gene patents is small but potentially significant. In this area of biotechnology, which is advanced through global research efforts, jurisdictional differences in approaches to patentability can complicate both research collaborations and the translation of innovations into clinical use. Where the UPC can promote a clear, consistent and logically defensible approach to common questions, it may be hoped that moves towards useful harmonisation might be possible.

30.4 Conclusion

Gene patents continue to be endlessly fascinating, not only to scientists and patent lawyers, but also in the public imagination. Although the patents which were initially the subject of concern, such as for expressed sequence tags and isolated disease genes, have long since expired, science continues to advance. New fields of research, with their associated inventions continue to be developed. Genetics is an established field of scientific endeavour, and patents in this field will continue to be filed into the future.

Although the particular legal questions have moved on from questions about the eligibility of patenting isolated DNA sequences, difficult questions around ethics, morality and access remain. The European patent system must continue to address these questions into the future. Perhaps more interestingly, the international divergence in approach to key questions around gene patent eligibility and scope has opened up in recent years. The UPC may arguably provide scope for this divergence to be explored, and for some degree of consistency and coherence in approach to be developed.

---

93 See for example Intellectual Property Owners Association, Proposed Amendments to Patent Eligible Subject Matter Under 35 U. S.C. § 101, Feb. 7, 2017, <http://www.ipo.org/wp-content/uploads/2017/02/20170207_IPO-101-TF-Proposed-Amendments-and-Report.pdf> (accessed 16 December 2022); American Bar Association, Letter to Michelle K. Lee, Supplemental Comments Related to Patentable Subject Matter Eligibility, Mar. 28, 2017, <https://www.americanbar.org/content/dam/aba/administrative/intellectual_property_law/advocacy/advocacy-20170328-comments.authcheckdam.pdf> (accessed 16 December 2022).
94 Dreyfuss, Nielsen and Nicol (n 4).

Aisling McMahon

31 Decision-makers, institutional influences and the role of ethical issues in the patenting of biotechnological inventions in Europe: enter the unitary patent system

Introduction

After many years of discussions and (other failed) proposals around establishing a unitary patent system in Europe,[1] the current Unitary Patent system is set to commence in June 2023.[2] There is much anticipation around the implications of this new adjudicative system for the 'European' patent landscape.[3] Such implications will likely be varied and multifaceted and may take several years to fully discern. Yet, as with the introduction of any new system, it presents us with an opportunity to reflect on the opportunities and challenges ahead, and on how we would like to envisage the role of its new adjudicative body, the Unified Patent Court (UPC). As part of this, we must consider to what extent the UPC will engage with areas of contention in patent law and whether it will maintain or disrupt the status quo in such contexts.

This chapter focuses specifically on one long contested area, namely, the role of ethical considerations in patent decision-making for biotechnological inventions in Europe.[4] More specifically, the chapter examines to what extent the introduction of the

---

[1] For a discussion of the history of proposals for a unitary patent system, see: Christopher Wadlow, "An historical perspective II: the unified patent court" in: J Pila & Christopher Wadlow (eds) *The EU unitary patent system*. (OUP, 2015); Aurora Plomer, "A unitary patent for a (Dis)United Europe: the long shadow of history" (2015) 46(5) IIC 508; K Walsh, "Promoting Harmonisation Across the European Patent System Through Judicial Dialogue and Cooperation" (2019) 50 IIC 408.
[2] https://www.epo.org/applying/european/unitary.html correct at the time of writing January 2023.
[3] The word 'European' is used to denote the patent system within European Patent Organisation States, which includes all EU States and several non-EU States.
[4] There is an extensive body of literature examining the role of morality or 'ordre public' in European patent law, this includes: Derek Beyleveld and Roger Brownsword, Mice, Morality and Patents (Common Law Institute of Intellectual Property, 1993); Lionel Bently and Brad Sherman, "The Ethics of Patenting:

Aisling McMahon, Professor of Law, School of Law and Criminology, Maynooth University. I would like to thank Dr Karen Walsh, and the editors for this invitation and their helpful comments on this chapter. Any errors remain the authors own. Parts of this chapter draw on research conducted under the ERC *PatentsInHumans* project – This work is funded by the European Union (ERC, PatentsInHumans, Project No. 101042147). Views and opinions expressed are however those of the author only and do not necessarily reflect those of the European Union or the European Research Council Executive Agency. Neither the European Union nor the granting authority can be held responsible for them.

UPC– and the unitary patent system more generally – has the potential to influence the current interpretative approach for how ethical issues are considered in the patenting of biotechnological inventions in Europe. It puts forward the case for why a renewed conversation is urgently needed around what normative role ethical issues *should* play in European patent law.

The chapter makes three main arguments. First, section one argues – as I have discussed elsewhere[5] – that whilst the role of ethical issues is contested in many fields of patent law, there is a clear emphasis on the need for ethical issues to be considered within the EU's Biotechnology Directive 98/44EC (hereafter 'the Directive'). Thus, at a legislative level, I argue that there is a clear mandate for ethical issues to be considered in the patenting of biotechnological inventions. Second, and relatedly, in section two, the chapter highlights that despite this legislative mandate, at a supranational level, multiple adjudicative bodies are involved in the interpretation of these ethical provisions across the EU, European Patent Organisation (EPOrg),[6] and now the UPC contexts. The system was already institutionally complex,[7] and the UPC introduces a further interpretative community within European patent decision-making.[8] As a result, more bodies will be interpreting how ethical issues are considered in the patent grant stage for biotechnological inventions. It further fragments the supranational European patent adjudicatory land-

---

Towards a Transgenic Patent System" (1995) 3 Medical Law Review 275; Peter Drahos, "Biotechnology Patents, Markets and Morality" (1999) 21(9) European Intellectual Property Review 441; Margo Bagley, "Patent First, Ask Questions Later: Morality and Biotechnology in Patent Law" (2003–2004) 45 William and Mary Law Review 469; Oliver Mills, Biotechnological Inventions: Moral Restraints and Patent Law (revised edn, Ashgate Publishing, 2010); Ana Nordberg, "Patents, Morality and Biomedical Innovation in Europe: Historical Overview, Current Debates on Stem Cells, Gene Editing and AI, and de lege ferenda Reflections" in Daniel Gervais (ed.), Fairness, Morality and Ordre Public (Edward Elgar Publishing, 2020); Karen Walsh and Naomi Hawkins, "Expanding the Role of Morality and Public Policy in European Patent Law" in Paul Torremans (ed.), Intellectual Property and Human Rights (4th edn, Wolters Kluwer, 2021).

5 Aisling McMahon, 'Institutions, Interpretive Communities and Legacy in Decision-Making: A Case Study of Patents, Morality and Biotechnological Inventions' in: Edward S Dove & Niamh Nic Shuibhne (eds), *Law and Legacy in Medical Jurisprudence: Essays in Honour of Graeme Laurie* (Cambridge University Press, 2022).

6 For a discussion of role of the EPOrg and EU in interpreting ethical issues related to the patentability of human embryonic stem cell technologies, and institutional tensions which may arise: see: Antonina Bakardjieva-Engelbrekt, 'Institutional and Jurisdictional Aspects of Stem Cell Patenting in Europe (EC and EPO): Tensions and Prospects' in Aurora Plomer and Paul Torremans (eds), *Embryonic Stem Cell Patents in Europe: European Law and Ethics* (Oxford University Press 2009).

7 See discussion in Bakardjieva-Engelbrekt, ibid.

8 On the idea of interpretative communities in this context, see: Drahos (n 5), 441–2. This concept is developed and discussed further in: McMahon (n 6); Aisling McMahon, *The Morality Provisions in the European Patent System: An Institutional Examination* (PhD thesis, University of Edinburgh 2016); Aisling McMahon, 'An Institutional Examination of the Implications of the Unitary Patent Package for the Morality Provisions: A Fragmented Future Too Far?' (2017) 48 *IIC* 42.

scape,⁹ heightening the potential for institutional tensions.¹⁰ Accordingly, with the UPC's introduction, this section argues that a renewed and much deeper interdisciplinary conversation is urgently needed around what role ethical considerations *should* have at patent grant stage for biotechnological inventions in Europe. Finally, third, in section three, I argue that the need for this discussion is heightened because science continues to rapidly develop, thus, the ethical issues presented by patent applications for emerging biotechnological inventions are likely to increase. This in turn will pose complex questions for existing frameworks.

The chapter concludes in section four arguing that the addition of the UPC must give us pause to reflect upon how ethical considerations *are currently,* and *should in future be,* considered within the European patent system for biotechnological inventions. Within such discussions, it is vital that we are cognisant of the important role of decision-making actors, *of who decides*, on how the ethical provisions within the Directive are interpreted and operating in practice. Moreover, given the fragmented landscape applicable, it is vital that there is greater institutional dialogue across and between the relevant European patent institutions on this issue in Europe.¹¹

31.1 Patenting biotechnological inventions in Europe: the embedding of ethical considerations within the Biotechnology Directive 98/44/EC

The role that 'ethical' considerations should play in patent grant decisions, particularly, for biotechnological inventions has long been contested within Europe.¹² The term 'ethical' could be used to relate to a range of issues – this chapter uses the term in a broad sense to refer to potential concerns related to the use of a patent right, and/or to the development or use of the proposed invention for which a patent is granted or sought, in

---

9 McMahon, 2017, ibid.
10 This idea of institutional tensions in the European patent framework in the EU and EPO context is discussed in: Bakardjieva-Engelbrekt, (n 7).
11 On institutional dialogue more generally in the European patent context, see: Karen Walsh, *Fragmentation and the European Patent System* (Hart Publishing 2022); Karen Walsh, 'Promoting Harmonisation Across the European Patent System Through Judicial Dialogue and Cooperation' (2019) IIC 50, 408–440. Karen Walsh, Handbook Chapter.
12 Discussions include: Beyleveld and Brownsword (n 5); Mills (n 5); Bentley and Sherman (N 5); Justine Pila, 'Adapting the Ordre Public and Morality Exclusion of European Patent Law to Accommodate Emerging Technologies' (2020) 38 *Nature Biotechnology* 555; Amanda Warren-Jones, 'Identifying European Moral Consensus: Why Are the Patent Courts Reticent to Accept Empirical Evidence in Resolving Biotechnological Cases?' (2006) 28 *European Intellectual Property Review* 26.

terms of the impact of this right or use of the related invention on, for example, humanity, animal life, and the environment we live in.[13]

There are a range of differing views around the role, scope and purpose – if any – of ethical considerations in patent grant decision-making in Europe.[14] Arguments for embedding such considerations in patent law for biotechnological inventions include concerns about commodification of life, human dignity, and the potential impact of patents on access/development/use of biotechnologies.[15] In contrast, others view the patent system as being a technical or inert field,[16] or one which is not configured to engage with ethical considerations.[17] The purpose of this chapter is not to provide a normative framework for how ethical issues *should* be framed in this context, nor is it to provide a normative argument for how the 'European' patent system should engage with ethical issues *per se*. Instead, it argues that although there are multiple contestations around the role of ethical issues at patent grant stage in Europe, the Directive offers a clear mandate for ethical issues to be considered in patenting biotechnological inventions.[18]

31.1.1 Drafting of the Biotechnological Directive and ethic

The main legal text applicable to patenting technologies generally within the 'European' patent system is the European Patent Convention (EPC), this applies to all fields of inventions, and was originally adopted in 1973. It is not an EU text, instead it applies to 38 Contracting States, which include all EU States. As biotechnologies developed, uncertainties arose about the patentability of biotechnologies in Europe, and fears grew that Europe would fall behind other jurisdictions.[19] To address this, the EU sought to adopt legislation on the patenting of biotechnologies culminating in the Directive.[20] The Directive's negotiations took over ten years,[21] and during this time concerns were raised about the

---

[13] Ethical considerations could be raised at various levels around the use of a patent right or use/development of the patented technologies. For a discussion, see: also: Cliona Kelly and Rachel Claire Brady, 'Research Ethics and the Patent System' (2022) 44(4) EIPR 209–220.
[14] This is discussed in McMahon (n 6).
[15] See discussion in Mills, (n 5). This is discussed further in: Aisling McMahon, 'The 'Ethical' Regulation of Novel Being Technologies: The Potential Role for Patents as Drivers, Blockers and Ethical Guiders' In: David Lawrence & Sarah Morley (eds). *Novel Beings: Regulatory Approaches for a Future of New Intelligent Life*. (Edward Elgar 2022).
[16] See discussion of arguments in: Bently and Sherman (n 5).
[17] See discussion, in Mills (n 5).
[18] See also McMahon (n 6).
[19] Gerard Porter, 'The Drafting History of the European Biotechnology Directive' in Aurora Plomer and Paul Torremans (eds), *Embryonic Stem Cell Patents in Europe: European Law and Ethics* (Oxford University Press 2009).
[20] Ibid.
[21] Ibid.

ethical issues posed by patenting biotechnological inventions. This focus on ethical concerns within the drafting process, and the final directive text only passed after the draft was amended including to address such issues,[22] arguably highlights the concrete role that ethical considerations were viewed as playing by those involved in the legislative process.

31.1.2 Ethical provisions and the Directive

Notably, the Directive's final text contains several provisions which embed ethical considerations within the patenting of biotechnological inventions in Europe.[23] One of the most discussed provisions is Article 6 of the Directive. Art 6(1) states that inventions "shall be considered unpatentable where their commercial exploitation would be contrary to *ordre public* or morality; however, exploitation shall not be deemed to be so contrary merely because it is prohibited by law or regulation." This so-called general morality provision is similar to the general morality provision within Art 53(a) of the EPC.

However, Art 6(2) of the Directive is a new addition. It lists four categories of biotechnological inventions as unpatentable based on Art 6(1),[24] which denoted areas of contention at the time that the Directive was drafted (late 1980s-1998). However, Art. 6 (2)'s list is not exhaustive. It states: "On the basis of paragraph 1, the following, **in particular,** shall be considered unpatentable:" [emphasis added]. The word 'in particular' here denotes inventions falling within these categories are automatically excluded,[25] but other categories could also be excluded from patentability, if considered to fall within the general exclusion under Art 6(1). Recital 38 confirms this, and it also states that: "whereas processes, *the use of* which offend against human dignity... are obviously also excluded from patentability" [Emphasis added]. Importantly, within this recital, the focus appears to be not just on ethical objections to the *patentability* of a technology, but also ethical objections to the *'use'* of the technology which a patent is applied for. Thus, whilst Article 6(1) highlights that patents are excluded where the 'commercial exploitation' of an invention is against *ordre public*/morality, this recital suggests consideration also of the *use* of the technology/process.

Alongside the morality provisions, there are several other references to ethical issues within the Directive. These include, Art 5(1) which states: "The human body, at the various stages of its formation and development, and the simple discovery of one of its elements,

---

22 The first draft was rejected, see discussion in Porter (ibid).
23 This is discussed in detail in: McMahon (note 6).
24 These are: (a) processes for cloning human beings; (b) processes for modifying the germ line genetic identity of human beings; (c) uses of human embryos for industrial or commercial purposes; (d) processes for modifying the genetic identity of animals which are likely to cause them suffering without any substantial medical benefit to man or animal, and also animals resulting from such processes.
25 See discussion in McMahon (note 6).

including the sequence or partial sequence of a gene, cannot constitute patentable inventions." This provision suggests legislators were concerned about the ethical issues posed by potential patent applications related to the human body, and sought to exclude patents being granted directly over the human body or its parts.[26] Furthermore, several other recitals – which provide guidance on how the legislation is to be interpreted – refer to the need to take ethical considerations into account. These include Recital 16 which refers to the need to apply patent law in a manner that respects "the dignity and integrity of the person,"[27] and Recital 43 which refers to fundamental human rights.

Considered together, these provisions arguably embed a consideration of ethical issues posed by the patentability, development, and use of biotechnologies within the Directive. Accordingly, regardless of broader contestations around whether ethical issues *should* be embedded in patent law, within the EU context reading the Directive's text literally, there are clear references to, and thus, arguably, a clear mandate for ethical issues to be considered in patenting biotechnologies.

31.2 Applying the directive's ethical provisions in Europe: interpretative communities, institutional overlaps & influences

Having said this, in practice, the effect of these legal provisions depends on how they are interpreted and applied by the relevant decision-making bodies within the 'European' patent system.[28] At a regional level a complex and overlapping institutional framework applies in this context, and the introduction of the UPC (in its current form) further complicates this framework. Thus, this section argues that it must give us pause to consider how these ethical provisions *should* apply, and relatedly, to what extent the institutional frameworks within European patent law are conducive to this aim.

31.2.1 Ethical provisions within the Directive & practical interpretation – pre-UPC

Prior to the coming into force of the UPC, the European patent system for how ethical provisions in the Directive are applied already involved a complex overlap of EPOrg and EU functions. This is because even though the Directive is an EU text, the European Patent Office (EPO) is the main patent grant body in Europe. Therefore at a regional level,

---

26 See also, recital 21–22. The effect of this provision has been narrowed by Art 5(2).
27 See also recital 39.
28 McMahon (n 6).

it is the Examining Divisions and Boards of the EPO, not the decision-making bodies within the EU, that have the most significant role in interpreting how these provisions apply on a day-to-day basis.[29] Under the 'European' patent system – prior to the UPC system coming into effect – there is no unitary 'European' patent per se. Instead, there is a single application route to apply for patents in a range of the 38 EPC Contracting States. An applicant would apply to the EPO, for a patent, and if granted would obtain a bundle of national patents this is the so-called 'classic European patent' route. Under this process, it is the EPO bodies that consider the application's compatibility with the patentability requirements, including considering, the ethical exclusions against patentability. Furthermore, post-grant the EPO has Opposition Proceedings which is a mechanism to challenge a patent at the regional level soon after it is granted, providing an additional avenue for EPO interpretative influence over how such provisions are applied.[30]

In contrast, the EU's adjudicative body, the Court of Justice of the European Union (CJEU), is only involved in adjudicating how such ethical provisions in the Directive are interpreted in a narrow range of circumstances such as, for example, if a preliminary reference by a national EU Member State is made about the interpretation of the Directive. However, such preliminary reference cases are relatively rare in practice in this context, and certainly would not afford the EU the same level of day-to-day practical interpretative influence over how the ethical provisions of the Directive are applied, as the EPO adjudicatory bodies have.

Moreover, the EPO is not an EU entity, and its Contracting States include all EU States, but also non-EU States. After the Directive was adopted, the EPO adopted it as supplementary interpretation for the EPC.[31] Thus, the bodies of the EPO are in theory, informed by these provisions. However, the EPO is not legally bound to follow the EU's approach. Moreover, as will be discussed below, considerable discretion applies for decision-making bodies in relation to setting the threshold and contours of the ethical provisions within the Directive, this widens the potential significance of decision-makers' influence in this context.

31.2.2 Institutional overlaps & ethical considerations – enter the UPC

The supranational institutional complexity in the current system is increased by the UPC's commencement because rather than offering a single patent system for EU States, the new unitary patent and UPC will exist alongside the current EPO and national systems. Moreover, the UPC does not have its own patent grant body, instead such appli-

---

29 See also discussions in: Bakardjieva-Engelbrekt (n 7), 227; McMahon 2016 (n 9); McMahon 2017 (n 9).
30 There are also avenues to challenge patents for each national patent granted, at the national level, this is beyond the scope of this paper.
31 Rule 26, Implementing Regulations to the EPC.

cants need to apply under the EPO's single application route system for this. Thus, the EPO remains the patent grant body for unitary patents. If the application is granted, it is converted into a European patent with unitary effect, and potentially, also other relevant patents will be granted for States who have not signed the Agreement on a Unified Patent Court (AUPC),[32] depending on the application. However, the key difference is that if granted, the UPC will have jurisdiction over any unitary patents and also for 'classic' European patents granted in States which have signed up to the AUPC.[33]

Thus, once this system commences, it will lead to a scenario where several different overlapping types of patent routes, and differing avenues/implications in terms of which decision-making actor adjudicates over the patent post-grant within Europe. These will include, the possibility of: (1) an application to the national patent office in an EPC Contracting State for a national patent whose post grant life is adjudicated over by the national State; (2) an application to the EPO for a European patent with unitary effect whereby the jurisdiction for this patent after grant would be dealt with by the UPC; (3) an application to the EPO for a bundle of patents in EPC Contracting States where post grant each patent is dealt with by the national State for non-AUPC States or in cases where applicants have opted out for the transitional period, and if some of these are applied for in States which have signed/ratified the AUPC the post grant jurisdiction of these patents is overseen by the UPC.[34] It will also be possible, to apply for a combination of these under the EPO route e.g. a single application to the EPO for patents in a range of non-AUPC States alongside a European patent with unitary effect for relevant AUPC States.

As noted, transitional periods will apply after the new system comes into effect which means that applicants can opt-out of the unitary patent system for EPO granted patents in AUPC Contracting States for a certain period, currently proposed as seven years.[35] During the transitional period, where applicants opt-out such European patents will fall under the jurisdiction of the national States, rather than the UPC.[36]

At the post-grant stage, the UPC will have a role in interpreting the ethical provisions within the European patent system, for patents within its jurisdiction such as, if a patent is challenged under revocation proceedings.[37] Currently, revocation proceedings are considered by national courts. After the UPC enters into force, revocation pro-

---

[32] Council Agreement on a Unified Patent Court (2013/C 175/01).
[33] This is unless applicants have opted out of the UPC system during the transitional period.
[34] See McMahon 2017, (n 9), p 51 citing: Hilty RM, Jaeger T, Lamping M, Ullrich H, "The unitary patent package. Twelve reasons for concern" *Max Planck Institute for Intellectual Property and Competition Law*, (17 October 2012).
[35] This is correct at time of writing January 2023.
[36] See: Art. 83(3) AUPC; see also: Luke McDonagh, Exploring perspectives of the unified patent court and unitary patent within the business and legal communities. (UK IPO 2014) at 9.
[37] Art 138(1)(a)EPC states that one ground for revocation is that "(a) the subject-matter of the European patent is not patentable under Articles 52 to 57;" under this it could be argued that a patent should not have been granted on the basis of ethical issues at stake.

ceedings would fall under its remit for unitary patents and for patents that are granted by the EPO in States which have signed and ratified the AUPC (provided applicants have not opted out during the transitional period). All non-EU States including the UK will fall outside this jurisdiction because only EU States can participate in the unitary patent system. Hence, revocation actions for such States remain under the jurisdiction of their national States. Furthermore, whilst the UPC is not an EU court per se, it has a link with, and may refer questions, to the CJEU aimed at ensuring EU law is applied in a consistent manner.[38]

Alongside this, opposition proceedings under the EPO system will remain possible for all patents granted by the EPO, including patents with unitary effect. As highlighted elsewhere,[39] if a patent is rendered invalid by the UPC, this would only apply to patents in States party to the AUPC, and would not apply to that patent in other EPC Contracting States. This could create further potential for institutional divergence and tensions in the context of how ethical issues are considered for biotechnological inventions and more generally.

Accordingly, once the UPC comes into effect, the ethical provisions within the Directive will be considered at a supranational level by three entities under the following main avenues: the EPO in considering patentability of inventions at patent grant stage, and challenges under opposition/appeal proceedings; the UPC will have a role in deciding matters of revocation for unitary patents and European patents granted by the EPO in AUPC Contracting States; and the CJEU will retain a role in providing guidance on preliminary rulings if the UPC or national courts request this, this could include guidance on questions raised about the interpretation of ethical provisions within the Directive. Thus, three overlapping supranational bodies will be involved in the interpretation of these provisions – each with differing institutional features and differing compositions of applicable State parties.

31.2.3 Interpretative communities and the UPC's role in interpreting ethical provisions within the Directive

Given this context, it is important to consider, to what extent and how this institutional change might influence how ethical considerations are applied within the European patent system. One could argue that because the legal text – the Directive – applies to various extents in all frameworks, as EU law has primacy within the UPC, and the EPO has adopted the Directive as supplementary interpretation for the EPC, all such bodies should, in theory, be applying the text in a similar manner. However, this section ques-

---

38 Art. 21 AUPC., See McMahon 2017 (n 9), 60.
39 McMahon 2017, (n 9) 52.

tions this by highlighting the importance of the institutional influences at play.[40] It argues that: (1) as much discretion is left to decision-making actors on these provisions, and (2) due to the differing institutional features of each decision-making framework they will have their own distinct interpretative community for the interpretation of provisions.[41] This in turn, means the three supranational decision-making actors involved could lead to differing approaches on these provisions, and heightened potential for institutional tensions within the system.[42]

31.2.3.1 Ethical issues, discretion & the interpretative role of decision-makers in the European patent system

If we consider the ethical provisions in the Directive, due to their wording and the concepts within them -around which there is limited consensus – many of these provisions require decision-making actors to exercise discretion in interpreting them. Essentially, such provisions are open-textured and decision-making actors, put the flesh on the bones of such provisions in their application.[43] For instance, take Art 6(1) of the Directive. To exclude a technology from patentability under this provision, decision-makers would need to assess to what extent its 'commercial exploitation' is contrary to 'ordre public' or 'morality'. This is not a straightforward assessment and decision-makers have considerable latitude in assessing what counts as 'commercial exploitation', 'ordre public' and 'morality'. Furthermore, even for the listed exclusions under Art 6(2), technologies are rapidly evolving, and thus, the legal text has not always kept pace with the science. Thus, decision-makers must exercise discretion in how these provisions apply. This is evident in cases involving whether technologies involving the creation of a human embryonic stem cells or parthenotes would be patentable given the exclusion under Art 6(2)(c).[44] Similarly, other ethical provisions in the Directive's text refer to concepts such as dignity and human rights – assessing to what extent granting patents over biotechnologies or using/developing biotechnologies may impact human rights/dig-

---

40 See also McMahon 2017, (n 9).
41 Drahos (n 5).
42 This concept was discussed in the context of the EPO/EU and hESC patents by Bakardjieva-Engelbrekt (n 7).
43 See discussion of such open textured principles in: Hart HLA, *The concept of law*. (Oxford University Press, 1961) 199–200, as cited in: McMahon, 2017 (n 7), 56; see also discussion in Warren-Amanda Warren Jones, *Taming Scary Monsters with morality: An assessment of the morality criterion in European and UK Patent law in the context of human and animal biotechnology*, (PhD Thesis, Cardiff University, 2002), 50.
44 Wisconsin Alumni Research Foundation (WARF) (G002/06), Decision of the Enlarged Board of Appeal 25 November 2008; n Case C-34/10 Brustle v. Greenpeace eV [2011] E.C.R. I-9821, and Case C-364/13. International Stem Cell Corporation v. Comptroller General of Patents, Designs and Trade Marks, Judgment of the Court, Grand Camber, 18 December, 2014.

nity also requires decision-makers to exercise discretion reinforcing decision-makers interpretative role in such contexts.

As an aside, another important issue in terms of questions of discretion in this context, is that Member States have been recognised as having a margin of discretion in applying the general morality provision under Art 6(1).[45] This 'scope for manoeuvre' is provided to take account States different social and cultural contexts applicable and which Member States are better placed to understand.[46] However, the European patent with unitary effect is unitary in character "i.e. providing uniform protection and having equal effect in all the participating Member States. Consequently, a European patent with unitary effect should only be limited, transferred or revoked, or lapse, in respect of all the participating Member States ..."[47] This unitary character suggests that for such patents there is no avenue for accommodating divergence between States on moral issues related to the patentability of biotechnological inventions and is likely another issue which will need to be considered as the UPC comes into effect.[48]

31.2.3.2 Institutional influences and overlapping EPO, CJEU and UPC functions: interpretating ethical provisions in the Directive

Moreover, as I have argued elsewhere,[49] institutional theories suggest that within any decision-making framework, there will be both legally constraining influences and persuasive influences on decision-making actors which, in turn, may affect how decision-makers interpret legal provisions in practice. Legally constraining factors include the legal competences of that body as contained within its founding legal text and prior case law which may create binding precedents. Whilst persuasive influences include the composition of decision-making actors within that body, as evidence suggests that if such actors come from a similar background e.g., from scientific/technical fields, where ethical issues are either rarely examined within their remit, or marginalised, such actors may continue this status quo when they are required to engage with such provisions. If bodies such as the EPO, CJEU or UPC are called upon to determine the application of any of the provisions which embed ethical considerations within the Directive for patentability, they will arguably each consider the text of such provisions by filtering these through their own distinct institutional lens to give an application of such provisions.[50]

---

45 Case C-377/98 Netherlands v. European Parliament and Council, Judgment of the Court, 9 October, 2001,
46 Ibid, para 37–38.
47 Recital 7 of Regulation 1257/2012.
48 McMahon, 2017 (n 9) 62–65.
49 McMahon 2016; McMahon 2017 (n 9).
50 McMahon 2016, note 9.

In contexts where legal provisions require decision-makers to exercise limited discretion[51]– the institutional influence may have limited effect. However, in cases where discretion needs to be exercised, decision-making bodies are more likely to be constrained and persuaded to apply provisions in line with institutional frameworks within that decision-making body.

Furthermore, in terms of the institutional frameworks applicable, each of these three supranational bodies share some similarities, but also key differences. For example, both the EPO and UPC will be comprised of primarily scientific and technical experts, and where legal experts sit on these bodies, they are likely to be experts within patent law, and hence, drawn largely from commercial practice. Such individuals may likely have limited broader engagement with ethical considerations related to the patentability of biotechnologies previously. This in turn may reinforce a likelihood for such actors to engage in a light touch manner with such provisions/questions. Indeed, the EPO in cases involving the ethical provisions to date, has demonstrated an acute reluctance to engage deeply with ethical issues related to the patentability of biotechnological inventions.[52] In contrast, the CJEU is a generalist legal court composed of legal experts drawn from all legal fields and may likely have broader experience in engaging with questions related to human rights, ethics etc. – and relatedly, less familiarity with specific aspects of patent law which may bring other issues.[53] Based on these features one might predict that the UPC may be likely to adopt a similar light touch approach to the ethical considerations as the EPO has to date. Having said that, much will depend on to what extent the UPC refers questions to the CJEU.[54] This may give the CJEU greater involvement in the field and greater influence over these and other provisions. Furthermore, although the UPC is not an EU supranational court per se, as noted, EU law has primacy within the UPC, and this may influence how it deals with these ethical provisions – only time will tell how the UPC will impact this area.

In short, at a supranational adjudicatory level, the role of ethical considerations in patent grant decisions for biotechnological inventions involves a complex institutional landscape and mesh of functions including the EU and EPOrg and UPC actors. Thus, even though the Directive is an EU legislative text, the EPO is the primary body which interprets the law in practice. To date, the EPO has had the main role in guiding the interpretation of these provisions in everyday patent practice and has done so in a light touch manner. The EPO will continue to have a key role under the unitary patent system as it remains the patent grant body for unitary patents. Nonetheless, the UPC will now also have a role at post-grant stage should questions on the ethical provisions related to pa-

---

51 For example, under Art 6(2) provisions whereby if an invention falls squarely within the definition of the provision it is automatically excluded.
52 See discussion in: McMahon 2016 (n 9); Walsh and Hawkins (n 5).
53 See discussion in Brinkhof J, Ohly A, Towards a unified patent court in Europe. In: Ohly A, Pila J (eds) The Europeanization of intellectual property law. (Oxford University Press 2013) at 215.
54 See also McMahon 2017, (n 9) 60–62.

tents over biotechnological inventions arise before it. How the UPC will engage with these provisions remains unknown, but it will likely be affected by the institutional framework which exists within the UPC, and which differs to both the CJEU and EPO frameworks. This opens new possibilities for divergent interpretations and demands a much more joined up approach and conversation around the role of ethical provisions within and across these institutional frameworks/actors.

31.3 Technological developments and the need for a renewed conversation on the role ethical issues should play within the European patent system

Alongside the increasing institutional complexity in the European patent system, which the UPC system will exacerbate, the scientific field for biotechnologies is constantly advancing. Accordingly, the ethical issues posed by patent grant (and use) of emerging biotechnologies are likely to intensify in the coming years as the nature of biotechnologies continue to develop at pace. These include, for example, advances in developing immunotherapies, such as CAR-T;[55] advances in gene-editing technologies such as CRISPR; and the potential for biotechnologies to be used to develop novel being technologies including using those created via biotechnologies that may resemble humans but not quite be human.[56] A myriad of ethical questions arise over the patentability of such technologies, including re-igniting questions around commodification of the body, around whether such patents would infringe on human dignity, and the broader (bio)ethical questions around the role of patents in encouraging the development of contentious biotechnologies, and around the impact of such patents on access to health-related biotechnologies.

Moreover, within the patent field, there is now also a growing focus on patents potential broader governance functions.[57] Patents give rightsholders the right to stop others using an invention for generally 20 years. However, this in turn allows right-

---

[55] See also: Luis Gil Abinader, and Jorge L Contreras, The Patentability of Genetic Therapies: CAR-T and Medical Treatment Exclusions Around The World" (2019) 34(4) *American University International Law Review* 705.

[56] David Lawrence & Sarah Morley (eds), *Novel Beings: Regulatory Approaches for a Future of New Intelligent Life.* (Edward Elgar 2022).

[57] Aisling McMahon, "Biotechnology, Health and Patents as Private Governance Tools: The Good, the Bad and the Potential For Ugly?" (2020) 3 *Intellectual Property Quarterly* 161; Shobita Parthasarathy, "'Use the Patent System to Regulate Gene Editing'" (25 October 2018) 562 *Nature* 486; Duncan Matthews, et al, "The Role of Patents and Licensing in the Governance of Human Genome Editing: A White Paper" (2021) Queen Mary Law Research Paper No. 364/2021; Naomi Scheinerman and Jacob S. Sherkow, "Governance Choices of Genome Editing Patents" (2021) 3 Frontiers in Political Science No. 745898; Jacob Sherkow, Eli Y. Adashi and Glenn Cohen, "Governing Human Germline Editing Through Patent Law" (2021) 326(12) *Journal of the American Medical Association* 1149.

sholders to dictate the terms of access to the invention, and to shape how technologies are used and developed. How patent rights act as governance devices and affect the development, use and access to biotechnologies pose further ethical issues, which may be exacerbated as such technologies develop.

Furthermore, at a practical level, the Directive marks its 25th year in 2023 and many provisions of this legal text related to ethical issues have been outpaced by scientific developments.[58] This could result in further challenges arising before the adjudicative bodies in Europe, which could require difficult decisions. It could also potentially, in the not-so-distant future, result in pressure for legislative change to amend the Directive or Implementing Regulations to the EPC, addressing ethical issues, depending on how technologies develop.

These developments will place further pressure on the EPO, EU, and now UPC to consider how they engage with ethical considerations posed by patents – and how they are used – over biotechnologies in future. This adds further impetus for a renewed interdisciplinary conversation on the role that ethical considerations should play within the European Patent system, involving dialogue across the EPO, UPC and CJEU and with relevant stakeholders.

31.4 Concluding thoughts

In short, even though the role of ethical issues in patent law generally is contested, various provisions within the text of the Directive demonstrate a recognition of the need to consider ethical issues in the patenting of biotechnological inventions within EU States. However, how such provisions play out in practice depends on how they are interpreted by the decision-making actors involved. In this context, at a supranational level, the European system within which such ethical provisions for biotechnological patents apply, is institutionally complex. It involves the overlap of EPO, EU, and now UPC decision-making bodies. Moreover, it remains to be seen how the UPC, and the unitary patent system more generally, will engage with such provisions – only time will tell. There is potential it will offer greater more nuanced engagement with ethical issues in this context, but it is also plausible that the UPC will maintain the status quo light touch approach to such provisions, akin to the EPO's approach to date.

This chapter argues that, given the increasing institutional complexity which the UPC brings, and given the increasing ethical issues likely to arise in the patenting of biotechnologies due to the pace of scientific developments, the time is long over-due for a renewed conversation on the role of ethical issues in this area. It is vital that this conversation takes places across the EPO, EU, UPC institutions and that it involves input from relevant stakeholders and interdisciplinary experts in order to consider what role ethi-

---

[58] For example, Art 6(2) provisions have required interpretation in light of scientific developments.

cal issues are *currently playing* in the patenting of biotechnologies, what is the intended role that *ethical issues should* play in this context in light of obligations within the Directive and other applicable legal instruments, and importantly, within such contexts, what is the role of the various adjudicatory bodies involved in achieving this.

Gail E Evans
32 The UPC and the FRAND injunction

In the near future patentees holding European Patents or Unitary patents will be able to choose between litigation in a national court or the Unified Patent court (UPC).[1] In the early years of the UPC, there is likely to be some uncertainty as to the choice of court, particularly where the litigation involves FRAND encumbered patents.[2] FRAND encumbered patent infringement has become associated with the parties' use of strategic dynamics to improve their respective positions when negotiating a licensing agreement.[3] For its part a patentee, possibly a patent assertion entity (PAE) with an international patent portfolio, in pursuit of higher royalties, may 'hold up' implementers by seeking an injunction for patent infringement, which if granted, would effectively oblige the defendant to close operations in the jurisdiction. Indeed, having failed to conclude a licence with the implementer, the claimant who seeks to exert pressure on the defendant to accept the terms of the licence by means of permanent injunction, may effectively end the litigation by closing the defendant's business. Moreover, in the event the patentee holds a unitary patent, the scope of a final injunction may extend throughout the European Union,[4] rendering the UPC's decision-making as to injunctive relief all the more critical.

---

[1] Regarding the Unitary Patent system and the Unified Patent Court, which will have jurisdiction over Unitary Patents and 'classic' European patents: a claimant will be able to bring an infringement action before a Local or Regional Division of a country where either (1) infringement has occurred or is threatened, or (2) at least one of the defendants is resident or has a place of business. If the country does not participate in a Local or Regional Division, the case can be brought in the Central Division: see EU regulations establishing the Unitary Patent system: No/1257/2012 (Unitary Patent) and No 1260/2012 (Translation Arrangements); and the Agreement on a Unified Patent Court (UPCA opened for signature in 2013) Arts. 32 and 33. The UPC is a Court common to seventeen EU Member States created by the UPCA opened for signature in 2013) which will enter into force after ratification by Germany. The commencement of the Unified Patent Court (UPC) is expected on 1 June 2023: https://www.unified-patent-court.org/; https://www.epo.org/.
[2] Fair, reasonable and non-discriminatory (FRAND): See the European Telecommunications Standards Institute (ETSI) Rules of Procedure, ETSI Intellectual Property Rights Policy (IPR Policy) 2022, Annex 6: Cl. 6.1, Availability of Licences. According to the FRAND undertaking a patentee is to provide licences to all those who participate in one or more telecommunications' standards.
[3] On the strategies of hold-up and hold-out see Optis Cellular Technology LLC & Ors v Apple Retail UK Ltd & Ors [2022] EWCA Civ 1411. See GE Evans 'Negotiating FRAND Encumbered Patent Licences' (JIPLP Vol.16 (10) 2021, 1091–1108).
[4] Unitary Patent: Reg. 1257/2012; classic European patents: UPCA, Art. 34: Decisions of the Court shall cover...the territory of those Contracting Member States for which the European patent has effect. To date, 16 countries have ratified the UPCA, namely Austria, Belgium, Bulgaria, Denmark, Estonia, Finland, France, Germany, Italy, Latvia, Lithuania, Luxembourg, Malta, the Netherlands, Portugal, Slovenia and Sweden.

Gail E Evans, (BA Hons, Dip.Ed, LLB, SJD) Centre for Commercial Law Studies, Queen Mary University of London, Reader in the Licensing of Intellectual Property.

https://doi.org/10.1515/9783110781687-032

The possibility of obtaining a pan-European injunction may well renew debate as to whether a standard essential patent (SEP) holder is entitled to an injunction, having previously undertaken to provide licences at fair and reasonable royalty rates.[5] For their part implementers may 'hold out' entering into a licence to the prejudice of patentees and, in view of the possible duration of litigation, may succeed in delaying payment until the market price of the patent falls, or worst case, until the patent in question expires. The problem is clearly identified in the parties' continued gaming of the litigation system in the matter of FRAND encumbered patent litigation, in particular, as recent litigation tends to show,[6] an implementer's unwillingness to commit to taking a licence.

The UPC may expect the claimant to argue that it is entitled to an immediate and unqualified injunction if the implementer does not commit to take a licence on FRAND terms. The defendant will counter-claim mounting a FRAND defence,[7] that the patentee is not entitled to an injunction in light of its failure to offer a licence on FRAND terms and, contrary to competition law, its abuse of a dominant market position. The UPC Agreement provides the court with a discretion as to whether it should order a final injunction in patent infringement suits.[8] In view of the controversy the FRAND undertaking brings to patent litigation and the differences in approach among the decisions of national courts in Europe,[9] it is important to consider the way in which the UPC may approach the grant of a final injunction. The court's determination will require an assessment of the circumstances in which it is appropriate to grant injunctive relief in respect of the infringement of a SEP, and in the final analysis, whether damages would be a more proportional remedy.

Although it was originally a party to the UPCA and took part in the Unitary Patent enhanced procedure, the UK has withdrawn from the UPC system (and the EU) and UPs will not cover the UK. C.f. A UK [Standard Essential Patent] has limited territorial scope and UK courts will generally only determine disputes concerning the infringement and validity of UK or [European Patent (UK)] patents. Unwired Planet International Ltd & Anor v Huawei Technologies Co Ltd & Anor (Rev 1) [2018] EWCA 2344 [52].

5 See S Barazza, 'Licensing Standard Essential Patents, Part Two: The Availability of Injunctive Relief' (2014) 9 Journal of Intellectual Property Law & Practice, 552–564.

6 See Unwired Planet International Ltd & Anor v Huawei Technologies (UK) Co Ltd & Anor [2020] UKSC 37; Optis Cellular Technology LLC & Ors v Apple Retail UK Ltd & Ors [2022] EWCA Civ 1411; Interdigital Technology Corporation & Ors v Lenovo Group Ltd (FRAND Judgment – Public Version) [2023] EWHC 539; and Sisvel v Haier, FRAND-Einwand I, German Federal Court of Justice, 2020, KZR 36/17 (English translation provided by the firm of Arnold Ruess: https://www.arnold-ruess.com).

7 It is likely that the UPC will be involved in the litigation of a FRAND encumbered patent when the FRAND defence is raised in infringement proceedings: Art. 32 (1)(a) UPCA.

8 UPCA Art. 63(1).

9 Note that the UPCA allows a defendant to file a counterclaim for revocation of the patent in an infringement claim (Art. 32 (e) UPCA). The Local and Regional Divisions, having heard the parties, have the option of hearing both claims in a single case, as is the practice in almost all of the UPC member states. Further see P Cappuyns & N Al Ganim, 'Four times FRAND: An Analysis of Recent Judgments from the UK, Germany, the Netherlands and France, and Lessons for the Upcoming UPC System' (2022) 17 Journal of Intellectual Property Law & Practice, 946–961.

The UPC, according to permissible sources of law, must base its determination of final FRAND injunctions on the provisions of the UPC Agreement, European Union law, applicable international agreements and national law.[10] As to jurisdiction, a patentee may bring its infringement action before the UPC in a Member State where the infringement has occurred or where the defendant has a place of business. Non-EU based defendants, including a defendant that has a place of business in the UK, can be sued for infringement in the UPC.[11] Furthermore, for those patents that remain within the UPC jurisdiction, to the extent there is an issue of infringement in the UK, a parallel national case will be required in the UK. Moreover, patent litigation in relation to national patents will continue whether they are EPs designating the UK, or UK national patents, rendering the judgments of UK courts persuasive before the developing jurisprudence of the UPC. As a result, it might be anticipated that the UPC will base its decisions not only on the national jurisprudence of Member States, but also on that of non-contracting states, such as the UK, so far as it constitutes persuasive evidence of a consistency in the European approach to the grant of a final FRAND injunction.[12] Although the UK has withdrawn from the UPCA, its patent law remains relevant. The EU Enforcement Directive of 2004 as implemented in UK law is retained, as is the case law of the CJEU in the manner of its interpretation by UK courts.[13]

Therefore, based upon recent case law in the UK and Germany, the aim of this chapter is to examine whether a SEP holder who has undertaken to grant licences on FRAND terms, is entitled to a prohibitory injunction, once the court has found that the patent is valid, essential and has been infringed by an implementer. It will be argued that notwithstanding the FRAND undertaking,[14] once there is a finding of patent validity and infringement, the law will allow the UPC little discretion to refuse a permanent injunction, whether on the basis of the remedy's proportionality or the claimant's alleged breach of competition law.

---

10 UPCA, sources of law Art. 24. Further see M Marfe, A Reetz, C Pecnard, R Fruscalzo & R van der Velden 'The Power of National Courts and the Unified Patent Court to Grant Injunctions: a Comparative Study' (2015) 10 Journal of Intellectual Property Law & Practice, 180–190.
11 UPCA, Art. 33 (1)(b): '…the local division hosted by the Contracting Member State where the defendant or, in the case of multiple defendants, one of the defendants has its residence, or principal place of business, or …its place of business, or the regional division in which that Contracting Member State participates.'
12 L Bently & R Arnold, 'Conditional Injunctions: 'The New FRAND Injunction in Unwired Planet Int'l Ltd v Huawei' in JL Contreras & M Husovec (eds), *Injunctions in Patent Law Trans-Atlantic Dialogues on Flexibility and Tailoring* (CUP 2022); see also P Treacy & M Hunt, 'Litigating a 'FRAND' patent licence: the Unwired Planet v Huawei judgment' (2018) 13 (2) Journal of Intellectual Property Law & Practice, 124 at 130.
13 EU Withdrawal Act 2018, European Union (Withdrawal) Act 2018 s.6: re: interpretation of retained EU law: 'retained case law' means '(b) retained EU case law'.
14 The FRAND undertaking: ETSI (European Telecommunications Standards Institute) IPR Policy: Clause 6.1 states relevantly, that when an essential patent relating to a particular standard (SEP) is brought to the attention of ETSI, the Director-General of ETSI shall request the owner to give within three months an undertaking that it is prepared to grant licences on fair, reasonable and non-discriminatory terms.

In the exposition of this argument, the chapter is organised as follows. Part One considers the discretion of the UPC to grant a final injunction under the UPCA and in accordance with its primary source of law, under the EU Enforcement Directive. Further, given the broad, equitable nature of the discretion within English law, by way of comparison, the first part of the chapter considers the approach of English courts to the grant of an injunction. Part Two examines the impact of the FRAND undertaking on the UPC's discretion to grant a final injunction, turning first to its expression and interpretation within the ETSI. IPR Policy and secondly to its role within the exercise of the court's discretion. Subsequently, given the use of strategic gaming within European FRAND litigation, Part Two examines the use of an injunction to defeat hold-out strategies. Part Three evaluates the adequacy of damages as an alternate remedy, where the grant of an injunction might cause the defendant implementer 'disproportionate harm'. In light of recent UK and German cases, Part Four analyses the FRAND defence whereby an implementer will counter-claim that the patentee in bringing an infringement action and requesting a final injunction, is abusing its dominant position in the market in breach of competition law. Part Five evaluates the contention that if the defendant is a willing licensee there should be no entitlement to an injunction, by contrasting the cases of Samsung whose conduct as a matter of competition law, was found to be an abuse of market dominance; and those of Unwired Planet and Sisvel where in patent suits, the defendants were found unwilling to make an unconditional commitment to take a licence on FRAND terms. The chapter concludes by affirming the hypothesis that based upon an analysis of recent case law in the UK and Germany, once there is a finding of patent infringement, the court is unlikely to withhold a FRAND injunction.

32.1 The discretion of the UPC to grant a final injunction

Pursuant to Article 63(1) of the UPCA,[15] following a finding of liability for patent infringement,[16] the Unified Patent Court 'may grant an injunction against the infringer aimed at prohibiting the continuation of the infringement.[17] According to Art. 24 of the UPCA, when hearing a case brought before the UPC for a permanent injunction the primary

---

[15] See also Rules of Procedure, July 2022, Rule 118.
[16] Article 25 UPCA: substantive patent law provisions relating to direct infringement.
[17] When Article 63(1) UPCA is considered in the context of the provisions governing court powers pursuant to Part III Chapter V, the UPC's powers do not exist *ex officio*. Instead, an action must be 'brought to' the UPC (Arts 47(1)–(4) UPCA) in order that the court may exercise its powers. The right under the patent is a private right from which a standing to sue is derived. As a general rule, the auxiliary verb 'shall' is used for such provisions that the legislator considers to be strict law, i.e. without conferring any discretion for the court to decide.

source of law will be European Union law.[18] Therefore, we will first consider the application of EU law to patent enforcement, before turning to the impact of the FRAND undertaking on the exercise of the UPC's discretion in granting a final injunction. Article 11 of the Directive on the enforcement of intellectual property rights (Enforcement Directive) similarly requires Member States to ensure that, where a court makes a finding of infringement, it 'may issue' an injunction aimed at prohibiting the continuation of the infringement.[19] Article 3 of the Enforcement Directive ostensibly identifies the elements of that discretion so far as it provides[20] that remedies are to be not only be fair and equitable', but also 'effective, proportionate and dissuasive.'[21] The Court of Justice of the European Union has stressed that Article 3 requires courts to consider the proportionality of injunctions to restrain infringements of intellectual property rights.[22]

If the words 'may grant an injunction' in Art. 63 UPCA allows the UPC some discretion in granting a FRAND injunction, then questions arise to the character and scope of that order. Consistent with such a discretion, an implementer may argue that since the claimants' only interest in the SEPs is in obtaining reasonable royalties, and that interest can be fully recognised by an award of damages instead of an injunction, it follows that such an award is the appropriate and proportionate remedy. Indeed, Article 12 of the Enforcement Directive provides that the courts of Member States may order damages to be paid the claimant, if grant of a final injunction would cause the defendant 'disproportionate harm' and if monetary compensation 'appears reasonably satisfactory'. Thus, it is only when considering damages as an alternative remedy, that Article 12 would permit such a weighing up of interests.[23]

32.1.1 The English courts and the discretionary grant of an injunction

Under English law, an injunction is an equitable remedy, one that is at the discretion of the court. Taking account of the greater historic breadth of the English courts' discretion

---

18 Art. 25 UPCA: (1) '... when hearing a case brought before it under this Agreement, the Court shall base its decisions on: (a) Union law, including Regulation (EU) No 1257/2012 and Regulation (EU) No 1260/2012.'
19 In doing so, the Member States fulfilled the obligation of Art. 44 TRIPS, that is to confer on their judicial authorities the 'authority' for granting injunctions (Recitals 4 and 5 of the Enforcement Directive).
20 Arts. 3 and 12 of Directive 2004/48/EC on the Enforcement of Intellectual Property Rights ('The Enforcement Directive').
21 Art. 3(2) Enforcement Directive.
22 See e.g. Case C-275/06 Productores de Música de España (Promusicae) v Telefónica de España SAU [2008] ECR I-271 at [68]; Case C-360/10 Belgische Vereniging van Auteurs, Componisten en Uitgevers CVBA (SABAM) v Netlog NV [2012] ECR I-0000 at [34].
23 The TRIPS Agreement provides limited exceptions to intellectual property rights, which would permit the court a discretion to refuse an injunction, provided that such exceptions do not unreasonably conflict with a normal exploitation of the patent.

in granting an injunction, by way of persuasive authority, let us consider their approach to assessment.[24] Consistent with EU law, the High Court in HTC v Nokia states explicitly that the criteria to be applied are those laid down by Article 3 of the Enforcement Directive that is, efficacy, proportionality and dissuasiveness.[25] Although the text of Art. 3 appears to suggest a balance of convenience, the English courts have found that in the case of a permanent injunction, the analysis cannot be so characterised.

It is only in special circumstances that the court will exercise its discretion to award damages in lieu of an injunction. Only if the case is one in which it would be grossly oppressive to the defendant to grant an injunction would damages in substitution for an injunction be awarded.[26] In other words, the effect of the grant of the injunction would be grossly disproportionate to the right protected. As the use of the word 'grossly' suggests, the grant or refusal of a final injunction is not a question of the balance of convenience.[27] This is because, in the case of a final injunction the scope of the court's discretion relates closely to the finding of infringement and the exclusivity of the patentee's rights.

English jurisprudence acknowledges that the effect of refusing an injunction to restrain future infringement involves a deprivation of its intellectual property rights.[28] Both the civil and the common law are consistent in establishing that the claimant is *prima facie* entitled to an injunction to restrain the defendant from invading the patentee's legal right. Following a finding of infringement, it is also possible to see the same reluctance to deprive the patentee of its property rights by withholding a final injunction, in cases of FRAND encumbered patent litigation. Nevertheless, in exercising its discretion to grant a final injunction, the court will take account of the FRAND undertaking. We

---

[24] Section 50 of the Senior Courts Act 1981 provides: 'Where the Court of Appeal or the High Court has jurisdiction to entertain an application for an injunction or specific performance, it may award damages in addition to, or in substitution for, an injunction or specific performance'.

[25] Although the United Kingdom did not expressly implement Arts. 3 or 12 of the Directive, the powers of the courts under general law are generally sufficient to ensure compliance with the principle of proportionality and where appropriate, to permit damages to be awarded instead of an injunction. The principles of English law as to the grant of an injunction are considered to embody the principle of proportionality as it is used in the Enforcement Directive with reference to intellectual property rights. See Vestergaard Frandsen A/S v Bestnet Europe Ltd [2011] EWCA Civ 424 at [56]; Virgin Atlantic Airways Ltd v Premium Aircraft Interiors Group [2009] EWCA Civ 1513, [2010] at [23]-[25] Jacob LJ approved Pumfrey J's test in Navitaire Inc v EasyJet Airline Co Ltd (No. 2) [2005] EWHC 282 (Ch), [2006] as being consistent with Article 3 of the Enforcement Directive. C.f German law, see M Stierle & F Hofmann, 'The Latest Amendment to the German Law on Patent Injunctions: The New Statutory Disproportionality Exception and Third-Party Interests' (2022) 71 GRUR International, 1123–1137.

[26] See Shelfer v City of London Lighting Co Ltd [1895] 1 WLR 287 per AL Smith LJ.

[27] Navitaire Inc v EasyJet Airline Co Ltd (No. 2) [2005] EWHC 282 (Ch), [2006] [104].

[28] See in contrast, the classic German, Italian and French positions on the issue in See P Cappuyns & N Al Ganim, 'Four times FRAND: An Analysis of Recent Judgments from the UK, Germany, the Netherlands and France, and Lessons for the Upcoming UPC System (2022) 17 Journal of Intellectual Property Law & Practice, 946–961.

turn therefore to the nature and impact of the FRAND undertaking on the patentee's entitlement to an injunction following a finding of liability for infringement.

32.2 The FRAND undertaking and the court's discretion to grant a final injunction

To appreciate the impact of the FRAND undertaking on the UPC's discretion to grant a final injunction, we turn first to its expression and interpretation within the ETSI. IPR Policy; and secondly to the part it plays within the exercise of such discretion. The ETSI undertaking requires Members who have declared their patents as essential to a standard, to give an irrevocable undertaking in writing that they are prepared to grant irrevocable licences on FRAND terms and conditions.[29] For SEPs, a licence is required because it is not possible on technical grounds to make or operate equipment or to use methods which comply with the standard, without committing an infringement.[30] As the result, industry operators who make or operate equipment which complies with a standard have no alternative without infringing one or more essential patents. Despite the FRAND undertaking resembling a licence of right, the UK Supreme Court did not interpret the IPR Policy as prohibiting the patentee from seeking an injunction where it establishes that an implementer is infringing its patent. The possibility of the grant of an injunction is considered a necessary component of the balance which the IPR Policy seeks to strike, in that it serves to ensure that an implementer has a strong incentive to negotiate and accept FRAND terms for use of the owner's SEP portfolio.[31]

The strategic dynamics of FRAND licensing are characterised on the one hand, as one of 'hold-up' in reference to the negotiating disadvantage faced by licensees for whom there is no feasible non-infringing alternative. Antitrust cases such as European Commission's proceeding against Samsung,[32] show that the ETSI undertaking does not necessarily deter patentees from holding out for a higher price. On the other hand, cases

---

[29] ETSI Rules of Procedure, ETSI Intellectual Property Rights Policy (IPR Policy) Annex 6: Cl. 6.1.
[30] See the ETSI definition of 'IPR' in cl. 15(7): '"IPR" shall mean 'any intellectual property right conferred by statute law…other than trademarks:' ETSI IPR Policy.
[31] See P Cappuyns & N Al Ganim, 'Four times FRAND: An Analysis of Recent Judgments from the UK, Germany, the Netherlands and France, and Lessons for the Upcoming UPC System (2022) 17 Journal of Intellectual Property Law & Practice, 946–948.
[32] Case AT.39939, Samsung, Enforcement of UMTS Standard Essential Patents, Antitrust Procedure Council Regulation (EC) 1/2003 European Commission Brussels, C(2014) 2891 Final [87]: with its invitation to negotiate, Samsung should have provided details of its proposed licensing terms including: '(i) the relevant Mobile standards; (ii) the Mobile SEPs that Samsung claimed were infringed; (iii) the value these Mobile SEPs contributed to the standards; and (iv) the requested royalty rate, including the underlying calculation method used by Samsung.' Further on willingness to negotiate see Sisvel v Haier, FRAND-Einwand I, German Federal Court of Justice, 2020, KZR 36/17 [93–100].

such as Unwired Planet v Huawei and Sisvel v Haier, show that the ETSI undertaking does not deter licensees from 'holding out' for a lower royalty rate or a licence of more limited territorial scope. Indeed, both strategies, 'hold-up' and 'hold-out' have seen the parties have recourse to litigation to dispute both the essentiality of the patent and the FRAND royalty rate.[33] In determining whether to grant the patentee an injunction and the conditions of a FRAND injunction, courts are well aware that both SEP holders and implementers may be attempting to game the system in their favour. Both parties, may prefer to litigate rather than engage constructively in the negotiation process.[34]

The court must therefore be able to enforce its determination against both parties, when the parties cannot agree FRAND terms.[35] On the one hand, implementers can rely on the FRAND undertaking as a contractually enforceable 'stipulation pour autrui' under French law, the governing law of the ETSI IPR Policy.[36] On the other hand, if the SEP holder does not offer FRAND terms, it is in breach of contract and is likely to be denied an injunction when seeking relief from patent infringement.[37] By the same token the implementer will lose the benefit of the FRAND undertaking, if it does not commit to accept a court-determined licence.[38] For example, Optis was attempting to enforce a number of European Patents (UK) relating to 3G and 4G standards, UMTS (3G) and LTE (4G), against Apple, a company implementing the technology in their iPhone and iPad devices.

Although Optis requested an unqualified injunction, the High Court preferred to grant a FRAND injunction, which requires an implementer to either enter into a court-determined licence or accept an injunction. Thus, at such time when the terms of the li-

---

[33] Unwired Planet International Ltd & Anor v Huawei Technologies Co Ltd & Anor (Rev 1) [2018] EWCA 2344 [88] (Lord Kitchin).

[34] Unwired Planet International Ltd & Anor v Huawei Technologies Co Ltd & Anor (Rev 1) [2018] EWCA 2344 [5]. On FRAND as a process see PG Picht, 'Unwired Planet/Huawei: A seminal SEP/FRAND Decision from the UK' (2017) 66 GRUR Int 569, 568 -579: commenting that the decision of the High Court in Unwired Planet is significant in its determination that 'FRAND' has not only a 'content component' but also a 'process component' which focuses on the way in which the parties conduct themselves during negotiations for a licensing agreement.

[35] Optis Cellular Technology LLC & Ors v Apple Retail UK Ltd & Ors [2022] EWCA Civ 1411 [73].

[36] UK Supreme Court. Art. 1205 of the French Civil Code concerns the 'stipulation pour autrui' which states that: 'A person may make a stipulation for another person. One of the parties to a contract (the 'stipulator') may require a promise from the other party (the 'promisor') to accomplish an act of performance for the benefit of a third party (the 'beneficiary'). While the enforceability of the FRAND undertaking in French law is not a clear cut question, the interpretation rests largely on the FRAND undertaking being expressed as 'irrevocable' within the IPR Policy and that qualification itself being based on grounds of public policy.

[37] Unwired Planet International Ltd v Huawei Technologies Co. Ltd & Anor [2017] EWHC 711 [657–668].

[38] In Unwired Planet [2017] EWHC 2988, the HC in the exercise of its discretion, did not grant the injunction on the day the judgement was handed down but granted the parties additional time to conclude a licence in accordance with the conditions set by the court. See also Optis Cellular Technology LLC & Ors v Apple Retail UK Ltd & Ors [2021] EWHC 2564: granting a FRAND injunction; affirmed in Optis Cellular Technology LLC & Ors v Apple Retail UK Ltd & Ors [2022] EWCA Civ 1411.

cence are finally settled by the court, Apple can either rely on Optis' FRAND undertaking, or be subject to an immediate injunction. It is within the English court's discretion to grant a more limited form of injunction than that requested by the claimant. However, while the UK Supreme Court begins its analysis with the contractual nature of the FRAND undertaking as an enforceable obligation, the German court, takes account of it as an implementer's right to a licence when set against a patentee's abuse of dominance under Article 102 TFEU. Accordingly, before the German courts, it is not a question of the patentee's breach of a contractual obligation to offer the implementer a licence that gives cause for withholding an injunction, but the patentee's abuse of a market dominant position.

Notwithstanding, the German and UK courts are consistent as their general approach to injunctive relief in cases of FRAND patent infringement. When the parties cannot agree FRAND terms, both the UK Supreme Court and the German Federal Court of Justice take the approach that the court must be able to enforce its determination if necessary, by the grant of an injunction. Whether the court begins its assessment with a patentee's breach of contract or competition law, if the patentee fails to take the necessary steps to enable a willing implementer to enter into a FRAND licence, it is likely to be denied injunctive relief, as the chapter's ensuing consideration of the FRAND defence will show.

32.2.1 Use of the FRAND injunction to defeat hold-out strategies

The FRAND undertaking has not deterred implementers from employing a 'hold-out' strategy, an obstructive strategy designed to put the patentee in a detrimental position by delaying the conclusion of a FRAND licence.[39] In granting an injunction, the UPC is also likely to be concerned by an implementer's continued 'holding-out' for more favourable terms of agreement or worst case, until the patent at issue, expires. The facts in Sisvel v Haier represent a particularly egregious example of delaying tactics. Sisvel acquired the patent in suit, declared essential to ETSI's GSM.[40] Sisvel offered Haier a global portfolio licence, as Haier was allegedly infringing the claimant's patent by manufacturing and selling mobile phones that implemented the GSM standard.[41]

---

39 Unwired Planet International Ltd & Anor v Huawei Technologies Co Ltd & Anor (Rev 1) [2018] EWCA 2344 [5].
40 Defendant Haier distributed and sold mobile phones and tablets in Germany; in 2014 it offered these devices at an exhibition in Berlin: Sisvel v Haier, FRAND-Einwand I, German Federal Court of Justice, 2020, KZR 36/17 [3]. The mobile telephones and tablets attacked by the claimant supported GPRS (General Packet Radio Service). This is an extension of the GSM standard (Global System for Mobile Communications Standard). The European Telecommunication Standard Institute (ETSI) is responsible for both standards: Sisvel v Haier, FRAND-Einwand I, German Federal Court of Justice, 2020, KZR 36/17: [3].
41 Sisvel v Haier, FRAND-Einwand I, German Federal Court of Justice, 2020, KZR 36/17 [78].

When the parties were unable to agree on the terms of a licence, Sisvel sued Haier for infringement. The Federal Court of Justice found that correspondence from the defendant stating, 'As long as you remain unwilling to specify the way in which your patents ... could be infringed... we are not able to further amend our offer,' indicated the use of delaying tactics. Although, the patentee must provide the infringer with sufficient information, the court held that this duty does not go beyond what one party might reasonably provide in negotiations for a portfolio licence. As in the giving of notice of infringement, it is sufficient to explain those embodiments of the invention indicating the features of the claims allegedly infringed. In Sisvel, after more than three years, the defendant Haier remained insistent that the claimant submit claim charts for the patent portfolio. The court found that the defendant's unwillingness to improve its offer constituted evidence that the defendants were less interested in expediting negotiations than in further delaying them, all the more so, given the near end of the term of the patent in suit.

In fact, delay indicating an unwillingness to license, will affect the likelihood of the court granting an injunction. In such an egregious example, the Federal Court of Justice reasoned that the longer an implementer delays concluding an agreement, the stronger its duty to rectify the delay by expediting negotiations. Although the FRAND undertaking endures despite an implementer's ostensible unwillingness to take a licence, this does not mean, the court found, that such delay will impact upon the FRAND defence as to the claimant's abuse of dominance. Following such delay, an injunction may well be granted unless the patentee acts abusively by pursuing the claim despite the implementer's belated willingness to license.

Likewise, the English High Court in TQ Delta v. ZyXel[42] found the defendants to have engaged in hold-out where the SEPs in suit were due to expire in several months, and ZyXel failed to commit unconditionally to taking a licence and before FRAND terms could be settled by the court. Of course it might be argued that, in the event the implementer's 'hold out' tactic is due to a patent nearing the end of its life, the defendant's willingness to settle the dispute on payment of a cash sum might be reflected in an award of damages. However, the High Court in TQ Delta having found the licensee's conduct intentional, concluded that depriving the patentee of an injunction would be unjust. Generally speaking, where the duration of the patent has yet to run, an order for an injunction will be considered sufficient to persuade an infringer, who wishes to remain in the market, to accept a FRAND licence.

Finally, adopting similar reasoning to the German Federal Court of Justice, the English Court of Appeal in Optis v Apple, found that although the FRAND undertaking entitles the implementer to take a licence at any time, delay in electing to take a licence, will increase the prospect of an injunction. This is because Clause 6.1 of the ETSI IPR policy cannot be read as allowing an implementer to take the benefit of the patentee's FRAND

---

[42] TQ Delta v. ZyXel Communications, [2019] EWHC.

undertaking, without the corresponding burden of taking a licence. Recall that in the case of Optis, the High Court had ordered a FRAND injunction against the defendant to restrain Apple from infringement. In dismissing appeals by both parties, the Court of Appeal observed that Apple's behaviour in declining to commit to take a court-determined licence, once it had been held liable for patent infringement, and its pursuit of an appeal, constituted a form of hold out. The court found that the patentee is entitled to an injunction unless and until the implementer undertakes to take a licence on the terms subsequently determined by the court to be FRAND.

32.3 The discretion to award damages as an alternate and adequate remedy

The UPC has the power to consider awarding damages as an alternative remedy where the grant of an injunction would cause the defendant 'disproportionate harm'.[43] The Enforcement Directive allows the court a discretion to refuse to grant an injunction, where to do so would not be effective, proportionate and dissuasive. The resulting burden on the defendant is a heavy one.[44] The principles which are applicable to the assessment of damages in lieu of an injunction are essentially the same as those which are applicable to the assessment of damages for past acts of infringement. Those damages would be assessed as the sum which would have been agreed between a willing licensor and a willing licensee in respect of those infringing acts which had actually been committed by the defendant.[45]

As to the more difficult assessment of future compensation, this might be assessed as the sum which would be agreed between a willing licensor and a willing licensee for those future acts of infringement which the defendant might commit. The quantum of such damages will be the amount of money which could reasonably have been asked by the claimant for its consent to the infringing acts of the defendant.[46] Where damages are awarded in lieu of an injunction, they are assessed once and for all, in respect of all future infringements, so that any further such claim would be disallowed as *res judicata*.[47]

Licensing a FRAND patent is a voluntary transaction. Notwithstanding the FRAND undertaking to license the invention, it remains the patentee's right, enforceable by law,

---

43 Art. 12 Enforcement Directive.
44 Art. 3 Enforcement Directive.
45 Vringo Infrastructure, Inc v ZTE (UK) Ltd & Anor [2013] EWHC 1591 [37] and [43] regarding the nature of such a hypothetical negotiation.
46 Force India Formula One Team Ltd v 1 Malaysia Racing Team [2012] EWHC 616 29 at [386]: re: principles for the assessment of damages.
47 Ibid [391] re: damages in substitution for the grant of an injunction.

to decide who shall and who shall not exploit its patented invention.[48] The UPC is likely to be very cautious before making an order which might be considered tantamount to a compulsory licence,[49] when international law only provides a narrow scope for compulsory licensing.[50] According to the TRIPS Agreement, there are very limited circumstances in which patentees can be compelled to grant licences of their patents.[51] In Optis v Apple[52] the High Court found that damages would not be an adequate remedy. *Prima facie*, the SEP owner would be prejudiced by having an injunction withheld. The High Court found that having to wait for over a year for proceedings in other jurisdictions to be concluded before the injunction is granted in the UK, would constitute a form of potential hold-out, which would be detrimental to the patentee. In fact the High Court likened such a period of waiting to an unjustified compulsory licence.[53]

Therefore, when evaluating the likely commercial consequences, as far as the patentee is concerned, damages in lieu are unlikely to be considered an adequate remedy. Likewise, a defendant implementer that is holding-out for more favourable terms, would effectively have no incentive to conclude a FRAND licence. Moreover, the determination made by the UPC will have future commercial repercussions on the worldwide licensing of FRAND patents. If the SEP-holder were confined to damages, implementers who were infringing SEP patents would have an incentive to continue infringing until, patent by patent, and country by country, they were compelled to pay royalties.[54] Given the high cost of litigation, it is most unlikely to be commercially practical

---

[48] Classic EP: Article 64 EPC: Rights conferred by a European patent: 'A European patent shall...confer on its proprietor in each Contracting State in respect of which it is granted, the same rights as would be conferred by a national patent granted in that State.' UK Patents Act, 1977 s. 60: 'a person infringes a patent ... if ... [without the consent of the proprietor] where the invention is a product, he makes, disposes of, offers to dispose of, uses or imports the product or keeps it whether for disposal or otherwise.' Article 5 Regulation 1257/2012, uniform protection for unitary patents: i.e. 'the right to prevent any third party from committing acts against which that patent provides protection throughout the territories of the participating Member States... defined by the law applied to European patents with unitary effect in the participating Member State whose national law is applicable to the European patent with unitary effect'.
[49] HTC Corporation v Nokia Corporation [2013] EWHC 3778 [29–32] per Arnold J.
[50] TRIPS Art. 31; UK Patents Act 1977 ss. 48 – 48B; HTC Corporation v Nokia Corporation [2013] EWHC 3778 [29] per Arnold J.
[51] In *Evalve v Edwards* [2020] EWHC 513 (Pat) the High Court considered the question of the court's discretion in granting or withholding a final injunction; it stresses the adverse effects on patentees of being subjected to, effectively, a compulsory licence for which there is no specific statutory basis.
[52] Optis Cellular Technology LLC v Apple Retail UK Ltd [2021] EWHC 2564 [104]: the High Court observed that the view of the UKSC was also of 'high relevance to competition law'...[once the court] proceeds to the determination of FRAND terms. See also Unwired Planet International Ltd v Huawei Technologies (UK) Co Ltd [2020] UKSC 37 [164]: as a matter of patent infringement: the FRAND undertaking prevents an injunction being used to secure an excessive royalty.
[53] Optis Cellular, ibid [333].
[54] Unwired Planet International Ltd & Anor v Huawei Technologies (UK) Co Ltd & Anor [2020] UKSC 37 [167].

for a SEP holder to seek to negotiate patent licences country by country, just as it may be prohibitively expensive. Damages in lieu may thereby encourage 'hold out' tactics. There would be no prospect of any effective injunctive relief being granted, provided implementers agreed to pay the royalties in respect of their activities in any particular country once those activities had been found to infringe.

Thus, the UK Supreme Court, having considered whether it would be disproportionate to enforce an injunction that would exclude the defendant's products from the UK market, concluded to the contrary that it would not be fair nor reasonable to expect a patentee to negotiate licences or bring proceedings territory by territory. Taking into account the disadvantage to the patentee in awarding damages in lieu, the UK Supreme Court made it clear that the court would normally grant an injunction against the infringement of a FRAND encumbered patent. At which point in proceedings, an implementer can choose to invoke the contractual right to a licence under the ETSI IP Policy,[55] or submit to an injunction if it wishes to remain operating within the jurisdiction.

32.4 Withholding an injunction based on the FRAND defence of abuse of dominance

In advancing a FRAND defence the defendant seeks to persuade the court that an injunction for patent infringement should be withheld, because the patentee is abusing its dominant position in the market.[56] The FRAND defence is based upon Art. 102 of the Treaty on the Functioning of the European Union (TFEU), which prohibits any abuse of dominant position in so far as it may affect trade between Member States.[57] In bringing evidence, the defendant will identify factors indicative of such abuse having occurred

---

[55] ETSI Intellectual Property Rights Policy (IPR Policy) 2022, Annex 6: Cl. 6.1 [FRAND undertaking]. As to the implementer's choice see Interdigital Technology Corporation & Ors v Lenovo Group Ltd (FRAND Judgment – Public Version) [2023] EWHC 539 [537].
[56] C.f. the Orange-Book-Standard Case No KZR 39/06, 2009, Bundesgerichtshof) concerning CD-R and CD-RW technologies: a defendant may plead that the patentee is abusing its dominant position in the market, if the patentee refuses to conclude a patent licence agreement with a 'willing' defendant on fair terms, but the defendant has the burden of offering evidence that the patentee was given an opportunity to grant a licence on fair terms. Advocate General Wathelet sought to distinguish FRAND patents based on the patentee's undertaking to ETSI: Case C-170/13, Huawei Technologies Co. Ltd v ZTE Corp., ZTE Deutschland GmbH CJEU 2015 [48]. Further see B Lundqvist, 'The interface between EU competition law and standard essential patents: from Orange-Book-Standard to the Huawei case' (2015) 11 European Competition Journal 381 at 387–88.
[57] Treaty on the Functioning of the European Union (TFEU), Article 102: 'Any abuse by one or more undertakings of a dominant position within the internal market or in a substantial part of it shall be prohibited as incompatible with the internal market in so far as it may affect trade between Member States.' See the UK Competition Act 1998, s. 18 to the same effect.

during the course of the negotiations, in particular the claimant's insistence in offering a global licence; the bundling of SEPs and non SEPs; excessive royalty rates and; commencing an action for patent infringement without notice.[58] Enforcing a standard essential patent is not anti-competitive in and of itself, but under special circumstances, seeking an injunction based on a standard essential patent against a third party that is unconditionally willing to conclude a licence, is not permitted.[59]

There is a presumption that a SEP holder with a 100 % market share holds a dominant position,[60] given that standard-setting tends to eliminate pre-existing competition for the technology. For the purpose of assessing dominance the relevant market is the market for the licensing of each SEP, so the SEP owner has 100 % of each such market.[61] Dominance being a rebuttable presumption, it is possible to rebut with evidence such as that relating to the impact of the FRAND undertaking and detriment due to the implementer's tactical delay in entering into a licence.[62] Moreover, in Sisvel v Haier the court stated that an abuse of market power would only result from the refusal of access to the invention or from unreasonable conditions of access to it, from which the patentee was not prepared to diverge even at the end of the negotiating phase.[63]

The CJEU provided a 'safe harbour' or an exemption for patentees from claims of abuse dominance in Huawei v ZTE, by setting out a phased plan for negotiating a licence, before a patentee can seek an injunction.[64] The interpretation of the CJEU's judgment in Huawei v ZTE by national courts raises questions concerning the scope and operation of

---

58 Unwired Planet International Ltd v Huawei Technologies Co. Ltd & Anor [2017] EWHC 711 [671–785]; Optis Cellular Technology LLC & Ors v Apple Retail UK Ltd & Ors [2021] EWHC 2564 [303–315]; see also Koninklijke Philips N.V. v Asustek Computers Inc, 2019 Court of Appeal of the Hague, Case No. 200.221.250/01 [4.150–166].
59 Sisvel v Haier, FRAND-Einwand II, German Federal Court of Justice, 2020, KZR 35/17 [64] (English translation by the firm of Bardehle Pagenberg: https://media.bardehle.com) citing Case C-170/13, Huawei Technologies Co. Ltd v ZTE Corp., ZTE Deutschland GmbH CJEU 2015 at [71]: the FCJ stated that a claimant does not abuse its dominant market position by seeking injunctive relief, when the defendant is not sufficiently willing to enter into a licence; and on the entitlement of the SEP patentee to damages see ibid [134–35]. Further see A Jones & R Nazzini, 'The Effect of Competition Law on Patent Remedies', in B Biddle, JL Contreras, BJ Love, and NV Siebrasse, eds. *Patent Remedies and Complex Products* Cambridge University Press, 2019, Ch 6, pp. 202–238 at 219–220.
60 Dominant position defined: Case 27/76 *United Brands v Commission* [1978] ECR 2017 at [65]; in Huawei v ZTE the CJEU started from the existence of a dominant position in its decision: [43]; on the assessment of dominance and the relevant factors see: Unwired Planet International Ltd v Huawei Technologies Co Ltd (Rev 1) [2018] EWCA 2344 [213–19]; Unwired Planet International Ltd v Huawei Technologies Co. [2017] EWHC 711 [806]. Further see Commission Communication on the assessment of dominance: 2009/C 45/02 [12].
61 Case AT.39985 – Motorola – Enforcement of GPRS Standard Essential Patents Antitrust Procedure Regulation 1/2003, 2014 [468].
62 Opinion of Advocate General Wathelet Case C-170/13, Huawei Technologies Co. Ltd v ZTE Corp., ZTE Deutschland GmbH CJEU 2014 [88].
63 Sisvel v Haier, FRAND-Einwand II, German Federal Court of Justice, 2020, KZR 35/17 [54].
64 See Case C-170/13, Huawei Technologies Co. Ltd v ZTE Corp., CJEU 2015 [61–69].

the FRAND defence. We will examine the nature of the safe harbour, before assessing the factors relating to abuse of dominance, notably, commencing an action for patent infringement without notice. Finally, we consider how the UPC might interpret the CJEU's judgment in Huawei v ZTE, in view of the approach of the UK and German courts to the scheme set out for negotiating a FRAND licence.

32.4.1 Huawei v ZTE: a 'safe harbour' from abuse of dominance

In assessing the FRAND defence, the UPC will therefore refer to the authority of the CJEU judgment in ZTE v Huawei.[65] In that case Huawei brought an action for patent infringement against ZTE in Germany. The defendant counter-claimed that the action for an injunction constituted an abuse of a dominant position, since ZTE was willing to negotiate a licence. The German District Court of Düsseldorf asked the CJEU for clarification on the use of injunctive relief and other remedies in patent infringement proceedings in the context of standard-essential patents. In the first place, the CJEU held that a SEP holder who has given a FRAND undertaking does not abuse its dominant position by seeking an injunction. In this the CJEU made it clear that there is no prohibition against seeking an injunction simply because a patent in question is standard-essential. However, the court identified a number of conditions that the patentee must satisfy before an injunction can be ordered. The SEP holder must evince a willingness to license, having previously: (a) alerted the implementer of the infringement by specifying the way in which the patent has been infringed and; (b) presented the implementer with a specific, written offer for a licence, specifying the royalty and the way in which it is to be calculated.[66]

By the same token, the CJEU held that a defendant can only rely on a FRAND defence against the claimant's motion for injunctive relief, if a number of requirements are met. The court stressed the need for the implementer to show a willingness to conclude a licensing agreement on FRAND terms. Indeed, the implementer may maintain the defence as to the abusive conduct, only if it has submitted to the SEP holder, promptly and in writing, a specific counter-offer that corresponds to FRAND terms.[67] In ZTE, the CJEU

---

65 UPCA, sources of law Art. 24.
66 M. Leistner characterises the CJEU's scheme for FRAND negotiating as a 'clear and simplified sequential structure [that] allows patent holders and implementers to reasonably foresee which necessary steps they have to take in order to avoid being charged with abusive behaviour': M Leistner, 'FRAND Patents in Europe in the Post-Huawei Era: A Recent Report from Germany', in *SEPs, SSOs and FRAND: Asian and Global Perspectives on Fostering Innovation in Interconnectivity*, K-C Liu, RM Hilty (eds), Taylor & Francis 2019, chapter 15.
67 Case C-170/13, Huawei Technologies Co. Ltd v ZTE Corp., CJEU 2015 [66]. If the counter-offer is rejected the implementer has to provide appropriate security, in accordance with commercial practice, e.g. by providing a bank guarantee: [67]. Where there is no agreement on the FRAND terms following a counter-offer, the parties may agree that the amount of the royalty should be determined by an independent third party.

equates the undertaking to make a FRAND offer with compliance under Art 102 TFEU, so far as the conduct of the SEP holder must not be considered to disrupt negotiations, as to do so would amount to evidence of an unwillingness to negotiate a licence in good faith. Likewise, the defendant implementer may raise a FRAND defence against the claim for an injunction, provided that it has submitted to the patentee, promptly and in writing, a specific counter-offer that corresponds to FRAND terms.

32.4.2 The importance of giving the implementer notice of patent infringement

The patentee that fails to give notice to, or consult with, an alleged infringer before seeking an injunction, may be found abusive, with the result that the claimant will be denied an injunctive relief. According to the CJEU the SEP holder who considers that the SEP is the subject of an infringement cannot, without infringing Article 102 TFEU, bring an action for a prohibitory injunction against the alleged infringer without notice or consultation. In other words, the notice requirement provides a positive obligation on a SEP holder to give notice to, or consult with, the alleged infringer prior to taking legal action or otherwise fall foul of Art. 102.[68] The patentee bears the burden of notifying the implementer of the alleged infringement,[69] by first alerting the alleged infringer of the infringement, and in so doing, designating the SEP and specifying the way in which it has been infringed.

Both the UK Supreme Court and the German Federal Court of Justice focused on the purport of notice as a requirement, rather than risk prejudicing the patentee with a requirement of compliance with certain formalities.[70] Thus, in the case of Unwired Planet v Huawei, following a finding that the defendant had infringed two of Unwired Planet's SEPs, the defendant unsuccessfully argued that Unwired Planet should be denied an injunction because the patentee had failed to give notice in commencing proceedings for infringement before making an offer of a licence with FRAND terms. The Supreme Court in Unwired Planet affirmed that commencing suit for infringement, including the claim for an injunction, was not an abuse of Unwired's dominant position.[71] The Supreme

---

68 Unwired Planet International Ltd & Anor v Huawei Technologies Co Ltd & Anor (Rev 1) [2018] EWCA 2344 [251–254].
69 Case C-170/13, Huawei Technologies Co. Ltd v ZTE Corp., CJEU 2015 [60] and [71].
70 Re: the differences in past decisions of the German courts: Prof. Picht wrote of the decisions of some German courts that accord with the limited scope of the scheme in Huawei (CJEU), while other decisions provide more flexibility in their approach: PG Picht, 'Unwired Planet/Huawei: A seminal SEP/FRAND Decision from the UK' (2017) 10 JIPLP 2017, 876 at 879.
71 Unwired Planet International Ltd v Huawei Technologies Co. Ltd & Anor [2017] EWHC 711 [755]: the High Court rejected the defendant's argument that it was sued before FRAND terms were offered, giving it a defence to the claim for an injunction, as being founded on a narrow interpretation of Huawei v ZTE.

Court held that the form of notice is not prescriptive and will depend upon the circumstances of each case.[72] The facts revealed that Unwired Planet had provided the key terms of its offer to Huawei several weeks after commencing proceedings for patent infringement, followed by further negotiations.[73] Additionally, in view of the fact that the defendant had failed to make an unqualified offer to accept a licence on FRAND terms, the injunction remained in place.[74] Similarly, in Sisvel the Federal Court of Justice took the view that notice is intended to inform the implementer of the infringement and draw attention to the necessity of taking a licence. In giving notice, the patentee is not required to provide detailed technical or legal explanations of the alleged infringement.[75]

32.4.3 Assessing 'abuse of dominance'

A breach of Art. 102 is an all-factor assessment as to the aggregate effect of the alleged abuses.[76] The major stages in the analysis involve the factors relating to the course of the parties' private negotiation for a FRAND patent licence. The FRAND undertaking is largely characterised by the conduct of the parties during the negotiating phase. For example, evidence good faith during negotiations might be indicated by an implementer's attempt to obtain information about the SEP owner's portfolio and comparable licences.[77] On the other hand, a patentee's refusal to negotiate could increase the likelihood of litigation and may lead to the implementer agreeing to pay royalties which are too high. In sum, when it comes to assessing the FRAND defence, both UK and German courts have adopted a flexible approach to the negotiating scheme set out by the CJEU in Huawei v ZTE, so far as the scheme is considered to represent a standard of behaviour against which both parties behaviour can be measured, to decide in the circumstances of the case, if an abuse has taken place.[78] In the following sections, offering excessive royalty rates and other factors regarding the nature of the offer, including global licensing and bundling, as they impact upon the assessment of abuse, will be considered in turn.

---

72 Unwired Planet International Ltd v Huawei Technologies (UK) Co Ltd [2020] UKSC 37 [151].
73 Ibid [152].
74 Unwired Planet International Ltd v Huawei Technologies Co. Ltd & Anor [2017] EWHC 711 [753].
75 Notice of infringement using 'claim charts' is not mandatory: Sisvel v Haier, FRAND-Einwand I, German Federal Court of Justice, 2020, KZR 36/17 [85].
76 Optis Cellular Technology LLC & Ors v Apple Retail UK Ltd & Ors [2021] EWHC 2564 [311–12].
77 Unwired Planet International Ltd & Anor v Huawei Technologies (UK) Co Ltd & Anor [2020] UKSC 37 [144]; Optis Cellular Technology LLC & Ors v Apple Retail UK Ltd & Ors [2021] EWHC 2564 [314].
78 Unwired Planet International Ltd & Anor v Huawei Technologies (UK) Co Ltd & Anor [August, 2020] UKSC 37 [744]; and Sisvel v Haier, FRAND-Einwand II, German Federal Court of Justice, 2020, KZR 35/17 [59].

32.4.3.1 Offering a global licence

Following the negotiating scheme set down by the CJEU,[79] the defendant must show that the SEP holder failed to present the implementer with an initial, written offer. In the case of Unwired Planet, the UK Supreme Court took a flexible, fact dependent approach to assessment. Although Unwired Planet had not presented Huawei with a detailed, written offer prior to issuing proceedings, the court accepted that it had provided the defendant with the key terms of a licence offer several weeks after the commencement of proceedings, followed by a counter-offer and further negotiations.[80]

Defendant Huawei further argued that Unwired Planet had abused its dominant position by persisting in the offer of a global licence. The UK Supreme court rejecting this contention, found that the offer of a global licence was not inherently likely to distort competition. The court identified a number of factors that should be taken into account, notably, the size and geographical scope of the patent portfolio. Unwired Planet's patent portfolio covered only forty two countries, but the Supreme Court held it impractical, not to say inconsistent with the FRAND obligation, to have to agree separate licences, including the management of royalty payments.[81] Likewise, in Sisvel v Haier the German Federal Court of Justice recognised that a worldwide licence might be FRAND and that portfolio licensing does not necessarily constitute an abuse of dominant position.[82]

32.4.3.2 Bundling SEPs and non-SEPs

It is not contrary to competition law on tying and bundling to make an offer that includes SEPs and non-SEPs, provided that there is no evidence that the patentee is trying to use the market power conferred by the SEPs to secure a licence under the non-SEPs.[83] In order to prevent an action being regarded as an abusive, in the circumstances of the case, there should be a reasonable balance between the interests concerned.[84] For example, assuming Huawei had asked Unwired Planet to separate the SEPs from the non-SEPs and it had refused, that might have indicated the action of a patentee who was seeking to use the market power given by the SEPs to tie in a further licence under its non-SEP portfo-

---

[79] Case C-170/13, Huawei Technologies Co. Ltd v ZTE Corp., ZTE Deutschland GmbH CJEU 2015 [63–69].
[80] Unwired Planet International Ltd & Anor v Huawei Technologies (UK) Co Ltd & Anor [August, 2020] UKSC 37 UPSC [157].
[81] Unwired Planet International Ltd & Anor v Huawei Technologies (UK) Co Ltd & Anor [August, 2020] UKSC 37 [166 168].
[82] Sisvel v Haier, FRAND-Einwand I, German Federal Court of Justice, 2020, KZR 36/17 [78].
[83] Unwired Planet International Ltd v Huawei Technologies Co. Ltd & Anor [2017] EWHC 711 [785–787].
[84] Unwired Planet International Ltd & Anor v Huawei Technologies (UK) Co Ltd & Anor [August, 2020] UKSC 37 [151–2].

lio.[85] In fact, the record of negotiations showed that Unwired Planet had been willing to discuss an offer separating SEPs from non-SEPs.[86] As a result, the Supreme Court rejected Huawei's submission that the offer could not be FRAND if it amounted to bundling.[87]

32.4.3.3 The reasonableness of the royalty rate

Recall that in raising the defence of abuse of dominance, the implementer will argue that the patentee only made offers far in excess of FRAND royalties. A crucial issue concerning the FRAND undertaking and possible abuse of dominance will concern the reasonableness of the royalty rate. To succeed in the defence of abuse, the defendant must argue that in the circumstances of the case there is discrimination below the FRAND benchmark rate and most importantly, also show that the offer of allegedly excessive royalty rates has caused competitive harm. For example, in the case of Unwired Planet, Huawei argued that as a relevant comparator, it was entitled to the lower worldwide royalty rate that Unwired had previously agreed with Samsung. However, the Supreme Court did not consider differential royalty rates *per se* to be either unreasonable or discriminatory.[88] As the English Court of Appeal acknowledged, price discrimination is not inherently anti-competitive, stating that 'an effects-based approach to non-discrimination is appropriate'.[89] In this view the UK Supreme Court is in agreement with the German Federal Court of Justice in Sisvel v Haier. The German court similarly held that SEP holders are allowed to offer different FRAND rates to different licensees.[90] In Sisvel the Federal Court of Justice took the view that the 'dominant patentee' is not obliged to grant licences in the manner of a 'uniform tariff' or one which effectively grants 'equal conditions to all users'.[91]

However, in the matter of the court's calculation of a FRAND royalty rate, the UK and German courts differ. The Supreme Court approved the use of the benchmark method of assessment as non-discriminatory, because it is applicable to all licensees seeking the same kind of licence and it constitutes a measure of the intrinsic value of the portfolio, regardless of the identity of the licensee.[92] Nevertheless, the Federal Court of Justice

---

85 Unwired Planet International Ltd v Huawei Technologies Co. Ltd & Anor [2017] EWHC 711 [788].
86 Ibid [788–789].
87 Unwired Planet International Ltd & Anor v Huawei Technologies (UK) Co Ltd & Anor [2020] UKSC 37 [165].
88 Ibid [107].
89 Unwired Planet International Ltd & Anor v Huawei Technologies Co Ltd & Anor (Rev 1) [2018] EWCA 2344 [197].
90 Sisvel v Haier, FRAND-Einwand I, German Federal Court of Justice, 2020, KZR 36/17 [102].
91 Ibid [81].
92 Unwired Planet International Ltd & Anor v Huawei Technologies (UK) Co Ltd & Anor [2020] UKSC 37 [107]. See further SEPs Expert Group' stating that non-discrimination requires the licensor to treat similarly situated parties in a similar manner: at pp. 13 – 14.

declined to determine a FRAND royalty rate, taking the view that it was neither appropriate nor feasible for the court to do so, given that royalty rates are normally set by the market under complex commercial circumstances. Specifically, the Federal Court of Justice stressed the 'decisive importance' of the parties conducting their negotiations in a 'serious and goal-oriented' manner in good faith within a 'contractual relationship' to achieve a price that is determined as the result of 'negotiated market processes'.[93] In so doing, the reasoning of the Federal Court of Justice is consistent with that of the CJEU in Huawei v ZTE, that the implementer who wishes to rely on the abusive nature of an action for a prohibitory injunction has a duty to respond diligently to the patentee's offer, in good faith and in accordance with commercial practice, a point which must be established on the basis of objective factors.[94] In sum, while the UK Supreme Court and the German Federal Court of Justice differed over the role of the court in calculating a suitable royalty, their approval of differential royalty rates serves to illustrate the similarity of their approach to the FRAND defence.

32.5 No entitlement to an injunction where the defendant is a willing licensee

Assuming the defendant is a willing licensee, then the patentee may not entitled to obtain an injunction.[95] For example, Samsung had given a FRAND undertaking, but nevertheless sought a permanent injunction against Apple for infringement of its SEPs. In an antitrust procedure, the Commission concluded that Samsung's action raised issues as to a possible breach of Art. 102.[96] Following the scheme of the CJEU, together with its invitation to negotiate, Samsung should have provided details of the licensing terms on offer and the royalty rate, including the method of royalty calculation.[97] Samsung's conduct was seen as all the more open to abuse of dominance, where the implementer was able to show that it remained willing to enter into a licence for Samsung's SEPs on FRAND terms.[98]

In the case of Samsung the European Commission appeared to regard the suit for patent infringement and the request for a prohibitory injunction as contrary to Arti-

---

93 Sisvel v Haier, FRAND-Einwand I, German Federal Court of Justice, 2020, KZR 36/17 [81].
94 Case C-170/13, Huawei Technologies Co. Ltd v ZTE Corp., ZTE Deutschland GmbH CJEU 2015 [65–66].
95 Vringo Infrastructure, Inc v ZTE (UK) Ltd & Anor [2013] EWHC 1591 2013 HC [43].
96 Case AT.39939, Samsung, Enforcement of UMTS Standard Essential Patents, Antitrust Procedure Council Regulation (EC) 1/2003 European Commission Brussels, C(2014) 2891 Final [52] and [63].
97 Ibid [87].
98 Ibid [122]. Further see T Muller and V Henke, 'Patent Enforcement as a Violation of Antitrust Law: EU Commission decisions in Samsung and Motorola' (2014) 9 (11) Journal of Intellectual Property Law & Practice, Vol. 9, 939.

cle 102, where that action relates to a SEP, the patentee has given a FRAND undertaking and the infringer remains willing to negotiate a FRAND licence, even if the terms cannot be agreed. As defendant ZTE was willing to negotiate, this approach would have made Huawei's action for an injunction unlawful under Article 102.[99] In Huawei v ZTE, the CJEU stressed the importance of the parties' showing in their negotiations a willingness to conclude a licensing agreement on FRAND terms. Indeed, the implementer may maintain the argument as to the abusive conduct of the patentee, only if it has submitted to the SEP holder, promptly and in writing, a specific counter-offer that corresponds to FRAND terms. To be shown to be a willing licensee, the implementer has an obligation to react 'diligently… in accordance with recognised commercial practices in the field and in good faith'.[100]

32.5.1 Proof of an implementer's 'willingness' to enter into a FRAND licence

As to the nature of 'willingness', when the CJEU referred to licensee ZTE expressing a willingness to conclude a licence agreement on FRAND terms, the court appeared to refer to a willingness which is unqualified.[101] The German Federal Court of Justice in Sisvel v Haier speaks of the need for an implementer to show a serious and unconditional willingness to take a licence by declaring clearly and unequivocally its willingness to conclude a licence agreement with the patentee on FRAND terms.[102] Consistent with this view, in the cases of both Unwired Planet and Sisvel v Haier, the UK and German courts stressed the inconsistency of tactical delay on the part of an implementer and willingness to licence. The Supreme Court found that if either party implementer or SEP holder, is engaging in tactical delay, they are not what a court would call 'willing', in so far as they are not willing to negotiate in good faith.[103] The Federal Court of Justice found defendant Haier to have employed delaying tactics in its approach to the negotiations.[104] Claimant Sisvel was granted an injunction because Haier had failed to express an 'unconditional willingness' to take a licence on FRAND terms.

---

[99] Case C-170/13, Huawei Technologies Co. Ltd v ZTE Corp., ZTE Deutschland GmbH CJEU 2015 [71]. Further see S Lawrance, F Brooks, 'Unwired Planet v Huawei: The UK Court of Appeal Upholds FRAND Determination' (2019) 10(3) Journal of European Competition Law & Practice, 180–186.
[100] Ibid [65].
[101] Ibid [101]; Unwired Planet International Ltd v Huawei Technologies Co. Ltd & Anor [2017] EWHC 711 [806].
[102] Sisvel v Haier, FRAND-Einwand I, German Federal Court of Justice, 2020, KZR 36/17 [83]; likewise Birss J, Unwired Planet, ibid [708].
[103] Unwired Planet International Ltd & Anor v Huawei Technologies (UK) Co Ltd & Anor [2020] UKSC 37. [103]. Unwired Planet, EWHC [806].
[104] Sisvel v Haier, FRAND-Einwand I, German Federal Court of Justice, 2020, KZR 36/17 [98].

The breadth of willingness presents the implementer with a high burden of proof. Proof of willingness to enter into a FRAND licence may be indicated by evidence that as soon as it received notice from the patentee of the intention to commence infringement proceedings, the implementer without delay gave notice that it was willing to take a licence on FRAND terms. Moreover, the implementer must show that it continued to express such willingness throughout the course of the negotiating phase in a timely manner. The German Federal Court of Justice stated that defendant Haier's declaration of willingness more than one year after the first infringement notification, did not meet the requirements for an infringer willing to obtain a licence within a reasonable period of time.[105]

Furthermore, the implementer must not be shown to have conditioned its willingness to take a FRAND licence on: a. resolving issues of validity; or b. the allegedly high price of the patent at issue; or c. territorially, the global reach of the licence.[106] Regarding the issue of the patent's validity, both UK and German courts recognise an implementer who claims to be willing to license on condition that the patent is found valid, may be in fact simply holding out or seeking to delay agreeing to licence. The Court of Appeal in Optis v Apple affirmed that the implementer had to commit to take a licence once there was a finding of validity and infringement in order to avoid an injunction. Nevertheless, the court further held that a failure to do so did not permanently deprive the implementer of the right to a FRAND licence in view of the FRAND undertaking to ensure implementers have world-wide access to the relevant standards.

Secondly, as to the price of the patent, according to the CJEU a SEP holder must have shown a willingness to license, having previously presented the implementer with a specific, written offer for a licence, specifying the royalty and the way in which it is to be calculated. Nevertheless, as to the timeliness of such evidence, the German Federal Court of Justice found that a letter from the defendant Haier that required the claimant to explain how the price on offer had been calculated was not in itself sufficient. The court stated that the undertaking to specify the method of royalty calculation, would only exist after the defendant had expressed a serious willingness to license.[107]

Thirdly, given the size and territorial scope of Unwired Planet's patent portfolio, the Supreme Court concluded that a willing licensor and a willing licensee with global sales

---

[105] Ibid [92]; further see evidence of a willingness to licence on the part of an implementer [93–96]: e.g. an e-mail letter from the IP director of the defendant's parent companies, because it merely expressed the hope of a formal negotiation, failed to satisfy the need for an unconditional expression of willingness to take a licence.

[106] The licensee may reserve the right to challenge validity and infringement in parallel to or after signing a licence: Case C-170/13, Huawei Technologies Co. Ltd v ZTE Corp., ZTE Deutschland GmbH CJEU 2015 [69]; Sisvel v Haier, FRAND-Einwand I, German Federal Court of Justice, 2020, KZR 36/17 [96]; Sisvel v Haier, FRAND-Einwand II, German Federal Court of Justice, 2020, KZR 35/17 [95]. Note that unlike the German bifurcated system, the UPCA allows a defendant to file a counterclaim for revocation of the patent in an infringement claim (Art. 32 (1) (e) UPCA).

[107] Sisvel v Haier, FRAND-Einwand I, German Federal Court of Justice, 2020, KZR 36/17 [99].

like those of Huawei would negotiate a global licence.[108] Similarly, Unwired Planet succeeded in showing to the court's satisfaction that it had been willing to license Huawei on whatever terms the court determined were FRAND, whereas the defendant had only been prepared to take a regional licence. In all, to succeed in a FRAND defence, the implementer must adduce strong evidence that it is willing to take a licence on whatever terms are considered by the court or possibly an arbitrator, to be FRAND.[109]

32.6 Conclusion: FRAND injunctions, consistency of decision-making and arbitration

Based upon recent case law in the UK and Germany, the foregoing chapter set out to examine how the UPC may determine that a SEP holder, who has undertaken to grant licences on FRAND terms, is entitled to a prohibitory injunction. Our analysis has shown that despite the courts having some discretion in the grant of an injunction, once there is a finding of patent infringement, the court is unlikely to refuse a FRAND injunction. This is because the strategic dynamics of negotiating and litigating a FRAND licence run counter to the likelihood of the court withholding an injunction, either on the basis of disproportionate harm to the defendant or a successful FRAND defence.[110] In this regard, both UK and German courts incline to the view that withholding an injunction to restrain infringement of a patent, which has been found valid, essential and infringed will tend to promote hold out and leave the patentee with an inadequate remedy. Moreover, in FRAND disputes, our analysis found that damages were unlikely to be considered an adequate, alternative remedy.

Further, so far as the judgments of the UK and German courts may be considered representative, the foregoing analysis has revealed that the UPC is likely to benefit from a general consistency in the approach of European national courts to the interpretation of the discretionary grant of a FRAND injunction. Two particular features of FRAND patent jurisprudence are indicative of a growing consistency in analytical approach, the FRAND injunction and the FRAND defence. Deploying a permanent injunction cannot fully address the problem of an implementer's hold out or continuing disagreement over a FRAND royalty rate. When the parties fail to agree terms, a FRAND injunction presents

---

[108] Unwired Planet International Ltd & Anor v Huawei Technologies (UK) Co Ltd & Anor [2020] UKSC 37 [UKSC, [29]. ibid EWHC [538] – [543]. Ibid, Sisvel [78].
[109] A 'strong reason is required to justify withholding an injunction. The assumed fact that Optis have abused a dominant position by disrupting meaningful negotiations prior to launching this litigation does not provide such a reason: Optis Cellular Technology LLC & Ors v Apple Retail UK Ltd & Ors [2022] EWCA Civ 1411 [94].
[110] Optis Cellular Technology LLC & Ors v Apple Retail UK Ltd & Ors [2021] EWHC 2564 [320]; Optis Cellular Technology LLC & Ors v Apple Retail UK Ltd & Ors [2022] EWCA Civ 1411 [64] and [92].

an implementer with a choice to enter into a court-determined licence, or be subject to an immediate injunction. Both courts would agree that the availability of a reasonable and non-discriminatory royalty rate means that the price on offer should be available at a fair market price for any participant.[111]

In the matter of the FRAND defence both UK and German courts adopt a consistent approach to assessment. To succeed in a FRAND defence, the defendant needs to show evidence that as soon as it received a notice of infringement, it was willing to take a licence on FRAND terms. In both jurisdictions, proof of the defendant's willingness to negotiate a licence is the key element in the assessment of abuse of dominance.

However, where the two courts differ is in the appropriate manner of enforcing their respective determinations. The UK courts have found a court determined licence to be a necessary step in addressing the problem of hold-out, where an implementer has not shown a willingness to commit unconditionally to enter into a FRAND licence.[112] In contrast, the Federal Court of Justice would consider an implementer's willingness to seriously negotiate the terms of a licence, in particular the royalty rate as critical, given its reference to achieving a royalty that is determined as the result of 'negotiated market processes'.[113]

In the alternative, remedying liability for past infringement and addressing the FRAND undertaking might be satisfied if the UPC were to grant a FRAND injunction and require the parties to arbitrate the terms of a FRAND licence, in particular the scope of the territorial grant of rights and the reasonableness of the royalty rate.[114] Failing such a court order, to avoid leaving the patentee without a FRAND licence, the Court of Appeal has suggested that ETSI might include the arbitration of disputes over FRAND licences as a legally enforceable element of its Intellectual Property Rights Policy.[115]

---

111 Sisvel v Haier, FRAND-Einwand I, German Federal Court of Justice, 2020, KZR 36/17 [81]; Sisvel v Haier, FRAND-Einwand II, German Federal Court of Justice, 2020, KZR 35/17 [71]; and Unwired Planet International Ltd & Anor v Huawei Technologies (UK) Co Ltd & Anor [2020] UKSC 37 [114].
112 Optis Cellular Technology LLC & Ors v Apple Retail UK Ltd & Ors [2021] EWHC 2564 [362]; affirming, Optis Cellular Technology LLC & Ors v Apple Retail UK Ltd & Ors [2022] EWCA Civ 1411 [94]: 'The only obstacle Apple face is their own unwillingness to commit to taking a Court- Determined Licence before the terms have been finally determined.' Unwired Planet International Ltd v Huawei Technologies Co. Ltd & Anor [2017] EWHC 711 [803]. C.f. Interdigital Technology Corporation & Ors v Lenovo Group Ltd (Public Version) [2023] EWHC 539 [957]: Lenovo was prepared to give an undertaking to take a licence thereby avoiding an injunction.
113 Sisvel v Haier, FRAND-Einwand I, German Federal Court of Justice, 2020, KZR 36/17 [81]; Sisvel v Haier, FRAND-Einwand II, German Federal Court of Justice, 2020, KZR 35/17 [71].
114 The CJEU suggested that where the parties continue to dispute a FRAND royalty rate they may request that the amount of the royalty be determined by an independent third party. Case C-170/13, Huawei Technologies Co. Ltd v ZTE Corp., ZTE Deutschland GmbH CJEU 2015 [68]. Art. 35 UPCA establishes an arbitration centre with seats in Ljubljana and Lisbon. During an interim procedure the UPC may inquire as to the possibility of settlement by arbitration, using the facilities of the centre: Art. 52(2) UPCA.
115 Optis Cellular Technology LLC & Ors v Apple Retail UK Ltd & Ors [2022] EWCA Civ 1411 [115].

Index

Agreement on Trade Related Aspects of Intellectual Property (TRIPS) 172
appeals 4–5, 213, 244–245, 255, 281, 414, 424, 466, 481, 543
arbitration XXVI, 41, 129–151, 226–227, 298, 317, 322, 325, 327, 333, 336, 397, 399, 406, 410, 555–556

biotechnology 7, 47, 53, 172, 181, 505, 510, 515
Bolar exemption 120, 122, 250

civil proceedings 408
claim construction 26, 39, 99
claims 5, 10–14, 30–31, 33, 38–39, 41, 45, 51, 57, 69, 71, 91, 99, 104, 145, 175, 177, 182–183, 201–202, 206, 237, 258–259, 261, 269, 313, 320–323, 326, 336, 351–353, 356–357, 361, 364, 378, 420, 434, 441, 460, 467, 498–500, 507, 534, 542, 546, 554
competition law XXIX, 113, 259, 264, 339–344, 346–352, 440, 478, 480, 495, 510, 534–536, 541, 544–545, 550
constitutionality 84
Court of Justice of the European Union (CJEU) XXVI–XXVII, 91, 123, 205, 246, 440, 523
cross-border litigation XXV, 30–31, 34, 36, 41

Enforcement Directive XXVI, 35, 59–60, 62, 66–67, 71–76, 79, 85–87, 90, 113, 170, 172, 179, 183, 266, 289, 295, 311, 393, 478–479, 481, 483–484, 487–489, 494, 535–538, 543
ethics 499, 502, 504, 513–515, 528
European Patent V, VII, XXV, XXVIII–XXXI, 3–6, 8–9, 17–20, 24, 27, 29, 43, 49, 97, 99–100, 105–106, 111, 142–143, 163, 169–173, 180, 186, 193, 195–196, 198–201, 203, 205, 210, 213, 222, 235–239, 241–242, 246–247, 250, 253–254, 256, 258, 267, 271, 283, 285, 320, 340, 350–351, 355–357, 359, 363–365, 368–369, 371, 378–379, 425, 449–461, 463–464, 467–474, 479, 494–495, 498, 500, 504–506, 513–514, 517–520, 522, 529–530, 533, 540
European Patent Convention (EPC) V, XXV, 3, 8, 43, 99–100, 111, 205, 235, 425, 479, 520
European patent system VII, XXV–XXVI, 0, 40, 58, 80, 100, 221, 224–225, 231, 235, 237, 239, 246, 285, 449, 451, 461, 463–465, 468, 470–475, 514–515, 519, 522, 524–526, 529
European Union law 11, 104, 210, 247, 535, 537

fair XXIX, XXXI, 14, 53, 86, 150, 179, 187, 228, 253, 294, 342, 347, 355, 361, 374, 381, 482–484, 491, 499, 510, 534–535, 537, 545, 556
fair, reasonable and non-discriminatory (FRAND) 533

gene patents XXXI, 498–500, 502–504, 506–507, 509–513, 515

human rights 4, 82, 228, 315, 317, 321–322, 326, 335–336, 522, 526, 528

infringement XXVII–XXVIII, 0, 25, 28–39, 41, 59–63, 65, 67–69, 71, 75, 80, 84–93, 99, 103, 106–108, 111, 116–118, 120, 125, 134, 137–139, 145, 154, 158–160, 170–172, 174, 176–177, 179, 183, 186, 189, 191–195, 198–199, 201–203, 205, 225, 229, 238, 245, 250–251, 255–256, 258–265, 269–273, 277–278, 281–282, 285–286, 294–296, 298, 301–304, 306–308, 310–312, 321, 342, 345, 349–350, 352, 358, 371, 375, 378, 388–389, 391–393, 402, 411–417, 419, 423–427, 429–445, 450–451, 456, 458–460, 463, 465, 467–469, 471–472, 474, 485–489, 491–493, 533–543, 545–549, 552, 554–556
innovation XXIX–XXX, 15, 44, 52, 58, 80, 88, 93–94, 98, 115, 122, 125, 253, 259, 264–265, 274, 276, 307, 344, 355–356, 363, 365–367, 372–375, 378–379, 381–384, 387–389, 391, 395–396, 469, 483, 498–499, 502, 507–509, 515

licensing 81, 119, 135, 150, 178, 263, 265, 273, 277, 343, 345, 351, 373, 385, 388, 390, 462, 504, 510–511, 533, 539–540, 544, 546–547, 549–550, 552–553
litigation VII, XXV–XXVI, XXVIII, XXX, 7–8, 14, 23–25, 27–28, 30–31, 34, 36–38, 40–41, 60–61, 63–64, 66, 68, 72, 74, 76, 82, 84, 86–88, 93, 103, 129, 134, 149, 169, 173–174, 183, 190, 193, 195–196, 199, 205, 219, 226–227, 232, 234, 236, 241, 245, 247, 262–264, 273, 278, 281–283, 285–286, 294–295, 298–299, 301, 303–305, 307–308, 313–314, 327, 346–347, 349, 369, 410–412, 415, 418–421, 423, 428, 432, 436–440, 445, 451, 454, 459, 468, 482–483, 490, 499, 501–502, 507, 533–536, 538, 540, 544, 549, 555

mediation XXX, 130–139, 141–142, 144–146, 149–150, 226–227, 298, 397–402, 404–410
medicinal products XXVI, 110, 121, 124, 153–156, 159, 170, 275–276, 346, 367, 379–380, 386–387, 479

novelty XXVI, 10, 53, 56, 97, 99–100, 103–104, 106–107, 184, 260, 376, 426, 502

patent applications 18, 21, 24–25, 97, 100, 235–236, 246, 307, 348–349, 364, 454, 456, 467, 501, 519, 522
plant varieties 15, 110, 125, 171, 217, 260, 381
plausibility XXV–XXVI, 43–58
products of nature 515
proportionality XXVI, XXVIII, 70–71, 79–80, 83–87, 89–91, 93–94, 231, 266, 278, 290, 293–296, 299, 367, 388, 391, 393, 396, 484, 494, 535, 537–538

public interest 6, 86–87, 89, 234, 265, 276, 316, 334, 390–391, 484, 510–511, 513

research exemption 118–119, 154, 276, 383

Supplementary Protection Certificate (SPC) 124, 245

territoriality 17–18, 38, 170–171, 351

Unified Patent Court (UPC) V, XXV, XXVII, 80, 111, 132, 169, 238, 254, 423, 449, 457, 463, 478, 517, 533

Printed in the USA
CPSIA information can be obtained
at www.ICGtesting.com
LVHW082340150324
774517LV00005B/698